Learning
Microsoft® Works 4
for Windows® 95

Belis / Blanc

To Our Families

Stephen, Craig, David and Mom
and to my extended family, Dale Roth and Gloria Jackelow
Alan, Pamela, Jaime and Mom

Thank you for all your patience, devotion and support during this project.
We could never have done it without you.

A special thank you to our dear friend, colleague and confidant,
Shirley Dembo for her continued support and directions.

Thanks also to Carol Havlicek for her contribution to this project.

Project Manager
Rosemary O'Connell Shmavonian
New York, NY

Technical Editors
Carol Havlicek
Long Beach, NY

Maria Reidlebach
New York, NY

English Editors
Mary Mendola
Accord, NY

Rebecca Fiala
Cambridge, MA

Layout and Design
Adrion Smith
New York, NY

Paul Wray
New York, NY

TABLE OF CONTENTS

Works Basics   **2**

    The Keyboard
    The Mouse
    Universal Features
    Buttons
    Access Microsoft Works for Windows
    Mouse and Keyboard Methods
    Works Task Launcher

WORD PROCESSOR   **5**

Lesson 1: Create, Save and Print Documents

Exercise 1 6
    Access the Word Processor
    Word Processor Screen Parts
    Select Menu Items
    Pull-Down Menus
    Access from Pull-Down Menus
    Exit Works
Exercise 2 10
    Select Menu and Submenu Items
    Change View Modes
Exercise 3 13
    Help
    Zoom Feature
Exercise 4 16
    Defaults
    Create a New Document
    Close a New Document
    Save a New Document
Exercise 5 19
    The Tab Key
    Customize the Toolbar
Exercise 6 21
    Insertion Point Movements
    Scroll a Document
Exercise 7 24
    Create a Business Letter
    Print Preview
Exercise 8 28
    Use the Date and Time Feature
    All Caps
    Print a Document
Exercise 9 32
    Lesson 1 – Summary

Lesson 2: Edit Documents

Exercise 10 33
    Proofreaders' Marks
    Open a Previously Stored Document
    Insert/Typeover Text
    Update a Document
Exercise 11 37
    Delete Text
    Select Text
    Undo Editing

Exercise 12 40
    Typing Replaces Selection
    Show All Characters
    Delete Characters
    Combine Two Paragraphs into One
    Delete Tabs
Exercise 13 43
    Modified-Block Letter
    Non-Breaking Space
Exercise 14 45
    Lesson 2 – Summary

Lesson 3: Text Alignments and Enhancements; Language Tools

Exercise 15 46
    Alignment Options (Left, Center and Right)
Exercise 16 49
    Spell Check
    Justify Text
Exercise 17 52
    Bold, Underline and Italics
    Create Bulleted Lists
    Change Bullet Style
    Remove Bullets
Exercise 18 56
    Font, Font Size and Color
    Create a Memorandum
Exercise 19 60
    Thesaurus
    Word Count
    Easy Text
Exercise 20 64
    Remove Typestyles
    Remove Bullets
Exercise 21 66
    Lesson 3 – Summary

Lesson 4: Margins, Indents and Spacing

Exercise 22 68
    Create a One-Page Report
    Change Margins
    Change Line Spacing
    Add a Space Before/After a Paragraph
Exercise 23 73
    Indents (First Line, Hanging and Quotation)
    Increase/Decrease Indent Levels
    Undo Indents
Exercise 24 77
    Numbered Lists
    Easy Formats
Exercise 25 81
    Move Text (Drag and Drop, Cut and Paste)
    Save As a New File
Exercise 26 84
    Edit an Easy Format
    Rename a File

Exercise 27 86
   Copy Text (Copy and Paste; Drag and Drop)
   Copy Formats
Exercise 28 89
   Customize an Indent
   Non-Breaking Hyphen
Exercise 29 93
   Prepare a Resume
Exercise 30 95
   Lesson 4 – Summary

Lesson 5: Editing and Formatting;
Multiple-Page Documents;
File Management
Exercise 31 97
   Find Text
   Find Special Characters
Exercise 32 100
   Find and Replace Text
   Find and Replace Special Characters
   Hyphenation
Exercise 33 104
   Hard vfs. Soft Page Breaks
   Second Page Headings
   Print Selected Pages
Exercise 34 107
   Letters with Special Notations
   Bookmarks
Exercise 35 110
   Footnotes
Exercise 36 113
   Print a Footnote at the End of the Document
   Edit a Footnote
Exercise 37 116
   Create Headers and Footers
   Edit Headers and Footers
   Page Numbers
Exercise 38 120
   Page Numbers
   Superscripts and Subscripts
Exercise 39 123
   Cut and Paste Text from One Page to
      Another Using Go To
   File Management (Create a Folder, Send a File
      to Another Location, Delete a File)
Exercise 40 126
   Lesson 5 – Summary

Lesson 6: Columns, Tabs and Tables
Exercise 41 128
   Columns
Exercise 42 131
   Add a Title to a Column Layout
   Move Around in Columns
Exercise 43 133
   Tabs
   Change Tab Settings
   Tabular Columns
Exercise 44 137
   Leaders
   Move and Change Tabs

Exercise 45 140
   Create a Table
   Enter Text in a Table
   Edit a Table Cell
   Gridlines
   Column Headings
Exercise 46 143
   Change Alignment
   Change Format
   Add/Delete Columns or Rows
Exercise 47 146
   Adjust Column Width
   Resize a Table
Exercise 48 149
   Lesson 6 – Summary

Lesson 7: Advanced Text Enhancements;
Draw; ClipArt
Exercise 49 151
   Lines and Paragraph Borders
Exercise 50 154
   Create a Report Cover Page
   Page Borders
   Shading
Exercise 51 157
   Insert ClipArt
   Resize a Graphic
   Move a Graphic
   Delete a Graphic
Exercise 52 162
   Create a Letterhead
Exercise 53 164
   Text Wrap Feature
   Newsletters
Exercise 54 167
   Microsoft Draw
   Create a Drawing
Exercise 55 171
   Copy a ClipArt or Drawing
   Edit a ClipArt or Drawing
Exercise 56 175
   WordArt
Exercise 57 179
   Use Note-It
Exercise 58 182
   Lesson 7 – Summary

SPREADSHEET   **185**

Lesson 1: Create, Save and Print a Spreadsheet
Exercise 1 186
   Introduction to the Spreadsheet Tool
   Start a Spreadsheet
   Spreadsheet Screen Parts
   Move Around in a Spreadsheet
Exercise 2 189
   Enter Labels
   Make Simple Corrections
   Save and Exit
Exercise 3 191
   Enter Values
   Numeric Labels

Edit Cell Contents
Clear a Cell
Exercise 4.. 193
   Adjust Column Width
   Print a Spreadsheet
   Change Margins and Orientation
   Print Gridlines
Exercise 5.. 196
   Lesson 1 – Summary

Lesson 2: Formulas; Format Spreadsheets

Exercise 6.. 197
   Use Formulas
Exercise 7.. 199
   Use Formulas
Exercise 8.. 200
   Open and Resave a File
   Select Cells in the Spreadsheet
   Ranges
   Change Alignments (Values and Labels)
Exercise 9.. 204
   Format Values
Exercise 10.. 207
   Copy Data
   Copy Formulas (Relative Reference)
Exercise 11.. 209
   Copy a Formula (Absolute Condition)
   Repeat an Entry
Exercise 12.. 211
   Lesson 2 – Summary

Lesson 3: Functions

Exercise 13.. 212
   Functions
   AVG (Average) Function
Exercise 14.. 214
   Sum Function
   Autosum
Exercise 15.. 216
   Count, Min and Max Functions
   Fill Series
Exercise 16.. 219
   Built-In Functions
   Change Column Width
Exercise 17.. 221
   IF Statements
Exercise 18.. 223
   IF Statements
Exercise 19.. 225
   Freeze Titles
Exercise 20.. 227
   Hide Columns and Rows
   Easy Calc
Exercise 21.. 230
   Lookup
   Vertical Lookup
Exercise 22.. 234
   Horizontal Lookup Function
   Protect Data
Exercise 23.. 236
   Lesson 3 – Summary

Lesson 4: Format, Edit and Enhance Spreadsheets

Exercise 24..238
   Insert, Delete and Move Columns and Rows
   Move and Copy Information
   Paste Special
Exercise 25..242
   Name Ranges
Exercise 26..245
   Sort Information
Exercise 27..248
   Enhance the Spreadsheet (Font, Font Size, Typestyle)
Exercise 28..250
   Borders
   Patterns
Exercise 29..253
   AutoFormat
Exercise 30..255
   Lesson 4 – Summary

Lesson 5: Create and Enhance Charts

Exercise 31..257
   Create a Single Series Bar Chart, a Line Chart and a Pie Chart
   Change Titles
   Rename Charts
   Save Charts
Exercise 32..263
   Create a Multiple-Series Bar Chart
   Charting Toolbar
   Change a Chart Type
   Stacked Bar Chart
   Print a Chart
Exercise 33..267
   Edit the Spreadsheet Data
   Edit a Series Range
   Edit a Legend
   Display/Hide a Legend
   Duplicate a Chart
Exercise 34..270
   Data Labels
   Gridlines
   Explode a Pie Chart
Exercise 35..273
   Change Font, Font Size and Typestyle
   Change Color, Pattern and Markers
   3-D Charts
Exercise 36..276
   Lesson 5 – Summary

DATABASE   279

Lesson 1: Create and Save a Database File

Exercise 1..280
   Introduction to the Database
   Plan a Database
   Create a Database File
   Save a Database File
Exercise 2..283
   View Modes

Exercise 3...285
   Create and Save a Database File
Exercise 4...285
   Create and Save a Database File
Exercise 5...286
   Lesson 1 – Summary

Lesson 2: Edit and Print a Database File

Exercise 6...287
   Open a File
   View Modes
   Enter Records
   Correct a Field Entry
   Field Width
   Record Height
Exercise 7...291
   Modify the Form
   Move a Field
   Copy Data
   Use Fill Series
Exercise 8...298
   Open a Database File
   Modify the Form
   Enter Records
   Copy Data
Exercise 9...299
   Page Setup
   Add Headers and/or Footers
   Print Preview
   Print
   Show and Print Selected Records
Exercise 10...303
   Edit Record or Field Data
   Insert a Record
   Delete a Record
Exercise 11...307
   Edit a Record
   Insert and Delete a Record
Exercise 12...308
   Lesson 2 – Summary Exercise 12A
   Lesson 2 – Summary Exercise 12B

Lesson 3: Filters; Format a Database

Exercise 13...312
   Locate a Specific Record
   Wildcards
   Find and Replace
   Use Filters to Search a Database
   Create a Filter
   Results of a Filter
   Display All Records
Exercise 14...318
   Relational Operators
   View a Filter
   Delete a Filter
   Rename a Filter
Exercise 15...321
   View Filters
   Delete Filters
   Rename Filters
Exercise 16...322
   Apply a Previously Created Filter
   Format a Database

Exercise 17...327
   Apply a Previously created Filter
   Format the Database
Exercise 18...328
   Lesson 3 – Summary Exercise 18A
   Lesson 3 – Summary Exercise 18B

Lesson 4: Reports

Exercise 19...333
   Sort Database Records
Exercise 20...336
   Sort Database Records
Exercise 21...337
   Create a Report
   The Report Definition Screen (Report View)
   Preview a Report
Exercise 22...341
   Modify a Report
   Format a Report
   Access a Report
   Rename a Report
   Delete a Report
Exercise 23...349
   Sort and Group Report Data
   Display Statistic Summaries within Each Group
Exercise 24...357
   Group and Sort Data
   Use Shading in a Report
Exercise 25...360
   Create a Report Based on the Results of a Filter
Exercise 26...364
   Lesson 4 – Summary

INTEGRATION   371

Exercise 1...372
   Windowing
   Maximize a Window
   Minimize a Window
   Resize a Window
   Multiple Windows (Cascade Tile)
   Restore a Window
   Close a Document Window
Exercise 2...376
   Copy Text from One Word Processing Document
      to Another
Exercise 3...378
   Integrate Word Processing and Spreadsheet Files
      (Copy and Paste, Drag and Drop)
Exercise 4...380
   Embed an Existing Spreadsheet
Exercise 5...382
   Embed an Existing Chart
Exercise 6...384
   Embed a New Spreadsheet
Exercise 7...386
   Link Word Processing and Spreadsheet Documents
   Edit a Link
   Change a Source
Exercise 8...390
   Integrate Database Files and Reports

Exercise 9.................................... 393
   Merge Word Processing and Database Documents
   Create Form Letters
   Print Merge
Exercise 10................................... 399
   Merge Selected Records
Exercise 11................................... 402
   Create and Print a Single Envelope
Exercise 12................................... 405
   Create and Merge Envelopes
Exercise 13................................... 408
   Create and Print Labels
Exercise 14................................... 411
   Integration – Summary

TASKWIZARDS AND TEMPLATES   413

Exercise 1.................................... 414
   Create a Letterhead with a TaskWizard
   Integrate a Letterhead with a Letter
   Create a Template
Exercise 2.................................... 418
   Address Book TaskWizard
Exercise 3.................................... 421
   Grade Book TaskWizard
Exercise 4.................................... 423
   Brochure TaskWizard
Exercise 5.................................... 425
   TaskWizards and Templates– Summary

COMMUNICATIONS   429

Exercise 1....................................430
   Introduction to Communications
   Begin a Communications Session
Exercise 2....................................433
   Adjust Settings
   Save Settings
Exercise 3....................................439
   Send Information
   Send Text
   Send Files
   Send a Fax
   End a Session
Exercise 4....................................444
   Answer a Call
   Receive and Save Incoming Text
   Capture Text
   Receive Files
   Information Services/Bulletin Boards
Exercise 5....................................448
   Communications – Summary

LOG OF EXERCISES

Lesson	Exercise	Filename	On Disk As	Solution File
Word Processing				
WP – 1	4	WARE	—	WP WARE.4S
	5	WORKS	—	WP WORKS.5S
	6	DIVE	—	WP DIVE.6S
	7	APPLY	—	WP APPLY.7S
	8	BLOCK	—	WP BLOCK.8S
	9	GOOD	WP GOOD.9	WP GOOD.9S
WP – 2	10	WARE	WP WARE.10	WP WARE.10S
	11	WORKS	WP WORKS.11	WP WORKS.11S
	12	APPLY	WP APPLY.12	WP APPLY.12S
	13	BLOCK	WP BLOCK.13	WP BLOCK.13S
	14	GOOD	WP GOOD.14	WP GOOD.14S
WP – 3	15	NEWS	—	WP NEWS.15S
	16	COMPANY	WP COMPANY.16	WP COMPANY.16S
	17	DIVE	WP DIVE.17	WP DIVE.17S
	18	MEMONEWS	—	WP MEMONEWS.18S
	19	MEMO	WP MEMO.19	WP MEMO.19S
	20	MEMONEWS	WP MEMONEWS.20	WP MEMONEWS.20S
	21	REPORT	WP REPORT.21	WP REPORT.21S
WP – 4	22	BULLETIN	—	WP BULLETIN.22S
	23	INDENT	—	WP INDENT.23
	24	STUDY	WP STUDY.24	WP STUDY.24S
	25	INDENT	WP INDENT.25	
		INDENT 1	—	WP INDENT1.25S
	26	BULLETIN	WP BULLETIN.26	
		BULLETIN BOARD	—	WP BULLETIN BOARD.26S
	27	MEMO	WP MEMO.27	WP MEMO.27S
	28	DIVE	WP DIVE.28	WP DIVE.28S
	29	RESUME	—	WP RESUME.29S
	30	BATS	WP BATS.30	WP BATS.30S
WP – 5	31	BULLETIN BOARD	WP BULLETIN BOARD.31	WP BULLETIN BOARD.31S
	32	STUDY	WP STUDY.32	WP STUDY.32S
	33	NYC	WP NYC.33	WP NYC.33S
	34	PREVIEW	WP PREVIEW.34	WP PREVIEW.34S
	35	SCORPION	WP SCORPION.35	WP SCORPION.35S
	36	INFO	WP INFO.36	WP INFO.36S
	37	VOYAGE	WP VOYAGE.37	WP VOYAGE.37S
	38	UP AND DOWN	WP UP AND DOWN.38	WP UP AND DOWN.38S
	39	PREVIEW	WP PREVIEW.39	WP PREVIEW.39S
		PREVIEW 2	—	
		EDUCATION FILMS	—	
	40	DIVE	WP DIVE.40	
		DIVING	—	WP DIVING.40S
WP – 6	41	ETIQUETTE	—	WP ETIQUETTE.41S
	42	COOK	—	WP COOK.42S
	43	PRESIDENTS	—	WP PRESIDENT.43S
	44	TABLE OF CONTENTS	—	WP TABLE OF CONTENTS.44S
		TABLE OF CONTENTS 2	WP TABLE OF CONTENTS.44	WP TABLE OF CONTENS 2.44S
	45	COURSES	—	WP COURSES.45S
		COURSES 2	WP COURSES.45	WP COURSES 2.45S

Lesson	Exercise	Filename	On Disk As	Solution File
Word Processing *(continued)*				
WP – 6	46	BASEBALL	—	WP BASEBALL.46S
		BASEBALL 2	WP BASEBALL.46	WP BASEBALL 2.46S
	47	OFFICER	—	WP OFFICER.47S
	48	DELIVERY	—	WP DELIVERY.48S
		DELIVERY 2	WP DELIVERY.48	WP DELIVERY 2.48S
WP – 7	49	OFFICER	WP OFFICER.49	WP OFFICER.49S
	50	COVER	—	WP COVER.50S
	51	WORLD ONLINE	WP WORLD ONLINE.51	WP WORLD ONLINE.51S
	52	SOCK	—	WP SOCK.52S
	53	PACK	—	WP PACK.53S
	54	HAPPY	WP HAPPY.54	WP HAPPY.54S
	55	TELECOPY	—	WP TELECOPY.55S
	56	ETIQUETTE	—	
		CYBERNEWS	—	WP CYBERNEWS.56S
	57	JETS	—	WP JETS.57S
	58	NHS	—	WP NHS.58S
Spreadsheet				
SS – 1	2	DAILY	—	SS DAILY.2S
	3	SALES	—	SS SALES.3S
	4	SALARY	—	SS SALARY.4S
	5	REPAIR	SS REPAIR.5	SS REPAIR.5S
SS – 2	6	PRICE	—	SS PRICE.6S
	7	WAGES	—	SS WAGES.7S
	8	REPAIR	SS REPAIR.8	SS REPAIR.8S
	9	PRICE	SS PRICE.9	SS PRICE.9S
	10	SALARY	SS SALARY.10	SS SALARY.10S
	11	DAILY	SS DAILY.11	SS DAILY.11S
	12	UNIVERSITY	—	SS UNIVERSITY.12S
SS – 3	13	EXAM	—	SS EXAM.13S
	14	SALES	SS SALES.14	SS SALES.14S
	15	WOOD	SS WOOD.15	SS WOOD.15S
	16	BONUS	—	SS BONUS.16S
	17	TESTSUM	—	SS TESTSUM.17S
	18	COMM	—	SS COMM.18S
	19	BONUS	SS BONUS.19	SS BONUS.19S
	20	PLAY	—	SS PLAY.20S
		PLAY 2	—	SS PLAY 2.20S
	21	HOME	—	SS HOME.21S
	22	ZONE	—	SS ZONE.22S
	23	VIDEO	—	SS VIDEO.23S
SS – 4	24	SALARY	SS SALARY.24	
		SALARY COMPARE	—	SS SALARY COMPARE.24S
	25	EXAM	SS EXAM.25	SS EXAM.25S
	26	COMM	SS COMM.26	
		COMM1	—	SS COMM1.26S
		COMM2	—	SS COMM2.26S
	27	BONUS	SS BONUS.27	SS BONUS.27S
	28	WOOD	SS WOOD.28	SS WOOD.28S
	29	SALARY	SS SALARY.29	
		SALARY 2	—	SS SALARY 2.29S
	30	FOLIO	—	SS FOLIO.30S
SS – 5	31	HS	—	SS HS.31S
	32	HS	SS HS.32	SS HS.32S
	33	BONUS	SS BONUS.33	

Lesson	Exercise	Filename	On Disk As	Solution File
Spreadsheet (continued)				
SS – 5		BONUS2	—	BONUS2.33S
	34	FINER FUNDS	—	SS FINER FUNDS.34S
	35	GROW	—	SS GROW.35S
	36	BUSINESS COURSES	—	SS BUSINESS COURSES.36S
Database				
DB – 1	1	STUDENT	—	DB STUDENT.1S
	2	MEMBER	—	DB MEMBER.2S
	3	STORES	—	DB STORES.3S
	4	INVENTORY	—	DB INVENTORY.4S
	5	PROGRAM	—	DB PROGRAM.5S
DB – 2	6	MEMBER	DB MEMBER.6	DB MEMBER.6S
	7	STUDENT	DB STUDENT.7	DB STUDENT.7S
	8	STORES	DB STORES.8	DB STORES.8S
	9	MEMBER	DB MEMBER.9	DB MEMBER.9S
	10	STUDENT	DB STUDENT.10	DB STUDENT.10S
	11	STORES	DB STORES.11	DB STORES.11S
	12A	INVENTORY	DB INVENTORY.12	DB INVENTORY.12S
	12B	PROGRAM	DB PROGRAM.12	DB PROGRAM.12S
DB – 3	13	MEMBER	DB MEMBER.13	DB MEMBER.13S
	14	STORES	DB STORES.14	DB STORES.14S
	15	INVENTORY	DB INVENTORY.15	DB INVENTORY.15S
	16	STORES	DB STORES.16	DB STORES.16S
	17	PROGRAM	DB PROGRAM.17	DB PROGRAM.17S
	18A	PROMOTE	—	DB PROMOTE.18S
	18B	STOCK	—	DB STOCK.18S
DB – 4	19	INVENTORY	DB INVENTORY.19	DB INVENTORY.19S
	20	STOCK	DB STOCK.20	DB STOCK.20S
	21	STORES	DB STORES.21	DB STORES.21S
	22	INVENTORY	DB INVENTORY.22	DB INVENTORY.22S
	23	PROGRAM	DB PROGRAM.23	DB PROGRAM.23S
	24	PROMOTE	DB PROMOTE.24	DB PROMOTE.24S
	25	STOCK	DB STOCK.25	DB STOCK.25S
	26	TEACHER	—	DB TEACHER.26S
Integration				
	1	DIVE	IN DIVE.1	
		MEMO	IN MEMO.1	
		NYC	IN NYC.1	
	2	MEMO	IN MEMO.2	
		DIVE	IN DIVE.2	
		NYC	IN NYC.2	
		HOTELS	—	IN HOTELS.2S
	3	REPORT	IN REPORT.3	
		SALES	IN SALES.3	
		REPSALES	—	IN REPSALES.3S
	4	FINER FUNDS	IN FINER FUNDS.4	IN.FINER INVEST.4S
	5	BONUS2	IN BONUS2.5	
		GOOD	IN GOOD.5	
		GOODBAR	—	IN GOODBAR.5S
	6	TELECOPY	IN TELECOPY.6	
		TELEMEMBER	—	IN TELEMEMBER.6S
	7	EXAM	IN EXAM.7	
		EXAM REP 3	—	IN EXAM REP 3.7S

Lesson	Exercise	Filename	On Disk As	Solution File
Integration (*continued*)				
		EXAM 4	—	IN EXAM 4.7S
		EXAM REP 4	—	IN EXAM REP 4.7S
	8	INVENTORY	IN INVENTORY.8	
		DB INVENTORY	—	IN DB INVENTORY.8S
	9	SOCK	IN SOCK.9	
		MEMBER	IN MEMBER.9	
		SPORTS	—	IN SPORTS.9S
	10	JETS	IN JETS.10	
			IN STUDENT.10	
		ACCEPT	—	IN ACCEPT.10S
	11	BLOCK	IN BLOCK.11	IN SELF.11S
		SELF	—	
	12	ACCEPT	IN ACCEPT.12	IN ACCEPT.12S
	13	SPORTS	IN SPORTS.13	IN SPORTS.13S
	14	LH COMM	—	IN LH COMM.14S
		PROMOTE	IN PROMOTE.14	IN PROMOTE.14S
		PROMOTE 2	—	IN PROMOTE 2.14S
Wizards and Templates				
	1	LH GLOBAL	—	WW LH GLOBAL.1S
		DIVING	WW DIVING.1	
		LH DIVE	—	WW LHDIVE.1S
	2	ADDRESS BOOK	—	WW ADDRESS BOOK.2S
		SAMPLE ADDRESS BOOK	—	
	3	COMPUTER LITERACY PER. 1	—	WW COMPUTER LITERACY PER 1.3S
	4	BROCHURE	—	WW BROCHURE.4S
	5	PAPER COMPANY	—	WW PAPER COMPANY.5S
		COVER LETTER	—	WW COVER LETTER.5S
Communications				
	3	ETIQUETTE	CO ETIQUETTE.3	
	5	COMM SUMMARY	—	COMM SUMMARY.5S

Word Processor

WP Exercise File Name	Exercise	Page
APPLY	7	26
	12	41
BASEBALL	46	144
BATS	30	95
BLOCK	8	30
	13	43
BULLETIN	22	70
	26	85
BULLETIN BOARD	26	85
	31	98
COMPANY	16	50
COOK	42	131
COURSES	45	141
COVER	50	155
CYBERNEWS	56	177
DELIVERY	48	149
DIVE	6	22
	17	54
	28	90
	40	126
DIVE 2	40	126
DIVING	40	126
ETIQUETTE	41	129
	56	177
GOOD	9	32
	14	45
HAPPY	54	169
INDENT	23	75
	25	82
INFO	36	114
JETS	57	180
MEMO	19	62
	27	87
MEMONEWS	18	58
	20	64
NEWS	15	47
NHS	58	182
NYC	33	105
OFFICER	47	147
	49	152
PACK	53	165
PRESIDENTS	43	136

WP Exercise File Name	Exercise	Page
PACK	53	165
PRESIDENTS	43	136
PREVIEW	34	108
	39	124
REPORT	21	66
RESUME	29	93
SCORPION	35	111
	35	111
SOCK	52	162
STUDY	24	78
	32	102
TABLE OF CONTENTS	44	138
TELECOPY	55	173
UP AND DOWN	38	121
VOYAGE	37	118
WARE	4	18
	10	35
WORKS	5	19
	11	38
WORLD ONLINE	51	159

Spreadsheet

SS Exercise File Name	Exercise	Page
BONUS	16	220
	19	226
	27	248
	33	268
BUSINESS COURSES	36	276
COMM	18	223
	26	246
COMM1	26	246
COMM2	26	246
DAILY	2	190
	11	210
EXAM	13	213
	25	243
FINER FUNDS	34	271
FOLIO	30	255
GROW	35	274
HOME	21	232
HS	31	261

SS Exercise File Name	Exercise	Page
	32	265
PLAY	20	228
PLAY 2	20	228
PRICE	6	198
	9	206
REPAIR	5	196
REPAIR	8	202
SALARY	4	195
	10	207
	24	240
	29	254
SALARY 2	29	254
SALARY COMPARE	24	241
SALES	3	192
	14	214
TESTSUM	17	222
UNIVERSITY	12	211
VIDEO	23	236
WAGES	7	199
WOOD	15	217
	28	251
ZONE	22	235

Database

DB Exercise File Name	Exercise	Page
INVENTORY	4	285
	12	308
	12	310
	15	321
	19	335
	22	345
MEMBER	2	284
	6	289
	9	301
	13	315
PROGRAM	5	286
	12	311
	17	327
	23	352
PROMOTE	18	328
	24	358
STOCK	18	332
	20	336
	25	361
STORES	3	285
	8	298
	11	307

DB Exercise File Name	Exercise	Page
	14	320
	16	325
	21	340
STUDENT	1	282
	7	294
	10	305
TEACHER	26	364

Integration

IN Exercise File Name	Exercise	Page
ACCEPT	10	400
	12	406
BLOCK	11	403
BONUS2	5	383
DIVE	1	375
	2	376
EXAM	7	388
EXAM REP 3	7	388
EXAM REP 4	7	388
EXAM 4	7	388
FINER FUNDS	4	380
FINER INVEST	4	381
GOOD	5	383
GOODBAR	5	383
HOTELS	2	377
INVENTORY	8	391
	8	391
JETS	10	400
LH COMM	14	411
MEMBER	9	396
MEMO	1	375
	2	376
NYC	1	375
	2	376
PROMOTE	14	411
PROMOTE 2	14	411
REPORT	3	378
REPSALES	3	378
SALES	3	378
SELF	11	403
SOCK	9	396
SOCK.9	9	396
SPORTS	9	396
	13	409
TELECOPY	6	384
TELEMEMBER	6	385

Wizards and Templates

WW Exercise File Name	Exercise	Page
DIVING	1	416
LHDIVE	1	416
SAMPLE ADDRESS BOOK	2	419
ADDRESS BOOK	2	419
COMPUTER LITERACY PER. 1	3	422
BROCHURE	4	423
PAPER COMPANY	5	425
COVER LETTER	5	426

Communications

WW Exercise File Name	Exercise	Page
INFO	3	442
ETIQUETTE	3	443
COMM SUMMARY	5	448

About Microsoft® Works 4.0 for Windows 95

Microsoft® Works 4.0 for Windows® 95 is an **integrated program** that incorporates a number of tools, or applications, in one package. These tools can be used separately or they can be used together to produce professional-looking documents.

The information created in one tool can be shared with the other tools. For instance, a spreadsheet can be incorporated into a memo that was created in the Word Processor. Such sharing is called **integration**. In addition, you can enhance the appearance of the memo by adding pictures, borders and patterns. The four major tools in Microsoft Works are:

Word Processor

You use this tool to create letters, memos and other typed documents. Word processing documents can be enhanced by integrating information from other tools or by adding graphic elements to improve their appearance and emphasize your message.

Spreadsheet

Spreadsheets are worksheets that let you add, subtract, multiply, divide and much more. In this tool, you can create financial records for both personal and business use. The appearance of all spreadsheets can be enhanced by adding a variety of graphic elements, such as borders and shading. In addition, you can present your spreadsheet data graphically by creating charts using the Works charting feature.

Database

Databases are like huge filing cabinets that organize your information so you can find it more easily. For example, you can create address lists and arrange them in alphabetical or numerical order and then create labels and form letters using the lists. You can calculate values in the Database tool, search for specific information and report it using the tool's reporting capabilities, which allow you to sort, group and present the data with a variety of visual enhancements.

Communications

The Communications tool lets you connect your computer to the outside world. To use this feature, you need a modem, a device that lets you communicate with other computers and connect to on-line information services and bulletin boards.

How to Use this Book

Each exercise contains four parts:

Notes	explain the Microsoft Works concept and application being introduced.
Exercise Directions	tell how to complete the exercise.
Exercise	lets you apply the new concept.
Mouse and Keystroke Procedures	outline the mouse actions or keystrokes necessary to complete the exercise.

✓ NOTE: *Keystrokes and mouse actions are provided only when a new concept is being introduced. Therefore, if you forget the mouse/keystroke procedures necessary to complete a task, you can use the Help feature or the book's index to find the procedures.*

Before you begin working on the exercises in Lesson 1 of the Word Processor tool, read the Works Basics section that follows this introduction. Works Basics introduces the keyboard and mouse, tells you how to set started with Works and provides other preliminary information.

Universal Features

Toolbars, commands, keystrokes and menus are similar in each application. Some functions operate the same way in all the different tools. We call these operations Universal Features. They are indicated by a globe graphic 🌐 when introduced in each section.

The Data and Solutions Disks

Data and solutions disks may be purchased separately from DDC Publishing. You may use the data files on the data disk to complete an exercise without keyboarding lengthy text or data. However, exercise directions are given for both data disk and non-data disk users. Exercise directions will include a keyboard icon to direct non-data disk users as well as a disk icon to direct data disk users. For example, a typical direction might read: Open ⌨ **BLOCK**, or open 💾 **WP BLOCK.3.**

In order to maintain the integrity of the data disk, make a backup copy.

The solutions disk may be used to compare your work with the final version or solution on disk.

A directory of data disk and solutions disk files by exercise are listed in the Log of Exercises, and an alphabetical list of files is given in the Directory of Documents.

The Teachers' Manual

While this text can be used as a self-paced learning book, a comprehensive teachers' manual is available, containing the following:

- Lesson objectives
- Exercise objectives
- Related vocabulary
- Points to emphasize
- Exercise settings
- Solutions

Works Basics

Works Basics

■ The Keyboard ■ The Mouse ■ Universal Features ■ Buttons
■ Access Microsoft Works for Windows ■ Mouse and Keyboard Methods ■ Works Task Launcher

NOTES:

The Keyboard

In addition to the alphanumeric keys found on typewriters, computers contain:

■ **Function Keys** (F1 through F12) that perform special functions and are located across the top of an enhanced keyboard and on the side of a regular keyboard.

> ✓ NOTE: An enhanced keyboard has 12 function keys while a regular keyboard has 10.

■ **Modifier Keys** (two each: Shift, Alt, and Ctrl) that are used with other keys to select certain commands. To use a modifier key with another key, you must hold down the modifier key while you tap the other key.

■ **Numeric Keys** that allow you to enter numbers quickly when the Num Lock key (located above the 7/Home key) is pressed. When Num Lock is OFF, the arrow keys and other application keys found on the numbers (Home, PgUp, End, PgDn) are activated.

■ **Escape (Esc) Key** is used to cancel some commands.

■ **Enter Keys** (most keyboards have two) that are used to move the insertion point to the next line or may be used to complete a command.

■ **Insertion Point Movement Keys** (Arrows, Home, End, Page Up, Page Down) that move the insertion point (the blinking marker indicating where the next character keyed will appear) through the text in the direction indicated by the key.

The Mouse

■ When the **mouse** is rolled on the tabletop, a corresponding movement of the mouse pointer occurs on screen. The mouse pointer will not move, however, if the mouse is lifted up and placed back on the tabletop.

■ The mouse pointer changes its shape to signal different functions. When the mouse is pointing anywhere on the document window screen, it looks like an "I" ($\mathcal{I}$); but when the mouse is pointing to a menu item or border area, it changes to an arrow ( ).

Function Keys   Enter Key

Cursor Keys   Numeric Keypad

The following mouse terms and corresponding actions will be used throughout the book:

TERM	ACTION
Point	Roll the mouse in any direction until the pointer is on a specific item.
Click	Quickly press and release the mouse button. Use the *left* mouse button unless otherwise instructed.
Right-click	Quickly press and release the right mouse button.
Double-click	Press and release the mouse button twice in rapid succession.
Drag	Press and hold down the mouse button while rolling the mouse.

Below is a list of mouse pointer shapes and uses you may encounter:

SHAPE	DESCRIPTION
[I]	Appears when mouse pointer is placed within document text. Indicates where you will begin typing. This shape is referred to as the I beam.
[⇖]	Appears in menus, the Toolbar and the Ruler bar. Selects a menu item, clicks a button, places or removes tabs or drags tabs to new positions. Also used for dragging margins or indent symbols to new locations or for moving graphic images in documents.
[⧖]	Appears when you are requested to wait for an operation to be completed before continuing.
[⇗]	Appears when you move the pointer into the selection bar along the left edge of the screen or the left edge of a table. Selects (highlights) a line, paragraph or the whole document.
[⬌⬍]	Appears when the pointer is placed on the line separating columns in a spreadsheet or database. Changes column widths and heights.
[⬌]	One of these shapes appears when the pointer is on a window border. Changes the size of the window by dragging.
[RESIZE]	Used when trying to resize a linked or embedded object. Click the object and drag when the resize cue appears.

Universal Features

There are a number of features in Microsoft Works that operate exactly the same way in the Word Processor, Spreadsheet, Database and Communications tools. Because of this uniformity, we have chosen to call these operations **Universal Features.** They will be noted with a globe graphic 🌐 when they are introduced in each section. These **Universal Features** are listed below:

- Accessing Help
- Closing a file
- Creating a file
- Dialing a telephone number
- Exiting Works
- Opening an existing file
- Previewing a document
- Saving procedures
- Viewing two parts of a file at once
- Scrolling
- Selecting menu/submenu items

Buttons

Buttons (also known as **icons**) are graphic images representing a command or function that can be accessed when clicked with the mouse.

Access Microsoft Works for Windows

You can use the mouse or the keyboard to operate in Microsoft Works.

At the Windows 95 Screen

MOUSE USERS	KEYBOARD USERS
Click Start	Ctrl+Esc
Click Programs	P

The right arrow after Programs signifies that another menu will open.

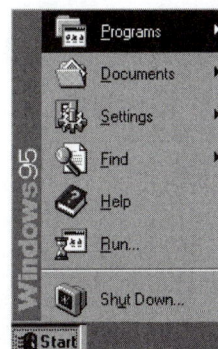

■ To Enter Microsoft Works 4.0 Folder:

MOUSE USERS	KEYBOARD USERS
Click Microsoft Works 4.0 icon.	Use down arrow to access Works 4.0 icon.

🖿 Accessories ▶	🖳 MS-DOS Prompt
🖿 Aldus ▶	📑 The Microsoft Network
🖿 America Online ▶	💻 Windows Explorer
🖿 Applications ▶	
🖿 C-2 Office Gear ▶	
🖿 Corel5 ▶	
🖿 Cwc ▶	
🖿 DesignCAD 2-D for Windows ▶	
🖿 Labels PLUS! ▶	
🖿 Lotus Applications ▶	Microsoft Works
🖿 Microsoft Office ▶	4.0 folder icon
🖿 Microsoft Publisher 2.0 ▶	
🖿 Microsoft Works 4.0 ▶	
🖿 Microsoft Works for Windows ▶	
🖿 Norton AntiVirus ▶	
🖿 Paint Shop Pro ▶	
🖿 Psp ▶	
🖿 Startup ▶	
🖿 Verbatim Sampler ▶	
🖿 WinFax PRO 3 ▶	
🖿 WPWin 6.1 ▶	

■ To Open Microsoft Works 4.0:

MOUSE USERS	KEYBOARD USERS
Double click Microsoft Works program icon.	Use right arrow to access Works 4.0 icon.

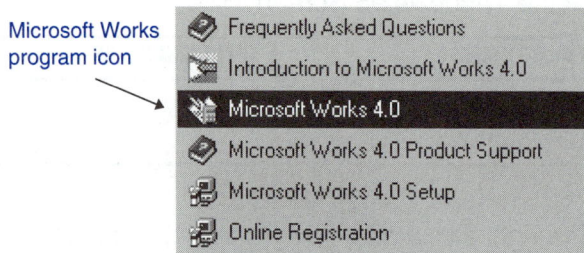

Microsoft Works program icon

🔍	Frequently Asked Questions
📄	Introduction to Microsoft Works 4.0
📝	Microsoft Works 4.0
📄	Microsoft Works 4.0 Product Support
🖥	Microsoft Works 4.0 Setup
🖥	Online Registration

■ If this is the first time you are using Works, the Welcome to Microsoft Works screen appears. It is advisable to go through this ten-minute introduction. If you wish to skip the introduction, click Done. The introduction can be accessed at a later time by choosing it from the Help menu.

Works Task Launcher

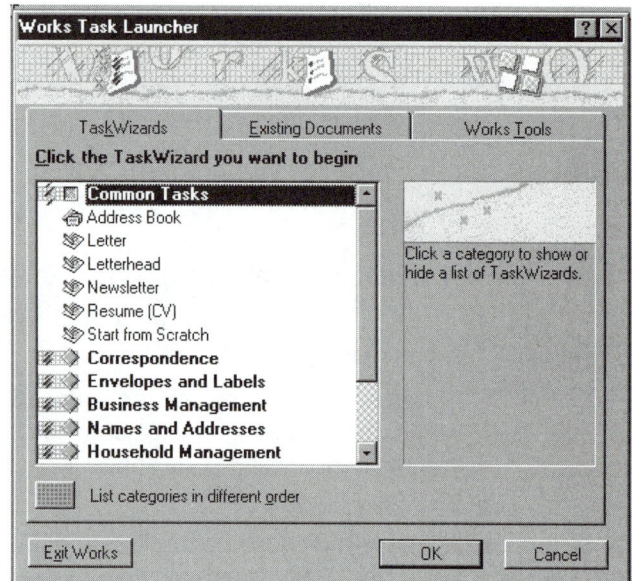

```
Works Task Launcher                              [?][X]

   TaskWizards    │  Existing Documents  │  Works Tools
Click the TaskWizard you want to begin
┌──────────────────────────────┐  ┌──────────────┐
│ 📋 Common Tasks            ▲ │  │              │
│   📕 Address Book            │  │              │
│   📝 Letter                  │  │ Click a category to show or │
│   📝 Letterhead              │  │ hide a list of TaskWizards. │
│   📝 Newsletter              │  │              │
│   📝 Resume (CV)             │  │              │
│   📝 Start from Scratch      │  └──────────────┘
│ ⚙ Correspondence            │
│ ⚙ Envelopes and Labels      │
│ ⚙ Business Management       │
│ ⚙ Names and Addresses       │
│ ⚙ Household Management    ▼ │
└──────────────────────────────┘
   ▦   List categories in different order

  Exit Works              │   OK   │  │ Cancel │
```

■ The **Works Task Launcher** provides access to all tools and a variety of options. From this screen you can:

- Click the TaskWizards tab to quickly create a document through a series of guided steps.

- Click the Existing Documents tab to see a list of documents that have been previously created.

- Click the Works Tools tab to open a blank document in either Word Processor, Spreadsheet, Database or Communications.

■ To select an option on this screen, either click the desired option using the mouse, or press the underlined letter in the desired tool icon.

Word Processor

LESSONS 1 - 7

Lesson 1: Create, Save and Print Documents

Lesson 2: Edit Documents

Lesson 3: Text Alignments and Enhancements; Language Tools

Lesson 4: Margins, Indents and Spacing

Lesson 5: Editing and Formatting; Multiple-Page Documents; File Management

Lesson 6: Columns, Tabs and Tables

Lesson 7: Advanced Text Enhancements; Draw; ClipArt

EXERCISE **1**

■ **Access the Word Processor** ■ **Word Processor Screen Parts**
■ **Select Menu Items** ■ **Pull-Down Menus** ■ **Access from Pull-Down Menus** ■ **Exit Works**

NOTES:

Access the Word Processor

■ **To access the Word Processor**: Click the Works Tools tab, click the Word Processor button from the Microsoft Works Task Launcher as shown below:

```
Works Task Launcher                    [?][X]

    TaskWizards    Existing Documents    Works Tools
Click one of the Works tools

  [ ]  Word Processor
       ·Create letters, memos, form letters, and mailing labels

  [ ]  Spreadsheet
       ·Do budgeting and calculations, create charts and graphs

  [ ]  Database
       ·Create address books, lists and reports

  [ ]  Communications
       ·Send and receive documents with your modem

  [Exit Works]              [   OK   ]  [ Cancel ]
```

■ The word processing screen shown at the bottom of this page displays.

Word Processor Screen Parts

■ The following are the screen parts included on every new word processing screen:

• The Title bar, located at the top of the screen, indicates the application window and the name of the program (Microsoft Works). The Title bar for the smaller window indicates the name of the document (Unsaved Document 1). When you create a word processing document, Works automatically labels the document. If it is the first document, Works labels it Unsaved Document 1.

• The Menu bar, located below the application Title bar, contains a group of selections that let you perform most Microsoft Works tasks. Within each main menu item are numerous submenu commands.

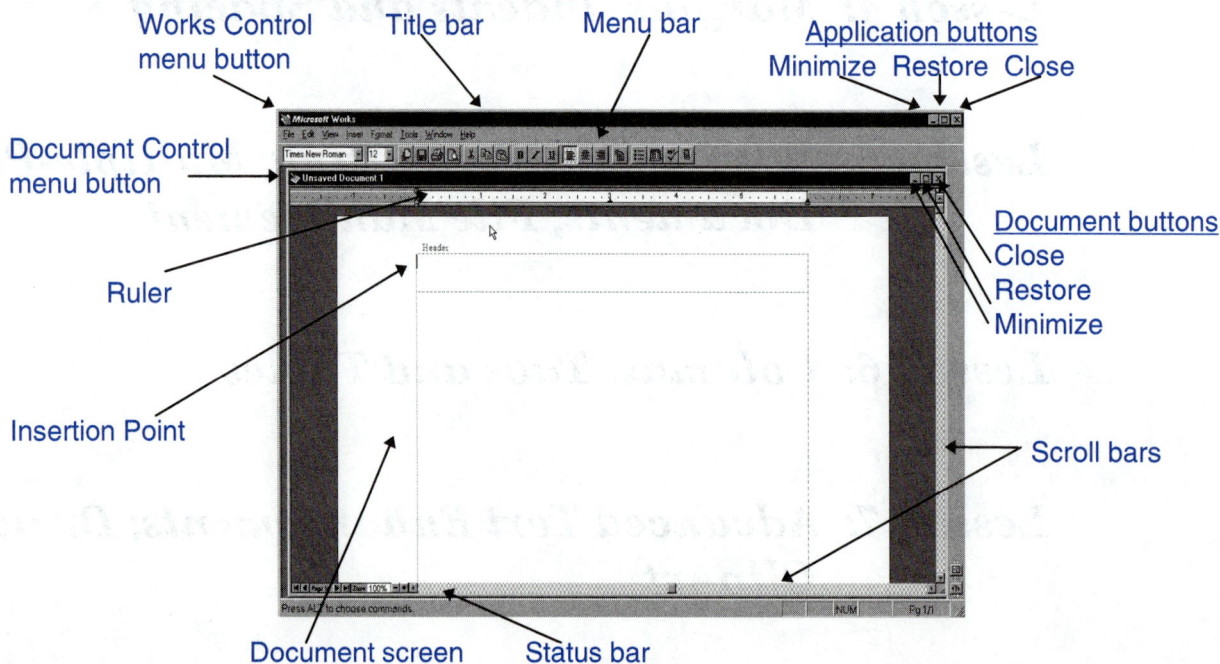

Works Control menu button   Title bar   Menu bar   Application buttons Minimize Restore Close

Document Control menu button

Ruler

Insertion Point

Document buttons Close Restore Minimize

Scroll bars

Document screen   Status bar

- A **Control menu button** is located at the left end of the Title bars. Click the Control menu button on the document Title bar to close the document window and click the Control menu button on the application Title bar to close Microsoft Works. You can also use the **Close button** [X] at the right of the Title bars to close the document or program, respectively.

To close the desired window:

MOUSE USERS	KEYBOARD USERS
To Close a Document Window: Click the X at the top right of the document Title bar or click the Control box at the left of the document Title bar.	Ctrl + F4
To Close Microsoft Works: Click the X at the top right of the application Title bar or click the Control box at the left of the application Title bar.	Alt + F4

- The **minimize** [_], **restore** [⊡] and **maximize** [□] buttons are located at the right end of the Title bars. When you access a new word processing screen, the application Title bar contains the name of the program on the left and the minimize, restore and close buttons on the right. The document Title bar contains the document name on the left and the minimize, maximize and close buttons on the right. Click the minimize button to reduce the window to a task button on the Taskbar. Click the maximize button to make the window as large as possible. Click the restore button on the maximized window to return the window to its previous size. When you restore a maximized window, the restore button is replaced with the maximize button.

  ✓ NOTE: *When a document screen is maximized, there is one Title bar containing both the program and document names. The Menu bar now contains the minimize, restore and close buttons for the document window.*

- The **insertion point** is the blinking marker that appears in the upper left-hand corner of the screen. It indicates where the next character to be keyed appears.

- The **Toolbar**, located below the menu bar, contains buttons (which have symbols or graphic images on them representing a command or function) that execute functions. The Toolbar is accessible only with the mouse. Use the Toolbar as a shortcut to execute a command.

  ✓ NOTE: *Microsoft Works lets you customize your Toolbar with those features you use most often by adding and/or rearranging the buttons. Customizing the Toolbar is covered In Exercise 5.*

You can hide or display the Toolbar to make more room on your screen.

When you point to a button on the Toolbar, and hold the mouse still, an explanation of the button's function is displayed.

The Toolbar buttons will be explained as they are introduced in the lessons.

- The **Ruler bar**, located beneath the Toolbar, displays the margins, indents and tab settings. Above the ruler and to the left of the Toolbar, you will find the font and font size display. The font and font size at the insertion point are displayed.

- The **document screen**, or **text area**, is the large white part of the screen on which you create and edit your documents.

- The **Status bar**, located below the text area at the bottom of the screen, gives page location in the document, the zoom factor, menu commands, keys that are locked and information for each tool. It also indicates whether you are working in Insert or Overtype mode.

  ✓ NOTE: *When text is typed in Insert mode, it advances to the right of the insertion point. When text is typed in Overtype mode, it replaces existing text.*

- The **Scroll bars** appear along the right side of the window (vertical scroll bar) and across the bottom of the window (horizontal scroll bar). They allow you to see parts of the document that are not currently visible on the screen.

Select Menu Items

- You may use the keyboard, the mouse or a combination of both to select menu items. Keyboard shortcut keys may also be used to accomplish tasks.

  To access a menu:

  Use the mouse to point to a menu item and click once.

  OR

  Press Alt + underlined letter to choose a menu and make a selection.

  OR

  Click a button on the Toolbar.

  OR

  Press keyboard shortcut keys.

Pull-Down Menus

- Once a main menu item is accessed, a pull-down menu appears listing additional options.

FILE MENU

File	
New...	Ctrl+N
Open...	Ctrl+O
Close	Ctrl+W
Save	Ctrl+S
Save As...	
Page Setup...	
Print Preview	
Print...	Ctrl+P
Send...	
Exit Works	

Access Commands from Pull-Down Menus

- As with accessing main menus, there are a number of ways to issue a command in a pull-down menu. You can:

  Use the mouse to point to the item and click once.

OR

Press the underlined letter.

OR

Press the keyboard shortcut keys shown to th right of word commands.

- Procedures for completing a task will be illustrated as follows throughout this text:

EXIT MICROSOFT WORKS

Quick keys → *ALT + F4*

Mouse actions
1. Click **File** .... [Alt]+[F]   Key-
2. Click **Exit Works** .... [X]   stroke

- Mouse actions are illustrated on the left.

- Keyboard commands are illustrated on the right.

- Keyboard shortcut keys are illustrated below the heading.

- You may use whichever method you find most convenient.

Exit Works

- It is important to exit the program properly. This will insure that you have the opportunity to save or update documents that might still be active in the Works program.

- Again, there are a number of ways to exit Microsoft Works:

  Select Exit from the File menu.

  OR

  Double-click the Control menu button.

  OR

  Click the Close button at the right of the Title bar.

  OR

  Click the Control menu button, then select Close.

  OR

  Press Alt+F4.

EXERCISE DIRECTIONS:

. Click the Word Processor icon from the Works Task Launcher Tools screen.

. Roll the mouse on the tabletop (or mousepad) up, down, left and right.

. Point to File and click once (or press Alt+F) to select this menu item.
Note the selections on the pull-down menu.

. Click off the menu (or press ESC) to close the File menu.

. Point to Edit and click once (or press Alt+E) to select this menu item.
Note the selections on the pull-down menu.

. Press right arrow twice to close Edit menu and open Insert menu.
Note the selections on the pull-down menu.

. Click off the menu (or press ESC to close the Insert menu).

8. Select each remaining Menu bar item using any method.
Note the drop-down selections on each.

9. **Hide the Toolbar:**

a. Select View from the Menu bar.
Note the selections on the pull-down menu.

b. Click on Toolbar option.
Note Toolbar is hidden.

10. **Display the Toolbar:**

a. Select View from the Menu bar.

b. Click on Toolbar option.
Note Toolbar is displayed.

c. Point to each Toolbar button.
Note the explanations under each button.

11. Exit the Microsoft Works program.

NOTE: *Mouse action procedures are indicated on the left; keyboard procedures are indicated on the right; shortcut keys (if any) are indicated below title. You may use the mouse, the keystrokes, or a combination of both.*

REATE A NEW WORD ROCESSING DOCUMENT

FROM WORKS TASK LAUNCHER–

lick **Word Processor** .... `Alt` + `W`

🌐 SELECT A MENU ITEM

1. Click menu item .. `Alt` + *underlined letter*
2. Click submenu item ..... *underlined letter*

🌐 CLOSE A MENU

Click off the menu .... `Alt` or `Esc`

HIDE TOOLBAR

1. Click **View** .... `Alt` + `V`
2. Click **Toolbar** .... `T`

   ✓*NOTE:* *To display Toolbar, repeat procedure.*

🌐 EXIT MICROSOFT WORKS

Alt + F4

1. Click **File** .... `Alt` + `F`
2. Click **Exit Works** .... `X`

OR

1. Click Microsoft Works **Control-menu button** .... 🗔
2. Click **Close** .... `C`

OR

Click Works **Close button** .... `X`

EXERCISE **2**

■ **Select Menu and Submenu Items** ■ **Change View Modes**

NOTES:

Select Menu and Submenu Items

■ In Exercise 1, you selected Menu bar items. Once selected, each menu item provided a **pull-down submenu**.

■ Note the pull-down menu which appears when <u>V</u>iew is selected:

View
Normal
✔ Page Layout
✔ Toolbar
✔ Ruler
All Characters
Header
Footer
Footnotes
Zoom...

■ Some options are dimmed, while others appear black. **Dimmed options** are not available for selection at this time, while black options are.

■ A **check mark** next to a pull-down item means that the option is currently selected.

■ An item followed by an **ellipsis** (...) opens a dialog box.

■ A **dialog box** requires you to provide additional information to complete a task.

■ Note the dialog boxes at right. The Open dialog box (Illustration A) appears after <u>O</u>pen is selected from the <u>F</u>ile menu; the Font dialog box (Illustration B) appears after <u>F</u>ont and Style is selected from the F<u>o</u>rmat menu.

ILLUSTRATION A

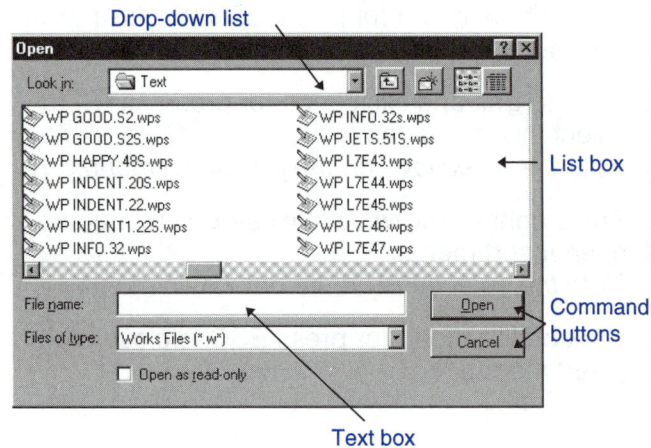

Drop-down list

List box

Command buttons

Text box

ILLUSTRATION B

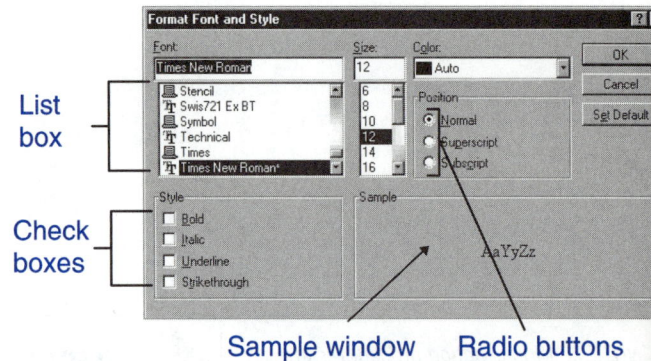

List box

Check boxes

Sample window   Radio buttons

■ A dialog box contains different ways to ask you for information. The following appear in Illustration A:

• A text box is a location where you key in information.

• A command button performs an action or closes the dialog box without performing the action. One button is preselected and is indicated by a dark border. Notice Open is th preselected action in Illustration A above.

- A list box displays a list of selections. Use the up/down arrows to scroll through the list.

- A **drop-down** list is marked with a down arrow. Clicking the arrow causes a short list of options to appear. Choose one of the options on the list.

The following appear in Illustration B:

- A **radio button** is a round button which is part of a group of options. Only one option in the group may be selected at a time.

- A **check box** is a small square box where options may be selected or deselected. An "X" in the box indicates the option is selected.

- A **sample window** shows the effect of a selected item.

To move around a dialog box:

Use the Tab key

OR

Use Shift+Tab to move backwards.

To select an item:

- Press the underlined letter of an item.

  ✓ NOTE: Press Alt+underlined letter to select
              the command button.

- Click the item, then click OK.

OR

Tab to the item, then press the Enter key.

**To exit a dialog box
without making a selection:**

Click cancel.

OR

Press Esc.

Change View Modes

- Microsoft Works gives you the option of displaying your screen in two different view modes. You access the following views by clicking the View menu.

Page Layout View
This is the default view. This view shows how your document will look when it is printed. It displays the headers, footers and columns as well as all formatting and inserted objects.

Normal View
Normal view will display your document with formatting and inserted objects; however, it may not display the document as it will look when it is printed. Headers and footers will display only on the first page.

VIEW MENU

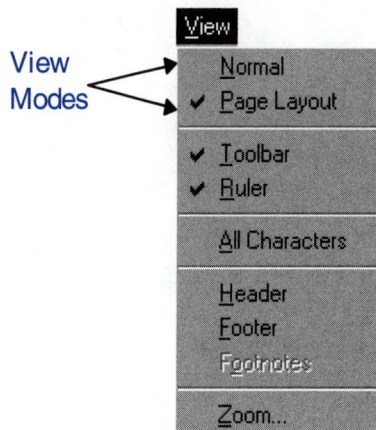

View
Modes

In this exercise, you will create a new document, explore various options and exit Works.

EXERCISE DIRECTIONS:

1. Create a new document for the Word Processor with the Works Task Launcher.

2. Type your name at the insertion point.

3. Select <u>V</u>iew from the Menu bar.

4. Change your display view to <u>N</u>ormal view.

   Note the difference from <u>P</u>age Layout view.

5. Select <u>V</u>iew from the Menu bar and return to <u>P</u>age Layout view.

6. Select <u>V</u>iew from the Menu bar.

7. Display the Tool<u>b</u>ar.
   - ✔ *NOTE:* *If it is already displayed, just note the checkmark. This indicates that the option has been selected.*

8. Select <u>F</u>ile from the Menu bar.

9. Select <u>P</u>rint.
   - ✔ *NOTE:* *A first-time help screen will appear if the Print command has never been previously selected.*

10. Note the dialog box selections. Use the Tab key to move around the dialog box, or click to select an option.

11. Exit the Print dialog box (click Cancel or press Esc).

12. Select <u>F</u>ormat from the Menu bar.

13. Choose <u>F</u>ont and Style.

14. Click any item in the Font Face List other than the one currently highlighted.
    Note the new display in the Sample window.

15. Exit the Font box without making changes (click Cancel or press Escape).

16. Exit Microsoft Works (click <u>F</u>ile, click E<u>x</u>it Works).

CHANGE VIEW MODES

1. Click **<u>V</u>iew** .... `Alt`+`V`
2. Click desired mode:

   Normal .... `N`

   <u>P</u>age Layout View .... `P`

EXERCISE **3**

■ **Help** ■ **Zoom Feature**

NOTES:

Help

■ The **Help** feature displays information about a command, or presents the proper actions or keystrokes to complete a task. There are two Help areas: the main Help screen and the Help window.

■ The main Help screen may be accessed by clicking Help on the Menu bar or by pressing Alt+H. The following pull-down menu options will assist you.

> Help
> Contents...
> Index...
>
> Introduction to Works...
> How to use Help
> Show Help
> Launch Works Forum
>
> About Microsoft Works

Contents
Allows you to choose from a list of help topics that are specific for each tool. Click the desired tool to access the folders containing the information. A folder icon next to the topic indicates there are additional related topics. Click a folder icon to get the desired information or to access a listing of more detailed folders.

Index
Offers a listing of all Help topics. Click on the desired topic to display additional folders or the information you desire. If you don't see the topic you want, you can enter a word or phrase in the text box, and the Help feature will search it for you.

Introduction to Works
Provides a ten-minute tutorial that covers the basic elements as well as new features in the Works 4.0 program.

How to use Help
Gives information on how the Help system works.

Hide Help
Closes the Help screen. When Help is hidden, the option changes to Show Help.

Launch Works Forum
Connects you to the Works Forum which is a bulletin board you can use when you subscribe to the Microsoft Network. This bulletin board offers information, software and the exchange of ideas with other Works users.

About Microsoft Works
Provides system status information.

■ The Help window is automatically displayed to the right of your document window when you create a new document.
> ✓ NOTE: *This Help screen can be reduced to an icon to provide more room for the document window.*

■ The information displayed in the Help window is specific to the tool being used (Word Processor, Spreadsheet, Database, Communications). The active word processing document and the related Help screen are shown on the next page in Illustration 1.

ILLUSTRATION 1

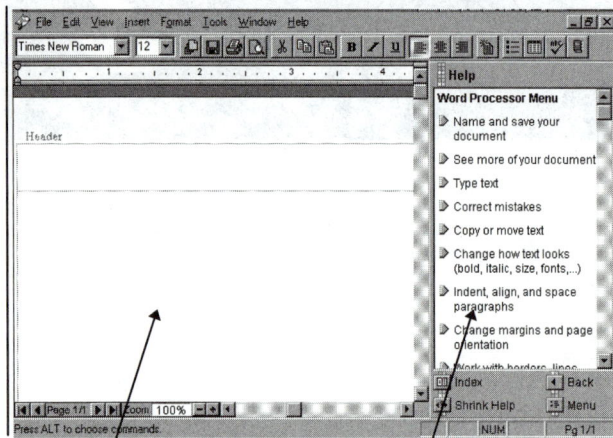

Document Window   Help screen

- This Help feature leads you through a progression of Help windows to get to the specific instructions you need. Refer to Illustrations 2 and 3 below:

ILLUSTRATION 2   ILLUSTRATION 3

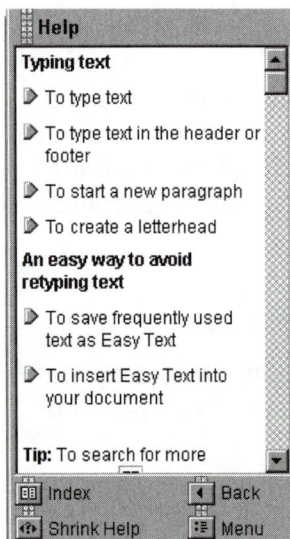

- Click the task you wish to accomplish in Illustration 1.
- Click the topic you need information for in Illustration 2.
- Follow the step-by-step instructions in Illustration 3.
  - ✓ NOTE: You can scroll through the Help window to access additional information.

- The **More Info** tab provides access to the Overview feature, background information, troubleshooting and other related information.

- The four icons on the bottom of the Help window allow you to:
  - access the Index of Works Help topics.
  - access the previous Help window.
  - shrink the Help window.
  - access the current tool's help menu.

- If you do not wish to have the Help window open, you can close it by clicking on the Shrink Help icon located at the bottom of the Help window. Doing this reduces the Help window to a vertical bar located to the right of the document window. Click the icon again to restore it.

- Help may also be accessed from a dialog box. To display information related directly to the dialog box options, click the question mark in the upper-right corner of the dialog box and then click a button or a setting in the dialog box.

- Works also has a first-time help feature. When a task is performed for the first time, a help screen displays. This feature can be turned off by accessing Options in the Tools menu, selecting the View tab and deselecting Show first-time help.

- To exit Help:

  Click Close.

  OR

  Press ESC.

  OR

  Click Help, click Hide Help.

  - ✓ NOTE: Choosing Hide Help also closes out the Help window to the right of your document window.

🌐 Zoom Feature

- You can increase or decrease the size of the active document window using the Zoom feature on the Status bar. You can click the minus or plus sign to increase or decrease the magnification, or you can choose a magnification option from the pop-up list shown on the next page.

```
Whole Page
Page Width
Margin Width
50%
70%
100%
150%
200%
400%
Custom
```
Zoom 100% − + ◄

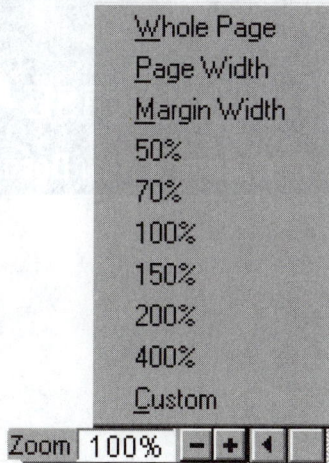

■ You may have only a partial view of your document when using the Help feature. Use the Zoom feature to reduce the document window while working in the Help menu.

> *In this exercise, you will explore the Help feature and practice using the Zoom feature.*

EXERCISE DIRECTIONS:

1. Create a new document for the Word Processor.

2. Select Help from the Menu bar.

3. Select Contents.

4. When the pointer becomes a hand, select Word Processor.

5. Select Word Processor basics.

6. Select Get Help.

7. Read through the various Help folders.

8. When finished, close Help Topics window.
   ✓ NOTE: The Word Processor Menu Help screen is at the right.

9. Using the minus sign on the Zoom feature, change the zoom factor to 50%.

10. Click the number in the Zoom box to access the pop-up list.

11. Click Page Width.

12. Repeat to view additional zoom factors.

13. Select File.

14. Select Exit Works.

🌐 **GET HELP**

F1

1. Click **Help** .... Alt + H
2. Click desired help option:
   - **Contents** C
   - **Index** I
   - **Introduction to Works** .... N
   - **How to use Help** .... U
   - **Hide Help** .... H
   - **Launch Works Forum** L
   - **About Microsoft Works** .... A

To shrink the Help window:

   Click **Shrink Help** icon .... 🔳

To close the main Help screen:

   Click **Close** .... Alt + C
   OR
   Press **ESC** .... Esc
   OR
   1. Click **Help** .... Alt + H
   2. Click **Hide Help** .... H

🌐 **ZOOM FEATURE**

   Click minus sign .... −
   to reduce window.
   OR
   Click plus sign .... +
   to increase window.
   OR
   1. Click zoom factor to access pop-up list.
   2. Select desired zoom factor

EXERCISE **4**

■ **Defaults** ■ **Create a New Document** ■ **Close a New Document** ■ **Save a New Document**

NOTES:

Defaults

■ **Defaults** are preset conditions within the program. Settings such as margins, tabs, line spacing, typestyle, type size and text alignment are automatically set by Microsoft Works.

- **Margins** are set at 1.25" on the left and right, and 1" on the top and bottom. (Microsoft Works assumes you are working on a standard 8.5" x 11" sheet of paper.)

- **Tabs** are set 0.5" apart.

- **Font** is set to Times or Courier, depending on your printer.

  ✓ *NOTE: The fonts and type sizes available are dependent on your printer.*

- **Type size** is set to 12 point.

- **Text alignment** is set to left.

■ Defaults may be changed at any time, and as many times as desired, throughout a document.

Create a New Document

■ When you first open Works, the Works Task Launcher dialog box appears. There are three tabs or areas within the Task Launcher. Any of the tools can be opened at this point. To begin a new word processing document, you need to click on the Works Tools tab and then click on Word Processor. A tool can be accessed by using the mouse, by pressing the underlined letter or by tabbing to the icon and pressing Enter. A clean screen will then appear.

■ Page Layout is the default view mode and the header and footer text boxes are displayed.

■ Headers and footers will be covered in a later lesson.

■ Immediately under the header text box you will see the flashing insertion point. You can begin typing your text at the insertion point.

■ As text is typed, it automatically advances to the next line. This is called **word wrap**. It is only necessary to use the Enter key at the end of a short line or to begin a new paragraph.

■ Use the Backspace key to correct immediate errors to the left of the insertion point.

Close a New Document

■ Most documents are saved on a disk for future use. However, you do not necessarily need to save all documents. If you want to discard your document, you can click the document close button ☒ at the right side of the Menu bar. Microsoft Works will ask if you want to save your work. Responding No closes your document and brings you to the Works Task Launcher.

■ You may also close your document by selecting Close from the File menu bar. Again, Microsoft Works asks if you wish to save your work. Respond No to close without saving.

Save a New Document

■ When you **save** a document as a new file, you must be aware of where the document is being saved. A disk is like a file cabinet. If you wish to save your file in a particular drawer in the cabinet, you must specify the **folder** (known as directory in former versions of Windows).

- When saving a file, you must indicate the **drive letter** where your disk resides (a, b or c) and/or the folder on the disk where you want your document to be saved. You must also assign a **filename**. For example: C:\MSWORKS\WARE will save your file in drive C (hard drive), folder MSWORKS, under the filename WARE.

  ✓ NOTE: *A **colon** separates drives from folders and filenames; a **backslash** (\) separates folders from subfolders and filenames.*

- Filenames may be written in upper- or lowercase and may contain up to 255 characters. Filenames may also contain spaces. You may include an optional **file extension** of three characters. The extension may be used to further identify your document. The filename and extension are separated by a **period**.

  EXAMPLE: WARE.WPS

  ✓ NOTE: *It is recommended that your filenames be relevant so that you can easily identify your files.*

- The following extensions are used in Works to identify whether the document is a word processing, spreadsheet, database or communications document. The extension is not displayed. The asterisks represent the filename.

• Word Processor	*.wps
• Database	*.wdb
• Spreadsheet	*.wks
• Communications	*.wcm
• All files	*.*
• Works files	*.w*

- You may save a document by selecting <u>S</u>ave from the <u>F</u>ile menu or by clicking the Save button on the Toolbar as shown below:

Save button

Times New Roman 12 | B / U

- When you save a document for the first time, the following dialog box appears:

Access other directories   Up one level

Save As

Save in: Lesswp

Basics
L1e1
l1e2
L1e3
L1e4

File name: L1e4   Save

Save as type: Works WP   Cancel

☐ Create Backup Copy   Template...

Type file name here   Shows the type of file

- After saving your document, you can keep the document on the screen and continue working, or you can clear the screen by selecting **Close** from the <u>F</u>ile menu. If the document was not modified since the last save, Works will automatically return you to the Task Launcher.

- After saving your document for the first time, you can save the document again by selecting <u>S</u>ave from the <u>F</u>ile menu or by clicking the Save button on the Toolbar.

  CAUTION: Save often to prevent losing data.

- Documents may also be saved using the Save As command. This command is generally used when you want to save your document under a different filename or in a different drive/folder.

In this exercise, you will type a paragraph and Zoom it to various magnifications. You will also save and close the document.

EXERCISE DIRECTIONS:

1. Create a new document for the Word Processor.

2. Type the first paragraph of the exercise, allowing the text to word wrap to the next line.

3. Correct only immediate errors using the Backspace key.

4. After completing the document, view the document in the following magnifications using the Zoom feature on the Status bar.
    a. Change to Whole Page.
    b. Change to 200%.
    c. Change to 100%.

5. Close the file without saving it.

6. Begin the exercise again, and complete it. Press the Enter key twice to begin a new paragraph.

7. Save the exercise; name it **WARE**
    ✔ *NOTE:*   *If saving on a disk, indicate the drive where the disk resides before keying the document name.*
    EXAMPLE: A:WARE

    If saving on a hard drive, it is only necessary to key the document filename. The file will be automatically stored in the folder displayed in the Save in text box in the Save or Save As dialog box.

8. Close the document window.

Hardware means the physical equipment being used. The computer, the printer, the monitor, and the keyboard are all considered hardware.

Software is the program that instructs the hardware to perform specific functions. Software is then used to perform either word processing, database, spreadsheet, or other applications.

🌐 CLOSE WITHOUT SAVING

1. Click **File** .... Alt + F
2. Click **Close** C
3. Click **No** .... N

🌐 SAVE AND CONTINUE

Ctrl + S

1. Click **File** .... Alt + F
2. Click **Save** .... S
3. Type document filename .... *filename*
4. Click **Save** .... Alt + S

🌐 SAVE AND CLEAR SCREEN

1. Click **File** .... Alt + F
2. Click **Close** C
3. Click **Yes** .... Y
    ✔ *NOTE:*   *If document was not modified since last save, Works will automatically return you to the Task Launcher.*
4. Type filename .... *filename*
5. Click **Save** .... Enter

🌐 SAVE AND EXIT MICROSOFT WORKS

Alt + F4

1. Click **File** .... Alt + F
2. Click **Exit Works** X
3. Click **Yes** when asked .... Y
    to save changes
4. Type filename .... *filename*
5. Click **Save** .... Enter

EXERCISE 5

■ **The Tab Key** ■ **Customize the Toolbar**

DEFAULT TOOLBAR

Times New Roman | 12 | [toolbar buttons]

NOTES:

The Tab Key

■ Tabs are used to indent the first line of a paragraph. Double-spaced text requires a paragraph indent; single-spaced text can have either indented paragraphs or blocked paragraphs. You will use indented paragraphs for the exercise in this lesson.

■ Tab stops are preset 0.5" apart. Each time the Tab key is pressed, the insertion point advances 0.5".

■ The default tab may be changed at any time and as many times as desired throughout a document. Thus, if you wanted to tab 0.8" instead of 0.5", this could be done. Changing tab settings will be presented in Lesson 6, Exercises 43 and 44.

🌐 Customize the Toolbar

■ The Toolbar comes with a series of **buttons** that are shortcuts for executing a function. Each tool has its own preset series of buttons. Some buttons are universal, while others are specific to the active tool.

■ Because users work differently, Works allows changes to the default Toolbar (shown above) so you can customize it with the functions you most commonly use. You can add, delete or move buttons to make those most often used more accessible.

In this exercise, you will customize the Toolbar to include the Page Layout view and Normal view buttons.

EXERCISE DIRECTIONS:

1. Create a new document for the Word Processor.

2. Begin the exercise at the top of your screen.

3. Type the exercise, allowing the text to word wrap to the next line.
   ✓ NOTE: *Press the Enter key twice to begin a new paragraph and press the Tab key once to indent the paragraph.*

4. Correct only immediate errors using the Backspace key.

5. Click on Tools and click Customize Toolbar.

6. Click View under Categories.

7. Drag the Page Layout and Normal buttons directly onto the Toolbar to the left of the Bold button.

8. Click OK.

9. Click the Normal button 📃.
   Note the difference in the document's appearance.

10. Click on the Page Layout button 📃.
    Note the difference in the document's appearance.

11. Click Tools, Customize Toolbar.

12. Click Reset.

13. Click OK.

14. Save the exercise; name it **WORKS**. Use the **Save** button 💾 on the Toolbar.

Another term for computer programs is "software."   There are many software packages out on the market today. Software is available for just about every interest--business, science, education, as well as for personal use and entertainment.

Microsoft Works is an example of an integrated software package. This program offers you word processing, spreadsheets, database, and communications capabilities. The advantage of this type of program is that the information in each of these applications can be shared, so there is no need to rekey it.

In addition, Microsoft Works for Windows 95 also has many features to enhance the appearance of your work. These features include Word Art, Clip Art and Drawing which add special effects and graphics to your documents.

TAB

1. Press **Tab** .... `Tab`

    Insertion point moves in .5"

2. Type text .... *text*

CUSTOMIZE THE TOOLBAR

1. Click **T**ools .... `Alt`+`T`
2. Click **C**ustomize .... `C`
3. Click C**a**tegories............................. `A`
4. Click desired category:
    - File
    - Edit
    - View
    - Insert
    - Format
    - Tools
    - Window
5. Drag button to or from Toolbar.
6. Click **OK**...................................... `Enter`

RESET THE TOOLBAR

1. Click **T**ools .... `Alt`+`T`
2. Click **C**ustomize Toolbar........ `Alt`+`C`
3. Click **R**eset...................................... `E`
4. Click **OK**................................... `Enter`

EXERCISE **6**

■ **Insertion Point Movements** ■ **Scroll a Document**

NOTES:

■ This exercise will give you more practice keyboarding text that wraps, using the Tab key and saving a document. Be sure to keyboard text exactly as shown since it will be used in a later exercise for additional editing practice.

■ After keyboarding this and the next few exercises, you will practice moving the insertion point through the document. This is an essential skill for correcting errors.

Insertion Point Movements

■ As noted earlier, the **insertion point** is the blinking vertical bar that shows you where you are in your document.

■ You may move the insertion point using the keyboard or the mouse:

Mouse Users:

Move the mouse pointer to where you want to place the insertion point. Then, click the *left* mouse button.

Keyboard Users:

Press the arrow key in the direction you wish the insertion point to move. You may use the arrow keys located on the numeric keypad, or (depending on your keyboard) the separate arrow keys located to the left of the keypad. You can move the insertion point more quickly from one point on the document to another using special key combinations (*see **Insertion Point Movement Keystrokes**, page* 23).

✓ *NOTE:*   *In this exercise, and throughout this book, if keystrokes are separated by a plus (+), hold down the first key as you tap the next key.*

For example, if a keystroke procedure looks like the following:

Ctrl + Page Down

*Hold down the Ctrl key while you **tap** the Page Down key.*

■ The insertion point will only move through text, spaces or codes. The insertion point stops moving when the end or beginning of your document is reached.

Scroll a Document

■ To move the insertion point to a part of the document that does not appear on the screen, you can scroll your document vertically or horizontally. This operation allows you to view text or data that did not previously fit on the display. You can scroll using the mouse or the keyboard.

Scroll bars
Universal for all Microsoft Works tools. They are the gray bars with arrows at the opposite ends that appear on the right side (vertical scroll bar) and bottom (horizontal scroll bar) of the screen. You can move up or down (or side to side) in a document by pointing to a scroll bar or **scroll arrow** and clicking the mouse button.

Vertical scroll bar
Used to move up or down through a document. Clicking near the top of the vertical scroll bar allows you to view screens nearer to the beginning of the document; clicking near the bottom of the scroll bar allows you to view screens nearer to the end of the document.

Vertical scroll box
Located on the vertical scroll bar, it may be dragged up or down to move quickly toward the beginning or end of the document.

Vertical scroll arrows
Located at the top and bottom of the vertical scroll bar. Click to move up or down one line at a time. Clicking and holding the scroll arrows will allow continuous scrolling.

Horizontal scroll bar
Used to move the document left or right on the screen. Clicking near the left side of the horizontal scroll bar allows you to view one screen to the left; clicking on the right side of the scroll bar allows you to view the next screen to the right.

Horizontal scroll box
Located on the horizontal scroll bar, it may be dragged left or right to move more toward the left or right.

Horizontal scroll arrows
Located on the left and right of the horizontal scroll bar. Click to move left or right one column at a time. Clicking and holding the scroll arrows will allow continuous scrolling.

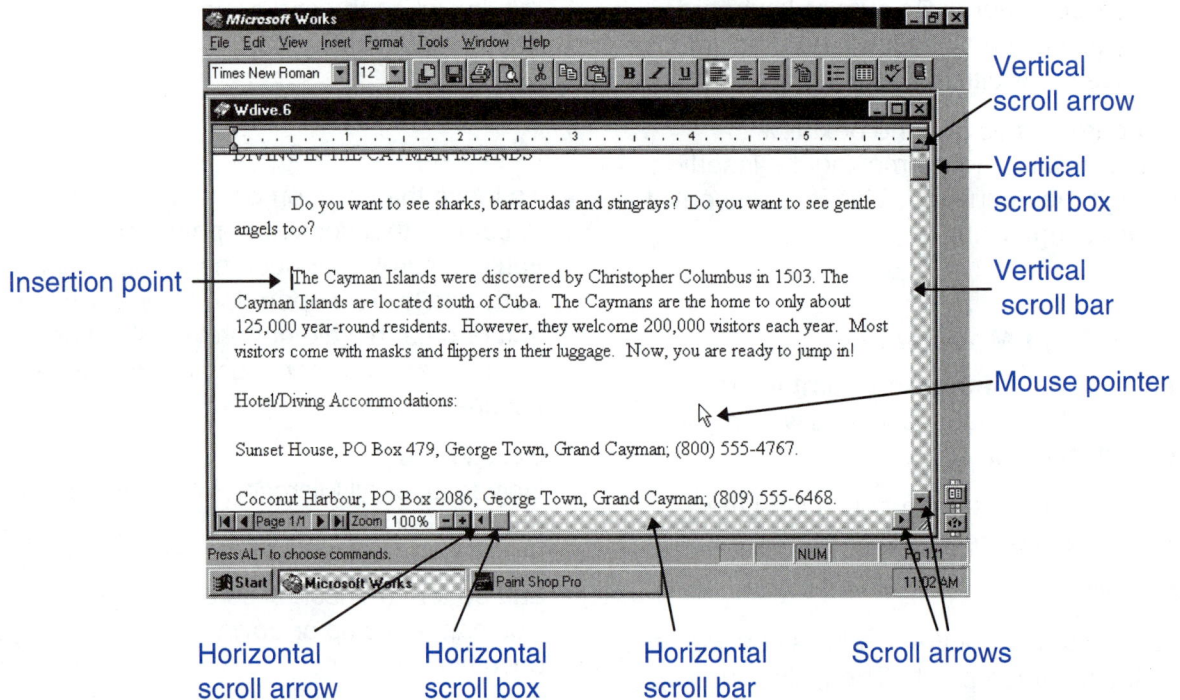

Vertical scroll arrow

Vertical scroll box

Insertion point

Vertical scroll bar

Mouse pointer

Horizontal scroll arrow

Horizontal scroll box

Horizontal scroll bar

Scroll arrows

In this exercise, you will type text with tabs and practice scrolling through a document.

EXERCISE DIRECTIONS:

1. Create a new document for the Word Processor.

2. Begin the exercise at the top of your screen directly under the header section.

3. Keyboard the exercise on the next page *exactly as shown*.

4. Press the Enter key twice between paragraphs and press the Tab key once to indent the first line of the paragraphs.

5. Correct only immediate errors by using the Backspace key.

6. Change the magnification to margin width.

7. After completing the exercise, move the insertion point through the document as follows:
   One line up/down
   One character right/left
   Previous word
   End of screen
   Beginning of line
   End of line

8. Use the vertical scroll arrows to scroll your page up and down.

9. Save the exercise using the Save button 🖫 on the Toolbar; name it **DIVE**.

10. Close the document window.

DIVING VACATIONS
DIVING IN THE CAYMAN ISLANDS

Do you want to see sharks, barracudas and stingrays? Do you want to see gentle angels too?

The Cayman Islands were discovered by Christopher Columbus in 1503. The Cayman Islands are located south of Cuba. The Caymans are the home to only about 125,000 year-round residents. However, they welcome 200,000 visitors each year. Most visitors come with masks and flippers in their luggage. Now you are ready to jump in!

Hotel/Diving Accommodations:

Sunset House, PO Box 479, George Town, Grand Cayman; (809) 555-4767.

Coconut Harbor, PO Box 2086, George Town, Grand Cayman; (809) 555-6468.

SCROLL

Click up, down, left and right arrows on the scroll bar until desired text is in view, or click and drag the scroll box up/down to move the window quickly.

INSERTION POINT MOVEMENT KEYSTROKES

To Move	Press
One character left	←
One character right	→
One line up	↑
One line down	↓
Previous word	Ctrl + ←
Next word	Ctrl + →

Beginning of line	Home
End of line	End
One paragraph up	Ctrl + ↑
One paragraph down	Ctrl + ↓
One window up	Page Up
One window down	Page Down
Beginning of window	Ctrl + Page Up
End of window	Ctrl + Page Down
Beginning of document	Ctrl + Home
End of document	Ctrl + End

EXERCISE **7**

■ **Create a Business Letter** ■ **Print Preview**

NOTES:

Create a Business Letter

- There are a variety of letter styles for business and personal use.

- The parts of a business letter and the vertical spacing of letter parts are the same regardless of the style used.

- A **business letter** is made up of eight parts:

  date

  inside address (to whom and where the letter is going)

  salutation

  body

  closing

  signature line

  title line

  reference initials (the first set of initials identifies the person who wrote the letter; the second set of initials identifies the person who typed the letter.)

- Whenever you see **yo** as part of the reference initials in an exercise, substitute *your* *own* initials.

- The letter style illustrated in this exercise is a **modified-block** business letter, since the date, closing, signature and title lines begin at the center point of the paper. Most business letters are printed on letterhead paper.

- In the inside address, there are two spaces between the state abbreviation and the zip code.

- A letter generally begins 2.5" down from the top of a page. If the letter is long, it may begin 2" from the top. If the letter is short, it may begin beyond 2.5".

- Works does not indicate the vertical position on the page. Therefore, you will need to press the Enter key to place your insertion point at the appropriate location for the dateline.

- Be aware of the following information when using the Enter key to produce a specific top margin.

  - The line spacing is a function of the font size. For example, pressing the Enter key 6 times in 12 point will produce approximately one inch of vertical space. If you are using a larger font size, pressing the Enter key 6 times will give more than one inch of space.

  - The default top margin is 1". Therefore, to produce a 2" top margin, you need to press the Enter key 6 times. To produce a 2.5" top margin, you need to press the Enter key 9 times (6 times = 1", 3 times = 0.5").

    ✓ NOTE: *An exact top margin can be set in the Page Setup area. This will be taught in a later lesson.*

- Margins and the size of the characters (**font size**) may also be adjusted to accommodate longer or shorter correspondence. Changing margins and font size will be covered in a later lesson.

🌐 Print Preview

- Preview is used to see how a word processing document, spreadsheet or database appears printed. The Print Preview shows all features such as headers/footers, graphics, imbedded objects and the format of the document.

- In this exercise, you will use the Print Preview to check the placement of the letter on the page.

- The standard view in the preview screen lets you see an entire page. Other views allow you to enlarge the image.

  ✓ NOTE: *You can only view the document in the Preview; you cannot edit.*

- To see how your letter will appear on a page:

  Click the Print Preview button 🔳 on the Toolbar.

  OR

  Select Print Pre_view from the _File menu.

- There are many options available on the Print Preview screen shown below. They are as follows:

P_revious
Click to view a previous page.

N_ext
Click to view the next page.

Zoom _In
Click to enlarge the document so that it is easier to read and find errors. You can zoom in two levels. You can also enlarge the view by clicking directly on the previewed document.

✓ *NOTE:* *The mouse pointer changes to a magnifying glass in the preview screen.*

Zoom _Out
Click to bring you back one view level.

P_rint
Click to print the document.

C_ancel
Click to bring you back to the document window.

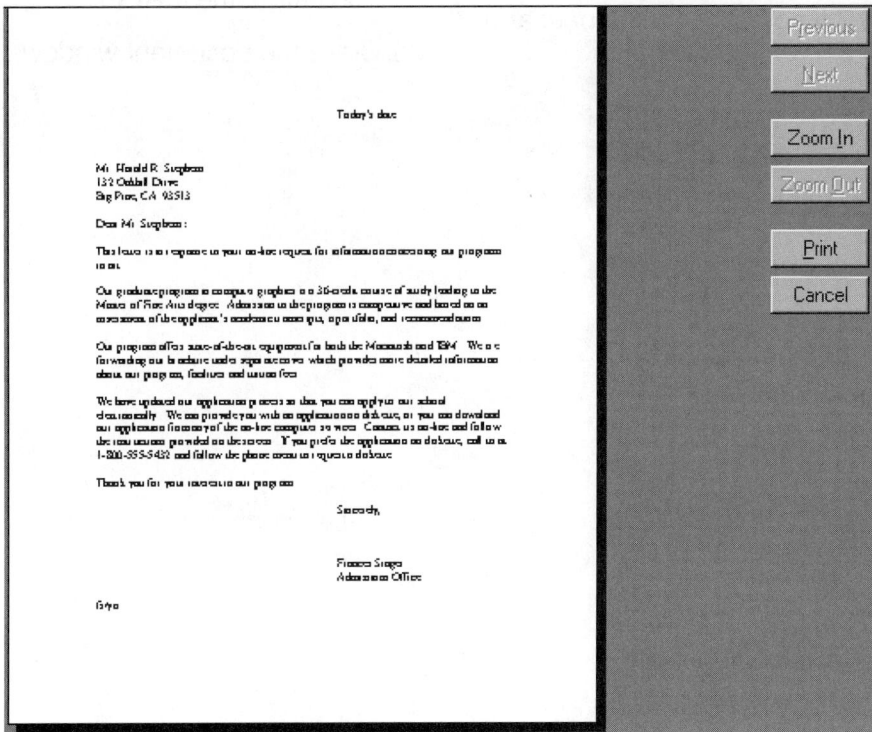

> *In this exercise, you will create a modified-block business letter and use Print Preview to view the document.*

EXERCISE DIRECTIONS:

1. Create a new document for the Word Processor.

2. Keyboard the letter as directed. Correct only immediate errors using the Backspace key.

3. Use the default margins and tabs.

4. With your insertion point at the top of the screen, press the Enter key 6 times to begin the date 2" from the top.

   ✓ *NOTE: This measurement can vary with the font you are using. If 6 returns does not give an exact 2" top margin, adjust the number of returns accordingly.*

5. Press the Tab key 7 times to begin the *date* and *closing* at position 3.5" on the ruler.

6. Press the Enter key between parts of the letter as directed in the exercise.

7. After completing the exercise, use the scroll bar to scroll your page up.

8. Preview your work using the Print Preview button on the Toolbar.

   ✓ *NOTE: Make adjustments to the vertical placement as needed. Practice zooming in and zooming out in the Print Preview screen.*

9. Save the exercise using the Save button on the Toolbar; name it **APPLY**

10. Close the document window.

🌐 **PRINT PREVIEW**

Click **Print Preview** icon .... 🔲
on the Toolbar.

OR

1. Click **File** .... Alt + F

2. Click **Print Preview** V

PREVIEW OPTIONS

Click **Zoom In** .... Alt + I
OR
Click **Zoom Out** .... Alt + O

EXIT PREVIEW

Click **Cancel** .... Esc

2"

Tab 7 x
→   →   →   →   →   →   →   Today's date

4x

Mr. Harold R. Stephens
132 Oakhill Drive
Big Pine, CA 93513
↓2x

Dear Mr. Stephens:
↓2x

Tab 1x →   This letter is in response to your on-line request for information concerning our programs in art.
↓2x

Tab 1x →   Our graduate program in computer graphics is a 36-credit course of study leading to the Master of Fine Arts degree. Admission to the program is competitive and based on an assessment of the applicant's academic transcripts, a portfolio, and recommendations.
↓2x

Tab 1x →   Our program offers state-of-the-art equipment for both the Macintosh and IBM. We are forwarding our brochure under separate cover which provides more detailed information about our program, facilities and tuition fees.
↓2x

Tab 1x →   We have updated our application process so that you can apply to our school electronically. We can provide you with an application on diskette, or you can download our application from any of the on-line computer services. Contact us on-line and follow the instructions provided on the screen. If you prefer the application on diskette, call us at 1-800-555-5432 and follow the phone menu to request a diskette.
↓2x

Tab 1x →   Thank you for your interest in our program.

↓2x
Sincerely,

4x

Tab 7 x
→   →   →   →   →   →   →   Frances Singer
Admissions Office
↓2x

fs/yo

EXERCISE **8**

■ **Use the Date and Time Feature** ■ **All Caps** ■ **Print a Document**

NOTES:

Use the Date and Time Feature

■ This exercise requires you to prepare another letter. The letter style is called **block**. This style is very popular because all parts of the letter begin at the left margin and there is no need to tab the date and closing. The spacing between the various parts of the letter remains the same as in the modified-block format. This time, however, when you type the date, you will use the Date and Time feature.

■ The Microsoft Works Date and Time feature enables you to insert the current date or time into your document automatically.

■ To insert the date and time, click Insert on the Menu bar as shown:

• Click Date and Time and the following formats are displayed:

• Choose the desired format.

• The format January 1, 1996 is preferred for formal business letters.

■ Every time you open, print or preview the document, the date and time are updated.

✓ *NOTE:* *If you do not want the date and time updated, deselect the Automatically Update When Printed checkbox in the Insert Date and Time dialog box.*

🌐 All Caps

■ Pressing the Caps Lock key once allows you to type all capital letters without holding down the Shift key. Only letters are changed by the Caps Lock key.

■ When the Caps Lock key has been pressed, the word CAPS appears in the status line at the bottom of your screen alerting you that you are in uppercase mode. Also, the Caps Lock Light on your keyboard will be lit.

CAUTION: If you happen to press the shift key when you are in Caps Lock mode, you will get a lowercase letter.

To end uppercase mode:

Press the Caps Lock key again.

Print a Document

- Microsoft Works allows you to print a page of a document, the full document or a range of pages within a document.

- When printing for the first time in a session, a first-time help screen appears. If you feel you do not need this assistance, check "Don't display this message in the future."

- Check to see that the printer is turned on, the paper is loaded and the ready light is lit. There are several ways to access print:

Click the Print button 🖨 on the Toolbar.

OR

Select <u>P</u>rint from the <u>F</u>ile menu shown below.

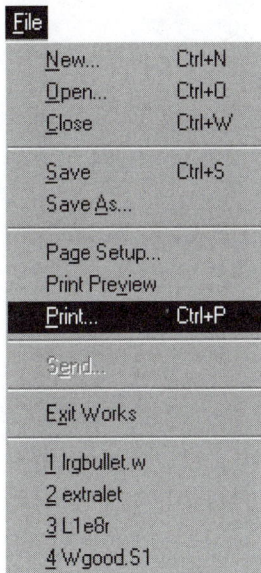

```
File
  New...          Ctrl+N
  Open...         Ctrl+O
  Close           Ctrl+W

  Save            Ctrl+S
  Save As...

  Page Setup...
  Print Preview
  Print...        Ctrl+P

  Send...

  Exit Works

  1 lrgbullet.w
  2 extralet
  3 L1e8r
  4 Wgood.S1
```

OR

Press Ctrl+P.

- The following dialog box appears:

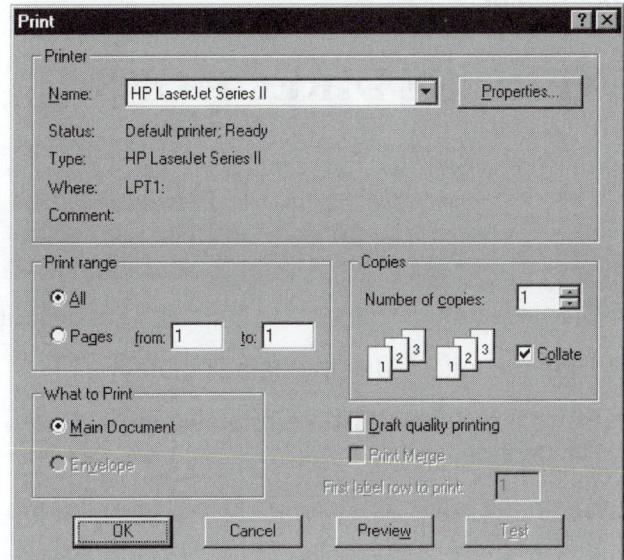

- There are a number of options available. They are:

Printer
Click drop-down box to select another printer.

Properties
Choose to display options affecting paper size, source, orientation as well as graphic print options.

Print range
Select <u>A</u>ll to print entire document or Pa<u>g</u>es to print certain pages within the document. If you wanted to print only the third page of a five-page document, you would choose Pa<u>g</u>es, then type 3 in the <u>f</u>rom box and 3 in the <u>t</u>o box.

Copies
Indicate the number of copies you want printed and whether to collate them or not.

What to Print
Choose which section of the document you want printed.

- Once all the print options are specified, click OK to start printing.

- You can cancel printing, if desired, by clicking Cancel in the Printing display box that appears. Once the data is transferred to the Windows 95 print queue, you will need to access the Print Queue window to pause or cancel the print job.

> *In this exercise, you will create a block letter using the Date and Time feature and print the document.*

EXERCISE DIRECTIONS:

✓ *NOTE:* *Directions are given for 12 point type size. Be sure your default type size is set to 12 point to minimize discrepancies between your document and the one shown in the exercise. Check the type size setting indicated on Toolbar.*

1. Create a new document for the Word Processor.

2. Type the letter. Use the default margins.

3. Correct only immediate errors using the Backspace key.

4. Begin the letter approximately 2.5" from the top of the page.

   ✓ *NOTE:* *This measurement can vary according to the font you are using. If nine returns do not give an exact 2.5" top margin, then adjust the number of returns accordingly.*

5. Click Insert, click Date and Time.

6. Select the format - January 1, 1996.

7. Use the Caps Lock key to type CONGRATULATIONS in the first paragraph.

8. Supply the appropriate year in paragraph one.

9. After completing the exercise, use the scroll bar to scroll your page up.

10. Preview your work.

11. Save the exercise (use File, Save); name it **BLOCK**.

12. Print the document by clicking the Print button on the Toolbar.

INSERT DATE

Ctrl + D (prints current date)

1. Click **Insert** .... Alt + I

2. Click **Date and Time** .... D
   Choose desired option

3. Click **Insert** .... Alt + I

🌐 **PRINT**

Ctrl + P Enter

Click **Print** button on Toolbar .... 🖨

OR

1. Click **File** .... Alt + F

2. Click **Print** .... P

3. Click **OK** .... Enter

2.5"

Today's date

4x

Mr. Thomas Walen
Updike Mechanics Company
23 Clogg Avenue
Atlanta, GA 30315

2x

Dear Mr. Walen:

2x

CONGRATULATIONS! You have been nominated as the outstanding office employee
of the month beginning November 4, 199- through November 30, 199-.

2x

The Committee that made your selection requires that you submit a photograph of
yourself to your supervisor so that we can display your picture in the company's executive
offices.

2x

Updike Mechanics is proud of your accomplishments. We look forward to honoring you
at our ANNUAL AWARDS DINNER on December 3.

2x

Sincerely,

4x

Paulette Manning
President

2x

PM/YO

EXERCISE **9**

Lesson 1 – Summary

In this exercise, you will create and print a block letter from unarranged copy.

EXERCISE DIRECTIONS:

1. Create a new document for the Word Processor, or open **WP GOOD.9**

2. Use the default margins and tabs.

3. Begin the date approximately 2.5" from the top of the page.

4. Key the letter below in **block style**. Correct only immediate errors using the Backspace key.

5. Use the automatic date feature to insert the current date.

6. Preview the copy.

7. Print one copy.

8. Save the document, name it **GOOD**.

9. Close the document window.

   ✓NOTE: *The proofreaders' mark for a new paragraph is ⁋.*

Today's date Mr. Jack Smith, President 481 Madison Avenue New York, NY 10022 Dear Jack: The promotion we ran from January - June was extremely profitable for the company and rewarded outstanding members of the sales staff as well. Total sales for the month were $45,788.44. ⁋Three of our salespersons exceeded $9,000.00, qualifying them for the higher 3 percent bonus. Janice Olson had the highest sales, followed by Hugh Robertson. Lois Chen did well also. ⁋Events like this motivate the staff to be more effective and to reach sales levels they were unaware they could attain. It is a pleasure to compensate these exceptional employees with this bonus. Sincerely, Deborah Wilson Sales Manager dw/yo

- **Proofreaders' Marks** ■ **Open a Previously Stored Document**
- **Insert/Typeover Text** ■ **Update a Document**

NOTES:

Proofreaders' Marks

- Before a file can be revised or edited, it must be opened from the disk and placed on the screen.

- A document is revised when corrections need to be made. **Proofreaders' marks** are markings on a document that indicate errors that need to be corrected. These markings are often abbreviated in the form of symbols. As each proofreaders' mark is introduced in an exercise, it will be explained and illustrated.

- A document containing proofreaders' marks is referred to as a **rough-draft**. After revisions are made, the completed document is referred to as a **final copy**.

🌐 Open a Previously Stored Document

- **To open a document:**

  –FROM THE TASK LAUNCHER–

  Click the Existing Documents tab on the Task Launcher as shown below to display the documents you recently used. Double-click the desired document.

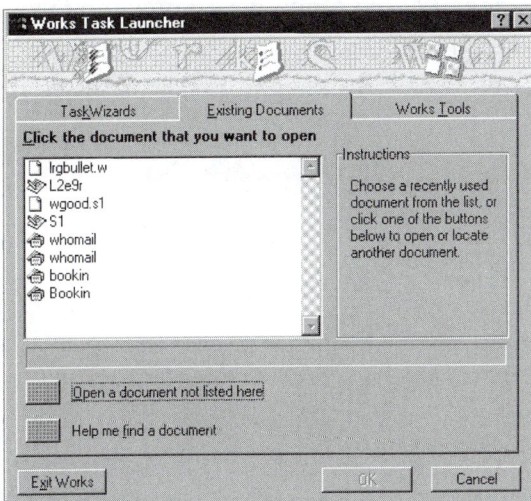

OR

If your document is not listed in the Existing Documents dialog box, click **Open a document not listed here** to display the Open dialog box.

OR

- Click **Help me find a document** to display the **Find Files** dialog box below.

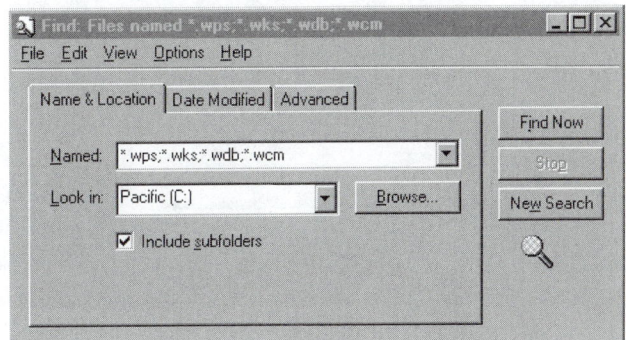

- Type the name of the document in the **Named** text box and then enter the drive to be searched in the **Look in** text box. If you cannot find the file, you can use the other options that allow you to search for specific text, size or type of file.

  –FROM WITHIN WORKS–

- Click File on the Menu bar.

- If the file was recently opened, it will appear on the list at the bottom of the File menu. Click once on its name to open the document.

File
New...   Ctrl+N
Open...   Ctrl+O
Close   Ctrl+W

Save   Ctrl+S
Save As...

Page Setup...
Print Preview
Print...   Ctrl+P

Send...

Exit Works

Recently used files
{
1 L2e9
2 L1e6
3 wbats.s4s
4 L1e5
}

OR

Click Open to access the Open dialog box shown below.

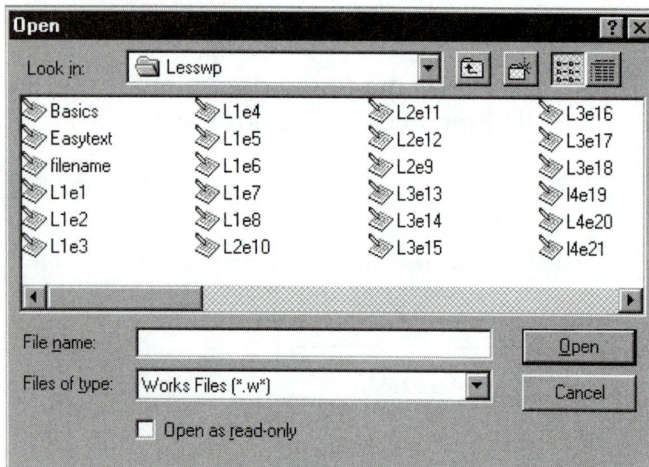

Open

Look in: Lesswp

Basics	L1e4	L2e11	L3e16
Easytext	L1e5	L2e12	L3e17
filename	L1e6	L2e9	L3e18
L1e1	L1e7	L3e13	l4e19
L1e2	L1e8	L3e14	L4e20
L1e3	L2e10	L3e15	l4e21

File name: _____ [Open]

Files of type: Works Files (*.w*) [Cancel]

☐ Open as read-only

■ There are a number of features to help access your document from the Open dialog box:

Look in
Lists the current folder. Click the down arrow to see the hierarchy of drives and folders on your computer. From the drop-down list, click the desired folder. Double click your file once it appears in the box below or click the file name and click Open.

The icon identifies the type of file.

word processing

spreadsheet

database

communications

Open dialog box buttons
Click [icon] to open a folder one level up in the hierarchy.

Click [icon] to create a new folder.

Click [icon] for a list of folder or files.

Click [icon] for folder/file information.

File name
Provides space for you to specify the file you want. If the file is in a different folder or drive, use the backslash to separate the drive, folder and filename. You can use the asterisk (*) as a wildcard to see all files in the folder. For example, to see all the files in the Document folder in drive C you would enter:

C:\Document*.*

All files in the folder will display.

Files of type
Lists the types of files. Use this to narrow the list of files in a folder to those that were created in a particular file format. For example, narrow the list to see only Works word processing, spreadsheet or database files or files created in another program. If you wish to see every file in a folder, you would choose **All Files** from the drop-down list.

Open as read-only
Allows you to view the document without making any changes.

✓ NOTE: If you need help, click the question mark, then click the area of the dialog box in question.

If you click the right mouse button in the workspace of the Open dialog box, the following menu appears:

View   ▶
Arrange Icons ▶
Line up Icons
Paste
Paste Shortcut
New   ▶
Properties

Move the mouse pointer to View, Arrange Icons, and New to open their cascading menus.

Insert/ Overtype Text

- **Inserting** is adding text to an existing document while **Overtype** is replacing text as you type.

- **To make corrections:**

  - Use the insertion point movement keys to move to the point of correction.

    OR

    Use the mouse to click at the point of correction.

  - Type the desired text.

- Text is inserted immediately before the insertion point when Insert is on. Insert is the default and the program is automatically in Insert mode when started. When typing inserted text, the existing text moves to the right. When inserting a word, the space following the word must also be inserted.

To create a new paragraph in existing text:

  - Place the insertion point to the left of the first character in the new paragraph.

  - Press the Enter key twice.

- Another way to edit text is to type over the existing text with new text. Works calls this method **Overtype**. Overtype is a correction method that is used for an exact letter-for-letter replacement. For example, if you wanted to change the name "Smith" to "Jones," you might use this feature.

To put Works in Overtype mode:

- Press the Insert key once.
  Note the Status bar – OVR is displayed

- Type the desired text.

  ✓ NOTE: In this mode, existing text does not move to the right; it is typed over. Text is automatically adjusted after insertions have been made.

- When finished, press the **Insert** key again.

  ✓ NOTE: Once you have finished typing over your text, you MUST immediately press the Insert key again to go back into Insert mode so you don't lose additional text as you type.

- The proofreaders' mark for insertion is: ∧

- The proofreaders' mark for a new paragraph is: ⁋

🌐 Update a Document

- When a file is opened and revisions are made, the revised or updated version must be resaved. When a document is resaved, the old version is replaced with the new version. Works lets you update your document with or without confirmation.

- If you select Save from the File menu or click the Save button, your document will be saved without confirmation and you can continue working.

- If you close your file or exit, Works asks if you wish to save your changes. If no changes were made, Works just closes the file.

In this exercise, you will open a previously typed document and edit it by using both insert and overtype modes.

EXERCISE DIRECTIONS:

1. Open ⌨**WARE**, or open 💾**WP WARE.10**.

2. Make the indicated insertions.

3. Use the Overtype mode to insert "display" over "monitor" in the first paragraph and "computer" over "hardware" in the second paragraph.

4. Type the handwritten paragraph as the third paragraph.

5. Print one copy.

6. Close your file; save the changes.

actual   *and other peripherals*

Hardware means the physical equipment being used. The computer, the printer, the ~~monitor~~, and the keyboard are all considered hardware.

display   *computer*

Software is the program that instructs the ~~hardware~~ to perform specific functions. Software is then used to perform either word processing, database, spreadsheet, or other applications.

desktop publishing

¶ These components range widely in both price and capabilities; therefore, be aware of your computer needs before purchasing a computer system.

🌐 OPEN A SAVED DOCUMENT

1. Click **File** .... `Alt`+`F`
2. Click **Open** .... `O`
3. Click **Look in** .... `Alt`+`I`
4. Select desired drive/folder.
5. Click **File name**.
6. Type filename to open .... *filename*
   OR
   Click filename in list.
7. Click **Open** .... `Enter`

   ✔ *NOTE:* *You can also double-click a filename in the file list to open the file without clicking Open.*

INSERT TEXT

1. Use cursor keys to place insertion point one character to the left of where text is to be inserted.
   OR
   a. Place mouse pointer one character to the left of where text is to be inserted.
   b. Click once.
2. Type text .... *text*

OVERTYPE

1. Place insertion point where text is to be overwritten.
2. Press **Insert** key .... `Ins`
   to enter OVR mode.

3. Type text .... *te*
4. Press **Insert** key .... `Ins`
   to exit OVR mode.

🌐 SAVE CHANGES (WITHOUT CONFIRMATION)

Ctrl + S

Click **Save** button on Toolbar. .... 🖫
OR
1. Click **File** .... `Alt`+`F`
2. Click **Save** .... `S`

■ **Delete Text** ■ **Select Text** ■ **Undo Editing**

NOTES:

Delete Text

■ Deleting is the process of removing text and spaces. The procedures for deleting vary depending on what is being deleted.

■ The proofreaders' mark for deletion is: ℘

The proofreaders' mark for do not delete is: .....
or *stet*

To delete a character to the left of the insertion point:

Press the Backspace key.

To delete a character to the right of the cursor:

Press the Delete key.

Select Text

■ To delete a block of text, (words, lines, paragraphs), you must select the text by **highlighting.** You can use the mouse or the keyboard, or a combination of both to highlight.

Mouse Users:

Click and drag the mouse over the desired text.

✓ *NOTES:* *Works automatically highlights a word at a time while you are dragging.*

This feature can be turned off by clicking Tools, Options, and clearing the Automatic word selection check box.

Mouse Shortcuts:

• You can quickly highlight words and larger sections of text with the mouse.

• When you move the mouse pointer into the space at the left margin, the mouse pointer changes to the shape of an arrow pointing upward toward the top right of the screen. Below is a screen showing the mouse pointer.

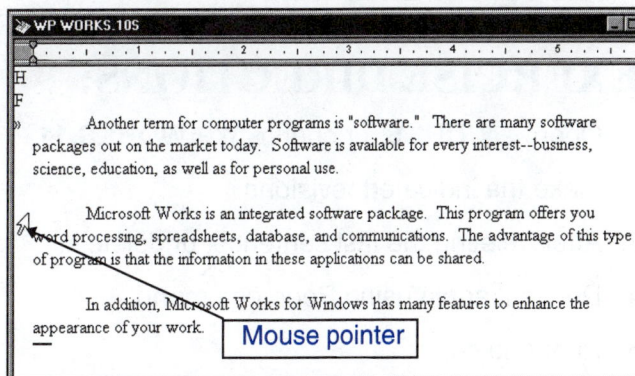

WP WORKS.105

Another term for computer programs is "software." There are many software packages out on the market today. Software is available for every interest--business, science, education, as well as for personal use.

Microsoft Works is an integrated software package. This program offers you word processing, spreadsheets, database, and communications. The advantage of this type of program is that the information in these applications can be shared.

In addition, Microsoft Works for Windows has many features to enhance the appearance of your work.

Mouse pointer

• Click the left mouse button while the pointer is in this area to highlight the entire line of text opposite the pointer. Hold the left mouse button and drag the mouse pointer up or down in the left margin to select as many lines of text as you wish.

Keyboard Users:

Press **F8** to place Works in Extend Selection mode. This anchors the insertion point and allows you to use the cursor movement keys to highlight or select text in any direction from the insertion point.
*Note the status bar – **EXT** is displayed.*

OR

Hold down the Shift key while pressing the cursor movement keys to highlight text.

To cancel a selection:

Click the mouse anywhere outside the selection.

OR

Press Esc + arrow key.

To delete highlighted text:

Press the Delete key or the Backspace key.

OR

Click Edit, Clear.

OR

Click the Cut button on the Toolbar.

OR

Press Ctrl+X.

🌐 **Undo Editing**

■ Text may be restored after it has been changed. In order to undo the change, you must immediately select Edit, Undo Editing after making the change.

✓ NOTE: After undoing a change, the Undo Editing command becomes the Redo Editing command allowing you to restore the change.

In this exercise, you will delete text from a previously typed paragraph and use Undo and Redo to restore and re-delete text.

EXERCISE DIRECTIONS:

1. Open 📺**WORKS**, or open 💾**WP WORKS.11**.

2. Make the indicated revisions.

3. After deleting the last sentence, undelete it.

4. Delete it again using Redo command.

5. Print one copy.

6. Close your file; save the changes.

✓ NOTE: While Works offers a number of ways to select and delete text, the keystrokes on the next page represent the most efficient selection and deletion techniques. You may experiment with those methods and use the one you find most comfortable.

Another term for computer programs is "software." There are many software packages out on the market today. Software is available for ~~just about~~ every interest—business, science, education, as well as for personal use ~~and entertainment~~.

Microsoft Works is an ~~example of an~~ integrated software package. This program offers you word processing, spreadsheets, database, and communications ~~capabilities~~. The advantage of this type of program is that the information in ~~each of these~~ applications can be shared, ~~so there is no need to rekey it~~.

In addition, Microsoft Works for Windows 95 also has many features to enhance the appearance of your work. ~~These features include Word Art, Clip Art and Drawing which add special effects and graphics to your documents.~~

Undo the deletion of the last sentence
Redo the deletion of the last sentence

SELECT TEXT (HIGHLIGHT)

USING MOUSE METHOD

1. Position insertion point at beginning of text to select.
2. Hold down left mouse button and drag over text.
3. Release mouse button.

To select a word:

1. Place insertion point anywhere on word.
2. Double-click the left mouse button.

To select a sentence:

1. Place mouse pointer in desired sentence.
2. Press **Ctrl** and click .... `Ctrl`+click

To select a paragraph:

1. Place mouse pointer in left margin opposite desired paragraph.
2. Double-click.

To select an entire document:

1. Place mouse pointer in left margin
2. Press **Ctrl** and click .... `Ctrl`+click

   OR

1. Click **Edit** .... `Alt`+`E`
2. Click **Select All** .... `L`

USING KEYBOARD METHOD

F8 + any arrow

   OR

Shift + any arrow

1. Position insertion point to the immediate left of text to select.
2. Hold down **Shift** .... `Shift`

   OR

   Press **F8** .... `F8`
3. Press desired option:

TO SELECT	PRESS
One character left	`←`
One character right	`→`
One line up	`↑`
One line down	`↓`
To end of line	`End`
To start of line	`Home`
To end of word	`Ctrl`+`→`
To start of word	`Ctrl`+`←`
Top of screen	`Page Up`
Bottom of screen	`Page Down`
To end of paragraph	`Ctrl`+`↓`
To start of paragraph	`Ctrl`+`↑`
To end of document	`Ctrl`+`End`
To beginning of document	`Ctrl`+`Home`

CANCEL SELECTION

Esc + any arrow

Click anywhere outside the selection.

DELETE

Delete a Character:

1. Place insertion point immediately to the *left* of character or space to delete.
2. Press **Delete** .... `Del`

   OR

1. Place insertion point to the *right* of character to delete.
2. Press **Backspace** .... `Backspace`

Delete a Block of Text:

1. Select (highlight) block of text to delete.
2. Click **Cut** button .... ✂

   OR

   Press **Delete** .... `Del`

   OR

   Press **Backspace** .... `Backspace`

UNDO EDITING

Ctrl + Z (Alt + Backspace)

1. Click **Edit** .... `Alt`+`E`
2. Click **Undo Editing** .... `U`

RESTORE

Ctrl + Z (Alt + Backspace)

1. Click **Edit** .... `Alt`+`E`
2. Click **Redo Editing** .... `R`

EXERCISE **12**

■ **Typing Replaces Selection** ■ **Show All Characters** ■ **Delete Characters**
■ **Combine Two Paragraphs into One** ■ **Delete Tabs**

NOTES:

Typing Replaces Selection

■ Typing replaces selection combines two steps into one. It allows you to replace the selected text as you type, thereby eliminating the need to delete the text first.

✓ *NOTE:* *This option can be turned off. Click Tools, Click Options, Click Editing tab, Click Typing replaces selection.*

Show All Characters

■ As a document is created in Works, special characters are inserted. These characters are not displayed on the screen, but can be revealed when necessary. These characters are:

Hard return represented by a paragraph symbol (¶)

Tab represented by an arrow (→)

Space represented by a small centered dot (·)

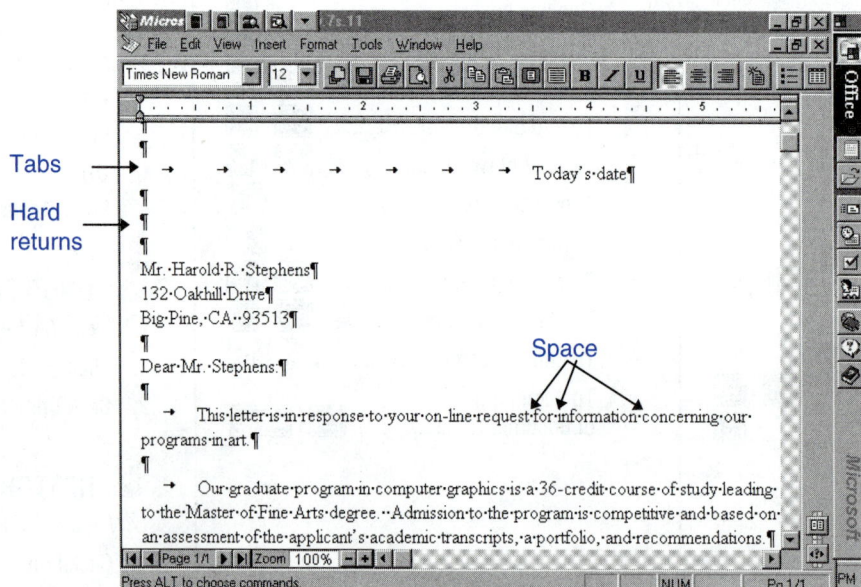

■ When the characters are displayed the **All Character** item is checked in the menu. An example of a document with symbols displayed is shown below.

Delete Characters

- Deleting the paragraph symbol (¶) allows you to combine paragraphs, while deleting the Tab (→) symbol allows you to block paragraphs.

- You can change letter styles by deleting these various characters.

Combine Two Paragraphs into One

- Paragraphs are separated by returns (two in single-spaced documents and one in double-spaced). You must delete these hard returns between the paragraphs in order to combine them. Returns are represented on the screen by the paragraph symbol (¶).

✓ NOTE: If the paragraph symbols are not displayed, you can display them as previously explained.

To delete the paragraphs:

Highlight the blank space (or the paragraph symbols if displayed) that separate the paragraphs and press the **Delete** key.

OR

Place the cursor at the end of the paragraph after the period, and press the **Delete** key as many times as necessary to bring the paragraphs together.

Delete Tabs

- To change a modified-block letter to block style, you would have to delete the tabs that precede the date until the date aligns with the left margin. Tabs are represented on the screen by the Tab symbol (→).

To delete the tabs:

Place the cursor at the left margin (to the left of the indent) and press the **Delete** key.

OR

Use the mouse to highlight the blank space (or the tab symbols if displayed) to the left of the date and press the **Delete** key.

In this exercise, you will make changes to a previously typed letter using **Typing replaces selection** *and display the non-printing characters.*

EXERCISE DIRECTIONS:

1. Open 🖮**APPLY**, or open 🖫**WP APPLY.12**.

2. Display the characters.

3. Make the indicated deletions.

4. Immediately undelete the last deleted sentence.

5. Use *Typing replaces selection* to make the following changes:
   - 2nd paragraph: .....*Our* **to** *The*
   - 4th paragraph ....*provide* **to** *offer*
     .... *instructions provided* **to** *directions*

6. Print one copy.

7. Close the file; save the changes.

SHOW ALL CHARACTERS

. Click **View**...........................Alt+V

. Click **All Characters**.......................A

To hide codes:

. Click **View**...........................Alt+V

. Click **All Characters**.......................A

DELETE

To delete character:

1. Place insertion point to the left of code to delete

2. Press **Delete**................................Del

To delete returns:

1. Highlight the space between paragraphs (or ¶ symbols if displayed).

2. Press **Delete**...............................Del

To delete tabs:

1. Highlight the space before the indent (or → symbols if displayed).

2. Press **Delete**...............................Del

Today's date

Mr. Harold R. Stephens
132 Oakhill Drive
Big Pine, CA 93513

Dear Mr. Stephens:

This letter is in response to your on-line request for information concerning our programs ~~in art~~. *no* ¶

The
~~Our~~ graduate program in computer graphics is a 36-credit course of study leading to the Master of Fine Arts degree. Admission to the program is competitive and based on an assessment of the applicant's academic transcripts, a portfolio, and recommendations.

~~Our program~~ offers state-of-the-art equipment for both the Macintosh and IBM. We are forwarding our brochure under separate cover which provides more detailed information about our program, facilities and tuition fees.

offer
We have updated our application process so ~~that~~ you can apply to our school electronically. We can ~~provide~~ you ~~with~~ an application on diskette, or you can download our application from any of the on-line computer services. Contact us on-line and follow the ~~instructions provided~~ on the screen. If you prefer the application on diskette, call us at 1-800-555-5432 and follow the phone menu to request a diskette.

directions
~~Thank you for your interest in our program.~~

Sincerely,

Frances Singer
Admissions Office

fs/yo

Immediately undelete the last deleted sentence.

■ **Modified-Block Letter** ■ **Non-Breaking Space**

NOTES:

Modified-Block Letter

■ Moving the date and closing to 3.5" on the Ruler will make this a **modified-block letter**. To do this, place the insertion point to the left of the first letter of the date and press the Tab key as many times as necessary to bring the text to 3.5".

Non-Breaking Space

■ To prevent two or more words from splitting during word wrap, a **hard** or **non-breaking space character** can be inserted between words. This feature is particularly necessary when keyboarding first and last names, dates, equations and time.

■ When the special characters are displayed, a small raised circle between the words identifies the non-breaking space.

■ When inserting a non-breaking space between two existing words, you must either highlight the space between the two words you don't want broken or delete the original space between the words.

■ Click Insert, Special Character to access the Special Character dialog box below.

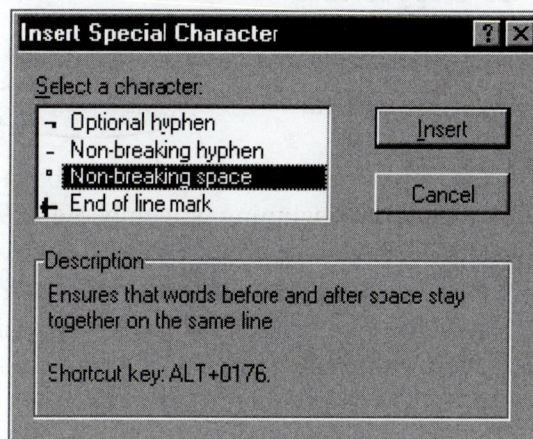

Insert Special Character   [?] [X]

Select a character:
- → Optional hyphen
- - Non-breaking hyphen
- ▫ Non-breaking space
- ← End of line mark

[Insert]

[Cancel]

Description
Ensures that words before and after space stay together on the same line

Shortcut key: ALT+0176.

■ The proofreaders' mark for moving text right is: ⌐

The proofreaders' mark for lowercase is: /

The proofreaders' mark for uppercase is: ≡

The proofreaders' mark for inserting a non-breaking space is: △

In this exercise, you will revise text, inserting hard spaces where indicated, and practice insertion and deletion.

EXERCISE DIRECTIONS:

1. Open **BLOCK**, or open **WP BLOCK.13**.

2. Make the indicated revisions; insert a hard space where you see the hard space symbol.

3. Delete the last deleted sentence, then immediately undelete it.

4. Convert ANNUAL AWARDS DINNER to lowercase with initial caps using the overtype method.

5. Print one copy.

6. Close the file; save the changes.

3.5" (tab 7 times)

Today's date →

Accounting Department

T.

Mr. Thomas Walen
Updike Mechanics Company
23 Clogg Avenue
Atlanta, GA 30315

Dear Mr. Walen:

, Mr. Walen

CONGRATULATIONS! You have been nominated as the outstanding office employee of the month beginning November 4, 199- through November 30, 199-. We made the selection based on the recommendations of your supervisors.
The Committee ~~that made your selection~~ requires ~~that~~ you submit a photograph of yourself to your supervisor ~~so that~~ we ~~can~~ display your picture ~~in~~ the company's ~~executive offices~~.

will then   throughout   O

Selection   immediate   , Mr. Quinn.

Updike Mechanics is proud of your accomplishments. ~~We look forward to honoring you at our ANNUAL AWARDS DINNER on December 3.~~

Sincerely,

→ 3.5" (tab 7 x)

Paulette Manning
President

PM/YO

Immediately undo deletion of last sentence

INSERT A NON-BREAKING SPACE TO NEW TEXT

Ctrl + Shift + Spacebar

1. Type first word .... *word*
2. Click **Insert** .... Alt + I
3. Click **Symbol** .... S
4. Select **Special Character** tab .... S
5. Click **Non-breaking space** .... ↓, ↑
6. Click **Insert** .... Alt + I
7. Click **Close** .... ↵
8. Type next word. .... *word*

INSERT A NON-BREAKING SPACE TO EXISTING TEXT

1. Position insertion point to the left of existing space between the words.
2. Press Delete to delete the space..... De
3. Repeat steps 2-4 at right.

EXERCISE 14

Lesson 2 – Summary

In this exercise, you will recall a document, edit and save it.

EXERCISE DIRECTIONS:

1. Open 📠**GOOD** using the Find Files feature, or open 💾**WP GOOD.14**.

   HINT: *From the Works Task Launcher, click Existing Documents, click Help me find a document, enter appropriate information in the dialog box to find file.*

2. Make the indicated revisions.

3. Print one copy.

4. Resave the document.

5. Close the document window.

Today's date ———————————————————→

Mr. Jack Smith, President   *Bit-Byte Computer Company* ←
481 Madison Avenue
New York, NY 10022

Dear Jack:

The *sales* ∧ promotion we ran from January - June was extremely profitable for the company and rewarded outstanding members of the sales staff as well. Total sales for the ~~month~~ were $45,788.44.   *six-month period*

Three of our salespersons exceeded $9,000.00, *in total sales* qualifying them for the higher 3 percent bonus. Janice Olson had the highest sales, followed by Hugh Robertson. Lois Chen did well also. *We will honor these salespeople at our next board meeting.*

Events like this motivate the staff to be more ~~effective~~ *productive* and to reach *higher* ∧ sales levels, ~~they were unaware they could attain.~~ It is a pleasure to compensate these exceptional employees with this bonus.

Sincerely,

Deborah Wilson
Sales Manager

dw/yo

EXERCISE 15

■ **Alignment Options (Left, Center and Right)**

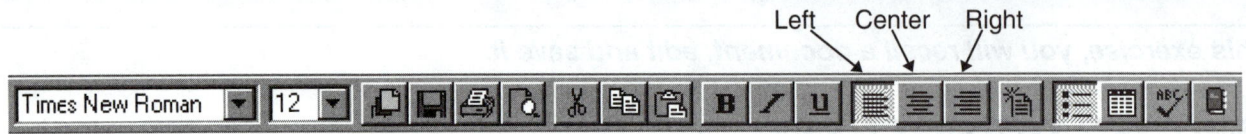

Left   Center   Right

| Times New Roman ▾ | 12 ▾ | 🗋 🖫 🖨 🔍 | ✂ 🗈 📋 | **B** *I* U̲ | ▤ ▤ ▤ | 🗈 ☷ ▦ | ✓ABC 🗐 |

NOTES:

🌐 Alignment Options

- **Alignment** refers to the arrangement of the lines. Works offers three alignments: left, center and right.

- Alignments can be changed using the keyboard or the mouse.

  To change alignments:

  - Click desired alignment button on the Toolbar (see above).

    OR

  - Use Quick keys for left, center and right alignments.

Left

- **Left alignment** is the default or standard alignment in most word processing programs. When text is left aligned, all lines are even on the left side only; the right side has uneven line endings.

- Left alignment is the default and needs to be chosen only when exiting from centering or right aligning text.

Center

- Works lets you center a single word, line, paragraph or an entire page between the left and right margins. Text can be centered before or after you type.

- All text typed after the center instruction will be centered. Therefore, you must make sure to return to left alignment to continue the document at the left margin.

- When centering text after it is typed, highlight the text to center and then give the center instruction. This procedure only centers the highlighted text.

- The proofreaders' mark for centering is:] [

Right

- **Right alignment**, or flush right, is a feature that aligns a single line (or part of a line) of text at the right margin. This feature is particularly useful when typing dates or creating invitations or business headings. You may right align before or after typing text.

- Exit the right alignment mode by choosing another alignment.

> *In this exercise, you will create a news release using left, right and center alignments.*

EXERCISE DIRECTIONS:

1. Create a new document for the Word Processor.

2. Begin the exercise at the top of the screen directly below the header.

3. Use the default margins.

4. Type the news release. Center and right align text as indicated.

5. Insert a non-breaking space where you see the Δ symbol.

6. Preview your document.

7. Print one copy.

8. Save the file; name it **NEWS**.

9. Close the document window.

LEFT ALIGN
trl + L

✓ NOTE: *This is the default. Use this procedure when exiting an alternate alignment.*

New Text

1. Place insertion point at beginning of line to left-align.

2. Click **Left-alignment** button .... ▤
   on Toolbar.

3. Type text...*text*

Existing Text

1. Select text to left align.

2. Click **Left-alignment** button .... ▤
   on Toolbar.

CENTER
Ctrl + E

New Text

1. Place insertion point at beginning of line to center.

2. Click **Center** button.......................... ▤
   on Toolbar.

3. Type text...*text*

4. Click **Left-alignment** button. .... ▤
   to return to left margin.

Existing Text

1. Select text to center.

2. Click **Center** button.......................... ▤
   on Toolbar.

RIGHT ALIGN
Ctrl + Shift + R

New Text

1. Place insertion point at beginning of text to right align.

2. Click **Right-alignment** button .... ▤
   on Toolbar.

3. Type text...*text*

4. Click **Left-alignment** button . ... ▤
   to return to left margin.

Existing Text

1. Select text to right align.

2. Click **Right-alignment** button .... ▤
   on Toolbar.

NEWS RELEASE
↓ 2x

For Immediate Release
↓ 2x

For more information contact: Andrea Rose
↓ 3x

NEW PRODUCTS TO INCREASE DESKTOP PUBLISHING PRODUCTIVITY
↓ 2x

Newtown, CT, July 1, 199-
↓ 3x

QUIRKY PRESS is full-featured page layout and document composition software that allows you to create professional looking documents by combining text and graphics from many popular word processing and graphics programs. You can use it to produce traditional office correspondence such as letters and memos, or create more complex documents such as advertising flyers, multi-page brochures and company newsletters.
↓ 2x

Text mode features include search and replace, spell checking, automatic error correction, a thesaurus and the ability to import files from many word processing programs. Graphics capabilities include drawing, importing graphic files and convenient scaling, cropping and placement.
↓ 2x

BEST SCANNER is a scanner which translates text and graphics into computer-usable files. Graphics can be scanned at a resolution as high as 600 dpi; photos at up to 256 levels of gray scale. Complete with OCR (optical character recognition) software, this unit will surely increase your productivity.
↓ 2x

The public is welcome to a demonstration of these new software items at the Computer Expo at the Nassau Coliseum on Sunday,∆July∆24,∆199-,∆from 9∆a.m. to 12∆noon.

EXERCISE 16

■ Spell Check ■ Justify Text

Spell check

NOTES:

🌐 Spell Check

■ Works' **Spell Check** has a dictionary of more than 110,000 words. It scans for words that are spelled, capitalized or hyphenated incorrectly in the Word Processor, Spreadsheet and Database tools. It also scans for repeated words.

■ You can spell check an entire document or a highlighted section of the document. Names and words not recognized by the dictionary will be identified as misspelled. You can also add these words to the dictionary so they will be accepted as correct in future checks.

■ Works has special purpose dictionaries (legal, medical and scientific) that can be purchased separately and installed.

■ **To change dictionaries:**

- Click Tools
- Click Options
- Click Proofing tab
- Select desired dictionary
- Click OK

■ If you have another dictionary installed on your computer, you can have Works use that dictionary instead.

■ Spell check can be accessed through the menus or by clicking on the Spell Check button on the Toolbar shown above.

■ Once the Spell Check is accessed, the following Spelling dialog box will appear:

Spelling: American English

Not in dictionary: doucment

Change to: document

Suggestions: document

Ignore   Ignore All

Change   Change All

Add   Suggest

Cancel

Spelling options
☑ Always suggest
☑ Ignore words in UPPERCASE
☑ Ignore words with numbers

Edit Custom Dictionary...

■ The Spelling dialog box gives you a number of options. You can:

Change to
Provides an area to type in the correct spelling.

Suggestions
Allows you to access the list of suggested spellings.

Ignore
Leaves the word unchanged.

Change
Changes only highlighted word.

Add
Adds the word to the dictionary.

Ignore All
Ignores all occurrences of the same word.

Change All
Changes all occurrences of the same word.

Suggest
Provides a list of possible spellings.

Always suggest
Always provides possible spellings.

Ignore words in UPPERCASE
Will not check capitalized words.

Ignore words with numbers
Will not check words containing numbers.

Edit Custom Dictionary
Allows you to add or delete words to the dictionary.

■ Spell check does not find errors in word usage (e.g., using *their* instead of *there*). Spell checkers, in general, are not a substitute for proofreading a document.

Justify Text

■ **Justifying text**, or justification, means all lines are even at the left and right margins. Justification may be changed before or after typing text.

■ You can customize the Toolbar to include the button for justification.

In this exercise, you will create an announcement using justify, center, left and right alignments as well as the Spell Check feature.

EXERCISE DIRECTIONS:

1. Create a new document for the Word Processor, or open 🖫**WP COMPANY.16**.

2. Use the default margins.

3. Keyboard the document exactly as shown, including the circled misspelled words.

4. Justify, center, left align and right align text as indicated.

5. Spell check your document. Accept all appropriate suggestions for changing spelling. *HINT: Deselect Ignore Words in UPPERCASE.*

6. Print one copy.

7. Save the exercise; name it **COMPANY**.

8. Close the document window.

🌐 SPELL CHECK
F7

1. Place insertion point where spell check should begin.

   OR

   Select a word or block of text to spell check.

2. Click **Spell Check** button .... [ABC✓]
   on Toolbar.

   OR

   a. Click **Tools** .... [Alt]+[T]

   b. Click **Spelling** .... [S]

   ✔ *NOTE: When the system encounters a word not found in its dictionary, the word is displayed in the Change to box and the insertion point will appear in the Change to box.*

3. Click **Ignore** to proceed .... [Alt]+[I]
   without changing the word.

   ✔ *NOTE: Click **Ignore All** to proceed without changing any occurrence of the word.*

OR

a. Edit word in **Change to** box .... [T]

b. Press **Enter** .... [Enter]

OR

Click **Change** .... [Alt]+[C]
to accept the suggested spelling and proceed with spell check.

OR

Click **Change All** .... [Alt]+[E]
to change all occurrences of the word.

OR

Click **Add** .... [Alt]+[A]
to add the word to the dictionary.

OR

a. Click **Suggest** .... [Alt]+[S]
   to see list of suggested spellings.

b. Click the desired suggestion.

c. Press **Enter** .... [Enter]

   ✔ *NOTE: Click **Always Suggest** to always provide a list of possible spellings.*

4. Click **OK** .... [Enter]
   when notified that the spell check is finished.

JUSTIFY TEXT
Ctrl + J

New Text

1. Place insertion point at beginning of text to justify.

2. Click **Format** .... [Alt]+[O]

3. Click **Paragraph** .... [P]

4. Click **Indents and Alignments** [Alt]+[I]

5. Click **Justified** .... [Alt]+[J]

Existing Text

1. Select text to justify.

2. Repeat steps 2-5 above.

Janet Reed is our (consultent) who can (advice) you about software companies and their products that can best meet the needs of those in the accounting and personal finance areas. In addition, she can evaluate your general office work flow and recommend hardware (configurations) and software to best serve your needs. Below is a brief list of software (companys) and the products they produce.

Justify

↓ *3x*

ACCOUNTING & PERSONAL FINANCE
SOFTWARE COMPANIES
Absolute Solutions
Check Mark Software
Computer Associates
Softview
Teleware
TimeSlips Corporation

Center

↓ *3x*

BUSINESS & PRESENTATION
SOFTWARE COMPANIES
Aldus
Borland
CE Software
Lotus
Microsoft
PowerUP!

↓ *3x*

Right justify

CALL 1-800-205-0831
ANY (BUISNESS) DAY
FOR INFORMATION
ABOUT
THE ABOVE COMPANIES
AND THEIR PRODUCTS

EXERCISE **17**

■ **Bold, Underline and Italics** ■ **Create Bulleted Lists** ■ **Change Bullet Style** ■ **Remove Bullets**

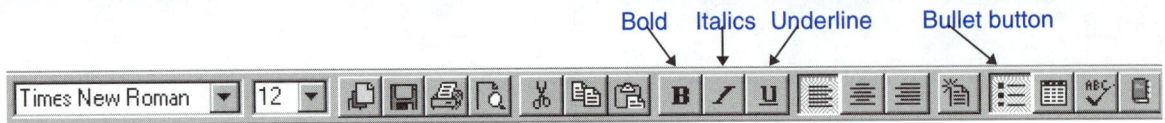

Bold   Italics   Underline   Bullet button

NOTES:

Bold, Underline and Italics

■ **Bold**, underline and *italics* are features used to enhance or emphasize text and are often referred to as **typestyles** or **appearance attributes**.

■ Text may be emphasized before keyboarding by first clicking the typestyle button. These features work as on/off toggle switches. You must choose the command to turn on the feature; then choose the same command to turn off the feature.

■ Existing text may be emphasized by selecting the text and then clicking the desired typestyle button.

■ Typestyles can be changed using the keyboard, the mouse or a combination of both.

To change typestyles:

• Click the desired style buttons on the Toolbar (*see above*).

    OR

• Click F**o**rmat and click **F**ont and Style. Then click desired style (*see below*).

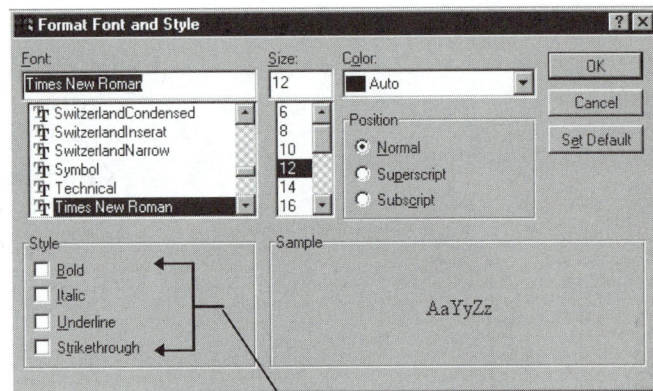

Typestyles

OR

• Use Quick keys for bold, italics and underline.

    ✓*CAUTION: To return to basic format style after applying the styles you want, reverse the procedure you used to apply the styles.*

■ The proofreaders' mark for bold is: 〰〰〰

The proofreaders' mark for underline is: ‗‗‗

Create Bulleted Lists

■ A **bullet** is a circle, square or diamond-shaped mark that is used to highlight points of information or itemize a list that does not need to be in any particular order. The bulleted list option inserts a bullet at the left margin (or the current indent) and then aligns the text with the default tab.

■ Works allows you to bullet text before or after typing.

To apply the bullet:

- Click the Bulleted List ▣ button on the Toolbar.

✓ *NOTE:* *The Toolbar Bulleted List button acts as an on/off toggle switch. One click creates the bullet and a second click removes it.*

OR

- Click Format, Paragraph.
- Click Indents and Alignment tab.
- Click Bulleted.
- Click OK.

■ The default format for the bulleted list is a hanging indent with the bullet at the left margin and the text indented 0.25". If you wish to customize the spacing between the bullet and the text, then follow the steps immediately above and make the desired changes in the Left and First-Line indent boxes. Check the sample box to see the results of your changes.

✓ *NOTE:* *Under Indentation, in the Left box, enter the desired distance between the bullet and the text and supply a corresponding negative number in the First line box. For example, if you want a list indented 0.5" from the left margin and want the bullet at the left margin, you would set the Left indent at 0.5" and the First line indent at -0.5".*

Change Bullet Style

■ The default bullet is a circle. However, Works allows you to select the shape and size of the bullet. You can choose the shape and size before or after typing the bulleted list. When changing the bullet style to an existing list, select the list before changing the style.

To change the appearance of the bullet:

- Click Format.
- Click Bullets.
- Click desired bullet.

- Select desired Bullet size by clicking the up/down arrow.
- Click Hanging indent, if desired.
- Click OK.

  Note the variety of bullet shapes available from the Bullet dialog box shown below. From this dialog box you can choose the bullet style, size and indent style. Your changes will be reflected in the Sample box.

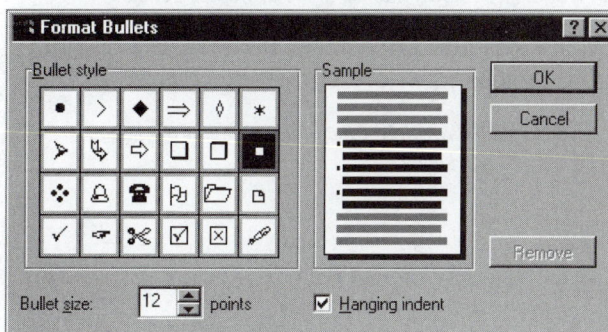

✓ *NOTE:* *You can also click the right mouse button and click Bullets to access the Format Bullets dialog box.*

Remove Bullets

■ You may accidentally create a bullet where you do not want one. If this should happen, you can remove the unwanted bulleted as follows:

a. Select the text containing the unwanted bullets.

b. Click Format.

c. Click Bullets.

d. Click Remove.

OR

a. Select the text containing the unwanted bullets.

b. Press Ctrl+Q.

■ It is recommended that you eliminate unwanted bullets from a list after you have completed typing the bulleted list.

> *In this exercise, you will revise a previously typed document by changing typestyles and adding a bulleted list.*

EXERCISE DIRECTIONS:

1. Open 🖥️**DIVE,** or open 💾**WP DIVE.17**.

2. Create a bulleted list of the hotels using the square bullet.

   ✓ *NOTE:* *Use Ctrl+Q to eliminate unwanted bullets.*

3. Make indicated revisions, bolding, underlining and italicizing where shown.

   ✓ *NOTE:* *Use whichever method you prefer to change typestyles.*

4. Spell check.

5. Preview your work.

6. Print one copy.

7. Close the file; save the changes.

🌐 BOLD

Ctrl + B

New Text

1. Place insertion point where bolding is to begin.
2. Click **Bold** button............................ **B**
3. Type text ....*text*
4. Click **Bold** button
   to discontinue bolding.................... **B**

Existing Text

1. Select text to bold.
2. Click **Bold** button............................ **B**

🌐 UNDERLINE

Ctrl + U

New Text

1. Place insertion point where underlining is to begin.
2. Click **Underline** button .... **U**
3. Type text ....*text*
4. Click **Underline** button .... **U**
   to discontinue underlining.
5.
Existing Text

1. Select text to be underlined.
2. Click **Underline** button .... **U**

🌐 ITALICIZE

Ctrl + I

New Text

1. Place insertion point where italicizing is to begin.
2. Click **Italics** button .... **I**
3. Type text ....*text*
4. Click **Italics** button .... **I**
   to discontinue italics.

Existing Text

1. Select text to be italicized.
2. Click **Italics** button .... **I**

CREATE BULLETED LISTS

Click **Bulleted List**......................... ☰
button on Toolbar.

New Text

1. Place insertion point where the bulleted list is to begin.
2. Click **Format**........................... Alt +O
3. Click **Paragraph** .... P
4. Click **Indents and Alignments** tab.
5. Click **Bulleted**........................ Alt +B
6. Click **OK**.................................... Enter

Existing Text

1. Select text to bullet.
2. Follow steps 2-6 above.

CHANGE BULLET SHAPE AND SIZE

1. Click **Format**........................ Alt +O
2. Click **Bullets**.................................. L
3. Click desired bullet.
4. Click desired **Bullet size**........ Alt +S
5. Type desired size................... *point size*
   OR
   Click up/down arrow for bullet size .. ▲▼

REMOVE BULLETS

Ctrl + Q

1. Highlight area containing unwanted bullets.
2. Click **Format**........................ Alt +O
3. Click **Bullets** .... Alt +L
4. Click **Remove** .... Alt +R

DIVING VACATIONS   *Center*
~~DIVING IN THE CAYMAN ISLANDS~~

⟵   Do you want to see sharks, barracudas and stingrays? Do you want to see gentle angels too?

Italics
⟵   The Cayman Islands were discovered by Christopher Columbus in 1503. ~~The~~ *and*
~~Cayman Islands~~ are located south of Cuba. The Caymans are the home to only about   *Justify*
125,000 year-round residents. However, they welcome 200,000 visitors each year. Most
visitors come with masks and flippers in their luggage. ~~Now, you are ready to jump in!~~

Hotel/Diving Accommodations:

■ **Sunset House**, PO Box 479, George Town, Grand Cayman; 1 (809) 555-4767.

■ **Coconut Harbour**, PO Box 2086, George Town, Grand Cayman; 1 (809) 555-6468.

■ Red Sail Sports, PO Box 1588, George Town, Grand Cayman; 1 (809) 555-7965.

■ Cayman Diving Lodge, PO Box 11, East End, Grand Cayman; 1 (809) 555-7555.

■ Anchorage View, PO Box 2123, East End, Grand Cayman; 1 (809) 555-4209.

Bold and underline hotel names and bullet each one.

■ **Font, Font Size and Color** ■ **Create a Memorandum**

NOTES:

🌐 Font, Font Size and Color

■ In Exercise 17, you used bold, underline and italics to emphasize text. Works allows you to further enhance your document by changing font, font size and color.

■ A **font** is the design of a character. Each font has a distinctive character that will make your document attractive and able to communicate a particular message. **Typeface** is often used as another name for font.

■ The fonts that are available to you depend on the printer you are using. There are basically three types of fonts: serif, sans serif and script.

Serif
Serif has "serifs," curves or edges extending from the ends of the letter: **R**, and is generally used for long text because it is more readable.

Sans serif
Sans serif is straight-edged: **R**, and is often used for headlines.

Script
Script looks like handwriting: *R*.

■ Each design has a name and each is used to convey a different feeling. While there are hundreds of varieties of each, Works includes those that will work with most printers. It is difficult to tell by the name which fonts are serif and which are sans serif. You can preview and select a font using either of the methods listed below:

To select a font:

• Click the down arrow on the Font box on the Toolbar.
• Click desired font from the drop-down list.
  OR
• Click Format.
• Click Font and Style.

• Click a font from the Font list box.
• Preview selected font in sample box.
• Click OK.

Either method allows you to view the font as it is displayed on the screen.

■ Works supports the use of True Type fonts. Using the True Type fonts permits your screen to more accurately display text the way it will appear when you print it. True Type fonts are identified by a double T [𝕋] in front of the font name in both the font box on the Toolbar and in the Font and Style dialog box. Note the font names in the dialog box below.

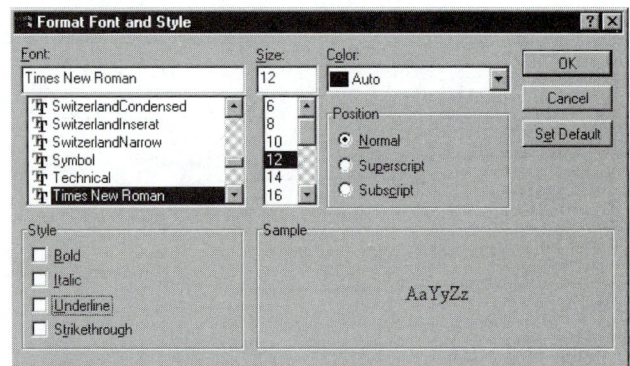

■ Fonts are available in a variety of sizes. Type size is measured in points (there are 72 points to an inch). Use 10 or 12 point type size for document text and larger text for headings and headlines. Works displays only the fonts and font sizes that are available for your printer. However, text can be displayed in different colors and font styles even if they are not supported by your printer.

- Font size can be changed in the Font Size box on the Toolbar or in the Format Font and Style dialog box.

  ✓ NOTE: *If your printer does not support certain font styles and color, the text will print in a substitute font and/or in black.*

- You can change font, font size and color before or after typing text. To change fonts and font size you can use the mouse, the keyboard or a combination of both. If you want to change the font, size and apply a typestyle (bold, italic, underline) at the same time, you should use the Format Font and Style dialog box.

  ✓ NOTE: *A document that contains many changes in fonts, font sizes, typestyles and colors becomes busy and difficult to read. Try to keep formatting changes to a minimum so that the text you want to emphasize stands out from the rest of the document.*

- The default font in Works is Times New Roman; the default size is 12 point. However, the default can be changed.

  To change the default:

  - Click Format.
  - Click Font and Style.
  - Make desired changes.
  - Click Set Default.
  - Click OK.
  - Click Yes when asked if you want to change the default.

- All future documents will be affected by this change. The active document and previous documents will not be affected.

- You cannot undo this change. To return to the previous default, you need to reselect the previous formats and follow the above procedure to set a new default.

Create a Memorandum

- The **memorandum**, or memo, is a written communication within a company. Companies create memos on blank paper or on letterhead (company stationery). Some use preprinted forms, while others create the memo form.

- A memo should begin 1" from the top of the page, which is the top of your screen. The word MEMORANDUM may be centered, as illustrated in the accompanying exercise, or it may be omitted, if desired.

- Memorandums are usually prepared with all parts beginning at the left margin. The guide words: TO: FROM: DATE: and RE: are aligned at the left margin. Tab appropriately after the colons to align the text following the guide words.

- Re (in reference to) is often used in place of the word "Subject."

- Double space between each part of the memorandum heading. The body of the memo is in single space and begins a double or triple space below the subject line.

- If copies are to be sent to others, a **copy notation** may be indicated as the last item on the page.

> *In this exercise, you will create a memorandum using various fonts, font sizes and typestyles. You will also create a bulleted list.*

EXERCISE DIRECTIONS:

1. Create a new document for the Word Processor.

2. Type the memorandum starting at the top of the screen under the header area, centering text where indicated.

3. Type the title MEMORANDUM in all caps in a sans serif font in 18 point bold. Press the Enter key twice after the title.

4. Type the guide words in all caps in the same sans serif font in 14 point bold.

5. Type the information following the guide words in a serif font in 12 point.

6. Type the paragraph text in the same serif font in 12 point.

7. Create a bulleted list of events as shown. Key event titles in the same sans serif font in14 point bold. Choose any desired color.

8. Spell check.

9. Preview your document.

10. Print one copy.

11. Save the exercise; name it **MEMONEWS**.

12. Close the document window.

CHANGE A FONT

Shift + Ctrl + F

✓ NOTE: If changing a font, font size or color of existing text, first select the text before performing the following procedures.

1. Click **F**ormat.......................... Alt + O
2. Click **F**ont and Style .... F
3. Click up/down arrows on side. .... ▲▼ of **F**ont list box to view font names
4. Click desired font.
5. Preview selected font in sample box.
6. Click **OK**...................................... Enter

OR

1. Click font name in **Font Name** text box on Toolbar.
2. Delete existing name and enter new font name........*font name*
3. Press **Enter** .... Enter

OR

1. Click down arrow in **Font Name** text box .... ▼ on Toolbar to view font names
2. Click desired font.

CHANGE A FONT SIZE

Shift + Ctrl + P

1. Click **F**ormat.......................... Alt + O
2. Click **F**ont and Style .... F
3. Click up/down arrows on side .... ▲▼ of **Size** box to view font sizes.
4. Click desired font size.

OR

1. Click **Font size box** .... 12 ▼ on the Toolbar.
2. Delete existing size and enter new font size .... *font size*

OR

1. Click down arrow on side of............. ▼ **Font size box** to view font sizes.
2. Click desired font size.

CHANGE A COLOR

1. Click **F**ormat.......................... Alt + O
2. Click **F**ont and Style .... F
3. Click **C**olor text box .... Alt + O to open pop-up list of colors.
4. Click up/down arrows .... ▲▼ to view colors.
5. Click desired color.

CHANGE DEFAULT FONT

1. Click **F**ormat.......................... Alt + O
2. Click **F**ont and Style .... F
3. Click desired font.
4. Click desired size.
5. Click **S**et Default .... Alt + E
6. Click **Y**es .... Y

MEMORANDUM

Set in sans serif 18 pt. bold

*Set guide words in
sans serif 14 pt. bold*

TO: The Staff

↓ 2x

FROM: Sarah Walesk   *— Set information in serif 12 pt.*

↓ 2x

DATE: Today's date

↓ 2x

RE: Computer Expo

↓ 3x

I strongly urge you to attend this year's Computer Expo. In four days, you'll pick up all the latest computer news and discover new ways to put your computer to work--in the office, in the lab, in the studio, in the classroom or in your home.

↓ 2x

Here are some of the events you can look forward to:

↓ 2x

- **Keynote Sessions**. These sessions will feature luminaries from the computer world who will offer you insights from industry.
- **Application Workshops**. Join a series of two-hour learning sessions which will provide guidelines, tips and "how-to's" on popular software packages.
- **Programmer/Developer Forums**. Veteran and novice computer users will brainstorm so you can learn about innovative advances and techniques.

↓ 2x   *italics*

If you are interested in attending, see *Derek Brennen* He will pre-register anyone from our company who wishes to attend. This will save you long lines at the show.

yo

*Bullet and set event names
in sans serif 14 pt. bold.
Use any desired color.*

NOTES:

Thesaurus

■ The **Thesaurus** feature provides approximately 200,000 meanings and synonyms for selected words. It also displays the parts of speech. It is a useful writing tool and helps to prevent repetitiveness in a document.

To access the Thesaurus:

• Click Tools, Thesaurus.

   OR

• Click Thesaurus button ▣ on Toolbar.

   ✓ NOTE: The Toolbar must be customized to include the Thesaurus button.

■ Once you access Thesaurus, a dialog box appears giving you several choices:

Looked up
Traces the words you looked up in one session.

Meanings
Displays different meanings for the selected word.

Replace with synonym
Displays selected synonym.

Replace
Replaces the word in your document with the selected synonym.

Look Up
Gives additional meanings and synonyms for word highlighted in dialog box.

Cancel
Closes the dialog box.

■ Once you are in the Meanings or Synonyms box, you can either click the desired word or use the arrows to locate on the desired word. Press **Enter** to select it.

Word Count

■ The **Word Count** feature adds the number of words in a block of text or an entire document. This feature is excellent for writers who must keep within a certain number of words for a particular assignment.

■ If you wish to count words in a section of text, you must highlight that area. If you do not highlight, the Word Count feature counts the words in the entire document. When the count is finished, a message box gives the results.

   ✓ NOTE: The Toolbar must be customized to include the Word Count button.

Easy Text

■ **Easy Text** allows you to reuse frequently used words or phrases without retyping them.   You type and format the text once, name it and recall it when needed. Some examples of uses for Easy Text are: addresses, standard paragraphs, complimentary closings and headings.

- Click <u>E</u>dit, Easy Text, <u>N</u>ew to access the New Easy Text dialog box below.

> Type Easy Text name here.

New Easy Text

Type a name for the Easy Text below:

[   ]

In the box below, type the text you want to store as Easy Text. Click Done when you are finished.

Easy Text contents

> Type Easy Text contents here.

Done
Cancel
<u>F</u>ormat...

Shortcut: Next time, type the text in your document and then highlight it before clicking the Easy Text command -- it will show up in the box above

- You must give a name for the Easy Text in the **Type a name for the Easy Text below:** text box. Remember the Easy Text names must be one word. Type the contents of the Easy Text in the **Easy Text contents** text box. It is important to include the correct spacing before, after and within the Easy Text. For example, in this exercise you must include the four returns after the title MEMORANDUM. In addition, when creating the Easy Text for the guidewords, include the two returns between each of the guidewords as well as the two returns after the last guideword.

- If you wish to format the Easy Text, click <u>F</u>ormat on the New Easy Text dialog box to access the **Easy Formats** dialog box above right. You can choose an existing format or click **New** to create an original format.

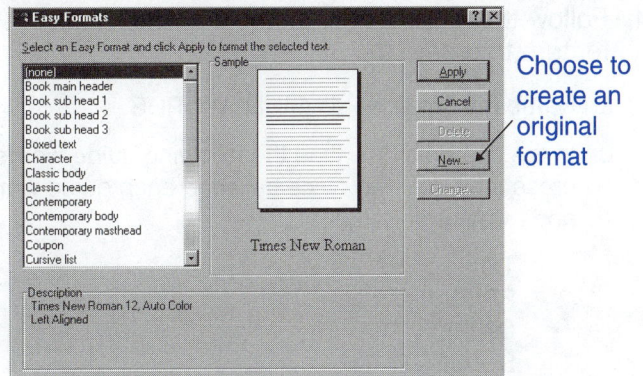

Easy Formats

Select an Easy Format and click Apply to format the selected text

[none]
Book main header
Book sub head 1
Book sub head 2
Book sub head 3
Boxed text
Character
Classic body
Classic header
Contemporary
Contemporary body
Contemporary masthead
Coupon
Cursive list

Sample

Times New Roman

Apply
Cancel
Delete
New...
Change

> Choose to create an original format

Description
Times New Roman 12, Auto Color
Left Aligned

- Click one or more of the format options in the **New Easy Format** dialog box shown below to change or create the format. Click <u>D</u>one once all formatting options are completed.

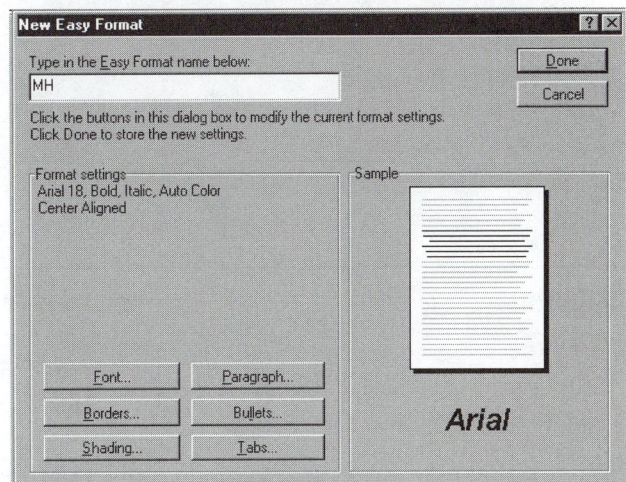

New Easy Format

Type in the Easy Format name below:

[MH]

Click the buttons in this dialog box to modify the current format settings. Click Done to store the new settings.

Format settings
Arial 18, Bold, Italic, Auto Color
Center Aligned

Sample

Arial

Done
Cancel

<u>F</u>ont...
<u>B</u>orders...
<u>S</u>hading...
<u>P</u>aragraph...
B<u>u</u>llets...
<u>T</u>abs...

- Once the Easy Text is created and formatted, you can choose <u>I</u>nsert to insert the Easy Text into the current document, or you can choose <u>C</u>lose and insert the Easy Text at a later time.

> *In this exercise, you will create a memorandum using Easy Text to insert guidewords. In addition, you will create a bulleted list, replace words using the Thesaurus and use the Word Count feature.*

EXERCISE DIRECTIONS:

1. Create a new document for the Word Processor, or open 💾**WP MEMO.19**.

2. Keyboard the memorandum starting at the top of the page.

3. Follow the steps listed here to use the Easy Text feature to create the title MEMORANDUM.

   a. Name the heading MEMOHEAD.

   b. Press the Enter key 4 times after typing the word MEMORANDUM in the <u>E</u>asy Text contents box.

   c. Create a new Easy Format; name it MEMO.

      • Click the <u>F</u>ont option and set the title in sans serif 18 point bold and italics.

      • Click the <u>P</u>aragraph option and select <u>C</u>enter Alignment.

4. Follow the steps below to use the Easy Text feature to create the guide words:

   a. Name the guide words GUIDEWORDS.

   b. In the contents box, type the following guide words; press the Enter key twice between each guide word and twice after SUBJECT:

      TO:
      FROM:
      DATE:
      SUBJECT:

   c. Create a new Easy Format; name it GW.

      • Click the <u>F</u>ont option and set the guide words to sans serif 12 point bold and italics.

5. Once the guide words are inserted, use the Tab key to appropriately align information after the colons. Set this text to serif in 12 point.

6. Create the bulleted list in sans serif 12 point bold. Use circle bullets.

7. Use the Thesaurus feature to replace the words in brackets. Be sure the tense of the new word is the same as the one it replaces.

8. Do a word count.

9. Spell check the document.

10. Save the file; name it **MEMO**.

11. Print one copy.

12. Close the document window.

THESAURUS

Shift + F7

1. Select word to be checked.
2. Click **Thesaurus** button on Toolbar .. `⊞`

OR

1. Click **T**ools .... `Alt`+`T`
2. Click **T**hesaurus .... `T`
3. Click **M**eanings .... `Alt`+`M`
4. Click desired meaning.
5. Click desired **S**ynonym .... `Alt`+`S`
   ✓NOTE: Use the arrows to see more.
6. Click **R**eplace .... `Alt`+`R`

   OR

   Press **Enter** .... `Enter`

   OR

   Click **Cancel** to .... `Esc`
   exit without replacing

WORD COUNT

1. Select text or entire document (no text selected).
2. Click **Word Count** .... `⊡`
   button on Toolbar

   OR

   a. Click **T**ools .... `Alt`+`T`

b. Click **W**ord Count .... `W`
   Message box appears with number of words in selection.
3. Click **OK** .... `Enter`

EASY TEXT

To Save Text as Easy Text

1. Click **E**dit .... `Alt`+`E`
2. Click **Easy Te**x**t** .... `X`
3. Click **N**ew .... `Alt`+`N`
4. Click in **Type a name for** .... `Alt`+`T`
   the Easy Text below text box
5. Type the name for the Easy Text ...*name*
   ✓NOTE: Easy Text names must be one word without any spaces.
6. Click in **Easy Text contents** ... `Alt`+`E`
   text box.
7. Type Easy Text contents........... *contents*
   ✓NOTE: Be sure to include all appropriate spacing.
8. Click **D**one .... `Alt`+`D`
9. Click **C**lose .... `Alt`+`C`

To Format Easy Text

1. Follow steps 1-7 above.
2. Click **F**ormat .... `Alt`+`F`

3. Click **N**ew .... `Alt`+`N`
4. Type in a name .... *name*
   for the new format.
5. Click one or more of the following format buttons:
   • **F**ont .... `Alt`+`F`
   • **B**orders .... `Alt`+`B`
   • **S**hading .... `Alt`+`S`
   • **P**aragraph .... `Alt`+`P`
   • **Bu**l**lets** .... `Alt`+`L`
   • **T**abs .... `Alt`+`T`
6. Make desired changes in each section.
7. Click **OK** to exit each format section.
8. Click **D**one .... `Alt`+`D`
   once all formatting is complete.
9. Click **A**pply .... `Alt`+`A`
10. Click **D**one .... `Alt`+`D`
11. Click **C**lose .... `Alt`+`C`

   OR

   Click **I**nsert .... `Alt`+`I`

To Insert Easy Text into a Document

1. Click **I**nsert .... `Alt`+`I`
2. Click **East Te**x**t** .... `X`
3. Click desired Easy Text
4. Press **Enter** .... `Enter`

*Use Easy Text - set in sans serif
18 pt bold and italics*

MEMORANDUM

*Use Easy Text - set
guide words in sans serif
12 pt. bold and italics*

↓ 4x

TO: All Managers Attending Computer Expo

↓ 2x

FROM: Robin McDonald

↓ 2x

DATE: Today's date

↓ 2x

SUBJECT: Hotel Discounts for Computer Expo Attendees

↓ 2x

The following San Francisco hotels have [agreed] to offer special discounted rates to all attendees of Computer Expo:

↓ 2x

- Fairmont Hotel
- Grand Hyatt
- Holiday Inn: Civic Center
- Hyatt Regency
- King George Hotel   *set in sans serif, 12 pt. bold*
- Mark Hopkins
- Nikko
- Villa Florence
- Westin St. Francis

When you call to make your reservation, [mention] that you're going to the Computer Expo at the Convention Center. There are only a limited number of rooms available at preferred rates, so plan early.

yo

Use circle bullets

■ **Remove Typestyles** ■ **Remove Bullets**

NOTES:

Remove Typestyles

- Bold, italics and underline may be removed by using the same procedure when applying these special character formats.

- You may remove character formatting individually, or you may remove *all* character formatting from a selected (highlighted) block of text by pressing Ctrl + Space. This is a useful feature when you wish to remove two or more formats in one step, such as bold, underline *and* italics.

Remove Bullets

- Removing the bullets will return the paragraph to the left margin with a five space first line indention. As noted in Exericse 17, bullets can be removed using Ctrl+Q.

- In this exercise, you are to remove character formatting and insert a separator line after the *Re*: line. A horizontal double line may be created by pressing and holding down the equal sign key (=).

> *In this exercise, you will edit a memo using previously created Easy Text. In addition, you will delete bullets and use the Thesaurus feature to replace words.*

EXERCISE DIRECTIONS:

1. Open 💬**MEMONEWS**, or open 💾**WP MEMONEWS.20**.

2. Change the memo heading using the Easy Text feature as follows:

   a. Select the current heading.

   b. Click I̲nsert.

   c. Click Easy Te̲xt and choose MEMOHEAD.

3. Make all other indicated revisions.
   - ✓ *NOTE:* *Use the same sans serif font for heading and guide words. Use the same serif font for text and event names.*

4. Create the horizontal, double line using the Equal Sign key. Make sure that the space above and below the line is equal.

5. Use Thesaurus to substitute words in brackets.

6. Spell check.

7. Preview your work.

8. Resave the document.

9. Close the document window.

CHANGE TYPESTYLES

Ctrl + B (Bold)
Ctrl + I (Italics)
Ctrl + U (Underline)
Ctrl + Space (to remove all typestyles)

1. Select text to be changed.
2. Click desired typestyle:
   - **Bold**.. `B`
   - *Italic*.. `I`
   - Underline .... `U`

REMOVE BULLETS

Ctrl+Q

1. Place insertion point within bulleted paragraph.
2. Click **F̲ormat**........................... `Alt`+`O`
3. Click **P̲aragraph** .... `P`
4. Click **B̲ulleted**................................. `B`
5. Click **OK** .... `Enter`

MEMORANDUM

Change heading to
Easy Text MEMOHEAD

Change to Easy Text
GUIDEWORDS

TO: The Staff

FROM: Sarah Walesk

DATE: Today's date

Bold the = sign

RE: Computer Expo

==

set 14 pt. bold

I strongly [urge] you to attend this year's Computer Expo. In four days, you'll pick up all the latest computer news and [discover] new ways to put your computer to work--in the office, in the lab, in the studio, in the classroom or in your home.

Here are some of the events you can look forward to:

Justify

- **Keynote Sessions** These sessions will feature luminaries from the computer world who will offer you insights from industry.
- **Application Workshops** Join a series of two-hour learning sessions which will provide guidelines, tips and "how-to's" on popular software packages.
- **Programmer/Developer Forums.** Veteran and novice computer users will brainstorm so you can learn about innovative advances and techniques.

Delete underline   *Delete italics*

If you are interested in attending, see Derek Brennen He will pre-register anyone from our company who wishes to attend. This will save you long lines at the show.

yo

Set all event names in serif
14 pt. bold and italics.

Delete bullets and add one
return between ¶'s

EXERCISE **21**

Lesson 3 – Summary

In this exercise, you will create a memorandum using previously created Easy Text, format font attributes, and use the Thesaurus, Spell Check and Word Count features to check your work.

EXERCISE DIRECTIONS:

1. Create a new document for the Word Processor, or open ⊟**WP REPORT.21**.

2. Begin typing at the top of the screen.

3. Create a memorandum from the text shown.

4. Select MEMOHEAD from Easy Text to create the memo heading.

5. Select GUIDEWORDS from Easy Text to create the guidewords.

6. Set the memo heading and guidewords in another color.
   ✓ *NOTE:* *If your printer does not support color, all text will print black.*

7. Set all body text to serif in 12 point.

8. Use the Thesaurus feature to replace bracketed words.

9. Spell check.

10. Do a word count.

11. Preview your document.

12. Print one copy.

13. Save the exercise; name it **REPORT**.

14. Close the document window.

Use Easy Text MEMOHEAD

MEMORANDUM

Use Easy Text
GUIDEWORDS

TO: Dennis Jones, Corporate Financial Manager

FROM: Susie Hand, Oceanview Branch Manager

DATE: Today's date

SUBJECT: Sales Comparison - Two Years

I have [compiled] the sales figures for the last two years of all computer items we have in stock. I assembled these figures from the data I have in my computers. Please review the information for accuracy and completeness.

I know you are [eager] to assemble the sales results from all the **Bit-Byte** computer stores to aid you in long-term planning for our organization. However, we must make sure our records are 100% correct before we can make any decisions concerning the future of our product lines.

Please let me know as soon as possible if any changes should be made.

sh/yo

- Create a One-Page Report ■ Change Margins
- Change Line Spacing ■ Add a Space Before/After a Paragraph

CUSTOMIZED TOOLBAR

Single-line spacing

Double-line spacing

NOTES:

Create a One-Page Report

- A report or manuscript generally begins 2" from the top of the page and is prepared in double space. Each new paragraph begins 0.5" from the left margin (tab once). The title of a report is centered and keyed in all caps. A double or quadruple space follows the title.

- Side margins vary depending on how the report is bound. For an unbound report, use margins of 1" on the left and right.

Change Margins

Left and Right Margins

- Since the default left and right margins are 1.25", you will need to change the margin settings in this exercise.

- Margins can be changed before or after typing text.

- There are two methods to change the margins in Works.

- Click File, Page Setup to change the margin settings for the entire document. Then, in the dialog box shown on the right, enter precise settings for each margin.

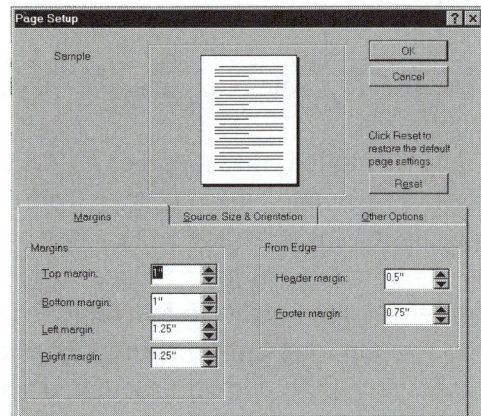

- The default unit of measure for margins is inches. You can specify another unit of measure by typing the abbreviation after the number:

  pi = picas
  cm = centimeters
  mm = millimeters

- Use the Ruler bar (illustrated on the next page) to change the margins for the entire document or a portion of the document. Using the Ruler bar to set margins lets you see the effects of margin changes as you make them. A left/right margin change affects text beginning with the paragraph in which the insertion point is placed. Therefore, to change margins for the entire document, place the insertion point at the beginning of the document.

(ruler image with measurements 1 2 3 4 5)

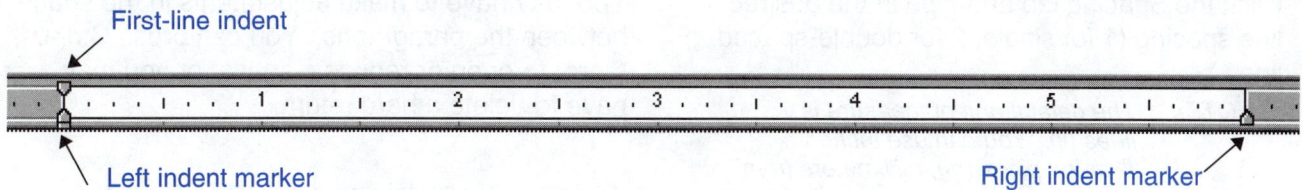

- There are two triangles at the left margin. The bottom triangle represents the left indent marker. The top triangle represents the **first-line indent marker**. To change the margin, click and drag (click and hold left mouse button) the bottom part of the marker (the top marker will move with it). Text will adjust to the new margins when the mouse button is released.

- For new text, make the changes before typing. For existing text, select text before changing margins, and drag the left and right margin markers to the desired position.

Top/Bottom Margins

- It is only necessary to change top and bottom margins if additional vertical space is needed on the document. Most documents should have at least a 1" top margin.

- Titles for reports begin 2" from the top of the page. Up to this point, you pressed the Enter key to achieve the 2" top margin. However, for one-page documents, you can set the top margin to 2" in the Page Setup dialog box.

- Setting the top margin in the Page Setup dialog box sets the margin for all pages in the document and would cause all pages to have a 2" top margin. Therefore, if you have a multiple-page document, you cannot use the Page Setup dialog box to set the top margin; you will have to press the Enter key to obtain the 2" top margin on the first page.

  ✔ NOTE: *Remember pressing the Enter key six times in 12 point gives approximately 1" of vertical space; pressing the Enter key three times equals 1/2". The size of the space produced by pressing the Enter key is a function of the font size. Pressing the Enter key six times in a larger font will produce a space larger than 1". If your title is in a font size larger than 12 point, click after the last letter in the title and set the font size to 12 point before pressing the Enter key six times.*

Change Line Spacing

- Use **line spacing** to specify the spacing between lines of text. The default line spacing is Auto. Auto allows Works to accommodate the largest character in a line.

- A line spacing change affects text from the insertion point forward. Line spacing may also be adjusted for selected text.

- Works offers a number of methods to change the line spacing:

  Click the line spacing buttons 🔲 and 🔲 on the Toolbar.

  ✔ NOTE: *You must customize the Toolbar to include these buttons as shown above.*

  OR

  Use keyboard shortcuts.
  Ctrl+1 for single spacing.
  Ctrl+5 for one and a half spacing.
  Ctrl+2 for double spacing.

  OR

- Click Format, Paragraph to access the Spacing dialog box illustrated below.

(Format Paragraph dialog box image: Indents and Alignment tab, Spacing tab; Indentation — Left: 2.5", Right: 0", First line: -2.5"; Alignment — Left, Center, Right, Justified; Sample; Bulleted checkbox; OK, Cancel buttons)

- Click the <u>S</u>pacing tab and type in the desired line spacing (1 for single, 2 for double-spaced lines.)

  ✓NOTE: *The default unit of measure is lines (li). You can use inches (" or in), picas (pi), millimeters (mm) or centimeters (cm) as a unit of measure. You can change the default unit of measure. Click Tools, Options, General tab and make desired selection.*

■ You can change the line spacing before or after typing the document.

■ If your line spacing is set for double spacing, press the Enter key once between paragraphs.

■ If you are making changes to the line spacing within a document (single to double, double to single), press the Enter key at least once before setting a new line spacing. Otherwise, the line spacing change will affect the current paragraph.

You may have to make adjustments in the space between the paragraphs. You can press Ctrl+0 (zero) to open or reduce a space, or you may have to delete a hard return.

Add a Space Before/After a Paragraph

■ You can also adjust the space between paragraphs by adding a space before or after a paragraph. Make the changes in the B<u>e</u>fore and <u>A</u>fter text boxes in the <u>S</u>pacing dialog box.

■ Use this feature to make the document easier to read, adjust the spacing between paragraphs or place emphasis on a specific paragraph. It is advisable to make these changes after the paragraph has been typed.

■ If you are using this method to create specific space between paragraphs, be careful not to put additional blank lines between the paragraphs.

In this exercise, you will create a one-page report and change the margins and spacing.

EXERCISE DIRECTIONS:

1. Create a new document for the Word Processor.
2. Set 1" left and right margins.
3. Set a 2" top margin in the Page Setup dialog box.
4. Keyboard the report on the right.
5. Key eight asterisks (*) before and after the heading.
6. Press the Enter key three times after the heading.
7. Double space the first paragraph.

8. Single space the second, third and fourth paragraphs.
9. Double space the fifth and sixth paragraphs.
10. Adjust spacing between paragraphs using Ctrl + 0 or by deleting blank lines between the paragraphs.
11. Spell check.
12. Preview your document.
13. Print one copy.
14. Save the exercise; name it **BULLETIN**.
15. Close the document window.

********ELECTRONIC BULLETIN BOARDS********

↓ *3x*

    Thousands of people across the nation are using computer bulletin boards. Through their

computers, they spend hours on line "talking" with other users, "discussing" topics ranging from

zoology to finding information about taxes or taxis, completing graduate courses, even

exchanging wedding vows. Some productive uses of bulletin boards are:

Set to single space ↘

A system set up by a hospital in West Virginia that offers detailed answers to medical questions
for people who don't want to travel great distances necessary to see a doctor.

A system created by a retired guidance counselor in Atlanta that provides current information on
scholarships and loans.

A system operated by a car expert in Las Vegas that lists thousands of collectors' cars.

Set to double space ↘

    Except for the fee of subscribing to a bulletin board, the cost of "talking" on your

computer is the same as talking on your phone, since phone lines are used for data transmission.

    The only equipment you need to connect to a bulletin board is a computer and a modem

connected to a telephone line. While most bulletin boards are free, some of the largest are

professional operations that charge a fee.

CHANGE MARGINS

1. Click **File** .... `Alt`+`F`
2. Click **Page Setup** .... `G`
3. Click **Left Margin** .... `Alt`+`L`
4. Key desired left margin .... *number*
5. Click **Right Margin** .... `Alt`+`R`
6. Key desired right margin .... *number*

   OR

1. Drag the left margin marker ⬚ to the desired location.
2. Drag the right margin marker ⬚ to the desired location.

CHANGE LINE SPACING

Ctrl + 1, Ctrl + 2, Ctrl + 5

1. Place insertion point within paragraph where line spacing change will begin.

   OR

   Select text to receive line spacing change.
2. Click **Format** .... `Alt`+`O`
3. Click **Paragraph** .... `P`
4. Click the **Spacing** tab.............. `Alt`+`S`
5. Type desired spacing in the **Line Spacing** text box .... `L`
6. Click **OK** .... `Enter`

   OR

   Click desired **Line spacing** ... ⬚ or ⬚ button on Toolbar.

ADJUST SPACING BETWEEN TWO PARAGRAPHS

1. Place insertion point in the second paragraph.
2. Press **Ctrl + 0** to reduce .... `Ctrl`+`O` space between the paragraphs.

ADD SPACE BEFORE OR AFTER A PARAGRAPH

1. Highlight the paragraph.
2. Click **Format** .... `Alt`+`O`
3. Click **Paragraph** .... `P`
4. Click the **Spacing** tab.............. `Alt`+`S`
5. Click **Before** .... `Alt` +`E`
6. Enter desired number of lines .... *number* you want inserted before the paragraph.
7. Click **After** .... `Alt`+`A`
8. Enter desired number of lines .... *number* you want inserted after the paragraph.
9. Click **OK** .... `Enter`

EXERCISE **23**

Indents (First Line, Hanging and Quotation)
Increase/Decrease Indent Levels ■ Undo Indents

NOTES:

Indents

■ An **indent** is a temporary adjustment to the margin. The indent feature allows you to indent a paragraph or the entire document from the left margin, the right margin or both margins.

■ Paragraphs may be indented before or after text is typed.

- To change the indent style for a block of text or the whole document, the desired text must be selected (highlighted).

- To change the indent style for a specific paragraph, the insertion point must be placed within the paragraph.

New paragraphs will contain the same indents as the current paragraph unless you remove or change the indent formatting.

Works offers several indent styles that work with the default tab settings. In addition, indents can be customized. This will be covered in a later lesson. The indents can be set using the Ruler bar or the Format, Paragraph menu.

First-Line Indent

This feature indents the first line in a paragraph at the default tab setting. Default tabs are set 0.5" apart. All other lines in the paragraph are left aligned.

First-line indents are set by dragging the **first-line indent marker** (the top left triangle) on the Ruler bar to the desired first-line indent position.

The sample following shows the positions of the markers for a first-line indent.

First-line indent

> Indents the first line in a paragraph according to the default tab setting. All other lines in the paragraph are left aligned.
>
> First-line indents may be set by dragging the **first-line indent marker** (the top left triangle) on the Ruler to the desired first-line indent position.

Left margin marker   Right margin marker

■ You can also change the first-line indent by choosing Format, Paragraph, Indents and Alignment tab. Select the First line box and type the measurement you want the first line indented from the left margin.

Hanging Indent

■ This feature aligns the first line of the paragraph with the left margin or indent, all other lines are indented according to the default tab setting. Below is an example of a **hanging indent**:

> *This paragraph is an example of a hanging indent. Note that all the lines in the paragraph are indented except the first line. This can be an effective way to emphasize paragraph text. This paragraph style is commonly used for bibliographies and to set up numbered lists.*

To set a hanging indent:

Click the bottom left triangle (left margin marker) on the Ruler bar, and drag both triangles to the desired tab setting. Once there, drag the top triangle (first-line indent marker) back to the margin or other desired setting. Your Ruler bar will appear as shown on the next page.

First-line indent marker

Left margin marker   Right margin marker

OR

Click Format, Paragraph, Indents and Alignment tab. Select the First line box and type a negative measurement to get the hanging indent.

OR

Press the shortcut key Shift+Ctrl+H once for each level of indent, or press Shift+Ctrl+M for each level of indent you wish to remove.

Quotation Style

■ Works uses the term **Quotation** for paragraphs that are indented equally from the left and right margins. Below is a sample of a quotation style indent. Note how this example (and the following examples) are indented from other paragraphs in this section.

> *This is a sample of a quotation style indent. Note that the paragraph is indented equally from both the left and right margins. This can be set either through the Format menu or by moving the margin markers on the Ruler.*

To set a quotation style indent:

Move the left and right margin markers on the Ruler bar to the desired location as shown below.

First-line indent marker

Left margin marker   Right margin marker

OR

Click Format, Paragraph, Indents and Alignment tab and click the up or down arrows to change the left or right indents.

Nested Paragraphs

■ A nested paragraph indents the text only on the left side. Below is an example of a nested style indent.

> *This is an example of a nested style indent. Note that the paragraph is indented only on the left side. The right side remains at the current right margin. You can set this indent by moving both the left margin and first-line indent markers on the Ruler, or by pressing Ctrl+M once for each level of indent you wish to achieve.*

To set a nested paragraph:

Press shortcut keys Ctrl+M once for each level of indent, or Press Shift+Ctrl+M for each level of indent you wish to remove.

OR

Click Format, Paragraph, Indents and Alignment tab and click the up or down arrows to change the left indent.

Increase/Decrease Indent Levels

■ Indent levels can be increased or decreased by using the Toolbar buttons as shown below. However, you must customize the Toolbar to make these buttons accessible.

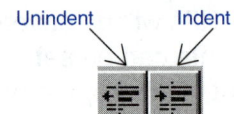

Unindent   Indent

Undo Indents

■ All indents can be undone by pressing Ctrl+Q. This action returns all lines within the paragraph to the original margins and line spacing.

■ You can also undo an indent in the Indents and Alignment dialog box.

- Click Format.

- Click Paragraph, click Indents and Alignment tab.

- Type a zero in the Indentation boxes for each indent option you want to undo.

EXERCISE DIRECTIONS:

1. Create a new document for the Word Processor.

2. Set 1" left/right margins in the Page Setup dialog box.

3. Display the Ruler bar.

4. Use the Tab key to indent the first line of the first three paragraphs.

5. Type the document in the default line spacing.

6. Prese the Enter key twice between paragraphs.

   ✓ NOTE: Proper form dictates that you press the Enter key twice between paragraphs when using single spacing and once in double spacing.

7. Set a 0.5" first-line indent on the Ruler bar before typing the fourth paragraph.

   ✓ NOTE: Be sure you press the Enter key twice between paragraphs. If you don't press the Enter key before beginning the next paragraph, the changes to the indent will affect the preceding paragraph.

8. Press the Enter key twice before beginning the fifth paragraph and press Ctrl+Q to end the first-line indent.

9. Type the fifth paragraph with a 0.5" hanging indent using Shift+Ctrl+H.

10. Press the Enter key twice to start the sixth paragraph, and press Ctrl+Q to end the hanging indent.

11. Type the sixth paragraph using a quotation style indent paragraph from the Format, Paragraph, Indents and Alignment dialog box. Change the left and right indents to 0.5".

12. Press the Enter key twice to start the seventh paragraph, and press Ctrl+Q to end the quotation style indent.

13. Type the seventh paragraph with a 0.5" nested indent using Ctrl+M.

14. Press the Enter key twice to start the eighth paragraph, and press Ctrl+Q to end the nested paragraph.

15. Type the eighth paragraph by pressing the bulleted list button on the Toolbar and then using the Indent button on the Toolbar to increase the indent.

   ✓ NOTE: If the Toolbar was not customized to contain the increase/decrease indent buttons, press Ctrl+M to increase the indent.

16. Press the Enter key twice to start the final paragraph, and press Ctrl+Q to end the bulleted list option.

17. Type the ninth paragraph by pressing the Tab key to indent the first line.

18. Change the line spacing as follows:

    a. Double space the first three paragraphs.

    b. Single space the fourth-eighth paragraphs.

    c. Double space the final paragraph.

19. Adjust spacing between paragraphs.

    ✓ NOTE: Use Ctrl+0 or delete returns as needed.

20. Save the exercise; name it **INDENT**.

21. Close the document window.

FIRST-LINE INDENT

1. Place insertion point where indent should begin.

2. Click **Format** .... Alt + O

3. Click **Paragraph** .... P

4. Click **First line** .... Alt + F

5. Type a value in the text box............ *value*

6. Click **OK** .... Enter

–USING RULER–

1. Place insertion point where indent should begin.

2. Drag first-line indent marker (top triangle) to the *right* to the desired first-line indent position.

HANGING INDENT

Shift + Ctrl + H

1. Click **Format** .... Alt + O

2. Click **Paragraph** .... P

3. Click **First line** .... Alt + F

4. Type a negative value in the text box....................... *value*

5. Click **OK** .... Enter

QUOTATION STYLE INDENT

1. Click **Format** .... Alt + O

2. Click **Paragraph** .... P

3. Click **Left** (under Indentations)........................ Alt + E

4. Type a value to indent .... *value*

5. Click **Right** .... Alt + G

6. Type a value to indent. .... *value*

7. Click **OK** .... Enter

–USING RULER–

1. Place insertion point where indent should begin.

2. Drag both left margin marker and first-line indent marker to the *right* to the desired position.

3. Drag right margin marker to the *left* to the desired position.

INCREASE/DECREASE INDENT LEVELS

Increase - Ctrl + M
Decrease - Shift + Ctrl + M

1. Click **Indent** button .... 🔲
   on Toolbar to increase indent

2. Click **Unindent** button .... 🔲
   on Toolbar to decrease indent.

REMOVE INDENTS
Ctrl + Q

1. Place insertion point where reset adjustments should begin.

2. Click **Format**.................... [Alt]+[O]
3. Click **Paragraph** .... [P]
4. Type a zero in the indent box for **each** indent you want to undo ... [0]

There are many ways to emphasize text. In addition to bolding, underlining, and italicizing words and phrases, you could set off the desired text from the rest of the document. This is done through the indent functions.

What are indents? **Indents** set a temporary adjustment to the margin settings. They can allow you to indent a paragraph or the entire document from the left margin, from the right margin or both.

A variety of indent styles are available in most current word processing programs. The following paragraphs describe the most commonly used indent styles. Each paragraph has been formatted in the style it describes.

A **first-line indent** has only the first line of the paragraph indented. All other lines of the paragraph are at the left margin.

A **hanging indent** is a format that indents all lines of the paragraph except the first line. It is used for bibliographies and to create numbered lists.

A **quotation-style indent** is used for paragraphs that are indented from both the left and right margins. When writing a report, use this style to format quotations of four or more lines.

A **nested-style indent** indents only from the left margin. The right margin is not indented in this format.

- A **bulleted list** is another feature that indents the paragraph and marks the beginning of the paragraph with a shaded circle.

In addition to the above indents, you can create custom indents for your document by dragging the indent markers on the ruler to the desired location.

NOTES:

Numbered Lists

■ In Works, a **numbered list**, also known as an **enumeration**, is created using the Hanging Indent feature.

To create a numbered list:

Press Shift+Ctrl+H, type the number and a period, then press the Tab key.

Easy Formats

■ Easy Formats simplify the process of formatting. Once you create a format, you can make it an Easy Format and reuse it when desired. The following format options can be applied to an Easy Format: font, borders, shading, paragraph, bullets and tabs.

■ Works provides a number of preset formats for headings, various document styles and indents. In addition you can create a new Easy Format or change an existing one.

To use an Easy Format:

- Click Format.

- Click Easy Formats.

- Click desired Easy Format from list as shown below.

- Click Apply.

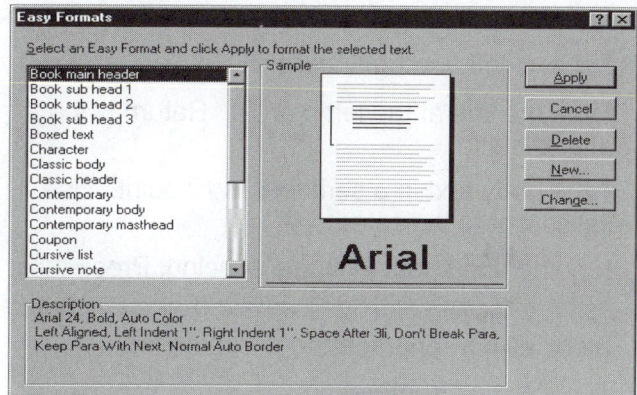

To create a new Easy Format:

- Follow steps 1-2 right.

- Click New.

- Make changes to desired options in New Easy Format dialog box shown below:

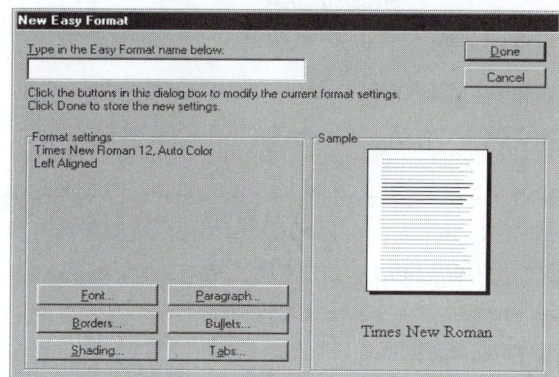

- Click Done.

- Click Apply.

  ✓ NOTE: *You can create an Easy Format from text that has been previously formatted. Select the desired formatted text, then select new from the Easy Format dialog box, provide a name for the new format, then click Done.*

In this exercise, you will create the one-page report shown in Illustration A. Once the document is created, you will apply an Easy Format and make all necessary adjustments to duplicate the document shown in Illustration B.

EXERCISE DIRECTIONS:

PART I

Instructions for Illustration A:

1. Create a new document for the Word Processor, or open 🗎**WP STUDY.24**.
   ✔ NOTE: *If opening data file WP STUDY.24, proceed to Part II.*

2. Set a 2" top margin.

3. Set a 1" left and right margin.

4. Type the title at the left margin. Return twice after the title.

5. Type body text in a serif font in 12 point. Use italics where indicated.

6. Key the document in single spacing. Press the Enter key twice between paragraphs.

7. Block all non-enumerated paragraphs.

8. To type the enumeration:
   a. Type the number and period at the left margin.
   b. Press Shift+Ctrl+H, press the Tab key, then type the enumerated text.
   c. Press the Enter key twice between enumerated paragraphs.
      ✔ NOTE: *Before typing the last paragraph, press the Enter key twice and turn off the enumeration by pressing Ctrl+Q.*

9. Spell check.

10. Preview your work.

11. Print one copy.

PART II

Make the following changes to the document so it resembles Illustration B:

1. Center the title in a sans serif 16 point bold font.

2. Indent the first line of all non-enumerated paragraphs using the Indented Paragraph option from the Easy Formats feature.

3. Double space the non-enumerated paragraphs.
   ✔ NOTE: *You will have to adjust the spacing between the paragraphs. Allow one blank line between each paragraph.*

4. Indent the enumerated paragraphs.
   HINT: *Highlight the enumerated paragraphs, press Ctrl+M to indent one level.*

5. Select the first enumerated paragraph and create a new Easy Format. Name it Enumeration.

6. Make necessary adjustments to the spacing between the paragraphs so they are consistent throughout the document.

7. Preview the document.

8. Save the document; name it **STUDY**

9. Close the document window.

NUMBERED LISTS

number, period, Shift + Ctrl + H, Tab

1. Click **F**o**rmat** .... `Alt`+`O`
2. Click **P**aragraph .... `P`
3. Click **I**ndents & **Alignment** tab .... `Alt`+`I`
4. Click **F**irst line .... `Alt`+`F`
5. Type a negative value in the text box. .... *value*
6. Click **OK** .... `Enter`

EASY FORMATS

To Use an Existing Easy Format

1. Click **F**o**rmat** .... `Alt`+`O`
2. Click **E**asy Formats .... `Alt`+`E`
3. Click desired Easy Format from list
4. Click **A**pply .... `Alt`+`A`

To create a new Easy Format

1. Follow steps 1-2 above.
2. Click **N**ew .... `Alt`+`N`
3. Type a name for the new Easy Format .... *name*
4. Make changes to desired format options in New Easy Format dialog box.
5. Click **D**one .... `Alt`+`D`

6. Click **A**pply .... `Alt`+`A`
   OR
   Click **C**lose .... `Alt`+`C`

To create a new Easy Format from formatted text

1. Select previously formatted text.
2. Click **F**o**rmat** .... `Alt`+`O`
3. Click **E**asy Formats .... `E`
4. Click **N**ew .... `Alt`+`N`
5. Type a name for the new Easy Format .... *name*
6. Click **D**one .... `Alt`+`D`
7. Click **A**pply .... `Alt`+`A`
   OR
   Click **C**lose .... `Alt`+`C`

HOW TO STUDY EFFECTIVELY

How do you study? If your studying consists of reading and rereading the material, you are not studying effectively.

In order to study productively, you must become actively involved in the process. Reading alone is passive involvement. In order to be actively involved, you should utilize as many senses as you can: sight, sound and touch, if possible. This means that in addition to reading the material, you should be writing, speaking and thinking about what you are studying.

Here are some helpful tips for studying effectively:

1. When studying from a text, prepare an outline of the material according to the structure of the text. Use the main topics and subtopics as the different levels of the outline.

2. Turn a section heading in the text into a question. For example, if the section heading in a history book reads: *Events leading to World War II*, you should rephrase it to read: *What were the events leading to World War II?* Read the section in the text to find the answer to the question. Once you have the answers, you can either write them down, say them to yourself, or better yet, do both.

3. Take good class notes. Keep a separate notebook for each class. Write the date and page number for each page you use. Teachers usually write the key points on the board or overhead. Wait to write each point until your teacher begins to talk about it. In this way, you will have room to fill in the details.

4. Read your notes after class. Your memory is fresh and you may be able to supply more details. Underline or highlight important points and write down questions and the key terms included in the lesson.

Good study skills not only help us achieve good grades in school, but they are invaluable tools that will allow us to be more productive in both our personal and professional lives.

HOW TO STUDY EFFECTIVELY

How do you study? If your studying consists of reading and rereading the material, you are not studying effectively.

In order to study productively, you must become actively involved in the process. Reading alone is passive involvement. In order to be actively involved, you should utilize as many senses as you can: sight, sound and touch, if possible. This means that in addition to reading the material, you should be writing, speaking and thinking about what you are studying.

Here are some helpful tips for studying effectively:

1.   When studying from a text, prepare an outline of the material according to the structure of the text. Use the main topics and subtopics as the different levels of the outline.

2.   Turn a section heading in the text into a question. For example, if the section heading in a history book reads: *Events leading to World War II*, you should rephrase it to read: *What were the events leading to World War II?* Read the section in the text to find the answer to the question. Once you have the answers, you can either write them down, say them to yourself, or better yet, do both.

3.   Take good class notes. Keep a separate notebook for each class. Write the date and page number for each page you use.   Teachers usually write the key points on the board or overhead. Wait to write each point until your teacher begins to talk about it. In this way, you will have room to fill in the details.

4.   Read your notes after class. Your memory is fresh and you may be able to supply more details. Underline or highlight important points and write down questions and the key terms included in the lesson.

Good study skills not only help us achieve good grades in school, but they are invaluable tools that will allow us to be more productive in both our personal and professional lives.

■ **Move Text (Drag and Drop, Cut and Paste)** ■ **Save As a New File**

DEFAULT TOOLBAR

Cut   Paste

| Times New Roman ▼ | 12 ▼ | 🗋 🖫 🖨 🔍 ✂ 🗐 📋 **B** *I* <u>U</u> ▤ ▤ ▤ 📰 ☷ ▦ ✓ 🗋 |

NOTES:

Move Text

■ You can move any portion of text to a new location within the same document or to another document.   Moving text to another document will be covered in the Integration section.

■ You can accomplish a move in all the Works tools through either the **drag and drop** procedure or the **cut and paste** procedure.

■ When moving a word or a sentence, be sure to move the space following the word or sentence. When moving a paragraph, make sure that the paragraph characters and any tab characters are moved along with the paragraph. Click <u>V</u>iew, **All Characters** when moving text that has hidden characters.

🌐 Drag and Drop

■ The drag and drop feature uses the mouse to move selected text. Once the selected information is dragged from its current location, it can then be dropped into another location within the same document, into another Works document, or into a document in another Windows application.

■ Drag and drop is best used to move small units of text.

■ Once text to be moved is selected, place the mouse pointer anywhere on the selected text. Note that the I-beam changes to a pointer with the word *drag* appearing . Click and hold the *left* mouse button as you drag the pointer to the new location. Note at this point that both the word *move* and the cursor appear . As you drag the selected text, the cursor is moving with you. Text does not move until you release the mouse. When you reach the new location, release the mouse button to drop the text into place. Works inserts the selected text at the insertion point.

> ✓ NOTE: *If your pointer changes to a circle with a diagonal line running through it, then the information cannot be moved using drag and drop.*

■ Cancel the drag and drop operation by pressing the Escape key.

■ If the text was not reinserted at the correct point, you can undo it (<u>E</u>dit, <u>U</u>ndo Drag and Drop). It is sometimes necessary to insert or delete spaces, returns or tabs after completing a move.

🌐 Cut and Paste

■ You can use the cut and paste method to move information in all the tools. The cut and paste method can use both the mouse and the keyboard while the drag and drop feature is only used with the mouse.

- Cut and paste is best used to move large units of text such as multiple lines or paragraphs. When text is cut, it temporarily disappears from the screen and is retained on the Clipboard, which is a temporary storage buffer.

- Information remains on the Clipboard until you cut or copy another selection (or until you exit Windows). Therefore, you can paste the same selection into many different locations.

- The proofreaders' mark for moving is : ⌒

Save as a New File

- When saved under a new filename, the original document remains intact. After saving, Works closes the original document, leaving the newly named document on the screen.

> *In this exercise, you will move text using cut and paste and drag and drop.*

EXERCISE DIRECTIONS:

1. Open **INDENT**, or open **WP INDENT.25**.

2. Move the paragraphs in the order indicated.
   ✔ NOTE: *Do not type the numbers.*

3. Use the cut and paste procedure for the first move.

4. Use the drag and drop procedure for the second move.
   ✔ NOTE: *Select View, All Characters before making revisions. Be sure you do not delete the paragraph symbol at the end of the third paragraph. If you delete it, you will lose the paragraph format.*

5. Make the indicated revisions.

6. Delete the current format for each of the bracketed paragraphs. Change all bracketed paragraphs to nested style.

7. Preview your document.

8. Print one copy.

9. Save as **INDENT1**.

10. Close the document window.

DRAG AND DROP

1. Select text to be moved.

2. Position mouse pointer on selected text.

3. Click and hold *left* mouse button.
   Pointer and DRAG appear.

4. Drag text to new location
   Cursor and MOVE appear.

5. Release mouse button.

CUT AND PASTE

Ctrl + X, Ctrl + V

1. Select text to move (cut).

2. Click **Cut** button on Toolbar .... ✂
   OR
   a. Click **Edit** .... `Alt`+`E`
   b. Click **Cut** .... `T`

3. Position insertion point where text is to be reinserted.

4. Click **Paste** button on Toolbar .... 📋
   OR
   a. Click **Edit** .... `Alt`+`E`
   b. Click **Paste** .... `P`

SAVE AS A NEW FILE

1. Click **File** .... `Alt`+`F`

2. Click **Save As** .... `Alt`+`A`

3. Type document filename .... *filename*

4. Click **Save** .... `Alt`+`S`

] INDENT STYLES [*Set sans serif, 18 pt. bold*

There are many ways to emphasize text. In addition to bolding, underlining, and italicizing words and phrases, you ~~could set off the desired text~~ *can indent* from the rest of the document. ~~This is done through the indent functions.~~

What are indents? **Indents** set a temporary adjustment to the margin settings. They ~~can~~ allow you to indent a paragraph or the entire document from the left margin, from the right margin or both. (*no #*)

A variety of indent styles are available in most current word processing programs. The following paragraphs describe the most commonly used indent styles. ~~Each paragraph has been formatted in the style it describes.~~

2 A **first-line indent** has only the first line of the paragraph indented. All other lines of the paragraph are at the left margin.

3 A **hanging indent** is a format that indents all lines of the paragraph except the first line. It is used for bibliographies and to create numbered lists, or enumerations.

5 A **quotation-style indent** is used for paragraphs that are indented from both the left and right margins. When writing a report, use this style to format quotations of four or more lines.

4 A **nested-style indent** indents only from the left margin. The right margin is not indented in this format.

1 • A **bulleted list** is ~~another~~ *a* feature that indents the paragraph and marks the beginning of the paragraph with a shaded circle.

In addition to the above indents, you can create custom indents for your document by dragging the indent markers on the ruler to the desired location.

Move #s in number order. DO NOT TYPE the numbers.

Reformat bracketed #s and change to nested style.

EXERCISE **26**

■ **Edit an Easy Format** ■ **Rename a File**

NOTES

Edit an Easy Format

■ You can change the specifications of an Easy Format. Choose the Easy Format you wish to make changes to, then choose the desired options you wish to include. You can <u>A</u>pply the changed format to the current document or you can <u>C</u>lose it and apply it at a later time.

Rename a File

■ In Windows 3.1, filenames were confined to 8 characters plus a three-digit extension. In Windows 95, a filename can contain up to 255 characters in either lower or uppercase, and may contain spaces.

■ Filenames can be changed from within the Open dialog box. Make sure the document you want to rename is **NOT** open. Click the file you wish to rename with the right mouse button and select Rena<u>m</u>e. The filename is now boxed and you can type the new name over the existing one. Press the Enter key to accept the new name.

■ The proofreaders' mark for inserting a space is: #

RENAME A FILE

F2

1. Make sure file to be renamed is not open.
2. Click **<u>F</u>ile** .... `Alt` + `F`
3. Click **<u>O</u>pen** .... `O`
4. Right click the desired file.
5. Select **Rena<u>m</u>e** .... `M`
6. Type new name in boxed area. ..... *name*
7. Press **Enter** .... `Enter`

EDIT AN EASY FORMAT

1. Click **F<u>o</u>rmat** .... `Alt` + `O`
2. Click **<u>E</u>asy Formats** .... `E`
3. Click Easy Format to change.
4. Click **Chan<u>g</u>e** .... `Alt` + `G`
5. Make desired changes to format options.
6. Click **<u>D</u>one** .... `Alt` + `D`
7. Click **<u>A</u>pply** .... `Alt` + `A`
   OR
   Click **<u>C</u>lose** .... `Alt` + `C`

In this exercise, you will edit an Easy Format and apply it, move and justify text and rename the file so that it has a more descriptive name.

EXERCISE DIRECTIONS:

1. Open ⌨ **BULLETIN**, or open 💾 **WP BULLETIN.26**.

2. Set 1.5" left and right margins.

3. Edit the ENUMERATION Easy Format to include a line before the paragraph.
   ✓ NOTE: See keystrokes on page 84.

4. Convert the single spaced paragraphs to a numbered list as follows:

   a. Highlight the paragraphs to be enumerated.

   b. Apply the newly revised ENUMERATION Easy Format.

   c. Type the number, period and press the Tab key.

5. Move the paragraphs, as directed, using any desired method.

6. Full justify double-spaced paragraph text.

7. Print one copy.

8. Close the file; save the changes.

9. Rename the file; name it **BULLETIN BOARD**.

10. Close the document window.

Set sans serif ↘
16 pt bold

```
********ELECTRONIC BULLETIN BOARDS********
```

Thousands of people across the nation are using computer bulletin boards. Through their computers, they spend hours on line "talking" with other users, "discussing" topics ~~ranging~~ from zoology to finding information about taxes or taxis, completing graduate courses, even exchanging wedding vows. Some productive uses of bulletin boards are:

→ .5"

1. A system set up by a hospital in West Virginia that offers detailed answers to medical questions for people who don't want to travel ~~great~~ distances ~~necessary~~ to see a doctor.
   long

2. A system created by a retired guidance counselor in Atlanta that provides current information on scholarships and loans.

3. A system operated by a car expert in Las Vegas that lists thousands of collectors' cars.

basic
Except for the fee of subscribing to a bulletin board, the cost of "talking" on your

Move ¶ and combine with previous ¶

computer is the same as talking on your phone, since phone lines are used for data transmission.

The only equipment you need to connect to a bulletin board is a computer and a modem connected to a telephone line. While most bulletin boards are free, some of the largest are professional operations that charge a fee.

EXERCISE **27**

■ **Copy Text (Copy and Paste; Drag and Drop)** ■ **Copy Formats**

DEFAULT TOOLBAR

Copy   Paste

NOTES:

Copy Text

■ **Copy and paste** and **drag and drop** are features that let you copy text from one location to another.

■ Copying leaves text in its original location while placing it in another location in the same document or another document.

> ✔NOTE: Copying text to another document will be covered in the Integration Section, page 376.
>
>   Moving removes text from its original location and places it elsewhere.

🌐 Copy and Paste

■ You can use the **copy and paste** method to copy information in all the tools. The copy and paste method can use both the mouse and the keyboard, while the drag and drop feature is only used with the mouse.

■ When text is copied, it will remain on the screen while a copy of it is placed on the clipboard.

🌐 Drag and Drop

■ Use the **drag and drop** method to copy selected text using your mouse.

■ Once the text to be copied is selected, place the mouse pointer anywhere on the selected text. Note the I beam changes to a pointer and the word *drag* appears. Press the Ctrl key while dragging text to the new location. Note the word *copy* appears as you drag. Then drop a copy of

the text into its new location by releasing the mouse button. Be sure to release the mouse button *before* releasing the Ctrl key.

■ Like moving, if the text is not copied properly, you can Undo it.

Copy Formats

■ In addition to copying text, you can copy character formats (fonts, font sizes and typestyles) and paragraph formats (margins, tabs, indents and line spacing).

To copy character formats:

• Select the text whose character or paragraph format you wish to copy.

• Click Edit.

• Click Copy.

• Select the text or paragraph you wish to copy the format to.

• Click Edit.

• Click Paste Special.

• Click Character style to copy the character format.

OR

Click Paragraph format to copy the paragraph format.

• Click **OK**.

> ✔NOTE: Immediately click Edit, Undo to restore the original format.

> *In this exercise, you will apply formatting to text and copy that format to other text. You will also copy and paste and drag and drop to rearrange information.*

EXERCISE DIRECTIONS:

1. Open ⌨**MEMO**, or open 💾**WP MEMO.27**.

2. Make all revisions as indicated.

3. Change memo heading to Book Antiqua. Retain the font size and typestyles.
   - ✓ NOTE: *If you do not have the Book Antiqua font, choose another serif font.*

4. Change the guide words and hotel names to Book Antiqua, 12 point bold. Remove the italics from the guide words. Copy new format to all guide words and hotel names.

5. Copy and move hotel information as indicated. Remember to select the space after your text so you copy the format codes as well.

6. Preview your document.

7. Print one copy.

8. Close the file; save the changes.

🌐 COPY AND PASTE
Ctrl + C, Ctrl + V

1. Select text to be copied.
2. Click **Copy** button on Toolbar........... 🖻
   OR
   a. Click **E**dit .... E
   b. Click **C**opy................................... C
3. Place insertion point to the left of where text is to be reinserted.
4. Click **Paste** button .... 🖺
   on Toolbar.
   OR
   a. Click **E**dit .... Alt + E
   b. Click **P**aste .... P

🌐 DRAG AND DROP

1. Select text to copy.
2. Position mouse pointer on selected text.
3. Press and hold **Ctrl** while clicking and holding *left* mouse button.
   Pointer and DRAG appear 🖱DRAG
4. Drag text to new location.
   Pointer and COPY appear 🖱COPY
5. Release mouse button.
6. Release **Ctrl** key.

COPY FORMATS

1. Select the text whose character or paragraph format you wish to copy.
2. Click **E**dit................................ Alt + E
3. Click **C**opy C
4. Select the text or paragraph to which you wish to copy the format.
5. Click **E**dit................................ Alt + E
6. Click **Paste S**pecial......................... S
7. Click **C**haracter style to C
   copy the character format.
   OR
   Click **P**aragraph format to .... P
   copy the paragraph format.
8. Click **OK** .... Enter

*Change memo heading to
a serif font.
Retain size and typestyle.*

MEMORANDUM

Change guide- words to a serif font and delete italics

TO: All Managers Attending Computer Expo

FROM: Robin McDonald

DATE: Today's date

Insert a divider line of asterisks (*)

SUBJECT: Hotel Discounts for Computer Expo Attendees ↓2

Set italics   ↓2

The following San Francisco hotels have decided to offer special discounted rates to all attendees of Computer Expo: *All hotels listed are within 20 minutes of the Convention Center.*

Apply new guideword format to hotel names

- **Fairmont Hotel**
- **Grand Hyatt**
- **Holiday Inn: Civic Center**
- **Hyatt Regency**
- **King George Hotel**
- **Mark Hopkins**
- **Nikko**
- **Villa Florence**
- **Westin St. Francis**

copy

explain   *attending*

When you call to make your reservation, ~~specify~~ that you're ~~going to~~ the Computer Expo at the Convention Center. There are only a limited number of rooms available at preferred rates, so plan early.

yo

#Hotels listed below offer free parking:
↓2
___
___
↓2

move

EXERCISE **28**

■ **Customize an Indent** ■ **Non-Breaking Hyphen**

NOTES:

Customize an Indent

■ You can customize the indent if the indent options are not suitable for your needs. This can be done using either the mouse or the keyboard.

■ You can set a custom indent either before or after typing text.

■ Custom indents can be set using the mouse or the keyboard.

Mouse users:

You can use the mouse to drag the markers on the Ruler bar to create a customized indent. The left margin marker and the first-line indent marker can be moved independently of each other.

Keyboard users:

You can also set a customized indent using one or more of the options in the Indents and Alignment dialog box shown below:

Left	Enter the amount you want indented from the left margin.
Right	Enter the amount you want indented from the right margin.
First line	Enter the amount you want the first line indented. The negative amount in the example to the right moves the first line to the left of the left margin marker. This gives a hanging indent.
Alignment	Choose whether you want the paragraph left, right, centered or justified.
Bulleted	Click in this box to insert a bullet and a tab at the beginning of the highlighted paragraph. Click again to deselect the bullet.

Format Paragraph   ? X

Indents and Alignment	Spacing

Indentation
Le_ft: 2.5"
Right: 1"
First line: -2.5"

Sample

OK
Cancel

Alignment
◉ Left
○ Center
○ Right
○ Justified

☐ Bulleted

Non-Breaking Hyphen

■ A non-breaking hyphen prevents a hyphenated word or number from breaking at the end of a line. This is especially useful when keying phone numbers, social security numbers or dates in the day-month-year format.

> *In this exercise, you will copy text, move text, set a customized hanging indent and insert non-breaking spaces.*

EXERCISE DIRECTIONS:

1. Open ⌨**DIVE**, or open 💾**WP DIVE.28**.

2. Set the left and right margins for 1".

3. Make the revisions indicated in Illustration A:

    a. Move hotel information so hotels are listed alphabetically.

    b. Copy hotel information as shown.

4. Reformat the text to look like Illustration B:

    a. Insert additional hotel information.

    b. Single space hotel information; double space between hotels.

    c. Format hotel name and hotel information using a customized hanging indent feature. Set the first-line indent at 0" on the Ruler bar; set the left-margin marker at 2.5".

    d. Delete the comma and space after each hotel name.

    e. Press the Tab key after each hotel name.

    f. Insert a non-breaking space in check-in and check-out times and after area codes.

    g. Insert a non-breaking hyphen in phone numbers.

5. Spell check.

6. Preview your document.

    ✓*NOTE: If document does not fit on one page, change the top and bottom margins to 0.5".*

7. Print one copy.

8. Close the file; save the changes.

CUSTOMIZE AN INDENT

—USING THE MOUSE—

Before typing text

1. Drag first-line indent marker, and left and right-margin markers to desired points.

2. Type text.

3. Press **Ctrl + Q** .... `Ctrl`+`Q` to return to default settings.

After typing text

1. Select paragraph to indent.

2. Drag first-line indent marker and left and right margin markers to desired points.

—USING THE KEYBOARD—

Before typing text

1. Click **F̲ormat**...........................`Alt`+`O`
2. Click **P̲aragraph** ....`P`
3. Click **I̲ndents and Alignment**...........`I`
4. Enter amount left margin is to be indented.
5. Enter amount right margin is to be indented.
6. Enter amount the first line should be indented.
7. Type text.
8. Press **Ctrl + Q** ....`Ctrl`+`Q` to return to default settings.

After typing text

1. Select paragraph to indent.
2. Follow steps 1-6 above.

NON-BREAKING HYPHEN

Ctrl + Shift + Hyphen

Before typing text

1. Click **I̲nsert**...................................`I`
2. Click **S̲pecial Character** ....`S`
3. Click **Select a character**........`Alt`+`S`
4. Click **Non-breaking hyphen**.
5. Click **I̲nsert**

After typing text

1. Delete existing hyphen or space....`Del`
2. Follows steps 2-5 above.

DIVING VACATIONS *Change to sans serif*
<u>Diving in the Cayman Islands</u>   *16 pt bold and italics*

Tab → Do you want to see sharks, barracudas and stingrays? ~~Do you want to see gentle~~ angels fish too?

delete italics

Tab → *The Cayman Islands* were discovered by Christopher Columbus in 1503 and are located south of Cuba. *The Caymans* are the home to only about 125,000 year-round residents.   *D.S.* However, they welcome 200,000 visitors each year. Most visitors come with masks and flippers in their luggage.

Delete underline — *Change to sans serif* Hotel/Diving Accommodations: *12 pt. bold and italics*   *Delete bold in all phone numbers.*

Delete all bullets and underlines. Place all hotel names in alphabetical order.

- <u>Sunset House</u>, PO Box 479, George Town, Grand Cayman; **(809) 555-4767**.

- <u>Coconut Harbour</u>, PO Box 2086, George Town, Grand Cayman; **(809) 555-6468**.

- <u>Red Sail Sports</u>, PO Box 1588, George Town, Grand Cayman; **(809) 555-7965**.   *copy*

- <u>Cayman Diving Lodge</u>, PO Box 11, East End, Grand Cayman; **(809) 555-7555**.

- <u>Anchorage View</u>, PO Box 2123, East End, Grand Cayman; **(809) 555-4209**.   *copy*

↓2

Hotels Offering Free Diving Instruction: ←— *Set in sans serif, 12 pt. bold and italic.*

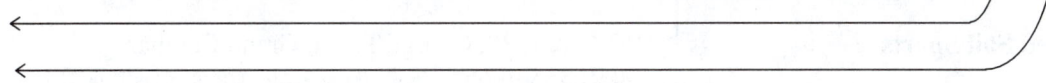

ILLUSTRATION B

DIVING IN THE CAYMAN ISLANDS

Do you want to see sharks, barracudas, stingrays and angelfish?

The Cayman Islands were discovered by Christopher Columbus in 1503 and are located south of Cuba. The Caymans are the home to only about 25,000 year-round residents. However, they welcome 200,000 visitors each year. Most visitors come with masks and flippers in their luggage.

Hotel/Diving Accommodations:

Anchorage View

PO Box 2123, East End, Grand Cayman; (809) 555-4209. Pool, four restaurants; check in 9 a.m., check out 2 p.m. Famous for outstanding view of the harbor from all rooms. Popular night spot among tourists and locals alike. *) Insert*

Cayman Diving Lodge

2.5"

PO Box 11, East End, Grand Cayman; (809) 555-7555. No pool, room service available; check in 10 a.m., check out 4 p.m. Basic accommodations, low rates. Diving expeditions three times daily at extra cost. *) Insert*

Coconut Harbour

PO Box 2086, George Town, Grand Cayman; (809) 555-6468. Pool, two restaurants; check in 10 a.m., check out 4 p.m. Free scuba exhibitions nightly. *) Insert*

Red Sail Sports

PO Box 1588, George Town, Grand Cayman; (809) 555-7965. Pool, three restaurants; check in 11 a.m., check out 3 p.m. Wind surfing and parasailing available at extra cost. *) Insert*

Sunset House

PO Box 479, George Town, Grand Cayman; (809) 555-4767. Pool, three restaurants; check in 11 a.m., check out 3 p.m. *) Insert*

Hotels Offering Free Diving Instruction:

Cayman Diving Lodge

PO Box 11, East End, Grand Cayman; (809) 555-7555. No pool, room service available; check in 10 a.m., check out 4 p.m. Basic accommodations, low rates. Diving expeditions three times daily at extra cost. *) Insert*

Sunset House

PO Box 479, George Town, Grand Cayman; (809) 555-4767. Pool, three restaurants; check in 11 a.m., check out 3 p.m. *) Insert*

EXERCISE **29**

■ **Prepare a Resume**

NOTES:

Prepare a Resume

■ A **resume** is a document which describes your background and qualifications. This document is used to gain employment. It is usually enclosed with a **letter of application** and sent to an employer, or it may be given to the employer during an interview.

■ Resume formats vary depending on the extent of your education and work experience. Most resumes are one or two pages long; however, one page is preferable.

■ Your most recent education and work experience should be listed first.

■ Resumes can be formatted using the hanging indent feature with customized indents. You can create an Easy Format for one section of the resume and then apply that Easy Format to other parts of the resume.

✓ *NOTE:* *You can use the Works TaskWizard to create a resume. See Works TaskWizards, page 413.*

In this exercise, you will create a resume and create and apply Easy Formats.

EXERCISE DIRECTIONS:

1. Create a new document for the Word Processor.

2. Set 1" left and right margins.

3. Begin the exercise at the top of the screen (1" top margin).

4. Type the resume without paragraph formatting. Upon completion, format the paragraphs as indicated.

5. Create an Easy Format for the objective as follows:
   a. Set the left indent at 2.0".
   b. Set the first-line indent at -2.0".
   c. Set the right indent at 0".

6. Name this new Easy Format OBJ.

7. Apply this format to the education and experience section.

8. Spell check.

9. Preview your work.

10. Print one copy.

11. Save the exercise; name it **RESUME**.

12. Close the document window.

JODY ABBATO ← *Set 16 point bold*
7652 Shore Road
Staten Island, NY 10314 ← *Set 12 point*
(718) 654-9870

↓ *3x*

Apply OBJ
Easy Format

CAREER OBJECTIVE: To secure a responsible management position with opportunities
for growth in a leading hotel chain.

↓ *2x*

EDUCATION
↓ *2x*

Sept. 1990 - June 1994   _Cornell University_, School of Hotel Administration, Ithaca,
NY 14850. Received a Bachelor of Science degree in Hotel
Administration with a 3.5 overall grade point average.

↓ *2x*

Sept. 1987 - June 1990   _Tottenville High School_, 100 Luten Avenue, Staten Island,
NY 10312.

↓ *2x*

SKILLS
↓ *2x*

IBM Personal Computer, knowledge of WordPerfect, Lotus and Paradox applications software.

↓ *2x*

EXPERIENCE
↓ *2x*

June 1993 - Aug. 1993   _**Mariott Hotel,**_ Broadway, NY 10012. Duties: Data entry
operator in accounting department.

↓ *2x*

June 1992 - Aug. 1992   _**Holiday Inn**_, Richmond Avenue, Staten Island, NY. Duties:
Worked in accounting department as assistant to manager.

↓ *2x*

ACTIVITIES
↓ *2x*

Tab →   Vice President of Cornell University Management Society
Tab →   Member of Cornell University Student Senate
Tab →   Staff reporter for Cornell University Management News

↓ *2x*

REFERENCES
↓ *2x*

*Indent
0.5" →*

Dr. Stanley Simon, Professor of Management, Cornell University, Ithaca, NY 14850
(325) 456-8765.
↓ *2x*
Ms. Maria Lopez, Manager, Holiday Inn, Richmond Avenue, Staten Island, NY 10314
(718) 876-3677.

EXERCISE **30**
Lesson 4 – Summary

In this exercise, you will create a one-page report with customized indents and line spacing.

EXERCISE DIRECTIONS:

1. Create a new document for the Word Processor, or open 🖫**WP BATS.30**.

2. Create a one-page report from the text in Illustration A.

3. Set 1" left and right margins.

4. Set a 2" top margin.

5. Format the report as shown in Illustration B:

   a. Double space the first three paragraphs.

   b. Single space bat species and their descriptions using a customized indent. Using the Ruler bar, set the left margin marker at 2.0", the first-line indent at 0.5" and indent the right margin 0.5".

c. Bold the bat species.

   ✓ NOTE: Your ruler should look like this:

   ` . . . ▽ . . . 1 . . . ┃ . . . 2 . . . ┃ . . . 3 . . ┃ . . 4 . . . ┃ . . 5 . . . ▲ . . 6 . . ┃`

6. Spell check.

7. Preview your work.

8. Print one copy.

9. Save the exercise; name it **BATS**.

10. Close the document window.

ILLUSTRATION A

BATS Do bats get in your hair? Do vampire bats exist? How blind is a bat? These are questions you might ask yourself if you were ever near a cave, an attic or another sheltered place. ⌗A bat is the only mammal that can fly. They usually stay in dark places, tend to live in colonies, come out only at night, and hang upside down when they are resting. As night approaches, they head for their feeding grounds. Bats have an excellent sense of smell and hearing and depend on these senses to navigate and find food at night. Bats eat large numbers of insects and are, therefore, valuable to people. ⌗The following is a description of several bat species: **Vampire Bats** These mammals feed on the blood of other animals and live in Central and South America. Vampire bats swallow about 1 tablespoon of blood a day. They leave their victims with a small wound which heals quickly, but these bats can carry rabies. **Brown Bats** They live in the United States in buildings and caves and have a wingspan of about 12 inches. **Free-Tailed Bats** These brown bats have a wingspan of up to 12 inches and live in colonies in the Southern United States and Mexico. **Red Bats** With a wingspan of 12 inches, these bats live alone in trees and fly south every winter. The male has bright red, white-tipped fur, while the female has a grayish red fur. ⌗Now to answer the questions asked earlier: Bats do not get tangled in people's hair. Bats tend to be frightened of people and will fly away. Bats are not blind. All species of bats can see, but they see very poorly, especially at night. But, vampire bats DO exist; they are one of several kinds of bat species which have been described here.

ILLUSTRATION B

BATS

Do bats get in your hair? Do vampire bats exist? How blind is a bat? These are questions you might ask yourself if you were ever near a cave, an attic or another sheltered place.

A bat is the only mammal that can fly. They usually stay in dark places, tend to live in colonies, come out only at night, and hang upside down when they are resting. As night approaches, they head for their feeding grounds. Bats have an excellent sense of smell and hearing and depend on these senses to navigate and find food at night. Bats eat large numbers of insects and are, therefore, valuable to people.

The following is a description of several bat species:

Vampire Bats	These mammals feed on the blood of other animals and live in Central and South America. Vampire bats swallow about 1 tablespoon of blood a day. They leave their victims with a small wound which heals quickly, but these bats can carry rabies.
Brown Bats	They live in the United States in buildings and caves and have a wingspan of about 12 inches.
Free-Tailed Bats	These brown bats have a wingspan of up to 12 inches and live in colonies in the Southern United States and Mexico.
Red Bats	With a wingspan of 12 inches, these bats live alone in trees and fly south every winter. The male has bright red, white-tipped fur, while the female has a grayish red fur.

Now to answer the questions asked earlier: Bats do not get tangled in people's hair. Bats tend to be frightened of people and will fly away. Bats are not blind. All species of bats can see, but they see very poorly, especially at night. But, vampire bats DO exist; they are one of several kinds of bat species which have been described here.

EXERCISE 31

■ Find Text ■ Find Special Characters

CUSTOMIZED TOOLBAR

Find

| Times New Roman | 12 |

NOTES:

Find Text

- The **Find** feature scans your document and searches for occurrences of specified words, phrases or special characters. Once the desired text or code is found, it can be edited or replaced.

- The Find feature will search text that follows the insertion point. Therefore, when searching an entire document, place the insertion point at the beginning of the document.

  ✓ *NOTE:*   *If you start your Find procedure in the middle of a document, Works will ask if you want to continue the search from the beginning of the document.*

- **Find** may be accessed from the **E**dit menu or by clicking the Find button on the Toolbar.

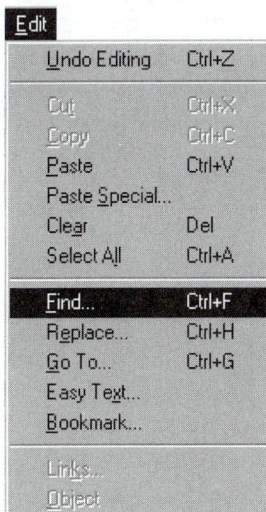

Edit	
<u>U</u>ndo Editing	Ctrl+Z
Cu<u>t</u>	Ctrl+X
<u>C</u>opy	Ctrl+C
<u>P</u>aste	Ctrl+V
Paste <u>S</u>pecial...	
Clea<u>r</u>	Del
Select A<u>l</u>l	Ctrl+A
<u>F</u>ind...	Ctrl+F
<u>R</u>eplace...	Ctrl+H
<u>G</u>o To...	Ctrl+G
Easy Te<u>x</u>t...	
<u>B</u>ookmark...	
Lin<u>k</u>s...	
<u>O</u>bject	

- The Find dialog box appears as shown below:

  - The word, phrase or special character to be found must be typed in the Find what text box.

  - To search for text exactly in the case it was typed (uppercase, lowercase or initial caps), select **Match case**.

  - The **Find whole words only** option may be selected to search for whole words only. For example, if you were searching for the word *the*, Works would not flag words in which "the" was a part of a word, like "**the**se," "**the**saurus," "**the**sis," etc.

Find Special Characters

- The Find feature can also find special characters. To find a special character, you must enter the appropriate code for that character. A list of special characters and their codes appears in the table below:

Tab	^T or click the ➡ button
End-of-line mark	^N
Nonbreaking space	^S
Page break	^D
Paragraph mark	^P or click the ¶ button
Caret	^^

Question mark	^?
Wildcard	?
White space between words	^W

- A wildcard code can be used to represent any character in a specific location within a word. For instance, to find both Cathy or Kathy, you would use ?athy, or to find any three-letter word beginning with an s and ending with an n,

you would use s?n. This last search would yield words like the following: sun, son, sin.

- Once a word is "found," it is highlighted. In order to begin a new search, you must deselect the highlighted word.

- In this exercise, you will search for the words shown in brackets. The Find feature will quickly place the insertion point on those words so you can use the Thesaurus feature to edit them.

> *In this exercise, you will search for text using the Find feature.*

EXERCISE DIRECTIONS:

1. Open ⌨**BULLETIN BOARD**, or open 💾**WP BULLETIN BOARD.31**.

2. Use the Find feature to search for each word marked in brackets. Then, using the Thesaurus feature, find a substitute for each bracketed word. Make sure the new word is in the same tense, number and person as the one it replaces. In addition, edit adjacent words as needed.

3. Use the wildcard feature to find *taxes* and *taxis*.

4. Print one copy.

5. Close the file; save the changes.

FIND TEXT/SPECIAL CHARACTERS

1. Place insertion point at top of document.

2. Click **Edit** .... `Alt`+`E`

3. Click **Find** .... `F`

   OR

   Click **Find** button on Toolbar. .... 🔍

4. Enter text to be searched in **Fin̲d what** text box. .... *text*

To find specific text:

   a. Click **Find w̲hole** .... `Alt`+`W`
      words only checkbox.

   b. Click **Match c̲ase** .... `Alt`+`C`
      check box.

To find special characters:

Enter special characters as follows:

- Tab .... ^T

   OR

   Click the Tab button .... ➡

- End-of-line mark .... ^N
- Nonbreaking space .... ^S
- Page break .... ^D
- Paragraph mark .... ^P

   OR

   Click the Paragraph button .... ¶

- Caret .... ^^
- Question mark .... ^?
- Wildcard .... ?
- White space between words .... ^W

5. Click **Fin̲d Next** to search ...... `Alt`+`F`
   for next occurrence.

6. Click **Cancel** if it finds .... `Esc`
   the word you want.

   OR

   Click **Fin̲d Next** to .... `Alt`+`F`
   continue the search.

   ✓ *NOTE:* *Deselect the current word before beginning a new search.*

********ELECTRONIC BULLETIN BOARDS********

Thousands of people across the nation are using computer bulletin boards. Through their computers, they spend hours on line "talking" with other users, "discussing" topics from zoology to finding information about taxes or taxis, [completing] graduate courses, even exchanging wedding vows. While most bulletin boards are free, some of the largest are professional operations that [charge] a fee.

Some productive uses of bulletin boards are:

Delete numbers and periods; replace with bullets.

1. A system set up by a hospital in West Virginia that offers detailed answers to medical questions for people who do not want to travel long distances to see a doctor.

2. A system created by a retired guidance counselor in Atlanta that provides current information on scholarships and loans.

3. A system operated by a car expert in Las Vegas that lists thousands of collectors' cars.

The only equipment you need to connect to a bulletin board is a computer and a modem connected to a telephone line. Except for the basic fee of [subscribing] to a bulletin board, the cost of "talking" on your computer is the same as talking on your phone, since phone lines are used for data transmission.

EXERCISE **32**

■ **Find and Replace Text** ■ **Find and Replace Special Characters** ■ **Hyphenation**

NOTES:

Find and Replace Text

■ The **Find and Replace** feature searches for and replaces specified words, phrases or special character codes.

■ You should save your work before doing a find and replace operation in case you make an error and accidentally replace needed text or codes.

■ Click <u>E</u>dit, <u>R</u>eplace to access the Replace dialog box below:

■ The Replace dialog box contains the following features:

Fi<u>n</u>d What
Type the text to be replaced.

<u>R</u>eplace With
Type the replacement text.

Find <u>w</u>hole words only
Allows you to look for a word as an entire word, not as part of a longer word. For example, if you wanted to find *keyboard,* Works would ignore *keyboarding*.

Match <u>c</u>ase
Allows you to look for text that matches the exact capitalization of the text entered in the Fi<u>n</u>d what textbox. For example, if you wanted to find *ALL CAPS*, Works would skip *All Caps*.

<u>F</u>ind Next
Skips the current occurrence and goes to the next occurrence of the word or code.

Cancel
Closes the dialog box before any changes are made.

Close
Closes the dialog box and saves the changes that have been made.

Replace <u>A</u>ll
Changes all occurrences of the word or code.

<u>R</u>eplace
Changes only specific occurrences of the word or code.

✓ *NOTE:* *When the search and replace is completed, Works will ask if you want to start searching from the beginning of the document.*

Find and Replace Special Characters

■ The following list contains the special characters and their corresponding codes that can be searched in a Works document:

Tab	^T
End-of-line mark	^N
Nonbreaking space	^S
Page break	^D
Paragraph mark	^P
Caret	^^
Question mark	^?
Any character	?
White space	^W

- If you wanted to replace any of the above special characters, you would enter the codes in the Find what textbox. If you were replacing with a special character, you would enter the code in the Replace with textbox.

Hyphenation

- Hyphenation produces a tighter right margin by dividing words that extend beyond the right margin rather than wrapping them to the next line. If the text is justified and hyphenated, the sentences will have smaller gaps between words.

- Works hyphenates a document with or without confirmation. When Works hyphenates a document it inserts an optional hyphen. Optional hyphens appear like this (⌐)and print only at the end of the line.

  ✓NOTE: It is advisable to hyphenate only after you have edited and spell checked your work.

- Click Tools, Hyphenation to access the Hyphenation dialog box below:

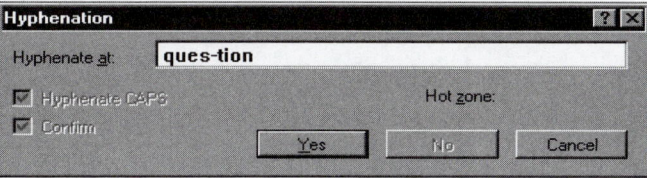

Hyphenation	? ☒
Hyphenate at:	ques-tion
☑ Hyphenate CAPS	Hot zone:
☑ Confirm	Yes No Cancel

Hyphenate at
Displays a word to be hyphenated and suggests a hyphenation. Use the directional arrows to position the hyphen at a different point in the word.

Hyphenate CAPS
Allows for hyphenation of words appearing in all caps.

Confirm
Displays each word to be hyphenated so that the suggested hyphenation can be reviewed. Click off this option to perform an automatic hyphenation.

Hot zone
Allows you to specify the right margin area to increase or decrease the raggedness of the right margin. A smaller number reduces the raggedness of the right margin; a larger number increases it.

No
Allows you to skip the current word and go on to the next word.

Cancel
Stops the hyphenation operation but leaves all existing hyphens.

- Use the Replace feature to remove hyphens either selectively or globally from a document. Type a ^ in the **Find what** textbox and leave the Replace textbox empty.

> *In this exercise, you will hyphenate a document and use the Replace feature to replace words and special characters.*

EXERCISE DIRECTIONS:

1. Open ▥**STUDY**, or open ▤**WP STUDY.32**.

2. Reset the top margin to 1.5".

3. Reset the right indent for the enumeration (numbered paragraphs) to 5.5" on the Ruler bar.

4. Justify the document.

5. Change the title to 20 point bold and italics.

6. Set the Hot Zone to 0.15".

7. Hyphenate the document using **C**onfirm.

8. Use the Replace feature to delete the numbers, periods and tabs in the enumerated paragraphs. Paragraphs should appear in the hanging indented style.

   ✓ HINT: *Enter ?.^t in the Fi**n**d what text box; leave the Re**p**lace with textbox empty.*

9. Make all revisions as indicated.

10. Insert the handwritten paragraph where shown and format for hanging indented style.

11. Use the Find feature to search for the words in brackets.

12. Use the Thesaurus to find a substitute for each bracketed word.

13. Use the **R**eplace feature to search **text** and replace with **textbook**. Follow the steps below:

    a. Use the **R**eplace option to change the first occurrence.

    b. Do not change the second occurrence.

    c. Use the Replace **A**ll option to change all other occurrences.

14. Spell check.

15. Preview your document.

16. Print one copy.

17. Close the file; save the changes.

REPLACE TEXT/SPECIAL CHARACTERS

1. Place insertion point at top of the document.

2. Click **E**dit .... `Alt`+`E`

3. Click **R**eplace .... `E`

4. Click **Fi**nd what text box......... `Alt`+`N`

5. Enter text or code to find.

6. Press **Tab**...................................... `Tab`

7. Enter replacement text or code.

8. Click **F**ind Next...................... `Alt`+`F`

9. Click **R**eplace .... `Alt`+`R`

   OR

   Click **Replace A**ll.................. `Alt`+`A`
   to change all occurrences of word or code.

10. Click **Clos**e .... `Alt`+`E`

HYPHENATION

1. Position insertion point where hyphenation is to begin.

2. Click **Tools** .... `Alt`+`T`

3. Click **Hyph**enation.......................... `H`

4. Click **OK** to perform prompted hyphenation .... `Enter`

5. Click **Yes** to accept suggested hyphenation point .... `Alt`+`Y`

   OR

   Click **No** to avoid hyphenating `Alt`+`N`

   OR

   Move arrows to desired hyphenation point and click **Yes**............... `Alt`+`Y`

   OR

   Click off **Confirm** to perform automatic hyphenation.......... `Alt`+`C`

6. Click **OK** when prompted that hyphenation is complete. .... `Enter`

REMOVE OPTIONAL HYPHENS

1. Click at the beginning of the document.

2. Click **Edit**............................... `Alt`+`E`

3. Click **R**eplace .... `E`

4. Click **Fi**nd what textbox.......... `Alt`+`N`

5. Type ^-.................................. `^` `-`

6. Leave **Repl**ace .... `Alt`+`P`
   textbox empty.

7. Click **Fi**nd Next...................... `Alt`+`F`

8. Click **R**eplace to remove........ `Alt`+`R`
   the optional hyphen and search for the next one.

   OR

   Click **F**ind Next to keep .... `Alt`+`F`
   the selected optional hyphen and find the next one.

   OR

   Click **Replace A**ll.................... `Alt`+`A`
   to remove all optional hyphens.

9. When finished, click **Clos**e ..... `Alt`+`E`

HOW TO STUDY EFFECTIVELY

*Change to 20 pt
bold and italics*

How do you study? If your studying consists of reading and rereading the material, you are not studying effectively.

In order to study productively, you must become actively involved in the process. Reading alone is passive involvement. In order to be actively involved, you should utilize as many senses as you can: sight, sound and touch, if possible. This means that in addition to reading the [material], you should be writing, speaking and thinking about what you are studying.

Here are some helpful tips for studying effectively:

Change right indent to 5.5"

Delete numbers periods and tabs.

1. When studying from a text, prepare an outline of the material according to the structure of the text. Use the main topics and subtopics as the different levels of the outline.

Change #s to hanging indented style

2. Turn a section heading in the text into a question. For example, if the section heading in a history book reads: *Events leading to World War II*, you should [rephrase] it to read: *What were the events leading to World War II?* Read the section in the text to find the answer to the question. Once you have the answers, you can either write them down, say them to yourself, or better yet, do both.

on an   projector

3. Take good class notes. Keep a separate notebook for each class. Write the date and page number for each page you use.   Teachers usually write the key points on the board or overhead. Wait to write each point until your teacher begins to talk about it. In this way, you will have [room] to fill in the details.

while   so

4. Read your notes after class, Your memory is fresh and you may be able to supply more details. Underline or highlight important points and write down questions and the key terms included in the lesson.

Good study skills not only help us [achieve] good grades in school, but they are invaluable tools that will allow us to be more productive in both our personal and professional lives.

Reread the material. Look back and carefully read any material you still don't understand. Always look for the main points, further details and questions you can answer as you reread.

EXERCISE **33**

■ **Hard vs. Soft Page Breaks** ■ **Second Page Headings** ■ **Print Selected Pages**

NOTES:

Hard vs. Soft Page Breaks

■ Works assumes you are working on a standard 8 1/2" x 11" page. Since Works uses default 1" top and bottom margins, there are exactly 9" of vertical space on a standard page for keyboarding text.

■ Therefore, when you enter more text than can fit on one page, Works automatically inserts small arrows (>>) at the left margin to indicate the end of one page and the start of another. The current page and the total number of pages are indicated at the far right in the status bar and on the left of the horizontal scroll bar.

> ✓ NOTE: In Page Layout view, each page is displayed separately.

■ When Works ends the page, this is referred to as an **automatic page break**.

■ You can also set your own page breaks by selecting Page Break from the Insert menu, or by pressing Ctrl+Enter. When you specify the page break, this is referred to as a **manual page break**. Text can still be added above the page break, but the manual page break will always begin a new page.

■ A manual page break may be deleted by moving the insertion point to the beginning of the line immediately following the page break, and pressing the Backspace key.

Second Page Headings

■ A multiple-page letter requires a heading on the second and succeeding pages. The heading should begin at 1" and include the name of the addressee (to whom the letter is going), the page number and the date.

■ Setting a top margin in Page Setup affects all pages in the document. Therefore, you must use a 1" top margin (the default), and press the Enter key to achieve a different top margin on the first page of the document.

Print Selected Pages

■ Works prints the entire document as the default. However, you may specify how much of the document you wish to print: the full document, current page, or a range of pages within a document.

To print selected pages:

Pages 2 and 3, or pages 3-5, for example.

• Select Print from the File menu.

• Select Pages.

• Specify the range by entering the first page of the range in the from box and the last page of the range in the to box.

To print one page of a multiple-page document:

• Specify the same page in the from and to text boxes.

Note the Print dialog box on the next page which indicates that only page 2 be printed.

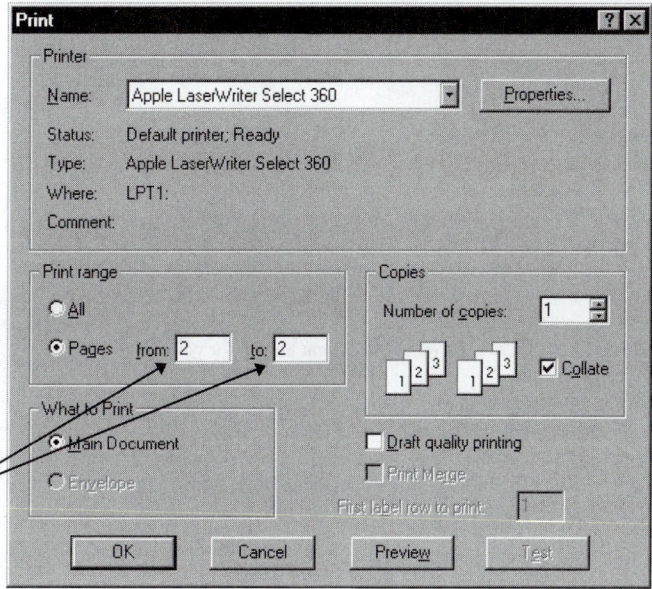

Print only page 2.

(Dialog box: Print)

In this exercise, you will create a two-page letter with a bulleted list and a numbered list. You will insert a hard page break, create a second-page heading and print the letter.

EXERCISE DIRECTIONS:

1. Create a new document for the Word Processor, or open 💾**WP NYC.33**.

2. Format the letter on the right in draft-block style.
   ✓ *NOTE: Draft copies must be double spaced.*

3. Set 1" left and right margins.

4. Begin the exercise approximately 2.5" from the top.
   ✓ *NOTE: Use the 1" default top margin and press the Enter key four times.*

5. Use the bulleted list feature to create the list on the first page.
   HINT: Press Ctrl+Q to eliminate unwanted bullets.

6. Use the Hanging Indent feature to create the enumeration on the second page.
   HINT: Use the Hanging Indent Easy Format.

7. Spell check.

8. Print one copy of pages 2 and 3.

9. Reset the line spacing to single.
   ✓ *NOTE: Make all necessary adjustments to the spacing. The date should begin at 2.5" from the top and there should be a double space between paragraphs.*

10. Insert a hard page break immediately after the fourth line in the seventh paragraph.

11. Type the second-page heading at the top of page 2. Press the Return key three times after the heading.

12. Print one copy of the full document.

13. Save the exercise; name it **NYC**

14. Close the document window.

INSERT HARD PAGE BREAK
Ctrl + Enter

1. Place insertion point where new page is to begin.
2. Click **Insert** .... Alt + I
3. Click **Page Break** .... B

DELETE HARD PAGE BREAK

1. Place insertion point immediately after hard page break line.
2. Press **Backspace** .... Backspace

PRINT SELECTED PAGES
Ctrl + P

1. Click **File** .... Alt + F

2. Click **Print** .... P
   OR
   Click **Print** button on Toolbar.
3. Click **Pages** .... Alt + G
4. Click **from** .... Alt + F
5. Enter a first page in range.
6. Click **to** .... Alt + T
7. Enter last page in range.

Today's date

Mr. Brendon Basler
54 West Brook Lane
Fort Worth, TX 76102-1349

Dear Mr. Basler:

I am so glad to hear that you might be moving to Manhattan. You asked me to write and tell you what it is like living in Manhattan. Since I have been a New Yorker for most of my life and love every minute of it, I will describe to you what it might be like for you to live here.

Use bulleted list feature.

- If you move to an apartment in Manhattan with a view, you might see the Empire State Building, the Metropolitan Life Tower, the Chrysler Building or even the Citicorp Center. Depending on where your apartment is located, you might even see the twin towers of the World Trade Center. The Brooklyn and Manhattan Bridges are off to the east and on a clear day you can see the Hudson River.

- Traffic in New York, as well as waiting in long lines at the post office and the movie theaters, can be very frustrating. However, after you have lived here for a short while, you will know the best times to avoid long lines.

- It is absolutely unnecessary and *very* expensive to own a car in Manhattan. The bus and subway systems are excellent modes of travel within the city.

- There is always something to do here. If you love the opera, ballet, theater, museums, art galleries, and eating foods from all over the world, then New York is the place for you.

Before you actually make the move, I suggest that you come here for an extended visit. Not everyone loves it here.

You mentioned that you would be visiting some time next month. I have listed on the next page some of the hotels (and their phone numbers) you might want to consider staying at while you are visiting. I have included those that would be in walking distance to your meeting locations. And, while you are attending your meetings, your family can take advantage of some of the sights and

Mr. Brendon Basler
Page 2
Today's date

shopping near your hotel. I have called the hotels to be certain they can accommodate you and your family. They all seem to have availability at the time you are planning to visit.

Use hanging indent feature.

1. **Plaza Hotel** - located at 59th Street and Central Park South at the foot of Central Park. 1-800-555-3000.

2. **The Pierre Hotel** - located at 61st Street and Fifth Avenue across the street from Central Park. 1-800-555-3442.

3. **The Drake Swissotel** - located at 56th Street and Park Avenue. 1-212-555-0900.

Of course, you realize that there are many other hotel options available to you. If these are not satisfactory, let me know and I will call you with other recommendations.

Good luck with your decision. When you get to New York, I will show you some of the sights and sounds of the city. Hopefully, you will then be able to decide whether or not New York City is the place for you.

Sincerely,

Pamela Davis

pd/yo

EXERCISE **34**

■ **Letters with Special Notations** ■ **Bookmarks**

NOTES:

Letters with Special Notations

■ Letters may include special parts in addition to those learned thus far. The letter in this exercise contains a mailing notation, a subject line and enclosure and copy notations.

■ When a letter is sent by a **special mail service** such as Express Mail, Registered Mail, Certified Mail or by hand (via a messenger service), it is customary to include an appropriate notation on the letter. The notation is placed a double space below the date and typed in all caps.

■ The **subject** identifies or summarizes the body of the letter. It is typed a double space below the salutation. A double space follows it. It may be typed at the left margin or centered in modified block style. **Subject** may be typed in all caps or in upper- and lowercase. **Re** (in reference to) is often used instead of **Subject**.

■ An **enclosure**, or attachment notation, is used to indicate that something besides the letter is included in the envelope. An enclosure or attachment notation is typed a double space below the reference initials and may be typed in several ways. A number indicates how many items are enclosed in the envelope.

ENC.	Enclosure	Enclosures (2)
Enc.	Encls.	Attachment
Encl.	Encls. (2)	Attachments (2)

■ If copies of the document are sent to others, a **copy notation** is typed a double space below the enclosure or attachment notation (or the reference initials if there is no enclosure or attachment notation). A copy notation may be typed in several ways:

Copy to	c:
Copy to	pc: (photocopy)

Bookmarks

■ A **Bookmark** is an invisible marker you can use to mark and return to any location within the document. This is a convenient feature if, for example, you need to leave your work to obtain additional information. When you return, you open the file, find the bookmark and quickly return to the place you marked.

■ You cannot set a bookmark during the actual typing. You can only set a bookmark into existing text. There must be text to the right of where you wish to place the bookmark; otherwise, the bookmark will move as you enter new text.

■ Name your bookmarks in the Bookmark Name dialog box shown below. A bookmark name can consist of up to 15 characters including blank spaces and punctuation. Click <u>E</u>dit, click <u>B</u>ookmark to access the dialog box.

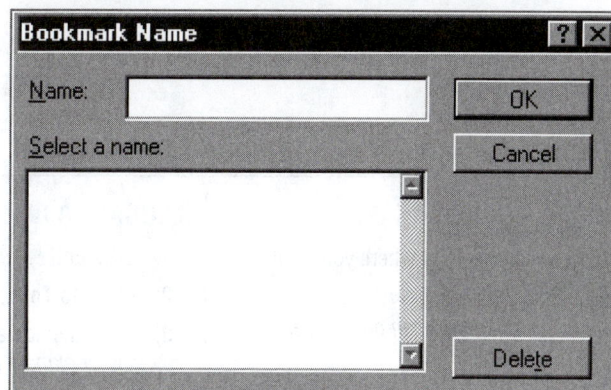

- Once your bookmark is created, you can jump to that location without having to move through the document. Your insertion point may be anywhere in the document when finding the bookmark.

- Use the Go To feature to access a bookmark. **To find your place using a bookmark**:
  - Click **E**dit.
  - Click **G**o To.
  - Click desired bookmark.
  - Click OK.

> *In this exercise, you will create a modified-block letter with special notations and set and find bookmarks.*

EXERCISE DIRECTIONS:

1. Create a new document for the Word Processor, or open 🖫**WP PREVIEW.34**.

2. Format the letter on the next page in modified-block style.

3. Use the default margins.

4. Begin the exercise approximately 2.5" from the top.

5. Double indent the quotation paragraphs 1" from the left and right margins.

   HINT: Create an Easy Format for the first quotation style paragraph and apply it to format the second one.

6. Set bookmarks where indicated; name the first one **1st Indent**, the second **3rd Indent** and the third **copyto**.

   ✓ *NOTE: You must type all the text first, then locate the insertion point where you want the bookmark and set it.*

7. Insert a manual page break where indicated, and include the second page heading.

8. Spell check.

9. Save the exercise; name it **PREVIEW**.

10. Find the first bookmark, **1st Indent**. Insert the following sentence at the bookmark location:

    Furthermore, they have captured the objects on film so true to life that anyone watching them is captivated.

11. Find the second bookmark, **3rd Indent**. Insert the following as the third indented paragraph:

    I will institute a program which will make schools throughout the country aware of their vocational potential.

12. Find the third bookmark, **copyto**. Insert a copy notation to Tien Lee.

13. Print three copies of page 1 and one copy of page 2.

14. Close your file; save the changes.

TO SET A BOOKMARK

1. Place insertion point where you want the bookmark.

   ✓ *NOTE: Bookmarks can only be set in existing text.*

2. Click **E**dit.................................. `Alt`+`E`

3. Click **B**ookmark .... `B`

4. Enter bookmark name in **Name** textbox .... *bookmark name*

5. Click **O**K................................... `Enter`

LOCATE A BOOKMARK

1. Click **E**dit.............................. `Alt`+`E`

2. Click **G**o To............................... `G`

3. Enter the name of bookmark to locate the *bookmark name*

   OR

   a. Click **S**elect...................... `Alt`+`S`

   b. Select name of bookmark to locate.

   c. Click **O**K .... `Enter`

DELETE A BOOKMARK

1. Click **E**dit.............................. `Alt`+`E`

2. Click **B**ookmark .... `B`

3. **S**elect name of bookmark to delete................. `Alt`+`S`

4. Click **D**ele**t**e....................... `Alt`+`T`

5. Click **C**lose .... `Alt`+`C`

Today's date

REGISTERED MAIL
↓ 2
Ms. Elizabeth DeKan
Broward College
576 Southfield Road
Marietta, GA 30068
↓ 2
Dear Ms. DeKan:
↓ 2
Subject: Educational Films for High Schools and Colleges
↓ 2
Thank you for your interest in the films that we have available for high school and college
students. We are pleased to send you the enclosed flyer which describes the films in
detail. Also enclosed is a summary of those films that have recently been added to our
collection since the publication of the flyer.

We will be sure to send the films in time for you to preview them. Please be sure to list
the date on which you wish to preview the films.

There have been many positive reactions to our films. Just three weeks ago, a group of
educators, editors and vocational experts were invited to view the films at the annual
EDUCATORS' CONFERENCE. Here are some of their comments:

Mr. William R. Bondlow, Jr., president of the National Vocational Center in Washington,
D.C. and editor-in-chief of Science Careers, said,

1" I like the films very much. They are innovative and a great
benefit to all those interested in the earth sciences as a
professional career. ⟵——— *create bookmark*   1"

Ms. Andra Burke, a leading expert presently assigned to the United States Interior
Department, praised the films by saying:

Ms. Elizabeth DeKan
Page 2
Today's date

1" They are a major educational advancement in career
placement, which will serve as a source of motivation for all
future geologists.   1"

A member of the National Education Center, Dr. Lawrence Pilgrim, also liked the films
and said, ⟵——— *create bookmark*

These are just some of the reactions we have had to our films. We know you will have a
similar reaction.

We would very much like to send you the films that you would like during the summer
session. You can use the summer to review them. It is important that your request be
received quickly since the demand for the films is great, particularly during the summer
sessions at colleges and universities throughout the country.

Cordially,

William DeVane
Executive Vice President
Marketing Department

wd/yo
Enclosures (2)

Copy to   Robert R. Redford
                 Nancy Jackson
                 ⟵——— *create bookmark*

EXERCISE **35**

■ **Footnotes**

NOTES:

Footnotes

- A **footnote** is used in a document to give information about the source of quoted or paraphrased material. The information includes the author's name, the publication, the publication date and the page number from which the quote was taken.

- Footnotes can also be used to make comments or clarify information in the body of the document.

- Footnotes are printed at the bottom of a page. A separator line separates footnote text from the text on the page.

- A **reference number** appears immediately after the quote in the text, and a corresponding footnote number appears at the bottom of the page. You can use symbols such as the asterisk (*) rather than numbers as the footnote mark.

- Place your insertion point where you want the reference in the body of the report. Click Insert, Footnote to access the Insert Footnote dialog box below.

- A numbered reference is the default marker. If you wish to use a symbol as the footnote marker, enter it in the Mark textbox.

- The **Footnote** feature automatically inserts the reference number after the quote, inserts the separator line, numbers the footnote and formats your page so that the footnote appears on the same page as the reference number.

- The actual note is typed at the bottom of the page in Page Layout view or in a footnote pane in Normal view. It is recommended that you use Page Layout view when working with footnotes. This view displays the document as it will look when printed. You will need to press the Enter key after each footnote to get a double space between notes.

  ✔ NOTE: To close the footnote pane in Normal view, click View, click Footnotes. Repeat the steps to open it.

- If you move a footnote, Works automatically repositions the footnotes in correct order. When a footnote is deleted, Works renumbers the remaining footnotes.

  ✔ NOTE: Another method of citing sources other than footnoting uses textual citations or parenthetical citations. This method inserts the author's last name and the page number in parentheses within the text. A bibliography entitled Works Cited is created on a separate page at the end of the report and provides complete information on the sources used.

Insert Footnote ? ✕

Footnote style
- ⦿ Numbered
- ○ Special mark
  - Mark: [   ]

[Insert]

[Cancel]

EXERCISE DIRECTIONS:

1. Create a new document for the Word Processor, or open 💾**WP SCORPION.35**.

2. Type the the report on the next page in double space.

3. Use the default left and right margins.

4. Set a 2" top margin in the Page Setup dialog box.

5. Type until you reach each reference number; use the Footnote feature to insert the reference number and the footnote text.

6. Set a Bookmark at the end of the second paragraph; name it **Spider**.

7. Spell check.

8. Find the Bookmark. Insert the following sentences at the Bookmark location:

   It belongs to a class of animals called arachnids, the same family that spiders, mites and ticks belong to. Scorpions live in warm countries in most parts of the world.

9. Print one copy.

10. Save the document; name it **SCORPION**.

11. Close the document window.

INSERT FOOTNOTES

1. Click **Insert** .... Alt+I
2. Click **Foot<u>n</u>ote** .... N
3. Click **<u>N</u>umbered** .... Alt+N

   OR

   a. Click **<u>S</u>pecial Mark** .... Alt+S
   b. Type character in **Mark** textbox. .... symbol
4. Click **Insert** .... Enter

✓ *NOTE:* In Normal view, a blank window appears displaying the separator line and the first assigned footnote number.

In Page Layout view, the insertion point moves to the bottom of the page under the separator line and to the right of the footnote number.

5. Keyboard the footnote text .... text
6. Press Enter key between .... Enter footnote entries.

TO RETURN TO DOCUMENT IN NORMAL VIEW

1. Click **<u>V</u>iew** .... Alt+V
2. Click **<u>F</u>ootnotes** .... O

   to close footnote pane and return to document.

THE SCORPION

What is the first thing you think of when you hear the word "scorpion"? Most people think of **sting**, **unsightly insect** or **poisonous**.

The scorpion is a small animal with a dangerous poisonous stinger in its tail. The scorpion is not an insect. ←—— *Create bookmark.*

Scorpions eat large insects and spiders, and are most active at night. "Scorpions capture and hold their prey with their pedipalps, which have teeth. They then stab the prey with their stingers."[1] ←——————————————————— *Reference markers*

The scorpion's stinger is a curved organ in the end of its tail. Two glands at the base give out a poison that flows from two pores. "Of the more than forty species of scorpions found in the United States, only two are considered to be harmful to people."[2]

Separator line

---

[1] Gottfried, et al., <u>Biology</u> (New Jersey: Prentice, 1983) 461.

[2] Gottfried, et al., 461.

←—— *Footnotes*

EXERCISE **36**

■ **Print a Footnote at the End of the Document** ■ **Edit a Footnote**

NOTES:

Print a Footnote at the End of the Document

■ By default, footnotes are printed at the bottom of the page on which they appear. However, you can specify that the footnotes appear at the end of the document or on a separate page.

■ **To print footnotes at the end of the document:**

- Click File, Page Setup.
- Click Other Options.
- Click Print footnotes at end text box.

  ✓ *NOTE:* *The format for the footnotes remains the same; the only difference is their placement within the document.*

■ You can place the footnotes on a separate page. Press the Enter key after the last line of the report and then insert a page break. You can head the new page with a centered title such as Citations.

Edit a Footnote

■ When you edit, add or delete footnotes, Works renumbers and reformats them as necessary.

■ Footnotes appear at the bottom of the page in Page Layout view. It is recommended that you work in this view because it displays the document as it will look when printed. If you are in Normal view, however, you must access the footnote pane in order to edit the footnotes.

■ **To edit a footnote in Normal view:**

- Click View, Footnotes.
- Edit appropriate footnote.
- Repeat the first two steps to close the footnote pane.

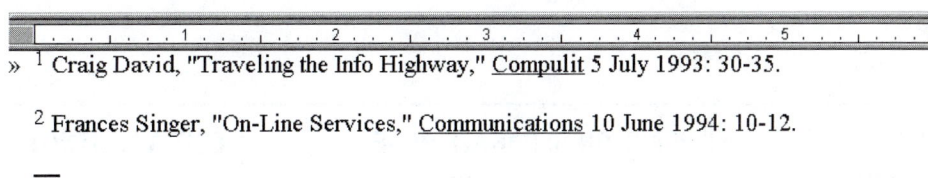

» [1] Craig David, "Traveling the Info Highway," Compulit 5 July 1993: 30-35.

[2] Frances Singer, "On-Line Services," Communications 10 June 1994: 10-12.

—

In this exercise, you will create a report with footnotes appearing on a separate page.

EXERCISE DIRECTIONS:

1. Create a new document for the Word Processor, or open ▭**WP INFO.36**.

2. Create the report on the following page in double space.

3. Set the left and right margins for 1".

4. Set the top margin for 2".

5. Type until you reach each reference number.

6. Use the <u>O</u>ther Options feature in the Page Setup dialog box to insert and print the footnotes at the end of the document.

7. Place the footnotes on a separate page. Center the title CITATIONS in a sans serif font in 14 point bold.

   ✓ NOTE: *You must press the Enter key before inserting the page break. If you don't, the last paragraph of the report will be centered.*

8. Spell check.

9. Edit footnote number 1. Change the page numbers to 30-35.

10. Print one copy.

11. Save the exercise; name it **INFO**.

12. Close the document window

PRINT FOOTNOTES AT THE END OF A DOCUMENT

1. Click **<u>F</u>ile** .... `Alt`+`F`
2. Click **Pa<u>g</u>e Setup** .... `G`
3. Click **<u>O</u>ther Options** .... `Alt`+`O`
4. Click **P<u>r</u>int footnotes at end** .. `Alt`+`R`
   Check mark appears in box.
5. Click **OK** .... `Enter`

PLACE ON SEPARATE PAGE

1. Follow steps 1-5 at left.
2. Place insertion point before footnotes begin.
3. Click **<u>I</u>nsert** .... `Alt`+`I`
4. Click **Page <u>B</u>reak** .... `B`

EDIT A FOOTNOTE

In Page Layout view:

1. Use scroll bar to access footnote area. .... `↓` `↑`
2. Edit as needed.

In Normal view:

1. Click **<u>V</u>iew** .... `Alt`+`V`
2. Click **<u>F</u>ootnotes** .... `O`
3. Edit as needed.

To return to document:

1. Click **<u>V</u>iew** .... `Alt`+`V`
2. Click **<u>F</u>ootnotes** .... `O`

INFORMATION HIGHWAY

Traveling on the information highway is similar to traveling on any interstate. There are signposts along the way to direct you, and you can leave the main highway at various intervals to explore the surrounding area. Once you are connected to an information highway, you can choose to inspect areas devoted to business, entertainment, travel, computers, as well as other subjects. The menus or icons provide the access to these special interest areas.

How do you become a traveler on an information highway? Your mode of transportation is a computer with a modem. "A modem is a device that allows you to send or receive information via the phone lines."[1] Before you can begin exploring the territory, you must purchase a ticket. On this highway, a ticket is your subscription to an on-line service. "An on-line service offers you bulletin boards, databases, electronic mail and more."[2]

Once you are traveling, you may never want to come home. There are so many areas to investigate. In addition to receiving information, you can send and receive messages and have an ongoing dialog with someone who shares a similar interest. If you are interested in expanding your software library, you can download programs or graphic files that have been provided by other users. Want to become a financial wizard? There are many areas where you can research information to obtain the latest investment results.

There is a world of information out there on the *highway*, and all you have to do is get on your computer, buy your ticket and begin your journey.

---

[1] Craig David, "Traveling the Info Highway," Compulit 5 July 1993: 20-25.

[2] Frances Singer, "On-Line Services," Communications 10 June 1994: 10-12.

EXERCISE **37**

■ **Create Headers and Footers** ■ **Edit Headers and Footers** ■ **Page Numbers**

NOTES:

Create Headers and Footers

■ A **header** is text (a chapter title, a date or a company name) which prints at the top of every page or every other page; a **footer** is text which prints at the bottom of every page or every other page.

■ You can use headers and footers to add page numbers, titles, dates, document names or other information to your document. In Works, headers and footers may contain one or more lines of text and may also include graphics.

■ In Page Layout view, headers and footers appear at the top and bottom of each page. It is recommended that you work in Page Layout view when using headers and footers. See the illustration below:

HEADER IN PAGE LAYOUT VIEW

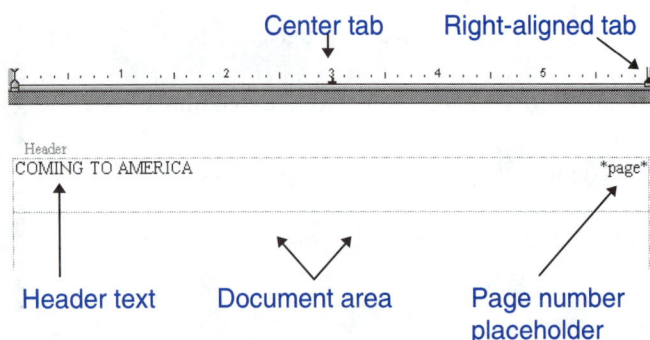

Center tab Right-aligned tab

Header
COMING TO AMERICA   *page*

Header text Document area Page number placeholder

■ To type the header or footer in Page Layout view, just click in the appropriate area on the page and type the desired header and/or footer text.

■ In <u>N</u>ormal view, Works places an H and F at the beginning of the document to identify the header and footer. Note the following illustration of the header and footer area in Normal view.

HEADER IN NORMAL VIEW

Header text Center tab Right-aligned tab

H COMING TO AMERICA   *page*
F
»

Beginning of document area Type footer text here Page number placeholder

■ To type the header or footer text in Normal view, click to the right of the H or F and type the desired header and/or footer text.

■ Text is automatically left-aligned. Works includes two preset tabs in each header/footer area: a center tab and a right-aligned tab. Note the tabs in the illustrations above. You can change these tabs to accommodate your needs for a particular document. If you change the margins, you will need to reset the tabs in the header and/or footer to the new center and right-aligned locations.

■ Header and footer text can be enhanced by applying all the formatting features available in the full Word Processor.

■ The header or footer margin is the space between the top or bottom edge of the paper and the header or footer area. The header and footer areas will expand automatically to include more text. They can take up to 1/3 of the page.

■ If you should need to change the header or footer margins, make sure that the header margin is smaller than the top margin, and the footer margin is smaller than the bottom margin. Otherwise, your header/footer information will not print.

To change header/footer margins:

- Click File, Page Setup.
- Click Margins tab.
- Click Header margin.

  OR

  Click Footer margin.
- Type new margin.

■ Headers and/or footers may be inserted before or after the document is typed.

Edit Headers and Footers

To edit a header/footer in Page Layout view:

- Click in the header/footer area.
- Edit as usual.
- Click in document area to exit header/footer.

To edit a header/footer in Normal view:

- Click the header/footer text.
- Edit as usual.
- Click in document to exit header/footer.

Page Numbers

■ Page numbers should be included on the second and succeeding pages of multiple-page documents. Page numbers can be included in headers and footers.

To insert a page number in a header/footer:

- Locate insertion point in header/footer.
- Click Insert.
- Click Page Number.

  ✓ NOTE: *A placeholder *page* appears. The page numbers will automatically number consecutively as the pages print.*

■ If you plan to insert a header on the left side of your pages, insert page numbers on the top right side or bottom of your pages. Be sure that your header/footer text does not overlap or appear too close to the page number.

■ Since headers/footers and page numbers should not appear on the first page of a multiple-page document, they must be suppressed.

To print headers/footers on all pages except page 1:

- Click File, Page Setup.
- Click Other Options tab.
- Click No header on first page.

  OR

  Click No footer on first page.
- Click OK.

■ Page numbers can be inserted before or after the text is typed.

> *In this exercise, you will create a two-page report with a header, page numbering and footnotes.*

EXERCISE DIRECTIONS:

1. Create a new document for the Word Processor, or open ⊟**WP VOYAGE.37**.

2. Type the report on the following page. Single space the two-line title. Press the Enter key twice after the title. Type the body of the report in double space.

   ✓ *NOTE:* *While the exercise is shown in single space, you are to use double space. Your printed document will result in two pages, and footnotes will appear on the same pages as reference numbers.*

3. Begin the exercise approximately 2" from the top of the page.

   ✓ *NOTE:* *Since this is a multiple-page document, you cannot set a 2" top margin. Press the Enter key to achieve the desired top margin on the first page.*

4. Set 1.5" left and right margins for the document.

5. Create the header DIFFICULTIES COMING TO AMERICA. Include a right-aligned page number as part of the header. Select No header on 1st page.

   ✓ *NOTE:* *Since the margins have been changed, the tabs in the header must be dragged to the new center and right aligned positions.*

6. Spell check.

7. Preview your document.

8. Edit the header. Delete DIFFICULTIES from the title.

9. Print one copy.

10. Save the exercise; name it **VOYAGE**.

11. Close the document window.

CREATE HEADERS/FOOTERS

1. Place insertion point in header/footer area.
2. Type header/footer text. .... *text*
3. Click in document area to exit header/footer.

TO PRINT WITHOUT A HEADER/FOOTER ON 1ST PAGE

1. Click **F**ile .... `Alt`+`F`
2. Click **Page Setup** .... `G`
3. Click **O**ther **O**ptions .... `Alt`+`O`
4. Click **N**o header on first page `Alt`+`N`

   OR

   Click No **f**ooter on first page.. `Alt`+`F`
5. Click **OK** .... `Enter`

EDIT HEADER/FOOTER

1. Click **V**iew .... `Alt`+`V`
2. Click **H**eader .... `H`

   OR

   Click **F**ooter .... `F`
3. Make desired changes.
4. Click in document area to return to document.

PAGE NUMBERS

1. Position the insertion point at desired location.
2. Click **I**nsert .... `Alt`+`I`
3. Click **P**age Number .... `P`

IMMIGRATION TO THE UNITED STATES
IN THE NINETEENTH CENTURY

The United States is sometimes called the "Nation of Immigrants" because it has received more immigrants than any other country in history. During the first one hundred years of U. S. history, the nation had no immigration laws. Immigration began to climb during the 1830s. "Between 1830-1840, 44% of the immigrants came from Ireland, 30% came from Germany, 15% came from Great Britain, and the remainder came from other European countries."[1]

The movement to America of millions of immigrants in the century after the 1820s was not simply a flight of impoverished peasants abandoning underdeveloped, backward regions for the riches and unlimited opportunities offered by the American economy. People did not move randomly to America but emanated from very specific regions at specific times in the nineteenth and twentieth centuries. "It is impossible to understand even the nature of American immigrant communities without appreciating the nature of the world these newcomers left."[2]

The rate of people leaving Ireland was extremely high in the late 1840s and early 1850s due to overpopulation and to the potato famine of 1846. "By 1850, there were almost one million Irish Catholics in the United States, especially clustered in New York and Massachusetts."[3]

Germans left their homeland due to severe depression, unemployment, political unrest, and the failure of the liberal revolutionary movement. It was not only the poor people who left their countries, but those in the middle and lower-middle levels of their social structures also left. "Those too poor could seldom afford to go, and the very wealthy had too much of a stake in the homelands to depart."[4]

Many immigrants came to America as a result of the lure of new land, in part, the result of the attraction of the frontier. America was in a very real sense the last frontier--a land of diverse peoples that, even under the worst conditions, maintained a way of life that permitted more freedom of belief and action than was held abroad. "While this perception was not entirely based in reality, it was the conviction that was often held in Europe and that became part of the ever-present American Dream."[5]

---

[1]Lewis Paul Todd and Merle Curti, Rise of the American Nation (New York: Harcourt, 1972) 297.

[2]John Bodner, The Transplanted (Bloomington: Indiana UP, 1985) 54.

[3]E. Allen Richardson, Strangers in This Land (New York: Pilgrim, 1988) 6.

[4]Richardson, 13.

[5]Richardson, 72.

EXERCISE 38

■ **Page Numbers** ■ **Superscripts and Subscripts**

CUSTOMIZED TOOLBAR

Superscript ——— Subscript

NOTES:

Page Numbers

■ Typically, page numbers are placed within the header or footer to keep the standard 1" top or bottom margin. However, page numbers may be included independently of the header/footer text.

■ Page numbers will print wherever the placeholder is inserted. Page numbers may be placed in any of the following locations: top left, top right, bottom left, bottom right, top center or bottom center of the page.

Superscripts and Subscripts

■ **Superscripts** are characters that are printed a half line above the normal typing line; **subscripts** are characters that are printed a half line below the normal typing line.

■ Superscripts and subscripts are commonly used in mathematical and scientific formulas as well as in footnoting.

■ The Footnote feature automatically creates the superscript. To raise or lower a character for any other purpose, it is necessary to use the Super/Subscript feature.

■ Superscripts/subscripts may be accessed through the Format Font and Style dialog box select Font and Style from the Format menu as shown below, or by selecting the superscript or subscript button on the Toolbar as shown above.

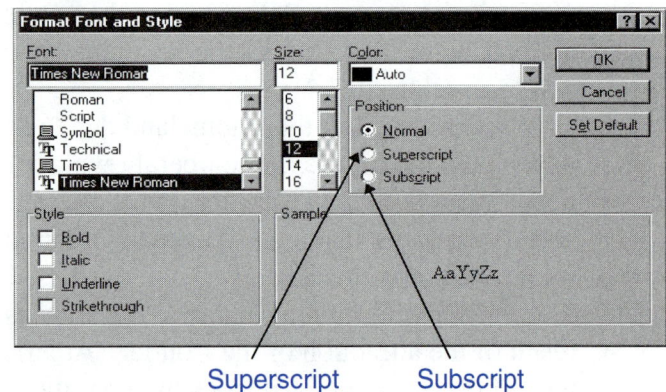

Superscript   Subscript

■ You can change to a superscript or subscript format before or after typing text.

■ You can return to the basic style by selecting the super or subscripted text and pressing Ctrl+Spacebar, or you can go to the Format Font and Style dialog box and click Normal.

In this exercise, you will prepare a multiple-page report with a header, footer and page numbers. You will use superscript and subscript text in the mathematical and scientific formulas.

EXERCISE DIRECTIONS:

1. Create a new document for the Word Processor, or open ▯**WP UP AND DOWN.38**.

2. Since this report will be left bound, set a 2" left margin. Set the right margin to 1".

3. Begin the report 2" from the top of the page.

4. Set the document for a sans serif font in 12 point.

5. Type the report title in single space. Type the report in double space.

   ✓*NOTES: Insert non-breaking spaces in the formulas.*

   Superscripted and subscripted characters print in full size.

6. Justify the document.

7. Create a header to include a page number at the top right of the second and succeeding pages. Do not print headers or page numbers on the first page.

8. Create the footer, SUPERSCRIPT/SUBSCRIPT, in sans serif 12 point bold and italics. Center the footer on the second and succeeding pages.

   ✓*NOTE: Since the margins have been changed, you will need to move the footer's center tab to the new centerpoint.*

9. Spell check.

10. Preview your document.

11. Print one copy.

12. Save the exercise; name it **UP AND DOWN**.

13. Close the document window.

PAGE NUMBERING

1. Place insertion point at desired location.
2. Click **Insert** .... Alt +**I**
3. Click **Page Number** .... **P**

SUPERSCRIPTS/SUBSCRIPTS

1. Place insertion point where superscript/subscript is to appear.

   OR

   Select character to format in superscript or subscript.

2. Click **Format** .... Alt +**O**
3. Click **Font and Style** .... **F**
4. Click **Superscript** .... Alt +**P**

   OR

   Click **Subscript** .... Alt +**C**
5. Click **OK** .... Enter

   OR

   Click **Superscript** x^2 or **Subscript** x_2 button on the Toolbar.

To return to normal text:

Ctrl + Spacebar

1. Click **Format** .... Alt +**O**
2. Click **Font and Style** .... **F**
3. Click **Normal** .... Alt +**N**
4. Click **OK** .... Enter

USING SUPERSCRIPTS AND SUBSCRIPTS
IN ALGEBRA AND CHEMISTRY

Superscripts and subscripts are commonly used in mathematical equations and scientific formulas. In algebra, superscripts are primarily used; while in science, subscripts are primarily used. Let's look at a few examples.

<u>Multiplication in Algebra - **Superscripts**</u>

Multiplication in algebra is usually demonstrated by writing two or more expressions together without a multiplication symbol. Example: a x b is written *ab*. Sometimes you may see a formula that is written ab^4. The little, raised number is called the **exponent**. It indicates the number of times a quantity is multiplied by itself. Therefore, a x a is written a^2. This is called the square of "a." It means that "a" is multiplied by itself. If you wanted to multiply a x a x a, the formula would be written a^3. This is called the cube of "a." If you wanted to multiply a x a x a x a, the formula would be written as a^4. A typical formula used to multiply an expression consisting of two or more terms by a single term or expression would look like this: $(5b^2c+2d)(3bd)$.

<u>Chemical Compounds in Chemistry - **Subscripts**</u>

In chemistry, chemical compounds have common names and are also represented by a formula. Many of the common names of chemical compounds are so familiar to us, yet the compound name sounds so scientific. For example, water is a chemical compound with which we are probably the most familiar. Its common name is "water" and it is represented by the formula H_2O. Laughing gas is another common name of a chemical compound. Its compound name is nitrous oxide and is represented by the formula N_2O. Baking soda, or sodium bicarbonate, is represented by the formula $NaHCO_3$. A compound which is not as familiar is ammonium hydroxide. However, when we look at the common name, it really is one we might have used: ammonia water. It is represented by the formula NH_4OH. Since you probably have used some of the compounds mentioned, you may be a chemist and not even know it!

EXERCISE **39**

■ **Cut and Paste Text from One Page to Another Using Go To**
■ **File Management (Create a Folder, Send a File to Another Location, Delete a File)**

NOTES:

Cut and Paste Text
from One Page to Another Using Go To

■ The procedure for cutting and pasting text from one page to another is the same as cutting and pasting text on the same page. However, when cutting and pasting text from one page to another, the **Go To** feature may be used to advance to the page where the text is to be reinserted quickly. As you learned in Exercise 34, the Go To command allows you to quickly locate a bookmark.

■ Go To is accessed from the Edit menu. Once the Go To dialog box appears, enter the desired page number in the text box, as shown below.

Page number

✓ *NOTE:* *After cutting and pasting the paragraph in this exercise, it may be necessary to move the second-page heading appropriately.*

File Management

Create a Folder

■ A folder is a location on your hard drive in which your files reside. Works saves your files to the MSWorks\Documents folder. Since all your documents are saved there, this folder can become very full making it difficult for you to locate or manage the files. Therefore, you may wish to create additional folders to make file management easier. You can create a folder to contain all documents related to a specific topic, a specific project, or you can create folders to save your spreadsheet, database and word processing documents separately.

■ You can create a new folder within the Documents folder or in another location. Click the Create New Folder icon from the Open dialog box shown below. A new folder is inserted in the workspace and is named *New Folder*. Type a name for the folder and the original text disappears. Press the Enter key to finalize the procedure.

Create new folder

Type folder
name here

■ Double-click the folder name to open the folder. All files will now be saved to this folder.

Send a File to Another Location

- This feature allows you to copy a file and send a file to another location from directly within Works. The file is retained in its current location and a copy can be sent to a number of locations: Floppy, Fax Recipient, Mail Recipient, My Briefcase.

  ✔ *NOTE:* *These locations may differ depending upon your computer's configuration.*

- Right-click the desired file in the Open or Save As dialog boxes, select Send To and choose the desired destination. Use this option to backup a file from your hard drive to the floppy drive. This feature will not work if the file is open.

Delete a File

- Files can be deleted from directly within Works. Right-click the desired file in either the Open or Save As dialog boxes, select Delete, then confirm that you want the file sent to the Recycle Bin. This feature will not work if the file is open.

  ✔ *NOTE:* *To permanently delete the file, you will need to empty the Recycle Bin.*

> *In this exercise, you will use the Go To command to move the insertion point quickly to a specific page in your document. Once the changes are made, you will save the document to a new folder and then use the right click options to rename, send and delete the file.*

EXERCISE DIRECTIONS:

1. Open ⌨**PREVIEW**, or open 💾**WP PREVIEW.39**.

2. Make the indicated revisions.

3. Use the Find feature to search for each word marked in brackets. Then, using the Thesaurus feature, substitute each word. Be sure replacement words maintain the same tense, number and person as the original words.

4. Print one copy.

5. Resave the file.

6. Using the Save As command, save the file as **PREVIEW 2**.

   ✔ *NOTE:* *The file is now saved under **PREVIEW** and **PREVIEW 2**.*

7. Create a new folder within the Works Documents folder (or other location as desired); name the folder **WP EXERCISES**.

8. Using the Save As command, save the file as **PREVIEW 2** in the new folder. Close the file.

9. Click File, Open and access the **WP EXERCISES** folder. Make the following changes to the **PREVIEW 2** file.

   ✔ *NOTE:* *Make sure **PREVIEW 2** is closed or you will not be able to perform the following operations.*

   a. Rename the file EDUCATION FILMS.

   b. Send EDUCATION FILMS to the floppy.

   c. Access the Works Documents directory (or the directory where you have been saving all your documents).

   d. Delete **PREVIEW 2**.

CUT AND PASTE USING GO TO

F5

1. Select text to be cut.
2. Click **Cut** button on Toolbar............ ✂
   OR
   a. Click **Edit**.................... Alt + E
   b. Click **Cut**........................... T
3. Click **Edit**........................ Alt + E
4. Click **Go To**........................ G
5. Type page number to go to. ...... *number*
6. Click **OK**........................ Enter
7. Place insertion point where text is to be reinserted.
8. Click **Paste** button on Toolbar......... 📋
   OR

a. Click **Edit**.................... Alt + E
b. Click **Paste**.................... P

CREATE A FOLDER

1. Click **File** .... Alt + F
2. Click **Open**........................ O
3. Click **Create New Folder** icon .... 📁
4. Type new folder name. ....*folder name*
5. Press the **Enter** key. .... Enter
6. Double click folder name to open.
7. Save desired files to new folder.

SEND A FILE

1. Click **File** .... Alt + F
2. Click **Open**........................ O

3. Right click the file you wish to send.
4. Click **Send To** .... N
5. Click desired destination

DELETE A FILE

1. Click **File** .... Alt + F
2. Click **Open**........................ Alt + O
3. Right click the file to delete.
4. Click **Delete**........................ D
5. Respond **Yes** to the .... Alt + Y
   message to delete the file.

   ✔ *NOTE:* *The file is sent to the Recycle Bin. To permanently delete the file, you will need to empty the Recyle Bin.*

← ———————————— Today's date

REGISTERED MAIL

Ms. Elizabeth DeKan
Broward College
576 Southfield Road
Marietta, GA 30068

Dear Ms. DeKan:

Subject: Educational Films for High Schools and Colleges

Thank you for your interest in the films that we have available for high school and college students. We are pleased to send you the enclosed flyer which describes the films in detail. Also enclosed is a [summary] of those films that have recently been added to our collection since the publication of the flyer.

Ⓐ *Move to next page*

We will be sure to send the films in time for you to preview them. Please be sure to list the date on which you wish to preview the films.

There have been many positive [reactions] to our films. Just three weeks ago, a group of educators, editors and vocational experts were invited to view the films at the annual EDUCATORS' CONFERENCE. Here are some of their comments:

Insert B →

Mr. William R. Bondlow, Jr., president of the National Vocational Center in Washington, D.C. and editor-in-chief of Science Careers, said:

> I like the films very much. They are innovative and a great benefit to all those interested in the earth sciences as a professional career. Furthermore, they have captured the objects on film so true to life that anyone watching them is captivated.

Ⓒ *Move to next page*

Ms. Andra Burke, a [leading] expert presently assigned to the United States Interior Department, praised the films by saying:

Ms. Elizabeth DeKan
Page 2
Today's date

Insert C →

> They are a major educational advancement in career placement, which will serve as a source of motivation for all future geologists.

Ⓑ *Move to page 1*

A member of the National Education Center, Dr. Lawrence Pilgrim, also liked the films and said:

> I will institute a program which will make schools throughout the country aware of their vocational potential.

These are just some of the reactions we have had to our films. We know you will have a similar reaction.

Insert A →

We would very much like to send you the films that you would like during the summer session. ~~You can use the summer to review them.~~ It is important that your request be received [quickly] since the demand for the films is great, particularly during the summer sessions at colleges and universities throughout the country.

← ———————————— Cordially,

William DeVane
Executive Vice President
Marketing Department

wd/yo
Enclosures (2)

Copy to   Robert R. Redford
           Nancy Jackson
           Tien Lee

EXERCISE 40
Lesson 5 – Summary

In this exercise, you will create a multiple-page, modified-block letter from existing text. You will use the header feature, change line spacing and justification, set bookmarks, use the replace feature and save the file to more than one location.

EXERCISE DIRECTIONS:

1. Open 🖛DIVE, or open 💾WP DIVE.40.

2. Create a two-page, modified-block letter from the document on the right.

3. Set left and right margins to 1".

4. Use the Header feature to create the header for the second page of the letter. Print the header on page 2 only.

5. Remove justification from the second paragraph.

   HINT: Select the paragraph and change to left justification.

6. Begin the date approximately 2.5" from the top of the page.

   ✓ *NOTE: Since this is a multiple-page document, you cannot set a top margin in the Page Setup. You will have to use the Return key to achieve the 2.5" top margin on the first page.*

7. Single space the text. Double space between paragraphs.

8. Create the first bookmark where indicated; name it **DEPTH**.

9. Make the remaining revisions.

10. After typing the closing to the letter, create the second bookmark where indicated; name it **SPOT**.

11. Find the first bookmark, **DEPTH**. Insert the following paragraph at the first bookmark location:

    Before you descend the depths of the ocean, it is important that you have a few lessons on the do's and don'ts of diving. Don't touch the coral, and don't come up to the surface too fast holding your breath. Now you are ready to jump in.

12. Find the second bookmark, **SPOT**. Insert the following paragraph at the second bookmark location:

    This is a great vacation spot. Let me know when you are ready to make reservations. Meanwhile, if you have any questions, please give me a call.

    ✓ *NOTE: Before typing the paragraph, you will need to press Ctrl+Q to end the customized hanging indent.*

13. Use the Replace feature to change all 10 a.m. check ins to 12 noon.

14. Preview the document and make all necessary adjustments to fit the letter on two pages.

15. Save the document as a new file (Save As); name it **DIVE 2**.

16. Print one copy.

17. Rename the file; name it **DIVING**.

18. Send a copy of **DIVING** to the floppy.

19. Close the document window.

Today's date

Mr. Kenyatta Belcher
80 Avenue C
Cambridge, MA 02138
↓2x

Dear Ken:
↓2x

SUBJECT:

Set in serif font 12-point bold

DIVING IN THE CAYMAN ISLANDS

Change to serif font
Delete italics
Change to 12 point

Do you want to see sharks, barracudas, stingrays and angelfish?

The Cayman Islands were discovered by Christopher Columbus in 1503 and are located south of Cuba. The Caymans are the home to only about 25,000 year-round residents. However, they welcome 200,000 visitors each year. Most visitors come with masks and flippers in their luggage. ← *Create "DEPTH" bookmark here*

Hotel/Diving Accommodations:

Anchorage View	PO Box 2123, East End, Grand Cayman; (809) 555-4209. Pool, four restaurants; check in 9 a.m., check out 2 p.m. Famous for outstanding view of the harbor from all rooms. Popular night spot among tourists and locals alike.
Cayman Diving Lodge	PO Box 11, East End, Grand Cayman; (809) 555-7555. No pool, room service available; check in 10 a.m., check out 4 p.m. Basic accommodations, low rates. Diving expeditions three times daily at extra cost.
Coconut Harbour	PO Box 2086, George Town, Grand Cayman; (809) 555-6468. Pool, two restaurants; check in 10 a.m., check out 4 p.m. Free scuba exhibitions nightly.
Red Sail Sports	PO Box 1588, George Town, Grand Cayman; (809) 555-7965. Pool, three restaurants; check in 11 a.m., check out 3 p.m. Wind surfing and parasailing available at extra cost.
Sunset House	PO Box 479, George Town, Grand Cayman; (809) 555-4767. Pool, three restaurants; check in 11 a.m., check out 3 p.m.

Hotels Offering Free Diving Instruction:

Cayman Diving Lodge	PO Box 11, East End, Grand Cayman; (809) 555-7555. No pool, room service available; check in 10 a.m., check out 4 p.m. Basic accommodations, low rates. Diving expeditions three times daily at extra cost.
Sunset House	PO Box 479, George Town, Grand Cayman; (809) 555-4767. Pool, three restaurants; check in 11 a.m., check out 3 p.m.

Create "SPOT" bookmark here →

Yours truly,

John Rogers
Travel Agent

jr/yo

Tab→ #Here are some hotel suggestions:

EXERCISE **41**

■ **Columns**

NOTES:

Columns

- The **Columns** feature allows text to flow from one column to another. The text flows down one column to the bottom of a page and then starts again at the top of the next column. This feature is particularly useful when creating newsletters, brochures, lists or articles.

- Columns may be created before or after typing.

- When you create a columns format, it applies to the entire document – except the headers and footers.

  ✓ *NOTE:* *If you want a heading across the columns, you must create it with the header/footer feature.*

- Select Columns from the Format menu to access the columns dialog box shown below.

  Format Columns   **? X**

  Number of columns: [1]   [OK]
  Space between: [0.5"]   [Cancel]

  ┌─Sample─────────┐
  │   │ Note: the
  │   ▓▓▓▓▓   │ column format
  │   ▓▓▓▓▓   │ applies to the
  │   │ entire
  │   │ document.
  └────────────────┘

  ☑ Line between columns

- You can indicate the desired number of columns and the space between those columns in the Columns dialog box above. The sample area will show you how your document will appear. You can also add a vertical line (**rule**) between the columns.

- Works determines the width of the columns based on the margins, number of columns, the page size and the amount of space specified between the columns.

  ✓ *NOTE:* *All columns are uniform in width; you cannot specify that one column be wider or narrower than the others.*

- To return to a single column layout, specify one column in the Number of columns text box.

  ✓ *NOTE:* *Multiple columns are best viewed in Page Layout view. You can only view one column in Normal view.*

In this exercise, you will create an article in a two-column format with a vertical line separating the columns.

EXERCISE DIRECTIONS:

1. Create a new document for the Word Processor.

2. Begin typing the document at the top of the screen.

3. Use the default margins. Set document for a serif 12 point font.

4. Create the article on the right using a two-column format. Use the default spacing between the columns.

5. Insert a vertical line between the columns.

   ✓ *NOTE:* *The vertical line will not appear until there is enough text to wrap to the second column.*

6. Double space the document.

7. Hyphenate the document.

8. Justify the document.

9. Spell check.

10. Preview your document.

11. Print one copy.

12. Save the exercise; name it **ETIQUETTE**.

13. Close the document window.

CREATE COLUMNS

1. Click **Format** .... Alt + O

2. Click **Columns** C

3. Click **Number of columns** ...... Alt + N

4. Enter desired number .... *number*

5. Click **Space between** .... Alt + S

6. Enter desired amount of space .... *number*

7. Click **Line between columns** to add a vertical line .... Alt + L

8. View changes in Sample box.

9. Click **OK** .... Enter

To undo columns:

1. Repeat steps 1-3.

2. Click **Number of columns** ...... Alt + N

3. Type **1** 1

4. Click **OK** .... Enter

People interact according to the unwritten rules of etiquette that have been handed down from generation to generation. Behaviors we take for granted are instilled in us at an early age. Take a moment and think about all the social customs we follow (or should follow) when we interact with others whether it be in person, on the phone, or driving a car.

Now comes the age of cyberspace with the arrival of the Internet and on-line services. Millions of people are using their computers to communicate in ways never thought possible. The information highway is an exciting place to find information and perhaps make new friends, but we do this in a vacuum. We don't hear the voice or see the facial expression that has traditionally helped us to convey our messages. Now we have only the written word, and we may sometimes forget that we are communicating with real people who have real live feelings. This could lead to a lapse in manners. As a result, there have been books and magazines written on the proper way to conduct yourself when communicating on-line.

One of the key points to remember when using a service or bulletin board is that there is a person at the other end of the computer, and we should apply the same standards to our on-line behavior that we follow in our daily lives. Ask yourself if your message is acceptable and if you would say this to someone in a face-to-face situation. Try to envision the person you're writing to so that the communication becomes more "human." Remember that anything you write takes on a life of its own. It can be saved and later forwarded to other users.

Be ethical, courteous, sensitive to others, and remember that your written word is your representative. If we all adhere to these general guidelines, then cyberspace will be a more pleasant place to visit.

EXERCISE **42**

■ **Add a Title to a Column Layout** ■ **Move Around in Columns**

NOTES:

Add a Title to a Column Layout

■ A columns format affects the entire document; therefore, you need to create the title in the header area.

  ✔ *NOTE:* *A title created in the header area will appear across the top of every page in a multiple-page document. If you want the title to appear only on the first page, you will need to create the title using the WordArt feature. See page 175 for WordArt.*

■ In this exercise, you will change the top margin to 2". Since this is a single-page document, you will change the top margin in the Page Setup dialog box.

■ Changing margins in the Page Setup dialog box affects every page. Consequently, if you set a 1.5" top margin in a multiple-page document, *every* page will begin at 1.5". Therefore, set the top margin in the Page Setup dialog box for single-page documents only. For multiple-page documents, use the Return key to customize a top margin on an individual page.

Move Around in Columns

■ You can use the mouse to locate the insertion point any place within the document. Use the left and right directional keys to move the insertion point within the column or to go from the bottom of one column to the top of the next. In addition, you can use the Page Up/Down keys, scroll bars, and other cursor movement keys as you do in single-column documents.

In this exercise, you will create a three-column article with a title.

EXERCISE DIRECTIONS:

1. Create a new document for the Word Processor.

2. Make the following changes in the Page Setup dialog box:

   a. Top Margin   2"
   b. Bottom Margin   1.5"
   c. Header Margin   1.25"

3. Use the header to create the following centered title: THE ART OF COOKING. Set the title to a serif font in 24 point; set the body text to a serif 12 point font.

4. Type the article on the right using a three-column format. Set the intercolumn space to 0.3".

5. Block indent the paragraphs. Set space after paragraph to 0.5".

  ✔ *NOTE:* *Access the Paragraph dialog box from the Format menu and make the changes to the spacing in the Spacing tab. Once you change this setting, do not press the Return key twice between paragraphs; this setting creates the space automatically.*

6. Preview your document.

7. Return to the beginning of the document and find the words in brackets. Use the Thesaurus feature to find substitutes for the words in brackets. Be sure the replacement word is in the same tense, number and person.

8. Spell check.

9. Print one copy.

10. Save the exercise; name it **COOK**.

11. Close the file.

THE ART OF COOKING

Preparing a meal requires skill and patience. The results may mean the difference between eating just to exist and the satisfaction that comes from one of the major pleasures of life.

Cooking is an art. Every recipe should be prepared with tender, loving care as one of the chief ingredients. A cook must develop a feeling for what each ingredient will do in a recipe.

An outstanding meal must be prepared with high-quality raw ingredients, cooked simply but perfectly to increase their natural flavor. It is important to plan your meal carefully. The menu should contain a contrast in textures, flavor and color. Salad should be served as a separate course.

Use the best natural foods of the season and plan menus around them. If at all possible, try to use fresh foods rather than packaged frozen items. If you have a garden, use the fresh garden vegetables and fruits whenever you can.

In the summer, it's a challenge to try to fit all the fruit--grapes, strawberries, raspberries, apricots, cantaloupes, watermelons, peaches, blueberries, blackberries, nectarines, cherries, and plums--into the menu. A fruit salad is always a welcome dessert on a hot day.

You might want to try to use fresh herbs like dill, parsley, basil, or tarragon. Or you might want to try a variety of garden lettuces and home-grown tomatoes like beefsteaks, plum and cherry-size.

In the fall and winter, there is a variety of foods that are available for your menu that will add zest to your meal. The apples, eggplant, cauliflower, pears, and chestnuts are wonderful ingredients for a meal.

In addition, you should try to use the ingredients that are good for your health. Some of the foods recently suggested in the news as being particularly beneficial are: leafy green vegetables such as broccoli and brussels sprouts, garlic, and low fat sources of protein such as fish and chicken.

When you are preparing a meal for guests, never serve a dish you have not prepared at least once or twice before.

To make your meal presentable, do not serve too much on the plate. Servings should be small. This way your guests will ask for second helpings.

Are you getting hungry?

EXERCISE 43

■ **Tabs** ■ **Change Tab Settings** ■ **Tabular Columns**

TOOLBAR WITH TAB BUTTONS

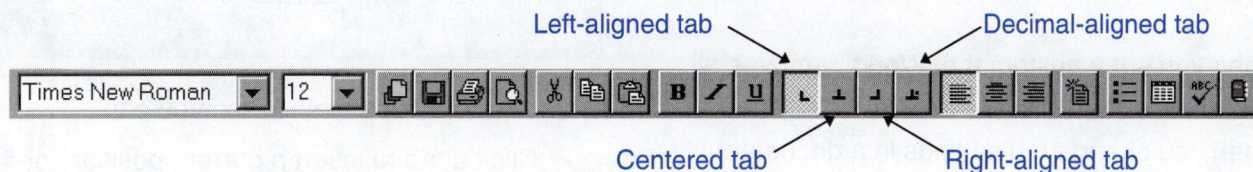

Left-aligned tab   Decimal-aligned tab

Centered tab   Right-aligned tab

NOTES:

Tabs

- Tabs are used for paragraph indents, aligning numbered items or aligning columns of information. However, it is more efficient to use either the table feature or the Spreadsheet tool to organize information into columns and rows.

    ✓ *NOTE:* *You can create a table in the Spreadsheet tool and then cut and paste or copy it to your word processing document. The integration of word processing and spreadsheets is covered in Integration, Exercise 4, page 380.*

- However, it is important for you to understand how tabs are set and the kinds of tab settings that are available since many tab types are used within a word processing document.

- The default tabs are located every 0.5" on the Ruler bar. Whenever you press the Tab key, the insertion point jumps to the next tab stop.

- In addition to the default tabs, you can create custom tabs at any location. There are four different tab types:

Left-aligned tab

Text moves to the right of the tab as you type. A left-aligned tab is the default.

EXAMPLE:

```
        XXXXXXX
        XXXX
        XXXXXX
```

Centered tab

Text centers at the tab stop.

EXAMPLE:

```
          XXXXXXX
           XXXX
          XXXXXXX
```

Right-aligned tab

Text moves to the left of the tab as you type.

EXAMPLE:

```
            XXXXX
          XXXXXXX
             XXXX
```

Decimal-aligned tab

Text typed before the decimal point (or other designated alignment character) moves to the left of the tab. Text typed after the decimal point moves to the right of the tab. The decimals stay aligned.

EXAMPLE:

```
        XXXXX.
       XXXXXX.X
        XXXX.XX
```

- Custom tabs are displayed on the Ruler bar with shapes that indicate the specific type of tab setting. See the Ruler bar on following page with four custom tab settings.

Centered tab marker

Right-aligned tab marker

Left-aligned tab marker

Decimal-aligned tab marker

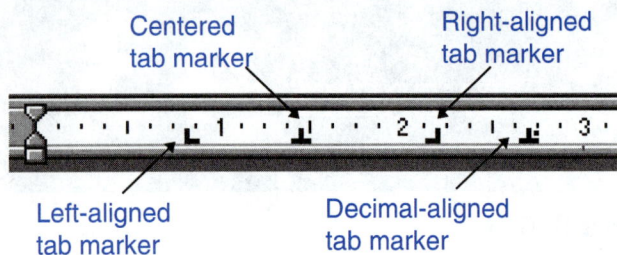

- When you set a custom tab, Works removes all default tabs to the left of that position.

- When you change tab settings in a document, changes take effect from that point forward.

- The Toolbar may be customized to include buttons for each tab style as shown at the beginning of the exercise.

Change Tab Settings

- Tabs can be set and deleted either by using the mouse or the Tabs dialog box which is accessed through the Format menu.

  —USING THE MOUSE—

  To set a new left-aligned tab:

  Click anywhere on the Ruler bar where a new tab is desired.

  To set a new centered, right or decimal-aligned tab:

  - Click the appropriate tab Toolbar button.

    ✓*NOTE:* *You must customize the Toolbar to include tab buttons.*

  - Click desired position on the Ruler bar.

  To delete a tab setting:

  Drag the tab marker off the Ruler bar.

  --USING THE TABS DIALOG BOX--

  To set/clear tabs:

  Double-click the desired location on the Ruler bar.

  OR

  - Click F*o*rmat.

  - Click Tabs to access the Tab dialog box shown the following illustration:

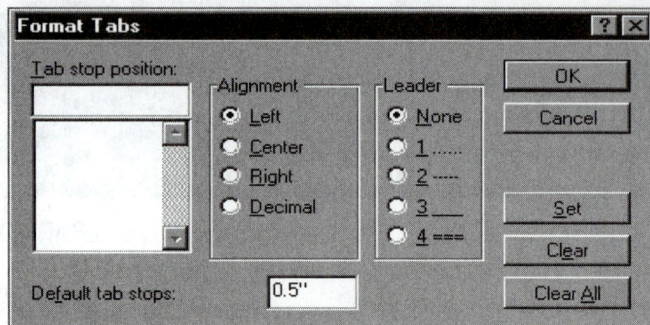

- Once in the Tabs dialog box, you can:

  - Click a tab to insert a current position, or specify a different one in the Tab stop position box.

  - Select desired Alignment.

  - Clear All tabs.

  - Clear a specific tab.

  - Change the Default tab spacing.

- Using the Tabs dialog box lets you set and clear tab positions and tab types in one operation. However, you cannot see the result of your changes until all settings have been made.

  ✓*NOTE:* *Double-clicking at the exact location on the Ruler bar is the best method to obtain the most exact tab location. This location is automatically displayed in the Tab stop position text box in the Tabs dialog box.*

Tabular Columns

- Tabs are best used to set up simple columns of data requiring no more than three columns. More complex tables, however, should be generated using the tables feature or the Spreadsheet tool. The tables feature will be discussed in Exercise 45 of this lesson; the Spreadsheet tool will be introduced in a later section.

- Tabular columns are generally horizontally centered between existing margins. The amount of space between the columns (intercolumn) can be adjusted to improve the attractiveness of the document. The following list is a guideline to determine the amount of space between the columns. Again, your document may require different spacing to improve readability or appearance.

  - two column   10 spaces
  - three column   8 spaces

- four column   6 spaces
- five + column   4 spaces

■ To determine where to set tabs so they appear horizontally centered, it is necessary to create a set-up line. The set-up line is a blueprint for setting tab stops. Use Normal view when creating a set-up line.

■ **To create a set-up line:**

- Center the longest line of each column and the space between the columns.

  ✓NOTE: *When using proportional fonts, the exact spacing specified in the above list might not yield the desired result. Therefore, you may have to increase or decrease the number of spaces between the column in the set-up line to achieve the desired intercolumn spacing.*

- Using the directional keys, move the insertion point to the first character in each column of the set-up line and click the Ruler bar in that location to set the tabs.

  HINT: *Scroll your screen up so your set-up line is directly below your Ruler.*

- Delete the set-up line.

- Press the Tab key once to type the first column, press the Tab key to type the second column, press Return and the Tab key to begin the second line.

SETTING TABS USING RULER

1. Click Ruler once at desired location to set left-aligned tab.

   OR

   a. Click desired tab style button on the Toolbar.
   b. Click desired location on Ruler bar.

SET TABS USING TABS DIALOG BOX

1. Double-click Ruler bar to set left, centered, right or decimal tabs.

   OR

   a. Click **F**ormat .... `Alt`+`O`
   b. Click **T**abs .... `T`

2. Click **T**ab stop position .... `Alt`+`T` text box.
3. Type desired position ....*number.*
4. Click desired alignment option:

       Left .... `Alt`+`L`
       Center .... `Alt`+`C`
       Right .... `Alt`+`R`
       Decimal .... `Alt`+`D`

5. Click **S**et .... `Alt`+`S`
6. Click **OK** .... `Enter`

DELETE TABS USING RULER

    Drag the tab marker off Ruler bar.

DELETE TABS USING TABS DIALOG BOX

1. Click **F**ormat .... `Alt`+`O`
2. Click **T**ab .... `Alt`+`T`

To clear a single tab:

1. Click desired tab to delete.
2. Click Cl**e**ar .... `Alt`+`E`

To clear all tabs:

1. Click Clear **A**ll .... `Alt`+`A`

TO SET DEFAULT TAB STOPS

1. Click **F**ormat .... `Alt`+`O`
2. Click **T**ab .... `T`
3. Click **Default tab stops** .... `Alt`+`F`
4. Enter desired interval ....*number*
5. Click **OK** .... `Enter`

> *In this exercise, you will create a two-column tabular document in which the first and second columns are left-aligned.*

EXERCISE DIRECTIONS:

1. Create a new document for the Word Processor.

2. Set a 2.5" top margin in the Page Setup dialog box. Use the default left and right margins.

3. To determine where tab stops should be set, create the set-up line:

   a. Center the longest line in each column, plus the intercolumn space (leave 10 spaces between columns).

   b. Use the directional keys or click the mouse to move the insertion point to the left of the first character in each column and click the Ruler bar to set a tab in that position.

   c. Delete the set-up line.

4. Center the title and subtitle lines. Press the Enter key three times after the subtitle. Format as desired.

5. Change to left alignment and type the table on the right.

6. Preview your document.

7. Print one copy.

8. Save the exercise; name it **PRESIDENTS**.

9. Close the document window.

Presidents of the United States
1901-1997

Theodore Roosevelt	1901-1909
William H. Taft	1909-1913
Woodrow Wilson	1913-1921
Warren G. Harding	1921-1923
Calvin Coolidge	1923-1929
Herbert C. Hoover	1929-1933
Franklin D. Roosevelt	1933-1945
Harry S. Truman	1945-1953
Dwight D. Eisenhower	1953-1961
John F. Kennedy	1961-1963
Lyndon B. Johnson	1963-1969
Richard M. Nixon	1969-1974
Gerald R. Ford	1974-1977
James E. Carter, Jr.	1977-1981
Ronald W. Reagan	1981-1989
George W. Bush	1989-1993
William J. Clinton	1993-

EXERCISE **44**

■ **Leaders** ■ **Move and Change Tabs**

NOTES:

Leaders

- A **leader** is a series of dots, dashes, double dashes or underlines that connect one column to another to keep the reader's eye focused.

- You can set leaders from the Tabs dialog box as shown below.

Set leaders here

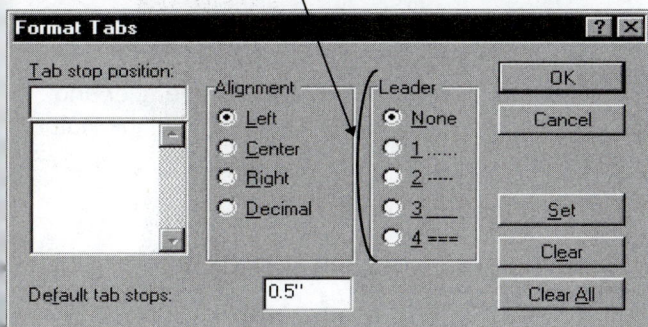

To set a tab with leaders:

- Move your insertion point to the desired tab location on the Ruler bar and double-click.

  ✔ *NOTE: You can set a left, center, decimal or right tab by selecting the appropriate tab style button on the Toolbar before clicking the desired tab location on the ruler.*

- Click desired alignment.

- Click desired leader style.

- Click Set.

- Click OK.

- After all tab settings are made, use the Tab key to advance to each column. The dot leaders will automatically appear between columns.

- You can set leaders before or after typing the table.

Move and Change Tabs

- When moving or changing a tab, you must first select the section of the document you want reformatted. If you are making a change that affects the entire document, click Edit, Select All.

To move a tab:

- Select text to reformat.

- Drag tab marker to new location on the Ruler.

To change a tab:

- Select text to reformat.

- Set new tab at desired location on Toolbar.

- Drag old tab off the Toolbar while text is still selected.

  ✔ *NOTE: You can move or change tabs in the Tabs dialog box as well. However, it is more efficient to change tabs on the Ruler bar because you can see the table reformat as the new tabs are applied.*

> *In this exercise, you will create a table of contents containing leaders and two left-aligned columns. You will then edit the format by changing the tab type and moving the tab settings.*

EXERCISE DIRECTIONS:

1. Create a new document for the word processor, or open 💾**WP TABLE OF CONTENTS.44**.

   ✓ *NOTE: If opening WP TABLE OF CONTENTS.44, proceed to step 10.*

2. Set a 2" top margin in the Page Setup dialog box. Set 1" left and right margins.

3. Clear all tabs.

4. Create a set-up line to format the table in Illustration A.

   a. Center the longest line in each column, plus the intercolumn space (leave 10 spaces between each column).

      ✓ *NOTE: You may have to increase or decrease the number of spaces between the columns to have them appear equally spaced.*

   b. Scroll your screen up to just below the Ruler bar.

   c. Place the insertion point to the left of the first character in the first column and set a left-aligned tab.

   d. Repeat for the second column.

   e. Choose the dot leader style for the second tab setting.

      ✓ *NOTE: Delete the set-up line*

5. Center the title in a 16 point bold font. Press the Enter key 3 times after the title.

6. Change to left alignment and type the table of contents in double spacing.

7. Preview your document.

8. Print one copy.

9. Save the exercise; name it **TABLE OF CONTENTS**.

10. Make the following changes to format the table in Illustration B.

    HINT: *Be sure to select the columnar section before changing or moving tabs.*

    a. Change the second tab to a right-aligned tab as follows:
       - Drag the second tab to the immediate right of the longest number in the second column.
       - Double-click the tab.
       - Change to right alignment.
       - Change the leader style to dashes.
       - Close the dialog box.

    b. Move the first tab 1" to the left on the ruler and move the second tab 1" to the right on the Ruler bar.

11. Preview the document.

12. Save the exercise; name it **TABLE OF CONTENTS 2**.

13. Print one copy.

14. Close the document window.

LEADERS

1. Click F**o**rmat........................ Alt + O
2. Click **T**abs .... T

3. Click appropriate leader style:

   None .... Alt + N
   1 .... Alt + 1
   2 .... Alt + 2
   3 .... Alt + 3
   4 .... Alt + 4

4. Click **Set**.............................. Alt + S
5. Repeat steps 3-4 for additional tabs.
6. Click **OK**.............................. Enter

TABLE OF CONTENTS

Introduction.................2 - 10

Computer Basics.........11 - 25

Word Processing.........26 - 100

Spreadsheets................101 - 175

Database.....................176 - 225

Communications.........226 - 260

Graphics.....................261 - 310

Glossary.....................311 - 320

Index.........................321 - 330

TABLE OF CONTENTS

Introduction ---2 - 10

Computer Basics-- 11 - 25

Word Processing--- 26 - 100

Spreadsheets -- 101 - 175

Database -- 176 - 225

Communications-- 226 - 260

Graphics -- 261 - 310

Glossary -- 311 - 320

Index -- 321 - 330

EXERCISE 45

■ **Create a Table** ■ **Enter Text in a Table**
■ **Edit a Table Cell** ■ **Gridlines** ■ **Column Headings**

NOTES:

Create a Table

■ In the previous exercises, you used tabs to create a table or a list. You can also create a table in the Works table feature. This feature organizes data in rows and columns and provides professional-looking formats for your table. It is more efficient to use this feature when creating multiple-column tables or tables that contain column headings.

■ A table consists of rows which run horizontally and columns which run vertically. The intersection of a row and column is called a **cell**. Note the example below of a table containing four columns and four rows.

Specify number of rows → | Specify number of columns →

Insert Table

Column↓		**Intersection of row and column**	
Row→		**Cell**	

■ The table feature sets up the table for you and automatically configures the table to fit within the existing margins. You define the table structure by entering the number of rows and columns in the Insert table dialog box shown below. Then, select your table format from the list of predefined formats. Each of these formats can be previewed in the Example box.

■ Select <u>T</u>able from the <u>I</u>nsert main menu to access the Insert Table dialog box shown at the top of the next column.

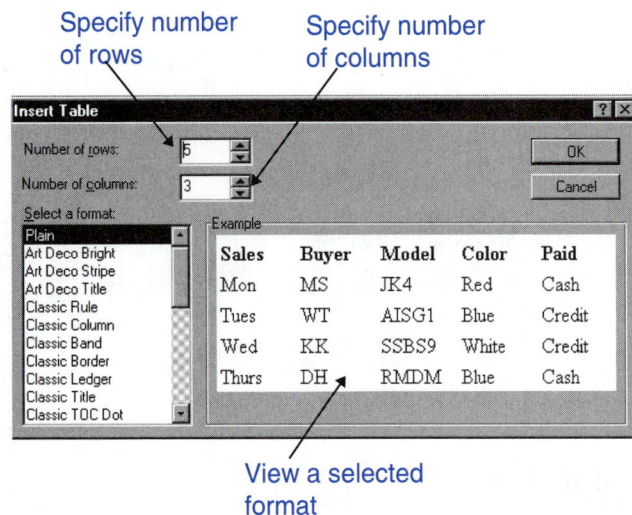

Specify number of rows | Specify number of columns

Insert Table

Number of <u>r</u>ows: 5
Number of columns: 3
<u>S</u>elect a format:
Plain
Art Deco Bright
Art Deco Stripe
Art Deco Title
Classic Rule
Classic Column
Classic Band
Classic Border
Classic Ledger
Classic Title
Classic TOC Dot

OK | Cancel

Example

Sales	Buyer	Model	Color	Paid
Mon	MS	JK4	Red	Cash
Tues	WT	AISG1	Blue	Credit
Wed	KK	SSBS9	White	Credit
Thurs	DH	RMDM	Blue	Cash

View a selected format

Enter Text in a Table

■ The table must be active in order to receive data. An active table will have a dark solid border.

■ You can move from cell to cell within the table by using the mouse, the Tab key or the directional arrows.

■ Once you are located in the desired cell, type text as you would in the Word Processor. You can use all the features to format the text as desired.

■ When the insertion point is located in a table cell, the bottom right of the Status bar reads EDIT. This signifies that the cell is ready to receive or edit data.

■ If the contents of the cell are larger than the width, the cell extends vertically to accommodate the text. Pressing Enter in a cell will also extend the cell vertically.

Edit a Table Cell

- Locate the insertion point in the cell that contains the text to edit. Highlight and edit text in a table cell as you do in a word processing document.

Gridlines

- Works allows you to set up **gridlines** to more easily read the data in the table. To display the gridlines, place the insertion point in the table and Click <u>V</u>iew, <u>G</u>ridlines.

Column Headings

- The table feature is particularly well suited for tables that require a column heading. **Column headings** identify the column information. These headings can be centered over the columns, or they can be aligned with the columns.

- The predefined table formats assume that the first row contains a heading. Therefore, this row is formatted differently from the remaining rows. If you do not wish to have a column heading, change the format of the first row so it is consistent with the remaining rows.

  ✓ NOTE: *Tables can also be created in the Spreadsheet tool and then copied to your word processing document.*

In this exercise, you will format a table with left-aligned columns.

EXERCISE DIRECTIONS:

1. Create a new document for the Word Processor, or open 🖫**WP COURSES.45**.

   ✓ NOTE: *If opening WP COURSES.45, proceed to step 12.*

2. Use the default left and right margins.

3. Set a 2" top margin in the Page Setup.

4. Center the title FALL COURSE OFFERINGS; format as desired. Press the Enter key twice after the title.

5. Create the table as shown using 6 rows and 4 columns.

6. Use the Plain predefined format.

7. Display the gridlines.

8. Type the table.

9. Preview your document.

10. Print one copy.

11. Save the document; name it **COURSES**.

12. Change the column headings to read:

    Course   Code   Time   Teacher

13. Center all column headings.

14. Delete the contents in the last row and replace with the following:

    Computer Graphics   CG1   1:00   P. Darby

15. Print one copy.

16. Save the document; name it **COURSES 2**.

CREATE A TABLE

1. Position insertion point where you want table to appear.
2. Click **Insert**............................ `Alt`+`I`
3. Click **Table**..................................`T`
4. Click **Number of rows** .... `Alt`+`R`
5. Enter desired number. ....*number*

   OR

   Click up/down arrow to select.........`▲`/`▼`
6. Click **Number of columns** ...... `Alt`+`C`
7. Enter desired number. ....*number*

   OR

   Click up/down arrows to select. ....`▲`/`▼`
8. Click **OK** ....`Enter`

ENTER TEXT IN A TABLE

1. Click cell to receive data.
2. Type text. ....*text*
3. Press **Tab** to advance to next cell... `Tab`

   OR

   Use directional arrows ..`↓``↑``→``←`

   OR

4. Click desired cell.

EDIT A TABLE CELL

1. Click desired cell.
2. Select text to be edited.

   OR

   Insert new text at insertion point.

DISPLAY GRIDLINES

1. Click **<u>V</u>iew**............................ `Alt`+`V`
2. Click **<u>G</u>ridlines** .... `Alt`+`G`
3. Repeat steps 1-2 to deselect Gridlines.

FALL COURSE OFFERINGS

Course Title	Course Code	Time of Class	Instructor
Database	DB3	10:30 A. M.	Winston
Spreadsheets	SS101	10:00 A. M.	Rosen
Presentations	PR1	11:00 A. M.	Grande
Desktop	DTP1	11:35 A. M.	Giordano
Word Processing	WP3	12 noon	Pilgrim

EXERCISE **46**

■ **Change Alignment** ■ **Change Format** ■ **Add/Delete Columns or Rows**

NOTES:

Change Alignment

■ Text is automatically left aligned as it is entered in a cell. Numbers are right aligned. The alignments can be changed before or after the data is entered.

■ You can change the alignment of a single cell, column(s), row(s) or the entire table. To change the alignment of a single cell, place the insertion point in that cell and make the desired change. If you are changing the alignment for an entire column or row, click the gray border of the column or row containing the data to be realigned. Once the area is highlighted, change the alignment as desired.

  ✓ *NOTE: The table must be active to accept any changes. An active table displays a solid blue border.*

Change Format

■ When you create the table, you designate a predefined format. You can customize the existing format by changing alignments, font, font sizes and typestyles, or you can replace the format with another predefined format. To choose another format, click the table to activate it, click Format, click AutoFormat, then make the desired selection.

Add/Delete Columns or Rows

■ You can insert or delete one or more rows and/or columns to an active table.

■ To add a row, place your insertion point in the row below where you want the new row to be inserted. Click Insert, Insert Row.

■ To add a column, place your insertion point to the right of where you want the new column to be inserted, click Insert, Insert Column.

■ When you add a row or column, you may have to make adjustments to the format so the inserted row or column is consistent with the existing table.

  ✓ *NOTE: You cannot create a row or column beyond the last row or column. You will have to create rows/columns before the last row/column and then move the text from the last row/column into the new area. You can use cut and paste or drag and drop.*

■ To delete a row or column, place your insertion point in the column or row to be deleted; click Insert, Delete Row or Delete Column.

In this exercise, you will create a three-column table. Once it is created, you will add a row of data and make changes to the format.

EXERCISE DIRECTIONS:

1. Create a new document for the Word Processor, or open 💾**WP BASEBALL.46**.

   ✔ *NOTE: If opening WP BASEBALL.46, proceed to step 10.*

2. Change top margin to 2".

3. Center the title and subtitles. Set the title to 18 point bold. Set the first line of the subtitle to 14 point and the second line to 12 point.

4. Press the Enter key three times after the subtitle.

5. Create a table containing 9 rows and 3 columns.

6. Choose Plain as the format.

7. Center the second and third column headings and column data.

8. Print one copy.

9. Save the file; name it **BASEBALL**.

10. Insert a row before Phil A. Soule. Add the following:

Cole Slaw	38	0.2992126

    ✔ *NOTE: Make sure the font and font size and alignment in the new row are consistent with existing data.*

11. Change the format to Contemporary Simple.

12. Preview the document.

13. Print one copy.

14. Save the file; name it **BASEBALL 2**.

15. Close the document window.

CHANGE ALIGNMENTS

Ctrl + L, Ctrl + E, Ctrl + R

1. Place insertion point in desired cell.
2. Click desired alignment button on Toolbar:
   a. **Left Align** .... 🔲
   b. **Center Align** .... 🔲
   c. **Right Align** .... 🔲
   OR
1. Select text to be aligned.
2. Click desired alignment button on Toolbar.

CHANGE FORMAT

1. Click table to activate.
2. Click **Format** .... Alt + O
3. Click **AutoFormat** .... M
4. Click desired format.
5. Click **OK** .... Enter

ADD ROWS/COLUMNS

1. Place insertion point where you want the row/column to be inserted.
2. Click **Insert** .... Alt + I
3. Click **Insert Row** .... R
   OR
   Click **Insert Column** C

DELETE ROWS/COLUMNS

1. Place insertion point in row/column to delete.
2. Click **Insert** .... Alt + I
3. Click **Delete Row** .... D
   OR
   Click **Delete Column** .... E

GOURMET PRODUCTS, INC.

THE GASTRONOMES BASEBALL TEAM
Player Hits and Averages for 199-

PLAYER	HITS	AVERAGE
Hal Ebitt	179	0.3260474
Chuck Latte	94	0.2368775
Ro Mana	106	0.2731959
Sal Monn	54	0.2352941
Mary Nara	130	0.1771855
Mary Nate	91	0.2241379
Mac E. Roni	80	0.2424242
Phil A. Soule	66	0.2920354

EXERCISE **47**

■ **Adjust Column Width** ■ **Resize a Table**

NOTES:

Adjust Column Width

■ When a **table** is inserted into a letter or memorandum, it can be indented from the existing margins. This indented format gives more emphasis to the table. In order to accomplish this, you will have to make adjustments to the **column width,** the table size or both.

■ Sometimes a table may contain too much space within a column causing the table to look uneven or awkward. You can adjust column widths to improve the appearance of the table.

Resize a Table

■ When a table is created, it is even with the existing margins. The table must be reduced in size to indent it within the margins of a letter or memorandum.

■ You must display the gray handles in order to resize the table. Click on the table once to display the handles. If you get a solid border, click outside the table and then click the table again. Note the following table displaying the gray handles.

NAME	POSITION
Stephen Richardson	President and CEO
Alan E. Ennis	Vice Chair, Board of Directors
Nicholas Stannis	Executive VP and CFO
Priscilla Carroll	VP--Director of Sales
Judy M. Blane	VP--Director of Marketing
Gladys R. Brown	Director
Kenneth Newman, Ph.D.	Director, Consultant
Donna Wolenski	Director
Norman Miller	Director

■ Once the table is **resized**, you can center it to space it evenly between the existing margins.

To center the table:

- Click to display the gray handles.
- Click the center button on the Toolbar.

  OR
- Press Ctrl+E.

In this exercise, you will create a memorandum with an inserted table and centered column headings.

EXERCISE DIRECTIONS:

1. Create a new document for the Word Processor.

2. Use the default margins.

3. Center the title MEMORANDUM in a sans serif font in 16 point bold. Press the Enter key 3 times and change to left alignment.

4. Set a left-aligned tab 1" from the left margin to align the text after the guide words.

5. Type the guide words in a sans serif font in 12 point bold. Type the information following the guide words in a serif 12 point font. Press the Enter key 3 times to begin the body of the memorandum.

6. Type the memorandum and table in a serif 12 point font. Double space before and after the table.

   ✓ *NOTE:* *In the last paragraph, you may need to insert a non-breaking space in Mr. Miller to keep the title and name together.*

7. Count up the number of rows to be included in the table. Include one blank row below the column heading.

8. Choose a table format that left aligns the column data.

9. Center the column headings.

10. Adjust the column width so the column headings are more closely aligned with the column data.

11. Center the table.

12. Preview the exercise.

13. Print one copy.

14. Save the file; name it **OFFICER**.

15. Close the document window.

ADJUST COLUMN WIDTH

1. Activate the table.

2. Click line located in the gray border area between the columns.

   ✓ *NOTE:* *Display the gridlines so you can see the vertical separation of the columns. Remember to deactivate the gridlines so they don't print.*

3. Drag the adjust tool .... to desired location.

RESIZE A TABLE

1. Click the table to display the gray handles.

   ✓ *NOTE:* *If the table has a solid border, click outside the table.*

2. Place your insertion point on one of the handles.

3. Drag the resize tool until the .... table is the desired size..

MEMORANDUM

TO: Management Vice Presidents

FROM: Carter Burlington

SUBJECT: Executive Officers of Technology, Inc.

DATE: Today's

The directors and executive officers of Technology, Inc. are listed in the table below. Brief summaries of their business experiences are outlined in a report that will be forwarded to you by the end of next week.

NAME	POSITION
Stephen Richardson	President and CEO
Alan E. Ennis	Vice Chair, Board of Directors
Nicholas Stannis	Executive VP and CFO
Priscilla Carroll	VP--Director of Sales
Judy M. Blane	VP--Director of Marketing
Gladys R. Brown	Director
Kenneth Newman, Ph.D.	Director, Consultant
Donna Wolenski	Director
Norman Miller	Director

Mr. Richardson and Ms. Brown are also members of the Executive Committee, while Mr. Miller and Ms. Blane are members of the Audit Committee.

yo

EXERCISE **48**

Lesson 6 – Summary

> *In this exercise, you will format a letter containing a four-column table with column headings.*

EXERCISE DIRECTIONS:

1. Create a new document for the Word Processor, or open 💾**WP DELIVERY.48**.

   ✓ *NOTE:* *If opening WP DELIVERY.48, proceed to step 12.*

2. Set 1" left and right margins.

3. Set a 2" top margin.

4. Create the full-block letter on the next page. Double space before and after the table.

5. Determine the number of rows and columns to be included in the table. Include one blank row below the column heading.

6. Create the table and choose Classic Border.

7. Resize the table and center it within the existing margins.

8. Spell check.

9. Preview the document.

10. Print one copy.

11. Save the document; name it **DELIVERY**.

12. Insert a column between columns 1 and 2 and add the following column heading and column data.

   ORDER NO.
   2651-988
   2787-333
   8861-123
   0098-234
   3450-344
   0098-888

13. Change the format to Prestige Column.

14. Change alignments as follows:

   a. Center all column headings.

   b. Center data in columns 2, 3 and 4.

15. Make adjustments to column widths and table size as needed.

16. Preview the document.

17. Print one copy.

18. Save the document; name it **DELIVERY 2**.

Today's date

Mr. Avram Issey
ABC Computer Company
785 Lighthouse Road
Portland, OR 98138

Dear Mr. Issey:

Listed below is our projected delivery schedule for the items you ordered. We agreed that it normally takes approximately six weeks from the day of purchase for you to receive your order. We are trying to make every effort to deliver on time.

We want you to know when shipments will be arriving so you can have someone there to accept them.

ITEM	DELIVERY DATE	QUANTITY
Laser Paper	February 01	220
Computer Cartridges	May 10	130
Printers	May 15	89
Monitors	May 16	10
Quad Speed CD Roms	June 01	108
Disk Drives	July 01	199

If there is a problem with any of the delivery dates, please phone me as soon as possible.   We will call you several days in advance if we expect a problem with the delivery time.

Sincerely,

Jackson Kellogg
Distribution Manager

jk/yo

EXERCISE **49**

■ Lines and Paragraph Borders

NOTES:

Lines and Paragraph Borders

■ You can enhance the appearance of your document by adding lines, borders and shadows around one or more paragraphs. **Borders** are used to emphasize important points, separate sections of a document or draw attention to a particular section of a document.

■ Borders follow the format of the paragraph. They extend from the left to the right margin or from the left to the right indent.

■ Click F̲ormat, B̲orders and Shading or click the right mouse button and select Borders and Shading. Once the Borders and Shading dialog box appears, click the Bor̲ders tab shown below.

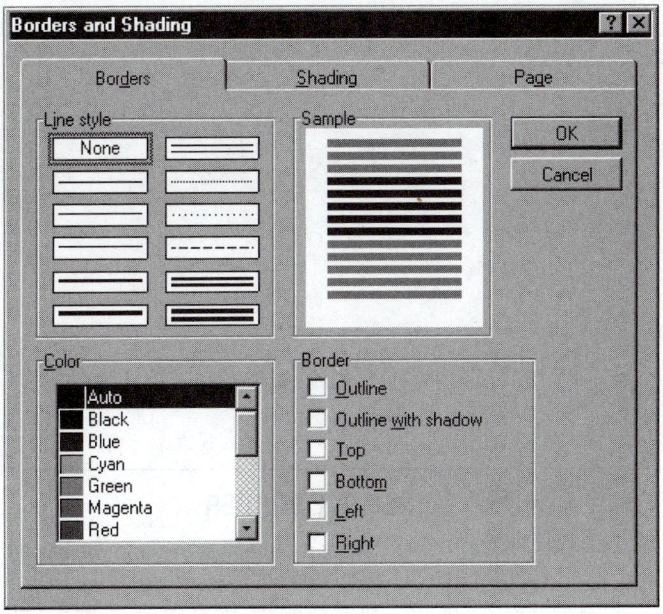

■ Borders can be formatted using a variety of options. You can make changes to the line style, line color and the location of the line. Your selection can be previewed in the Sample box.

■ To add a border to a single paragraph, you only need to place your insertion point in the paragraph before adding a border. To add a border to multiple paragraphs, you must select the paragraphs before adding a border.

■ You can add depth to your paragraph border by selecting the Outline w̲ith shadow option in the Borders and Shading dialog box shown on the left.

■ To remove a border, you must first select the paragraph and then click None in the Li̲ne Style column.

In this exercise, you will add borders and lines to a memorandum.

EXERCISE DIRECTIONS:

1. Open ▦**OFFICER**, or open ▦**WP OFFICER.49**.

2. From the top of the document, press the Enter key 3 times.

3. Select the title and enclose it in a double-line outline border with shadow.

4. Move the left-indent marker to 2" and the right-indent marker to 4" on the ruler.

5. Select the table to display the gray handles and place a single-line border on the top and bottom of the table.

6. Move the left-indent marker to 1" and the right-indent marker to 5" on the Ruler bar so the borders align with the table margins.

   ✓ *NOTE:* *You need to have the gray handles displayed on the table in order to change the size of the borders.*

7. Preview the document.

8. Print one copy.

9. Resave the document.

10. Close the document window.

ADD BORDER

1. Click **Format**......................... Alt+O
2. Click **Borders and Shading** .... B
3. Choose one of the following border options:
   - **Outline** .... Alt+O
   - **Outline with shadow** .... Alt+W
   - **Top**.................................... Alt+T
   - **Bottom**............................... Alt+M
   - **Left**................................... Alt+L
   - **Right** .... Alt+R

4. Choose a **Line style**. .... Alt+I
5. Choose a **Color**...................... Alt+C
6. Click **OK**.................................... Enter

INDENT BORDER

1. Follow steps 1-6, above and right.
2. Select the bordered text.
3. Move left and right indent markers on the Ruler bar to desired position.

REMOVE BORDER

1. Select paragraph or line from which you want borders removed.
2. Click **Format**......................... Alt+O
3. Click **Borders and Shading** .... B
4. Click **Line style** .... Alt+I
5. Click **None**
6. Click **OK**.................................... Enter

Enclose in double outline border
↙

MEMORANDUM

TO: Management Vice Presidents

FROM: Carter Burlington

SUBJECT: Executive Officers of Technology, Inc.

DATE: Today's

The directors and executive officers of Technology, Inc. are listed in the table below. Brief summaries of their business experiences are outlined in a report that will be forwarded to you by the end of next week.

NAME	POSITION
Stephen Richardson	President and CEO
Alan E. Ennis	Vice Chair, Board of Directors
Nicholas Stannis	Executive VP and CFO
Priscilla Carroll	VP--Director of Sales
Judy M. Blane	VP--Director of Marketing
Gladys R. Brown	Director
Kenneth Newman, Ph.D.	Director, Consultant
Donna Wolenski	Director
Norman Miller	Director

Mr. Richardson and Ms. Brown are also members of the Executive Committee, while Mr. Miller and Ms. Blane are members of the Audit Committee.

yo

Single-line border

■ **Create a Report Cover Page** ■ **Page Borders** ■ **Shading**

NOTES:

Create a Report Cover Page

■ A report must always be accompanied by a cover page. A cover page gives the following information:

- Title of the report

- Author of the report

- Date

- Class

- Teacher

■ Leave an equal amount of space between the various parts of the cover page. Use the format shown in the illustration on page 156 to format your cover page.

Page Borders

■ Page borders enclose the entire page within a border. The same options are available for page borders as for paragraph borders.

■ Click F**o**rmat, **B**orders and Shading, or click the right mouse button and choose Borders and Shading. Once the Borders and Shading dialog box appears, click the Page tab shown below.

■ Here, as with paragraph borders, there are a number of features available to enhance the page. You can specify the line type, the line color, shadowing and the distance between the border and the edge of the paper.

■ Your header may not fit within a page border. Check the Print Preview to see if this occurs. To correct this situation, access the Page tab above, and change the **T**op/bottom Distance from page edge to 0.3".

Shading

■ You can shade a paragraph, multiple paragraphs or an entire page. Shading adds a gray or colored pattern to the selected paragraphs. Shading can add a professional look to your document; however, a dark pattern can make the text difficult to read.

■ Click F**o**rmat, **B**orders and Shading and select the **S**hading tab to access the dialog box below:

See how pattern will look here

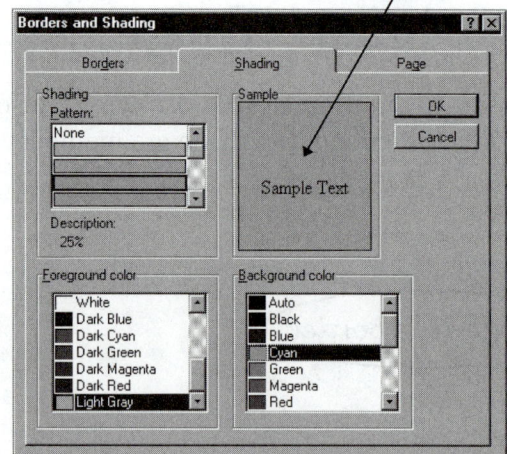

- All patterns require a foreground and background color. These can be chosen separately giving you a wide variety of shading options. Note the results of the various combinations in the <u>P</u>attern and Sample boxes.

- If you choose a colored pattern, it will display on the screen; however, the pattern will print in shades of gray if your printer does not support color.

> *In this exercise, you will create a cover for a paper written for a history class.*

EXERCISE DIRECTIONS:

1. Create a new document for the Word Processor.

2. Create the cover page shown on the following page.

3. Using the default font and font size, press the Enter key 7 times from the top of the screen.

   ✓ *NOTE: This instruction assumes you are using a 12 point font size. The distance between the lines is dependent on the font size. Six blank lines in 12 point gives less space than six blank lines in 20 point. You should be using the designated font size before returning to get the correct spacing between the sections.*

4. Center the title IMMIGRATION IN THE UNITED STATES in 20 point bold.

5. Press the Enter key 10 times while still in 20 point.

6. Center the following in 14 point bold:

   A Report by (*Use your name here*)

7. Press the Enter key 12 times while still in 14 point.

8. Center the following in single space and 12 point bold.

   Class: American History
   Teacher: Ms. Emma Grayshon
   Date: Today's Date

9. Enclose the title in a single-line border. Lightly shade the box.

   ✓ *NOTE: Place your insertion point in the title before selecting the border feature.*

10. Drag the indent markers on the Ruler Bar so the box is closer to the title. Try to duplicate the illustration as shown on the next page.

11. Select the entire document.

12. Enclose the cover page in a double-line border with shadow.

13. Print preview.

14. Make any necessary adjustments to the spacing between the three sections.

15. Preview again.

16. Print one copy.

17. Save the document; name it **COVER**.

PAGE BORDERS

1. Click **F<u>o</u>rmat** .... Alt + O
2. Click **<u>B</u>orders and Shading** .... B
3. Click **Pa<u>g</u>e** tab .... Alt + G
4. Select one or more of the following options:
   - Click desired **L<u>i</u>ne style** ..... Alt + I
   OR
     Use up/down arrows to select.
   - Click desired **<u>C</u>olor** .... Alt + C
   OR

Use up/down arrows to select.
   - Click **S<u>h</u>adow**.................... Alt + H
   - Click **Border first page only**................. Alt + F
   - Click **<u>L</u>eft/right**.................. Alt + L
     Type distance from left/right edge of page............*number*
   - Click **<u>T</u>op/bottom** .... Alt + T
     Type distance from top/bottom edge of page ....*number*
5. Click **OK** .... Enter

SHADING

1. Click **F<u>o</u>rmat** .... Alt + O
2. Click **<u>B</u>orders and Shading** .... B
3. Click **<u>S</u>hading** tab................. Alt + S
4. Choose from one or more of the following options:
   - Select desired **<u>P</u>attern** .... Alt + P
   - Select desired **<u>F</u>oreground** color .... Alt + F
   - Select **<u>B</u>ackground** color ... Alt + B
5. Click **OK** .... Enter

7 x

20 point bold

IMMIGRATION IN THE UNITED STATES

10 x

14 point bold

A Report by (*use your name here*)

12 x

12 point bold

Class: American History
Teacher: Ms. Emma Grayshon
Date: Today's date

EXERCISE **51**

■ **Insert ClipArt** ■ **Resize a Graphic** ■ **Move a Graphic** ■ **Delete a Graphic**

NOTES:

Insert ClipArt

■ Works provides a series of ready-made graphics known as ClipArt. You can select any graphic from the ClipArt Gallery to enhance a word processing or database document.

■ Click <u>I</u>nsert, Clip<u>A</u>rt to access the ClipArt Gallery dialog box below.

Categories	Selects the ClipArt by category so you do not have to scroll through the entire collection of pictures. Click the desired category to view the related clip art.
Pictures	Displays the ClipArt within the selected category. You may double-click the image to insert it into your document.
Insert	Inserts the picture into your document.
Close	Closes the ClipArt Gallery without inserting a picture.
Find	Locates a picture that meets criteria you specify.

| **Organize** | Allows you to update, edit and add pictures to the ClipArt Gallery. This feature allows you to add pictures from other software packages you have installed on your computer. |

Resize a Graphic

■ You can change the size of the picture to fit into the space you want. You can use a mouse or the Pictu<u>r</u>e command from the F<u>o</u>rmat menu to size a graphic.

■ To resize, move or delete a graphic, it must first be selected by clicking on the image. Once the image is selected, it appears in a rectangle with gray handles. Place the insertion point on one of these handles. When the resize tool appears, drag the mouse until the desired size is reached. Note the illustration below showing a graphic with the handles and resize tool displayed.

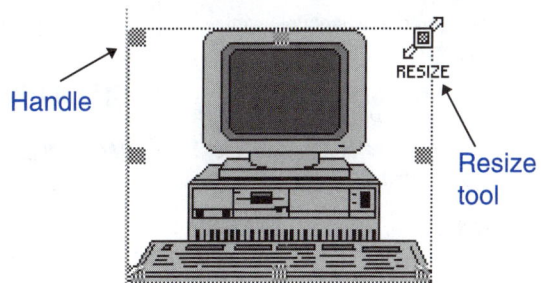

Handle

RESIZE

Resize tool

■ To keep the image in proportion as you change the size, drag a corner handle.

■ To stretch or shrink the image in height or width, drag the handles that appear in the center of the frame. Using this latter method will distort the image.

- You can also resize a graphic using exact measurements. Once you select the graphic to be resized, click the right mouse button and select Format Picture to access the Format Picture dialog box below.

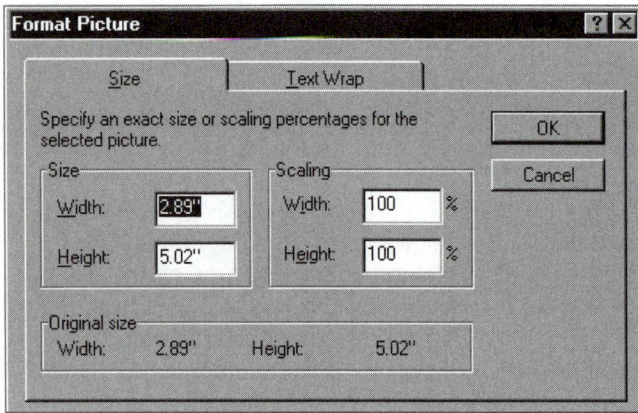

Format Picture		? X
Size	Text Wrap	

Specify an exact size or scaling percentages for the selected picture.

Size
Width: 2.89"
Height: 5.02"

Scaling
Width: 100 %
Height: 100 %

OK
Cancel

Original size
Width: 2.89"   Height: 5.02"

✔ *NOTE: You can also access this dialog box by choosing Picture from the Format menu.*

- You can specify the exact measurements for the height and width of the graphic, or choose the scaling feature to increase or decrease the picture's size by a desired percentage.

Move a Graphic

- You can drag the graphic only into an area on the page that already contains text, spaces or blank lines. A graphic cannot be moved beyond the last character on the page. Click View, All Characters to see where the last character appears.

- To move a graphic using the mouse, place the I beam in the center of the graphic. The I beam changes to the mouse pointer and the word drag appears ⬚. Click and hold the left mouse button as you drag the graphic; the word move appears ⬚.

- You can also move the graphic without using the mouse by using cut and paste.

- If you wish to change the graphic's alignment, position the insertion point before the graphic and press an alignment button. You can also move the graphic on a line by pressing the Tab key or the spacebar.

Delete a Graphic

- To delete a graphic, select the graphic (the gray handles appear) and press the Delete key.

INSERT CLIPART

1. Place insertion point where you want graphic to appear.

   ✔ *NOTE: You may press the Tab and/or Return key to place your insertion point in the desired location.*

2. Click **Insert**............................ Alt + I
3. Click **ClipArt** .... A
4. Click a **Category** .... Alt + G

   OR

   Press the down arrow to access other categories.

5. Double-click the desired graphic.

   OR

   a. Use arrow keys to select graphic.
   b. Click **Insert**............................ Enter

6. Press **End** key to place insertion point after the graphic..... End

SELECT A GRAPHIC

Click the graphic to display handles.

SIZE A GRAPHIC

Mouse Method:

1. Select the graphic.
2. Position mouse pointer on a handle, *the word resize appears.*

   ✔ *NOTE: Corner handles keep the proportion; center handles distort the graphic.*

3. Drag the mouse until graphic is desired size.

Exact measurement method:

1. Select graphic.
2. Click **Format**.......................... Alt + O
3. Click **Picture**................................. R
4. Click **Size** tab........................ Alt + S

5. Click **Width** (under Size)......... Alt + W
6. Enter desired width .... *number*
7. Click **Height**.......................... Alt + H
8. Enter desired height .... *number*
9. Click **OK**..................................... Enter

Scaling method:

1. Repeat steps 1-3 to the right.
2. Click **Width** (Under Scaling) ... Alt + I
3. Enter desired percentage.......... *number*
4. Click **Height**.......................... Alt + E
5. Enter desired percentage.
6. Click **OK**..................................... Enter

DELETE A GRAPHIC

1. Click graphic to delete.
2. Press **Delete** key .... Del

In this exercise, you will create a saying combining text and graphics. Once the document is completed, you will have resized and moved the graphics to new positions on the page.

EXERCISE DIRECTIONS:

ILLUSTRATION A

1. Create a new document for the Word Processor, or open 🖫**WP WORLD ONLINE.51**.

   ✓ *NOTE:* *If opening WP WORLD ONLINE.51, proceed to Illustration B.*

2. Use the default margins.

3. Type the following slogan in all caps using a serif font in 12 point bold.

   WITH MY COMPUTER, I HAVE THE WORLD ONLINE.

4. Press the Enter key twice.

5. Insert the following clip art graphics: computer, globe, phone receiver and cord. After a graphic is inserted, press the End key and then press the Enter key twice before inserting the next graphic.

   ✓ *NOTE:* *You may have identical images if you have added other ClipArt to your ClipArt Gallery. Be careful to select MSWorks ClipArt for this exercise because the images from the other software packages differ in size. Check the filename in the Gallery dialog box (C:\MSWORKS\CLIPART) to see if the image is a Works ClipArt image.*

6. Preview the document.

7. Print one copy.

8. Save the file; name it **WORLD ONLINE**.

ILLUSTRATION A

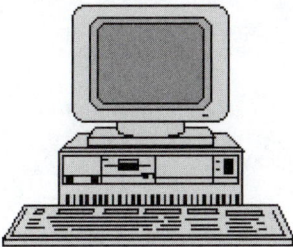

WITH MY COMPUTER, I HAVE THE WORLD ON LINE

ILLUSTRATION B

Follow the directions below to duplicate the solution on the next page.

✓ *NOTE:* *Because fonts, font sizes and typestyles are printer dependent, you may not be able to follow the exercise instructions exactly. Choose the font, font size and typestyle that is closest to the ones suggested in this exercise.*

1. Delete the word computer and use the mouse to move the computer graphic before the comma.

2. Press the Enter key twice after the comma.

3. Press the Enter key twice after the word HAVE.

4. Press the Enter key twice after the word THE.

5. Delete the words WORLD ONLINE.

6. Move the phone graphic to the right of the world graphic.

7. Format the words and graphics as follows:

   a. Select lines 1-3 including the spaces between the lines. Do not highlight the space after the third line.

   b. Center the selection in 60 point bold.

   c. Center the fourth line and make the following changes:

   - Select the globe and using the scaling option in the Size dialog box, resize it to 125% of its original width and height.

   - Select the phone graphic and using the mouse, resize it to approximately the same size as the globe.

8. Enclose the page in a single-line border.

9. Preview the document.

   ✓ *NOTE:* *Adjust the document as needed to duplicate the illustrated solution.*

10. Print one copy.

11. Resave the document.

WITH MY 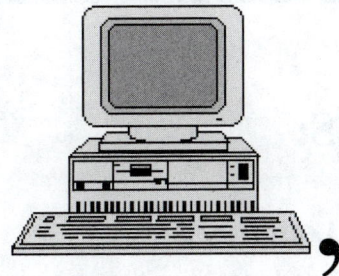,

I HAVE

THE

EXERCISE **52**

■ **Create a Letterhead**

NOTES:

Create a Letterhead

- A **letterhead** identifies the organization or person sending the letter and may contain the name, address, phone and fax number. Other identifying information may be included.

- The letterhead can be created using a variety of fonts, font sizes and ClipArt graphics. The letterhead area should be sized so there is enough blank space below it for the document.

- A letterhead is saved under its own name. Once a letter is added, the new document is saved under a different name. *(See Integrating Letterhead and Letter page 411.)*

  ✓ *NOTE:* *You can use the TaskWizards to create your own letterhead. See Wizards and Templates page 413.*

In this exercise, you will combine text with graphics to create a letterhead. To do this, you will first create the graphics as described in Exercise 51 and size it using the exact measurement feature.

EXERCISE DIRECTIONS:

1. Create a new document for the Word Processor.

2. Set the top margin to 0.5".

3. With your insertion point at the top of the screen, insert the soccer graphic from the Sports and Leisure category.

4. Use exact measurements to change the width and height of the graphic to 1.10".

5. Press the End key to place insertion point after the graphic.

6. Change to a sans serif 42 point bold font.

7. Type the company name in all caps. Press the spacebar twice between each of the words in the company name. Press the Enter key once after the company name.

8. Left align *SPORTING FOOTWEAR* and set in 14 point italics. Set a right-aligned tab on the same line at 6" on the Ruler bar.

9. Press the Tab key to right align the next two lines. Set them to 12 point. Be sure to deselect the italics.

10. Right align the phone number in 10 point bold.

11. Select the last line and create a double-lined bottom border.

12. Preview the document.

   ✓ *NOTE:* *Your copy may differ due to variations in font, font sizes and typestyles. Make necessary adjustments.*

13. Print one copy.

14. Save the document; name it **SOCK**.

SOCK IT TO ME

SPORTING FOOTWEAR

777 Mercedes Drive
Los Angeles, CA 90210
310 555-4398

EXERCISE **53**

■ **Text Wrap Feature** ■ **Newsletters**

NOTES:

Text Wrap Feature

■ Works offers two options for wrapping text around a graphic. They are demonstrated and explained below:

> This text is designed to show you how text flows around a graphic. The **In-line** option demonstrated here treats the graphic as if it were a ☎ character and places it on the same line as the text it immediately precedes and follows. The size of the graphic affects the line height. You may have to make adjustments to avoid awkward breaks in the line.

> This text is designed to show you how text flows around a graphic. The **Absolute** text wrap option demonstrated here wraps text around the graphic. Readjust the size and/or position of the graphic to avoid awkward breaks in the line.

■ Click Format, Text Wrap to access the Format Picture dialog box shown in fhe following illustration. Click the Text Wrap tab to make changes to your picture.

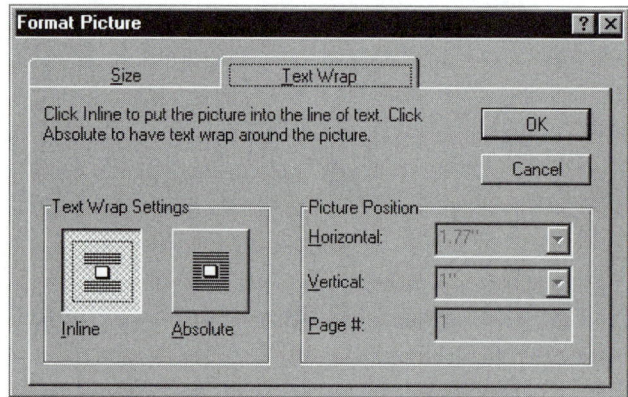

Format Picture dialog box (Size / Text Wrap tabs) — "Click Inline to put the picture into the line of text. Click Absolute to have text wrap around the picture." Text Wrap Settings: Inline, Absolute. Picture Position: Horizontal 1.77", Vertical 1", Page #: 1. OK / Cancel.

Newsletters

■ A **newsletter** is a document used by an organization to communicate information about an event, news of general interest or information regarding new products.

■ Newsletters consist of several parts:

Nameplate	May include the name of the newsletter, the organization publishing the newsletter and the logo (a symbol or distinctive typestyle used to represent the organization).
Dateline	Includes the volume number, issue number and the date.
Headline	Title preceding each article.
Byline	Located directly under the headline; it identifies the writer of the article.
Body text	The text of the article.

TEXT WRAP

1. Select the graphic.
2. Click **Format**........................... `Alt`+`O`
3. Click **Text Wrap**........................... `W`
4. Click on **Text Wrap** tab.......... `Alt`+`T`
5. Click **In-Line** to have graphic . `Alt`+`I` placed in line as a character.
6. Click **OK**....................................... `Enter`

   OR

   a. Click **Absolute** .... `Alt`+`A` to have text wrap around the graphic.

   b. Click **Horizontal** .... `Alt`+`H`

   c. Enter measurement to offset from left edge of paper. .... *number*

   d. Click **Vertical** .... `Alt`+`V`

   e. Enter measurement to offset from right edge of paper. ...... *number*

7. Click **OK**....................................... `Enter`

In this exercise, you will create a three-column newsletter containing ClipArt and a shaded, bordered paragraph.

EXERCISE DIRECTIONS:

1. Create a new document for the Word Processor.

2. Set the margins as follows:
   - Top Margin   1.5"
   - Bottom Margin   0.5"
   - Left and Right Margins   1.0"
   - Header/Footer   0.5"

3. Create the title in the header area. Center the title in sans serif 30 point bold.

4. Insert the palm tree graphic from the Plants category in ClipArt. Place it immediately to the left of the title. Size it to 50% in both width and height and use the In-Line text wrap option. Space once after the graphic to separate it from the title.

5. Press the Enter key once after the title.

6. Type the following information in sans seri 10 point bold and italics.

   Volume 2
   A Publication of Global
   Travel Summer, 199-

7. Format the dateline as follows:
   a. Left align the first part of the dateline.
   b. Press the Tab key once to center align the second part of the dateline.
   c. Set a right aligned tab at 6.5" on the Ruler bar.
   d. Press the Tab key once for the third part of the dateline.
   e. Make any necessary adjustments to the tab settings so the parts of the dateline are evenly spaced.

8. Place a single-lined bottom border under the header.

9. Place the insertion point in the document area and create the three-column newsletter at the right. Select the line feature to separate the columns.

10. Center each article's heading in serif 12 point bold.

11. Right align each byline in 8 point italics.

12. Type all paragraph text in serif 12 point. Set the first letter in each new paragraph to 16 point bold.

13. Use the following ClipArt where shown. Follow the instructions below to place the graphics.

    ✔ NOTE: If you have other Microsoft products installed on your computer, you may have more than one copy of each graphic. Be sure to use the Works version of the ClipArt; the other versions are different in size. Click the image and check the filename at the bottom of the Gallery dialog box. It should read: C:\MSWorks\Clipart\filename.

    a. Insert skiing. Use the mouse to scale it to 60% in width and 50% in height and place it as shown. Use the Absolute Text Wrap option to specify the following placement: horizontal 1.0", vertical 5.61". Make necessary adjustments to the Picture Position if the placement is awkward.

    b. Insert coffee. Use the Size dialog box to size it to 0.4" wide by 0.5" high, and place it as shown. Use the In-Line Text Wrap option.

    c. Insert daffodils. Use the mouse to scale it to 40% of its original size and place it as shown. Use the Absolute Text Wrap option and accept the Picture position settings. Make necessary adjustments if placement is awkward.

14. Set announcement at the end of the third column as follows:
    a. Set text in a sans serif 14 point bold font.
    b. Center the lines.
    c. Enclose the text in a single-line outline border.
    d. Fill the box with a light pattern.
       ✔ NOTE: Highlight the text before choosing the border. If each line is enclosed in a border, highlight the first line and clear the check from the bottom border in the Borders dialog box.

15. Enclose the entire page in a single-line outline border with shadow. Set the distance of the page border to .4" from the top/bottom edge of the page.

16. Spell check the document.

17. Preview your document.
    ✔ NOTE: Because available fonts and printers vary, your result may not appear exactly as the illustration.

18. Make any necessary adjustments to format the document attractively.

19. Save the document; name it **PACK**.

20. Close the document window.

VACATION TIPS

Volume 2   *A Publication of Global Travel, Inc.*   **Summer 199-**

Pack Right--Pack Light
By Stephen Michael

Never overpack when traveling. Dragging heavy suitcases around places a damper on even the most exciting vacation. However, with careful planning, this problem can be avoided.

Analyze your needs carefully. Will this trip be for business, pleasure or both? What kind of activities will be involved? Will you be playing golf, tennis or are you going skiing? More importantly,

what's the weather like where you're going? A bathing suit doesn't do you much good in Chile in August.

Plan a single-color scheme so you can mix and match to create several outfits with just a few pieces of clothing. Use accessories to dress up if needed.

When checking luggage on a plane, always keep a complete change of clothing and toiletries in your carry-on bag. Lost luggage can make all your careful packing a total waste of time. So that

prepacked carry-on can be a lifesaver.

Camping/Canoeing Weekend
By Susan Barry

Want to add some excitement to a weekend? Then try a combination camping/canoeing experience. This is a great adventure for a first-time camper and/or canoeist.

The West Bend River Outfitters are offering a weekend of camping and canoeing at various locations throughout the tri-state area. You don't need to know anything about camping. The river outfitters do all the work, all you do is PADDLE!

You arrive at the river late Friday evening to find your tent already set up. You awaken the next morning to the aroma of freshly

brewed coffee and bacon and eggs.

After this sumptuous beginning, you're off for a morning of fun and sun on the river. Although the river is usually calm at this time of the year, it may not always be clear sailing. The river guides are always with you, however, to lead

you through any white water you may encounter.

Time for lunch. The river outfitters meet you in a flower-filled meadow right off the riverbank where they set up a five-course

lunch. Who said roughing it was rough? A steak dinner over an open campfire is Saturday night's fare followed by square dancing and a hay ride.

Sunday morning arrives, and after another fabulous breakfast, you're ready for your last run down the river. Now you can paddle, upright an overturned canoe, and handle some moderate white water. You leave tired but exhilarated, and ready to tell your friends how you experienced nature firsthand--well, *almost* firsthand.

Next Month's Feature:

Vacationing in Hawaii

EXERCISE 54

■ **Microsoft Draw** ■ **Create a Drawing**

NOTES:

Microsoft Draw

■ **Microsoft Draw** is a drawing program that is included in Works. Like ClipArt, it can be used in both the Word Processor and Database tools. However, unlike ClipArt, which provided you with ready-made pictures, Draw enables you to:

- create your own drawings.

- import drawings from other applications.

- edit original, imported or ClipArt graphics.

Create a Drawing

■ Microsoft Draw is accessed through the Insert menu. When you access Draw, a separate screen appears as shown below.

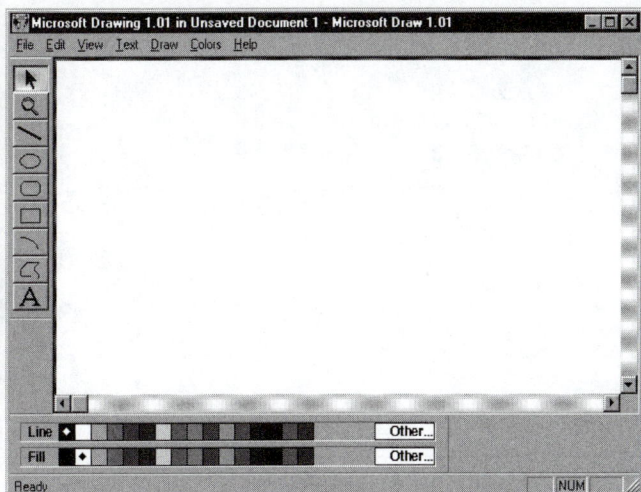

```
Microsoft Drawing 1.01 in Unsaved Document 1 - Microsoft Draw 1.01
File  Edit  View  Text  Draw  Colors  Help
```
```
Line                    Other...
Fill                    Other...
Ready                   NUM
```

■ Once you are in the Draw program, Works sets a placeholder for the drawing in the word processing document. This placeholder is displayed as a shaded gray area. After creating your drawing, it is inserted in your word processing document, replacing the placeholder.

■ Microsoft Draw has its own menus, drawing tools and on-line help.

✓ *NOTE:* *You can obtain help in Microsoft Draw by pressing F1.*

■ The following list contains the tools which appear on the left side of the Draw screen.

Pointer — Is used to select one or more objects. Once these objects are selected, they can be moved or resized.

Zoom — Increases or decreases the size of the image on the screen. To reduce the image, press Shift while clicking the magnifying glass.

Line — Draws a straight line. The mouse pointer turns into a **crosshair** $+$. Hold down the Shift key and drag the crosshair to get a straight line; hold down the Control key as you drag to draw the line from the center out.

Oval/Circle — Draws an oval. Draws a circle when you press Shift and drag the crosshair. Draws a circle from its center when you press the Shift + Control keys as you drag the crosshair.

Rounded Rectangle/ Square — Draws a rectangle with rounded corners. Draws a rounded square when you press Shift and drag the crosshair.

Rectangle/ Square — Same as above except corners are not rounded.

Arc — Draws an arc. Hold down Shift and drag the crosshair to get a 45 degree angle.

Freeform — Is used to draw freeform drawings. As you begin drawing, the crosshair turns into a pencil. When finished drawing with this tool, double-click to finish.

Text A
Is used to type up to 255 characters on a single line. The font, font size and typestyle can be changed.

✓ *NOTE:* *The exercises in this book give an introduction to the Draw program. Since the program is extensive and has many capabilities, it is advisable that you use the on-line Help to become familiar with all the features of Microsoft Draw.*

- To place your drawing in the word processing document:

  - Click File.

  - Click Exit and Return.

  - Click Yes to save changes.

- The drawing is now **embedded** in the word processing document at the insertion point. Embedding is a feature that allows you create or edit the graphic from within the Word Processor tool.

- The embedded graphic is saved with the word processing document.

- Draw provides an invisible **grid** to allow you to align objects precisely. All objects drawn on the Draw screen will snap to the nearest intersection on this grid. However, if the grid is on, you may not be able to place an object in an exact location. If the grid is causing this problem, click Draw, Snap to Grid to deselect the grid. This will not affect existing objects.

- The Draw program contains a **group** feature. This feature allows you to combine several objects into one image so it can be copied, moved or resized as a single entity. The face in this exercise consists of a number of independent objects that can be moved or resized individually. However, to resize or move the entire face, all the objects making up the face (mouth, nose, ears, etc.) will need to be grouped so they can be moved or resized as one unit.

To group an object:

- Click the arrow key and draw a dotted box around the objects to be grouped.

- Click Draw, Group.

  ✓ *NOTE: Four handles now appear around the grouped image.*

- Move, copy or resize as desired.

ACCESS MICROSOFT DRAW

1. Place insertion point where you want the graphic to be inserted.

2. Click **Insert** .... Alt + I

3. Click **Drawing** I

4. Click desired tool.

5. Place the crosshair where you want to draw.

6. Click and drag the mouse to achieve desired size and shape.

7. Release the mouse button.

8. Click in blank area of draw screen to deselect the object.

✓ *NOTE:* *The freeform tool allows you to draw both open and closed freehand drawings and open and closed polygons. To draw freehand, hold down the mouse button and drag. To draw polygons, click at various points and the lines will connect. In both cases, double-click when the shape is completed.*

9. Repeat for additional objects.

10. Click **File** .... Alt + F

11. Click **Exit and Return**. .... Alt + X

12. Click **Yes** to save changes. .... Y

    Drawing will be inserted at insertion point.

EXERCISE DIRECTIONS:

1. Create a new document for the Word Processor, or open ⊟**WP HAPPY.54**.

   ✓ NOTE: If opening WP HAPPY.54, proceed to step 3.

2. Type the letter at the right in full-block form.

3. Set the left and right margins at 0.75".

4. Start the date 1.5" from the top of the page.

5. After completing the letter, place the insertion point as indicated.

6. Access Drawing from the Insert menu. Maximize the Drawing window.

7. Create the child's face using the tools listed below. Your drawing may differ from the illustration.

   a. Click the circle/ellipse tool to draw the outline for the face.

   b. Start at the top left of the Draw screen and drag till the ellipse is approximately 2" in diameter.

   c. Click outside the ellipse to create the eyes.

   d. Use a small ellipse for the eye. Use a small circle or ellipse for the eyeball.

      ✓ NOTE: Deactivate the grid to get the eyeball in the center of the eye.

   e. Follow these steps to duplicate the eye so it will be equal in size to the first eye.

      • Click the arrow tool and draw a box around the completed eye.

      • Click Draw, Group.

      • With the grouped eye selected, click Edit, Copy.

      • Click Paste and move both eyes to the appropriate location.

   f. Use the line and freeform tools to create the nose.

   g. Use the arc tool for the ears. Follow these steps to duplicate and rotate the ear.

      • Draw the first ear.

      • With the handles displayed, click Edit, Copy.

      • Click Edit, Paste to duplicate the ear.

      • With the handles displayed on the second ear, click Draw, Rotate, Flip Horizontal.

      • With the handles still displayed, drag the ear to the correct location.

   h. Use the freeform tool for the mouth.

   i. Use the freeform tool for the hair.

   j. Use the line tool for the neck and shoulders.

   k. Use the text tool to type the child's name in a large font.

8. Click File and choose Exit and Return.

9. Click Yes when asked to update.

10. Once the graphic is embedded in the word processing document, resize it using the mouse.

11. Be sure there is a double space above and below the embedded graphic.

12. Center the graphic.

13. Enclose the graphic in a bold border. Decrease the width of the border (drag the left- and right-indent markers) so that it fits closely around the graphic.

14. Preview the document.

15. Print one copy.

16. Save the document; call it **HAPPY**.

Today's date

Mrs. Vera Proud
100 Chasmine Road
Wichita, KS 67208

Dear Mrs. Proud:

As a mother of a preschooler, you know how important it is to provide readiness activities to prepare your child for kindergarten. We, at Happy Land Preschool, offer programs that stress readiness in reading, writing, math, and computers. Today, your child's education is not complete without computer instruction.

Our classrooms are furnished with state-of-the-art computers equipped with the latest educational software. One of the programs the students particularly liked was a draw program. We asked the students to draw themselves and were delighted with the results. This program encourages them to express themselves and be creative. Here is a sample of a self-portrait done by one of our preschoolers.

Place insertion point and access Microsoft Draw.

TONY

If you are looking for a preschool that offers a fine education with state-of-the-art equipment and caring teachers, then please call us to arrange an appointment for a visit. We look forward to meeting with you soon.

Very truly yours,

Hector Menendez
Director

yo

EXERCISE **55**

■ **Copy a ClipArt or Drawing** ■ **Edit a ClipArt or Drawing**

NOTES:

Copy a ClipArt or Drawing

■ You may want more than one copy of a ClipArt graphic or drawing in your document. Note the copied computer graphic on the letterhead in this exercise on page 174. Once an object is inserted from ClipArt or Draw, you can copy it as many times as you need without having to switch back to the ClipArt gallery or Draw program.

■ You can copy an object as you do text by first selecting it. The handles will display. Once selected, use either drag and drop or Edit, Cut/ Edit Paste to copy.

Edit a ClipArt or Drawing

■ In addition to moving, resizing and copying ClipArt graphics and drawings, you can add other elements to the graphic, change the pattern, color or line style of an object, or flip or rotate the graphic or an object within the graphic. These changes to the ClipArt image are done in the Microsoft Draw program.

■ The computer ClipArt image used in the letterhead on page 174 has been copied, resized, rotated and altered to add text.

■ Illustrated below and to the right are several examples of editing changes made to a ClipArt graphic in Microsoft Draw.

This is a sample of ClipArt without editing changes.

Here the color was changed and the lines were changed to black.

Here a pattern was added and the line style was changed to 3 point.

Here the graphic was rotated (note the ribbon is on the right side of the box).

■ Since the ClipArt image is edited in the Draw program, you can use any of the tools available as if you were creating your own drawing.

To edit a ClipArt:

• Click Insert, Drawing.
• Click File from the Draw menu.
• Click Import Picture.
• Enter the correct drive and directory for the ClipArt files.
• Select desired ClipArt.

■ To edit the ClipArt graphic as a whole, you must **group** all the individual objects in the graphic. As explained in the last exercise, grouping allows you to combine objects in a drawing so they become a single object. Once an object has been grouped, four resize handles will appear around it. At this point, your editing changes will affect the entire object.

To edit a drawing:

- Double-click the drawing in the word processing document to access the Draw program.

- In the Draw screen, select desired elements to edit and make desired changes.

- Click File.

- Click Exit and Return.

- Choose Yes to save the drawing.

In this exercise, you will create a letterhead by combining ClipArt and Microsoft Draw objects. You will size, scale and copy the ClipArt and use Microsoft Draw to connect the two ClipArt objects.

EXERCISE DIRECTIONS:

1. Create a new document for the Word Processor.

2. Change the left and right margins to 1".

3. Make sure you are in the Page Layout view. Click in the header area.

4. Click Insert, Drawing.

5. Click Draw, click Snap to Grid to deselect it.

6. Click File, Import Picture and import the Ghost 1 ClipArt file.

   ✓ NOTE: *The location of the ClipArt files depends upon the folder in which the program was installed. Specify the correct drive and directory to access the Works ClipArt files.*

7. Click the text tool and click in the top left corner of the Draw screen to type the word ON. Once typed, Click outside the word to display the handles.

   ✓ NOTE: *If your text tool is not visible, resize the Draw window using the mouse or maximize the window.*

8. With the handles displayed, click the Text menu and make the following changes.

   a. Select Font and select a sans serif 8 point bold font.
   b. Select Center.

9. Click the white square on the Line palette.

   ✓ NOTE: *The words will disappear because they are in white. They will appear when they are dragged to the computer screen in step 10.*

10. Drag the word to the top of the computer screen in the graphic.

11. Repeat steps 7-10 for the word LINE.

12. Follow the directions below to extend the wire to the floor. Try to approximate the graphic in the solution.

   a. Choose the freeform tool and place the crosshair at the end of the wire.
   b. Hold down the mouse button and drag downward and slightly to the right (the crosshair turns to a pencil) to draw the wire.

13. Double-click to end the line.

14. Click the circle tool. Place the crosshair where the eye is. Hold down the Shift key and drag the circle as little as possible to cover the existing eye. Change the fill to black on the color palette.

15. Select the arrow tool, and draw a box around the graphic. Select Draw, Group.

16. Click File, Exit and Return. Click Yes to save the file.

17. Scale the graphic to 50%.

18. Copy the graphic.

19. Place insertion point to the right of the graphic.

20. Paste the graphic.

21. Double-click the second graphic to return to the Draw screen.

22. Click the Draw menu, select Rotate/Flip and Flip Horizontal.

   ✓ NOTE: *If Rotate/Flip is dimmed, click the graphic to display four handles. If you cannot get four handles, try grouping the graphic again.*

23. Exit and return to the letterhead saving the changes made to the graphic.

24. Place the insertion point between the two graphics.

25. Access Microsoft Draw.

26. Refer to the illustration and following the directions on the following page, draw a wire that will connect both computers.

   a. Select the freeform tool.

   b. Starting close to the bottom of the screen, draw a wavy line extending from the left to the right edge of the Draw screen window.

      ✓ NOTE: *Make any necessary adjustments to have the wire look connected to the two end computers. You may need to resize the wire or make changes to the wires attached to the computer graphics. Toggle between the Works and Draw screens to edit and view changes.*

27. Click above the newly drawn wire in the Draw screen.

28. Select the text tool and type TELECOPY CENTER. Format as follows:

   a. Set to a sans serif font in 26 point bold.
   b. Select a center alignment.

29. Return to the letterhead.

30. You may need to edit the graphics so the wires look more closely connected, and you may need to resize the graphics so they all fit on one line.

31. Select the entire header and enclose in a single-line outline border with shadow.

32. Click in the document area.

33. Set a right aligned tab at 6.37".

34. Type the address and phone numbers in a sans serif font in 10 point bold and italics.

35. Type the address; press the Tab key to type the phone number. Press the Enter key and type the second line of the address; press the Tab key to type the fax number.

36. Click in the footer area and press the Enter key once.

37. Type and center align the following slogan: "For All Your Computer and Copying Needs" in a sans serif font in 11 point bold and italics.

38. Place the insertion point in the space immediately above the slogan and insert a top single-line border.

39. Print Preview the document and make any necessary adjustments to more closely duplicate the illustrated solution.

40. Print one copy.

41. Save the file; name it **TELECOPY**.

COPY A CLIPART OR DRAW OBJECT

1. Click desired object to copy.

2. Place mouse pointer on graphic; *drag* appears. [DRAG]

3. Hold down Ctrl .... [Ctrl] while dragging the mouse, *copy* appears [COPY]

4. Move to new location.

5. Release the mouse button.

OR

1. Click desired object to copy.

2. Click **Edit**.............................. [Alt]+[E]

3. Click **Copy** .... [C]

4. Place insertion point at new location.

5. Click **Edit**.............................. [Alt]+[E]

6. Click **Paste** .... [P]

EDIT CLIPART GRAPHIC IN MICROSOFT DRAW

1. Click **Insert**............................. [Alt]+[I]

2. Click **Drawing** .... [I]

3. Click **File**............................. [Alt]+[F]

4. Click **Import Picture**...................... [I]

5. Enter correct drive and directory.

6. Click desired file.

   To have editing changes affect the entire graphic:

   a. Click arrow tool .... [↖]

   b. Draw box around graphic.

   c. Click **Draw** .... [Alt]+[D]

   d. Click **Group**............................... [G]

   ✓ NOTE: *Four resize handles should appear around the graphic.*

7. Make desired changes.

   a. Click **Draw** .... [Alt]+[D]

   b. Choose one or more of the following menu items:

   - **Patterns** .... [P]
   - **Line Style**.......................... [L]
   - **Frame**d .... [D]
   - **Filled**.............................. [F]
   - **Rotate** .... [O]

   To edit an object in the graphic:

   a. Click desired object.

   b. Handles should appear on object.

   c. Make desired changes.

8. Click **File**.............................. [Alt]+[F]

9. Click **Exit and Return** .... [X]

EDIT A DRAW OBJECT

1. Double-click Draw object.

2. Once in Microsoft Draw follow steps 7-9 above.

TELECOPY CENTER

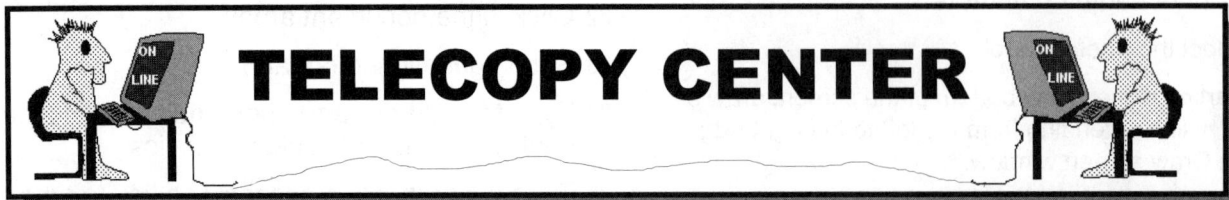

345 Northern Boulevard
Baldwin, NY 11755

Phone: 516-555-9843
Fax: 516-555-4596

For All Your Computer and Copying Needs

EXERCISE **56**

■ **WordArt**

WORDART TOOLBAR

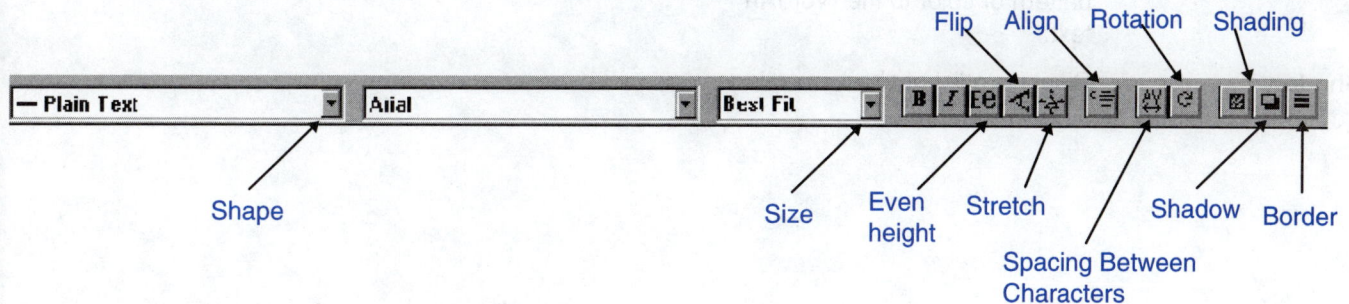

Flip   Align   Rotation   Shading

— Plain Text | Arial | Best Fit | B | I | Ee | ... | ... | ...

Shape   Size   Even   Stretch   Shadow   Border
                      height
                              Spacing Between
                              Characters

NOTES:

WordArt

■ **WordArt**, like Microsoft Draw, is an application that you can access directly from Works.

■ This feature can create striking text effects for flyers, letterheads, headings or logos. WordArt can also be used in the body text to make areas of your document more distinctive. You can curve, slant, stretch, rotate and add patterns, shade or shadow any text element.

✓ *NOTE:*   *The exercises in this book give an introduction to the WordArt program. Since the program is extensive and has many capabilities, it is advisable that you use the on-line Help to become familiar with all the features of the program.*

■ To access the WordArt application, select WordArt from the Insert menu. The WordArt application enables you to create an image which will then be inserted into the current document.

■ You enter your text in the **Enter Your Text Here** box as shown below. The gray area on the current document serves as a placeholder for the text.

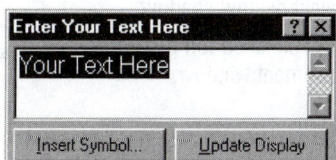

Enter Your Text Here   [?][X]

Your Text Here

[Insert Symbol...] [Update Display]

Your Text Here

■ WordArt has its own Toolbar, menu and on-line Help. Below is a list of WordArt Toolbar options.

✓ *NOTE:*   *Buttons which appear on other tools and have been previously introduced are not included in the list below:*

Shape	Allows you to choose the shape of your characters from a wide variety of options.
Size	Allows a choice of sizes. The Best Fit feature determines the best font size for the WordArt frame you've selected. When you use Best Fit, the font size changes when the frame is resized. If you choose a specific font size, however, your text will remain that size even if you resize the frame.
Even Height	Makes all letters the same height.
Flip	Turns words on their sides.
Stretch	Spreads the text both horizontally and vertically to fill the WordArt area.
Align	Aligns text in the WordArt area. The default alignment is center.

Spacing Between Characters	Provides options to adjusting the spacing between each letter or character. This is known as **kerning**.
Rotation	Provides options for turning the text.
Shading	Provides options for applying a pattern or color to the WordArt text.
Shadow	Displays a list of shadow options.

Border	Allows you to select a border for each character.

■ Once you have made all your desired changes, click the close button on the WordArt frame. You can also close the frame by clicking in the document area.

USING WORDART

1. Place insertion point where you want the WordArt text.
2. Click **Insert** .... Alt + I
3. Click **WordArt** .... Alt + W
4. Enter text in box.
5. Click **Font** box.
6. Select desired font.
7. Click **Size** box.
8. Select desired size.
9. Click **Shape** box.
10. Select desired shape.
11. Click **Format** .... Alt + T
12. Select desired option.
    Border .... E
    Select desired border.
    Shading .... H
    Select desired shading.
    Shadow .... W
    Select desired shadow.
13. Click close button to return to .... X document window.

    OR

    Click in the document window.

> In this exercise, you will open the Etiquette newsletter and add a nameplate using the WordArt feature.

EXERCISE DIRECTIONS:

1. Open ⌨**ETIQUETTE**, or open 💾**WP ETIQUETTE.56**.

2. Click in header area.

3. Click Insert and select WordArt.

4. Type CYBERSPACE ETIQUETTE in the text frame.

5. Click the shape list box and select Wave 2 (located in Row 2, Column 6).

6. Choose a sans serif font other than Arial. Select bold.

7. Click the Stretch button to fill the frame with the text.

8. Click the Spacing Between Characters button and set to loose.

9. Click Shading button and select the first shade in the second row.

10. Click the Shadow button and select the third shadow style.

11. Click the Border button and select Hairline.

12. Close the WordArt frame.

13. Use the mouse to stretch the WordArt frame to fill the header area. Use the lower-right sizing handle to retain proper proportions. The frame may drop below the header area.

14. While the frame is still selected, place a border under the WordArt frame. Select a double-line border from the Borders dialog box.

15. Click in the Footer area.

16. Type the dateline in the Footer area. Type Volume I at the left margin, press the Tab key twice to type today's date at the right margin. Type both in a serif 10 point italic font.

17. Enclose the Footer in an outline border and fill with a 20% fill pattern.

18. Enclose the entire newsletter in a page border with shadow. Decrease the Top/bottom Distance from the page edge to 0.3".

19. Preview the document.
    > ✔ NOTE: Depending on your printer, your header, footer or both may extend beyond the page border. To correct this, change your Header and Footer margins to 1" in the Page Setup.

20. Adjust the document as needed to approximate the illustration in this exercise.
    > ✔ NOTE: If your document goes on to two pages, change the Space between columns to 0.3" in the Columns dialog box.

21. Save the file under a new name; name it **CYBERNEWS**.

22. Print one copy.

23. Close the document.

CYBERSPACE ETIQUETTE

People interact according to the unwritten rules of etiquette that have been handed down from generation to generation.   Behaviors we take for granted are instilled in us at an early age. Take a moment and think about all the social customs we follow (or should follow) when we interact with others whether it be in person, on the phone, or driving a car.

Now comes the age of cyberspace with the arrival of the Internet and on-line services. Millions of people are using their computers to communicate in ways never thought possible. The information highway is an exciting place to find information and perhaps make new friends, but we do this in a vacuum. We don't hear the voice or see the facial expression that has traditionally helped us to convey our messages. Now we have only the written word, and we may sometimes forget that we are communicating with real people who have real live feelings. This could lead to a lapse in manners. As a result, there have been books and magazines written on the proper way to conduct yourself when communicating on-line.

One of the key points to remember when using a service or bulletin board is that there is a person at the other end of the computer, and we should apply the same standards to our on-line behavior that we follow in our daily lives. Ask yourself if your message is acceptable and if you would say this to someone in a face-to-face situation. Try to envision the person you're writing to so that the communication becomes more "human." Remember that anything you write takes on a life of its own. It can be saved and later forwarded to other users.

Be ethical, courteous, sensitive to others, and remember that your written word is your representative. If we all adhere to these general guidelines, then cyberspace will be a more pleasant place to visit.

EXERCISE **57**

■ **Use Note-It**

NOTES:

NOTE-IT

■ **Note-It** is a feature that allows you to add notes or reminders to your word processing or database documents. Works places a graphic or picture where the note is hidden. To read it, you double click the icon and the note appears.

■ Place the insertion point where you want the note and then select **Note-It** from the Insert menu. Select your picture, and enter the caption and message in the dialog box shown below:

■ Double-click the note to read it. The note appears at the top of the screen.

■ Click in the document area to close the note, or press the Enter key.

■ To delete the note, select it and press the Delete key.

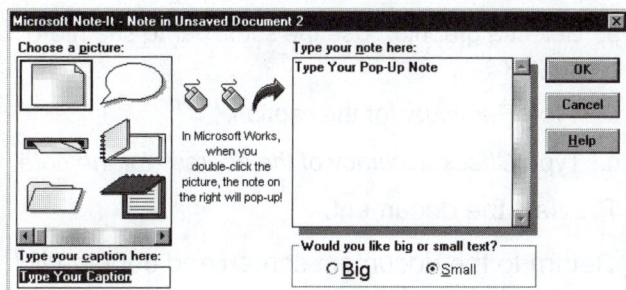

USE NOTE-IT

1. Place insertion point where you want to place the note.
2. Click **Insert**.......................... `Alt` + `I`
3. Click **Note-It**.................................. `E`
4. Select a picture for the note.
5. Enter a caption............................... *text*
6. Enter the text of the note.................. *text*
7. Select size of the text.
8. Click **OK** .... `Enter`

READ AND CLOSE A NOTE

1. Double-click the note to open it.
2. Click document area to close it.

   OR

   Press **Enter** .... `Enter`

DELETE A NOTE

1. Select the note.
2. Press **Delete**................................ `Del`

> *In this exercise, you will use WordArt, ClipArt and Microsoft Draw to create a letterhead.*

EXERCISE DIRECTIONS:

1. Create a new document for the Word Processor.

2. Set the top margin for .75".

3. Create the following footer in a serif 12 point bold font. Left align the footer; tab between parts to space attractively. Create a top and bottom border for the footer.

   > 301 Carman Road
   > New Meadows, NY 11554
   > (516) 555-3340

4. Click in the document area (under the header area) and use the WordArt feature to format NEW MEADOWS HIGH SCHOOL as follows:

   a. Select the Triangle (Inverted) shape.

   b. Select stretch to Frame.

   c. Select Best Fit.

   d. Select a Shadow effect for the text.

   e. Exit WordArt and size the frame so it extends from the left to the right margin.

      > ✓ NOTE: *Use the bottom right handle to resize. This keeps the letters in the correct proportion.*

   f. When done, click to the right of the frame and press the Enter key once.

5. To insert the lines and ClipArt:

   a. Use Microsoft Draw.

   b. Use the line tool and draw a diagonal line starting top left and dragging to bottom right. The line should be about 1-2 inches in length.

   c. Exit Draw and return to your document. Click Yes to save the drawing object. Click Format, Picture and size the line to measure exactly 2.5" in width and 0.34" in height. Place it under NEW MEADOWS.

   d. Insert the Plane ClipArt immediately after the line.

   e. Size it to exactly .77" in width and .31" in height.

   f. Copy the line and paste it under HIGH SCHOOL.

      > ✓ NOTE: *It will not be in the correct direction.*

   g. Double-click the line to edit it in Draw.

   h. Flip the vertical line so it resembles the line on the letterhead in this exercise.

   i. Make adjustments in the size as needed.

   j. When done, click to the right of the second line and press the Enter key once.

6. Use the WordArt feature to format the slogan *Home of the Jets* as follows:

   a. Choose same style as the main heading. Use the Best Fit option.

   b. Bold the slogan.

   c. Center the slogan.

   d. Center the WordArt frame under the school name and size accordingly.

7. Insert a Note-It after the slogan to remind yourself to check the accuracy of the address. Format as follows:

   a. Select a graphic. Use the scroll bar to see more graphics.

   b. Type *Reminder* for the caption.

   c. Type *Check accuracy of the address* for the note.

8. Preview the document.

9. Return to the document screen and double-click the icon to view the note.

   > ✓ NOTE: *The note appears at the top of the page.*

10. Delete the note.

11. Make any necessary adjustments so that the document resembles the letterhead.

12. Print one copy.

13. Save the file; name it **JETS**.

NEW MEADOWS HIGH SCHOOL

Home of the Jets

301 Carman Road   New Meadows, NY 11554   (516) 555-3340

EXERCISE **58**

Lesson 7 – Summary

In this exercise, you will create a four-column newsletter using WordArt, borders and shading and ClipArt.

EXERCISE DIRECTIONS:

1. Create the National Honor Society newsletter on the next page.
   - ✓ NOTE: *You may not be able to make an exact duplicate of the newsletter due to variations in fonts and printers. Make adjustments as needed to accommodate your system.*

2. Make the following changes in the Page Setup dialog box:
   a. <u>T</u>op margin .... 2.0"
   b. <u>B</u>ottom margin .... 0.75"
   c. Left/<u>R</u>ight margins .... 0.5"
   d. He<u>a</u>der .... 1"
   e. <u>F</u>ooter .... 0.75"

3. Create the nameplate and dateline in the header area. Use the WordArt feature to create the nameplate. Use a serif font in 9 point italics for the dateline.
   - HINT: *To have the date print at the right margin, you will need to move the right tab to the right indent marker on the Ruler bar.*

4. Insert a border under the dateline.

5. Create a four-column newsletter.

6. Format the first column as follows:
   a. Use WordArt to create the NATIONAL HONOR SOCIETY title using the bottom to top shape.
   b. Click the stretch button to have the text fill the WordArt frame.
   c. Extend the frame to fill most of the column as shown.
   d. Select the WordArt frame and insert a right-sided border.

   e. Insert the At the Top ClipArt and place it below the NATIONAL HONOR SOCIETY. Resize appropriately. You may use the Enter key to alter its position.
   f. Click to the right of the graphic and press the Enter key to access the top of column 2.

7. Center the first heading in a sans serif font in 20 point bold, and type the first paragraph in a serif font in 14 point.

8. Left align the headings for all other articles in a sans serif font in 14-point bold.

9. Type all articles in a serif font in 12 point.

10. Hyphenate the text selectively.

11. Justify all body text.

12. Insert additional ClipArt as shown:

   An Idea
   Gifts
   Daffodil
   - ✓ NOTE: *Use the edit, size and placement options to approximate the illustration in this exercise.*

13. Use the <u>B</u>order feature to set off various sections of the newsletter.

14. Print preview the document.

15. Make any necessary adjustments.

16. Print one copy.

17. Save the document; name it **NHS**.

18. Close the document window.

NHS NEWS

Publication of New Meadows H. S.

National Honor Society

NHS has another great year

As our school year draws to a close, we would like to highlight some of the events that contributed to our success this year.

Tutoring

Our faculty advisor, Mr. Bob McGuiness, had the inspiration to institute a tutoring program this year. Each of our NHS members signed up to offer their services during their lunch or free periods. This free service offered tutors in the math and science areas. Some of our members signed up to tutor in both subjects.

The tutoring service was advertised in all the classes. Students seeking tutoring were advised to come to the NHS office and connect with a tutor who fit into their schedule.

This was a truly successful program, and we hope to expand it to other subject areas next fall.

Christmas Hospital Visit

Two days before Christmas vacation, the **NHS** visited Long Island Hospital to deliver gifts to the children.

Our president, Philip D'Agostino, dressed as Santa Claus, padding his six-foot frame to fill out his Santa outfit. The children were so excited to see Santa Claus right there in the hospital.

This was a wonderful experience and our **NHS** members were as excited about giving the gifts as the children were to receive them.

Broadway Show and Dinner

Since this year was a smash hit, we decided to end it by seeing one. On May 1, we all boarded a chartered bus to Manhattan for dinner and a show.

Most of our members attended, and we were accompanied by our faculty advisor, school principal and a number of faculty members. A good time was had by all.

Good Luck!

At this time, we would like to offer our best wishes to the graduating class.

REMINDERS

- Car Wash - June 1 to benefit MADD. Main entrance to field from 7:30 a.m.-12 noon.
- Ushers needed for graduation. See Joanne Lang to sign up.

HAVE A GREAT SUMMER!!!

Spreadsheet

LESSONS 1 - 5

Lesson 1: Create, Save and Print a Spreadsheet

Lesson 2: Formulas; Format Spreadsheets

Lesson 3: Functions

Lesson 4: Format, Edit and Enhance
Spreadsheets

Lesson 5: Create and Enhance Charts

■ **Introduction to the Spreadsheet Tool** ■ **Start a Spreadsheet**
■ **Spreadsheet Screen Parts** ■ **Move Around in a Spreadsheet**

NOTES:

Introduction to the Spreadsheet Tool

■ The primary function of the **Spreadsheet tool** is to perform calculations. These calculations can involve mathematical, financial or scientific data. Some typical uses for spreadsheets are:

- household budgets
- income taxes
- inventories
- student grades

■ There are three types of data in a spreadsheet. They are:

Values	Any numeric data is considered a value, this includes numbers, dates and times.
Formulas	Equations that calculate the data. Functions are more complex formulas.
Labels	Non-numeric data which includes any heading or explanatory text.

■ In addition to performing mathematical calculations, spreadsheets can be used to create columns of text. In Lesson 6, Exercise 40, of the Word Processor section, you learned to set up columns of information using the Table feature. This feature is actually a spreadsheet that is embedded within a word processing document. You may also, however, set up the table directly in the Spreadsheet tool and then integrate it with other Works tools. (*See Integration, Exercise 3.*)

Start a Spreadsheet

■ You can create a spreadsheet when you start Works, while you are working in another spreadsheet or from other Works tools.

To access the Spreadsheet tool from the Works Task Launcher:

- Click Works <u>T</u>ools tab.
- Click the <u>S</u>preadsheet icon on the Microsoft Works Task Launcher shown below:

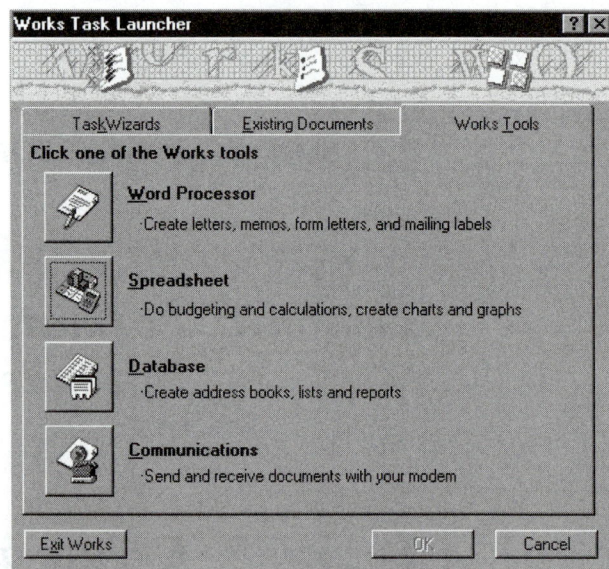

Spreadsheet Screen Parts

■ Once you access the spreadsheet, the following screen displays:

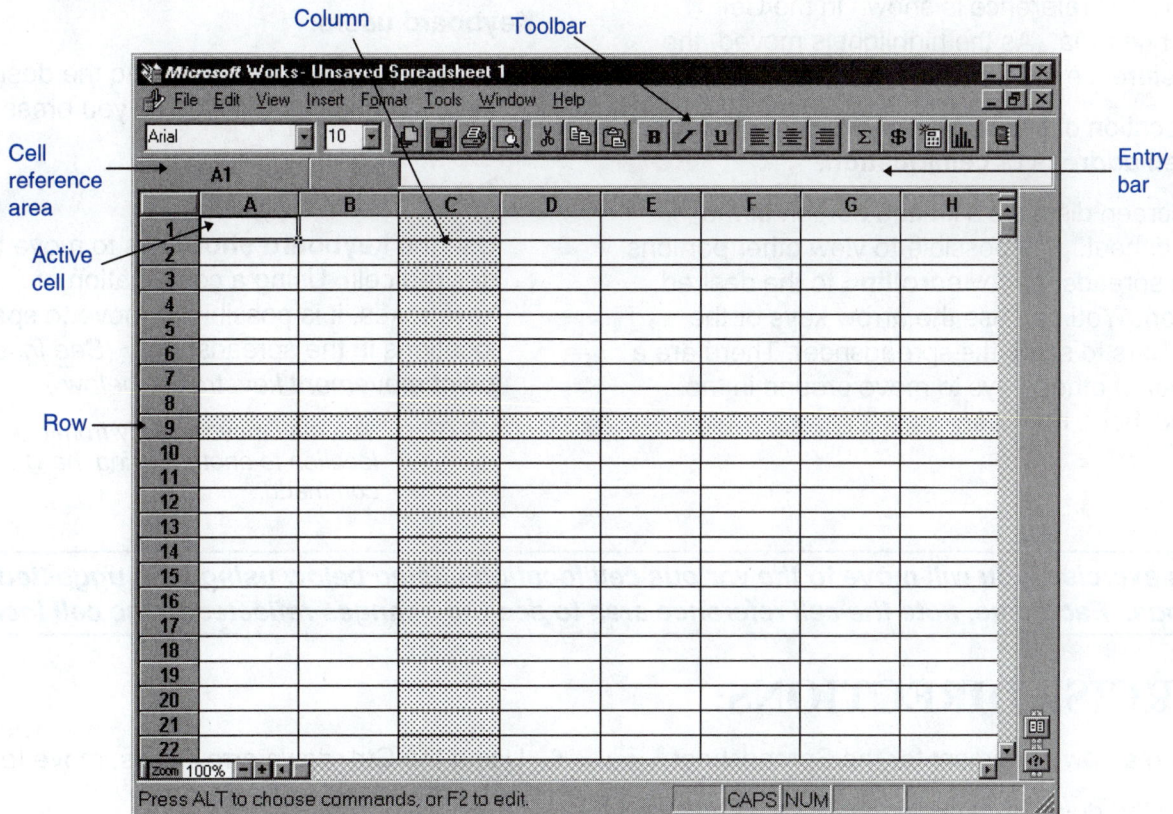

Column   **Toolbar**

Cell reference area

Entry bar

Active cell

Row

Microsoft Works- Unsaved Spreadsheet 1

File Edit View Insert Format Tools Window Help

Arial   10   B / U Σ $

A1

| | A | B | C | D | E | F | G | H |

Zoom 100%

Press ALT to choose commands, or F2 to edit.   CAPS NUM

■ The various parts of the spreadsheet screen are:

Columns   The vertical areas of the spreadsheet which are labeled with letters from A-Z. There are 256 columns.

Rows   The horizontal areas of the spreadsheet which are labeled with numbers. There are 16,384 rows.

Cell   Intersection of a row and a column. A cell is addressed by a letter and a number. For example, the cell where column A and row 1 intersect has the **cell address** A1.

Active cell   The highlighted cell. The heavy border around the cell shows it is **selected**.

Toolbar   The Toolbar contains shortcuts for the most commonly used spreadsheet functions.

Cell reference area   Reports the active cell location.

Entry bar   Displays the data in the active cell.

Cancel/Enter button ✕ ✓   Accepts or cancels the data in the Entry bar. Appears only when data is entered in the Entry bar.

■ Three mouse shapes appear in the spreadsheet. They are:

⇧   A **thick cross** in the work area.

I   An **I-beam** in the formula bar.

▣   An **arrow** in the menu area or Toolbar.

Move Around in the Spreadsheet

- When a spreadsheet is created, the active cell is A1. The highlight (heavy border) surrounds it, and the cell reference is shown in the Cell reference area. As the highlight is moved, the Cell reference area displays the new active cell.

- The location of the active cell is referred to as the **cell address** or **cell location**.

- The screen displays a limited portion of the spreadsheet. It is possible to view other portions of the spreadsheet by **scrolling** to the desired location. You can use the arrow keys or the scroll bars to scroll the spreadsheet. There are a number of other ways to move around in the spreadsheet, however.

Mouse users:

Point to the desired cell (your mouse shape is a thick cross) and click on it.

Keyboard users:

Use the arrow keys to move to the desired cell. The highlight moves as you press the arrow keys.

OR

Use the **keyboard shortcuts** to move to a desired cell. Using a combination of keystrokes, it is possible to move to specific locations in the spreadsheet. *(See insertion point movement keystrokes below.)*

✔ NOTE: *You may move directly from one cell location to another using the **Go to** command.*

In this exercise, you will move to the various cell locations listed below using the suggested methods. Each time, note the cell reference area to see the changes reflected in the cell location.

EXERCISE DIRECTIONS:

1. Create a new document for the Spreadsheet.

2. Using the down arrow key, move to cell A3.

3. Using the mouse, move to C6.

4. Using the F5 key, move to I26.

5. Using the Ctrl+Home keys, move to A1.

6. Using the Ctrl+down arrow keys, move to A16384.

7. Using the Ctrl+right arrow keys, move to IV16384.

8. Using the F5 key, move to A1.

9. Close the document window; do not save the changes.

INSERTION POINT MOVEMENT KEYSTROKES

Keyboard users:

MOVE:

Right (one cell) .... →

Left (one cell) .... ←

Down (one cell) .... ↓

Up (one cell) .... ↑

Specific cell .... F5 + *cell address*

Beginning of a row .... Home

End of a row .... End

✔ NOTE: *Use only if data is in the cells.*

Beginning of spreadsheet . Ctrl + Home

End of spreadsheet .... Ctrl + End

✔ NOTE: *Use the above procedure only if data is in the cells*

Up one block of data .... Ctrl + ↑

Down one block of data .... Ctrl + ↓

Left one block of data .... Ctrl + ←

Right one block of data .... Ctrl + →

Down one window .... Page Down

Up one window .... Page Up

Mouse users:

MOVE:

Click one cell to the left.

Click one cell to the right.

Click one cell up.

Click one cell down.

EXERCISE **2**

■ **Enter Labels** ■ **Make Simple Corrections** ■ **Save and Exit**

NOTES:

Enter Labels

■ The first character in a cell determines whether that cell entry is read as numeric data (value) or text (label).

■ A **label** is non-numeric data, as mentioned in Exercise 1. Labels are text and can be used for column headings, spreadsheet titles and descriptions in the spreadsheet.

■ Labels are automatically left aligned.

■ Each cell is ten characters wide. However, with proportionally spaced fonts, you may not be able to fit ten characters into a cell. The number of characters that fit into a cell varies with the font being used.

  ✓ NOTE: *It is possible, however, to enter a long label beyond the cell width if the cell to the right is blank.*

■ To type data into a cell, click the cell to contain the data. The clicked cell is now active and its cell location appears in the Cell reference area. Furthermore, this active cell is highlighted by a dark border. Use the Tab key or directional arrows to move to the next cell.

  ✓ NOTE: *You can set an option to automatically highlight the next cell in a column as soon as the Enter key is pressed. Click Tools, Options and click the Data Entry tab to select Move selection after Enter.*

Make Simple Corrections

■ As in the Word Processor tool, press the Backspace key to correct the data as it is entered.

■ If a correction is necessary after the data is completely entered, the correct entry may be retyped and entered again.

🌐 Save and Exit

See page 16, "Save a New Document." See page 18, "Save and Exit Microsoft Works."

  ✓ NOTE: *If you want to import your spreadsheet into a different spreadsheet program, you must save the spreadsheet in a format recognized by the other program. To do this, Click File, Save As, and click Save as Type in the dialog box. Select the desired format.*

In this exercise, you will create a spreadsheet for the Family Pharmacy by entering labels. Numeric data will be entered in Exercise 10.

EXERCISE DIRECTIONS:

1. Create a new document for the Spreadsheet.

2. Enter the labels in the exact cell locations shown in the illustration.

3. Use the Backspace key or Overtype method to correct errors.

4. Save the file; name it **DAILY**.

5. Close the document window.

	A	B	C	D	E	F	G
1	FAMILY PHARMACY						
2	DAILY SALES REPORT						
3							
4	DATE:						
5							
6							PERCENT
7	CODE	DEPARTMENT		SALES	TAX	TOTAL	OF TOTAL
8							
9	A	BEAUTY AIDS					
10	B	CANDY					
11	C	CARDS					
12	D	MEDICINE (OTC)					
13	E	TOILETRIES					
14	F	VITAMINS					
15	G	PRESCRIPTIONS					

ENTER ALPHABETIC LABEL

1. Click desired cell

   OR

   Press **directional arrow** keys .... ← →
   to place insertion point in ↑ ↓
   desired cell.

2. Type the label .... *label*

3. Press **Enter** .... ⏎

   OR

   Press **directional arrow** keys ... ← →
   in direction of next entry. ↑ ↓

   OR

   Click **Enter** button .... ☑
   on the Entry bar

EXERCISE **3**

■ **Enter Values** ■ **Numeric Labels** ■ **Edit Cell Contents** ■ **Clear a Cell**

NOTES:

Enter Values

- When a number or one of the symbols (=, +, -, ., @ or $) is entered as the first character in a cell, the entry is read as a **value**.

- Values are automatically right aligned.

- Since labels are left aligned and values are right aligned in a cell, column headings (which are labels) will not appear centered over numeric data. Note the illustration showing how data is aligned in the cells:

Left-aligned text

Right-aligned numeric value

Left-aligned numeric label

Numeric Labels

- You may want certain numbers, such as an I.D. number or an address, to be considered text. These are called **numeric labels**. Press the Shift key and the quotation mark key (Shift+ ") before you type the numbers; otherwise, the entry will be read as a value. The quotation mark (") appears only in the Entry bar, not in the cell.

  ✓ NOTE: *Works interprets an entry that contains a combination of numeric and alphabetic data as a label. An example of this would be a Social Security number containing hyphens (123-45-6789).*

Edit Cell Contents

- Data may be changed either *before* or *after* it has been entered in a cell.

- Before data is completely entered, use the Backspace key to correct errors while typing. You can also click the Cancel button to the left of the Entry bar ⊠.

- After data is completely entered there are several methods of correction:

  - You can overwrite the entire cell. Simply select the cell you wish to edit, re-type the value or label and press the Enter key. The new entry replaces the existing cell contents.

  - You can edit part of a cell entry. Select the cell to display the contents in the Entry bar (the mouse pointer changes to an I-beam), and position the I-beam where you wish to make a change. Click in the Entry bar and note the Status bar displays **EDIT**. Then, edit the entry using the Insert and Delete keys as you did in the Word Processor. Press the Enter key to accept the changes.

    ✓ NOTE: *You can customize how the data is edited. You can choose to edit only in the cells or only in the Entry bar. Click Tools, Options and click the Data Entry tab. Make the desired selections.*

Clear a Cell

- A cell can be cleared of its contents by selecting the cell and clicking Edit, Clear. As with any other deletion, you can also undo clearing a cell. Be sure that you select Edit, Undo Entry immediately after clearing the cell if you want to reinstate the data.

- The cell can also be cleared using the Delete key. You may select the cell to delete, then press the Delete key.

> *Your supervisor at the Bit-Byte Computer Company has learned that certain products have not sold well over the past two years. She wants you to prepare a spreadsheet showing the sales of selected products. After studying the data you prepare, she will decide which products to discontinue.*

EXERCISE DIRECTIONS:

1. Create a new document for the Spreadsheet.
   - ✓ NOTE: Do **not** type handwritten inserts at this point.

2. Enter the labels and values in the exact cell locations shown in the illustration.
   - ✓ NOTE: The ITEM NO. data is to be entered as a numeric label.

3. Use the Backspace key or Overtype method to correct errors.

4. Edit both lines of the title and the column heading as indicated by the handwritten instructions.

5. Clear cell B12. Undo clearing the cell.

6. Save the file; name it **SALES**.

7. Close the document window.

Insert hyphen

Insert —— *SALES*

Insert period

	A	B	C	D	E	
1	BIT BYTE COMPUTER COMPANY					Title (label)
2	INCOME - 2 YEARS					
3						
4	ITEM				NET	Column heading
5	NO	ITEM	YEAR 1	YEAR 2	CHANGE	(label)
6						
7	184008	Computers	73246.98	88004.56		
8	181008	Monitors	20567.4	18755.31		
9	183008	Printers	52349.76	55058.56		
10	180008	Scanners	35126.66	65845.9		
11	182008	Modems	7089.54	4800		
12	188008	Drives	35876.07	54987.37		
13	189008	Keyboards	35156.3	38779.29		

Numeric labels *Labels* *Values*

ENTER VALUES

1. Click desired cell.
2. Type value .... *value*
3. Press **Enter** .... ⏎
   OR
   Press **directional arrow** keys ... ← → ↑ ↓
   in direction of next entry.
   OR
   Click **Enter** Button .... ☑
   on the Entry bar.

ENTER A NUMERIC LABEL

1. Click desired cell.
2. Press **Shift** + " .... Shift + "
   (quotation mark)

3. Type numeric label .... *label*
4. Press **Enter** .... ⏎
   OR
   Press **directional arrow** keys ... ← → ↑ ↓
   in direction of next entry.
   OR
   Click **Enter** Button .... ☑
   on the Entry bar

EDIT A CELL
F2

1. Click desired cell.
2. Click item to edit on the Entry bar.
3. Edit as necessary.
4. Press **Enter** .... ⏎

CLEAR A CELL
Shift + Ctrl + H

1. Select cell to clear.
2. Click **Edit** .... Alt + E
3. Click **Clear** .... A
   OR
   Click **Cut** .... T
   OR
   Press **Delete** key .... Del

EXERCISE **4**

■ **Adjust Column Width** ■ **Print a Spreadsheet**
■ **Change Margins and Orientation** ■ **Print Gridlines**

NOTES:

Adjust Column Width

■ The following defaults are used in the spreadsheet tool:

Font	Arial
Size	10 point
Column width	ten characters

■ As mentioned in Exercise 2, since the number of characters that can fit into a cell are dependent on the font you choose, you might not be able to accommodate ten characters.

■ If labels are too long for the cell, they will either be extended into the next cell (if that cell is empty), or truncated (cut off) if the next cell contains an entry. The full label will be displayed in the Entry bar, however.

■ If values are too long to fit into the cell, a series of pound signs (###) appears.

■ There are a number of ways to adjust the column width. The simplest approach is to drag the line separating the columns in the border area. (*See the illustration below*.) Note the mouse changes shape and the word ADJUST appears.

■ Drag the ADJUST mouse pointer until the column is wide enough to accommodate the longest line.

✓ *NOTE: A fuller discussion on adjusting column size is presented in Exercise 16.*

Print a Spreadsheet

■ You may print the same way in the spreadsheet tool as you did in the Word Processor tool (*see page 30*). You can also change the margins, orientation and paper source and add headers/footers and page numbers the same way you did in the Word Processor tool.

■ If a spreadsheet is too large to fit on one page, reduce the margins and/or change the orientation to <u>L</u>andscape so the spreadsheet prints sideways.

✓ *NOTE: In some cases, you may be able to fit a spreadsheet on one page by decreasing the font size.*

Change Margins and Orientation

■ You can make changes to the spreadsheet format by changing the settings in any of the three tabs of the Page Setup dialog box: <u>M</u>argins; <u>S</u>ource, Size & Orientation; and <u>O</u>ther Options. The sample reflects the changes you make on the Margins tab.

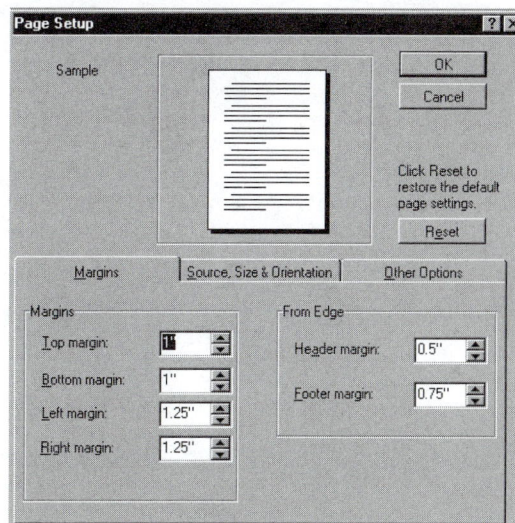

■ The Source, Size & Orientation tab of the Page Setup dialog box allows you to change the direction of the printout. Select Landscape orientation for large spreadsheets.

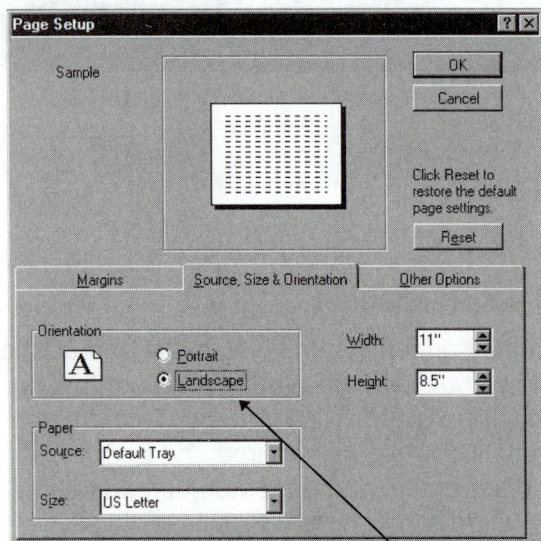

Use to print
large spreadsheets

Print Gridlines

■ Even though all spreadsheets are displayed with the gridlines as the default, they will *not* print with gridlines unless you specify that option. Click File, Page Setup and click the Other Options tab to display the following dialog box.

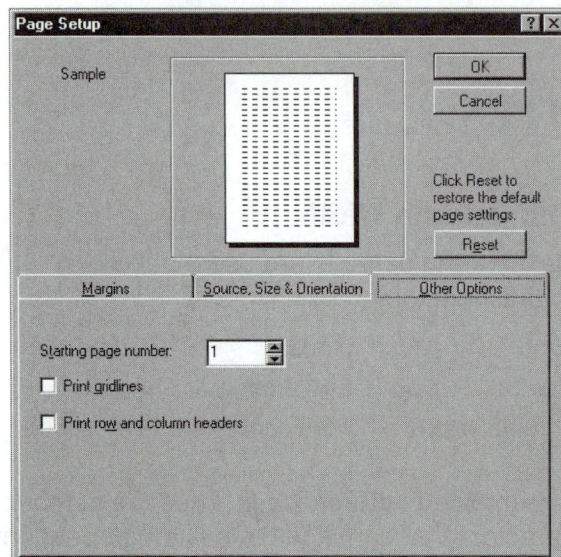

■ Make your selections in this dialog box to print the spreadsheet with gridlines as well as with the column and row headers (letters at the top of each column and numbers to the left of each row). These options may improve the readability of the spreadsheet.

■ You can preview your spreadsheet in Print Preview using the Zoom In feature to magnify your file.

✓ NOTE: You can display the spreadsheet without the grid by selecting View, Gridlines. Repeat the procedure to return the gridlines. This feature does not affect the printout.

In this exercise, you will create a payroll that shows salary information for employees in a company. GROSS PAY refers to total salary earned before taxes. NET PAY refers to salary received after taxes are deducted. F.I.C.A. (Federal Insurance Contributions Act) is a designation for Social Security tax and F.W.T. refers to Federal Withholding Tax.

EXERCISE DIRECTIONS:

1. Create a new document for the Spreadsheet.

2. Enter the labels and values in the exact cell locations shown in the illustration.

3. The employee identification numbers (in the ID NO. column) are to be entered as **numeric labels**.

4. Increase the size of Col B to accommodate the column heading EMPLOYEE.

5. Change left and right margins to 1".

6. Change the orientation to Landscape.

7. Click Other Options tab and select the Print gridlines check box.

8. Preview the spreadsheet to see if it fits on one page.

9. Save the file; name it **SALARY**.

10. Print one copy.

11. Close the document window.

	A	B	C	D	E	F	G	H
1	BURLINGTON NATIONAL BANK							
2	PAYROLL							
3								
4			HOURLY	HOURS				NET
5	ID NO.	EMPLOYEE	RATE	WORKED	GROSS	F. I. C. A.	F. W. T.	PAY
6								
7	12567	CARTER	5.55	15				
8	12750	FINCKEL	7.25	32				
9	12816	JAMISON	6.18	16				
10	12915	MILLS	4.66	28				
11	12345	POTTER	6.57	12				
12	12716	SAMUELS	8.65	21				

ADJUST COLUMN WIDTHS

1. Click line separating the column letter designations.

   Mouse pointer changes shape to ⊞.

2. Drag the line to desired location.

CHANGE MARGINS

1. Click **File** .... Alt + F
2. Click **Page Setup** .... G
3. Click **Margins** tab .... Alt + M
4. Make desired changes.
5. Click **OK** .... Enter

CHANGE ORIENTATION

1. Click **File** .... Alt + F
2. Click **Page Setup** .... G
3. Click **Source, Size & Orientation** tab .... Alt + S
4. Click **Portrait** .... Alt + P

   OR

   Click **Landscape** .... Alt + L
5. Click **OK** .... Enter

PRINT GRIDLINES

1. Click **File** .... Alt + F
2. Click **Page Setup** .... G
3. Click **Other Options** tab .... Alt + O
4. Click **Print gridlines** .... Alt + G
5. Click **OK** .... Enter

Mr. David Craig, owner of the Beldem Computer Supply Corporation, has asked you to prepare a summary of repairs that were completed during the week ending January 31.

EXERCISE DIRECTIONS:

1. Create a new document for the Spreadsheet, or open ⊟SS **REPAIR.5**.

2. Enter the labels and values in the exact cell locations shown in the illustration.

3. Enter the data in column B as numeric labels.

4. Change left and right margins to 1".

5. Change the orientation to Landscape.

6. Widen columns as needed to accommodate entries.

7. Check your spreadsheet on the Print Preview screen.

8. Edit the names in column A to read:

   H. Demba
   W. Grene
   E. Jackilo
   S. Okin
   R. Welsch

9. Save the file; name it **REPAIR**.

10. Print one copy with gridlines.

11. Close the document window.

	A	B	C	D	E	F	G	H
1	BELDEM COMPUTER SUPPLY COMPANY							
2	REPAIR RECORD -- WEEK ENDING JANUARY 31							
4								
5						TOTAL		
6			LABOR	LABOR		PARTS/	SALES	TOTAL
7	NAME	ID NO.	HOURS	COST	PARTS	LABOR	TAX	BILL
8								
9	Demba	106	3		98			
10	Grene	124	2.5		365			
11	Jackilo	098	4		234.95			
12	Okin	156	10		678.5			
13	Welsch	137	1.5		47.5			

■ **Use Formulas**

NOTES:

Use Formulas

■ A **formula** is an instruction to calculate a number and is entered in the cell where the answer should appear. As the formula is typed, it appears in the Entry bar. After it is entered, the answer is dispalyed in the **active cell** while the formula remains visible in the Entry bar.

■ Cell addresses, not the values themselves, are used to develop formulas. An equal sign (=) must precede a formula that begins with a cell address. The simple addition formula =C3+C5, for example, will add the values found in these cell locations. Any change to a value in these two cell locations will cause the answer to change automatically.

> ✓ NOTE: *Other spreadsheet programs may begin a formula with a plus sign (+). If you should use the plus sign to begin a formula, Works converts it to an equal sign.*

■ The standard mathematical operators used in formulas are:

+ Addition	- Subtraction
* Multiplication	/ Division

■ It is important to consider the **order of mathematical operations** when preparing formulas. Follow these rules when creating a formula:

- Operations enclosed in parentheses have the highest priority and are executed first.

- Exponential calculations are executed second.

- Multiplication and division operations have the next priority and are completed before any addition and subtraction operations.

- All other operations are executed from left to right in the order of appearance.

■ Look at the sample formula below:

=A1*(B1+C1)

In this formula,

- (B1+C1) is calculated first.

- That result is then multiplied by A1.

> ✓ NOTES: *If the parentheses were omitted, A1*B1 would have been calculated first and C1 would have been added to that answer. This would have given a different result.*
>
> *Multiplication and division formulas may result in answers with multiple decimal places. These numbers can be rounded off using a formatting feature.*

■ When using a **percentage** as a numeric factor in a formula, the percentage must be changed to a decimal or entered with the percent symbol. If you enter the percentage value followed by the percent sign (%), Works converts this entry to its decimal equivalent. Thus, you may, for example, enter either .45 or 45% to include .45 in a formula.

■ There are two methods of entering formulas; one uses the keyboard while the other uses the mouse. Use the method with which you are most comfortable.

■ Place the insertion point in the cell to contain the formula and type the equal sign (=).

Keyboard users:

- Enter the cell address and the mathematical operator, then enter the second cell address.

- Repeat for additional cells.

- Press the Enter key when done.

Mouse users:

- Click the first cell in the formula and enter the mathematical operator.

- Click the second cell in the formula.

- Repeat for additional cells.

- Press the Enter key when done.

   ✓ NOTE: The Status bar displays **POINT** when using this method.

In this exercise, LIST PRICE refers to the manufacturer's suggested retail price. DISCOUNT refers to a reduction from the list price. The SALES TAX percentage for this exercise is 8%.

Note the formula used to calculate SALES TAX: 8% has been changed to .08.

EXERCISE DIRECTIONS:

1. Create a new document for the Spreadsheet.

2. Enter the labels and values in the exact cell locations shown in the illustration.

3. Enter the appropriate formula in each cell using the first row as a guide:

   - Use the keyboard method for columns D and E.

   - Use the mouse method for column F.

4. Widen the columns as needed to accommodate entries.

5. Change the Page Setup options to print the gridlines.

6. Change the orientation to Landscape.

7. Save the file; name it **PRICE**.

8. Print one copy with gridlines.

9. Close the document window.

	A	B	C	D	E	F
1		LIST	DISCOUNT	SALE	SALES	TOTAL
2	PRODUCT	PRICE		PRICE	TAX	PRICE
3						
4	Red Gown	745	185	=B4-C4	=D4*0.08	=D4+E4
5	Blue Jacket	985	265			
6	Brown Slacks	395	98			
7						
8						

ENTER FORMULAS USING MATHE\MATICAL OPERATORS

1. Select cell to contain the formula.

2. Press = (equal sign) .... ▣

3. Select first cell .... ⬅️ ➡️ ⬆️ ⬇️
   of the formula

   OR

   Enter cell address .... *cell address* in the Entry bar.

4. Enter desired mathematical operator:

   - Addition .... ➕

   - Subtraction .... ➖

   - Multiplication .... *

   - Division.. /

5. Select next cell .... ⬅️ ➡️ ⬆️ ⬇️
   of the formula

   OR

   Enter the cell address .... *cell address* of next cell in formula in the Entry bar.

6. Repeat step 4.

7. Continue repeating steps 5 - 6 until last cell appears in formula.

8. Press **Enter** .... Ente

EXERCISE 7

■ Use Formulas

NOTES:

- A salesperson's salary is determined by adding the commissions earned on sales to the base salary.

- The commission rate is usually stated as a percent of sales.

- A percent may be entered as a percent or changed to its decimal equivalent. For example, 12% may be entered in the formula or it may be entered as .12, its decimal equivalent.

> *In this exercise, you will create a salary and commission report for Fashion Flair Dresses.*

EXERCISE DIRECTIONS:

1. Create a new document for the Spreadsheet

2. Enter the labels and values in the exact cell locations shown in the illustration.

3. Widen the columns as needed.

4. Enter the formulas in D7, D8 and D9 to find the COMMISSION for each salesperson.
   ✓ NOTE: The commission rate is 12% of sales.

5. Find TOTAL SALARY for each salesperson by adding the BASE SALARY to the COMMISSION.

6. Save the file; name it **WAGES**.

7. Print one copy with gridlines.

8. Close the document window.

	A	B	C	D	E
1	FASHION FLAIR DRESSES				
2	SALARY AND COMMISSION REPORT				
3	MARCH 19--				
4					TOTAL
5	SALESPERSON	BASE SALARY	SALES	COMMISSION	SALARY
6					
7	GAIL KELLY	525.25	5467.75		
8	SALLY MARTIN	655.75	8967.25		
9	LINDA SAMSONE	475.62	7698.75		

■ Open and Resave a File ■ Select Cells in the Spreadsheet
■ Ranges ■ Change Alignments (Values and Labels)

Task Launcher   Save   Left   Right

Center

NOTES:

🌐 Open and Resave a File

■ You can open and resave a spreadsheet file as you did in the Word Processor. (*See pages 33-35 to Update a Document.*)

Select Cells in the Spreadsheet

■ When you want to edit or change the format to a group of cells, you must first **select** the group.

■ You can use the mouse or the keyboard to select cells. Drag the mouse pointer over the desired cells, or use the F8 key and the directional arrows on the keyboard to select the cells. You can select a single cell, a group of cells, an entire column or row or the entire spreadsheet. The selected cells are highlighted with the first selected cell remaining white. The first cell is the active cell and its contents are displayed in the Entry bar.

■ You can select an entire column or row by clicking on the column letter or row number. Be careful when using this method because *all* cells in the column and row will be selected, not just the cells you have used. For example, if you click column letter A, all cells from A1 to A16384 highlight.

■ If you click the blank box in the header area as shown below, the entire spreadsheet highlights.

C8:C12		3
	A	B	C
1	BELDEM COMPUTER SUPPLY CO
2	REPAIR RECORD -- WEEK ENDIN(

Click to select entire spreadsheet

■ You can select cells by holding down the Shift key in combination with the arrow keys. For example, press Shift + right arrow to extend the highlight a cell at a time.

■ After selecting cells, the next command you choose affects all of them.

■ To deselect the cells, click outside the selected area or press one of the directional arrows.

Ranges

■ A group of selected cells is called a **range**. When a range is selected, it is displayed in the Cell reference area, and the contents of the first cell in the range are displayed in the Entry bar. For example, in the spreadsheet at the top of the next page, cells C8 through C12 are selected. The cell reference area displays C8:C12 (the range) and the Entry bar displays a 3 (the contents of the first cell in the range). Works uses the colon to separate the first cell in the range from the last cell in the range. The range reads C8 *through* C12.

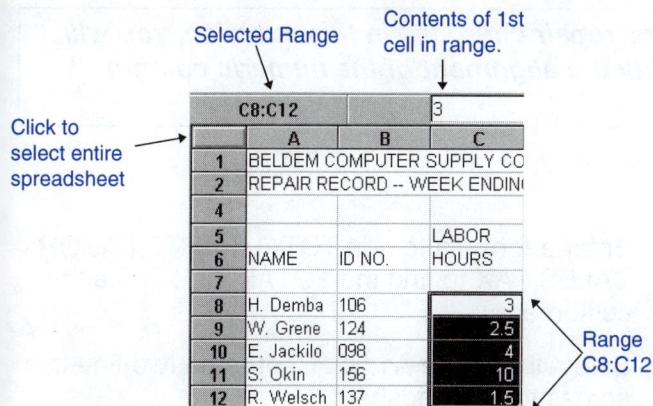

Selected Range / Contents of 1st cell in range. / Click to select entire spreadsheet / Range C8:C12

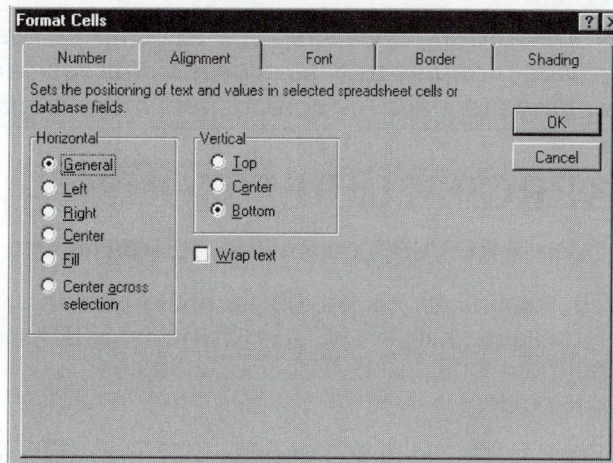

- You can format data in a column or row by first selecting a range then applying the desired format.

Change Alignments (Values and Labels)

- As mentioned in Exercise 2, when a spreadsheet is created, all labels (text) are left aligned while the values (dates, numbers and formulas) are right aligned. In addition, all entries are aligned at the bottom of the cell. Works calls this alignment **General**.

- The alignments of both values and labels can be changed to make the spreadsheet more attractive and readable. Column headings above numeric data may be centered or right aligned to improve the appearance of the spreadsheet.

- Long text entries can be formatted to wrap within the cell instead of extending into the next column.

- The vertical alignment within the cell can be changed to have the entry vertically aligned at either the top, bottom or center of the cell.

- Alignments can be changed *before* or *after* entering the data.

- The following tab in the Format Cells dialog box displays when the Format, Alignment options are selected:

General	Aligns text at the left and numbers at the right of the cell. This is the default setting.
Left	Aligns both text and numbers at the left of the cell.
Right	Aligns both text and numbers at the right of the cell.
Center	Centers the entry within the cell. If the entry is too long, it will be extended to the cells at the immediate left and right if they are empty.
Fill	Fills the cell with whatever is entered. If you enter an asterisk and then select Fill, the asterisk is repeated until the entire cell is filled.
Center across selection	Centers an entry within a selected range of cells. Excellent for centering titles in a spreadsheet.
Wrap text	Wraps the text within a cell instead of extending it to adjoining columns.

Vertical	**Top**	Aligns entry at top of the cell.
	Center	Aligns entry in the middle of the cell.
	Bottom	Aligns entry at bottom of the cell.

✓ NOTE: *The Toolbar contains Left, Right and Center buttons, and can be customized to include a Center across selection button.*

Mr. David Craig has asked you to compute customers' repair charges. In this exercise, you will provide formulas to determine the charges and modify the alignment of the numeric column headings to make the spreadsheet more readable.

EXERCISE DIRECTIONS:

1. Open ☰**REPAIR**, or open ⊟**SS REPAIR.8**.

2. The cost of labor is $40.00 per hour. Enter a formula to multiply LABOR HOURS by $40.00 per hour to find LABOR COST for each customer.

3. Enter a formula to add LABOR COST+PARTS to find TOTAL PARTS/LABOR for each customer.

4. Enter a formula to compute the sales tax at 8% of TOTAL PARTS/LABOR (use .08 in your formula) for each customer.

5. Enter a formula to add TOTAL PARTS/LABOR + SALES TAX to find the TOTAL BILL for each customer.

6. Select the range A1:H2. Center the two-line title across the spreadsheet.

7. Select the range C4:H6. Change to right alignment.

8. Resave the file.

9. Print one copy with gridlines.

10. Close the file.

	A	B	C	D	E	F	G	H
1	BELDEM COMPUTER SUPPLY COMPANY							
2	REPAIR RECORD -- WEEK ENDING JANUARY 31							
4						TOTAL		
5			LABOR	LABOR		PARTS/	SALES	TOTAL
6	NAME	ID NO.	HOURS	COST	PARTS	LABOR	TAX	BILL
7								
8	H. Demba	106	3		98			
9	W. Grene	124	2.5		365			
10	E. Jackilo	098	4		234.95			
11	S. Okin	156	10		678.5			
12	R. Welsch	137	1.5		47.5			

SELECT A RANGE

Select a Single Cell

Click cell.

OR

Use arrow key .... ← → ↑ ↓
to highlight cell

Select a Group of Cells

1. Click first cell in desired group.
2. Press left mouse button.
3. Drag to last cell in desired group.
4. Release left mouse button.

OR

1. Highlight first cell in desired group.
2. Press **F8** F8

✔ Note: Pressing **F8** places the spreadsheet into Extend mode and EXT displays in the Status bar. Once the operation is complete, the spreadsheet exits Extend mode and EXT is no longer displayed.

3. Use arrow keys .... ← → ↑ ↓
to select group.

Select a Row

✔ Note: The following methods will select the entire row through column IV.

1. Click row number.
2. Drag to select adjacent row(s).

OR

1. Highlight any cell .... ← → ↑ ↓
in desired row
2. Press **Ctrl + F8** .... Ctrl + F8

OR

1. Highlight any cell .... ← → ↑ ↓
in desired row.
2. Click **Edit** .... Alt + E
3. Click **Select Row** .... O

Select a Column

✔ Note: The following methods will select the entire column through row 16,384.

1. Click column letter.
2. Drag to select adjacent column(s).

OR

1. Highlight any cell .... ← → ↑ ↓
in desired column
2. Press **Shift + F8** .... Shift + F8

OR

1. Highlight any cell .... ← → ↑ ↓
in desired column
2. Click **Edit** .... Alt + E
3. Click **Select Column** .... M

Entire Spreadsheet

Ctrl + Shift + F8

Click box above row 1 and to left of column A.

To cancel selection:

Click outside the highlight.

OR

Press **ESC** and .... Esc + ← → ↑ ↓
any arrow key.

ALIGN ENTRIES

Left: Ctrl + L; Center: Ctrl + C;
Right: Ctrl + R

1. Highlight (select) range to align.
2. Click desired Toolbar alignment buttons:

   • Left Align.................................. 🔲
   • Center Align .... 🔲
   • Right Align .... 🔲

OR

a. Click **Format** .... Alt + O
b. Click **Alignment** .... A
c. Click desired setting(s) under Alignment:

   • **General** .... Alt + G
   • **Left**............................... Alt + L
   • **Center** .... Alt + C
   • **Right** .... Alt + R
   • **Fill** .... Alt + F
   • **Center across selection**. Alt + A
   • **Wrap text** .... Alt + W

d. Click desired settings under **Vertical:**

   • **Top**............................... Alt + T
   • **Center** .... Alt + E
   • **Bottom** .... Alt + B

e. Click **OK** .... Enter

■ **Format Values**

Percent   Currency

Comma

NOTES:

Format Values

■ You can change the appearance of numeric data to make it more attractive and readable by **formatting** it. Data can be formatted *before* or *after* typing. There are a number of formats available.

■ Number formats may be changed by selecting Format, Number to access the following tab in the Format Cells dialog box:

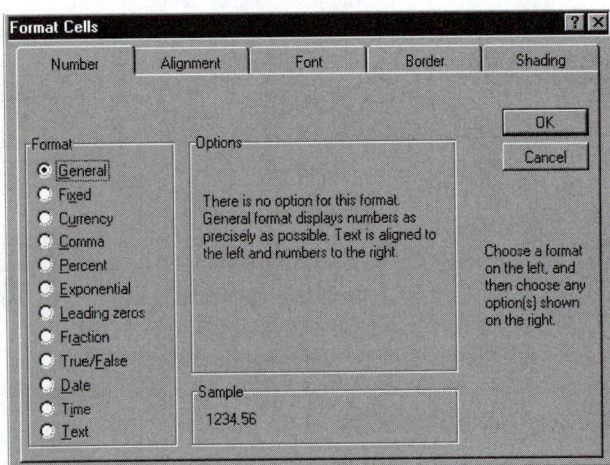

■ The Number tab in the Format Cells dialog box, shown above, gives you many options to format your numbers. As you choose different formats, the changes are displayed in the sample box. Click OK to accept the format.

■ The following options are available on the Number tab:

General   The default format displays the number as an integer or a decimal. Negative numbers display with a minus sign (-).

Fixed   Allows you to specify the number of decimal places. If you specify two decimal places, Works will round the number up accordingly.

Currency   Places a $ (dollar sign) before the number and includes commas as needed. The number of decimal places may be specified, and negative numbers can be displayed in red or in parentheses. A Toolbar button is available.

Comma   Places a comma in the number as needed. Negative numbers can be displayed in red or in parentheses. Customize the Toolbar to include the Comma format button.

Percent   Displays numbers as percentages. You can specify the number of decimal places. Customize the Toolbar to include the Percent format button.

Exponential   Is also known as *scientific notation*, and is typically used in engineering and other technical fields.

Leading Zeros	Allows you to use zeros before the actual number. Used in numbered forms, zip codes and in any number that requires zeros to come before the number.
Fraction	Allows you to display a number as a fraction. You can specify how you want the fraction displayed and whether or not it is to be reduced.
True/False	Zeros are displayed as FALSE, and non-zero numbers are displayed as TRUE.
Date	Allows you to display the date and specify the date format.
Time	Allows you to display the time and specify the time format.
Text	Allows you to enter numbers as text. All numbers entered with this feature will be left aligned. This feature is useful for entering social security numbers, phone numbers, zip codes or any identification number that uses special characters such as hyphens or parentheses. You have to set the format first. You cannot change numbers to text after they have been entered; they will have to be re-entered.

■ The default Toolbar displays the currency format. You can customize the Toolbar to display the Percent and Comma buttons. Note the customized Toolbar at the beginning of this exercise.

■ You can change the default number of decimal places. This decimal place format will apply only to numbers you enter *after* you have changed the setting. Numbers entered prior to the change will have to be reformatted.

> *In this exercise, you will provide a formula for the GRAND TOTAL and format money columns and column headings for the PRICE spreadsheet.*

EXERCISE DIRECTIONS:

1. Open ▦**PRICE**, or open ▤**SS PRICE.9**.

2. Using the Fixed number option, format all the money columns for two decimal places.

3. Enter the label GRAND TOTAL where indicated.

4. Enter a formula to add the TOTAL PRICE column to find GRAND TOTAL.

5. Using the Currency number option, format GRAND TOTAL for two decimal places.

6. Center all column headings.

7. Resave the file.

8. Print one copy with gridlines.

9. Close the file.

	A	B	C	D	E	F
1		LIST	DISCOUNT	SALE	SALES	TOTAL
2	PRODUCT	PRICE		PRICE	TAX	PRICE
3						
4	Red Gown	745	185	560	44.8	604.8
5	Blue Jacket	985	265	720	57.6	777.6
6	Brown Slacks	395	98	297	23.76	320.76
7						
8	GRAND TOTAL					

↑
Insert label

FORMAT DATA

Currency: Ctrl + 4   Percent: Ctrl + 5

1. Select cell or range to format.

2. Click **Format**.......................... Alt +O

3. Click **Number** .... N

4. Click desired format:

   • **General** .... G

   • **Fixed** X

   • **Currency**..................... U

   OR

   Click Currency button..................... $
   on Toolbar.

   • **Comma** C
   OR
   Click Comma button .... ,
   on Toolbar.

   • **Percent**..................... P
   OR
   Click Percent button................... %
   on Toolbar.

   • **Exponential** .... E

   • **Leading Zeros**................... L

   • **Fraction**................... A

   • **True/False** .... F

   • **Date** .... D

   • **Time**..................... I

   • **Text** .... T

5. Enter the number of decimal ..... *number* places (if applicable)

6. Click **OK**..................................... Enter

■ Copy Data ■ Copy Formulas (Relative Reference)

NOTES:

Copy Data

■ All data (labels, numeric labels, values and formulas) in a spreadsheet can be copied. Cell contents may be copied from one cell to another, or to a range of cells. Data can be copied horizontally or vertically.

■ As in the Word Processor tool, copying is accomplished by using copy and paste, or drag and drop. You can also copy to cells immediately below or the right of the cell containing the data to be copied. You can accomplish this using the Fill Down or Fill Right options found in the Edit menu shown below:

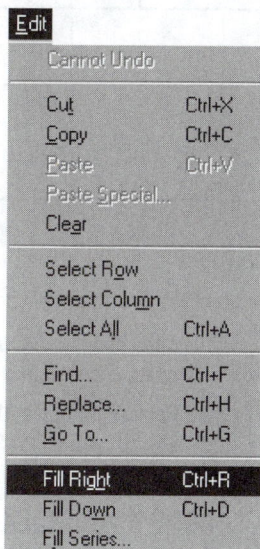

Edit	
Cannot Undo	
Cut	Ctrl+X
Copy	Ctrl+C
Paste	Ctrl+V
Paste Special...	
Clear	
Select Row	
Select Column	
Select All	Ctrl+A
Find...	Ctrl+F
Replace...	Ctrl+H
Go To...	Ctrl+G
Fill Right	**Ctrl+R**
Fill Down	Ctrl+D
Fill Series...	

■ You may add Fill Down and Fill Right buttons to the Toolbar. (*See page 19 for more information on customizing the Toolbar.*)

■ You can also copy data directly from within the spreadsheet. Click the entry you want to copy and point to the lower right corner of the cell. The pointer changes into the Fill mouse shape + FILL. Drag to highlight the cells you want to receive the copied data.

Copy Formulas (Relative Reference)

■ When a formula is copied, the cell addresses change relative to its new location. The formula performs the same operation using different data. Note the spreadsheet in this exercise. When copying the GROSS PAY formula for each employee, the formula multiplies the HOURLY RATE * HOURS WORKED but it uses the data specific to each employee.

In this exercise, you will prepare a payroll where Federal Withholding Tax is calculated using a fixed percentage. However, F.W.T. is actually determined using a table where the tax varies according to your salary and number of exemptions.

EXERCISE DIRECTIONS:

1. Open ▦**SALARY**, or open ▤**SS SALARY.10**.

2. Change the heading for column E to read GROSS PAY as indicated.

3. Enter a formula to calculate GROSS PAY for the first employee.

4. Copy the GROSS PAY formula for each employee.

   ✓ NOTE: Click each cell in the GROSS PAY column and refer to the Entry bar. Note the change in the formula from row to row. This is a **relative copy**; each formula reflects the location of the values it is calculating.

5. Enter a formula to calculate F.I.C.A. at 7.65%.

6. Copy the F.I.C.A. formula for each employee.

7. Enter a formula to calculate F.W.T. at 20%.

8. Copy the F.W.T. formula for each employee.

9. Enter a formula to calculate NET PAY.

   ✓ NOTE: You will need to add the deductions together before subtracting them from the GROSS PAY.

Refer to the order of mathematical operations rule in Exercise 6.

10. Copy the NET PAY formula for each employee.

11. Using the Fixed number option, format columns E-H for two decimal places.

12. Center all column headings.

13. Center the two-line title across the spreadsheet.

14. Resave the file.

15. Print one copy with gridlines.

16. Close the file.

	A	B	C	D	E	F	G	H
1	BURLINGTON NATIONAL BANK							
2	PAYROLL							
3								
4			HOURLY	HOURS	GROSS			NET
5	ID NO.	EMPLOYEE	RATE	WORKED	PAY	F. I. C. A.	F. W. T.	PAY
6								
7	12567	CARTER	5.55	15				
8	12750	FINCKEL	7.25	32				
9	12816	JAMISON	6.18	16				
10	12915	MILLS	4.66	28				
11	12345	POTTER	6.57	12				
12	12716	SAMUELS	8.65	21				

COPY USING COPY AND PASTE

Ctrl + C, Ctrl + V

1. Select cell or range to copy.

2. Click **Copy** button .... 🖹
   on Toolbar.

   OR

   a. Click **Edit**........................... Alt + E

   b. Click **Copy** C

3. Click cell or select range of cells to receive copied data.

   ✓NOTE: The formula can be copied to a location within the same file, to another file or to a completely different application. Works writes over any existing data in the cells to receive the formula.

4. Click **Paste** button .... 🖹
   on the Toolbar.

   OR

   a. Click **Edit**........................... Alt + E

   b. Click **Paste**................................. P

COPY USING DRAG AND DROP

1. Select cell or range of cells to copy.

2. Position mouse pointer on border of selected cell(s).

   Drag appears 📁 ; the cross changes to a pointer

3. Press and hold **Ctrl** while clicking and holding left mouse button.

4. Drag text to new location.

Copy appears 📁 ; the cross changes to a pointer.

5. Release mouse button.

6. Release **Ctrl** key.

COPY A FORMULA USING FILL DOWN OR FILL RIGHT

1. Enter the formula in the desired cell.

2. Select the cell containing the formula and all cells below, or to the right, where the formula is to be copied.

3. Click **Edit** .... Alt + E

4. Click **Fill Down** .... D
   if copying formula down

   OR

   Click **Fill Right** .... H
   if copying formula to the right.

EXERCISE **11**

■ Copy a Formula (Absolute Condition) ■ Repeat an Entry

NOTES:

Copy a Formula (Absolute Condition)

■ In some cases, a value in a formula must remain constant when copied to other locations. This is referred to as an **absolute condition**.

■ To identify a cell as an absolute value, a dollar sign ($) must precede both the column and row references for that cell.

■ In this exercise, we must divide each department's sales by the total to find each department's percentage of total sales.

Therefore, the total sales amount is a constant value in each line's formula. Note the formula indicated in the exercise. When this formula is copied, the total sales remains as a constant in every formula.

■ If a copied formula refers to empty cells, a zero (0) appears.

■ Formatting may be used to change decimal answers into a percentage format.

Repeat an Entry

■ You can repeat any entry or copy a formula across or down adjacent cells from within the spreadsheet.

■ If you repeat an entry or copy a formula to a cell that already contains data, Works replaces the existing data with the copied data.

ENTER FORMULAS FOR ABSOLUTE CONDITIONS

1. Click cell to .... ⬅ ➡ ⬆ ⬇
   contain formula.

2. Type = (equal sign) .... =

3. Highlight first .... ⬅ ➡ ⬆ ⬇
   cell of formula

   OR

   Type cell address .... *cell address*

4. Press **F4** (Absolute) F4
   if first cell to be calculated is absolute.

5. Type desired mathematical operator:

   • Addition .... +
   • Subtraction .... -
   • Multiplication .... *
   • Division .... /

6. Highlight next .... ⬅ ➡ ⬆ ⬇
   cell of formula.

7. Type cell address .... *cell address*

8. Press **F4** F4
   only if cell to be calculated is absolute.

9. Repeat steps 5-8 until last cell appears in formula.

10. Press **Enter** .... ⏎

REPEAT AN ENTRY/COPY A FORMULA

1. Click entry to be repeated or copied.

2. Click lower-right corner of cell.

3. Drag ＋FILL down rows or across columns.

4. Release mouse button.

In this exercise, you will complete the Family Pharmacy daily sales report by calculating sales, tax and total sales. To analyze each departmental sales, the owner requests an analysis showing the percentage each department's sales is of the total sales.

EXERCISE DIRECTIONS:

1. Open ⌨**DAILY**, or open 💾**SS DAILY.11**.

2. Enter Sales data, as shown below.

3. Enter a formula to calculate a 5% TAX on Beauty Aids.

4. Copy the TAX formula to each department *except* PRESCRIPTIONS.

5. Enter a formula to determine the TOTAL for Beauty Aids.

6. Copy the TOTAL formula for each department.

7. Enter the label TOTAL SALES in cell B17.

8. Enter a formula in cell D17 to calculate TOTAL SALES.

9. Copy the TOTAL SALES formula to cells E17 and F17.

10. Enter a formula as indicated using an absolute reference in the PERCENT OF TOTAL column.

11. Copy the PERCENT OF TOTAL formula for each department.

12. Copy the TOTAL SALES formula to find the total of the PERCENT OF TOTAL column.

13. Using the Fixed number option, format the money columns (D-F) for two decimal places.

14. Using the Percent number option, format the PERCENT OF TOTAL column for two decimal places.

15. Center the title over the spreadsheet.

16. Center Column A, B, D, E, F and G headings.
    - ✓ NOTE: Center Column B heading DEPARTMENT across columns B and C.

17. Resave the file.

18. Print one copy with gridlines.

19. Close the file.

	A	B	C	D	E	F	G
1	FAMILY PHARMACY						
2	DAILY SALES REPORT						
3							
4	DATE:						
5							
6							PERCENT
7	CODE	DEPARTMENT		SALES	TAX	TOTAL	OF TOTAL
8							
9	A	BEAUTY AIDS		2238.02			F9/$F$17
10	B	CANDY		543.98			
11	C	CARDS		326.85			
12	D	MEDICINE (OTC)		7654.83			
13	E	TOILETRIES		896.37			
14	F	VITAMINS		473.29			
15	G	PRESCRIPTIONS		7245.69			
16							
17		TOTAL SALES					

↑
Insert label

EXERCISE **12**

Lesson 2 – Summary

You are applying for employment in the Registrar's Office at Grande University under the work-study program. As part of the employment test, you are asked to prepare a summary of the student enrollment in each major the college offers.

EXERCISE DIRECTIONS:

1. Create a new document for the Spreadsheet listing each MAJOR and the NUMBER of students ENROLLED. Create an appropriate two-line title for the spreadsheet.

BUSINESS	8,700
COMMUNICATION ARTS	2,267
COMPUTER SCIENCE	3,000
ENGINEERING	1,460
MICROBIOLOGY	120
ZOOLOGY	900

2. Find:

   a. TOTAL ENROLLMENT

   b. What PERCENT each major is of the total ENROLLMENT. (Use a formula with an absolute reference.)

3. Widen columns as needed to accommodate column data.

4. Format values in NUMBER ENROLLED column for commas with no decimal places.

5. Format values in PERCENT OF ENROLLMENT column for two-place percents.

6. Right align all column headings over numeric data.

7. Center the two-line title over the spreadsheet.

8. Save the file; name it **UNIVERSITY**.

9. Print one copy with gridlines and column and row headers.

10. Close the document window.

EXERCISE **13**

■ **Functions** ■ **AVG (Average) Function**

NOTES:

Functions

■ A **function** is a built-in formula that performs a special calculation automatically.

■ Start functions with an equal sign (=) followed by the **function name** (in either upper- or lowercase), followed by an open parenthesis, the range to be affected and a close parenthesis.

■ A function may be used by itself, or it may be combined with other functions. Works provides many functions, some of which are used for statistical and financial analysis, while others are used in database operations. A function may be entered using the keyboard, the mouse or a combination of both.

> ✓ NOTE: *Only the most commonly used functions will be covered in this text.*

AVG (Average) Function

■ The **AVG function** averages values in a range. For example, to average the values in A4, A5 and A6, the formula would appear as: =AVG(A4:A6). The data the functions require you to supply are called **arguments**. For example, in =AVG(A4:A6), the data range A4:A6 is the argument.

> ✓ NOTE: *The beginning cell and ending cell in a range are separated by a colon. The range reads: A4 **through** A6.*

■ The following illustrates the various parts of a function.

function name   argument
↓   ┌───┴───┐
=AVG(A4:A6)

■ The equal sign begins the function. AVG is the function name. The range is the argument and is enclosed in parentheses.

> ✓ NOTE: *All functions follow the same format.*

You are teaching at New Meadows High School and you want to use a spreadsheet to record and compute your students' grades. In this exercise, you will prepare a spreadsheet showing the third quarter exam grades and averages for the students in your Advanced Information Processing class. In addition, you will calculate the average for each exam.

EXERCISE DIRECTIONS:

1. Create a new document for the Spreadsheet, entering the labels and values in the exact cell locations shown in the illustration.

2. Adjust column widths as needed.

3. Center the title across the spreadsheet.

4. Center column A heading.

5. Right align all numeric column headings.

6. Use the AVG function to average the students' test scores on the three exams. Copy the formula for each student.

7. Use the AVG function to average the scores for EXAM 1. Copy the formula to EXAM 2 and EXAM 3 columns.

8. Format all averaged values for fixed with two decimal places.

9. Save the file; name it **EXAM**.

10. Print one copy with gridlines.

11. Close the document window.

	A	B	C	D	E
1	ADVANCED INFORMATION PROCESSING				
2	THIRD QUARTER EXAM GRADES				
3					
4	STUDENT	EXAM 1	EXAM 2	EXAM 3	AVERAGES
5					
6	Burns	90	81	86	
7	Daniels	71	67	65	
8	Edwards	65	78	81	
9	Forbes	92	78	90	
10	Garner	91	71	95	
11	Yaro	91	34	88	
12					
13	AVERAGES				

AVERAGE FUNCTION

1. Place cursor in the cell where the answer should appear.

2. Press **=** (equal sign)....................▣

3. Type *AVG*...................................*AVG*

4. Type **(** (open parenthesis)..............▐

5. Type first cell .... *cell address* in range.

   OR

   Click first cell in range.

6. Type **:** (colon)................................▐

7. Type last cell .... *cell address* in range.

OR

Click last cell in range.

✓ NOTE: You omit steps 5-7 by selecting all cells in a range.

8. Type **)** (close parenthesis)..............▐

9. Press **Enter** ....⌁Enter⌁

EXERCISE 14

■ Sum Function ■ Autosum

Autosum
↓

NOTES:

SUM Function

■ The **SUM function** adds all the values in a range. To add the cells in B6, B7, B8 and B9, for example, the function is written:

=SUM(B6:B9).

Autosum

■ Because the SUM function is frequently used, Works provides the **Autosum** button on the Toolbar as shown above.

To use Autosum button:

• Select the cell where you want the result to appear.

• Click **Autosum** button on Toolbar.

Works selects a range of cells to include in the SUM function.

• Click Autosum again to agree to this range.

✓ *NOTE:* *If the range is incorrect, you can enter the correct cell range between the parentheses in the Entry bar and press Enter.*

Your supervisor wants to know the total sales of all computer products sold in YEAR 1 and YEAR 2. In addition, you are asked to supply a simple formula to find the difference between YEAR 1 and YEAR 2.

EXERCISE DIRECTIONS:

1. Open ⌨**SALES**, or open 💾**SS SALES.14**.

2. Center the title over the spreadsheet.

3. Right align all money column headings.

4. Type the word TOTAL in cell A15.

5. Using the =SUM function, total the YEAR 1 column. Copy the =SUM function to the YEAR 2 column.

6. In cell E7, provide a simple formula to subtract YEAR 1 from YEAR 2. Copy the formula to the remaining rows.

7. Format all money amounts to two decimal places.

8. Resave the file.

9. Print one copy with gridlines.

10. Close the file

	A	**B**	**C**	**D**	**E**
1	BIT-BYTE COMPUTER COMPANY				
2	SALES INCOME - 2 YEARS				
3					
4	ITEM				NET
5	NO	ITEM	YEAR 1	YEAR 2	CHANGE
6					
7	184008	Computers	73246.98	88004.56	
8	181008	Monitors	20567.4	18755.31	
9	183008	Printers	52349.76	55058.56	
10	180008	Scanners	35126.66	65845.9	
11	182008	Modems	7089.54	4800	
12	188008	Drives	35876.07	54987.37	
13	189008	Keyboards	35156.3	38779.29	
14					
15	TOTAL				

↑
Insert label

SUM FUNCTION

1. Select cell where answer should appear.
2. Type = (equal sign) .... 🔲
3. Type *SUM* .... *SUM*
4. Type **(** (open parenthesis) .... 🔲
5. Type first cell address .... *cell address*

   OR

   Click first cell.
6. Type **:** (colon) .... 🔲
7. Type last cell address .... *cell address*

OR

Click last cell.
8. Type **)** (close parenthesis) .... 🔲
9. Press **Enter** .... Enter

AUTOSUM BUTTON

Ctrl + M

1. Select cell where answer should appear.
2. Click **Autosum** button .... Σ
   on Toolbar.

3. Press **Enter** .... Enter
   to accept range.

   OR

   a. Type correct range .... *range*
      in Entry bar.
   b. Press **Enter** .... Enter

OR

1. Select cell where answer should appear.
2. Double-click **Autosum** button .... Σ
   on Toolbar.

EXERCISE **15**

■ **Count, Min and Max Functions** ■ **Fill Series**

NOTES:

Count, Min and Max Functions

■ **Count** counts all the non-blank cells in a range. Cells containing values, formulas or text are counted.

■ **Min** indicates the lowest value in a range.

■ **Max** indicates the highest value in a range.

Fill Series

■ Use the **Fill Series** feature to fill a range of cells with consecutive numbers or dates. The Fill Series feature allows you to create a series of numbers that are automatically increased by a specific amount.

■ Refer to the spreadsheet in this exercise. The first EMP. NO. is 101. When you use Fill Series, the other employee numbers in the column will be automatically entered with each number increasing by one (102, 103, 104 and so on). The default interval is one.

■ The Toolbar can be customized to include the Fill Series button.

To begin a series:

• Enter the first number in the cell.

• Select the range to contain the series.

✓ NOTE: Be sure to include the first number as the first cell in the range.

• Click Edit, Fill Series.

• Click the appropriate unit series in the dialog box above right.

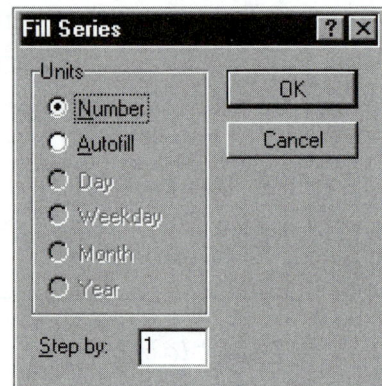

• Enter the desired Step by interval between the numbers or dates in the series. A positive number increases the series; a negative number decreases the series.

• Click OK to fill the series.

■ The following options are available in the Fill Series dialog box:

Number	Series of consecutive numbers.
Autofill	Fills the blanks in the selection with a series based on the information in the beginning cell.
Day	Series of consecutive days of the week including Saturdays and Sundays.
Weekday	Series of consecutive days of the week *excluding* Saturdays and Sundays.
Month	Series of consecutive months of the year.
Year	Series of consecutive years.
Step By	Allows you to indicate the interval between the numbers in the series.

✓ NOTE: To use the Day, Weekday, Month or Year option, your value must be entered in a date format.

In this exercise, you will create a spreadsheet for the **WOODWORKS FURNITURE COMPANY** showing employees' quarterly sales and commissions earned. Each ■ employee receives a 5% commission on sales.

EXERCISE DIRECTIONS:

1. Create a new document for the Spreadsheet, or open 💾**SS WOOD.15**.

2. Format the EMP. NO. column as text.

3. Adjust column widths as needed.

4. Center title across the spreadsheet.

5. Right align all numeric column headings.

6. Using the Fill Series, enter employee numbers beginning with 101 and stopping at 105.
   - ✔NOTE: For steps 7-10, copy the required data and formulas using the Edit, Fill Down command.

7. Copy the base salary to the remaining employees. (They all have the same base salary.)

8. Enter a formula to find the commission for the first employee. The commission rate is 5% of sales. Copy the formula to the remaining employees.

9. Enter a formula to find the quarterly salary for the first employee by adding the base salary and the commission for the quarter. Copy the formula to the remaining employees.

10. Use the SUM, AVG, MIN and MAX functions to find the TOTALS, AVERAGES, HIGHEST and LOWEST values. Copy the functions to each column.

11. Use the COUNT function to determine how many employees are listed in column B. The answer should be placed in cell C14.

12. Format all dollar amounts for commas with two decimal places.

13. Change the title to read: SALES AND SALARY QUARTERLY REPORT – APRIL - JUNE.
    - ✔NOTE: To edit the title, click cell A2 to have the title appear in the Entry bar. Then press F2 or click in the Entry bar to edit the title. Press Enter when finished.

14. Save the file; name it **WOOD**.

15. Print one copy with gridlines.

16. Close the document window.

	A	B	C	D	E	F
1	WOODWORKS FURNITURE COMPANY					
2	QUARTERLY SALES AND SALARY REPORT -- JANUARY - MARCH					
3						
4	EMP.		BASE		5%	QUARTERLY
5	NO.	NAME	SALARY	SALES	COMMISSION	SALARY
6						
7	101	ABRAMS, JUDY	1500	113456.67		
8		CHANG, PETER		150654.87		
9		LINSEY, KELLY		234765.36		
10		JOHNSON, LETOYA		89765.43		
11	105	RIVERA, TONY		287987.76		
12						
13		TOTALS		→	→	→
14		COUNT		→	→	→
15		AVERAGE		→	→	→
16		HIGHEST		→	→	→
17		LOWEST		→	→	→

FUNCTIONS (COUNT, MIN AND MAX)

1. Select cell where the answer should appear.
2. Type = (equal sign) .... ▣
3. Type name of desired function:
   - **COUNT** (count)...................... *COUNT*
   - **MAX** (maximum)........................ *MAX*
   - **MIN** (minimum) .... *MIN*
4. Type **(** (open parenthesis). .... ▣
5. Type or select range .... *range* to be calculated.
6. Type **)** (close parenthesis).............. ▣
7. Press **ENTER** .... Enter

FILL SERIES

1. Enter first value .... *value* of the series (number or date).
2. Press **Enter** .... Enter
3. Select first cell of........... ← → ↑ ↓ the series.
4. Select the range for the series.
5. Click **Edit**.............................. Alt + E
6. Click **Fill Series**........................... I

7. Click desired option:
   - **Number** .... N
   - **Day**...................................... D
   - **Weekday** .... W
   - **Month**.................................... M
   - **Year** .... Y
8. Click **Step by** .... S
9. Enter a value for the interval.......... *value* if other than one
10. Click **OK**................................. Enter

EXERCISE **16**

■ **Built-In Functions** ■ **Change Column Width**

NOTES:

Built-In Functions

■ Works provides a feature whereby you can have a function automatically inserted into the spreadsheet. You need to supply the appropriate cell locations.

■ Access the Insert Function dialog box shown below from the Insert menu. The dialog box contains categories for the types of functions. Click a Category or click All to see all the functions available in Works.

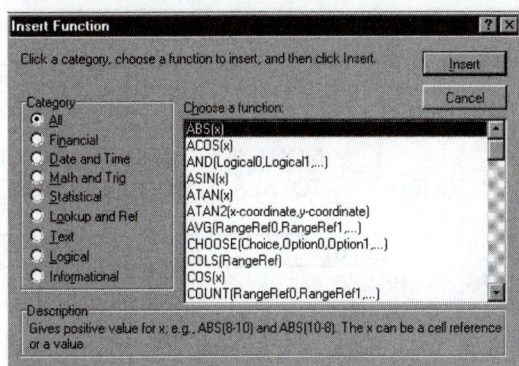

■ When you select a function in the dialog box, the description box describes what the function does and the function displays in the spreadsheet with placeholders.

■ For example, if you select the SUM function, its placeholder displays in the Entry bar as shown below:

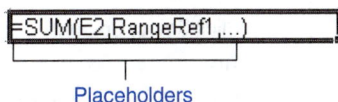

Placeholders

■ The *RangeRef0,RangeRef1,* are placeholders where you enter the cell references or ranges you wish to include in the formula.

■ If you are adding individual cells, separate each cell reference with a comma (,). If adding a range of cells, separate the beginning and ending cells with a colon (:). In both cases, be sure to close with the right parenthesis (close parenthesis) immediately following the last cell reference.

Change Column Widths

■ You learned to change column widths in Exercise 4, page 193 by dragging the column borders. You can also widen or reduce column widths by accessing the Column Width dialog box below.

■ To change column widths using the dialog box, click on the column letter to highlight the column to be changed. Click Format, Column Width to access the Column Width dialog box shown above. You can enter a specific column width in the textbox, select the Standard button to apply the standard column width or choose the Best Fit button to accommodate the longest entry in the column.

In order to determine how much of a bonus each salesperson at the Bit-Byte Computer Company will receive at the end of the year, you have been asked to prepare a monthly spreadsheet file listing each salesperson's monthly sales.

EXERCISE DIRECTIONS:

1. Create a new document for the Spreadsheet, entering labels and values in the exact cell locations shown in the illustration.

2. Center the titles over the spreadsheet.

3. Set the column widths as follows:
   - Column B = 13
   - Column C = 14
   - Column D = 13

4. Center all column headings.

5. Use Fill Series to place consecutive months starting with January 31.

   ✓ NOTE: The computer gives you current year.

6. Use the built-in functions to find the MONTHLY TOTALS, HIGHEST MONTHLY and the

LOWEST MONTHLY for each month. Copy the formula to each row as indicated.

   ✓ NOTE: Be careful not to include the monthly totals when looking for the MAX and MIN data.

7. Use the built-in functions to find the TOTALS, HIGHEST and LOWEST sales for each salesperson. Copy the formula to each column as indicated.

8. Format all money amounts to two decimal places.

9. Change the orientation to Landscape. Change the left and right margins to 1".

10. Save the file; name it **BONUS**.

11. Print one copy with gridlines.

12. Close the document window.

	A	B	C	D	E	F	G	H	I
1	SEMI-ANNUAL SALES REPORT								
2	JANUARY - JUNE								
3									
4	MONTH						MONTHLY	HIGHEST	LOWEST
5	ENDING	ROBERTSON	BELDEMBERG	HERNANDEZ	OLSON	CHEN	TOTALS	MONTHLY	MONTHLY
6									
7	1/31/95	2000	1540	1854	3222	2876			
8		1846	1100	856.23	1976	654.56			
9		1234.87	567.2	777.77	1287	2569.5			
10		3180	987.35	1345.54	876.5	1900			
11		843.75	1675	1234	2121.21	712			
12		876	398	1986	775	982.5			
13									
14	TOTALS		→	→	→	→	→		
15	HIGHEST		→	→	→	→	→	→	→
16	LOWEST		→	→	→	→	→	→	→

BUILT-IN FUNCTIONS

1. Select cell where you want function to appear.
2. Click **Insert** .... Alt + I
3. Click **Function** .... Alt + F
4. Click desired category:
   - **All** .... Alt + A
   - **Financial** .... Alt + N
   - **Date and Time** .... Alt + D
   - **Math and Trig** .... Alt + M
   - **Statistical** .... Alt + S
   - **Lookup and Ref** .... Alt + L

- **Text** .... Alt + T
- **Logical** .... Alt + L
- **Informational** .... Alt + I

5. Click desired function.
6. Click **OK** .... Enter
7. Select argument placeholders in Entry bar.
8. Click cells or range references.
   OR
   Type cell locations in Entry bar.
9. Press **Enter** .... Enter

CHANGE COLUMN WIDTHS

1. Click **Edit** .... Alt + E
2. Click **Select Column** .... M
   OR
   Click column letter to select column.
3. Click **Format** .... Alt + O
4. Click **Column Width** .... Alt + W
5. Enter desired width .... *number*
6. Click **OK** .... Enter

EXERCISE **17**

■ **IF Statements**

NOTES:

IF Statement

■ An **IF statement** is a logical function which sets up a conditional statement to test data. The truth or falsity of the condition will determine the results of the statement.

■ The format for an If statement is:

=IF(CONDITION,X,Y)

Note that the IF statement is preceded by an **equal sign** (=). If the condition is true, the function results in X; if the condition is false, the function results in Y.

In this exercise, the teacher uses an IF statement to determine the final grade depending on the final average. The passing grade is 71. Therefore, an IF statement can be used to test whether the final average is greater than 70.9. If the condition is true that the average is greater than 70.9, the student passes and the letter P is entered in the formula location. If the condition is false, the letter F is entered in the function

location. A breakdown of one of the IF statement formulas used in this problem is illustrated below:

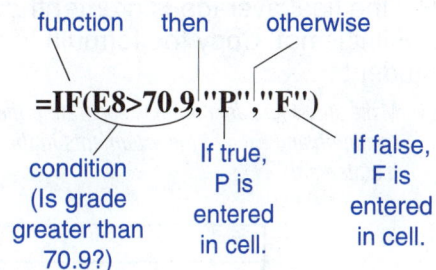

function then otherwise

=IF(E8>70.9,"P","F")

condition
(Is grade
greater than
70.9?)

If true,
P is
entered
in cell.

If false,
F is
entered
in cell.

■ If a label is to be used as an outcome of an If statement, it must be enclosed in quotes. Notice the position of the quotes in relation to the commas in the illustration above.

■ If statements use condition operators of:

= Equals	<> Not equal to
> Greater than	>= Greater than or equal to
< Less than	<= Less than or equal to

**ENTER FORMULAS WITH
IF STATEMENT**

1. Select cell to contain function.
2. Type **=** (equal sign) .... =
3. Type **IF** .... *IF*
4. Type **(** (open parenthesis) .... (
5. Type condition to meet.
6. Type **,** (comma) .... ,

7. Type the argument .... *argument* if the condition is true.
8. Type **,** (comma) .... ,
9. Type the argument .... *argument* if the condition is false.
10. Type **)** (closed parenthesis) ....)
11. Press **Enter** .... Enter

USE BUILT-IN IF FUNCTION

1. Click **Insert** .... Alt + I
2. Click **Function** .... F
3. Click **IF** function I
4. Click **OK** .... Enter
5. Replace placeholders with formula arguments.
6. Click **OK** .... Enter

In this exercise, you will calculate the FINAL GRADE and CREDITS GRANTED for Roberta Eastman's class based on a 71% passing grade by using If statements.

EXERCISE DIRECTIONS:

1. Create a new document for the Spreadsheet, entering the labels and values in the exact locations shown in the illustration.

2. Change the width of column A to 20. Adjust all other column widths as needed using any desired method.

3. Center the title over the spreadsheet.

4. Center all column headings.

5. Enter an IF statement for the first student in the FINAL GRADE column that will produce the letter P if the final average is greater than 70.9 and an F if it is not. Copy the formula to the other students.

   ✔ NOTE: Make sure there are commas separating the condition and each of the arguments in the If statement.

6. Enter an If statement for the first student in the CREDITS GRANTED column that will produce the number three (3) if the final average is greater than 70.9 and zero (0) if it is not. Copy the formula to the other students.

7. Format all grades to Fixed with one decimal point.

8. Center all entries in columns C and D.

9. Provide formulas for the NO. OF STUDENTS, CLASS AVERAGE, HIGHEST GRADE and LOWEST GRADE.

10. Save the file; name it **TESTSUM**.

11. Print one copy with gridlines.

12. Close the document window.

	A	B	C	D
1	FINAL AVERAGES			
2	BUSINESS MANAGEMENT 101			
3	MS. ROBERTA EASTMAN			
4				
5		FINAL	FINAL	CREDITS
6	STUDENT NAME	AVERAGES	GRADE	GRANTED
7				
8	Aaronson, M.	77.1		
9	Barnett, F.	82.3		
10	Costello, A.	81.8		
11	Dionesios, A.	76.1		
12	Einhorn, J.	63.7		
13	Ellenberg, L.	68.9		
14	Falstaff, S.	87.4		
15	Garcia, H.	77.4		
16	Hamway, R.	83.3		
17	Hawthorne, M.	58.6		
18	Ianelli, J.	73		
19	Jae Woo, K.	77.8		
20	Kelly, G.	90.6		
21				
22				
23				
24	NO. OF STUDENTS			
25	CLASS AVERAGE			
26	HIGHEST GRADE			
27	LOWEST GRADE			
28				

EXERCISE 18

■ **IF Statements**

NOTES:

IF Statements

■ An **IF statement** may be created to perform one calculation if a condition is true and perform another calculation if the condition is false.

■ When using the greater than condition, care must be taken to use the correct value. In this exercise, when testing if the sales are over $500,000, it is necessary to use >499,999 or >=500,000 in the formula so that a value of 500,000 is interpreted as a true condition.

> *In this exercise, you will find the commission on sales for agents working at the Interboro Real Estate Company. Interboro will give a .5% bonus to agents whose sales exceed $500,000.*

EXERCISE DIRECTIONS:

1. Create a new document for the Spreadsheet, entering the labels and values in the exact cell locations shown in the illustration.

2. Change left and right margins to 1".

3. Set width of column C to 11. Adjust other column widths as needed using any desired method.

4. Center the two-line title over the spreadsheet.

5. Align column headings attractively.
   ✓ *NOTE: Since text is left aligned and numbers are right aligned, the heading and the column data may be too far from each other. To improve readability of the spreadsheet, column headings should be closely aligned with the column data.*

6. Find COMM. (commission). Copy the formula to the remaining employees.

7. Find the BONUS for those agents who exceed $500,000 in sales.
   ✓ *NOTE: If SALES are greater than or equal to $500,000, compute a .5% bonus on sales; otherwise, enter zero.*

9. Find TOTAL COMPENSATION. Copy the formula to the remaining employees.

10. Format all money columns for Currency with no decimal places.

11. Format column E to Percent with two decimal places.

12. Total all money columns.

13. Save the file; name it **COMM**.

14. Print one copy with gridlines.

15. Close the document window.

	A	B	C	D	E	F	G
1	INTERBORO REAL ESTATE						
2	COMMISSION REPORT						
3							
4				COMM.			TOTAL
5	AGENT	LOCATION	SALES	RATE	COMM.	BONUS	COMPENSATION
6							
7	MARTIN	ELMHURST	640000	4.00%			
8	ROBERTS	JAMAICA	450000	3.00%			
9	CRIMMINS	ELMHURST	125000	3.00%			
10	LINDNER	JAMAICA	745000	4.00%			
11	WEEBLES	MASPETH	0	3.00%			
12	GARCIA	ELMHURST	550000	4.00%			
13	JACKSON	JAMAICA	210000	3.00%			
14	BOOKER	KINGSTON	435000	4.00%			
15	TROTTA	MASPETH	745000	4.00%			
16							
17	TOTALS						

EXERCISE **19**

■ Freeze Titles

NOTES:

Freeze Titles

- When working with a large spreadsheet, you will have to scroll either vertically or horizontally to see sections that do not fit into the display area. Identifying the data may become a problem because scrolling often causes the column and row headings to disappear from view.

- Therefore, you may wish to **freeze** your row and column headings so they are displayed regardless of the size of the spreadsheet and you no longer have to scroll back to identify your data.

- You can freeze rows and columns simultaneously. Click the first cell you do not want frozen. Once you select the command to freeze the titles, all cells above and to the left of the highlight are frozen.

- Frozen headings display with a bold line beneath the column headings and to the right of the row headings. In addition, frozen headings will also print on each page of a multiple-page spreadsheet.

	A	G	H	I
1				
2				
3				
4	MONTH	MONTHLY	HIGHEST	LOWEST
5	ENDING	TOTALS	MONTHLY	MONTHLY
6				
7	1/31/95	11492.00	3222.00	1540.00
8	2/28/95	6432.79	1976.00	654.56
9	3/31/95	6436.34	2569.50	567.20
10	4/30/95	8289.39	3180.00	876.50
11	5/31/95	6585.96	2121.21	712.00
12	6/30/95	5017.50	1986.00	398.00
13				
14	TOTALS	44253.98	15054.71	4748.26
15	HIGHEST	11492.00	3222.00	1540.00
16	LOWEST	5017.50	1976.00	398.00

Frozen Column Headings

Frozen Row Headings

FREEZE TITLES

1. Position highlight one row *below* or one column *to the right* of where the freeze is to occur.

2. Click **F**o**rmat** .... Alt + O

3. Click **Free**z**e Titles** .... Z

TO CLEAR FREEZE

a. Position highlight anywhere in the spreadsheet.

b. Repeat Steps 2-3 above.

All salespeople at the Bit-Byte Computer Company receive a bonus at the end of the month. Those whose monthly sales amount to $9000 or more receive a 3% bonus on sales; others receive 1%. Your supervisor would like you to include the bonus information on the BONUS spreadsheet you previously prepared.

In this exercise, you will use an If statement to calculate a bonus for sales personnel who have achieved $9000 or more in sales. In order to have the correct condition, it is necessary to use >8999 or >=9000 in the formula so that 9000 creates a true condition.

EXERCISE DIRECTIONS:

1. Open ⌨**BONUS**, or open 💾**SS BONUS.19**.

2. Freeze column A (place highlight in column B to freeze column A).

3. Enter the label BONUS where indicated in the illustration.

4. Enter an IF statement to calculate the BONUS for each salesperson based on the information provided.

5. Format Bonus amounts for 2 decimal places.

6. Clear the freeze.

7. Resave the file.

8. Print one copy with gridlines.

9. Close the file.

	A	B	C	D	E	F	G	H	I
1				SEMI-ANNUAL SALES REPORT					
2				JANUARY - JUNE					
3									
4	MONTH						MONTHLY	HIGHEST	LOWEST
5	ENDING	ROBERTSON	BELDEMBERG	HERNANDEZ	OLSON	CHEN	TOTALS	MONTHLY	MONTHLY
6									
7	1/31/95	2000.00	1540.00	1854.00	3222.00	2876.00	11492.00	3222.00	1540.00
8	2/28/95	1846.00	1100.00	856.23	1976.00	654.56	6432.79	1976.00	654.56
9	3/31/95	1234.87	567.20	777.77	1287.00	2569.50	6436.34	2569.50	567.20
10	4/30/95	3180.00	987.35	1345.54	876.50	1900.00	8289.39	3180.00	876.50
11	5/31/95	843.75	1675.00	1234.00	2121.21	712.00	6585.96	2121.21	712.00
12	6/30/95	876.00	398.00	1986.00	775.00	982.50	5017.50	1986.00	398.00
13									
14	TOTALS	9980.62	6267.55	8053.54	10257.71	9694.56	44253.98	15054.71	4748.26
15	HIGHEST	3180.00	1675.00	1986.00	3222.00	2876.00	11492.00	3222.00	1540.00
16	LOWEST	843.75	398.00	777.77	775.00	654.56	5017.50	1976.00	398.00
17									
18	BONUS		⟶	⟶	⟶	⟶			

↑
Insert label

EXERCISE **20**

■ **Hide Columns and Rows** ■ **Easy Calc**

Easy Calc

NOTES:

Hide Columns and Rows

■ In Exercise 19 you learned to freeze your column and row headings so you can easily identify data in a large spreadsheet.

■ You can also make a spreadsheet easier to read by **hiding** selected rows or columns. Once hidden, these columns and/or rows will not display or print. The numbers or formulas contained in the hidden cells, however, will continue to be used in the calculations.

■ You can hide a row or column by dragging the ADJUST mouse pointer ⬌. To hide a row, click on the lower border of the row heading and drag the ADJUST pointer until the row is no longer visible. To hide a column, click on the lower border of the column heading and drag the adjust pointer to the left until the column is no longer visible.

■ If you wish to hide multiple rows or columns, select the rows/columns to be hidden. Then reduce the Row Height or Column Width in the Format menu to 0 (zero).

■ Similarly, to show hidden columns or rows, select a range that contains the hidden columns or rows, click Format, and then click either Row Height or Column Width. The default column width or row height is displayed. When you click OK, the hidden areas reappear.

Easy Calc

■ The **Easy Calc** feature allows you to easily create a formula. Click the Easy Calc button on the Toolbar to access the dialog box shown above right.

✔ *NOTE:* *You can also access Easy Calc from the Tools menu.*

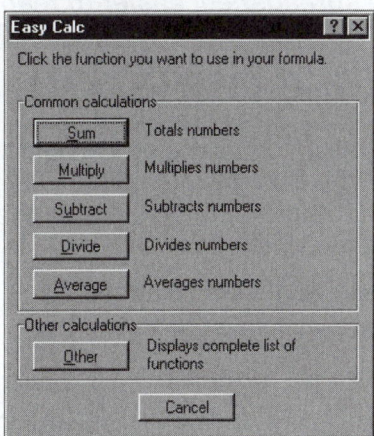

Click the appropriate button to use one of the five functions listed. To access a full list of Works functions, click the Other button. Once you select a function, a dialog box appears in which you can enter your data to create the formula. Note the illustration of the Easy Calc, SUM dialog box below.

Formulas display

Range displays

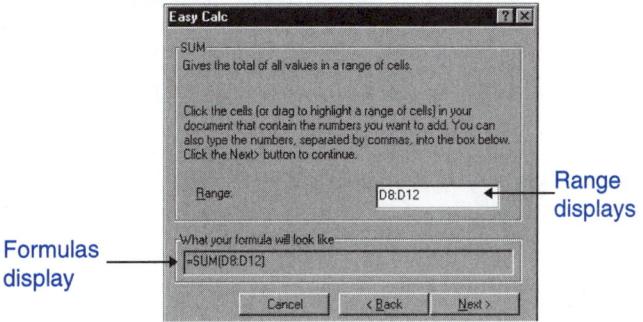

■ You can enter the range for your formula by typing it in the text box provided or by selecting the range using the mouse. If a cell reference is already displayed, delete it before entering the desired cell reference. If the dialog box is blocking your view of cells that you want to select, click the title bar and drag it to the side. Once the formula is complete, click Next. The following screen displays:

Click the cell or type the cell reference where you want to display the result and click Finish.

The athletic director has asked you to create a spreadsheet to calculate the statistics for the WOMEN'S COLLEGIATE BASKETBALL TEAM. You will use the Easy Calc feature to develop some of the formulas used in this spreadsheet. In addition, you will hide some of the columns to make the spreadsheet easier to read.

EXERCISE DIRECTIONS:

1. Create a new document for the Spreadsheet as shown in the illustration on page 229, entering labels and values in the exact cell locations shown in the illustration.

2. Set column widths as follows:

   column B: 15   column C: 11   column D: 9

   column E: 6   column F: 8   column G: 9

   column H: 8   column I: 8   column J: 8

3. Using the Fill Series option, complete the player numbers so they begin with 101 and end with 115.

4. Enter the data for each player as shown below:

PLAYER	POSITION	STATUS	AGE	FIELD GOALS	FREE THROWS	RBNDS	ASSTS
ALI	GUARD	FR	15	10	4	6	2
ALTOMARE	CENTER	FR	15	11	6	5	5
ANDERSON	CENTER	SR	18	13	6	11	9
BIRD	FORWARD	JR	17	14	9	4	11
CHANDRA	FORWARD	FR	15	7	4	3	3
CHU	GUARD	SO	16	6	2	2	3
COLCHESTER	GUARD	JR	17	8	2	5	3
GEORGIOS	GUARD	FR	15	4	4	4	2
HARRIS	FORWARD	SO	16	9	5	5	2
JORDAN	FORWARD	SR	18	13	11	8	7
KIEU	GUARD	SO	16	8	5	5	3
LEVINE	CENTER	SO	16	12	9	4	5
MINELLI	FORWARD	FR	15	10	8	6	3
PEREZ	GUARD	FR	15	6	2	1	0
ZHOU	GUARD	FR	15	5	4	2	2

5. Hide columns C-E.

6. Find POINTS for each player. (Each field goal is worth 2 points. Each free throw is worth 1 point.) Copy the formula to all players.

7. Using Easy Calc, find TOTAL for FIELD GOALS column. Copy the formula to all columns.

8. Using Easy Calc, find TEAM AVERAGES by entering a formula to find average of FIELD GOALS. Copy the formula to all columns.

9. Format the averages to two decimal places.

10. Find the highest number of goals in FIELD GOALS.

11. Copy the formula to all columns.

12. Find the lowest number of goals in FIELD GOALS. Copy the formula to all columns.

13. Center the titles across the spreadsheet.

14. Center all column headings.

15. Center the data in column A.

16. Change the orientation to Landscape.

17. Print Preview your spreadsheet, and make any adjustments to the column widths as needed.

18. Save the file; name it **PLAY**.

19. Print one copy with gridlines.

20. Unhide columns C-E.

21. Center column D data.

22. Save the file as **PLAY 2**.

23. Print one copy with gridlines.

24. Close the document window.

   ✓NOTE: *You will have two solutions; one hiding columns C- E, the other with all columns visible.*

	A	B	C	D	E	F	G	H	I	J
1	NORTH AMERICAN ACADEMY									
2	WOMEN'S COLLEGIATE BASKETBALL TEAM									
3	PLAYER STATISTICS									
4	DATE: JANUARY 10, 199-									
5										
6	PLAYER					FIELD	FREE			
7	NUMBER	PLAYER	POSITION	STATUS	AGE	GOALS	THROWS	RBNDS	ASSTS	POINTS
8										
9	101	ALI								
10		ALTOMARE								
11		ANDERSON								
12		BIRD								
13		CHANDRA								
14		CHU								
15		COLCHESTER								
16		GEORGIOS								
17		HARRIS								
18		JORDAN								
19		KIEU								
20		LEVINE								
21		MINELLI								
22		PEREZ								
23	115	ZHOU								
24										
25		TOTALS					→	→	→	→
26		AVERAGES					→	→	→	→
27		HIGHEST					→	→	→	→
28		LOWEST					→	→	→	→

HIDE COLUMNS AND ROWS

1. Click cell in column or row you want to hide.

   OR

   Select a range of columns or rows you want to hide.

2. Click **Format** .... Alt + O
3. Click **Row Height** .... H

   OR

   Click **Column Width** .... W
4. Type **0** (zero) 0
5. Click **OK** .... *Enter*

MOUSE USERS

1. Select the column or row to hide.
2. Drag the ADJUST mouse shape ...... ADJUST until column/row disappears

   ✓ *NOTE: You have to hide each row or column individually using this method.*

SHOW HIDDEN COLUMNS/ROWS

1. Select area that includes hidden columns/rows.
2. Click **Format** .... Alt + O
3. Click **Row Height** .... H

   OR

   Click **Column Width** .... W
4. Click **Best Fit** .... Alt + B

   OR

   Click **Standard** .... Alt + S
5. Click **OK** .... *Enter*

EASY CALC

1. Click **Tools** .... Alt + T
2. Click **Easy Calc** .... E

   OR

   Click **Easy Calc** button on Toolbar.

3. Click one of the following:
   - **Sum** .... S
   - **Multiply** .... M
   - **Subtract** .... U
   - **Divide** .... D
   - **Average** .... A
   - **Other** .... O
4. Enter cell range .... *cell range* in text box

   OR

   Select cell range in the spreadsheet.
5. Click **Next** .... Alt + N
6. Type cell address .... *cell address*

   OR

   Click cell to display result.
7. Click **Finish** .... Alt + F

■ **Lookup** ■ **Vertical Lookup**

NOTES:

Lookup

■ The **Lookup** function selects a value from a table and enters it into a location on the spreadsheet. For example, the Lookup function may be used to look up taxes on a tax table when developing a payroll, or to look up postage rates to complete a bill of sale.

■ The table containing the data to be looked up must be created in a blank or empty location on the spreadsheet. The Lookup formula is entered in a location on the spreadsheet that requires specific data from the table.

■ There are two ways to look up data depending on the way it is arranged: **vertically** or **horizontally**.

■ **=VLOOKUP** (vertical lookup) looks up data in a particular *column* in the table, while **=HLOOKUP** (horizontal lookup) looks up data in a particular *row* in the table. *(See Exercise 22, page 234, for more information on HLOOKUP.)*

Vertical Lookup

■ The function =VLOOKUP (lookup value, range reference, column number) has three components:

Lookup value is text, a value or a cell address of the item you are looking for and should be in the first column of the =VLOOKUP table. Numerical search items should be listed in ascending order.

Range reference is the range address or range name of the lookup table in which the search is to be made. If the lookup function is going to be copied later, the range should contain absolute references.

Column number is the position the column occupies in the lookup table range. The far left column has a position number of zero (0); the second column has a position number of one (1) and so forth.

✓ NOTE: *Column positions are counted from the left column in the range, not from the left column of the spreadsheet.*

■ For example, note the outlined lookup table in this exercise. To look up the mortgage payment for a mortgage amount of $105,000, at 9% for 25 years and enter it on the spreadsheet, a lookup formula would be created as follows:

lookup value   range reference   column number

=VLOOKUP(105000,B7:F14,3)

The lookup formula accesses the value from the table and returns 881.16 to the formula location.

■ If you need to look up more than one item, the formula should be entered using the cell address as the lookup value, not the value itself, so the formula can be copied later. In addition, the range should be made absolute so that the formula can be copied correctly. If you are using the cell reference instead of the column number, you will need to make that absolute as well.

EXAMPLE:

lookup value   range reference   column number

=VLOOKUP(E22,$B$7:$F$14,3)
OR
=VLOOKUP(E22,$B$7:$F$14,$E$15

- You can use the Easy Calc feature to create the VLOOKUP formula. Click Tools, Easy Calc to access the Easy Calc dialog box. Click Other to access the Insert Function dialog box shown below.

Select the VLOOKUP function from the list to access the EasyCalc VLOOKUP dialog box shown below.

Enter the value you want to lookup in the Lookup value text box. Enter the range of cells containing the table in the Range of cells textbox. Remember to make the range absolute if you are going to copy the formula. Enter the

number of columns to the right of the lookup value in the Columns to count text box. Click Next to access the Easy Calc Final result dialog box shown below:

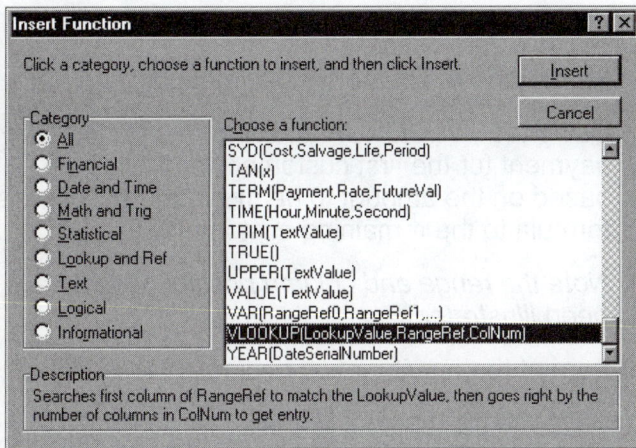

✓ NOTE: *Click the cell to contain the result, or type the cell reference in the Result at text box.*

Set Print Area

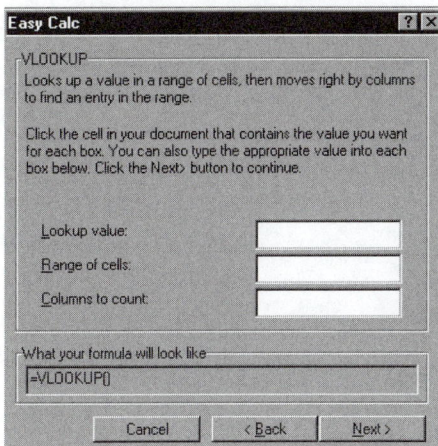

- There may be occasions where you wish to print only a section of a spreadsheet. In this exercise, you will print the bottom portion of the spreadsheet, but not the lookup table.

- To print a specific area, you must select that area and then click Set Print Area on the Format menu. The following message box appears:

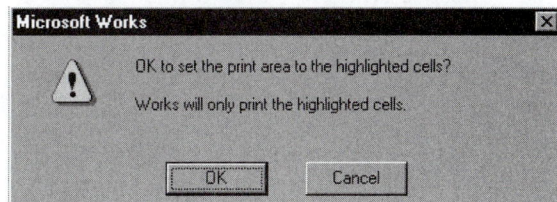

✓ NOTE: *Only the selected area will appear in the Print Preview screen.*

- You can deselect a print area by selecting the entire spreadsheet and resetting the print area as explained above.

In this exercise, you will create the following spreadsheet for the Home Money Depot. This spreadsheet contains the mortgage table and a spreadsheet to calculate the mortgage amount and the customer's monthly mortgage payment for 25 or 30 years. Use the Lookup function to enter mortgage payments depending upon the mortgage amount.

EXERCISE DIRECTIONS:

1. Create a new document for the Spreadsheet, including a table and enter the labels and values in the exact cell locations shown in the illustration.

2. Adjust column widths as needed using any desired method.

3. Center the titles in row 1 and row 17 over the spreadsheet. Center all column headings.

4. Set left and right margins to 1".

5. Format all money amounts to Fi<u>x</u>ed with two decimal places.

6. Find MORTGAGE AMOUNT by subtracting the down payment from the contract price. Copy the formula to the remaining customers.

7. Using the =VLOOKUP function, find the monthly payment for the first customer (for 25 years) based on the amount to be mortgaged. Copy the formula to the remaining customers.

   ✓ NOTE: Make sure you use absolute values for the range reference if the Lookup function is going to be copied later.

8. Format the result for two decimal places.

9. Using the =VLOOKUP function, find the monthly payment for the first customer (for 30 years) based on the amount to be mortgaged. Copy the formula to the remaining customers.

   Note the range and column position which have been illustrated.

10. Format the result for two decimal places.

11. Save the file; name it **HOME**.

12. Set the print area to rows 17-26.

13. Print one copy of the bottom portion of the spreadsheet in Landscape orientation with gridlines.

14. Close the document window.

	A	B	C	D	E	F	G	H	I
1	MORTGAGE PAYMENT TABLE AT 9%								
2									
3									
4	NUMBER OF YEARS		15	20	25	30			
5	INTEREST RATE		0.09	0.09	0.09	0.09			
6									
7	PRINCIPAL	100000	1014.27	899.73	839.20	804.62			
8		105000	1064.98	944.71	881.16	844.85			
9		110000	1115.69	989.70	923.12	885.08			
10		115000	1166.41	1034.68	965.08	925.32			
11		120000	1217.12	1079.67	1007.04	965.55			
12		125000	1267.83	1124.66	1049.00	1005.78			
13		130000	1318.55	1169.64	1090.96	1046.01			
14		135000	1369.26	1214.63	1132.92	1086.24			
15		0	1	2	3	4			
16									
17	HOME MONEY DEPOT								
18							MONTHLY	MONTHLY	
19			CONTRACT	DOWN	MORTGAGE		PAYMENT	PAYMENT	
20	CUSTOMER		PRICE	PAYMENT	AMOUNT		25 YEARS	30 YEARS	
21									
22	LOGENBERRY, K.		185000	80000					
23	MARTINS, D.		255000	120000					
24	POTTER, C.		320000	200000					
25	SANCHEZ, J.		195000	80000					
26	THOMPSON, I.		215000	105000					

Range reference B7:F14

Column number

Item to be looked up

Location for lookup formulas and results

LOOKUP

1. Select cell to contain function.
2. Type = (equal sign) .... 🖫
3. Type *VLOOKUP* (Vertical Lookup).

   OR

   Type *HLOOKUP* (Horizontal Lookup).
4. Type an **(** (open parenthesis) .... 🖫
5. Type cell address of .... *cell address* lookup value.

   OR

   Select cell containing lookup value.

   OR

   Type value .... *number* of the lookup value.
6. Type **,** (comma) .... 🖫

7. Type first cell reference ..... *cell reference* in the table.

   OR

   Click first cell in the table.
8. Type **:** (colon) .... 🖫
9. Type last cell reference ..... *cell reference* in the table.

   OR

   Click last cell in the table.
10. Type **,** (comma) .... 🖫
11. Type a number .... *number* representing the column or row number of the table where the value to be returned lies.

    ✔ *NOTE: First column or row in the table is always 0.*

12. Type **)** (close parenthesis) .... 🖫
13. Press **Enter** .... Enter

SET PRINT AREA

1. Select area to be printed.
2. Click **Format** .... Alt + O
3. Click **Set Print Area** .... S
4. Click **OK** .... Enter

DESELECT PRINT AREA

1. Select entire spreadsheet.
2. Repeat steps 2-4, above.

EXERCISE **22**

■ **Horizontal Lookup Function** ■ **Protect Data**

NOTES:

Horizontal Lookup Function

■ While =VLOOKUP looks up data in a particular *column* in the table, =**HLOOKUP** looks up data in a particular *row* in the table.

The function =**HLOOKUP** (lookup value, range reference, row number) uses the same format and contains the same three arguments (parts) as =VLOOKUP:

Lookup value is text, a value or a cell address of the item you are looking for (**search item**) and should be in the first row of the =HLOOKUP table. Numerical search items should be listed in ascending order.

Range reference is the range address of the lookup table in which the search is made.

Row number is the position the row occupies in the lookup table range. The top row has a position number of zero (0); the second row has a position number of one (1) and so forth.

■ You can enter the HLOOKUP function manually, or you can use the Easy Calc feature to develop the formula.

Protect Data

■ It is possible to protect an entire spreadsheet, individual cells or a range of cells from accidental changes or unauthorized use.

■ Click Format, Protection to access the Format Protection dialog box shown below.

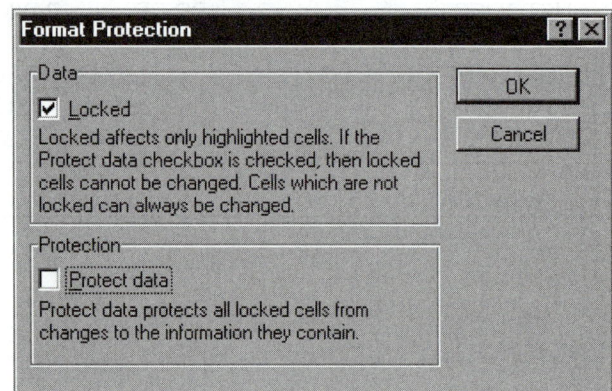

■ All cells are locked in a new spreadsheet, but the lock has no effect unless Protect is turned on. To keep certain cells accessible in a protected file, however, these cells must be unlocked *before* the file is protected. Works protects only those cells that are locked.

■ If someone tries to edit or change a protected cell, you will get a message that the cell cannot be changed.

HORIZONTAL LOOKUP

See Exercise 21 for keystrokes (page 233).

PROTECT DATA

1. Select cell or cell range to protect.
2. Click **F**ormat........................ Alt + O
3. Click **P**rotection............................. R

4. Click **L**ock............................. Alt + L
   Check mark appears.
5. Click **P**rotect Data .... Alt + P
   Check mark appears.
6. Click **OK**.................................... Enter

✓ *NOTE:* *The menu commands that cannot be used when a file is protected are automatically dimmed.*

To Unprotect Cells:

1. Select cell or range of cells where you want to allow changes.
2. Click **F**ormat .... Alt + O
3. Click **P**rotection .... R
4. Click **L**ocked L
   Check mark disappears.

In this exercise, you will create a spreadsheet listing daily sales. As an employee of the Regal Catalog Sales Company, you are to compute the sales tax and shipping charges for all packages. Using =HLOOKUP, you will compute the postage and sales tax required, depending on the zone to which the package is being shipped.

EXERCISE DIRECTIONS:

1. Create a new document for the Spreadsheet, entering the labels and values in the exact cell locations shown in the illustration.

2. Adjust column widths as needed.

3. Align column headings to improve the readability of the spreadsheet.

4. Center the titles in rows 1, 2 and 20 across the spreadsheet.

5. Use =HLOOKUP to find POSTAGE (based on the zone). Copy the formula to the remaining items using an absolute reference in the table range.

6. Use the Easy Calc feature to develop the HLOOKUP function to find the TAX RATE (based on the zone). Copy the formula to the remaining items using an absolute reference in the table range.

7. Find the SALES TAX and TOTAL SALE. Copy formulas to the remaining items.

   ✓ HINT: Sales tax is not charged on postage.

8. Format all money columns for two decimal places.

   To protect the lookup table:
   - Select the range A20:H23.
   - Make sure both the Locked and Protect data features are checked.

   To test protection:
   Try to edit an entry in the rate table.

9. Save the file; name it **ZONE**.

10. Print one copy of the top portion of the spreadsheet with gridlines.

11. Close the document window.

	A	B	C	D	E	F	G	H
1	REGAL CATALOG SALES							
2	JUNE 20, 199-							
3								
4					TAX	SALES	TOTAL	
5	CAT. NO.	PRICE	ZONE	POSTAGE	RATE	TAX	SALE	
6								
7	G23546	59.95	1					
8	V38765	65.49	3					
9	M65498	29.95	2					
10	T43769	43.98	4					
11	C65873	16.89	5					
12	X34598	98.78	6					
13	T23098	35.89	5					
14	G65980	54.99	3					
15	W45687	36.67	6					
16	A87654	89.67	1					
17	M65498	29.95	4					
18	D67843	43.65	3					
19								
20	POSTAGE AND SALES TAX RATES							
21	ZONE		1	2	3	4	5	6
22	POSTAGE		4	4.5	5	5.5	6	6.5
23	SALES TAX RATE		0.08	0.06	0	0.04	0.05	0.07

EXERCISE DIRECTIONS:

1. Create a new document for the Spreadsheet, entering the labels and values in the exact cell locations shown in the illustration.

2. Set 1" left and right margins.

3. Change the orientation to Landscape.

4. Center the three-line title over the spreadsheet.

5. Center all column headings.

6. Adjust column widths as needed.

7. Format all dollar amounts to two decimal places.

8. Use the Fill Series feature to enter ITEM NO. 2-11.

9. Place the highlight in cell B8, and freeze the column and row headings.

10. Create a simple multiplication formula to find the SALES PRICE. Copy the formula as indicated in the illustration.

11. Enter a formula using an IF statement that will give a 10% discount for any item in the QUANTITY column that has sold more than five units. There is no discount for selling five or fewer units. Copy the formula as indicated.

12. Enter a simple formula to find the NET AMOUNT. Copy the formula as indicated.

13. Use the Autosum feature to determine the TOTAL in cell F21. Copy the formula as indicated.

14. Use the COUNT formula to find the total number of items in the invoice.

15. Hide columns D-F.

16. Use the Easy Calc feature to develop the formulas for AVERAGE, MIN and MAX. Copy the formulas as indicated.

17. Show all hidden columns and unfreeze the titles.

18. Preview the spreadsheet and make any necessary adjustments to fit it on one page.

19. Save the file; name it **VIDEO**.

20. Print one copy with gridlines.

21. Close the document window.

	A	B	C	D	E	F	G	H
1	A. C. T. NOW							
2	Access Computer Technology							
3	Video and VideoDisc Programs							
4								
5	INVOICE #12954							
6								
7	ITEM NO.	ID NO.	DESCRIPTION	QUANTITY	UNIT PRICE	SALE PRICE	DISCOUNT	NET AMOUNT
8								
9	1	EVR-345	Exploring Virtual Reality	2	125			
10		TEL-897	Telecommunications	5	89.98			
11		INT-865	Exploring the Internet	10	149			
12		CG-897	Computer Graphics	20	129.95			
13		CAD-804	Computer Assisted Design	10	129.95			
14		ACC-932	Computer Accounting	25	125.95			
15		PRE-128	Presenting Presentations	12	139.95			
16		SUI-674	Sweet Suites	15	359.95			
17		ANI-345	Animation	5	245.5			
18	↓	BBB-129	Bulletin Board Basics	3	69.95			
19	11	ETQ-375	Internet Etiquette	8	59.95	↓	↓	↓
20								
21	TOTALS						→	→
22	COUNT							
23	AVERAGE						→	→
24	MAX						→	→
25	MIN						→	→

NOTES:

Insert, Delete and Move Columns and Rows

■ Columns and/or rows may be inserted, deleted or moved to change the format of a spreadsheet or to add, remove or rearrange data.

■ When a column or row is inserted, a blank area is created. Existing columns or rows shift to allow for the newly created space.

■ When a column or row is deleted, all data in that column or row is also eliminated. It is therefore recommended that you save the spreadsheet *before* you insert, delete or move data so you can retrieve the original spreadsheet in the event of an error.

■ Inserting, deleting or moving data can affect formulas. Be sure formulas are correct after an insert, delete or move operation.

Move and Copy Information

■ You can move or copy a single cell or a range of cells in much the same way you moved or copied text in the Word Processor tool. Moving or copying data can be accomplished by using a combination of cutting and pasting to the target location, or highlighting the range and dragging it to the target location (known as **drag and drop** and **drag and copy**).

CAUTION: *When moving data, be sure that the area of the spreadsheet to receive the data is blank or contains unimportant information. Works overwrites any existing data.*

■ The format of the data as well as the formulas will be moved or copied along with that data.

Paste Special

■ In addition to copying data and formulas, you may want to copy the result of a formula but not the formula itself. In addition, you can add, copy and subtract the values in a cell using the Paste Special command on the Edit menu. When you copy data into a cell or range that already contains data, the new data replaces the existing data. However, when pasting using the Paste Special command, you can add or subtract the data from the existing data in the cells. Note the illustration of the Paste Special dialog box below.

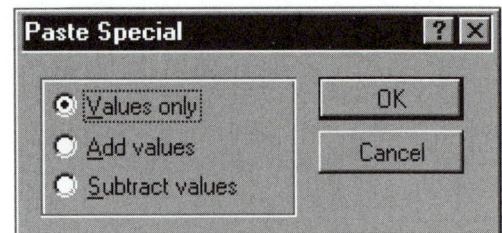

INSERT COLUMNS/ROWS

1. Click column letter to select where new column is to be inserted.

   OR

   Click row number to select where new row will be inserted.

   ✔ *NOTE:* *To insert more than one column or row, click on the column letter or row number and select adjacent columns or rows.*

2. Click **I**nsert .... `Alt` + `I`
3. Click **Insert R**ow .... `R`

   OR

   Click **Insert C**olumn .... `C`

   ✔ *NOTE:* *New columns will be placed to the left of the highlighted columns. New rows will be placed above the highlighted rows.*

DELETE COLUMNS/ROWS

1. Click column letter to select column to be deleted.

   OR

   Click row number to select row to be deleted.

   ✔ *NOTE:* *To delete more than one column or row, click on the column letter or row number and select adjacent columns or rows.*

2. Click **I**nsert .... `I`
3. Click **D**elete Row .... `D`

   OR

   Click **D**elete Column .... `E`

MOVE AND COPY INFORMATION

Cut & Paste

CTRL + X, CTRL + V

Copy & Paste

CTRL + C, CTRL + V

1. Select cell or range to move or copy.
2. Click **E**dit .... `Alt` + `E`
3. Click **Cu**t .... `T`

   OR

   Click **C**opy .... `Alt` + `C`

   ✔ *NOTE:* *You may also use the Cut or Copy Toolbar buttons.*

4. Select cell or range to paste data.

   ✔ *NOTE:* *You only have to specify the top left cell. The range can be in the same file, another file or a different application. However, Works will write over existing data.*

5. Click **Paste** button .... 🗐 on Toolbar.

   OR

   a. Click **E**dit .... `Alt` + `E`
   b. Click **P**aste .... `P`

MOVE INFORMATION WITH DRAG AND DROP

1. Select range to cut or copy.
2. Move cross ⊡ to edge of cell or selected range so it changes shape to a pointer.
3. Hold down mouse button and drag range to new location.
4. Release mouse button when outline of range is in desired location.

COPY/PASTE WITH DRAG AND DROP

1. Select cell or range to copy.
2. Move cross ⊡ to edge of cell or selected range so it changes shape to a pointer.
3. Press **Ctrl** and drag range ...... `Ctrl` +*drag* to new location.
4. Release mouse button when outline and range are in desired location.

PASTE SPECIAL

1. Select data to copy.
2. Click **E**dit .... `Alt` + `E`
3. Click **C**opy .... `C`
4. Select cell or range in which to paste data.
5. Click **E**dit .... `Alt` + `E`
6. Click **Paste S**pecial .... `S`
7. Click one of the following options:
   - **V**alues only .... `Alt` + `V`
   - **A**dd values .... `Alt` + `A`
   - **S**ubtract values .... `Alt` + `S`
8. Click **OK** .... `Enter`

In this exercise, you will insert and delete columns and rows as well as move information to edit the Burlington National Bank payroll spreadsheet. In addition, a new payroll spreadsheet will be created below the existing one for the new pay period.

EXERCISE DIRECTIONS:

1. Open ⌨**SALARY**, or open ▭**SS SALARY.24**.

2. Edit the two-line title as illustrated.

3. Make the following changes as shown in the illustration:

   a. Insert a new column A.

   b. Select only the data in new column C and move it to column A. Make sure you do not select the entire column.

   c. Center the two-line column title across the spreadsheet following these steps:

      - Click cell B2 and select the two-line title.

      - Click Format and change Alignment to Left.

      - Drag the two-line title to cell A1 (or use cut and paste to move the title).

      - Recenter the two-line title across the spreadsheet.

   d. Enter the label S.S. NO. as the column heading in column C. Center the heading.

   e. Enter Social Security numbers as follows:

CARTER:	069-65-4532
FINCKEL:	123-75-7623
JAMISON:	107-53-6754
MILLS:	103-87-5698
POTTER:	127-78-0045
SAMUELS:	043-67-7600

   f. Enter the labels TOTALS and AVERAGES and provide formulas where indicated.

   g. Format results in rows 14 and 15 for two decimal places.

   h. Adjust widths of columns A and C as needed.

   i. Copy the entire May 15 payroll, including the title, to a new location below the existing spreadsheet. Leave one blank row between the spreadsheets.

4. Make the following changes on the bottom payroll:

   a. Edit the title to read: FOR THE WEEK ENDING MAY 22, 199-

      ✓ NOTE: *Click cell B18 to display the title in the Entry bar.*

   b. Delete the row containing data for FINCKEL.

   c. Insert a row where necessary to maintain alphabetical order for a new employee named NELSON.

   d. Enter the following information for NELSON:

ID NO.:	12967
S.S. No.:	146-93-0069
Hourly Rate:	$6.25

   e. Edit the HOURS WORKED as follows:

CARTER:	22
JAMISON:	33
MILLS:	21
NELSON:	16
POTTER:	18
SAMUELS:	28

   f. Copy payroll formulas to complete NELSON's data.

5. Resave the file.

6. Print one copy with gridlines to fit on a page.

7. Set the top and bottom margins to .75".

8. Enter the following title in cell A33: Gain or Loss in Net Pay

9. Copy the employee names from the May 22 payroll to cells A35:A40.

10. Copy the May 22 NET PAY values for all employees. Use the Paste Special command and select the Values only option to paste the results in cells B35:B40.

11. Copy the appropriate May 15 NET PAY values for each individual employee as follows:

    a. Copy each individual's NET PAY separately. Do not do this in a range.

    b. Do not copy FINCKEL's data.

    c. Hide rows and columns as needed so the NET PAY column is close to the Gain or Loss in Net Pay column.

    d. Use the Paste Special command and select the Subtract values option to paste the results in each individual's cell. Make sure you match the correct NET PAY with the appropriate employee.

    e. Clear the data for NELSON in cell B38.

f. Format the results for two decimal places.

12. Set the print area to print cells A33:B40. Print one copy.

13. Reset the print area to the entire document and show all hidden rows and columns before saving. *(See Spreadsheet Lesson 3, Exercise 20 to display hidden rows/columns.)*

14. Save the file as **SALARY COMPARE**.

15. Print one copy of the entire spreadsheet with gridlines.

16. Close the document window.

Insert new column A *Move to column A* *Insert label* S.S. NO. PAYROLL

	A	B	C	D	E	F	G	H
1					BURLINGTON NATIONAL BANK			
2					PAYROLL FOR THE WEEK ENDING MAY 15, 199-			
3								
4			HOURLY	HOURS	GROSS			NET
5	ID NO.	EMPLOYEE	RATE	WORKED	PAY	F. I. C. A.	F. W. T.	PAY
6								
7	12567	CARTER	5.55	15	83.25	6.37	16.65	60.23
8	12750	FINCKEL	7.25	32	232.00	17.75	46.40	167.85
9	12816	JAMISON	6.18	16	98.88	7.56	19.78	71.54
10	12915	MILLS	4.66	28	130.48	9.98	26.10	94.40
11	12345	POTTER	6.57	12	78.84	6.03	15.77	57.04
12	12716	SAMUELS	8.65	21	181.65	13.90	36.33	131.42
13								
14	TOTALS					⟶	⟶	⟶
15	AVERAGES					⟶	⟶	⟶
16								
17								
18								
19								
20								
21								
22								

Copy entire spreadsheet

EXERCISE **25**

■ **Name Ranges**

NOTES:

Name Ranges

- It is often easier to use a descriptive name for a cell or range of cells rather than the cell or range reference. For example, when averaging the exam grades for EXAM 1 as shown in the illustration, you may simply name the range for first exam grades as EXAM1 and create the formula =AVG(EXAM1) rather than use the traditional formula =AVG(B6:B11).

- To create a named range, select the cells then click Insert, Range Name to access the dialog box shown below.

Name range here

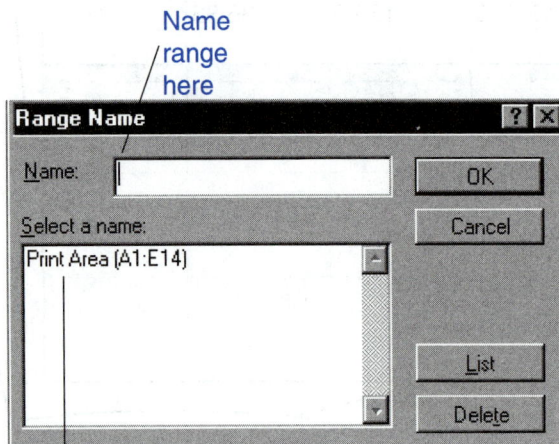

Other named ranges

- The following features are available in the Range Name dialog box:

Name	Names should not be more than 15 characters long. The name can use any combination of letters, numbers, spaces or symbols, and can be in either upper- or lowercase letters or a combination of both.
Select a name:	Lists all the range names with their accompanying ranges that are contained in the spreadsheet.
Delete	Allows you to delete a range name in the list.
List	Inserts a list that shows all the range names you created for the spreadsheet. Be careful to insert this list into an empty area. If there is data in the selected location, the list overwrites it. This feature allows you to keep track of your range names for each spreadsheet.

- When you delete or insert columns or rows in your spreadsheet, the cell references in the named range are automatically updated to reflect the change.

- You can assign a range name for this list to access it easily using the Go To command. Click Edit, Go To and type the name of the range. When you click OK, the highlight moves to the first cell in the named range.

- You can add, change or delete a named range at any time.

  ✓ NOTE: *You cannot Undo deleting a named range.*

In this exercise, you will open the EXAM spreadsheet and add the data for the fourth exam. Your supervisor also wants a listing of the grades showing the highest and lowest exam grades as well the final grade.

EXERCISE DIRECTIONS:

1. Open **EXAM**, or open **SS EXAM.25**.

2. Insert a row after the two-line title.

3. Edit the column heading in column E as shown in the illustration.

4. Insert a column for the fourth examination; label it EXAM 4.

5. Enter the following exam grades for EXAM 4:

Burns	88
Daniels	38
Edwards	87
Forbes	82
Garner	80
Yaro	74

6. Find the average for EXAM 4.

7. Enter the following label in column G: GRADE. Provide a formula for this column that will place PASS in the cell if the average is 65 or above, or place a FAIL if the grade is below 65.

   ✓ NOTE: Enclose the labels P and F in quotation marks. Copy the formula to the other rows.

8. Insert two rows in alphabetic sequence to include the new students, Hawkins and Lopez. Enter the following exam grades for these new students:

Hawkins:	87, 94, 78, 85
Lopez:	98, 83, 91, 78

9. Copy the formulas for STUDENT AVERAGES to the two new rows.

10. Edit the formulas for STUDENT AVERAGES to reflect the addition of the fourth exam.

11. Format all new data and labels so they are consistent with existing formats.

12. Center all column headings and center title over the spreadsheet.

13. Name the following ranges:

B7:B14	EXAM 1
C7:C14	EXAM 2
D7:D14	EXAM 3
E7:E14	EXAM 4

14. Enter the labels LOWEST and HIGHEST in cells A17 and A18, respectively.

15. Provide formulas for the lowest and highest exam using the named ranges in the formula.

16. In cell A20, enter the label: TABLE OF NAMED RANGES

17. Create a table listing named ranges beginning with cell A21.

18. Print one copy of the spreadsheet with gridlines.

19. Delete the named ranges for EXAM 1 and EXAM 2.

20. Close the file; save the changes.

Insert column for
EXAM 4
↓

	A	B	C	D	E
1	ADVANCED INFORMATION PROCESSING				
2	THIRD QUARTER EXAM GRADES				
3					STUDENT←
4	STUDENT	EXAM 1	EXAM 2	EXAM 3	AVERAGES
5					
6	Burns	90	81	86	85.67
7	Daniels	71	67	65	67.67
8	Edwards	65	78	81	74.67
9	Forbes	92	78	90	86.67
10	Garner	91	71	95	85.67
11	Yaro	91	34	88	71.00
12					
13	AVERAGES	83.33	68.17	84.17	78.56
14					

Insert row

Insert 2 rows

NAME A RANGE

1. Position the highlight in the cell or range you want to name.
2. Click **Insert**.............................. `Alt`+`I`
3. Click **Range Name** .... `N`
4. Accept name Works suggests

   OR

   Enter a name ....*name*
   up to 15 characters long.

   ✓*NOTE:* *Works suggests a name only if there is text in the selected range, or above, or to the left of the selected range.*

5. Click **OK**...................................... `Enter`

INSERT A RANGE NAME INTO A FORMULA

1. Type the formula up to the point where you would normally enter a cell reference.
2. Type the range name instead of the cell reference.
3. Finish the formula.
4. Click **OK**...................................... `Enter`

CREATE AND INSERT A LIST OF RANGE NAMES

1. Position the highlight where you want the list to appear.
2. Click **Insert**.............................. `Alt`+`I`
3. Click **Range Name** .... `N`
4. Click **List** .... `L`
5. Click **OK**...................................... `Enter`

DELETE A RANGE NAME

1. Click **Insert**........................... `Alt`+`I`
2. Click **Range Name** .... `N`
3. Click range name to delete.
4. Click **Delete**................................. `T`
5. Click **OK**...................................... `Enter`

EXERCISE 26

■ Sort Information

NOTES:

Sort Information

- It is always easier to find information when it is arranged in some sort of logical order. Works provides the **Sort** feature so you can arrange the data in your spreadsheets either alphabetically or numerically.

- You can specify whether you want the information arranged in either **ascending** order (A-Z, 1-9) or **descending** order (Z-A, 9-1).

  An ascending sort on text and numbers sorts the text first and then the numbers. A descending sort on the same information lists numbers first.

- A **single-level sort** arranges the data in a single column. Works allows you to sort just the selected column or to keep all the rows together as the data is sorted. A one-level sort may be accomplished in the accompanying spreadsheet by organizing the data in numeric order on the information contained in column C (SALES).

To perform a one-level sort

- Select the column or entries in the column to sort.

- Click Tools, Sort.

  ✓ NOTE: A first-time help screen appears. You can choose not to display it in the future.

- Click Sort only the highlighted information.

  OR

  Click Sort all the information.

  ✓ NOTE: This is the more widely used option.

- Click OK.

- Select the column to sort by.

- Click Ascending.

  OR

  Click Descending.

- Click Header row to ignore the first row if it is a heading.

  OR

  Click No header row to have all rows sorted.

- Click Sort.

- A **multiple-level sort** arranges data in the most important column first. Then the data in the other column(s) is sorted. Works allows you to have up to a three-column sort. A two-level sort on the spreadsheet in this exercise can be accomplished by performing the first sort on column B (LOCATION) and then a second (secondary) sort on column A (AGENT). Works first arranges the LOCATION in alphabetical order, and then alphabetizes the AGENT names of any employees within the same location. *(See sample of secondary sort below.)*

Secondary sort   Primary sort

KIM	BAYSIDE
CRIMMINS	ELMHURST
GARCIA	ELMHURST
MARTIN	ELMHURST
SINGER	FOREST HILLS
JACKSON	JAMAICA
LINDNER	JAMAICA
ROBERTS	JAMAICA
BOOKER	KINGSTON
TROTTA	MASPETH
KHALFAN	REGO PARK

Alphabetical order within each location

To perform a multiple-level sort

- Select entries to sort.

- Follows steps for one-level sort.

- In Sort dialog box, click Advanced.

- Click Sort by to sort the first column in either ascending or descending order.

- Click Then by to sort the second column.

- Click Then by to sort the remaining column.

- Click Header row to ignore the first row if it is a header.

  OR

  Click No header row to have all rows sorted.

- Click Sort

■ If there are formulas in the sorted information, Works will adjust the relative cell references after sorting.

In this exercise, you will recall the INTERBORO REAL ESTATE COMMISSION REPORT and add information. Once the new information is included, you will be asked to perform two sorts and save the spreadsheet under different names.

EXERCISE DIRECTIONS:

1. Open ⌨**COMM**, or open ▭**SS COMM.26**.

2. Insert three rows and add the following information:

KHALFAN	REGO PARK	255000	3.00%
KIM	BAYSIDE	666000	4.00%
SINGER	FOREST HILLS	355000	3.00%

3. Copy formulas to calculate COMM., BONUS and TOTAL COMPENSATION for the three new rows.

4. Format all new data and labels so they are consistent with existing formats.

5. Delete the row containing the information for WEEBLES.

6. Name the following ranges:

C7:C17	SALES
E7:E17	COMM
F7:F17	BONUS
G7:G17	COMP

7. Recalculate TOTALS using named ranges.

8. Enter the following labels:

A20	AVERAGES
A21	LOWEST
A22	HIGHEST

9. Adjust column widths as necessary.

10. Provide formulas to calculate the AVERAGE, LOWEST and HIGHEST values in the COMM., BONUS and TOTAL COMPENSATION columns.

11. Create a table listing named ranges starting in A25.

12. Format the spreadsheet as needed.

13. Perform the following sorts, then save the worksheet under a different name as directed.

    One-Level Sort:

    - Sort the spreadsheet by SALES in descending order to see the highest priced houses listed first.
      - ✓ NOTE: Remember to sort all the data, not just the highlighted column.

    - Save the file as **COMM1**.

    - Print one copy with gridlines to fit on one page.

    Two-Level Sort:

    - Sort the spreadsheet in ascending order by LOCATION, and then in ascending order by AGENT name.

    - Save the file as **COMM2**.

    - Print one copy with gridlines to fit on one page.

14. Close the document window.

	A	B	C	D	E	F	G
1	INTERBORO REAL ESTATE						
2	COMMISSION REPORT						
3							
4				COMM.			TOTAL
5	AGENT	LOCATION	SALES	RATE	COMM.	BONUS	COMPENSATION
6							
7	MARTIN	ELMHURST	$640,000	4.00%	$25,600	$3,200	$28,800
8	ROBERTS	JAMAICA	$450,000	3.00%	$13,500	$0	$13,500
9	CRIMMINS	ELMHURST	$125,000	3.00%	$3,750	$0	$3,750
10	LINDNER	JAMAICA	$745,000	4.00%	$29,800	$3,725	$33,525
11	WEEBLES	MASPETH	$0	3.00%	$0	$0	$0
12	GARCIA	ELMHURST	$550,000	4.00%	$22,000	$2,750	$24,750
13	JACKSON	JAMAICA	$210,000	3.00%	$6,300	$0	$6,300
14	BOOKER	KINGSTON	$435,000	4.00%	$17,400	$0	$17,400
15	TROTTA	MASPETH	$745,000	4.00%	$29,800	$3,725	$33,525
16							
17	TOTALS		$3,900,000		$148,150	$13,400	$161,550

Insert rows *Delete row*

Add labels A20 AVERAGES
A21 LOWEST
A22 HIGHEST

SORT

One-Level sort

1. Select entries to sort.
2. Click **Tools** .... Alt + T
3. Click **Sort** .... R
4. Click **Sort only the highlighted information.** .... Alt + O

   OR

   Click **Sort all the information.** Alt + R
5. Click **OK** .... Enter
6. Select the column to sort by.
7. Click **Ascending** .... Alt + A

   OR

   Click **Descending** .... Alt + D

8. Click **Header row** .... Alt + H
   to ignore the first row if it is a heading.

   OR

   Click **No header row** .... Alt + N
   to have all rows sorted.
9. Click **Sort** .... Alt + O

Multiple-Level sort

1. Select multiple columns to sort.
2. Repeat steps 2-5, **One-Level Sort**, above.
3. Click **Advanced** .... Alt + V
4. Click **Sort by** .... Alt + S
   to sort the first column.

5. Click **Ascending** .... Alt + A

   OR

   Click **Descending** .... Alt + D
6. Click **Then by** .... Alt + T
   to sort the second column.
7. Click **Then by** .... Alt + B
   to sort the remaining column.
8. Click **Header row** .... Alt + H
   to ignore the first row if it is a heading

   OR

   Click **No header row** .... Alt + N
   to have all rows sorted.
9. Click **Sort** .... Alt + O

EXERCISE 27

■ **Enhance the Spreadsheet (Font, Font Size, Typestyle)**

Font   Font size   Bold   Underline

Italics

NOTES:

Enhance the Spreadsheet

■ As in the Word Processor, you can change the appearance of printed data (text, numbers, symbols) by changing the font, font size and typestyle.

  In the Word Processor section you learned to apply these enhancements by using the keyboard, mouse or a combination of both. Because Works is an integrated program, you are able follow the same procedures in the spreadsheet.

■ You can apply font, font size and typestyle changes to a cell, range, column, row or an entire spreadsheet.

■ To change the fonts, font sizes, colors and/or typestyles of existing data, you must first select the cell or range of cells you wish to change.

■ The Spreadsheet Toolbar contains typestyle buttons (bold, italics and underline) as well as font and font size drop-down lists.

■ The default font is Arial and the default font size is 10 point. If you have a large spreadsheet that you want to print on one page, you can select a smaller font size to decrease the size of the spreadsheet.

Your supervisor is presenting the sales data from the semi-annual sales report at the next sales department meeting. She will be projecting the spreadsheet onto a screen and has asked you to improve the attractiveness and readability of the data.

EXERCISE DIRECTIONS:

1. Open ⌨**BONUS**, or open 🖫**SS BONUS.27**.

2. Change the entire spreadsheet to a serif font.

3. Change the orientation to Portrait.

4. Make necessary changes to font size, margins and column widths so that spreadsheet fits on one page.

5. Change title and subtitle to 12 point bold and italics.

6. Change all column headings to bold.

7. Preview the spreadsheet.

8. Resave the file.

9. Print one copy with gridlines.

10. Close the file.

   ✓ *NOTE: If you are changing the font, font size, color or typestyle to existing text, first select the text before performing the following procedures.*

12 pt. bold and italics

Bold column headings

	A	B	C	D	E	F	G	H	I
1				SEMI-ANNUAL SALES REPORT					
2				JANUARY - JUNE					
3									
4	MONTH						MONTHLY	HIGHEST	LOWEST
5	ENDING	ROBERTSON	BELDEMBERG	HERNANDEZ	OLSON	CHEN	TOTALS	MONTHLY	MONTHLY
6									
7	1/31/94	2000.00	1540.00	1854.00	3222.00	2876.00	11492.00	3222.00	1540.00
8	2/28/94	1846.00	1100.00	856.23	1976.00	654.56	6432.79	1976.00	654.56
9	3/31/94	1234.87	567.20	777.77	1287.00	2569.50	6436.34	2569.50	567.20
10	4/30/94	3180.00	987.35	1345.54	876.50	1900.00	8289.39	3180.00	876.50
11	5/31/94	843.75	1675.00	1234.00	2121.21	712.00	6585.96	2121.21	712.00
12	6/30/94	876.00	398.00	1986.00	775.00	982.50	5017.50	1986.00	398.00
13									
14	TOTALS	9980.62	6267.55	8053.54	10257.71	9694.56	44253.98	15054.71	4748.26
15	HIGHEST	3180.00	1675.00	1986.00	3222.00	2876.00	11492.00	3222.00	1540.00
16	LOWEST	843.75	398.00	777.77	775.00	654.56	5017.50	1976.00	398.00
17									
18	BONUS	299.42	62.68	80.54	307.73	290.84			

Decrease font size to fit on one page

CHANGE FONT

Shift + Ctrl + F

1. Click **Format** .... `Alt`+`O`
2. Click **Font and Style**...................... `F`
3. Select a font from the **Font** .... `↓``↑` drop-down list box.
4. Preview selected font in sample box.
5. Click **OK** .... `Enter`

OR

1. Click Toolbar **Font** box .... `▼`
2. Delete existing name............. *font name* and type desired font name.
3. Press **Enter** .... `Enter`

OR

1. Click down arrow next to **Font** box.... `▼` on Toolbar.
2. Double-click desired font name.

CHANGE FONT SIZE

Shift + Ctrl + P

1. Click **Format** .... `Alt`+`O`
2. Click **Font and Style**...................... `F`
3. Choose a size from the **Size** list box . `▼`
4. Double click desired font size.

OR

1. Click **Size** box .... `Shift`+`Ctrl`+`P` on Toolbar
2. Delete existing size...................*font size* and enter new font size.

OR

1. Click down arrow on **Font Size** box . `▼`
2. Double-click on desired font size.

CHANGE TYPESTYLES (BOLD, ITALICS, UNDERLINE)

Ctrl + B, Ctrl + I, Ctrl + U

1. Place highlight where typestyle change is to begin.
2. Click **Format** .... `Alt`+`O`
3. Click **Font and Style**...................... `F`
4. Make desired changes.
5. Click **OK** .... `Enter`

OR

6. Click desired Toolbar button(s):

   • **Bold** .... `B`

   • **Italics**... `/`

   • **Underline**................................... `u`

7. Type data .... *data*
8. Click appropriate Toolbar button to discontinue typestyle

   OR

   Select desired range, then apply desired typestyle.

■ **Borders** ■ **Patterns**

NOTES:

Borders

- Adding **visual enhancements** to a spreadsheet presents the information more attractively, improves the readability and focuses the reader's attention on certain areas.

- The **Border** feature allows you to:
  - add lines on the top, bottom, right or left of a cell or range of cells.
  - outline a cell or range of cells.
  - add color to your border.

- It may be difficult to see a border if the gridlines are turned on. You can eliminate the gridlines on the screen, on the printout or both.

- Before placing a border, you must select the desired cell or range of cells to be outlined. Click Format, Border to access the tab shown below.

- While the cell contents can be deleted, borders can only be **cleared** by selecting the border option you want to remove. Click the cell you wish to clear and access the Borders tab. Deselect each border option you want to remove.

  ✓ NOTE: *If desired, you can customize the Toolbar to display the Border button.*

Patterns

- Works allows you to fill an area of a spreadsheet with a **pattern** or **color**.

- You must first select the cell or range in which you wish to place a pattern. Click Format, Shading to access the Shading tab shown below.

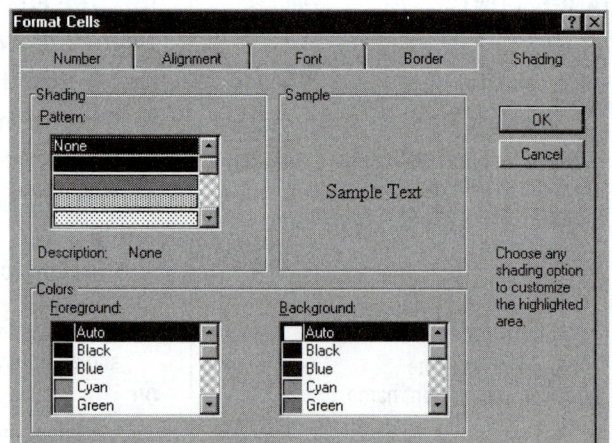

- A solid pattern is the default. You can change the pattern, foreground color or background color of a cell, range of cells or the entire spreadsheet. Be careful to select a pattern that does not adversely affect the readability of the data. Check the result in the sample box before finalizing your changes.

> *Your supervisor recognizes your abilities at designing and enhancing the department's spreadsheets and has asked that you prepare the WOODWORKS FURNITURE COMPANY SALES AND SALARY REPORT (WOOD file) for her next presentation. She asks that you add borders and patterns to improve the spreadsheet's appearance.*

EXERCISE DIRECTIONS:

1. Open 🖳WOOD, or open 🖫SS WOOD.28.

2. Compare Illustration A with the updated spreadsheet in Illustration B. Make the changes to your spreadsheet as indicated below so that it looks like Illustration B:

   a. Center all column headings.

   b. Center column A data.

   c. Format columns C-F for Commas (,) with two decimal places.

   d. Adjust column widths as needed.

   e. Change title and subtitle to a serif 12 point bold font.

   ✓ NOTE: Click cell A1 to edit title; select cell B1 for subtitle.

   f. Outline title and subtitle.

   g. Bold column headings.

   h. Include wide lines below column headings.

   i. Italicize column B data for rows 7-11.

   j. Select a light shade for column D data for rows 7-11.

   k. Select a medium-shade for column E data for rows 7-11.

   l. Select a darker-shade for column F data for rows 7 11.

   m. Include a vertical line between columns C and D.

   n. Include a single line below columns C-F data.

   o. Include a double line below TOTALS.

   p. Insert a blank row below TOTALS.

   q. Eliminate the gridlines on the display.

3. Preview the spreadsheet.

4. Resave the file.

5. Print one copy *without gridlines* to fit on one page.

6. Close the file.

ILLUSTRATION A

EMP. NO.	NAME	BASE SALARY	SALES	5% COMMISSION	QUARTERLY SALARY
	WOODWORKS FURNITURE COMPANY				
	SALES AND SALARY QUARTERLY REPORT -- APRIL-JUNE				
101	ABRAMS, JUDY	1500.00	113456.67	5672.83	7172.83
102	CHANG, PETER	1500.00	150654.87	7532.74	9032.74
103	LINSEY, KELLY	1500.00	234765.36	11738.27	13238.27
104	JOHNSON, LETOYA	1500.00	89765.43	4488.27	5988.27
105	RIVERA, TONY	1500.00	287987.76	14399.39	15899.39
	TOTALS	7500.00	876630.09	43831.50	51331.50
	COUNT	5			
	AVERAGE	1500.00	175326.02	8766.30	10266.30
	HIGHEST	1500.00	287987.76	14399.39	15899.39
	LOWEST	1500.00	89765.43	4488.27	5988.27

ILLUSTRATION B

WOODWORKS FURNITURE COMPANY				
SALES AND SALARY QUARTERLY REPORT -- APRIL-JUNE				

EMP. NO.	NAME	BASE SALARY	SALES	5% COMMISSION	QUARTERLY SALARY
101	ABRAMS, JUDY	1,500.00	113,456.67	5,672.83	7,172.83
102	CHANG, PETER	1,500.00	150,654.87	7,532.74	9,032.74
103	LINSEY, KELLY	1,500.00	234,765.36	11,738.27	13,238.27
104	JOHNSON, LETOYA	1,500.00	89,765.43	4,488.27	5,988.27
105	RIVERA, TONY	1,500.00	287,987.76	14,399.39	15,899.39
	TOTALS	7,500.00	876,630.09	43,831.50	51,331.50
	COUNT	5			
	AVERAGE	1,500.00	175,326.02	8,766.30	10,266.30
	HIGHEST	1,500.00	287,987.76	14,399.39	15,899.39
	LOWEST	1,500.00	89,765.43	4,488.27	5,988.27

BORDERS

1. Select cell or range of cells.
2. Click **F**o**rmat** .... Alt + O
3. Click **B**order .... B
4. Click desired border option:
   - **Outline** .... Alt + O
   - **Top** .... Alt + T
   - **Bottom** .... Alt + M
   - **Left** .... Alt + L
   - **Right** .... Alt + R
5. Click desired **Line Style** .... Alt + I
6. Click **Color** .... Alt + C
7. Click desired color.

   ✓NOTE: *Borders print in black unless you have a color printer.*

8. Click **OK** .... Enter

REMOVE BORDERS

1. Select cell or range of cells from which borders are to be removed.
2. Click **F**o**rmat** .... Alt + O
3. Click **B**order .... B
4. Click border style you want to remove.
   - **Outline** .... Alt + O
   - **Top** .... Alt + T
   - **Bottom** .... Alt + M
   - **Left** .... Alt + L
   - **Right** .... Alt + R
5. Repeat for each border to be removed.
6. Click **OK** .... Enter

SHADING

1. Select cell or range of cells.
2. Click **F**o**rmat** .... Alt + O
3. Click **Sh**ading .... D
4. Click arrow .... Alt + P
   on **Pattern** drop down list.
5. Click desired pattern.

   ✓NOTE: *The color of the solid pattern is determined by the foreground color.*

6. Click **OK** .... Enter

REMOVE PATTERN

1. Repeat steps 1-3, **Shading**, above.
2. Click on **Pattern** box .... Alt + P
3. Click **None**.
4. Click **OK** .... Enter

EXERCISE **29**

■ AutoFormat

NOTES:

AutoFormat

- The **AutoFormat** feature allows you to choose from ready-made formats for your spreadsheet. This is a quick and efficient method of enhancing your spreadsheet.

- You may wish to select a specific format to emphasize one area of a spreadsheet. The AutoFormats can be applied to a cell, range of cells or an entire spreadsheet. All areas to be formatted must be selected before applying the desired format.

- The available formats offer different fonts, font sizes, typestyles, borders and other features to make your spreadsheet more attractive. You make your format selection from the AutoFormat dialog box shown below:

- The Example box displays the format you have chosen.

- You can remove the format by immediately selecting Undo from the Edit menu.

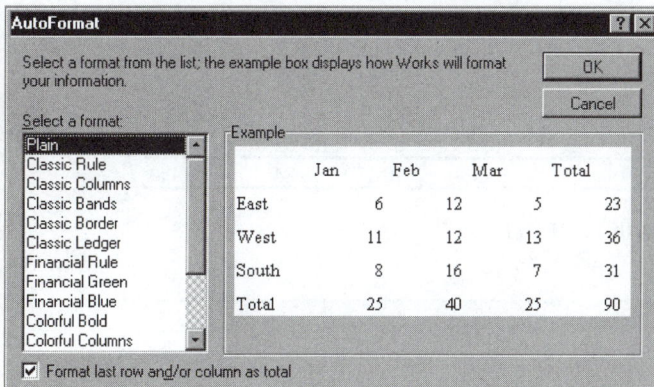

AutoFormat [? ✕]

Select a format from the list; the example box displays how Works will format your information.

| OK |
| Cancel |

Select a format:

| Plain |
| Classic Rule |
| Classic Columns |
| Classic Bands |
| Classic Border |
| Classic Ledger |
| Financial Rule |
| Financial Green |
| Financial Blue |
| Colorful Bold |
| Colorful Columns |

Example

	Jan	Feb	Mar	Total
East	6	12	5	23
West	11	12	13	36
South	8	16	7	31
Total	25	40	25	90

☑ Format last row and/or column as total

AUTOFORMAT

1. Select area to apply format.
2. Click **Format** .... Alt + O
3. Click **AutoFormat** .... M
4. Choose desired format.

REMOVE AN AUTOFORMAT

Ctrl + Z

NOTE: *To return to original format, you must select Undo command immediately after applying the format. Otherwise, you will have to close the document and reopen it.*

1. Click **Edit** .... Alt + E
2. Click **Undo Format** .... U

> *In this exercise you will use the AutoFormat feature to enhance the Burlington National Bank Payroll.*

EXERCISE DIRECTIONS:

1. Open 🖳**SALARY**, or open 🖫**SS SALARY.29**.

2. Make the following changes to the spreadsheet.

   a. Bold the main title and subtitle in both spreadsheets.

   b. Change all two-line column headings in both spreadsheets to one-line column headings as shown in the illustration.

   c. Delete the blank rows created by this change.

   d. Adjust all column widths as needed.

3. Select the first spreadsheet starting in row 4, cells (A4:I14).

4. Access AutoFormat and click Colorful Columns.

5. Select second spreadsheet starting in row 20, cells (A19:I29).

6. Access AutoFormat and click Classic Columns.

7. Eliminate the gridlines on display.

8. Preview the spreadsheet.

9. Save the file as **SALARY 2**.

10. Print one copy *without gridlines* to fit on one page.

11. Close the document window.

	A	B	C	D	E	F	G	H	I
1				BURLINGTON NATIONAL BANK PAYROLL					
2				FOR THE WEEK ENDING MAY 15, 199-					
3									
4	*EMPLOYEE*	*ID NO.*	*S. S. NO.*	*HOURLY RATE*	*HOURS WORKED*	*GROSS PAY*	*F. I. C. A*	*F. W. T.*	*NET PAY*
5									
6	CARTER	12567	069-65-4532	5.55	15	83.25	6.37	16.65	60.23
7	FINCKEL	12750	123-75-7623	7.25	32	232.00	17.75	46.40	167.85
8	JAMISON	12816	107-53-6754	6.18	16	98.88	7.56	19.78	71.54
9	MILLS	12915	103-87-5698	4.66	28	130.48	9.98	26.10	94.40
10	POTTER	12345	127-78-0045	6.57	12	78.84	6.03	15.77	57.04
11	SAMUELS	12716	043-67-7600	8.65	21	181.65	13.90	36.33	131.42
12									
13	TOTALS					805.10	61.59	161.02	582.49
14	AVERAGES					134.18	10.27	26.84	97.08

Colorful columns

	A	B	C	D	E	F	G	H	I
15									
16				BURLINGTON NATIONAL BANK PAYROLL					
17				FOR THE WEEK ENDING MAY 22, 199-					
18									
19	EMPLOYEE	ID NO.	S. S. NO.	HOURLY RATE	HOURS WORKED	GROSS PAY	F. I. C. A.	F. W. T.	NET PAY
20									
21	CARTER	12567	069-65-4532	5.55	22	122.10	9.34	24.42	88.34
22	JAMISON	12816	107-53-6754	6.18	33	203.94	15.60	40.79	147.55
23	MILLS	12915	103-87-5698	4.66	21	97.86	7.49	19.57	70.80
24	NELSON	12967	146-93-0069	6.25	16	100.00	7.65	20.00	72.35
25	POTTER	12345	127-78-0045	6.57	18	118.26	9.05	23.65	85.56
26	SAMUELS	12716	043-67-7600	8.65	28	242.20	18.53	48.44	175.23
27									
28	TOTALS					884.36	67.65	176.87	639.83
29	AVERAGES					147.39	11.28	29.48	106.64

Classic columns

EXERCISE **30**

Lesson 4 – Summary

As an active investor in the stock market, you would like to evaluate your portfolio each month.

EXERCISE DIRECTIONS:

- In order to create the spreadsheet in this exercise, you will need to know the following terms:

Cost	The amount you paid for a stock or bond.
Commission	The fee paid to the broker for selling you the stock.
Market Value	The current price of a traded security.
Portfolio	A group of investments in stocks and/or bonds.
Percent of Portfolio	The percent of each stock's value to the total portfolio's value. For example, if the entire portfolio is worth (at the current market value) $40,951.00, and the Rainbow Fund stock is worth $8,826.00, then it represents 21.55% of the entire portfolio. (Divide the individual stock's current market value by the current market value of the entire portfolio.)
Profit or Loss	Determined by subtracting the cost of the stock from the current market value. Unfortunately, this can result in a negative number.
Percent of Profit/Loss	Represents the percent of profit or loss for each stock within the portfolio. This is determined by dividing the profit and loss for each stock by the cost of the stock.

1. Create a new document for the Spreadsheet entering the labels and values in the exact cell locations shown in the illustration.

2. Adjust column widths as necessary.

3. Change the left and right margins to 0.5".

4. Name the following ranges:

F8:F13	TOTAL
H8:H13	CMV
I8:I13	$PL

5. Find:
   a. TOTAL COST
   b. CURRENT MARKET VALUE
   c. $ PROFIT OR LOSS
   d. % PROFIT OR LOSS for each stock (based on TOTAL COST)
   e. Totals of TOTAL COST, CURRENT MARKET VALUE, $ PROFIT OR LOSS columns (use named ranges to calculate totals)
   f. % PROFIT OR LOSS for the entire portfolio
   g. % OF PORTFOLIO (based on total CURRENT MARKET VALUE)
   h. % OF PORTFOLIO column total

6. Format appropriately.

7. Enhance the spreadsheet using a variety of borders, patterns, fonts, font sizes and typestyles.

8. Sort the spreadsheet by the DATE BOUGHT, starting with the most recent date.

9. Save the file; name it **FOLIO**.

10. Print one copy *without gridlines* in Landscape mode.

11. Close the document window.

Questions:

   a. Which stock is most profitable? Least profitable?

   b. Which stock represents the largest percentage of the portfolio? Smallest percentage?

   c. What is your recommendation for future sales/purchases of your currently held stocks?

	A	B	C	D	E	F	G	H	I	J	K
1				(YOUR NAME)							
2			MONTHLY PORTFOLIO ANALYSIS - OCTOBER, 199-								
3											
4	DATE	STOCK	QUANTITY	UNIT	COMMISSION	TOTAL	CURRENT	CURRENT	$ PROFIT	% PROFIT	% OF
5	BOUGHT	NAME		COST		COST	UNIT	MARKET	OR LOSS	OR LOSS	PORTFOLIO
6							PRICE	VALUE			
7											
8	2/13/95	RAINBOW FUND	300	23.54	0		29.42				
9	3/25/94	KAISER AL.	100	15.25	35		14.75				
10	7/22/93	CAPT. MOTORES	150	64.75	127.5		55.5				
11	11/14/92	TEX INC.	250	43	135.76		56				
12	1/18/93	GTTE	125	32	48.25		31				
13	5/5/93	IBBM	50	95	52.55		89				
14											
15		TOTALS									

EXERCISE **31**

■ **Create a Single Series Bar Chart, a Line Chart and a Pie Chart**
■ **Change Titles** ■ **Rename Charts** ■ **Save Charts**

New Chart

NOTES:

Create a Single Series Bar Chart, a Line Chart and a Pie Chart

■ **Charts** are a way of visually presenting spreadsheet data. This visual or graphic representation helps you see trends and relationships more clearly.

■ Works includes 12 basic chart types: area charts, bar charts, line charts, pie charts, stacked line charts, X-Y scatter charts, radar charts, combination charts, 3-D area charts, 3-D bar charts, 3-D line charts and 3-D pie charts.

■ In this book you will learn to create and modify the three most common types of charts.

Bar Chart
Uses rectangles to represent the relationship between two or more values in the spreadsheet. The height of each bar is proportional to its corresponding value.

Line Chart
Uses data points to represent the values in the spreadsheet. Trends are easily illustrated since lines connect the data points and show changes over time.

Pie Chart
Uses a circle that is divided into segments to show the relationship of each value in a data range to the entire data range. The size of each wedge represents the percentage each value contributes to the total

■ Each chart may contain the following elements:

Axes
There are two axes, the horizontal x-axis and the vertical y-axis.

The horizontal **x-axis** represents items or categories being compared, such as time periods, products or persons. This axis contains the category labels that identify the data being compared. The category labels are obtained from the spreadsheet row or column labels.

The vertical **y-axis** represents the unit of measurement used for comparison. The scale numbers are entered automatically, based on the data (value (Y) series) being charted.   Pie charts do not have axes and may have only one value (Y) series.

Legends
Serve as keys to interpret the chart. A legend appears at the bottom of a chart and identifies the markers representing the data. Pie charts do not have legends. Use labels to identify the slices.

Labels
There are two types of labels. **Data labels** identify data points in a chart; **category labels** identify the type of data represented along the x-axis. (*Data labels are presented in Exercise 34.*)

Scale
Displays the units of measurement, the minimum and maximum number and the intervals between the numbers.

Titles

Identify the chart contents. There are main titles, subtitles, x-axis titles and y-axis titles. The New Chart feature allows you to create a main title. All other titles can be entered once the chart is created.

■ Charts are directly related to the data in a spreadsheet. Works uses the selected data range(s) in a worksheet to create a chart.

Note the spreadsheet data and its relationship to the various chart elements for each type of chart.

SPREADSHEET DATA

	A	B	C
1	CARSON CORNERS HIGH SCHOOL			← Title
2	STUDENT POPULATION			← Subtitle
3				
4		MALES		← Legend
5	FRESHMEN	175		
6	SOPHOMORES	255		← First value (Y) series
7	JUNIORS	235		
8	SENIORS	205		

Category labels

BAR CHART

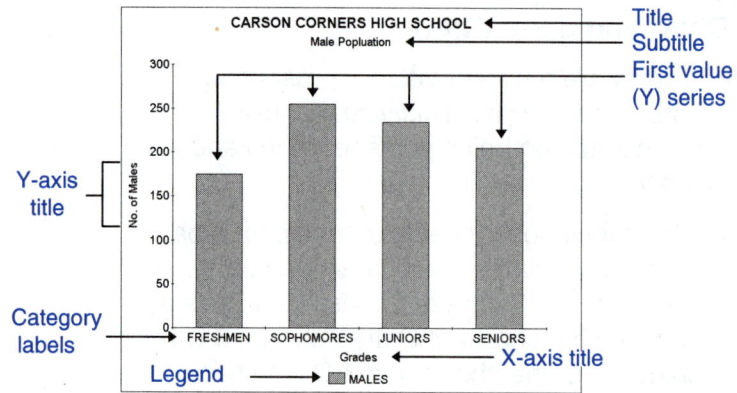

LINE CHART

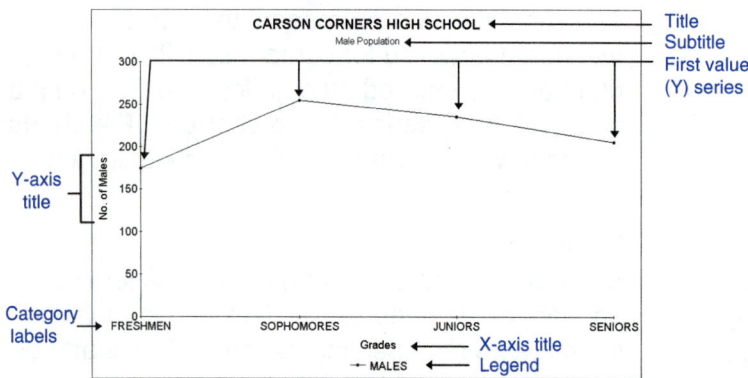

PIE CHART

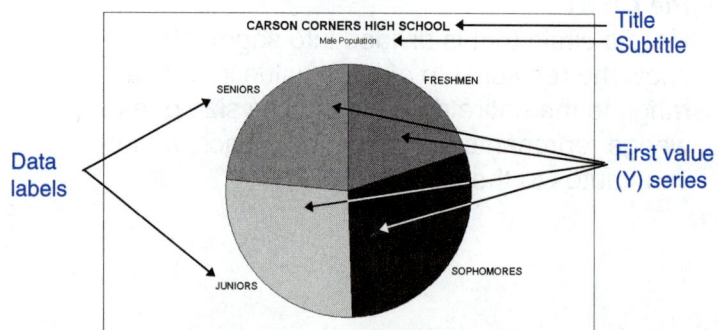

- To create a new chart, select the desired range and click the New Chart button on the Toolbar *(see illustration, page 257)*. Works automatically charts the selected data.

If you select the column or row headings when defining the data to use in the chart, those headings are used to create labels and a legend for the chart.

The spreadsheet's orientation determines how your column or row headings will be used. In general, if the selected value series is in a column, the row labels serve as category labels (see Illustration A below). If the value series is in a row, the column headings serve as category labels (see Illustration B below).

ILLUSTRATION A

CARSON CORNERS HIGH SCHOOL	
STUDENT POPULATION	
	MALES
FRESHMEN	175
SOPHOMORES	255
JUNIORS	235
SENIORS	205

Selected value series in a column

ILLUSTRATION B

	FRESHMEN	SOPHOMORES	JUNIORS	SENIORS
MALES	175	255	235	205

Value series in a row

To create a chart:

- Select the data in the spreadsheet to be included in the chart.
- Click <u>T</u>ools.
- Click Create <u>N</u>ew Chart.

    OR

Click the New Chart button on the Toolbar

✓NOTE: *Works automatically creates a bar chart.*

- Click OK to accept the chart.

OR

Make changes in the dialog box shown below.

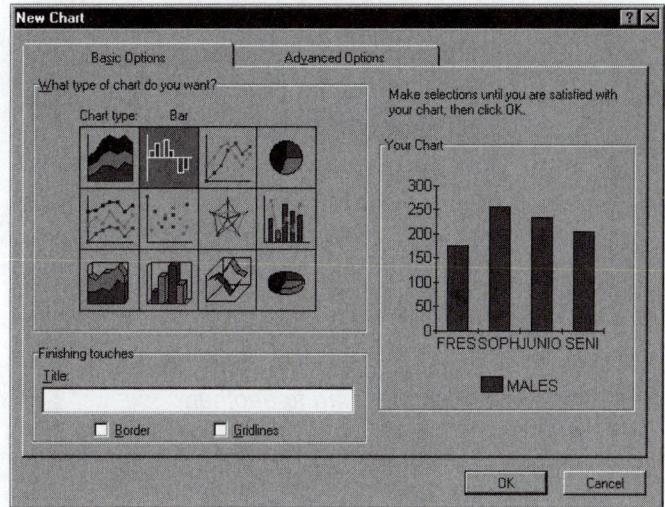

- The New Chart dialog box allows you to make the following changes to the chart:

  - Choose the chart type.
  - Provide a chart title.
  - Add a border or gridlines.
  - Choose advanced features to:

    Alter the way the spreadsheet is organized.

    Create a legend.

    Create category labels.

- When Works creates a chart, it uses the number of rows and columns to determine the layout of that chart. However, you can change the program-determined layout. In addition, you can create a subtitle, axis titles and further enhance the chart after it is created.

Change Views

■ You can easily switch between the chart and its related spreadsheet. If more than one chart was created for the spreadsheet, click Vıew, Chart to access the following dialog box. Select the desired chart from the list.

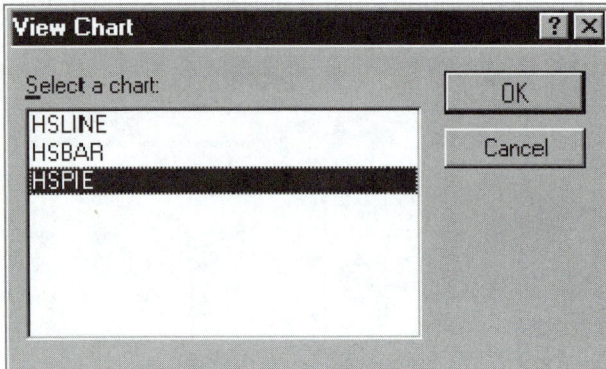

```
View Chart                              ? X
Select a chart:
HSLINE                          [  OK  ]
HSBAR
HSPIE                           [ Cancel ]
```

✓ NOTE: You can also press Ctrl+F6 to switch from one chart to another.

Change Titles

■ Once the chart is generated, you can change the title you entered in the New Chart dialog box. In addition, you can supply a subtitle, x-axis title and y-axis title.

✓ NOTE: If the titles do not fully display, place the highlight on a corner of the window and drag the double-sided arrow to stretch the window to the necessary size.

Rename Charts

■ Works automatically names charts as they are created (Chart 1, Chart 2, etc.), which makes them easy to locate and manipulate. Chart names can, however, be changed to make them more descriptive.

Save Charts

■ Charts are saved with their corresponding spreadsheets. You can create and save up to eight charts for every spreadsheet.

CREATE A CHART FROM A SINGLE SERIES (DATA RANGE)

1. Create (or open) the spreadsheet from which the chart is to be made.
2. Highlight (select) range to chart.
3. Click **New Chart** button .... [lll.] on the Toolbar.
   OR
   a. Click **Tools** .... Alt + T
   b. Click **Create New Chart** .... N
4. Click desired chart type .... Alt + W from list in **New Chart** dialog box.
   ✓ NOTE: A bar chart is the default.
5. Click **Title** text box. .... Alt + T
6. Type the title .... title as desired.
7. Click **Border** .... Alt + B if desired.
8. Click **Gridlines** .... Alt + G if desired.
9. Click **Advanced Options** ...... Alt + V if desired.
10. Check sample box to see if spreadsheet is charted correctly.
11. Click **OK** .... Enter
    Chart is displayed.

CHANGE TITLES

1. Click **Edit** .... Alt + E
2. Click **Titles** .... T
3. Click **Chart Title** C
4. Type a title .... Title as desired.
   OR
   Change existing title.
5. Click **Subtitle** .... Alt + S
6. Type a subtitle .... Subtitle as desired.
7. Click **Horizontal (X) Axis** ..... Alt + O
8. Enter a title for the X axis. ...... title
9. Click **Vertical (Y) Axis** ...... Alt + V
10. Enter a title for Y axis. .... title
11. Click **Right Vertical Axis** ..... Alt + R
12. Enter a title for the right Y axis ..... title
13. Click **OK** .... Enter
14. Click **File** .... Alt + F
15. Click **Close** C

(RE)NAME CHARTS

Works automatically assigns a name to any chart you create (e.g., [Chart1]). Use this procedure to change the name to something more descriptive.

1. Click **Tools** .... Alt + T
2. Click **Rename Chart**.
3. Click on chart to rename.
4. Click **Type a name below:** ..... Alt + T
5. Enter new name .... name up to 15 characters.
6. Click **Rename** .... Alt + R
7. To rename other charts repeat steps 3-5.
8. Click **OK** .... Enter

CHANGING VIEWS

1. Click **View** .... Alt + V
2. Click **Chart** C
3. If more than one chart, click desired chart.
4. Click **OK** .... Enter
5. Click **View** .... Alt + V
6. Click **Spreadsheet** .... S

In this exercise, you will create a bar chart, a line chart and a pie chart using Works automatic charting feature with titles showing student population data for the Carson Corners High School. Check your results with the illustrated solutions following the Exercise Directions.

EXERCISE DIRECTIONS:

1. Create a new document for the Spreadsheet, entering the labels and values in the exact cell locations shown in the illustration.

2. Select cells A4:B8, and create a *bar chart*.

3. Enter the following chart title: CARSON CORNERS HIGH SCHOOL

4. Add a Border.

5. Click Advanced Options tab and organize your chart is as follows:
   - Series goes Down
   - First row contains Legend text
   - First column contains Category labels

6. View the chart layout in the sample box, then click OK.

7. Click Edit, Titles and edit the chart as follows:
   Subtitle: Male Population
   Horizontal (X) Axis: Grades
   Vertical (Y) axis: No. of Males

8. Check your result with Solution A.

9. Close the chart.

10. Repeat steps 2-7 to create a *line chart*.

11. Check your result with Solution B

12. Close the chart.

13. Repeat steps 2-7 to create a *pie chart*.

14. Check your result with Solution C.

15. Close the chart.
    ✓ NOTE: A pie chart does not contains axes.

16. Edit the chart names as follows:
    - Change the name of Chart 1 to HSBAR.
    - Change the name of Chart 2 to HSLINE.
    - Change the name of Chart 3 to HSPIE.

17. Save the file, name it **HS**.
    ✓ NOTE: The three charts will be saved with the spreadsheet.

18. Close the document window.

	A	B	C
1	CARSON CORNERS HIGH SCHOOL		
2	STUDENT POPULATION		
3			
4		MALES	
5	FRESHMEN	175	
6	SOPHOMORES	255	
7	JUNIORS	235	
8	SENIORS	205	

ILLUSTRATED SOLUTION A
BAR CHART

CARSON CORNERS HIGH SCHOOL
Male Population

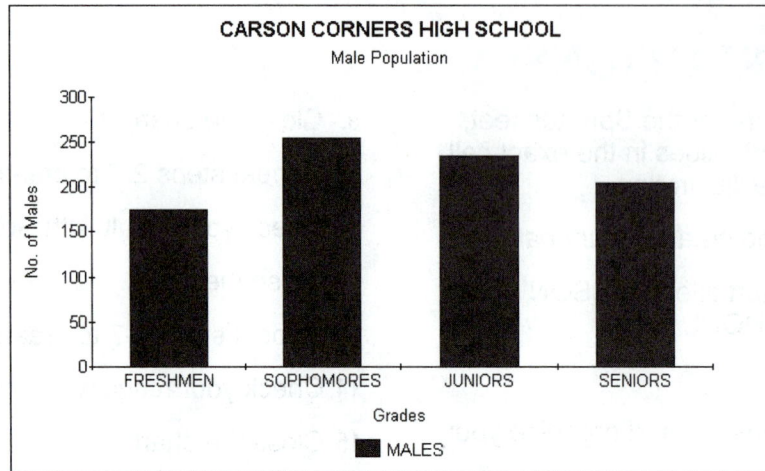

ILLUSTRATED SOLUTION B
LINE CHART

CARSON CORNERS HIGH SCHOOL
Male Population

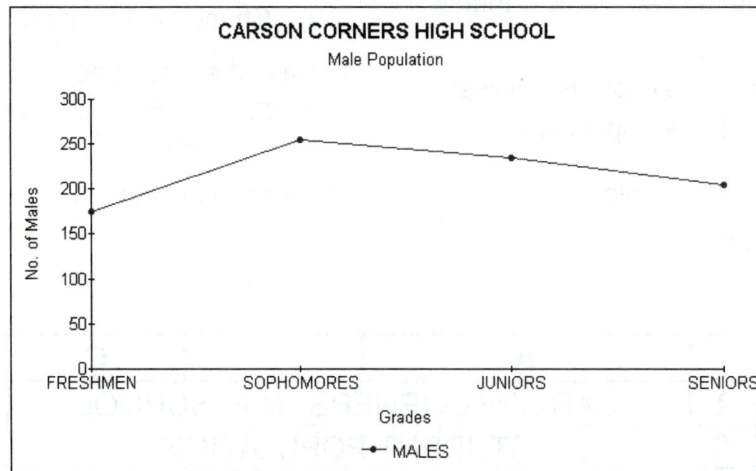

ILLUSTRATED SOLUTION C
PIE CHART

CARSON CORNERS HIGH SCHOOL
Male Population

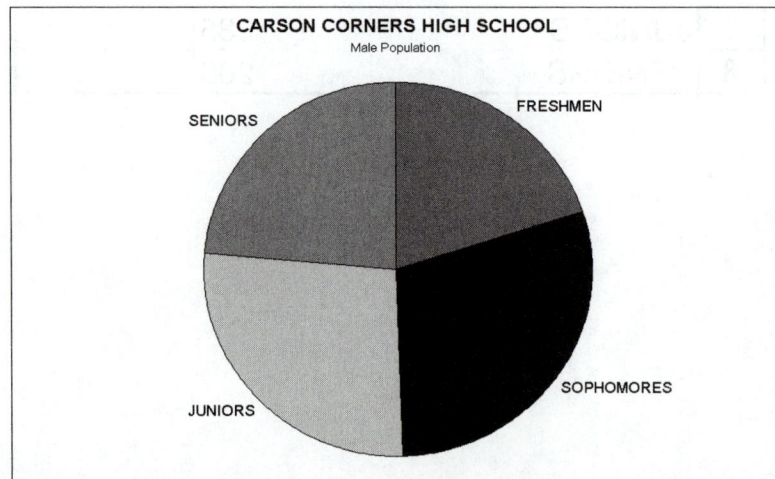

EXERCISE **32**

- Create a Multiple-Series Bar Chart ■ Charting Toolbar
- Change a Chart Type ■ Stacked Bar Chart ■ Print a Chart

Bar Chart | Pie Chart | Mixed Chart | 3-D Bar Chart | 3-D Pie Chart | Address Book

Line Chart | Scatter Chart | 3-D Area Chart | 3-D Line Chart | Go to 1st series

NOTES:

Create a Multiple-Series Bar Chart

- **Multiple-series charts** are used to compare sets of values to one another. Works allows you to chart up to six value (Y) series.

  The spreadsheet example shown below has row labels in column A as the category x series, and the numeric data in columns B and C as value (Y) series 1 and Value (Y) series 2, respectively.

- Legends are created automatically if legend text is included in the selection. In addition, legend placement and the labels may be changed or edited. The legends in the spreadsheet illustrated below are in cells B4 and C4. Note the relationship between the spreadsheet data (ILLUSTRATION A) and the bar chart (ILLUSTRATION B) below.

Charting Toolbar

- The **Charting Toolbar** provides shortcuts for many charting commands. These buttons are identified on the Toolbar illustrated above. Many other Toolbar functions on the Charting Toolbar are universal, however, and are used in all the Works tools.

  Furthermore, as with all Works Toolbars, this Toolbar can be customized to include additional charting features.

SPREADSHEET ILLUSTRATION A

	A	B	C
1	CARSON CORNERS HIGH SCHOOL		
2	STUDENT POPULATION		
3			
4		MALES	FEMALES
5	FRESHMAN	175	185
6	SOPHOMORES	255	240
7	JUNIORS	235	220
8	SENIORS	205	215

Category labels — First value (Y) series — Second value (Y) series — Legend

BAR CHART ILLUSTRATION B

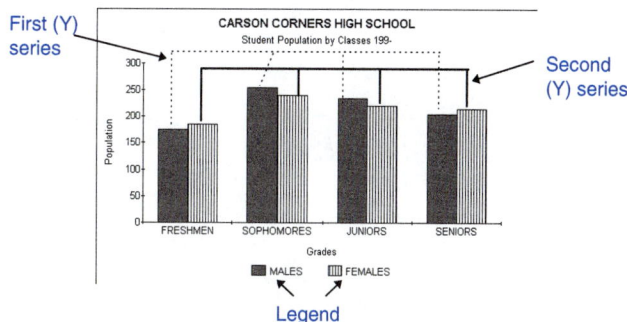

CARSON CORNERS HIGH SCHOOL
Student Population by Classes 199-

First (Y) series — Second (Y) series — Legend — MALES — FEMALES

Change a Chart Type

- You can change the chart type after it has been automatically created. When you change a chart type, the original chart is replaced.

  ### To change the chart type:

  - Display chart to be changed.
  - Click desired chart type button on the Toolbar.
  - Click desired chart type in the Chart type dialog box.
  - Click Variations, if desired.
  - Click desired Variation.
  - Click OK.

Stacked Bar Chart

- A **stacked bar chart** is a form of bar chart that shows the total effect of several sets of data. Each bar consists of sections representing values in a range, and each color or pattern in a bar represents a value. Legends are, therefore, essential to explain the sections of the bar. Each bar represents 100% of a category. See Illustration C below.

STACKED BAR CHART
ILLUSTRATION C

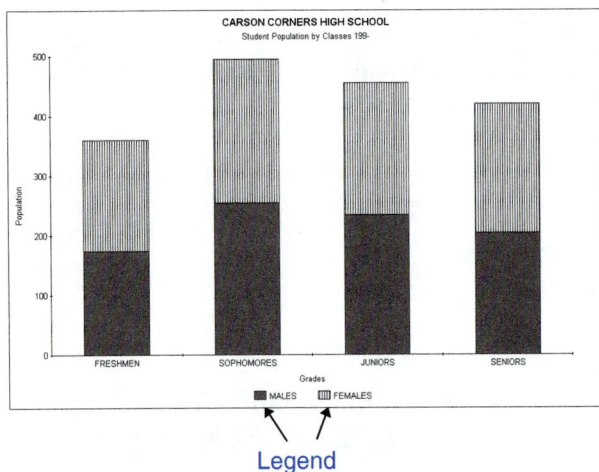

CARSON CORNERS HIGH SCHOOL
Student Population by Classes 199-

Legend

Print a Chart

- Before printing a chart, you should check that all settings in the Page Setup dialog box are correct. As in the other Works tools, changes to the settings in the Page Setup dialog box are reflected in the sample box.

  The Other Options tab lets you size the chart. You can choose one of the following options:

  - Screen size
  - Full page, keep proportions
  - Full page (default)
    - ✓NOTE: The last option (Full page, the default) stretches the chart so that it occupies most of the page.

- Once all the settings are acceptable, you can print your chart. The universal printing command is the same as in all the other Works tools.

- You can also check Properties from the Print dialog box. Here you can specify settings such as resolution, paper size, paper source and paper orientation. Any changes made in the Properties dialog box become the default settings and the Page Setup settings change to match them. Conversely, any changes made in Page Setup dialog box will be reflected in the Properties dialog box as well.

- You can view your chart exactly as it will print. This is an excellent feature to use when printing a color chart on a black and white printer. Click View, Display as Printed. Check to see that the patterns Works selected to replace the colors are different from one another.

In this exercise, you will open the Carson Corners High School population statistics, include additional data and prepare several charts. The principal wants to compare the number of males and females registered in each grade.

EXERCISE DIRECTIONS:

1. Open ✎**HS**, or open ⊟**SS HS.32**.

2. Enter new data in column C, as shown in the illustration.

3. Select cells A4:C8, and create a *bar chart*.

4. Make the following changes in the Ba<u>s</u>ic Options tab:
   - <u>T</u>itle: CARSON CORNERS HIGH SCHOOL
   - Add a <u>B</u>order.

5. Click Ad<u>v</u>anced Options tab and organize your chart as follows:
   - Series goes <u>D</u>own
   - First row contains <u>L</u>egend text
   - First column contains <u>C</u>ategory labels

6. Once the chart is displayed, add the following titles:
   - Subtitle: Student Population by Classes 199-
   - X-axis title: Grades
   - Y-axis title: Population

7. Check your result with illustrated Solution A.

8. View the chart using the Display as Printed option.

9. Rename the chart **HS BAR2**.

10. Print the bar chart using the Full page, <u>k</u>eep proportions option in the Page Setup dialog box.

11. Change bar chart to a *standard line chart*.

12. Check your result with Solution B.

13. Rename the chart **HS LINE2**.
    ✓ NOTE: This line chart replaces the bar chart.

14. Print the line chart using the <u>F</u>ull page option.

15. Change the line chart to a *stacked bar chart*.
    ✓ NOTE: You will need to click <u>V</u>ariations tab in the Chart Type dialog box to access the stacked bar chart.

16. Check your chart with Solution C.

17. Rename the chart **HS STACK**.

18. Print the stacked bar chart using <u>F</u>ull page, keep proportions.

19. Close the file; save the changes.

	A	B	C
1	CARSON CORNERS HIGH SCHOOL		
2	STUDENT POPULATION		
3			
4		MALES	FEMALES
5	FRESHMEN	175	185
6	SOPHOMORES	255	240
7	JUNIORS	235	220
8	SENIORS	205	215

Add new data

SOLUTION A

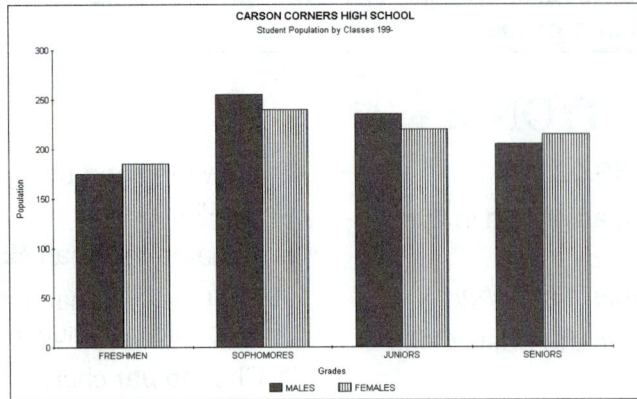

SOLUTION B

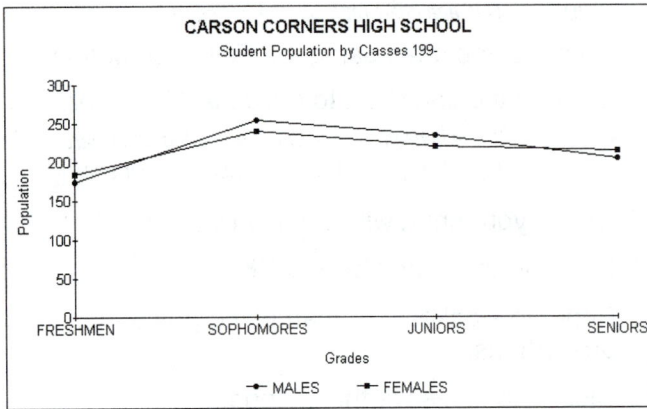

SOLUTION C

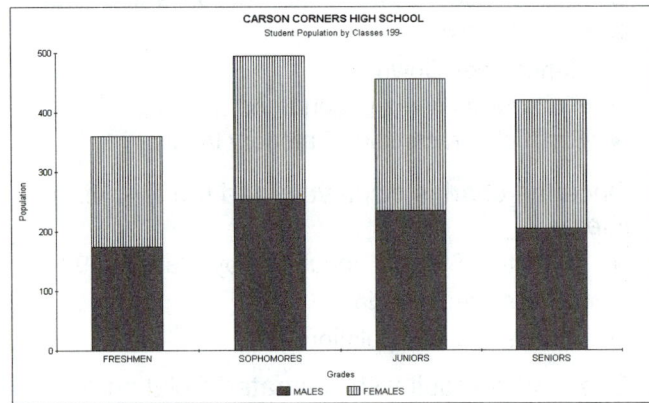

CREATE CHART FROM MULTIPLE SERIES (DATA RANGE)

1. Select range or series you wish to chart.
2. Click the **New Chart** button .... 📊 on the Toolbar.
   OR
   a. Click **Tools** .... Alt + T
   b. Click **Create New Chart** .... N
3. Click desired chart type .... Alt + W from list in **New Chart** dialog box.
4. Click **Title** text box. .... Alt + T
5. Type the title...................................*title* as desired.
6. Click **Border** .... Alt + B if desired.
7. Click **Advanced Options** .... Alt + V if desired.
8. Check sample box to see if spreadsheet is charted correctly.
9. Click **OK**...................................... Enter
   Chart is displayed.

CHANGE A CHART TYPE

1. Display chart to change.
2. Click desired chart type button on Toolbar.
   OR
   a. Click **Format** .... Alt + O
   b. Click **Chart Type** C
3. Click **Variations**...................... Alt + V if you want to see additional charts.
4. Click **OK**.. Enter

CHANGE PAGE SETUP

1. Display the chart.
2. Click **File** .... Alt + F
3. Click **Page Setup**............................ G
4. Click **Other Options** tab .... Alt + O
5. Click one of the following options:
   - **Screen Size**........................ Alt + C
   - **Full page, keep**.................. Alt + K
     proportions
   - **Full Page**.......................... Alt + U

To return to default Page Setup:

   Click **Reset**........................... Alt + E

EXERCISE **33**

■ **Edit the Spreadsheet Data** ■ **Edit a Series Range**
■ **Edit a Legend** ■ **Display/Hide a Legend** ■ **Duplicate a Chart**

NOTES:

Edit the Spreadsheet Data

■ The chart and its related spreadsheet are **linked**. The chart is automatically altered whenever a cell is changed in the spreadsheet. For example, if the category labels on the x-axis needed to be abbreviated, you would make the spreadsheet the active window and edit the labels. The changes are then made simutaneously in the spreadsheet.

Edit a Series Range

■ Works automatically creates the chart from the range of cells you select. It reads the selected data and determines the x- and y-series ranges. However, you may find that you may need to make adjustments to either the x-series, y-series or both series ranges. Some instances that may require a change to the series are:

- adding data to a spreadsheet
- deleting data in a spreadsheet
- correcting a wrong range reference
- charting non-adjacent values

■ You can add, delete or change the desired y-series range references in the series text boxes, or you can copy the data from the spreadsheet and paste it in the desired series text box. If you want to chart areas of the spreadsheet that are not adjacent, enter the range(s) for the desired data in the Value (Y) Series text boxes as shown in the Edit Series dialog box illustrated on the left below.

Edit a Legend

■ When creating a chart, if the range you select includes row or column headings, Works automatically uses that text to create a legend for the chart. If you did not select the headings, however, then Works creates a generic legend using Series 1, Series 2, etc., for the legend text.

■ You can edit the legend created by the Automatic Charting Feature. You can type in the text you want to use as the legend, delete the legend or hide the legend. Remember that pie charts do not have legends; labels are used instead to identify the pie slices.

■ Click Edit, Legend/Series Labels to access the dialog box illustrated below.

- Click the Auto series labels check box to use generic legends. Otherwise, enter the cell reference or type the text you want to use as the legend in the Value Series textboxes.

Display/Hide a Legend

- If a legend is created through the Automatic Charting feature, it is displayed as the default. You may choose to display or not display the legend after it is created. If you do not want a legend, click the **Don't use** check box in the Edit Legend/Series Labels dialog box.

Duplicate a Chart

- You may need to copy a chart. For instance, suppose you created a bar chart and now also need a line chart. If you change your existing bar chart to a line chart, however, you will lose the bar chart. Therefore, you need to duplicate the bar chart and change the copy to a line chart. In this way, you will have both charts.

The titles and legends in a duplicate chart remain the same as in the original chart. Edit them as needed.

You are scheduled to conduct a sales meeting next week where you will compare the sales for each salesperson during January - June using a series of charts. You created the chart, but there were errors in the data and one salesperson was omitted. You have obtained the correct information, and must now edit the chart. Your bar chart will display the data for each time period and the line chart will display the sales for each salesperson.

EXERCISE DIRECTIONS:

1. Open 💾**BONUS**, or open 🖫**SS BONUS.33**.

2. Select the range A7:E12, and create a *line chart*.

3. Enter the following chart title: SEMI-ANNUAL SALES REPORT

4. Add a Border.

5. View the chart in the sample box, then click OK. *Chart is displayed.*

6. Add the following titles:
Subtitle:	January - June 199-
X-axis title:	Month Ending
Y-axis title:	Sales

7. Switch to the spreadsheet and change the data in the following cells as indicated:
C12:	250.00
D10:	1750.00
E7:	4500.00

8. View the chart.

9. You realize that you accidentally omitted the data in F7:F12 for Chen.

10. View your line chart if is not on the screen. Click Edit, Series and enter the cell range for Chen's data at the 5th value Y series.

11. You decide that a legend giving each salesperson's name might make the chart more readable. Edit the existing legend as follows:

   a. Deselect the Auto series labels.

   b. Use the cell references from the column headings (range B5:F5). Enter the individual cell reference for each salesperson starting with B5 for the 1st Value Series, C5 for the 2nd Value Series and so on.

12. View the chart without legends. Restore the legends.

13. Rename the chart **BONUSLINE**. Compare to Solution A.

14. Print the line chart in landscape orientation using Full page, keep proportions.

15. Duplicate the chart and change to a bar chart.

16. Name the chart **BONUSBAR**.

17. You will change the direction of the data by editing the series as follows:

   a. The Value Y Series text boxes will read B7:F7, B8:F8, B9:F9, B10:F10, B11:F11, B12:F12

   b. The Category X Series text box will read: B5:F5

18. Use the data in the range A7:A12 for the legend inserting each cell reference separately.

19. Change the x-axis title to Salesperson.

20. Compare your result to Solution B.

21. Print the bar chart in Landscape orientation using Full page, keep proportions.

22. Save the file; name it **BONUS2**.

23. Close the document window.

SOLUTION A

SEMI-ANNUAL SALES REPORT
January - June 199-

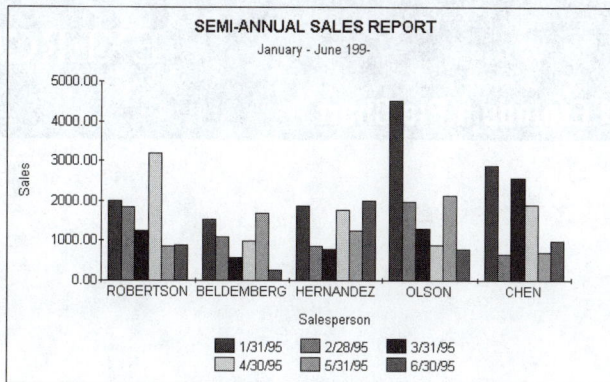

SOLUTION B

SEMI-ANNUAL SALES REPORT
January - June 199-

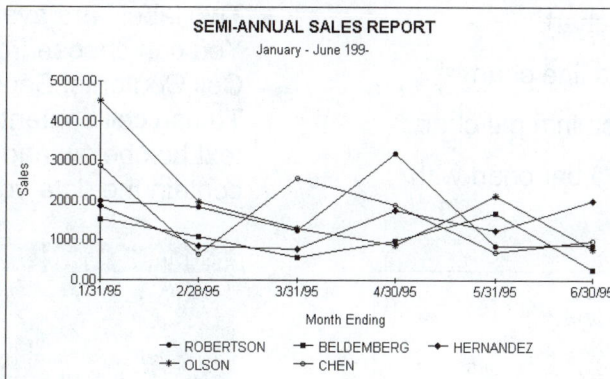

EDIT THE SPREADSHEET DATA

1. Change to Spreadsheet view.
   a. Click **View**.......................... Alt + V
   b. Click **Spreadsheet**....................... S
2. Make changes to data in cells.
3. Change to Chart view.
   a. Click **View**.......................... Alt + V
   b. Click **Chart**................................. C
4. Choose chart you wish to view.
5. Click **OK** .... Enter
6. Note the change reflected in the chart.

   ✔NOTE: *You cannot add another data range in this manner. In order to add another data range, you will need to Edit a Series Range as explained below.*

EDIT A SERIES RANGE

1. View the desired chart.
2. Click **Edit**................................ Alt + E

3. Click **Series** .... S
4. Click desired y-series range.
5. Enter new range references .... *range references*
6. Click **Category (X) Series** ...... Alt + C
7. Enter correct range references .... *range references*
8. Click **OK** .... Enter

EDIT A LEGEND

1. View desired chart.
2. Click **Edit**.............................. Alt + E
3. Click **Legend/Series Labels**............. L
4. Deselect the **Auto series label** box. .... Alt + U
5. Click desired Value Series.
6. Enter cell reference ....*cell reference* of data to use as a legend, or type in the data
7. Click **Use as legend**.............. Alt + L
8. Click **OK** .... Enter

HIDE/RESTORE A LEGEND

✔NOTE: *After a chart is created, the legend is displayed as the default.*

To hide a legend:

1. Click **Edit**............................... Alt + E
2. Click **Legend/Series Labels**............. L
3. Click **Don't use**...................... Alt + D

To display a legend:

1. Repeat steps 1 and 2 above.
2. Click **Use as legend**.............. Alt + L

DUPLICATE A CHART

1. Click **Tools**............................ Alt + T
2. Click **Duplicate Chart**....................... U
3. Click chart to duplicate.
4. Duplicate chart appears; rename as desired.

■ Data Labels ■ Gridlines ■ Explode a Pie Chart

NOTES:

Data Labels

- **Data Labels** identify a specific value and are placed on charts as follows:
  - On top of the bar in a bar chart.
  - Next to the data points in a line chart.
  - At the side of each pie slice in a pie chart.

Note the illustration below of a bar chart with data labels displayed.

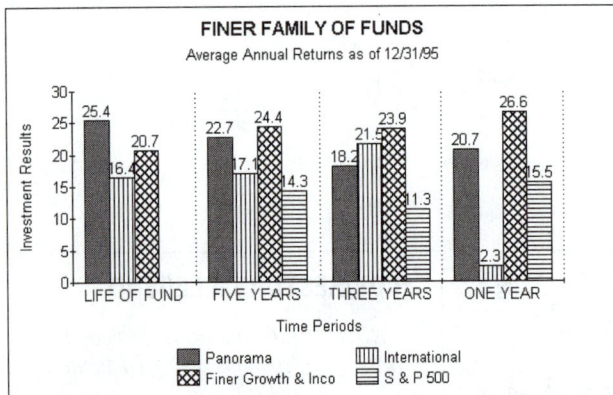

FINER FAMILY OF FUNDS
Average Annual Returns as of 12/31/95

- You can add data labels to any y-series range. However, data labels are not available in 3-D charts.

- You can add data labels to a bar or line chart by typing the range references for the data labels in the appropriate Value (Y) Series text boxes shown in the illustration below.

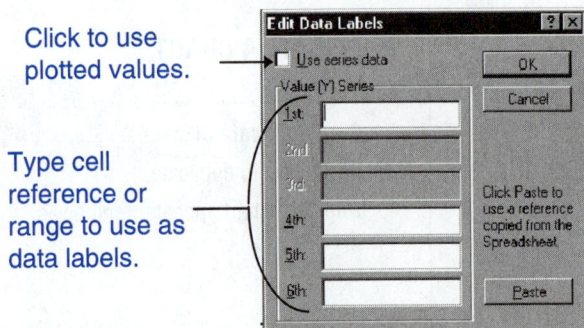

Click to use plotted values.

Type cell reference or range to use as data labels.

- Click the Use series data check box if you want to use the plotted values as the data labels.

- Two labels are available for each pie slice. You can choose from Values, Percentages, Cell Contents, Sequential Numbers or None. To use cell contents, click in the Cell Range text box below and enter the range of cells that contain the data you wish to use as labels.

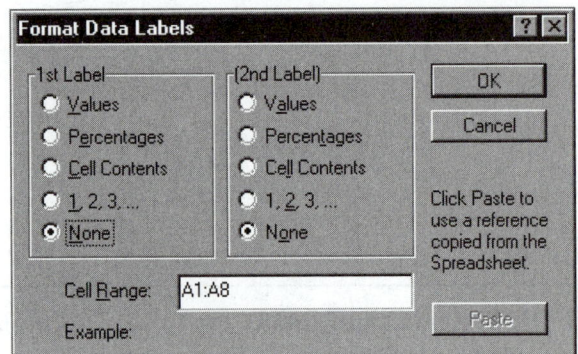

CAUTION: *Don't overuse data labels. They can clutter the screen and create confusion.*

Gridlines

- **Gridlines** are used to clarify the data points on a chart. You can use horizontal gridlines, vertical gridlines or both.

Explode a Pie Chart

- Individual slices may be **exploded** (separated) from the whole pie. For example, the following diagram illustrates a pie chart showing the five-year returns for the Finer Family of Funds. The Finer Growth & Income slice has been exploded.

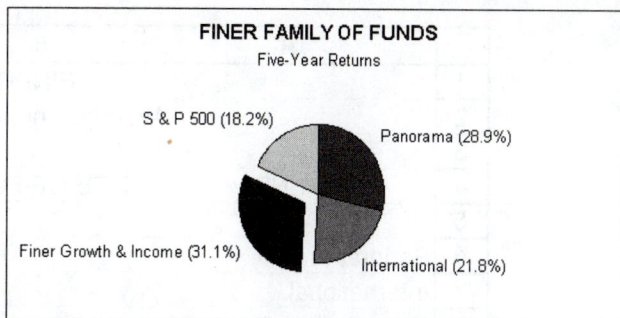

FINER FAMILY OF FUNDS
Five-Year Returns

S & P 500 (18.2%)
Panorama (28.9%)
Finer Growth & Income (31.1%)
International (21.8%)

As the financial analyst for Mr. David Craig, you periodically meet with him to review his investment portfolio. He has asked you for data on the Finer Family of Funds. In preparation for your meeting, you are to prepare a spreadsheet comparing the funds over time. In addition, to further enhance your presentation, you will present the data in both a bar and pie chart.

EXERCISE DIRECTIONS:

1. Create a document for the Spreadsheet, entering the labels and values in the exact cell locations shown in the illustration. In addition:
   - Center the title across the spreadsheet.
   - Center all column headings.

2. Select cells A6:E9 and create a *bar chart* for the Finer Family of Funds.

3. Add the following title: FINER FAMILY OF FUNDS, and select the Border option.

4. Make sure you have the following Advanced Options selected:
   - Select across for the Series Direction.
   - First column contains Legend text.
   - First Row contains Value Y Series.

5. View the chart layout in the sample box.

6. Include the following titles:
   - Subtitle: Average Annual Returns as of 12/31/95
   - X-axis title: Time Periods
   - Y-axis title: Investment Results

7. Click Use series data to create the data labels.

8. Edit the Series to include B4:E4 as the category (X) series.

9. Create horizontal gridlines and view the chart. Check your results with illustrated Solution A. Make necessary adjustments to duplicate the illustration.

10. Name the chart **FINER BAR**.

11. Print the bar chart using landscape orientation, keep proportions.

12. Select the data for the FIVE YEAR RETURN only.

13. Create a *pie chart* using the following title: FINER FAMILY OF FUNDS

14. Add a border.

15. Create a subtitle: Five-Year Returns

16. Include two data labels showing the names of the stocks and the percentages. You will have to enter the cell references for the stock names in the Cell Range text box.

17. Explode the pie slice with the largest return.

18. View the chart and check your result with illustrated Solution B. Make any necessary adjustments to duplicate the illustration.

19. Rename the chart **FINER PIE**.

20. Answer the following questions:
   a. Which fund gave the highest return?
   b. How did each of the Finer Family of Funds compare to the S + P 500 for each time period?
   c. Why would you compare your funds to the S + P 500?
   d. Would you invest in the International fund? Substantiate your reason by referring to the data in the chart.

21. Print the pie chart using the full page option.

22. Save the file; name it **FINER FUNDS**.

23. Close the document window.

	A	B	C	D	E
1	FINER FAMILY OF FUNDS				
2	Average Annual Total Returns as of 3/31/95				
3					
4	FUND	LIFE OF FUND	FIVE YEARS	THREE YEARS	ONE YEAR
5					
6	Panorama	25.4	22.7	18.2	20.7
7	International	16.4	17.1	21.5	2.3
8	Finer Growth & Income	20.7	24.4	23.9	26.6
9	S & P 500	NO DATA	14.3	11.3	15.5

SOLUTION A – BAR CHART

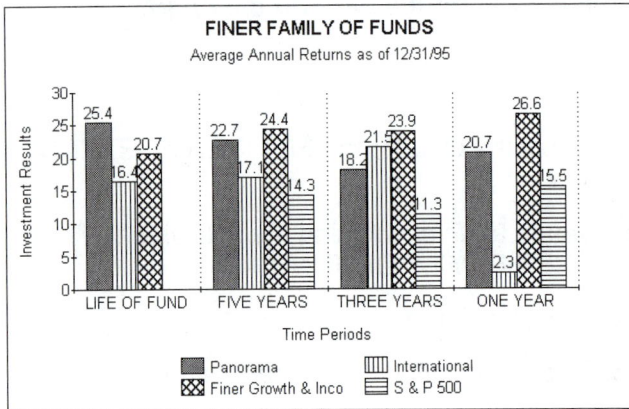

FINER FAMILY OF FUNDS
Average Annual Returns as of 12/31/95

SOLUTION B – EXPLODED PIE CHART

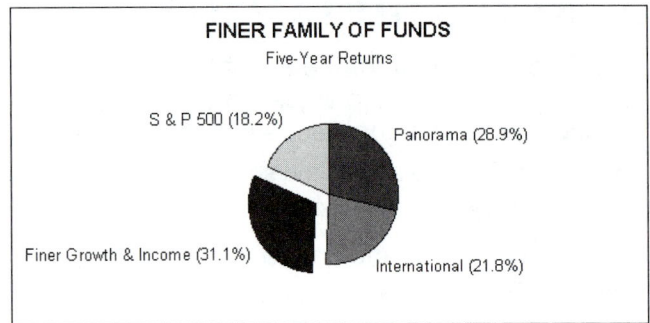

FINER FAMILY OF FUNDS
Five-Year Returns

DATA LABELS

1. Click **Edit** .... `Alt`+`E`
2. Click **Data Labels** .... `D`
3. Click **Use series data** .... `Alt`+`U`
   to use data in selected series.

   OR

   Enter **Value Y Series** ...... `Alt` + *number*
   data to use as data labels.

   ✓ *NOTE: You must deselect* **Use series data** *to use this second option.*

4. Click **OK** .... `Enter`

GRIDLINES

1. Click **Format** .... `Alt`+`O`
2. Click **Horizontal (X) Axis** .... `H`
   OR
   Click **Vertical (Y) Axis** .... `V`
3. Click **Show gridlines** .... `G`

ELIMINATE GRIDLINES:

Repeat steps 1-3, above.

EXPLODE PIE CHART

1. Click **Format** .... `Alt`+`O`
2. Click **Shading and Color** .... `D`
3. Click desired Y series values to explode.
4. Click **Explode slice** .... `Alt`+`E`
5. Click **Format** .... `Alt`+`F`
6. Click **Close** .... `Alt`+`C`

RETURN SLICE TO PIE:

1. Repeat steps 1-3, above.
2. Click **Explode Slice** .... `Alt`+`E`
   to return slice.

EXERCISE **35**

- **Change Font, Font Size and Typestyle**
- **Change Color, Pattern and Markers** ■ **3-D Charts**

NOTES:

Change Font, Font Size and Typestyle

- You can change font, font size, font color and typestyle in the Charting feature just as you did in the Word Processor and Spreadsheet tools. Changes in the text can often improve the readability and attractiveness of your chart.

- The format of the chart's main title, subtitle and x- and y-axis titles can be changed without affecting the other titles. The data labels, legends, category labels and the y-axis scale all use the same format. Changing the format of one changes the format for all the others.

- Click the area to be changed and once the handles are displayed, choose the font, font size and typestyle you desire. If you don't select an area, the data labels, legends, category labels and y-axis scale will all be changed.

- You can make changes to the font, font size or typestyle using the Toolbar, or you may prefer to work through the Format, Font and Style dialog box shown below.

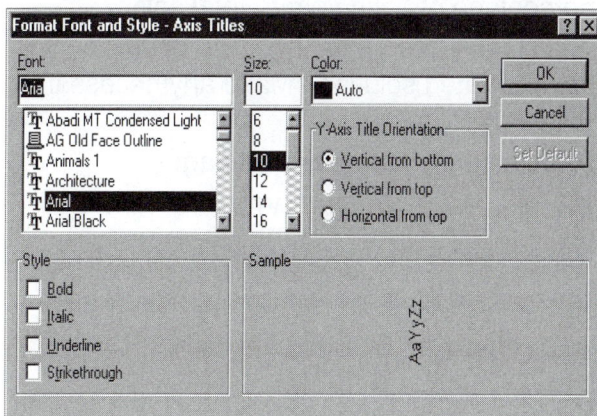

- You can also make changes to the Y-Axis Title Orientation in the Format Font and Style dialog box illustrated above. Select the y-axis title in the chart. Once the gray handles are displayed,

click the desired Orientation in the dialog box shown above. Look at the sample box to see the result of your selection.

Change Color, Pattern and Markers

- The **colors** displayed in a newly created chart are assigned by Works. Each y-series is assigned a different color that is preset by the program. You can customize the chart by changing the colors or assigning a pattern to the y-series in the chart. You can customize the Toolbar by adding a Shading and Color button.

- **Data markers** are used in line charts to identify the actual value from the spreadsheet. The data marker uses circles, squares or some other shape to mark the actual point on the line. The markers can be changed to identify the data more readily.

- To change colors, shading or markers, click Format, Shading and Color to access the Format Shading and Color dialog box.

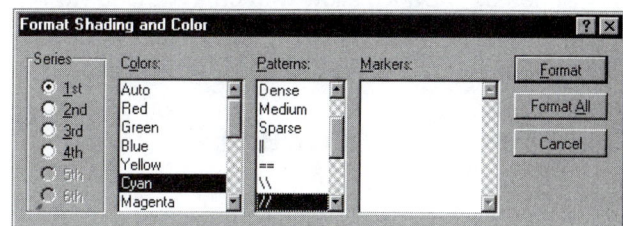

3-D Charts

- After you create a chart, you can transform it into a 3-D chart. You can transform area, bar, line or pie charts

  ✓ NOTE: *Data labels cannot be used in 3-D bar or line charts. Don't use 3-D if you need the precise information provided by data labels.*

In this exercise, you will create a spreadsheet to compare the performance of the Graphics Arts 2000 to that of its competitors over the past three years. You will create a variety of charts to illustrate the data.

EXERCISE DIRECTIONS:

1. Create a new document for the Spreadsheet, entering the labels and values in the exact cell locations shown in the illustration.

2. Create a *bar chart* with a border.

3. Create the following titles in the font and size indicated.
   - Title: SALES COMPARISON (sans serif 16 point bold and italics)
   - Subtitle: Graphic Arts 2000 vs. Competitors (sans serif 9 point)
   - X-axis: Omit
   - Y-axis: Units Sold (sans serif 9 point bold)

4. Change the Y-Axis Title Orientation in the Format Font and Style dialog box to Horizontal from top.

5. Change to a *3-D bar chart*.

6. Rename the chart **GROW3D**.

7. View your chart and compare your results with the illustrated solution. Make any necessary adjustments.

8. Print the 3-D bar chart using Full page, keep proportions.

9. Duplicate the chart.

10. Change to a *regular bar chart* and change the color of the bars as follows:
    - Series 1: Cyan with slanting (//) diagonals.
    - Series 2: Magenta with plus signs (++).
    - Series 3: Dark Yellow with dark slanting (\\) diagonals.

11. Add data labels using the Use series data option.

12. Rename the chart **GROWBAR**.

13. View your chart and compare your results with the illustrated solution. Make any necessary adjustments.

14. Print the bar chart using Full page, keep proportions.

15. Create a *line chart* using the same titles. Format titles as follows:
    - Change main title to serif 14 point bold.
    - Change other titles to serif 10 point italics.

16. Change the markers as follows:
    - Series 1: filled circle
    - Series 2: filled box
    - Series 3: filled diamond

17. Rename the chart **GROWLINE**.

18. View your chart and compare your results with the illustrated solution. Make any necessary adjustments.

19. Print the line chart using the Full page option.

20. Create a *pie chart* to measure Graphics Arts sales over three years.

21. Set up the titles attractively, using a variety of enhancements.

22. Select a different pattern for each slice.

23. Explode the slice which represents the greatest number of sales.

24. Include data labels to identify the year and percentage of each year to total sales.

25. View your chart and compare your results with the illustrated solution. Make any necessary adjustments.

26. Print the pie chart using Full page.

27. Rename the chart **GROWPIE**.

28. Save the file; name it **GROW**.

29. Close the document window.

SPREADSHEET

	A	B	C	D
1	SALES COMPARISON			
2	GRAPHIC ARTS 2000 VS. COMPETITORS			
3				
4		YEAR 1	YEAR 2	YEAR 3
5	GR ARTS	475	900	1200
6	COM GR	650	500	450
7	BETA DES	800	350	350

SOLUTIONS

GROW3-D

SALES COMPARISON
Graphic Arts 2000 vs Competitors

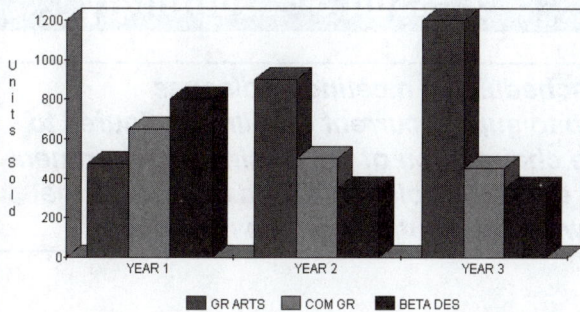

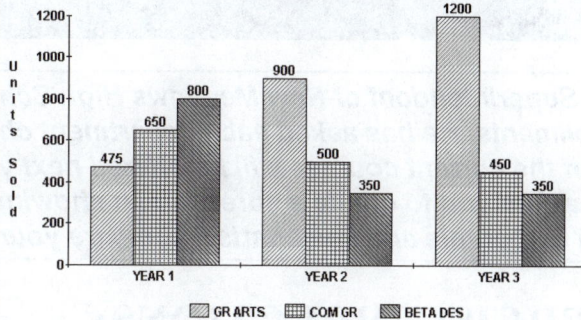

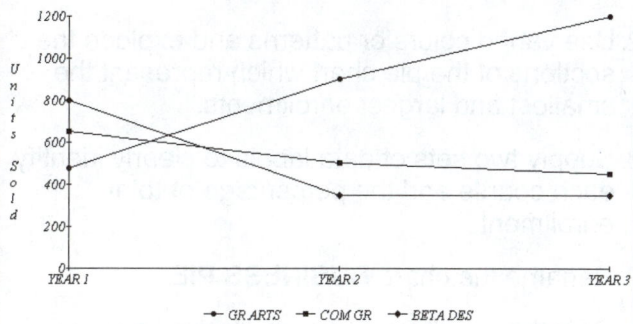

Units Sold (axis, 0–1200)
YEAR 1   YEAR 2   YEAR 3

■ GR ARTS   ■ COM GR   ■ BETA DES

GROWBAR

SALES COMPARISON
Graphic Arts 2000 vs. Competitors

Units Sold (axis, 0–1200)

YEAR 1: 475, 650, 800
YEAR 2: 900, 500, 350
YEAR 3: 1200, 450, 350

▨ GR ARTS   ▨ COM GR   ▨ BETA DES

GROWLINE

SALES COMPARISON
Graphic Arts 2000 vs. Competitors

Units Sold (axis, 0–1200)
YEAR 1   YEAR 2   YEAR 3

—■— GR ARTS   —■— COM GR   —◆— BETA DES

GROWPIE

GRAPHIC ARTS 2000
Three-Year Sale Record

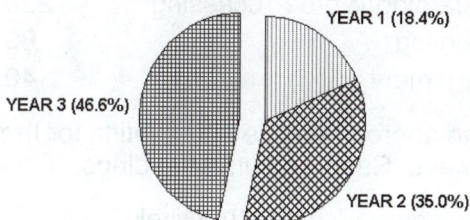

YEAR 1 (18.4%)
YEAR 2 (35.0%)
YEAR 3 (46.6%)

CHANGE FONT, FONT SIZE AND TYPESTYLE

Ctrl + B (bold), Ctrl + U (underline), Ctrl + I (italics)

1. Click title or label to edit.
2. Click **F**ormat .... `Alt`+`O`
3. Click **F**ont and Style .... `F`
4. Make desired changes.
5. Click **OK** .... `Enter`

CHANGE COLORS, PATTERNS AND MARKERS

1. Click **F**ormat .... `Alt`+`O`
2. Click Sha**d**ing and Color .... `D`
3. Click desired options
   ✔ NOTE: Markers are available for line charts only.
4. Click **F**ormat. .... `Alt`+`F`
   to activate change to one range.
   OR
   Click Format **A**ll. .... `Alt`+`A`
   to activate changes to all series
5. Click **C**lose .... `Alt`+`C`

BORDERS

1. Click **F**ormat .... `Alt`+`O`
2. Click **B**order .... `B`

DELETE BORDER:

Repeat Steps 1-2 above.

3-D CHART

1. Click **F**ormat .... `Alt`+`O`
2. Click **3**-D .... `3`

RETURN TO 2-D

Repeat Steps 1-2 above.

EXERCISE **36**

Lesson 5 – Summary

The Superintendent of New Meadows High School has scheduled a meeting to discuss enrollments. He has asked each department chairperson to supply current enrollment figures to see if the current courses will be offered next year. The chairperson of the Business Department has asked you to create a spreadsheet showing current course enrollments, and to convert the data to bar, pie and line charts. Compare your results with the solutions on the next page.

EXERCISE DIRECTIONS:

1. Create a new document for the Spreadsheet, entering the following labels and values:

Introduction to Occupations	230
Computer Literacy/Applications	120
Keyboarding/Word Processing	220
Accounting	80
Management	40

2. Create an appropriate title and subtitle for the spreadsheet. Supply column headings.

3. Format the spreadsheet attractively.

4. Save the file; name it **BUSINESS COURSES**.

5. Using the Automatic Charting feature, prepare a single-series *bar chart*.
   ✓ *NOTE: Use Down as the direction for the series.*

6. Include appropriate title, subtitle, and x- and y-axis titles. Change the font, font size and typestyle to enhance the titles.

7. Create data labels for each bar to give the exact number of students

8. Use all available features to format the chart attractively.

9. Name the chart **BUSINESS BAR**.

10. Print the bar chart using Full page, keep proportions.

11. Using the Automatic Charting feature, create a *pie chart* using the same title and subtitle. Use all available features to format the chart attractively.

12. Use varied colors or patterns and explode the sections of the pie chart which represent the smallest and largest enrollments.

13. Supply two sets of data labels to clearly identify each course and the percentage of total enrollment.

14. Rename the chart **BUSINESS PIE**.

15. Print the pie chart using any desired options.

16. Create a *line chart*. Make sure this chart shows the difference in enrollment in each class.

17. Supply appropriate titles using a variety of font sizes, and typestyles to enhance the chart.
    ✓ *NOTE: The x-axis labels may be too long. You can accommodate them by either reducing the font size or abbreviating the label text in the spreadsheet.*

18. Include appropriate titles, legends and markers as needed to enhance and clarify the chart's data. Change to 3-D and supply both vertical and horizontal gridlines.

19. Rename the chart **BUSINESS LINE**.

20. Print the 3-D chart using desired options.

21. Close the file; save the changes.

BUSINESS BAR

BUSINESS DEPARTMENT ENROLLMENT

September - June 199-

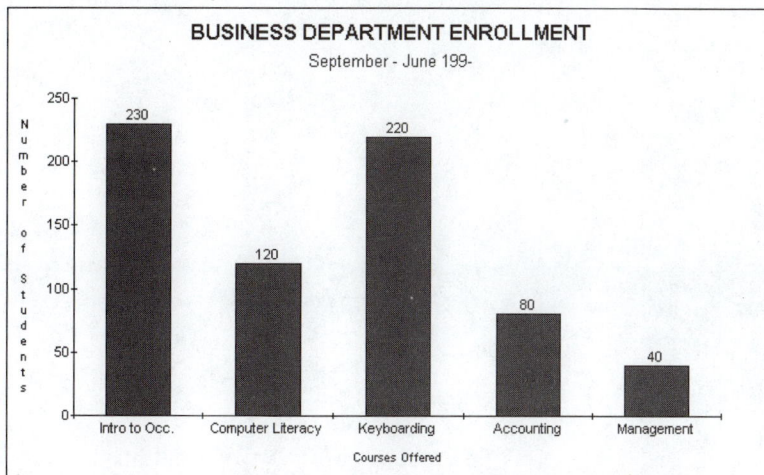

BUSINESS LINE

BUSINESS DEPARTMENT ENROLLMENT

September - June 199-

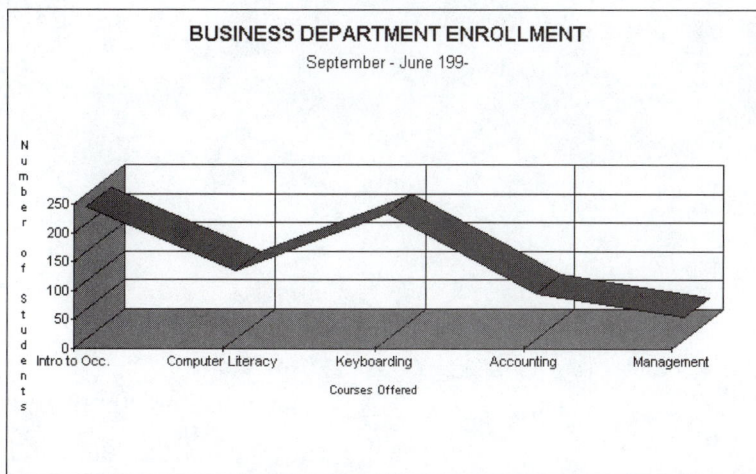

BUSINESS PIE

BUSINESS DEPARTMENT ENROLLMENT

September - June 199-

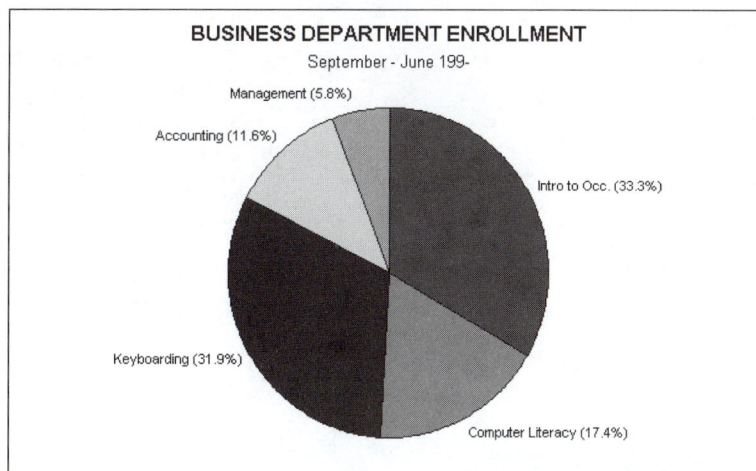

Database

LESSONS 1 - 4

Lesson 1: Create and Save a Database File

Lesson 2: Edit and Print a Database File

Lesson 3: Filters; Format a Database

Lesson 4: Reports

WARNING: *Computer information is confidential. Respect that confidentiality and access information only when authorized. It is a criminal offense to retrieve or view information from a private or limited-access computer or database without authority. It is also illegal to make copies of software programs. Breaking the laws governing computer use, either through ignorance or with criminal intent, could earn you a steep fine or even a prison term.*

■ **Introduction to the Database** ■ **Plan a Database**
■ **Create a Database File** ■ **Save a Database File**

NOTES:

Introduction to the Database

■ A **database** is a collection of related information which helps you collect and organize records. A typical database would be found in a school. Information relating to students, teachers and administrators would each be kept in a separate file. Think of a computer "file" as a file drawer in an office filing cabinet. See illustration below:

■ Each drawer in the "filing cabinet" contains folders. On a computer, the folder is called a **record**. A record lists information about one person or one thing. Therefore, a file is composed of many records. In the example illustrated below, the STUDENTS file would contain a record for each student in the school. See typical record below:

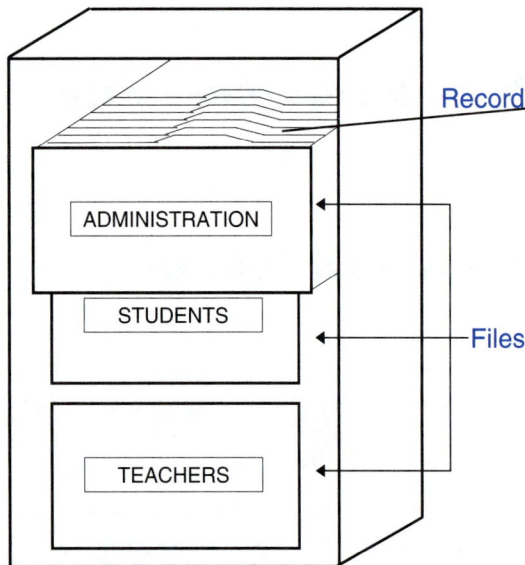

■ The record contains items of information. Each item is referred to as a **field**. There are two parts to a field, the **field name** and the **field contents**. See record below:

Plan a Database

- Before creating a database on the computer, you should plan which fields you want to include – that is, what type of information the database should include and what field names you wish to use. Plan your database on paper first.

- When planning a database, write the field names that would best identify the information you will enter as field contents. When your plan is complete, you are ready to enter your field names into the computer.

- Break the data up into small units that you might want to sort on or use separately. For example, FIRST *and* LAST gives you more flexibility than NAME.

Create a Database File

- To launch the database tool, select <u>D</u>atabase from the Works Task launcher.

- In the Create Database dialog box which follows, create the fields for your new database by typing the name in the <u>F</u>ield name text box and clicking <u>A</u>dd.

- The **Create Database** window appears so you can create the fields for your new database.

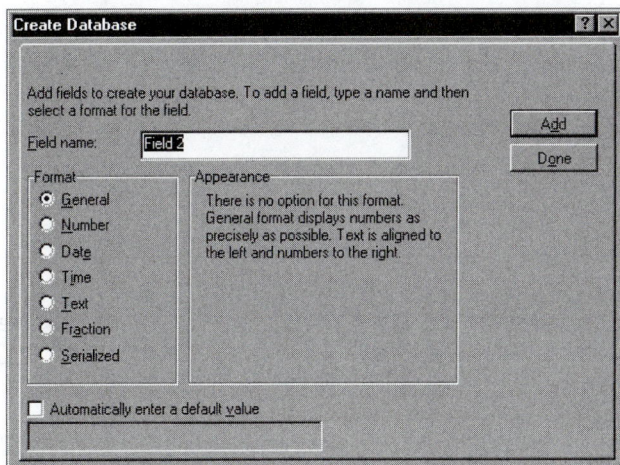

- Each field name may contain up to 15 characters including blank spaces and punctuation. Works automatically adds a colon to the end of your field name to distinguish it as a field name.

- After the field name is typed, you have an opportunity to select a **format** for that field. Formats display numerical data in different ways. If no format is chosen when the field is created, the <u>G</u>eneral format will be applied. General format displays numbers as precisely as possible. Text is aligned to the left and numbers to the right. (Other formats will be detailed in Exercise 16.)

- After all field names have been created, clicking D<u>o</u>ne will display the structure (or design) for your database. Note the database below which contains field names for the STUDENT file that you will create in Exercise 1:

Save a Database File

- After a database file has been created, it must be named and saved. You may then retrieve it at a later time to enter data into the fields. You may use the long file name feature just as you did in the Word Processor and Spreadsheet tools. Works adds a .wdb extension to the saved file, but you will not see that extension in your filename.

> *Your school wants to create a database listing students who apply for school activities and clubs. You will create the form for this database.*

EXERCISE DIRECTIONS:

1. Create a new database file.

2. Use the field names indicated below:

   LAST
   FIRST
   ADDRESS
   CITY
   ST
   ZIP
   M/F
   GRAD YR
   COUNSLR

3. Save the file; name it **STUDENT**.

4. Close the document window.

CREATE A DATABASE FILE

1. Click **File** .... `Alt`+`F`
2. Click **New** .... `N`
3. Choose **Database** .... `Alt`+`D`
   from Works Task Launcher.
4. Type first field name .... *name*
   in the **Field** name text box.
5. Click on the desired format for the field
   - **General** .... `Alt`+`G`
   - **Number** .... `Alt`+`N`
   - **Date** .... `Alt`+`E`
   - **Time** .... `Alt`+`I`
   - **Text** .... `Alt`+`T`
   - **Fraction** .... `Alt`+`A`
   - **Serialized** .... `Alt`+`S`

✓ *NOTE: When you select a format, some options may appear in the Appearance section. If any options appear, select the ones you want.*

6. Click **Add** .... `Alt`+`D`
7. Repeat steps 4-6 for each field name to be included in the database.
8. Click **Done** .... `Alt`+`O`
   Your file is presented in List view.

SAVE DATABASE FILE

1. Click **File** .... `Alt`+`F`
2. Click **Save** .... `S`
   OR
   Click **Save As** .... `A`
3. Type filename .... *text*
4. Click **Save** .... `Enter`

■ **View Modes**

NOTES:

View Modes

■ Works allows you to see your information in different **views**. In the previous exercise, after entering your desired field names into the Create Database dialog box, your new database appeared on the screen in **List view**. This view displays data as a table of columns and rows.

■ Each row in the table is a record; each column contains a field name (column heading) and eventually contain the field contents (column of data).

LIST VIEW

Field names

Field data area

■ A database file can also be viewed as a **form**. After the database is created you can switch to **Form view** by selecting Form from the View menu. Note the database form above right.

FORM VIEW

Field names

Field data area

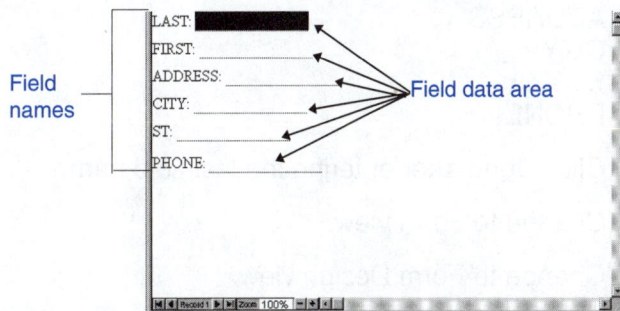

■ Works adds a colon at the end of field names and a line representing each field's width. Form view represents the structure (or design) of the individual records in your database file.

■ Works also provides you with a **Form Design view**. You can use this view to create a form that you wish to design. This view allows you to use all the formatting features available in Works such as font style, appearance, color and size, graphics (including WordArt, ClipArt, Note-It and Microsoft Draw) and Borders and Patterns.

FORM DESIGN VIEW

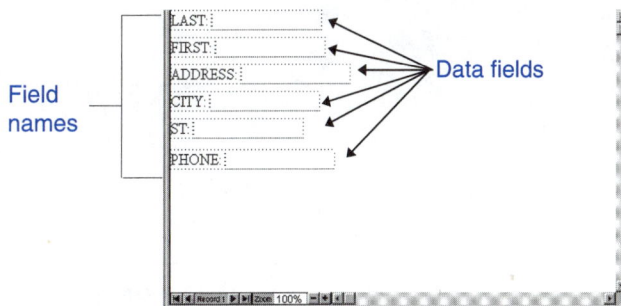

Field names

Data fields

■ Views will be further reviewed in Exercise 6.

> *You are the president of HUG, a computer users' group. One of your responsibilities is to send announcements and annual reports to the membership. To make your mailings easier, you have decided to create a name and address file for your group. In this exercise, you will create a new database. You will then view the database structure in Form and Form Design Views.*

EXERCISE DIRECTIONS:

1. Create a new database file.

2. Use the field names indicated below:

   LAST
   FIRST
   ADDRESS
   CITY
   ST
   PHONE

3. Click D**o**ne after entering the last field name.

4. Change to Form view.

5. Change to Form Design view.

6. Change back to List view.

7. Save the file; name it **MEMBER**.

8. Close the document window.

CHANGE VIEW MODES

F9

1. Click **V**iew .... Alt + V
2. Click **L**ist L
   OR
   Click **F**orm .... F
   OR
   Click **Form D**esign .... D

EXERCISE 3

■ Create and Save a Database File

Bit Byte Computer Stores, Inc. has opened numerous branches throughout the United States during the last several months. In order to keep track of the branches and the cities in which the branches are located, you have been asked to create a database.

EXERCISE DIRECTIONS:

1. Create a new database file.

2. Use the field names indicated below:

   BRANCH
   CITY
   ST
   STAFF

3. Save the file; name it **STORES**.

4. Close the document window.

EXERCISE 4

■ Create and Save a Database File

In order to keep track of equipment purchased by your department, your employer has asked you to create an inventory database.

EXERCISE DIRECTIONS:

1. Create a new database file.

2. Use the field names indicated below:

   ITEM
   MFG
   MODEL
   COST
   PURDATE
   WTY

3. Save the file; name it **INVENTORY**.

4. Close the document window.

EXERCISE **5**

Lesson 1 – Summary

Your department is responsible for ordering and evaluating software products. To keep track of the types of software you order, their prices and where they are stored, you have been asked to set up a database.

EXERCISE DIRECTIONS:

1. Create a new database file.

2. Use the field names indicated below:

   TITLE
   TYPE
   OS
   PRICE
   PURDATE
   STORED

3. Save the file; name it **PROGRAM**.

4. Close the document window.

EXERCISE 6

■ Open a File ■ View Modes ■ Enter Records
■ Correct a Field Entry ■ Field Width ■ Record Height

NOTES:

Open a File

- A previously saved file can be opened for the purpose of entering records.

- If you wish to open only database files, you may choose Works DB (*.wdb) from the Files of Type options in the Open dialog box.

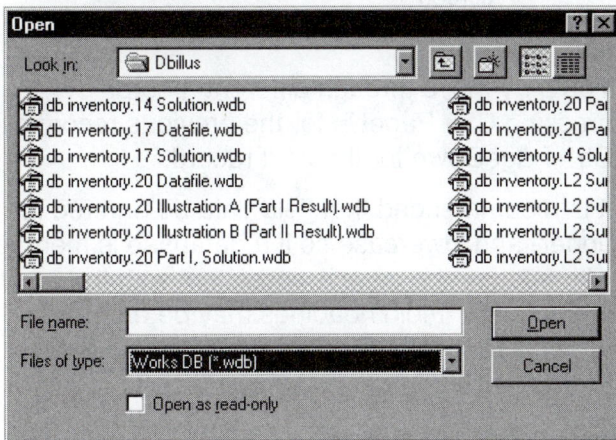

- A **record** is a collection of related data items. A record can be compared to a folder in a file drawer.

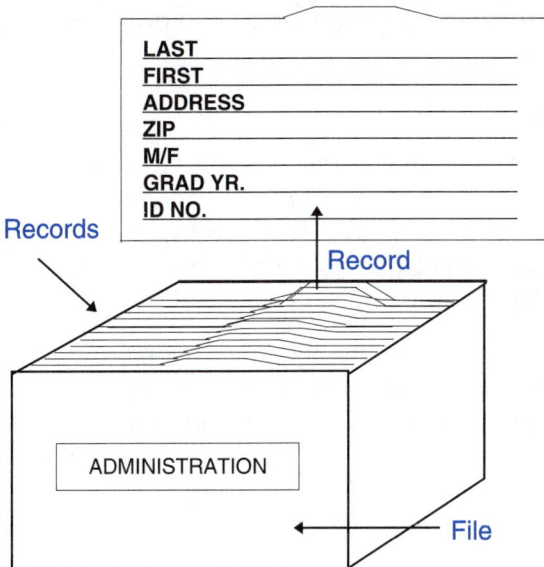

- In this exercise, you will fill out a form for each member of **HUG**. Each form is a record about one person.

View Modes

- As noted in Exercise 2, you may view your form in List view, Form view or Form Design view. **Form view** displays your records one at a time. (Data may be entered in this view.)

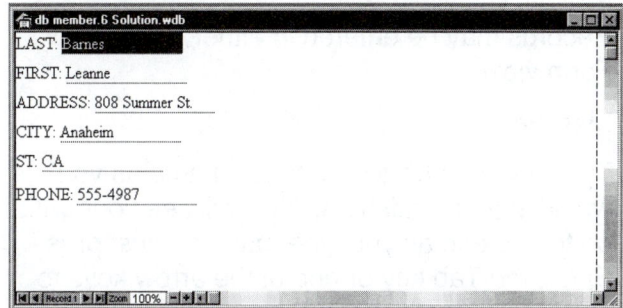

- **List view** displays the form in a column and row format, similar to a spreadsheet grid. This view may be used to display several records at once. In this format, one row contains the data of a single record. Data may be entered in this view.

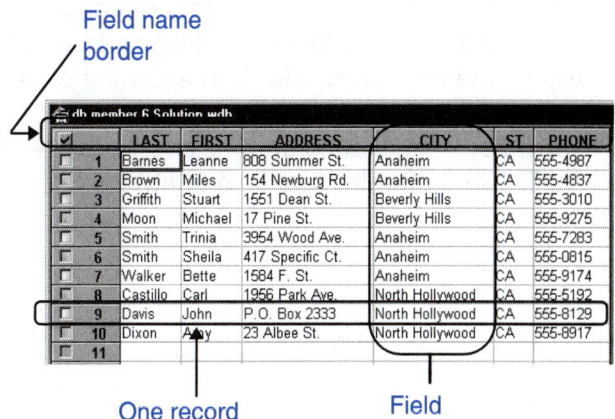

- **Form Design view** allows you to arrange your fields on the form, resize them, reformat them, create and insert graphics or enhance the appearance of the form. You can select font, alignment and numeric formats as well as add borders, patterns or colors. Data may *not* be entered in this view.

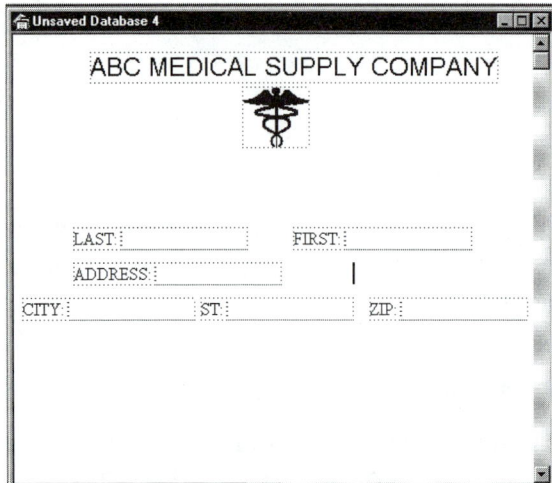

Enter Records

- Records may be entered in either List view or Form view.

List View

Type the data below each field name as you would in a spreadsheet. You will see your data on the screen as you type, but you must press Enter, the Tab key or one of the arrow keys to enter data into the cell. Press the Tab key or one of the arrow keys to advance from column to column. After entering data in the last column, press the Tab key to advance to the first column of the next row.

Form View

Type the data on the line provided next to each field name. You will see your data on the screen as you type but you must press Enter, the Tab key or one of the arrow keys to enter the data into the space provided. Press the Tab key or arrow keys to advance from field to field. Press the Tab key after the last field to advance to the next record.

The horizontal scroll bar shows the record number displayed on the screen. To move through different records in Form view, click the appropriate button in the horizontal scroll bar as illustrated below.

- You may move through different records by pressing Ctrl+PageUp for the previous record or Ctrl+PageDown for the next record.

- It is recommended that field data be entered in upper- and lowercase so if a database is merged with a letter, the case is consistent with the body of the letter. Field headings may be entered in uppercase to distinguish them from field data.

Correct a Field Entry

- As in the Spreadsheet tool, if you make an error while keyboarding an entry, use the Backspace key to correct it. If you have already advanced to another field, click in the field or press Shift+Tab, then retype the entry and press Enter.

Field Width

- As you enter data, you may find that the data exceeds the field width. *Alphabetical data* that exceeds the field width is truncated while *numerical data* displays as a series of number signs (####).

- Field widths may be changed as needed after the database has been created. Field widths may be changed in List view or Form Design view.

- In List view the default width is ten characters. However, the width expands automatically to accommodate the length of the field name you enter. In Form view, the default field size is twenty characters.

To change field width in Form Design view:

Drag the small white box in the lower right corner of the selected field to the desired width.

OR

Use the menus (Format, Field Size).

To change field width in List view:

Drag the field name border to a desired width (as you did in spreadsheets).

OR

Use the menus (Format, Field Width).

OR

Double-click the field name which automatically sets the field width to accommodate the longest entry in the field. This is called the **Best Fit** feature.

Record Height

- The default record height is 1 line high. However, field height may be changed.

To change record height in List view:

- Point to the lower border of the *record number*.
- When the pointer changes to a double-headed arrow, drag the border to the desired height.

OR

- Select the rows to receive the row height change.
- Use the menus (Format, Record Height, Row Height).

> *Now that you have created the form (structure) for your HUG membership database, you are ready to enter the information from your membership list into the database.*

EXERCISE DIRECTIONS:

1. Open ▦**MEMBER**, or open ▤**DB MEMBER.6**.

2. From the notebook page illustrated below, enter the information for each person into your form in List view.

3. Use the Best Fit feature to adjust column widths to accommodate the longest entry in each field.

4. Change the row heights to 14.

5. Correct errors.

6. Close the file; save the changes.

HUG MEMBERSHIP LIST					
California Members					
Leanne	Barnes	808 Summer St.	Anaheim	CA	555-4987
Miles	Brown	154 Newburg Rd.	Anaheim	CA	555-4837
Stuart	Griffith	1551 Dean St.	Beverly Hills	CA	555-3010
Michael	Moon	17 Pine St.	Beverly Hills	CA	555-9275
Trinia	Smith	3954 Wood Ave.	Anaheim	CA	555-7283
Sheila	Smith	417 Specific Ct.	Anaheim	CA	555-0815
Bette	Walker	1584 F. St.	Anaheim	CA	555-9174
Carl	Castillo	1956 Park Ave.	North Hollywood	CA	555-5192
John	Davis	P.O. Box 2333	North Hollywood	CA	555-8129
Amy	Dixon	23 Albee St.	North Hollywood	CA	555-8917

OPEN A DATABASE FILE

1. Click **File** .... Alt + F
2. Click **Open** .... O
3. Type the name of the document to be opened. .... *text*
   OR
   Click document name in list.
4. Click **Open** .... O

CHANGE VIEW MODES

F9 for Form view
Shift+F9 for List view

1. Click **View** .... Alt + V
2. Click desired view mode:
   - **Form** .... F
   - **List** L
   - **Form Design** .... D

ENTER RECORDS

In List View

1. Type data in desired location .... *text*
2. Press **Tab** .... Tab
   OR
   Press arrow keys .... ↓ ↑ → ←
   OR
   Press **Enter** .... Enter
   This will not move you to the next field.
3. To advance to next record (row):
   Press **Tab** from the last field in the current record .... Tab
   OR
   Click in the first column of the new record
   OR
   a. Press the **Home** key .... Home
   b. Press the **Down Arrow** key .... ↓

In Form View

1. Type data on line next to field name .*text*
2. Press **Tab** .... Tab
   OR
   Press the **Down Arrow** key .... ↓
3. To advance to the next record (form)
   Press **Tab** .... Tab
   OR
   Press **Enter** .... Enter
   OR
   Use appropriate icons on horizontal scroll bar to move between records
   - **Current Record** .... Record 20
     (shows record on screen)
   - **Next Record** .... ▶
   - **Previous Record** .... ◀
   - **First Record** .... ◀◀
   - **Last Record** .... ▶▶
   OR
   Use shortcut keys to stay in current field and move between previous and next record
   - **Previous Record** .... Ctrl + Page Up
   - **Next record** .... Ctrl + Page Down

CHANGE FIELD WIDTH

In Form Design View

1. Click **Format** .... Alt + O
2. Click **Field Size** .... Z
3. Click **Width** .... W
4. Type desired width .... *number*
5. Click **OK** .... Enter
OR
Drag white box at end of selected field to desired width.

In List View

1. Click **Format** .... Alt + O
2. Click **Field Width** .... W
3. Type desired width .... *number*
   OR
   Click desired automatic fit
      Standard .... S
      Best Fit .... B
4. Click **OK** .... Enter
   OR
   Drag field name border to desired width.
   OR
   Double-click field name to adjust field width automatically (after data is entered).

CHANGE RECORD HEIGHT

In List View

1. Click **Format** .... Alt + O
2. Click **Record Height** .... H
3. Click **Row Height** .... R
4. Type desired Height .... *number*
5. Click **OK** .... Enter
OR
Drag field number border to desired height.

SET OPTION TO MOVE TO NEXT ROW WITH ENTER

In List View

1. Click **Tools**. .... Alt + T
2. Click **Options** .... O
3. Click **Data Entry tab** .... Alt + Y
4. Click **Move selection after Enter** .... Alt + L
5. Click **Enter** .... Enter

EXERCISE **7**

■ Modify the Form ■ Move a Field ■ Copy Data ■ Use Fill Series

NOTES:

Modify the Form

Add a Field

■ After a database has been created, you might realize that you want to include another field. Or, you might want to delete a field that is no longer important to your database. Fields may be added or deleted in either List view or Form Design view. (*Fields cannot be added or deleted in Form view.*)

■ It does not matter where on the form you insert the field. You can move it wherever you desire (*see Move a Field, page 292*). The field created in the Form Design view displays to the right of the last field when you change to List view.

To add a field in Form Design view.

• Position insertion point anywhere on the form.

• Type the new field name, followed by a colon and press Enter.
  The Insert Field dialog box appears.

• Choose a Format.

• Click OK.

• Click <u>F</u>ield from the <u>I</u>nsert menu.

• Type the new field name, up to 15 characters.

• Choose a Format.

  ✓ NOTE: *Formatting a database field will be covered in detail in Exercise 15.*

• Click OK.

To add a field in List view:

• Click a field name to the left or right of where you wish to add the new field (the selected field will highlight).

• Select <u>I</u>nsert Field from the <u>R</u>ecord menu.

• Choose <u>1</u> Before to add the new field to the left of the highlighted field or <u>2</u> After to add the new field to the right of the highlighted field.

• Type the new field name (without colon).

• Choose a Format.

• Click A<u>d</u>d.

• Repeat these steps for each new field you wish to add.

• Click D<u>o</u>ne when you have added all desired new fields.

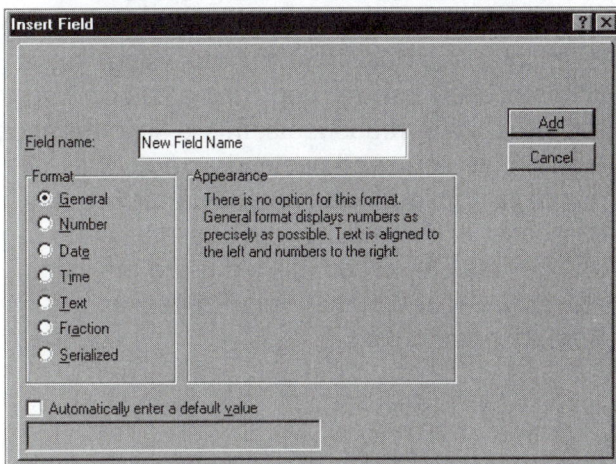

Field added in List view

OR

• Position insertion point anywhere on the form.

■ Adding a field in List view has one major disadvantage: When you add a field in List view, and then change to Form view, the new field will appear at the top of the form, overlaying the first field in the form.

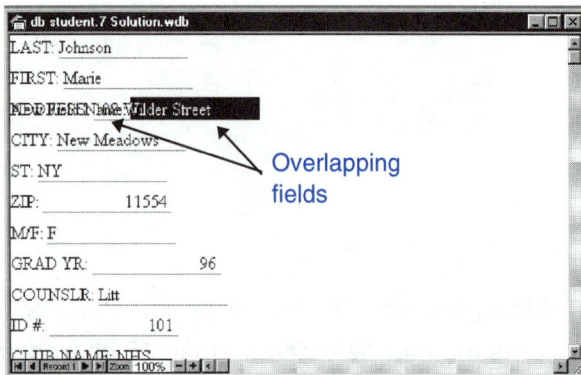

■ To remove the overlap and make the field usable, you must move the field. *It is suggested, therefore, that you add new fields in Form Design view, then change to List view if you prefer to enter data in that mode.*

Delete a Field

To delete a field in Form Design view:

- Click the field name to select the entire field to delete.
- Press the Delete key.
- Select OK to confirm the deletion.

To delete a field in List view:

- Click the field name to select the entire field to delete.
- Select Delete Field from the Record menu.
- Select OK to confirm deletion.

Move a Field

■ A field may be moved to any part of the record in List view or Form Design view.

To move a field in Form Design view:

- Select Form Design from the View menu.
- Click the field name to highlight the field to move.
- When the pointer changes to an arrow with the word *drag* under it, drag the field to the desired location.

■ When you change the location of the field in Form Design view, it will not affect the location of the field in List view.

To move a field in List view, you may use either drag and drop or cut and paste.

Use Cut and Paste

- Click field name to select entire column.
- Select Cut from the Edit menu.
- Select OK to confirm the deletion.
- Click the field name to the right of where the moved text is to be inserted (this will highlight the column).
- Select Paste from the Edit menu. The text will appear to the left of the highlighted column.

Use Drag and Drop

- Click the field name to select the entire field to move.
- When the pointer changes to an arrow with the word *drag* under it, click and hold the mouse button again.
- The word *drag* changes to the word *move* and a bold line with a cross bar at the top appears to help guide your move.
- Drag the field to the desired location.

■ Changing the field location in List view will not affect the location of the field in Form view or Form Design view.

Copy Data

■ In the Spreadsheet and Word Processor sections, you learned to copy data from one location to another. In word processing, this is accomplished through copy and paste or drag and drop. In spreadsheets, this is accomplished through the copy and paste, drag and drop, fill down, fill right or fill series procedures. In database, copying data from one location to another may be accomplished using the same procedures used in the Word Processor and Spreadsheet tools.

- Copy, Paste and Fill options may be selected from the Edit menu:

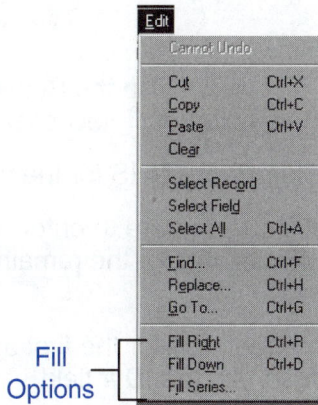

Fill Options

Copy and Paste

To copy data using Copy and Paste:

- Click entry to be copied or highlight multiple entries to be copied.
- Select Copy from the Edit menu.
- Click in the destination cell.
- If copying multiple entries, click the cell in which you want the copied data to begin.
- Select Paste from the Edit menu.

To copy data using the drag procedure:

- Click entry to be copied or highlight multiple entries to be copied.
- Point to the border of your selection until an arrow appears with the word *drag* under it.
- Hold down the Ctrl key.
- Hold your left mouse button down–the word *drag* will change to the word *move.*
- Drag your selection to the desired location.

Fill Down, Fill Right

- Click the cell containing the data to be copied.
- Click and hold the left mouse button.
- Highlight all cells below or to the right of where the data is to be copied.
- Click Edit.
- Click Fill Right or Fill Down to complete the procedure.

✓CAUTION: *When using a Fill option, do not click the column header to highlight the column. Click only the entry to be copied and drag down to highlight only those locations to receive the copied data.*

If you highlight the entire column, you will fill 32,000 records, creating a huge database that takes a long time to fill and uses a huge amount of memory.

Use Fill Series

- The Fill Series feature allows you to enter sequential numbers, days, weekdays, months and/or years in any increment you set in the **Step by** text box.

Fill Series

- Click List from the View menu.
- Click the field where you want to start the series.
- Type the starting number or date.
- Press Enter.
- Drag down or to the right to highlight where you want Works to fill in the series.
- Click Fill Series from the Edit menu.
- Under Units, click the unit you want for the series.
- In the **Step by** box, type a different number if you want the series to increase by more than 1.
- Click OK.

Fill as Number

Fill as Date

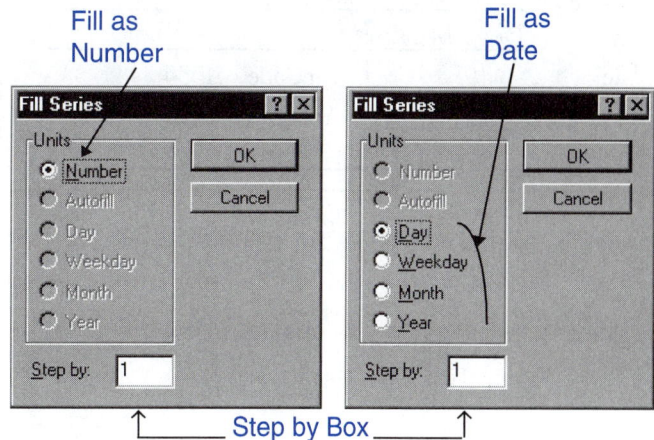

Step by Box

> *In this exercise, you will enter information into the STUDENT database you created.*

EXERCISE DIRECTIONS:

1. Open ⌨**STUDENT**, or open 💾**DB STUDENT.7**.

2. Change to Form view.

3. Enter the record for the first applicant (Form #1, Marie Johnson) from the application form illustrated. Enter only the last two numbers of the year of graduation.

4. Enter the records for the remaining applications. Enter the information from the forms in numerical order as indicated in the upper left hand corner of each form.

5. Change to List view.

6. Use the Best Fit feature in each field to adjust the column widths to accommodate the longest entry in each field.

7. Change to Form Design view.

8. Add 2 new fields: CLUB NAME and ID #. Move these Fields into usable locations on the form.

9. Change to List view. Use the Best Fit feature to widen the new columns if necessary.

10. Enter the Club Name NHS for the first record.

11. Use the Fill Down feature to enter NHS in the CLUB NAME column for the remaining applicants.

12. Enter the number 101 for the first applicant (*Marie Johnson*) in the ID # field.

13. Use the Fill Series feature to enter the ID #s sequentially for all the other applicants.

14. Move the CLUB NAME column after the ZIP CODE column.

15. Correct errors.

16. Close the file; save the changes.

Form #: 1   **KENNEDY HIGH SCHOOL**
2098 LUTEN AVENUE
NEW MEADOWS, NY 11554

"Home of the Dragons"

Name of Club to which you are applying   NHS

Last Name   Johnson   First Name   Marie
Address   108 Wilder Street
City   New Meadows
State   NY   ZipCode   11554
M/F   F   Year of Graduation   96
Counselor   Litt

Form #: 2   **KENNEDY HIGH SCHOOL**
2098 LUTEN AVENUE
NEW MEADOWS, NY 11554

"Home of the Dragons"

Name of Club to which you are applying   NHS

Last Name   Harris   First Name   Richard
Address   34 Desmond Avenue
City   New Meadows
State   NY   ZipCode   11554
M/F   M   Year of Graduation   96
Counselor   Litt

Form #: 3

KENNEDY HIGH SCHOOL
2098 LUTEN AVENUE
NEW MEADOWS, NY 11554

"Home of the Dragons"

Name of Club to which you are applying NHS

Last Name Russo   First Name Ron
Address 22 Hapins Lane
City New Meadows
State NY   ZipCode 11554
M/F M   Year of Graduation 98
Counselor Lifton

Form #: 6

KENNEDY HIGH SCHOOL
2098 LUTEN AVENUE
NEW MEADOWS, NY 11554

"Home of the Dragons"

Name of Club to which you are applying NHS

Last Name Freeman   First Name Keisha
Address 5 Winding Way
City New Meadows
State NY   ZipCode 11554
M/F F   Year of Graduation 97
Counselor Cohen

Form #: 4

KENNEDY HIGH SCHOOL
2098 LUTEN AVENUE
NEW MEADOWS, NY 11554

"Home of the Dragons"

Name of Club to which you are applying NHS

Last Name Lakhani   First Name Deepa
Address 87 Pine Street
City New Meadows
State NY   ZipCode 11554
M/F F   Year of Graduation 98
Counselor Lifton

Form #: 7

KENNEDY HIGH SCHOOL
2098 LUTEN AVENUE
NEW MEADOWS, NY 11554

"Home of the Dragons"

Name of Club to which you are applying NHS

Last Name Yu   First Name Vicki
Address 888 Martin Court
City New Meadows
State NY   ZipCode 11554
M/F F   Year of Graduation 97
Counselor Cohen

Form #: 5

KENNEDY HIGH SCHOOL
2098 LUTEN AVENUE
NEW MEADOWS, NY 11554

"Home of the Dragons"

Name of Club to which you are applying NHS

Last Name Lopez   First Name Maria
Address 987 Stiles Street
City Westbury
State NY   ZipCode 11590
M/F F   Year of Graduation 97
Counselor Cohen

Form #: 8

KENNEDY HIGH SCHOOL
2098 LUTEN AVENUE
NEW MEADOWS, NY 11554

"Home of the Dragons"

Name of Club to which you are applying NHS

Last Name Rifsky   First Name Vlad
Address 109 Maple Lane
City New Meadows
State NY   ZipCode 11554
M/F M   Year of Graduation 98
Counselor Scalisi

Form #: 9   **KENNEDY HIGH SCHOOL**
2098 LUTEN AVENUE
NEW MEADOWS, NY 11554

"Home of the Dragons"

Name of Club to which you are applying   NHS

Last Name _Craig_   First Name _David_

Address _23 Oak Lane_

City _Westbury_

State _NY_   ZipCode _11590_

M/F _M_   Year of Graduation _98_

Counselor _Scalisi_

Form #: 11   **KENNEDY HIGH SCHOOL**
2098 LUTEN AVENUE
NEW MEADOWS, NY 11554

"Home of the Dragons"

Name of Club to which you are applying   NHS

Last Name _Ahman_   First Name _Waisif_

Address _234 Woodrow Street_

City _Westbury_

State _NY_   ZipCode _11590_

M/F _M_   Year of Graduation _96_

Counselor _Litt_

Form #: 10   **KENNEDY HIGH SCHOOL**
2098 LUTEN AVENUE
NEW MEADOWS, NY 11554

"Home of the Dragons"

Name of Club to which you are applying   NHS

Last Name _Kim_   First Name _Phil_

Address _11 Oak Lane_

City _Westbury_

State _NY_   ZipCode _11590_

M/F _M_   Year of Graduation _96_

Counselor _Cohen_

ADD A FIELD

In Form Design View

1. Position insertion point where you wish to insert new field.

2. a. Type new field name............... *name* followed by a colon.

   b. Press **ENTER** .... `Enter`
      The Insert Field dialog box appears.

   OR

   a. Click **Insert** .... `Alt`+`I`

   b. Click **Field** .... `F`
      The Insert Field dialog box appears.

   c. Type new field name .... *name* without the colon.

3. Choose a Format.

   • **General** .... `G`

   • **Number** .... `N`

   • **Date** .... `E`

   • **Time** .... `I`

   • **Text** .... `T`

   • **Fraction** .... `A`

   • **Serialized** .... `S`

4. Click **OK** .... `Enter`

In List View

1. Select the field name header to which you wish the new field to be adjacent.

2. Click **Record**. .... `Alt`+`R`

3. Click **Insert Field.** .... `I`

4. Choose **1 Before** .... `1`

   OR

   2 After .... `2`
   The Insert Field dialog box appears.

5. Type new field name .... *field name* in **F**ieldname text box.

6. Choose a Format:

   • **General** .... `G`

   • **Number** .... `N`

   • **Date** .... `E`

   • **Time** .... `I`

   • **Text** .... `T`

   • **Fraction** .... `A`

   • **Serialized** .... `S`

7. Click **Add**. .... `D`

8. Repeat steps 5-6 for each new field.

9. Click **Done**. .... `O`

DELETE A FIELD

In Form Design View

1. Select field to delete.

2. Press **Delete** key .... `Del`

3. Click **OK** .... `Enter`
   to confirm deletion.

In List View

1. Select field to delete.

2. Click **Record** .... `Alt`+`R`

3. Click **Delete Field** .... `E`

4. Select **OK** .... `Enter`
   to confirm deletion.

MOVE A FIELD

In Form Design View

1. Select field to move.

2. Place cursor in selection until arrow appears with the word *drag* under it.

3. Drag field to new location.

4. Release mouse button.

In List View

1. Select entire column to move.

2. Click **Edit** .... `Alt`+`E`

3. Click **Cut** .... `T`

4. Click **OK** to confirm deletion .... `Enter`

5. Click field header to the right of where text is to be inserted.

6. Click **Edit** .... `Alt`+`E`

7. Click **Paste** .... `P`

COPY DATA

In List View

–USING COPY AND PASTE–

1. Select row to be copied.
   OR
   Select field contents to be copied.

2. Click **Edit** .... `Alt`+`E`

3. Click **Copy** .... `C`

4. Click location to be copied to.

5. Click **Edit** .... `Alt`+`E`

6. Click **Paste** .... `P`

–USING DRAG AND DROP–

1. Click entry or select entries to be copied.

2. Move cursor to border of selection until arrow appears with the word *drag* under it.

3. Hold down **Ctrl** key

4. Drag selection to desired location

5. Release mouse button.

6. Release the **Ctrl** key.

–USING FILL DOWN–

1. Select entry to be copied.

2. Drag down *(include the entry)* to highlight locations to be filled.

3. Click **Edit** .... `Alt`+`E`

4. Click **Fill Down** .... `W`

–USING FILL RIGHT–

1. Select entry to be copied.

2. Drag right *(include the entry)* to highlight locations to be filled.

3. Click **Edit** .... `Alt`+`E`

4. Click **Fill Right** .... `H`

–USING FILL SERIES–

1. Click the field where you want to start the series.

2. Type the starting number or date .... *number or date*

3. Press **Enter** .... `Enter`

4. Drag down or to the right to highlight where you want Works to fill in the series.

5. Click **Edit** .... `Alt`+`E`

6. Click **Fill Series** .... `I`

7. Click unit you want for the series

   • **Number** .... `N`
     Autofill is not available in Database

   • **Day** .... `D`

   • **Weekday** .... `W`

   • **Month** .... `M`

   • **Year** .... `Y`

8. Type a different number in the **Step by** box .... `S`
   if you want the series to increase by more than one.

9. Click **OK** .... `Enter`

EXERCISE **8**

Your manager at Bit-Byte has just given you a list of the new branches and their locations. She has asked you to enter this information into your database. In addition, she realized that sales information and whether or not a branch has evening hours should have been included in the database. You will need to add two additional fields.

EXERCISE DIRECTIONS:

1. Open ⌨**STORES**, or open 💾**DB STORES.8**.

2. Add two new fields to the end of the database: SALES and EVE.

3. From the list below, enter the information for each branch into the database.
   - ✔ *NOTE:* *When entering money amounts, remember that if you enter the amount without a dollar sign, Works displays it in that exact form. If you add a dollar sign to an entry, all the numeric entries in that field, including those you add subsequently, will change to include the dollar sign.*

4. Use the Best Fit feature to adjust column widths to accommodate the new data.

5. Use copy and paste to enter Yes/No information into the EVE field locations.

6. Move the SALES column before the STAFF column.

7. Correct errors.

8. Change to Form Design view.

9. Move the SALES and EVE fields into a usable location on the form.

10. Move the SALES field before the STAFF field on the form.

11. Change back to List view.

12. Close the file; save the changes.

	BRANCH	CITY	ST	STAFF	SALES	EVE
1	Big Apple	New York	NY	15	789300	Yes
2	Pacific	Los Angeles	CA	14	685400	No
3	Sunset	San Francisco	CA	21	876988	No
4	Lakeview	Chicago	IL	15	755420	No
5	Peach Tree	Atlanta	GA	9	457800	Yes
6	Bean Town	Boston	MA	16	682450	Yes
7	Astro Center	Houston	TX	8	541000	No
8	Twin Cities	San Diego	CA	7	235420	Yes
9	Wheatland	Topeka	KS	12	352415	Yes
10	Oceanview	Providence	RI	6	433443	Yes

EXERCISE **9**

■ **Page Setup** ■ **Add Headers and/or Footers**
■ **Print Preview** ■ **Print** ■ **Show and Print Selected Records**

NOTES:

Page Setup

■ Before actually printing the database, you can use the Page Setup selection to choose certain printing options. These include:

- Changing margins.

- Changing the paper source, size and orientation.

- Printing with field labels (in List view) or field lines (in Form view).

- Printing with gridlines (in List view).

- Inserting page breaks between records (in Form view).

■ Page Setup options affect both Form view and List view. However, Other Options are different for the two views. In Form view, you can print the lines below the fields. You can also specify if you wish to print each record on a separate page, print all the items on the form, or only the data in the fields.

SOURCE, SIZE & ORIENTATION IN LIST VIEW

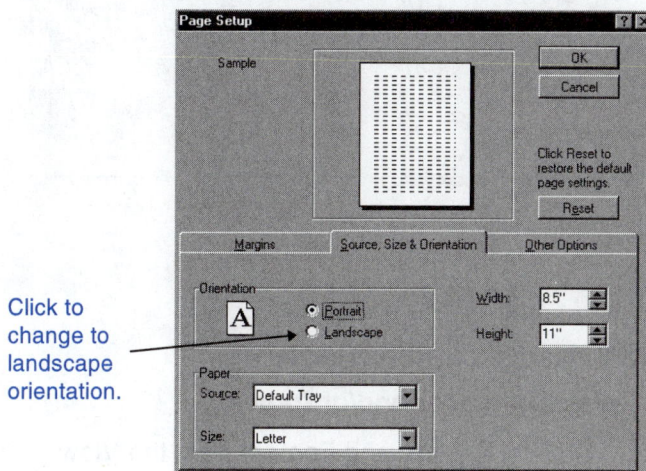

Click to change to landscape orientation.

OTHER OPTIONS IN LIST VIEW

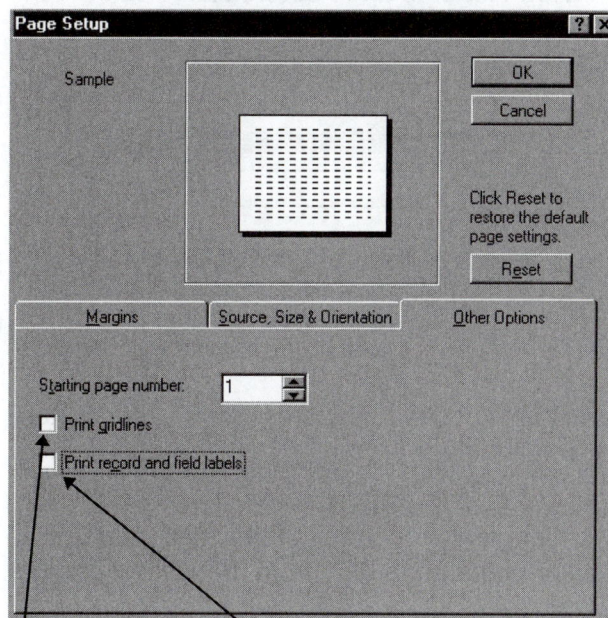

Click to print with guidelines

Click to print with record and field labels

OTHER OPTIONS IN FORM VIEW

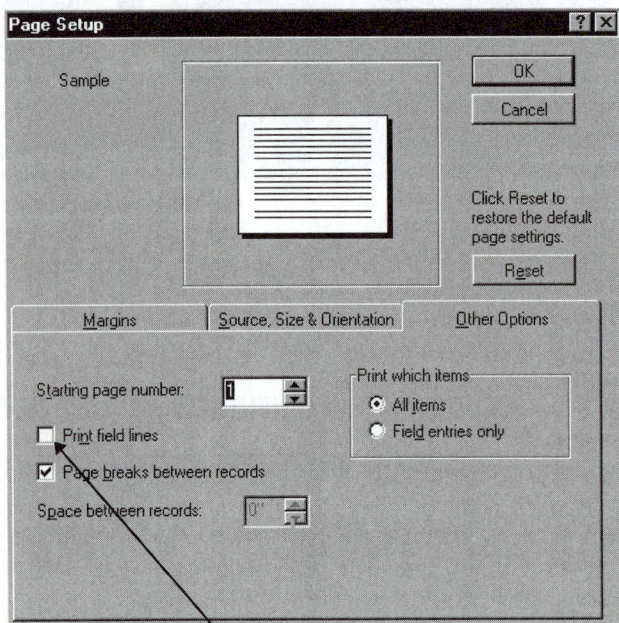

Click to print
field lines.

Add Headers and/or Footers

To add a header and/or footer:

- Select Headers and Footers from the View menu.

- Type the desired header and/or footer in the View Headers and Footers dialog box which follows.

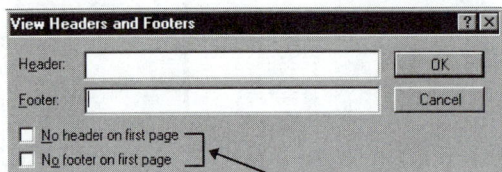

- Click OK.

Click to suppress header or
footer on the first page.

- You may choose to suppress the header/footer on the first page by clicking the desired check box in the Headers and Footers dialog box.

- Headers and/or footers automatically align in the center of the page, 0.5" from the top or bottom of the page.

Print Preview

- To see how your records will print before actually printing them, you may use the Print Preview option. This option also allows you to view multiple pages, change the view magnification, or print a single copy of the document. Headers and footers display in this view.

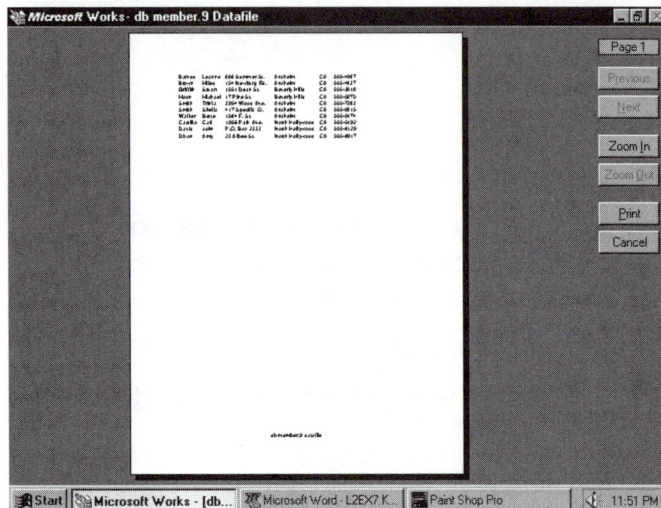

To Access Print Preview

Select Print Preview from the File menu.

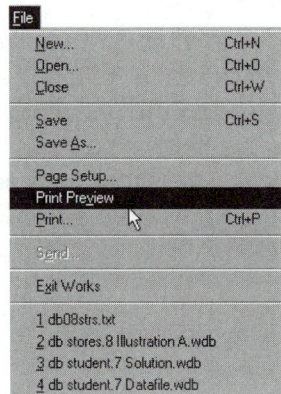

OR

Click the Print Preview button on the Toolbar.

Print

- Records may be printed in Form view or in List view. In Form view, you print each record on a separate page; in List view, you print multiple records all on one page displayed in a table format.

To print the database:

- Click Print from the File menu.
- Click OK.

Print One Selected Record

You may print one selected record from the database in Form view by selecting Print from the File menu and specifying that you wish to print the Current record only.

Show and Print Selected Records

You may show and print selected records by marking them. This is done in List view only. In a later lesson, you will learn how to search the database, select certain records that meet a condition or conditions, and print them.

To Show and Print Selected Records:

- Mark record(s) by clicking the check box next to the record number of each record you want to mark.

Check boxes

Click →
to mark →
records

✓		LAST	FIRST	ADDRESS	CITY	ST	PHONE
☐	1	Barnes	Leanne	808 Summer St.	Anaheim	CA	555-4987
☐	2	Brown	Miles	154 Newburg Rd.	Anaheim	CA	555-4837
☐	3	Griffith	Stuart	1551 Dean St.	Beverly Hills	CA	555-3010
☐	4	Moon	Michael	17 Pine St.	Beverly Hills	CA	555-9275
☐	5	Smith	Trinia	3954 Wood Ave.	Anaheim	CA	555-7283
☐	6	Smith	Sheila	417 Specific Ct.	Anaheim	CA	555-0815
☐	7	Walker	Bette	1584 F. St.	Anaheim	CA	555-9174
☐	8	Castillo	Carl	1956 Park Ave.	North Hollywood	CA	555-5192
☐	9	Davis	John	P.O. Box 2333	North Hollywood	CA	555-8129
☐	10	Dixon	Amy	23 Albee St.	North Hollywood	CA	555-8917
☐	11						
☐	12						
☐	13						
☐	14						
☐	15						
☐	16						
☐	17						
☐	18						

Zoom 100%

- Click Show, 3 Unmarked Records, from the Record menu to show unmarked records.

OR

Click Show, 2 Marked Records from the Record menu to show marked records.

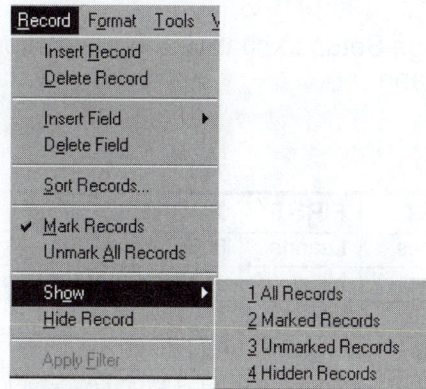

Record Format Tools
Insert Record
Delete Record

Insert Field ▶
Delete Field

Sort Records...

✔ Mark Records
Unmark All Records

Show ▶ | 1 All Records
Hide Record | 2 Marked Records
Apply Filter | 3 Unmarked Records
| 4 Hidden Records

- Print the database with only the desired records showing.

In order to use the HUG membership database for mailings, it is necessary to include a zip code for each member. Since certain mailings apply only to a particular professional group, it would be helpful to include a field that will identify a person's profession. This will enable you to send information to one particular group, rather than to everyone on your list. In this exercise, you will add two new fields (ZIP and PROF) and print selected records.

EXERCISE DIRECTIONS:

1. Open ⌨MEMBER, or open 💾DB MEMBER.9.

2. Select List view.

3. Add two new fields to the end of the database: ZIP and PROF.

4. Add the highlighted data to the existing database.

5. Use the Best Fit feature to adjust column widths to accommodate the new data.

6. Move the ZIP field after the ST field.

7. Correct any errors.

8. Change to Form Design view.

9. Move the ZIP and PROF fields into a usable location on the form.

10. Change to List view.

11. Mark the records of the doctors. (*Determine for yourself which professions would be associated with a Doctor.*)

12. Show only the unmarked records (without the Doctors).

13. Use Page Setup to change the orientation to Landscape.

14. Create a header: HUG MEMBERSHIP LIST - FIRST DRAFT

15. Use Page Setup to print with Record Field Labels and Gridlines.

16. Preview the page.

17. Print the database with only the unmarked records showing (without the Doctor records).

18. Show all the records.

19. Close the file; save the changes.

	LAST	FIRST	ADDRESS	CITY	ST	PHONE	ZIP	PROF
1	Barnes	Leanne	808 Summer St.	Anaheim	CA	555-4987	92803	Student
2	Brown	Miles	154 Newburg Rd.	Anaheim	CA	555-4837	92804	Accountant
3	Griffith	Stuart	1551 Dean St.	Beverly Hills	CA	555-3010	90210	Lawyer
4	Moon	Michael	17 Pine St.	Beverly Hills	CA	555-9275	80210	Teacher
5	Smith	Trinia	3954 Wood Ave.	Anaheim	CA	555-7283	92803	Student
6	Smith	Sheila	417 Specific Ct.	Anaheim	CA	555-0815	92803	Chiropractor
7	Walker	Bette	1584 F. St.	Anaheim	CA	555-9174	92803	Lawyer
8	Castillo	Carl	1956 Park Ave.	North Hollywood	CA	555-5192	91615	Banker
9	Davis	John	P.O. Box 2333	North Hollywood	CA	555-8129	91615	Student
10	Dixon	Amy	23 Albee St.	North Hollywood	CA	555-8917	91615	Orthopedist

PAGE SETUP

1. Click **File** .... Alt + F
2. Click **Page Setup** .... G
3. To change margins:
   a. Select **Margins** tab .... Alt + M
   b. Set desired margins.
4. To change orientation:
   a. Select **Source, Size and** .. Alt + S
      Orientation tab.
   b. Click desired orientation:
      • **Portrait** .... P
      • **Landscape** L
5. To print with gridlines and/or field labels:
   a. Select **Other Options** .... Alt + O
      on file folders.
   b. Click to select option (place x in check box or select radio button):
   In List View
      • **Print gridlines** .... G
      • **Print record and field labels** ... C
   In Form View
      • **Print field lines** .... N
      • **Print breaks between records.** B
         • **All items** I
         • **Field entries only** .... D
6. Click **OK** .... Enter

HEADERS AND FOOTERS

1. Click **View** .... Alt + V
2. Click **Headers and Footers** .... H
3. Type desired header
   in **Header** text box .... Alt + E
   AND/OR
   Type desired footer
   in **Footer** text box .... Alt + F
   To print without header/footer on first page:
      Select **No header on** .... Alt + N
      first page check box.
      AND/OR
      Select **No footer on** .... Alt + O
      first page check box.
4. Click **OK** .... Enter

PRINT PREVIEW

1. Click **File** .... Alt + F
2. Click **Print Preview** V

PRINT

Ctrl + P

1. Click **File** .... Alt + F
2. Click **Print** .... P
3. Click **OK** .... Enter

PRINT ONE SELECTED RECORD

1. Click **View** .... Alt + V
2. Click **Form** .... F
3. Click **File** .... Alt + F
4. Click **Print** .... P
5. Click **OK** .... Enter

SHOW AND PRINT SELECTED RECORD(S)

IN LIST VIEW

1. Mark record to be hidden ..... ☑ 1
   by clicking the check box
   next to the record number.
2. Click **Record** .... Alt + R
3. Click **Show** .... O
4. Click **3 Unmarked Records** 3
   OR
   Click **2 Marked Records** 2
5. Click **File** .... Alt + F
6. Click **Print** .... P
7. Click **OK** .... Enter

DISPLAY ALL RECORDS

1. Click **Record** .... Alt + R
2. Click **Show** .... O
3. Click **1 All Records** 1

EXERCISE **10**

■ **Edit Record or Field Data** ■ **Insert a Record** ■ **Delete a Record**

NOTES:

Edit Record or Field Data

■ Editing data that has already been entered in a field can be done only in List view or Form view, not in Form Design view.

To edit the data in a cell:

- Select the cell containing the data you wish to edit.
- Press the F2 key. This will give you a cursor within that field.
- Make desired changes to the data using functions you used in the Word Processor tool (backspace, delete and add new text).
- Press Enter.

To replace the entire contents of a data cell:

- Select the cell containing the existing data.
- Type the new data. (As soon as you start typing, your new data will replace the current data).
- Press Enter.

■ If you want to leave a record or field cell empty, select the cell and:

Click Clear from the Edit menu.

(Edit menu shown)

Edit
Cannot Undo
Cut   Ctrl+X
Copy   Ctrl+C
Paste   Ctrl+V
Clear
Select Record
Select Field
Select All   Ctrl+A
Find...   Ctrl+F
Replace...   Ctrl+H
Go To...   Ctrl+G
Fill Right   Ctrl+R
Fill Down   Ctrl+D
Fill Series...

OR

Press the Spacebar, then the Enter key.

OR

Press the Delete key, then the Enter key.

Delete the Contents of a Record or Field

■ Deleting the contents of a record or field without replacing it can be done only in List view. This will not affect the structure of the record or field.

Select the row number or field name containing the data, then click Clear from the Edit menu.

OR

Select the row number or field name containing the data, press the Delete key, then the Enter key.

Insert a Record

■ Records may be added in either Form view or List view, not in Form Design view.

In List View

To add a record to the end of the database:

- Select the appropriate cell in the last row (below the last record).
- Type the new record.

☑		LAST	FIRST	ADDRESS	CITY
☒	1	Johnson	Marie	108 Wilder Street	New Meadows
☒	2	Harris	Richard	34 Desmond Avenue	New Meadows
☒	3	Russo	Ron	22 Hapins Land	New Meadows
☒	4	Lakhani	Deepa	87 Pine Street	New Meadows
☒	5	Lopez	Maria	987 Stiles Street	Westbury
☒	6	Freeman	Keisha	5 Winding Way	New Meadows
☒	7	Yu	Vicki	888 Martin Court	New Meadows
☒	8	Rifsky	Vlad	109 Maple Lane	New Meadows
☒	9	Craig	David	23 Oak Lane	Westbury
☒	10	Kim	Phil	11 Oak Lane	Westbury
☒	11	Ahman	Waisif	234 Woodrow Street	Westbury
☐	12				
☐	13				

Click cell in last row to insert new record to end of database.

- Use the Tab key, Shift+Tab key or arrow keys to move from field to field.

To add a record anywhere in the database other than the end:

- Click the row number below where you wish to add the new record.

- Select Insert Record from the Record menu.

- Type the new record.

In Form View

To add a record to the end of the database:

- Click the Last Record button (located to the left of the Zoom Control).

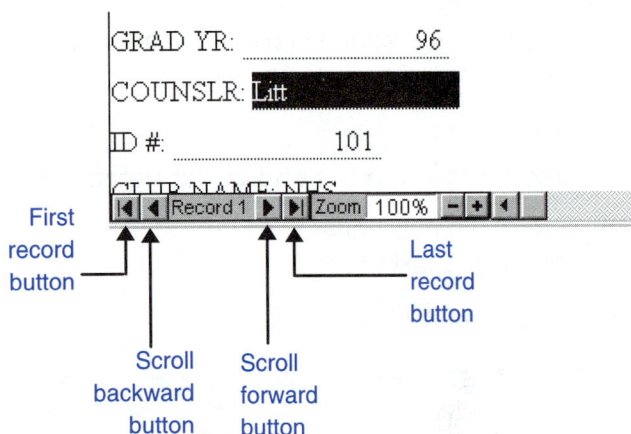

- Use the Tab key or Shift+Tab to get to the first field in the blank record if necessary.

- Type the new record.

To add a record anywhere in the database other than the end:

- Scroll to the record that you want to follow the new record.

- Select Insert Record from the Record menu.

- Works will provide a blank form for you to type a new record.

- Works renumbers all records below the new one, regardless of the view used when adding the new record.

Delete a Record

- Records may be deleted in either Form view or List view, not in Form Design view.

To delete a record in List view:

- Click the row number to select the entire record.

- Select Delete Record from the Record menu.

To delete a record in Form view:

- Scroll to the record you wish to delete.

- Select Delete Record from the Record menu.

- If after you delete a record, you realize that you made a mistake, you can undo your action by selecting Undo Delete Record from the Edit menu.

   ✓ NOTE: You can only undo the last action performed.

Several students are no longer being considered for membership in the National Honor Society (NHS) and several new students have just submitted applications. You have also discovered several errors in the records. You will need to edit your database to reflect these changes. Applications have just been received for the Academy of Finance Program. You will need to add these to your database.

EXERCISE DIRECTIONS:

1. Open ▧STUDENT, or open ▨DB STUDENT.10.

2. The students listed below have applied for admission to the Academy of Finance Program (AF). Add their records to the database. *(Their ID #s start with 201. Use the Fill Series feature to enter their ID #s.)*

	LAST	FIRST	ADDRESS	CITY	ST	ZIP	CLUB NAME	M/F	GRAD YR	COUNSLR	ID #
12	DeLorenzo	Kristin	871 River Road	New Meadows	NY	11554	AF	F	96	Litt	201
13	Chasin	Matthew	99 Bridle Lane	New Meadows	NY	11554	AF	M	98	Lifton	202
14	Wilkinson	Chad	2 Token Court	New Meadows	NY	11554	AF	M	98	Lifton	203
15	Rivers	Ebony	33 Pine Street	New Meadows	NY	11554	AF	F	96	Litt	204
16	Juliani	Jennifer	78 Token Court	New Meadows	NY	11554	AF	F	96	Litt	205

3. Ron Russo is no longer being considered for membership in the NHS. Delete his record. (Once an ID # has been assigned it cannot be reassigned until the following school year, so his ID# will also be deleted. The next available ID # is 111.)

4. The students listed in the next table have applied for admission to the NHS. Add their records to the database.

	LAST	FIRST	ADDRESS	CITY	ST	ZIP	CLUB NAME	M/F	GRAD YR	COUNSLR	ID #
16	Choi	Wendy	7654 Hylan Blvd.	New Meadows	NY	11554	NHS	F	97	Cohen	112
17	Smith	Rick	9012 Hylan Blvd.	New Meadows	NY	11554	NHS	M	97	Cohen	113

5. Keisha Freeman's correct address is 5 Winding Woods Way. Correct her record.

6. Use the Best Fit feature in each field to readjust the column widths to accommodate the new data.

7. Mark the records of the NHS applicants.

8. Show only the unmarked records.

9. Use Page Setup to print in Landscape Orientation and with field labels and gridlines.

10. Preview your page.

11. Print the database without the NHS records (the unmarked records).

12. Show all the records in the database.

13. Close the file; save the changes.

EDIT RECORD OR FIELD DATA

To Edit Existing Data

–IN LIST OR FORM VIEW–

1. Select the cell containing data to edit.
2. Press **F2** *(cursor appears in cell)* .... `F2`
3. Make desired changes to data
4. Press **Enter** .... `Enter`

To Replace Existing Data

–IN LIST OR FORM VIEW–

1. Select the cell containing the data to replace
2. Type the new data ....*text*
3. Press **Enter**. .... `Enter`

To Delete the Contents of Record or Field Cell

–IN LIST OR FORM VIEW–

1. Select the cell containing the data to delete
2. a. Click **Edit** .... `Alt`+`E`
   b. Click **Clear** .... `A`
   OR
   Press the **Spacebar**.................. `Space`
   OR
   Press the **Delete** key .... `Del`

To Delete the Entire Contents of a Record or Field

–IN LIST VIEW–

1. Select the row number ...... *row number* containing the data.
   OR
   Select the field name .... *field name* containing the data.
2. Click **Edit** .... `Alt`+`E`
3. Click **Clear**.................................... `A`
   OR
   a. Press the **Delete** key................ `Del`
   b. Press **Enter** .... `Enter`

INSERT A RECORD

At the End of Database

–IN LIST VIEW–

1. Click the appropriate cell in the last row below the last record.
2. Type new record

–IN FORM VIEW–

1. Click **Last Record** button................. `▶|`
2. Press **Tab** .... `Tab`
   to the first field in blank record.
   (Shift+Tab and the arrow keys can also be used)
3. Type new record.
4. Press **Enter** .... `Enter`

Middle of Database

–IN LIST VIEW–

1. Click in the row number below the row where new record is to be inserted.
2. Click **Record**......................... `Alt`+`R`
3. Click **Insert Record** .... `R`
4. Type new record.
5. Press **Enter** .... `Enter`

--IN FORM VIEW--

1. Scroll to the record that you want to follow the new record.
2. Click **Record**......................... `Alt`+`R`
3. Click **Insert Record** .... `R`
4. Type new record on blank form

DELETE A RECORD

–IN LIST VIEW–

1. Click row number to select the entire record
2. Click **Record**......................... `Alt`+`R`
3. Click **Delete Record** .... `D`

--IN FORM VIEW--

1. Select record to delete.
2. Click **Record**......................... `Alt`+`R`
3. Click **Delete Record** .... `D`

UNDO

1. Click **Edit**............................. `Alt`+`E`
2. Click **Undo**................................... `U`

EXERCISE **11**

■ **Edit a Record** ■ **Insert and Delete a Record**

Bit-Byte has opened several new branches. In some branches, there have been personnel changes. The database file, therefore, will need to be updated.

EXERCISE DIRECTIONS:

1. Open 📼**STORES**, or open 💾**DB STORES.11**

2. Select List view.

3. The following new branches have been opened. Add them to the database.

4. Use the Best Fit feature to adjust column widths to accommodate the new data.

5. There have been changes in the number of employees in the following branches: Make the changes to the database.

Big Apple	20
Wheatland	11
Astro Center	12
Peach Tree	16
Sunset	13

6. The **Twin Cities** branch closed. Delete the record.

7. Use Page Setup to print in Landscape orientation, with field labels and without gridlines.

8. Preview your page.

9. Print one copy.

10. Close the file; save the changes.

	BRANCH	CITY˜	ST	SALES	STAFF	EVE
11	Liberty	Philadelphia	PA	423150	19	Yes
12	Seal City Center	Anchorage	AL	185420	6	No
13	Central States	San Diego	CA	144524	14	No
14	Federal Plaza	Washington	DC	245860	11	No
15	Desert View Mall	Phoenix	AZ	189252	8	Yes
16	Rocky Mountain	Denver	CO	102563	9	Yes
17	Southland	Mobile	AL	104566	7	No
18	River View Plaza	Atlanta	GA	215400	6	No
19	Dixieland	Atlanta	GA	352622	14	Yes
20	Iron City Plaza	Cleveland	OH	543233	13	No

Exercise 12A, Part I: In the past, computer equipment inventory records for your department were kept on inventory cards. In an earlier exercise, you created an inventory database. In this exercise, you will enter information from those cards into the database.

EXERCISE DIRECTIONS:

1. Open ▦**INVENTORY**, or open 🖫**DB INVENTORY.12**.

2. After the last field, add two new fields: ASSIGNED TO and SERIAL #.

3. Change to Form Design view.

4. Move the ASSIGNED TO and SERIAL # fields into a usable location on the form.

   ✔ NOTE: *It is advisable to make **ASSIGNED TO** the last field on the form and to move the **SERIAL #** field under the **COST** field. This will allow you to enter the equipment information more easily by using your TAB key.*

5. Change to either List view or Form view, whichever view you prefer for entering data.

6. From the inventory cards in Illustration A, enter the equipment information into the database. Follow the numeric order of the cards as you enter the data. Enter field data in upper- and lowercase letters, except where names are represented by initials (NEC, IBM, PS2). Use the month/year format for entering dates (6/96).

7. Change to List view.

8. Use the Best Fit feature to adjust column widths where necessary.

9. Use Page Setup to change the orientation to Landscape and to print with field labels and gridlines.

10. Preview your page.

11. Print one copy.

12. Save the file; do not close the database.

ILLUSTRATION A

Card #: 1	**ABC Company**	
	Equipment Inventory Card	
Item Description	Computer	
Manufacturer	IBM	
Model	PS2	
Cost	1248	Serial # 651178
Purchase date	6/95	
Under Warranty	Yes	
Assigned to	Accounting	

Card #: 2	**ABC Company**	
	Equipment Inventory Card	
Item Description	Printer	
Manufacturer	IBM	
Model	ExecJet II	
Cost	335	Serial # 55211
Purchase date	6/96	
Under Warranty	Yes	
Assigned to	Personnel	

Card #: 3	**ABC Company**
	Equipment Inventory Card

Item Description	Computer
Manufacturer	IBM
Model	Thinkpad
Cost 2199	Serial # 2059
Purchase date	6/96
Under Warranty	Yes
Assigned to	Personnel

Card #: 6	**ABC Company**
	Equipment Inventory Card

Item Description	Printer
Manufacturer	HP
Model	LaserJet
Cost 1479	Serial # 88842
Purchase date	3/94
Under Warranty	No
Assigned to	Shipping

Card #: 4	**ABC Company**
	Equipment Inventory Card

Item Description	Hard Drive
Manufacturer	Conner
Model	CFS4 210MB
Cost 200	Serial # 12345
Purchase date	6/96
Under Warranty	No
Assigned to	Purchasing

Card #: 7	**ABC Company**
	Equipment Inventory Card

Item Description	Hard Drive
Manufacturer	Quantum
Model	LPS 40 170MB
Cost 199	Serial # 54219
Purchase date	3/96
Under Warranty	Yes
Assigned to	Accounting

Card #: 5	**ABC Company**
	Equipment Inventory Card

Item Description	Computer
Manufacturer	IBM
Model	Thinkpad 500
Cost 1399	Serial # 671150
Purchase date	6/96
Under Warranty	Yes
Assigned to	Accounting

Card #: 8	**ABC Company**
	Equipment Inventory Card

Item Description	Computer
Manufacturer	Canon
Model	Notebook 486
Cost 1889	Serial # 1445
Purchase date	1/96
Under Warranty	Yes
Assigned to	Shipping

> **Exercise 12A, Part II:** *Your company has acquired new equipment. These new purchases must be added to the inventory. When checking the database, you found several errors which needed to be corrected.*

EXERCISE DIRECTIONS:

If you closed the file from Exercise 12A, Part I, open **INVENTORY**

1. From the information below, add the new equipment purchases to the database.

2. Use the Best Fit feature to adjust the column widths if necessary to accommodate the new data.

3. The correct cost of the IBM PS2, purchased on 6/95 is 1348. Make the correction.

4. The Quantum Hard Drive is not under warranty. Make the correction.

5. The HP LaserJet printer, purchased on 3/94 is no longer in use. Delete the record from the database.

6. Mark the records where equipment has been assigned to Accounting.

7. Show only the marked records.

8. Print one copy of the marked records (Accounting records).

9. Show all records.

10. Unmark all records.

11. Print one copy of the entire database.

12. Close the file; save the changes.

ILLUSTRATION B

	ITEM	MFG	MODEL	COST	PURDATE	WTY	ASSIGNED TO	SERIAL #
9	Monitor	NEC	JGE/3V	539	12/96	No	Personnel	87098
10	Monitor	NEC	JGE	589	12/96	No	Accounting	11112
11	Modem	Intel	PCMCIA	115	1/96	No	Shipping	20098
12	Printer	Okidata	ML320	295	2/96	Yes	Shipping	98983
13	Printer	HP	DeskJet	429	11/96	Yes	Accounting	99911
14	Printer	HP	DeskJet	429	11/96	Yes	Personnel	22230
15	Computer	Canon	Notebook	2436	8/96	Yes	Personnel	98763
16	Computer	Canon	Notebook	2436	8/96	Yes	Purchasing	76666

Up to this time, you have kept a written log of your company's software purchases. Using the log page illustrated below, enter the records into the database you created in an earlier exercise.

EXERCISE DIRECTIONS:

1. Open the ⌨PROGRAM, or open 🖫DB PROGRAM.12.

2. Add a new field, SIGNED FOR, at the end of the database.

3. Change to Form Design view.

4. Move the SIGNED FOR field into a useable location on the form.

5. Change to Form or List view.

   ✔NOTE: You may enter the data in either form. Use the one you prefer.

6. From the March 11, 1996 log page illustrated below, enter the software information into the database.

7. If you entered the data in Form view, change to List View now.

8. Use the Best Fit feature to adjust column widths so that all the data shows.

   ✔NOTE: You may have to drag the column borders to widen columns that contain a long field name.

9. Use Page Setup to change the orientation to Landscape, and print with field labels and grid lines.

10. Preview your page.

11. Print one copy of the database.

12. Change to Form view.

13. Select the form listing ACCESSOR and print one copy of this record in Portrait Orientation.

   ✔HINT: After you access the Print Command, Click in the **Current Record Only** box so that only the one form prints.

14. Save the file, do not close the database.

15. Change to List view.

16. Mark the records of all Windows programs.

17. Show the unmarked records (Non-Windows Programs).

18. Print one copy of the unmarked records (Non-Windows Programs) in Landscape Orientation.

19. Show the marked records.

20. Print one copy of the database with only the marked records (Windows Programs) in Landscape orientation.

21. Show all records.

22. Unmark all records.

23. Close the file; save the changes.

	TITLE	TYPE	OS	PRICE	PURDATE	STORED	SIGNED FOR
1	Word-O	Word Processing	Windows	499.85	8/17/96	D230	C. Frances
2	Micro Words	Word Processing	Windows	459.8	6/14/96	D230	C. Frances
3	Word-O-D	Word Processing	DOS	499.85	5/18/96	D235	R. Steven
4	Word-O-2	Word Processing	OS/2	499.85	2/20/96	D235	R. Steven
5	Tulip 5	Spreadsheet	Windows	594.2	3/21/96	D238	A. Edward
6	Exceller	Spreadsheet	Windows	594.2	3/21/96	D238	A. Edward
7	Accessor	Database	OS/2	550.5	12/15/96	A114	I. Hans
8	Info Base	Database	DOS	488.88	12/15/96	A114	I. Hans
9	BBS	Communication	OS/2	111.5	1/20/95	D230	C. Frances
10	Officemate	Integrated	Windows	479.95	3/15/95	D238	A. Edward
11	Harword	Graphics	Windows	299.95	1/30/95	D230	C. Frances
12	Pagemarker	Desktop	Windows	399.4	2/15/95	A114	I. Hans
13	Peaches	Accounting	DOS	115.95	2/15/95	B205	C. Julian
14	Quick	Accounting	DOS	42.5	3/1/95	B205	C. Julian
15	Paradoxy	Database	Windows	144.95	3/1/95	A114	I. Hans

■ **Locate a Specific Record** ■ **Wildcards** ■ **Find and Replace**
■ **Use Filters to Search a Database** ■ **Create a Filter** ■ **Results of a Filter** ■ **Display All Records**

NOTES:

Locate a Specific Record

■ A database may be searched in either Form view or List view to find a record. You may wish to find a specific record to get information or to edit it.

To find a specific record:

• Select <u>F</u>ind from the <u>E</u>dit menu.

• In the Find dialog box, indicate the **search value** (specific item) you wish to find. For example, if you want to find the record of Miles Brown, one of the members in your membership list, you might indicate that you are looking for "Brown" (LAST name) or "Miles" (FIRST name). Or, suppose you did not know the name of the person you were looking for, but you knew that the person was a Chiropractor. By typing "Chiropractor" in the Fi<u>n</u>d what text box, the first record of a person in that profession displays.

• Select Next <u>r</u>ecord or <u>A</u>ll records

In List view, selecting Next <u>r</u>ecord leaves the entire database visible on the screen and places the pointer on the located record. Selecting <u>A</u>ll records displays only those records that match your search. In Form view, only a single record displays on the screen regardless of whether Next <u>r</u>ecord or <u>A</u>ll records is chosen.

• Press Shift F4 to find the next record with the same value (another Chiropractor, for example).

■ It is important to select Sh<u>o</u>w, <u>1</u> All Records from the Record menu before beginning a new search. Otherwise, Works will search only the records currently displayed.

■ When typing the search item in the Find dialog box, you may type it in upper- or lowercase letters. Works disregards case when searching for an item.

■ When searching for <u>A</u>ll Records, the Status bar indicates the record number you are looking at and the number of records found out of the total number of records in the database.

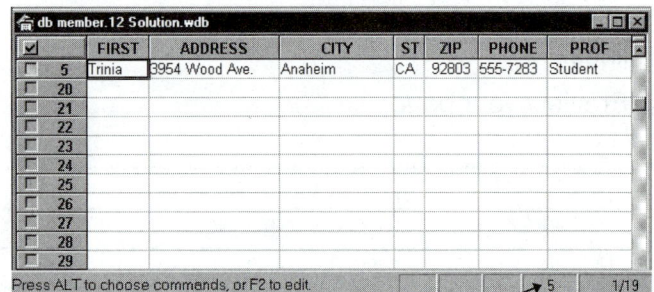

Record number you are viewing.

Number of records out of the total that match the Find specified.

Wildcards

■ A **wildcard** is a symbol used in a search value to substitute for unknown characters. There are two wildcard symbols that broaden the find command: The asterisk (*) and the question mark (?).

- An **asterisk** (*) is used to indicate an unknown group of characters in a specific position. For example, if you were searching for a particular name but were certain of only the first two letters, you would indicate the search value Br*. This will not only find records in which the last names begin with *Br,* but will also find any records which have a *Br* combination within the field data. Therefore, records with the names *Br*own, *Br*ickman and A*br*aham would display.

- The **question mark** (?) is used to substitute for an unknown single character in a specific position. If you were searching for a particular name, but were uncertain of one character in the name, the search value would be entered as Br?wn. This would find records with *any* letter in the question mark location.

Find and Replace

- In List view, the find and replace feature works the same way in database as in the Word Processor and Spreadsheet tools. You can find an item and replace it with another.

To find and replace:

- Select Replace from the Edit menu.

  In the Replace dialog box which appears, indicate the search value you wish to find and what you will be using to replace it.

- Click Records to search across rows; click Fields to search down columns.

- Click Replace All to replace all occurrences without confirmation; click Find Next to confirm each replacement.

  ✓ *NOTE:* *When using the Find Next option, the dialog box remains on the screen, making it difficult to see what record has been found. It is recommended that you move the dialog box to a corner of the screen. (Click, hold and drag the Title bar of the dialog box).*

Use Filters to Search a Database

- Filters are used to search a database for more than one item of information located in more than one field. For example, to find members of your organization that live in North Hollywood, Beverly Hills or Anaheim who are either students or lawyers, you may use a filter.

- When you use a filter, the database hides any records that do not apply. The resulting database can be printed, sorted, edited and so on as if it were a full database file.

Create a Filter

To create a filter in either List or Form view:

- Select Filters from the Tools menu.

- Works prompts you to enter a filter name for each new filter you create. The default name of *Filter 1* is offered. A filter name may use up to 15 characters or spaces. You can recall a filter at any time and apply it again or modify it. You may have up to 8 filters per database.

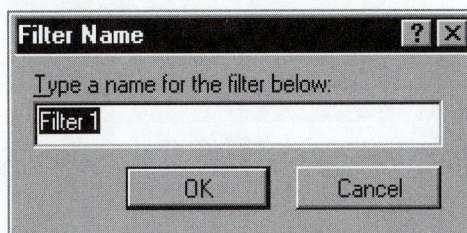

- Click OK.

- In the Filter dialog box which follows, you may enter up to five search criteria. Defining a combination of search criteria is referred to as creating a **filter sentence**.

- To create a filter sentence, you must enter certain information in the Filter dialog box:

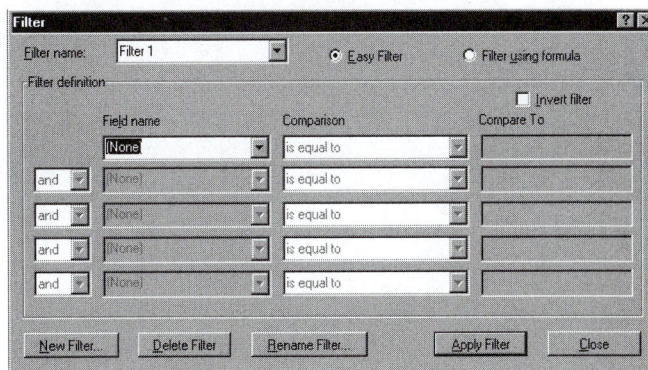

- **Field Name:** Enter the field where the information to be searched is contained. A drop-down list provides the field names in your database.

- **Comparison:** Choose how to compare the field.

  Using the default, **is equal to**, results in an exact match to the item you enter in the Compare To text box.

  A drop-down list provides other **relational operators** (which will be explained in detail in Exercise 14) to set the criteria for your search.

- **Compare To:** Enter the item to be searched.

- Specify **And** or **Or** (**Logical Operators**) as part of the search criteria. **And** narrows the number of records found; **Or** expands the number of records found. For example, to display records of those people who live in Anaheim *or* North Hollywood *and* who are students, note the Filter sentence below in which the *And* and *Or* operators are used:

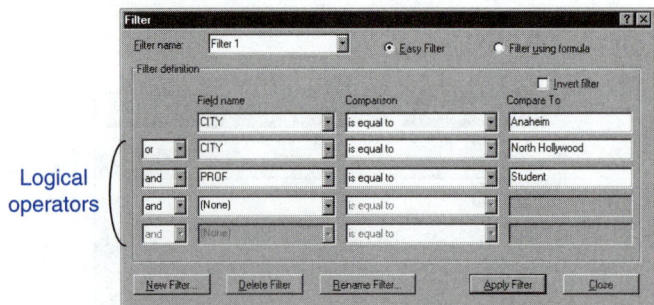

- **Or** will include people who live in either city (expands the search); **And** will include only students who meet the previous criteria (narrows the search).

- Click **Apply Filter** to see the results of the search.

Results of a Filter

- In List view, only those records that match the filter sentence will display. In Form view, you will have to page through the records to see the results. The records that do not match the criteria are hidden. To see only the hidden records, select Show, 4 Hidden Records from the Record menu. Repeat this procedure to see selected records.

Display All Records

- After applying filters, you will probably want to return your database to its original state. To display all records, change to List view and select Show, 1 All Records from the Record main menu.

Several new members have joined HUG, your computer users' group. In addition, you have been notified that several members have changed their names because of marriage, others have new telephone numbers and some members have moved. In this exercise, you will add new members' names, as well as find and edit existing members' records. After updating your database, you can generate information that would be helpful when mailings are made to the membership.

EXERCISE DIRECTIONS:

1. Open 🖮MEMBER, or open 💾DB MEMBER.13

2. From the information below, add the new members to the database. Use the Best Fit feature if necessary to widen the columns to accommodate the new data.

	LAST	FIRST	ADDRESS	CITY	ST	ZIP	PHONE	PROF
11	Kendall	Gale	15 Imperial Way	Beverly Hills	CA	90210	555-9888	Teacher
12	Dagger	Janice	27 Ocean Ave.	Anaheim	CA	92804	555-7777	Orthopedist
13	Chow	Michael	88 Riverside Dr.	Culver City	CA	90311	555-7655	Accountant
14	Wagner	David	879 Beverly Dr.	Beverly Hills	CA	90210	555-6676	Banker
15	Smith	Cleo	90 Rodeo Dr.	Beverly Hills	CA	90210	555-2222	Student
16	Anderson	Carolyn	666 Santa Ana Dr.	Culver City	CA	90312	555-9988	Lawyer
17	Ramaz	Naznine	9012 Wilshire Blvd.	Beverly Hills	CA	90210	555-2211	Teacher
18	Yakar	Winston	776 Prince Lane	North Hollywood	CA	91615	555-0000	Student
19	Mancuso	Mary	12 Pacific Ct.	North Hollywood	CA	91615	555-7773	Banker

3. Locate the record for *Michael Moon*. Make the following changes on his record:
   a. His new address is 32 Oak St.
   b. His new phone number is 555-8750.

4. Locate the record for Bette Walker. Make the following changes on her record:
   a. Her new name is Bette Walker-Sim.
   b. Her new address is 1745 River St., located in North Hollywood, 91615.
   c. Her new phone number is 555-8520.

5. Locate the record for Sheila Smith. Change her phone number to 555-7284.

6. Save the changes.

7. Using Edit, Find (click All Records) search the database for the answers to the following questions.
   ✓ NOTE: Write the answers in your notebook or print the displayed answers.
   a. Which members live in Anaheim?
   b. Which members live in Beverly Hills?
   c. Which members are Lawyers?
   d. Which members are Students?

8. Using filters, search the database for the answers to the following questions.
   ✓ NOTE: It is recommended that you use each question number as the Filter Name.
   a. Which members live in Beverly Hills and are Teachers? (Suggested Filter Name: 8A)
   b. Which members live in North Hollywood and are Bankers? (Suggested Filter Name: 8B)
   c. Which members have a last name beginning with "D" and live in North Hollywood? (Suggested Filter Name: 8C)

9. Display all records.

10. Insert a field to the left of **LAST**; give it the field name **TITLE**.

11. Enter titles for each member in your database as shown on the next page.

(Continued)

	TITLE	LAST	FIRST	ADDRESS	CITY	ST	ZIP	PHONE	PROF
1	Ms.	Barnes	Leanne	808 Summer St.	Anaheim	CA	92803	555-4987	Student
2	Mr.	Brown	Miles	154 Newburg Rd.	Anaheim	CA	92804	555-4837	Accountant
3	Mr.	Griffith	Stuart	1551 Dean St.	Beverly Hills	CA	90210	555-3010	Lawyer
4	Mr.	Moon	Michael	32 Oak St.	Beverly Hills	CA	80210	555-8750	Teacher
5	Ms.	Smith	Trinia	3954 Wood Ave.	Anaheim	CA	92803	555-7283	Student
6	Ms.	Smith	Sheila	417 Specific Ct.	Anaheim	CA	92803	555-7284	Chiropractor
7	Ms.	Walker-Sim	Bette	1745 River St.	North Hollywood	CA	91615	555-8520	Lawyer
8	Mr.	Castillo	Carl	1956 Park Ave.	North Hollywood	CA	91615	555-5192	Banker
9	Mr.	Davis	John	P.O. Box 2333	North Hollywood	CA	91615	555-8129	Student
10	Ms.	Dixon	Amy	23 Albee St.	North Hollywood	CA	91615	555-8917	Orthopedist
11	Ms.	Kendall	Gale	15 Imperial Way	Beverly Hills	CA	90210	555-9888	Teacher
12	Ms.	Dagger	Janice	27 Ocean Ave.	Anaheim	CA	92804	555-7777	Orthopedist
13	Mr.	Chow	Michael	88 Riverside Dr.	Culver City	CA	90311	555-7655	Accountant
14	Mr.	Wagner	David	879 Beverly Dr.	Beverly Hills	CA	90210	555-6676	Banker
15	Ms.	Smith	Cleo	90 Rodeo Dr.	Beverly Hills	CA	90210	555-2222	Student
16	Ms.	Anderson	Carolyn	666 Santa Ana Dr.	Culver City	CA	90312	555-9988	Lawyer
17	Ms.	Ramaz	Naznine	9012 Wilshire Blvd.	Beverly Hills	CA	90210	555-2211	Teacher
18	Mr.	Yakar	Winston	776 Prince Lane	North Hollywood	CA	91615	555-0000	Student
19	Ms	Mancuso	Mary	12 Pacific Ct.	North Hollywood	CA	91615	555-7773	Banker

12. Change to Form Design view and move the fields down so that the **TITLE** field can be moved above the **FIRST** field.

13. Change back to List view.

14. Create a footer: 1996-97

15. Set the left and right margins to 0.5".

16. Print one copy of the database in Landscape orientation.

17. Close the file; save the changes.

LOCATE A SPECIFIC RECORD

1. Open database to be searched.
2. Click **Edit**................................. `Alt`+`E`
3. Click **Find**................................. `F`
4. In **Find What** text box .... `N`, *text*
   type an item in the record (search value)
   you wish to find.

   ✓ *NOTE:* *Use a wildcard, asterisk*
   (*) or question mark (?),
   in the search value if you
   do not know how to spell
   the item name.

5. Click **Next record** .... `Alt`+`R`
   to leave the entire database visible on
   the screen (in List view).

   OR

   Click **All records** .... `Alt`+`A`
   to display only those records that match
   the search (in List view).
6. Click **OK**................................. `Enter`
7. Press **Shift F4** to find .... `Shift`+`F4`
   next record with the same value.

To display all records:

1. Click **Record** .... `Alt`+`R`
2. Click **Show**................................. `O`
3. Click **1 All Records** .... `1`

CHOOSE A SPECIFIC FIELD TO SEARCH

1. Click **Edit**................................. `Alt`+`E`
2. Click **Go To** .... `G`

   OR

   Press the **F5** key. .... `F5`
3. Type the desired field
   name in **Go To** text box.. `Alt`+`G`, *text.*

   OR

   Click on **Select a field** .... `S`
4. Click on Field to be searched .... `↓`
5. Click **OK** .... `Enter`
6. Follow steps for locating a specific
   record. Search will be limited to only
   the selected field.

FIND AND REPLACE

1. Open database and select List view.
2. Click **Edit**................................. `Alt`+`E`
3. Click **Replace**................................. `E`
4. Click **Find What** .... `Alt`+`N`, *text*
   text box; type text to find.
5. Click **Replace With** .... `Alt`+`P`, *text*
   text box; type text to replace.
6. Choose how to Search.
   - **Records** .... `Alt`+`O`
   - **Fields**................................. `Alt`+`I`
7. Click **Find Next** .... `Alt`+`F`
   to confirm each replacement.

   OR

   Click **Replace All** .... `Alt`+`A`
   to replace without confirmation.

USE FILTERS TO SEARCH A DATABASE

To create a filter

1. Open the database you wish to search.
2. Click **Tools** .... `Alt`+`T`
3. Click **Filters** .... `F`
4. Works will prompt you to name the
   filter. Type a name for your filter or
   accept the default name of
   Filter 1.............................. *text* or `Enter`
5. Click **OK** .... `Enter`

To enter the first criterion:

1. Click **Field Name** .... `Alt`+`L`
2. Click field on which to apply the filter.
3. Click **Comparison**. .... `Tab`
4. Select how to compare the field .... `↓`

   ✓ *NOTE:* *The default, is equal to, results*
   in an exact match to the item
   you enter in the Compare To
   text box.

5. Click **Compare To** .... `Tab`
6. Type item to be searched .... *text*

To enter the second criterion:

1. Click **and**...................................... `Tab`

   OR

   Click **or**... `↓`
2. Click **Field Name** .... `Alt`+`L`
3. Click on field to apply the filter to.
4. Click **Comparison** .... `Tab`
5. Select how to compare the field .... `↓`
6. Click **Compare To** .... `Tab`
7. Type item to be searched .... *text*

Repeats steps 1-7 above for additional
criteria.

APPLY A FILTER

Click **Apply Filter**........................ `Alt`+`A`
The Filter dialog box will close and save the
filter.

   ✓ *NOTE:* *Remember to Show All*
   Records before applying a
   new filter to your database.

DISPLAY ALL RECORDS

1. Click **Record** .... `Alt`+`R`
2. Click **Show**................................. `O`
3. Click **1 All Records** .... `1`

EXERCISE 14

■ Relational Operators ■ View a Filter ■ Delete a Filter ■ Rename a Filter

NOTES:

Relational Operators

- As indicated in the previous exercise, relational operators are used to set criteria for a search. In Exercise 13, you used the relational operator *is equal to* (the default) for all your searches.

- In this exercise, you will use other relational operators.

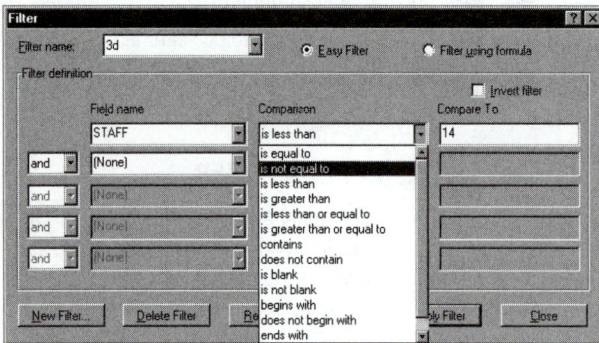

Relational operators

- Suppose you want to search the real estate database shown in Illustration A for different types of houses at various prices. Illustration B shows the information to be entered in the Filter dialog box to get the desired results.

ILLUSTRATION A

	TOWN	AVAIL	TYPE	ROOMS	PRICE
1	Springville	12/1/96	Colonial	10	345000
2	New Dorp	12/5/96	Ranch	8	300000
3	New Dorp	11/8/96	Ranch	7	285000
4	Springville	12/4/96	Colonial	8	301000
5	Brighton	1/9/97	Townhouse	5	185000
6	Annadale	1/19/97	Townhouse	6	199000
7	Brighton	1/31/97	Ranch	7	285000
8	Toten	2/10/97	Colonial	11	400000
9	New Dorp	2/1/97	Ranch	8	338000

ILLUSTRATION B

Field Name	Comparison (relational operator)	Relational operator symbol	Compare To	Desired results
TYPE	contains	=	ranch	All ranch-style houses
PRICE	is less than	<	400000	Houses priced less than $400,000
PRICE	is greater than	>	400000	Houses priced above $400,000
TYPE	does not contain	<>	ranch	All houses *except* ranch style
PRICE	is greater than or equal to	>=	400000	Houses priced at $400,000 or higher
PRICE	is less than or equal to	<=	400000	Houses priced at $400,000 or lower

View a Filter

- As each filter is created, it is identified by its filter name and becomes part of the database. To view a filter after it is created, or at a future time when the database is retrieved, access the Filter dialog box from the Tools menu and select the Filter Name you wish to view.

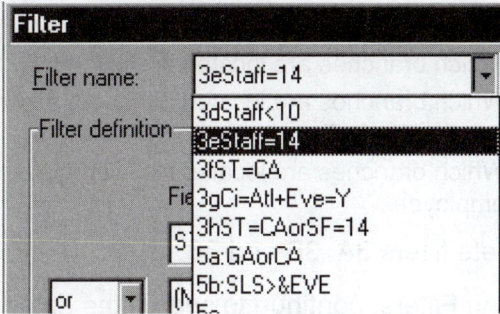

- In the Filter dialog box which follows, you can see the construction (or the filter sentence) of your selected filter.

Filter name   Filter sentence   Filter using formula

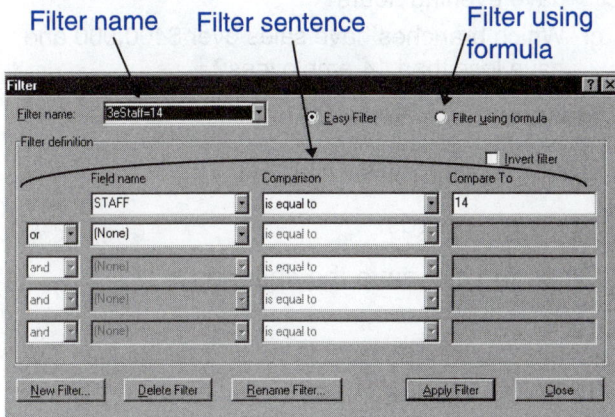

- To see the way the filter was constructed using relational operator symbols, click *Filter using formula* after choosing the filter you wish to view.

Delete a Filter

- Works permits you to create up to eight filters in a database. To create more than eight filters, you must delete others.

To delete a filter:

- Select the filter you wish to delete from the drop-down list in the Filter Name dialog box.

- Click Delete Filter.

Click Yes to ok the deletion.

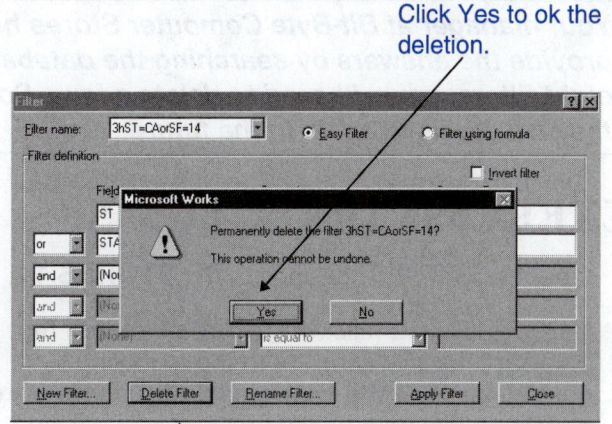

Click to delete filter you are viewing.

- Click Yes.

Rename a Filter

- Filters become part of the database, listed by filter name. If at any point you find it necessary to rename a previously created filter, you can do so by accessing the Rename Filter feature from the Filter dialog box.

To rename a filter:

- Select the filter you wish to rename from the drop down list in the Filter Name dialog box.

- Click Rename Filter button. *A Filter Name dialog box appears with the current filter name selected, as shown below.*

- Type the new filter name.

- Click OK.

Filter Name dialog box.

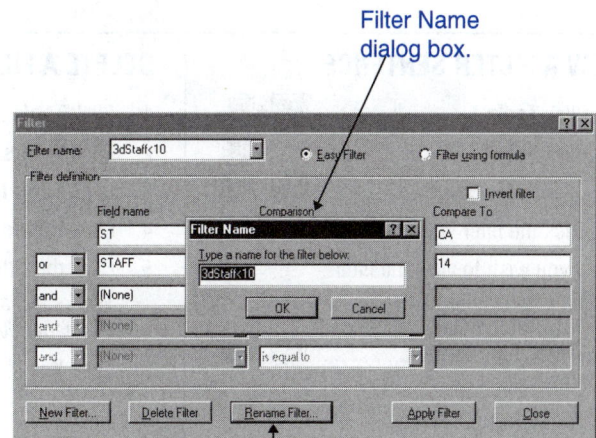

Click to rename filter

> *Your manager at Bit-Byte Computer Stores has many questions about branch stores. You can provide the answers by searching the database you developed. Since there will be more than eight filters, you will need to delete a few. Some queries will be given a descriptive name since they will be used again in the future.*

EXERCISE DIRECTIONS:

1. Open **STORES**, or open **DB STORES.14**.

2. Using Edit, Find (click All records), search the database for the answers to the following questions (write the answers in your notebook or print the displayed answers):

   a. Which branches have evening hours?

   b. Which branches are located in Atlanta?

   c. In what city is the Federal Plaza branch located?

   d. Which branch has sold $245,860 worth of merchandise.

      ✔ NOTE: *The value must be typed exactly as it is in the database. Check your database to see if your money amounts include a dollar sign. If the dollar sign is used in the data, it must be used in the search.*

3. Using Filters, search the database for the answers to the following questions:

   ✔ NOTE: *Name The filters with the number and letter of the question.*

   a. Which branches have sales less than $400,000?

   b. Which branches have sales greater than $400,000?

   c. Which branches have more than 10 employees?

   d. Which branches have less than 10 employees?

   e. Which branches have 14 staff members?

   f. Which branches are located in California?

   g. Which branches are located in Atlanta and have evening hours?

   h. Which branches are located in California or have 14 employees?

4. Delete filters 3A, 3B and 3C.

5. Using Filters, continue to search the database for the following information.

   a. Which branches are located in Georgia or California?

   b. Which branches have sales over $400,000 and have evening hours?

   c. Which branches have sales over $400,000 and have less than 14 employees?

6. Rename Filter 5A to GAandCA.

7. Rename Filter 5B to SLS>&EVE.

8. Show all records.

9. Close the file, save the changes.

VIEW A FILTER SENTENCE

1. Click **Tools** .... Alt + T
2. Click **Filters** .... F
3. Click **Filter Name** .... Alt + F
4. Click the filter you wish to view.

   If you wish to view the filter sentence using relational operator symbols, click **Filter using formula** .... Alt + U after steps 1-3

   To return to the Filter sentence using text, click **Easy filter** .... Alt + E

5. Click **Close** .... Alt + C to return to your database.

DELETE A FILTER

1. Click **Tools** .... Alt + T
2. Click **Filters** .... F
3. Click **Filter Name** .... Alt + F
4. Click **Delete Filter** .... Alt + D
5. Click the Filter Name you wish to delete.

   Works will ask you if you want to permanently delete this filter.

6. Click **Yes** .... Y

RENAME A FILTER

1. Click **Tools** .... Alt + T
2. Click **Filters** .... F
3. Click **Filter Name** .... Alt + F
4. Click **Rename Filter** .... Alt + R

   The Filter Name dialog box appears showing the currently selected filter name.

5. Type the new filter name in the Filter Name dialog box.

6. Click **OK** .... Enter

■ **View Filters** ■ **Delete Filters** ■ **Rename Filters**

Your company is preparing to purchase new computer equipment. Before doing so, management needs to know information about the current inventory. Your supervisor has asked you to respond to a survey by searching the inventory database.

EXERCISE DIRECTIONS:

1. Open ▦**INVENTORY**, or open ▭**DB INVENTORY.15**.

2. The Quantum hard drive *is* under warranty. Find the record (click Next <u>r</u>ecord) and make the change.

3. The correct model number for the Okidata printer is ML330RR. Find the record (click Next <u>r</u>ecord) and make the change.

4. Using <u>E</u>dit, <u>F</u>ind, (click <u>A</u>ll Records), search the database for answers to the following questions (write the answers in your notebook or print the displayed answers):

    a. List all computers.

    b. What equipment is manufactured by IBM?

    c. What equipment is manufactured by Canon?

    d. What equipment is assigned to Accounting?

    e. What equipment is under warranty?

5. Using Filters, search the database for the answers to the following questions:

    ✓*NOTE: Name the filters with the number and letter of the question.*

    a. What equipment costs more than $1,000 and is under warranty?

    b. Which printers are manufactured by HP?

    c. Where is the equipment assigned with the serial numbers 1445 and 76666?

    ✓*NOTE: Use **or** as the relational operator.*

    a. What model printers are Deskjet and are assigned to Personnel?

    b. What are the purchase dates of computers which are under warranty and cost less than $2,000?

6. View Filter 5A.

7. Rename Filter 5A. The new name is OVER 1000WTY.

8. Rename Filter 5B. The new name is HPPRINTERS.

9. Delete Filter 5C.

10. Show all the records

11. Print one copy of the database.

12. Close the file; save the changes.

■ **Apply a Previously Created Filter** ■ **Format a Database**

NOTES:

Apply a Previously Created Filter

■ Any time you retrieve a database, you can apply a filter you created previously. It is easier to select a filter if it was given a descriptive name. To view a filter, select **Filter name** from the Filter dialog box. Then, you can decide if you wish to apply it.

To apply a filter:

- Select Filters from the Tools menu.

- Click on the Filter name list box to display the previously created filters.

- The Filter sentence for that filter is displayed.

- Click Apply Filter.

Format a Database

Number Formatting

■ As in spreadsheets, database text/data may be changed to make it appear more attractive or readable. Format options may be accessed by selecting Field from the Format menu.

To format numerical data:

- Select Field from the Format menu as shown in the illustration that follows.

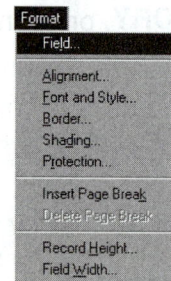

- The Format dialog box appears. Click the Number radio button.

- From the formats displayed in the Appearance list box.

  The default General format displays text and numbers as originally entered.

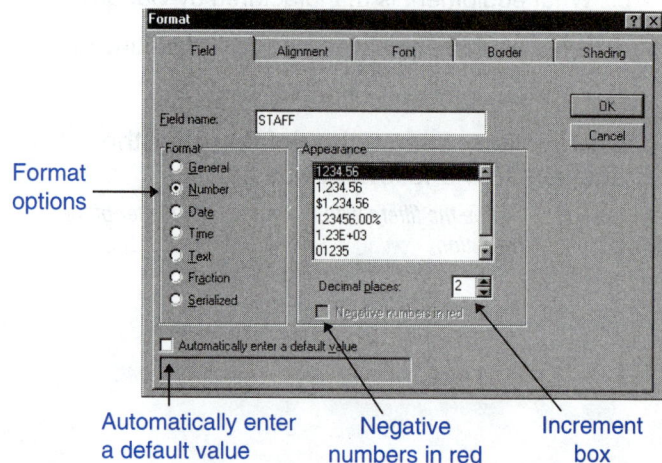

Format options → | ← Field name: STAFF

Automatically enter a default value | Negative numbers in red | Increment box

- If the desired formatting includes decimals, the increment box will display the default number of decimal places. You can change the number of decimal places by clicking in the **Decimal places** increment box.

- If the desired formatting includes leading zeros, the increment box will display the default number of digits. You can change the number of digits you want displayed by clicking in the **Number of digits** increment box.

- If the **Negative numbers in red** box is not dimmed, negative numbers will be enclosed in parentheses. If you have a color printer, they will be printed in red. If the Negative numbers in red box is dimmed, negative numbers will appear exactly as they are entered.

- To enter the same default information into all records, click the **Automatically enter a default value** check box, and type the information you want in the text box below

- If after formatting a numerical field, number signs appear (###), it means that the data is too wide for the field. In List view, double-click the field label at the top of the column to expand the width of the field to accommodate the longest entry. You can also position the cursor between the field labels until the cursor changes to a double-sided arrow. When the word *adjust* replaces the cursor arrow, hold down the right mouse button and drag to the right to widen the column

- When you have completed all number formatting options, click OK.

To format the date:

- Select Field from the Format menu.

- Click the Date radio button.

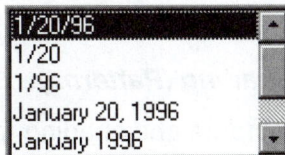

- Choose a date format from those displayed in the Appearance list box.

- Click OK.

To format the time:

- Select Field from the Format menu.

- Click the Time radio button.

- Choose a time format from those displayed in the Appearance list box.

- Click OK.

To format numeric data as text (numeric labels):

This option formats all entries as text (left-aligned) whether they are numbers, text, or both.

- Select Field from the Format menu.

- Click the Text radio button.

- Click OK.

To format numeric data as a fraction:

This options displays all entries as fractions in a format that you select from the Appearance list box. Example: 1.5 in 1/2 format displays as 1 1/2; 1.66 in 1/3 format displays as 1 2/3.

✓ NOTE: Fractions are automatically reduced (2/4 to 1/2) unless you check the Do not reduce check box.

- Select Field from the Format menu.

- Click the Fraction radio button.

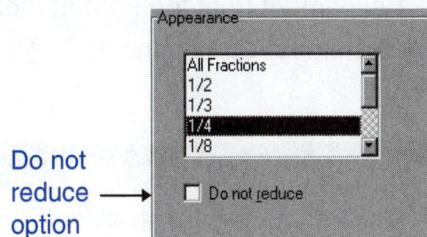

- Choose the format you wish to use.

- Click OK.

To format numeric data in serialized form:

This option assigns a unique number to each record. The number you assign to a record will stay with that record even if you move it. This option is useful if you need to obtain a consistent, unique identifier for each record.

- Select Field from the Format menu.

- Click the Serialized radio button.

- Choose Next value to set your starting value.

- Choose the Increment you wish your serialization to use.

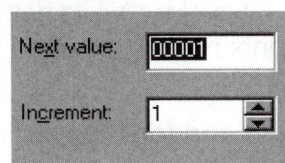

- Click OK.

Alignments

- When data is entered, it is formatted using **general alignment** in which text is aligned to the left of the field; numbers and dates are aligned to the right of the field. This is the default.

- In List view, fields (the entire column) may be aligned:

  - General, Left, Right or Center

  - Vertically (Top, Center or Bottom)
    (This is useful when you have assigned a cell or field height taller than a single line.)

  - The Wrap Text option wraps text within the cell or field.

- In Form Design view, field data may be aligned in the same way.

  ### To change the alignment of field data:

  - Select the Field to be aligned.
  - Select Alignment from the Format menu.
  - Choose the desired alignments.
  - Click OK.

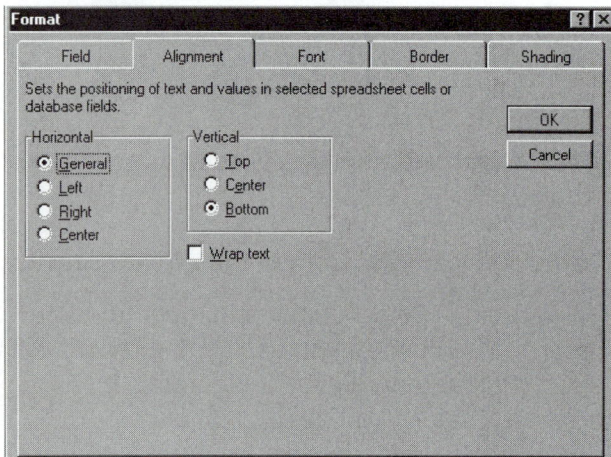

Font and Font Appearance (Size, Style and Color)

- Data may be enhanced by changing the font and appearance (size, style and color) using the same rules as in spreadsheets. Field data may be formatted in List view, while both field data and field headers may be changed in Form Design view.

  ### To change font and font appearance:

  - Select the field (or a cell within a field) to be affected.

    ✓ NOTE: *Any formatting to a cell within a field will affect the entire field.*

- Select Font and Style from the Format menu.

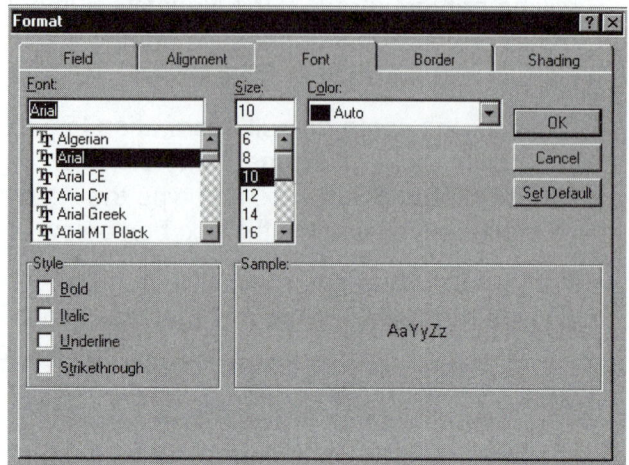

- Choose the desired font, as well as its size, style and color.
- Click OK.

  OR

  Click the appropriate button on the Toolbar:

Borders and Shading (Patterns)

- In List view, borders and shading (patterns) may be added to fields (the entire column) or to the entire database.

- In Form Design view, borders and shading (patterns) may be added to field labels or to field data (individual items.)

  ### To specify a border:

  - Select Border from the Format menu.

  - Choose the Border position, Line Style and Color from the choices in the Border dialog box.

  - Click OK.

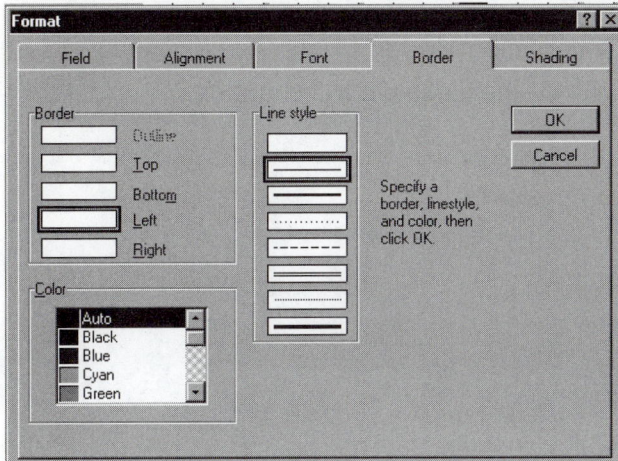

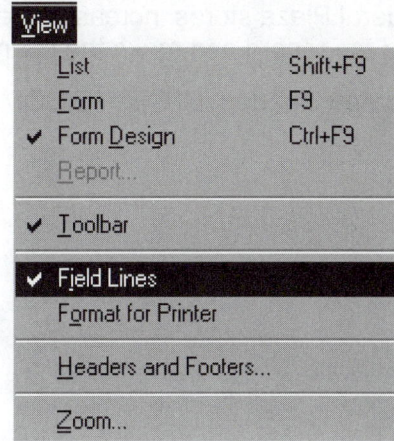

- In List view, Borders may be added only to entire fields; therefore, the border options Top, Bottom, Left and Right are available (the outline option is dimmed). An outline may be created by choosing all four positions. To better see the borders, turn off the gridlines by clicking Gridlines from the View menu.

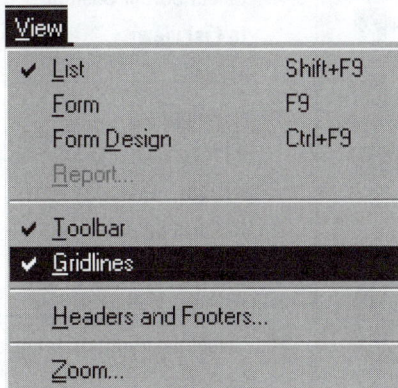

- In Form Design view, Borders may be added to field labels or field data; therefore, only the Outline option is available. To better see the border outline, turn off the field lines by clicking Field Lines from the View menu.

To specify Shading (patterns) in a database:

- Select Shading from the Format menu.

- Choose the Pattern and Colors (Foreground and Background) from the choices in the Shading dialog box.

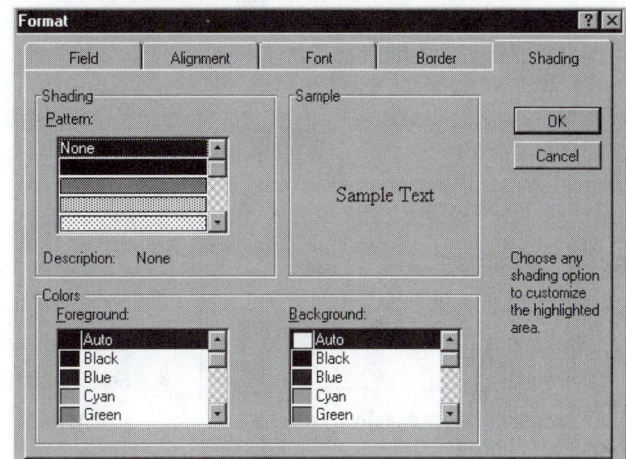

- Click OK.

Your manager needs a printout of California and Georgia stores. Since you did this search previously, you will apply the search again. In addition, you will apply formatting to make the data more attractive.

EXERCISE DIRECTIONS:

1. Open ☰STORES, or open 🖫DB STORES.16

2. Format the SALES field for currency with zero decimals. Adjust the column width if necessary.

3. Format the STAFF field for leading zeros with two digits.

4. Apply Filter GAandCA created in Exercise 13.

5. Create a header: GEORGIA AND CALIFORNIA STORES

6. Print one copy in Portrait orientation.

7. Display all records.

8. The Federal Plaza stores increased their staff to 14. Find the record and make the change.

9. Create a new header: BIT-BYTE COMPUTER STORES

10. Print one copy of the database in Portrait orientation.

11. Close the file; save the changes.

APPLY A PREVIOUSLY CREATED FILTER

1. Click **Tools**. .... `Alt`+`T`
2. Click **Filter**............................. `F`
3. Click down arrow in **Filter name** box .... `↓`
4. Click on filter you wish to apply. The filter sentence for the chosen filter appears.
5. Click **Apply Filter**................... `Alt`+`A`

FORMAT THE DATABASE

Number Formatting

1. Select data to be changed.
2. Click **Format**........................... `Alt`+`O`
3. Click **Field** .... `L`

   To format numbers exactly as entered and left aligned:

   Click **General** .... `Alt`+`G`

   To format numbers as desired:

   a. Click **Number** .... `Alt`+`N`

   b. Click desired number format and options (if applicable).

   To format the date as desired:

   a. Click **Date** .... `Alt`+`E`

   b. Choose desired format (scroll down for more)

   To format the time as desired:

   a. Click **Time**......................... `Alt`+`I`

   b. Choose desired format.

   To format numeric labels:

   a. Click **Text** .... `Alt`+`T`

To format numeric data as a fraction:

a. Click **Fraction**.................... `Alt`+`A`

b. Choose desired format.

To format numeric data in serialized form:

a. Click **Serialized** .... `Alt`+`S`

b. Choose the **Next** value ...... `Alt`+`X` you wish to use.

c. Choose the **Increment** ...... `Alt`+`C` you wish to use..... *choose increment*

4. Click **OK**...................................... `Enter`

ALIGNMENTS

1. Select data to receive alignment change.
2. Click **Format**........................... `Alt`+`O`
3. Click **Alignment**....................... `A`
4. Select desired alignment.
   - **General** .... `G`
   - **Left**...................................... `L`
   - **Right** .... `R`
   - **Center** .... `C`
   - **Top** .... `T`
   - **Center** (Vertically) .... `E`
   - **Bottom** .... `B`
   - **Wrap Text** .... `W`
5. Click **OK**..................................... `Enter`

FONT AND FONT APPEARANCE (SIZE, STYLE AND COLOR)

1. Select data to be changed.
2. Click **Format**........................... `Alt`+`O`
3. Click **Font and Style** .... `F`
4. Choose the desired font, size, style and color.
5. Click **OK**..................................... `Enter`

BORDERS

1. Select data to receive border/shading.
2. Click **Format**........................... `Alt`+`O`
3. Click **Border** .... `B`
4. Select Border position:

   In List view:
   - **Top** .... `T`
   - **Bottom** .... `M`
   - **Left**...................................... `L`
   - **Right** .... `R`

   In Form design view:

   Outline .... `O`

5. Click **Line** style list box. .... `Alt`+`I`
6. Select desired border line style.
7. Click **OK**................................... `Enter`
8. Click **Color** list box .... `Alt`+`C`
9. Select desired border line color.
10. Click **OK**................................... `Enter`

SHADING (PATTERNS)

1. Select data to receive border/shading.
2. Click **Format**........................... `Alt`+`O`
3. Click **Shading** .... `D`
4. Click desired pattern in **Pattern** list box....................... `P`
5. Click **OK**................................... `Enter`
6. Click **Foreground** color........... `Alt`+`F` list box (if desired).
7. Select desired foreground color.
8. Click **Background** color .... `Alt`+`B` list box (if desired).
9. Click desired background color.
10. Click **OK**................................... `Enter`

EXERCISE **17**

■ **Apply a Previously created Filter** ■ **Format the Database**

Your supervisor has asked you some questions about the software packages that your company has purchased. By searching the database, you will be able to provide the answers.

EXERCISE DIRECTIONS:

1. Open ⌨**PROGRAM**, or open 💾**DB PROGRAM.17**.

2. Using Edit, Find (click All records), search the database for answers to the following questions (write the answers in your notebook or print the displayed answers):

   a. Which word processing programs have we ordered?

   b. Which Windows programs have we ordered?

   c. How much did we pay for Quick software?

   d. What type of software is OfficeMate?

   e. What programs are stored in Room 238?

3. Using Filters, search the database for the answers to the following questions:

   ✔ NOTE: *Name the filters with the number and letter of the question.*

   a. Which word processing and spreadsheet programs do we have?

   b. Which software costs less than $300 and runs on Windows?

   c. Which database programs run on Windows and cost less than $300?

   d. Which software was purchased after April 1996?

4. Show all records.

5. View Filter 3a.

6. Rename Filter 3a. The new name is WP&SS

7. Format the PRICE field for currency.

8. Format the PURDATE field for Month, Day and Year (January 20, 1996). Adjust field width, if necessary.

9. Apply Filter WP&SS. Change all the room numbers for these records to D238.

   ✔ HINT: *Change the first record and then Edit, Fill Down.*

10. Show all records.

11. Left align PURDATE field items.

12. Create a header: SOFTWARE INVENTORY, 1995-96.

13. Using Page Setup, change the left and right margins to 0.5".

14. Print one copy of the database with gridlines and field labels in Portrait orientation.

15. Close the file, save the changes.

EXERCISE **18**

Lesson 3 – Summary Exercise 18A

The KAO Exercise Equipment Company opened last year in New York with three employees. Since then, the company has opened one store in Los Angeles, one in New Jersey and another in San Francisco, with a total of 21 employees. To keep track of personnel, you have been asked to create a database. In this exercise, you will create a database for the employees in your company. You will then search it to gather necessary information.

EXERCISE DIRECTIONS:

1. Create a new database file using the information in Illustration A.

   ✓ NOTE: *When creating the ZIP and ID NO fields, be sure to format both fields as text <u>before</u> entering the data (these items are numeric labels and should be left-aligned.)*

2. Enter the information for each person into the database.

3. Adjust column widths to accommodate the longest entry if necessary.

4. Add two new fields, ANNSAL and BRANCH.

5. Enter the highlighted information shown in Illustration B into the two new fields.

6. Format the WKSAL field for currency with two decimal places and the ANNSAL field for currency with no decimal places.

7. Move the BRANCH field after ZIP.

8. Search the database for answers to the following questions. Decide which search process (Edit, Find or Filters) to use. (Write the answers in your notebook or print the displayed answers):

   a. Which employees live in California?

   b. Which employees work in Los Angeles?

   ✓ HINT *Los Angles appears in two fields: the city the employee lives in and the city of the branch the employee works in. You must use a Filter that will specifically locate the information asked for!*

   c. When was Harriet Sawyer hired?

   d. In which branch does the vice president work?

   e. Which employees were hired after December 1992 and live in California?

   f. Which employees work in the Administration Department of a New York branch and earn over $350 a week?

   ✓ HINT: *Brooklyn, Manhattan, Bronx, Staten Island and Queens are all in New York. Employees of these branches must live in NY state. Use the ST field for your filter.*

   g. What are the names of the employees in the Sales and Stock Departments whose salary is greater than $400 a week?

   h. Which employees earn an annual salary of $20,500 or more and live in New York?

9. Rename Filter 9h: NYSAL.

10. Show all records.

11. Shade and bold ST and BRANCH fields. Use the lightest shade available.

12. Create a header: KAO EMPLOYEE LIST -- 1996.

13. Using Page Setup, set your left and right margins to 0.25".

14. Print one copy of the database with gridlines and field labels in Landscape orientation. Preview the database before you print it.

   ✓ NOTE: *If your database does not fit on one page, use your mouse to narrow the fields. If your database still does not fit on one page, change the font to a smaller size and then narrow your fields with your mouse again. If none of those options work, allow the database to print on two pages; include page numbers if you are printing on two pages.*

15. Save the file; name it **PROMOTE**.

16. Close the file; save the changes.

ILLUSTRATION A

	LAST	FIRST	ADDRESS	CITY	ST	ZIP	ID NO	HIRED	POSITION	DEPT	WKSAL
1	Accosta	Anthony	1314 13th Avenue	Brooklyn	NY	11219	13929	1/3/92	Assistant Manager	Sales	$454.81
2	Carson	George	2505 Benson Avenue	Brooklyn	NY	11236	14078	4/1/94	Administrative Assistant	Admin.	$389.76
3	Carson	Laurence	34 Flower Avenue	Merrick	NY	11566	14356	9/30/93	Assistant Supervisor	Stock	$355.77
4	Carson	Penn	2234 Montgomery Street	Brooklyn	NY	11213	14399	8/25/95	Sales Representative	Sales	$259.62
5	Gregonis	Dimitri	7200 Moore Avenue	Los Angeles	CA	90066	14395	5/15/95	Customer Service Rep	Admin.	$317.31
6	Hopkins	George	35 Gates Place	Tappan	NY	10983	14396	5/30/94	Inventory Supervisor	Stock	$391.35
7	Lee	Chin	62 Orange Court	LaHabra	CA	90631	13254	1/6/91	Vice President	Sales	$673.08
8	Lee	Michael	34 Woodrow Road	Staten Island	NY	10312	14295	5/1/92	Warehouse Coordinator	Stock	$509.62
9	Lee	Randy	8234 Cigna Lane	Laguna Beach	CA	92650	13298	5/15/93	Assistant Coordinator	Stock	$365.80
10	Martino	John	1001 Costa Drive	Berkley	CA	94704	14289	3/5/93	A/R Bookkeeper	Admin.	$403.85
11	Naidle	Adam	334 Roxbury Drive	Beverly Hills	CA	90210	14321	7/25/93	Senior Review Clerk	Sales	$301.35
12	Palmieri	Marie	2044 Waterview Drive	Edgewater	NJ	07020	14367	11/1/93	Senior Stock Clerk	Stock	$339.42
13	Parsons	Kyle	876 Rocky Point Drive	Yorktown Heights	NY	10598	14398	8/12/95	A/P Bookkeeper	Admin.	$360.58
14	Rogers	Jane	346 La Vista Road	Berkley	CA	94704	14024	2/15/92	Marketing Analyst	Sales	$432.69
15	Samtanai	Perkash	67 Main Street	Los Angeles	CA	90012	14354	9/1/93	Sales Rep, Level II	Sales	$259.62
16	Sawyer	Harriet	354 Marisol Road	Los Angeles	CA	90020	13290	5/1/91	Supervisor, Computer Operations	Admin.	$473.08
17	Tommie	Lori	344 Van Buren Drive	Baldwin Harbor	NY	11510	13852	11/1/91	Manager	Stock	$567.31
18	Valdez	Lina	344 Woodland Lane	Denby	CT	06418	14385	2/1/94	Payroll Supervisor	Admin.	$528.85
19	Viacomma	Maria	25433 Crown Street	Woodland Hills	CA	91365	14397	7/15/95	Executive Assistant	Admin.	$418.85
20	Watterson	Cathy	456 Adrienne Road	Staten Island	NY	10305	14269	12/15/92	Advertising Rep	Sales	$394.23
21	Wilson	Robert	34 Oak Place	E. Brunswick	NJ	08816	14235	11/1/92	Order Processing Clerk	Stock	$338.46

ILLUSTRATION B

	LAST	FIRST	ADDRESS	CITY	ST	ZIP	ID NO	HIRED	POSITION	DEPT	WKSALL	ANNSAL	BRANCH
1	Accosta	Anthony	1314 13th Avenue	Brooklyn	NY	11219	13929	1/3/92	Assistant Manager	Sales	$454.81	$23,650	Brooklyn
2	Carson	George	2505 Benson Avenue	Brooklyn	NY	11236	14078	4/1/94	Administrative Assistant	Admin.	$389.76	$20,267	Manhattan
3	Carson	Laurence	34 Flower Avenue	Merrick	NY	11566	14356	9/30/93	Assistant Supervisor	Stock	$355.77	$18,500	Manhattan
4	Carson	Penn	2234 Montgomery Street	Brooklyn	NY	11213	14399	8/25/95	Sales Representative	Sales	$259.62	$13,500	Manhattan
5	Gregonis	Dimitri	7200 Moore Avenue	Los Angeles	CA	90066	14395	5/15/95	Customer Service Rep	Admin.	$317.31	$16,500	Los Angeles
6	Hopkins	George	35 Gates Place	Tappan	NY	10983	14396	5/30/94	Inventory Supervisor	Stock	$391.35	$20,350	Bronx
7	Lee	Chin	62 Orange Court	LaHabra	CA	90631	13254	1/6/91	Vice President	Sales	$673.08	$35,000	Los Angeles
8	Lee	Michael	34 Woodrow Road	Staten Island	NY	10312	14295	5/1/92	Warehouse Coordinator	Stock	$509.62	$26,500	Queens
9	Lee	Randy	8234 Cigna Lane	Laguna Beach	CA	92650	13298	5/15/93	Assistant Coordinator	Stock	$365.80	$19,021	Los Angeles
10	Martino	John	1001 Costa Drive	Berkley	CA	94704	14289	3/5/93	A/R Bookkeeper	Admin.	$403.85	$21,000	San Francisco
11	Naidle	Adam	334 Roxbury Drive	Beverly Hills	CA	90210	14321	7/25/93	Senior Review Clerk	Sales	$301.35	$15,670	Los Angeles
12	Palmieri	Marie	2044 Waterview Drive	Edgewater	NJ	07020	14367	11/1/93	Senior Stock Clerk	Stock	$339.42	$17,650	Fort Lee
13	Parsons	Kyle	876 Rocky Point Drive	Yorktown Heights	NY	10598	14398	8/12/95	A/P Bookkeeper	Admin.	$360.58	$18,750	Manhattan
14	Rogers	Jane	346 La Vista Road	Berkley	CA	94704	14024	2/15/92	Marketing Analyst	Sales	$432.69	$22,500	San Francisco
15	Samtanai	Perkash	67 Main Street	Los Angeles	CA	90012	14354	9/1/93	Sales Rep, Level II	Sales	$259.62	$13,500	Los Angeles
16	Sawyer	Harriet	354 Marisol Road	Los Angeles	CA	90020	13290	5/1/91	Supervisor, Computer Operations	Admin.	$473.08	$24,600	Long Beach
17	Tommie	Lori	344 Van Buren Drive	Baldwin Harbor	NY	11510	13852	11/1/91	Manager	Stock	$567.31	$29,500	Manhattan
18	Valdez	Lina	344 Woodland Lane	Denby	CT	06418	14385	2/1/94	Payroll Supervisor	Admin.	$528.85	$27,500	Queens
19	Viacomma	Maria	25433 Crown Street	Woodland Hills	CA	91365	14397	7/15/95	Executive Assistant	Admin.	$418.85	$21,780	Los Angeles
20	Watterson	Cathy	456 Adrienne Road	Staten Island	NY	10305	14269	12/15/92	Advertising Rep	Sales	$394.23	$20,500	Manhattan
21	Wilson	Robert	34 Oak Place	E. Brunswick	NJ	08816	14235	11/1/92	Order Processing Clerk	Stock	$338.46	$17,600	Fort Lee

Move

The owner of Jane's Boutique, a local clothing store, has hired you to create an inventory system for her store. The clothing is arranged by style number, type of garment, color and size. This store specializes in junior sizes from 5 to 13. In this exercise, you will create a database to keep track of inventory and the number of garments on hand. You will then search it when customers call about availability of stock or when information is needed for reordering merchandise.

EXERCISE DIRECTIONS:

1. Create a new database file using the information in Illustration A.

   ✓ NOTE: *Although the STYLE field contains numeric labels, it is unnecessary to format it as text. Any combination of text and numbers will format as left-aligned text.*

2. Enter the information for each garment into the database using either List or Form view, whichever you prefer for data entry.

   ✓ Note: *BU stands for buttons.*

ILLUSTRATION A

	STYLE	TYPE	COLOR	J5	J7	J9	J11	J13	DATEMFG	BU
1	J8510	Skirt	Black	4	4	2	4	2	10/18/95	Yes
2	J5540	Blouse	White	5	6	6	4	3	11/12/95	Yes
3	J4309	Pants	Tan	2	12	12	3	4	11/17/95	Yes
4	J3254	Dress	Blue	4	15	16	12	14	7/16/95	Yes
5	J7654	Suit	Green	12	17	34	32	12	9/18/95	Yes
6	J7455	Blazer	Black	23	32	21	34	32	9/23/95	Yes
7	J3280	Dress	Yellow	5	7	4	5	12	11/17/95	No
8	J5532	Skirt	Purple	12	21	32	12	21	10/19/95	No
9	J4230	Pants	Gray	24	4	6	7	13	12/12/95	Yes
10	J5550	Blouse	Orange	12	24	43	25	4	8/21/95	Yes
11	J7676	Suit	White	9	6	5	3	7	7/22/95	Yes
12	J7405	Blazer	Yellow	12	32	32	23	21	10/8/95	Yes
13	J5555	Blouse	Green	13	32	45	6	9	6/19/95	No
14	J3290	Dress	Blue	23	32	33	23	12	11/17/95	No
15	J3317	Dress	White	3	6	7	3	4	1/7/96	Yes
16	J2222	Pants	Black	32	23	32	54	16	2/2/96	No
17	J3291	Dress	Red	17	21	35	32	18	10/8/95	No

3. Adjust column widths to accommodate the longest entry if necessary.

4. Change the field name DATEMFG to DATEORD.

(Continued)

5. Some garments come with accessory items and you will need to know the price of each garment, you must include two additional fields: PRICE and ACC (ACC stands for accessories). Adjust column width if necessary.

6. Enter the highlighted information shown in Illustration B into the two new fields.

ILLUSTRATION B

MOVE

	STYLE	TYPE	COLOR	JT	J7	J9	J11	J13	DATEORD	BU	PRICE	ACC
1	J8510	Skirt	Black	4	4	2	4	2	10/18/95	Yes	26	No
2	J5540	Blouse	White	5	6	6	4	3	11/12/95	Yes	18.59	No
3	J4309	Pants	Tan	2	12	12	3	4	11/17/95	Yes	44.5	No
4	J3254	Dress	Blue	4	15	16	12	14	7/16/95	Yes	61.99	Yes
5	J7654	Suit	Green	12	17	34	32	12	9/18/95	Yes	85.5	Yes
6	J7455	Blazer	Black	23	32	21	34	32	9/23/95	Yes	50.99	No
7	J3280	Dress	Yellow	5	7	4	5	12	11/17/95	No	59.44	Yes
8	J5532	Skirt	Purple	12	21	32	12	21	10/19/95	No	23.67	No
9	J4230	Pants	Gray	24	4	6	7	13	12/12/95	Yes	49.99	No
10	J5550	Blouse	Orange	12	24	43	25	4	8/21/95	Yes	23.99	No
11	J7676	Suit	White	9	6	5	3	7	7/22/95	Yes	106.99	Yes
12	J7405	Blazer	Yellow	12	32	32	23	21	10/8/95	Yes	48.5	No
13	J5555	Blouse	Green	13	32	45	6	9	6/19/95	No	19.99	No
14	J3290	Dress	Blue	23	32	33	23	12	11/17/95	No	56.88	Yes
15	J3317	Dress	White	3	6	7	3	4	1/7/96	Yes	62.65	Yes
16	J2222	Pants	Black	32	23	32	54	16	2/2/96	No	39.99	No
17	J3291	Dress	Red	17	21	35	32	18	10/8/95	No	48.25	Yes

7. Move the PRICE field after the J13 field.

8. The following items are no longer in stock Delete the records.

   ✓HINT   Use Edit, Find to locate the records quickly.

   - J3280
   - J7405
   - J2222

9. Format the PRICE field for currency with two decimal places.

(Continued)

10. The items shown in Illustration C were just purchased. Add them to the database.

ILLUSTRATION C

	STYLE	TYPE	COLOR	J5	J7	J9	J11	J13	PRICE	DATEORD	BU	ACC
15	J2121	Sweater	Brown	4	4	6	6	7	$29.99	2/7/96	Yes	No
16	J2123	Sweater	Olive	5	5	6	7	9	$35.75	2/7/96	Yes	No
17	J7699	Suit	Navy	12	10	10	8	7	$110.10	2/7/96	Yes	Yes
18	J9090	Vest	Red	23	22	22	25	25	$20.00	2/7/96	No	No
19	P214	Blouse	Red	5	6	8	9	9	$25.50	2/10/96	Yes	No
20	P232	Skirt	Black	5	5	5	5	7	$29.50	2/10/96	Yes	No
21	P287	Blazer	Navy	7	9	11	14	14	$75.50	2/10/96	Yes	No
22	P987	Skirt	Black	3	4	5	6	7	$30.75	2/10/96	Yes	Yes
23	P998	Skirt	Navy	2	4	4	5	7	$35.40	2/10/96	Yes	Yes
24	P999	Vest	Navy	6	6	7	7	7	$25.50	2/10/96	No	No
25	Q765	Blazer	Red	7	9	11	11	11	$60.99	2/10/96	Yes	Yes

11. Search the database for answers to the following questions. Decide which search process (Edit, Find or Filters) to use. (Write the answers in your notebook or print the displayed answers).

  a. What color is style number J7654?

  b. Which item is orange?

  c. Which item costs $19.99?

  d. Which items cost less than $46.50?

  e. Which items come with buttons?

    ✓ NOTE: BU is the code of Buttons.

  a. What are the style numbers for black blazers?

  b. Which dresses have accessories?

  c. Which skirts cost less than $40?

  d. How many items have more than 15 pieces in size J13?

  e. Which items are black, blue, navy or white?

  f. Which items were ordered after 10/31/95 and have 13 or more J7 items in stock?

12. Show all records.

13. Create a header: JANE'S BOUTIQUE -- Inventory as of March 1996

14. Using Page Setup, set the left and right margins to 0.5". Set a top margin of 1.5".

15. Print one copy of the database with gridlines and field labels in Landscape orientation.

16. Save the file; name it **STOCK**.

17. Close the document window.

EXERCISE **19**

■ **Sort Database Records**

NOTES:

Sort Database Records

■ The order in which records are entered is frequently not the order in which the user expects to locate and update records. Sorting allows you to rearrange the information so that you can look at it in different ways.

■ The reasons to sort a database are:

- To find information arranged in alphabetical or numerical order.

- To quickly see the largest or smallest number in a numerical field.

- To arrange information into groups (all people who live in Washington vs. San Diego, etc.).

- To find duplicate entries.

■ Database records can be sorted in either Form view or List view. It is easier to see the rearranged records in List view.

■ Sorting is accomplished in either **ascending** or **descending** order. Ascending order goes from the first to the last letter (A to Z); the smallest to the largest number (0 to 9); the oldest to the most recent date; or the earliest to the latest time. Descending order is the opposite.

To sort a database:

- Select Sort Records from the Record menu.

- In the Sort Records dialog box which follows, select the first field to be sorted from the *Sort by* drop-down list. This is called the **Primary Sort.**

- Click to indicate ascending or descending sort.

Click to list fields to sort

Click to choose desired order of sort

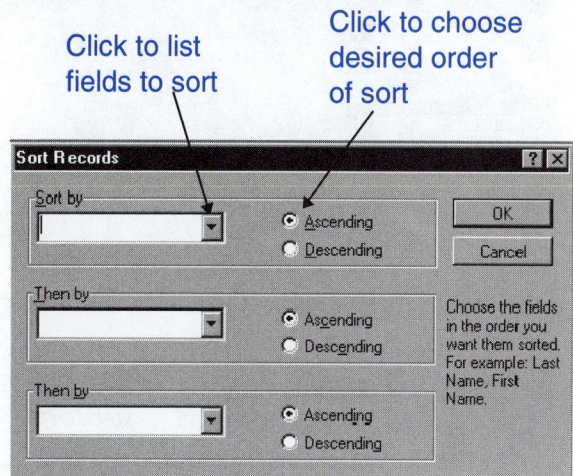

■ Works allow you to create two subsorts of the primary sort. In a subsort, records with identical items in the primary sort can be further sorted on the second field. In a second subsort, records with identical items in both the primary sort and first subsort are sorted again on the third field.

■ When you perform more than one search, the field name and sort direction (ascending or descending) of the first sort will still be selected when you access Record, Sort Records. It is important to replace any fields and sort direction remaining from the first sort.

■ The following fields were used to create a primary sort and two subsorts on the INVENTORY database:

Primary sort → First subsort → Second subsort →

Sort Records	? ×

Sort by
ITEM ▼ ○ Ascending ● Descending | OK | Cancel |

Then by
MFG ▼ ○ Ascending ● Descending

Then by
MODEL ▼ ● Ascending ○ Descending

Choose the fields in the order you want them sorted. For example: Last Name, First Name.

■ Note the results of the sort:

- All **Computers** in the **ITEM** field are grouped together.

- Records that contain identical items in the **ITEM** field are further grouped by the first subsort, the **MFG** field, in reverse alphabetical order (descending) within the primary sort.

- Records that contain identical items in both the **ITEM** and **MFG** fields are further sorted by the second subsort, the **MODEL** field, in alphabetical order (ascending) within the first subsort.

■ Each sort reshuffles the records. Therefore, if you wish to save the results of a particular sort, you must save the database using a new filename.

Primary sort ↓ *First subsort* ↓ *Second subsort* ↓

	ITEM	MFG	MODEL	COST	PURDATE	WTY	ASSIGNED TO	SERIAL #
1	Computer	Canon	Notebook	$2,436	8/96	Yes	Personnel	98763
2	Computer	Canon	Notebook	$2,436	8/96	Yes	Purchasing	76666
3	Computer	Canon	Notebook 486	$1,889	1/96	Yes	Shipping	1445
4	Computer	IBM	PS2	$1,348	6/95	Yes	Accounting	651198
5	Computer	IBM	Thinkpad	$2,199	6/96	Yes	Personnel	2059
6	Computer	IBM	Thinkpad 500	$1,399	6/96	Yes	Accounting	671150
7	Hard Drive	Conner	CFS4 210MB	$200	6/96	No	Purchasing	12345
8	Hard Drive	Quantum	LPS 40 170MB	$199	6/96	Yes	Accounting	54219
9	Modem	Intel	PCMCIA	$115	1/96	No	Shipping	20098
10	Monitor	NEC	FGE	$589	12/96	No	Accounting	11112
11	Monitor	NEC	FGE/3V	$539	12/96	No	Personnel	87098
12	Printer	HP	DeskJet	$429	11/96	Yes	Accounting	99911
13	Printer	HP	DeskJet	$429	11/96	Yes	Personnel	22230
14	Printer	IBM	ExecJet II	$335	6/96	Yes	Personnel	55211
15	Printer	Okidata	ML330RR	$295	2/96	Yes	Shipping	98983

It would be easier to find the information your manager has requested if the database were sorted. In this exercise, you will sort and subsort the database.

EXERCISE DIRECTIONS:

1. Open ⌨INVENTORY, or open 💾DB INVENTORY.19.

2. Format the COST field for currency with 0 decimal places.

3. Center align the WTY field.

4. Format the data in the SERIAL # field as text because serial #'s are numeric labels.

   ✓ NOTE: *Formatting a field containing numeric labels as text can only be done* before *the data is entered. Once it has been entered in General format, you can only change the alignment of the field through the number format options.*

5. Perform the following primary sorts *(Sort by)* to the database as follows:

   a. In ascending order by ITEM.
   b. In ascending order by ASSIGNED TO.
   c. In ascending date order by PURDATE.
   d. In descending order by COST.

6. Perform the following primary and subsorts *(Sort by, Then by, Then by)* to the database as follows:

   a. In alphabetical order by ITEM, alphabetical order by MFG, and ascending order by COST.
   b. In alphabetical order by MFG and alphabetical order by ITEM.
   c. In alphabetical order by ITEM and ascending (chronological) order by PURDATE.
   d. In alphabetical order by WTY, alphabetical order by ASSIGNED TO and ascending order by PURDATE.

7. Print one copy of this last sort.

8. Close the file, save the changes.

SORT RECORDS

1. Click **Records**........................ Alt + R
2. Click **Sort Records**........................... S
3. Select first field to **Sort by** ..... Alt + S from drop-down list.
4. Click to select type of sort:
   - **Ascending**........................... Alt + A
   - **Descending**........................ Alt + D

5. Select second field to sort by (**Then by**) from drop-down list.............. Alt + T
6. Click to select type of sort:
   - **Ascending**........................... Alt + C
   - **Descending**....................... Alt + E

7. Select third field to sort by (**Then by**) from drop-down list.............. Alt + B
   - **Ascending**........................ Alt + I
   - **Descending**...................... Alt + G
8. Click **OK**. .... Enter

■ **Sort Database Records**

Jane Blackwell, your boss at Jane's Boutique, has asked you to arrange the database so that she can provide inventory lists for store personnel. She wants the information arranged in alphabetical order for style, type and color choices. She also wants you to sort records by price and size to help customers choose clothing.

EXERCISE DIRECTIONS:

1. Open ⌨**STOCK**, or open 💾**DB STOCK.20**.

2. Perform each of the following primary sorts *(Sort by)* to the database as follows:

   a. In alphabetical order by TYPE.

   b. In alphabetical order by COLOR.

   c. In descending order by PRICE.

3. Perform each of the following primary and subsorts *(Sort by, Then by, Then by)* to the database as follows:

   a. In alphabetical order by COLOR and ascending order by PRICE within each color.

   b. In alphabetical order by TYPE, in alphabetical order by COLOR and descending order by PRICE.

   c. In ascending order by size J5, in alphabetical order by TYPE, and ascending order by PRICE.

   d. In alphabetical order by COLOR, in alphabetical order by TYPE, and ascending order by STYLE. Print one copy of this sort.

4. Close the file; save the changes.

■ **Create a Report** ■ **The Report Definition Screen (Report View)** ■ **Preview a Report**

NOTES:

Create a Report

■ Database reports allow you to present data in a customized way.

■ Standard reports are generated in columns. These reports contain a report title, fields to be included in the report (column headings) and rows of data listed in the order in which the file was last sorted.

■ Each column of the report corresponds to a field in the database.

■ Each row of the report corresponds to an individual record in the field.

■ Standard reports contain a report title, the fields to be included in the report and report statistics.

■ Like Filters, Reports become part of the database.

■ A sample report appears below. Note the title, field headings, records and summary statistics.

BIT-BYTE COMPUTER STORES/STAFF AND SALES DATA ← *Title*

CITY	ST	BRANCH	STAFF	SALES	
					← *Field headings*
Anchorage	AL	Seal City Center	6	$185,420	
Atlanta	GA	Dixieland	14	$352,622	
Atlanta	GA	Peach Tree	16	$457,800	
Atlanta	GA	River View Plaza	6	$215,400	
Boston	MA	Bean Town	16	$682,450	
Chicago	IL	Lakeview	15	$755,420	
Cleveland	OH	Iron City Plaza	13	$543,233	
Denver	CO	Rocky Mountain	9	$102,563	
Houston	TX	Astro Center	12	$541,000	
Los Angeles	CA	Pacific	14	$685,400	← *Records*
Mobile	AL	Southland	7	$104,566	
New York	NY	Big Apple	20	$789,300	
Philadelphia	PA	Liberty	19	$423,150	
Phoenix	AZ	Desert View Mall	8	$189,252	
Providence	RI	Oceanview	6	$433,443	
San Diego	CA	Central States	14	$144,524	
San Francisco	CA	Sunset	13	$876,988	
Topeka	KS	Wheatland	11	$352,415	
Washington	DC	Federal Plaza	14	$245,860	

TOTAL STAFF:	233	
TOTAL SALES:	$8,080,806	← *Summary statistics*
AVERAGE SALES:	$425,305	

■ Before creating a report, sort the data as you want it to appear in your report. *Sorting group data within the report will be introduced in Exercise 23.*

To create a new report:

• Select ReportCreator from the Tools menu.

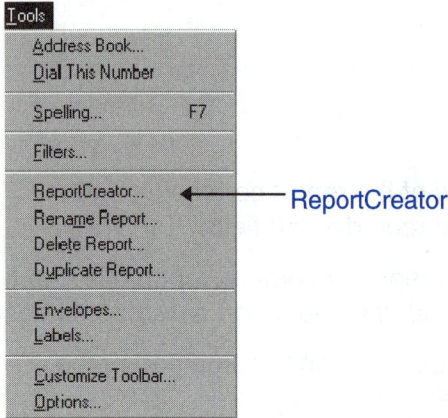

Tools
- Address Book...
- Dial This Number
- Spelling... F7
- Filters...
- ReportCreator... ← ReportCreator
- Rename Report...
- Delete Report...
- Duplicate Report...
- Envelopes...
- Labels...
- Customize Toolbar...
- Options...

■ In the Report Name dialog box that follows, give your report a name. The report name can include up to 15 characters including punctuation and spacing.

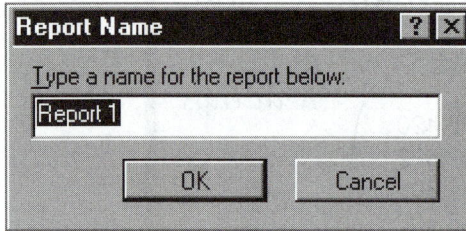

Report Name [?][X]

Type a name for the report below:

Report 1

[OK] [Cancel]

To add a title to a report:

• After you name your report and click OK, the ReportCreator dialog box appears displaying the Title tab.

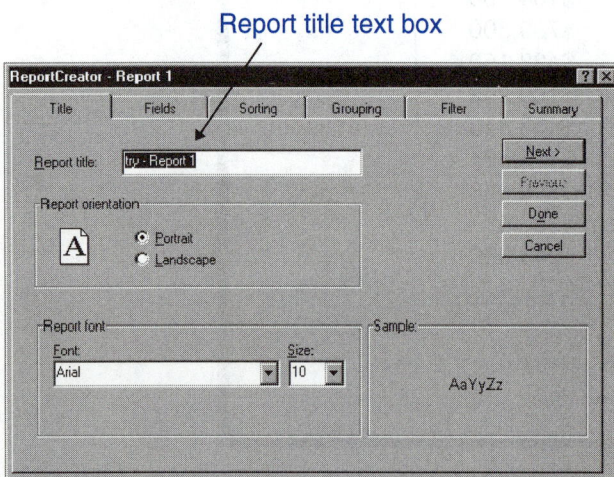

Report title text box

ReportCreator - Report 1 [?][X]

| Title | Fields | Sorting | Grouping | Filter | Summary |

Report title: try - Report 1

[Next >]
[Previous]
[Done]
[Cancel]

Report orientation

[A] ● Portrait ○ Landscape

Report font

Font: Arial   Size: 10

Sample: AaYyZz

• Enter a one-line title for your report in the Report title text box. The report title can be different from the report name. You can use up to 255 characters in the title. If you do not enter a title, Works creates one by combining your database filename with your report name.

✓ *NOTE:* *Clicking the Next or Previous button in any tab will bring you to the next or previous tab and record your choices.*

To select the fields to appear in the report:

• Click the **Fields** tab. Add the fields to be included in the order in which you wish them to appear in your report.

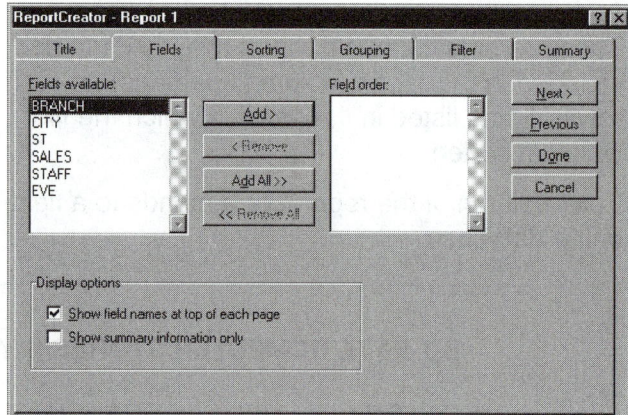

ReportCreator - Report 1 [?][X]

| Title | Fields | Sorting | Grouping | Filter | Summary |

Fields available:
BRANCH
CITY
ST
SALES
STAFF
EVE

[Add >]
[< Remove]
[Add All >>]
[<< Remove All]

Field order:

[Next >]
[Previous]
[Done]
[Cancel]

Display options
☑ Show field names at top of each page
☐ Show summary information only

■ It is recommended that you choose the default Display option, *Show field names at top of each page,* to add clarity to your report.

To add summary statistics to the report:

• Click the **Summary** tab. Click the appropriate statistic to print for each field in the report.

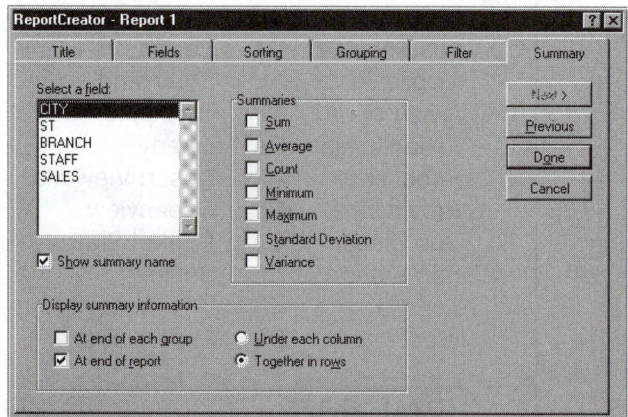

ReportCreator - Report 1 [?][X]

| Title | Fields | Sorting | Grouping | Filter | Summary |

Select a field:
CITY
ST
BRANCH
STAFF
SALES

Summaries
☐ Sum
☐ Average
☐ Count
☐ Minimum
☐ Maximum
☐ Standard Deviation
☐ Variance

☑ Show summary name

[Next >]
[Previous]
[Done]
[Cancel]

Display summary information
☐ At end of each group   ○ Under each column
☑ At end of report   ● Together in rows

• Click where you want the summary statistics to display.

• Click Done.

The Report Definition Screen (Report View)

- After clicking Done in the ReportCreator dialog box, you are prompted to preview your report or modify your report.

- If you choose Preview, Works displays the Print Preview screen, and you will see how your report will look when it is printed. If you choose Modify, Works shows Report view. In this view, the report definition screen appears, showing the formulas in the fields.

Row headers

- The left column on this screen contains row headers. The information in the columns relate to the row headers as follows:

  - **Title rows** (there are two) – contain one title which you can enter in the Title tab and one blank row for spacing.

  - **Headings** (there are two) – contain one heading representing field names and one blank row for spacing.

  - **Record row** – contains formulas for the fields to be included in the report.

  - **Summary rows** – contain labels and summary statistic formulas that you requested in the Summary tab.

- The report may be changed while in the Report Definition screen using the same methods used in the Word Processor and Spreadsheet.

- You can change margins, column headings (field titles), report instructions and column widths.

- You can also insert columns and rows and apply font and shading attributes to your data.

- Modifying and formatting a database report will be covered in more detail in Exercise 22.

Preview a Report

To see what your report will look like before you print it:

Select Print Preview from the File menu.

- As in spreadsheets, #### signs appearing in a column indicate that the column is too narrow for the data. If this occurs, return to the Report Definitions screen and widen the column using the methods learned earlier.

- If the title does not appear centered, move the title using the cut and paste procedures. Preview the report again after each formatting change to be certain that all data looks attractive.

- Print the report the same way you would print any Works document.

- Save a report by saving the database. All reports created within a database are saved along with it.

> *Your manager at Bit-Byte must submit reports to the president of the company. You have been asked to create these reports from your database.*

EXERCISE DIRECTIONS:

1. Open ▧**STORES**, or open ▧**DB STORES.21**.

2. Reformat the STAFF column to General (F**o**rmat, Fie**l**d, **G**eneral).

3. Sort the records alphabetically by CITY and BRANCH.

4. Create a report.

5. When prompted for a report name, name it **Stores.**

   ✓ NOTE: *This is not the title of the report; it is just an identifying name for the report within the database.*

6. Access the Title tab. Use the one-line title: BIT-BYTE COMPUTER STORES/STAFF AND SALES DATA

7. Access the *Fields* tab. Include the following fields in your report in this order:

   CITY
   STATE
   BRANCH
   STAFF
   SALES

8. Accept the default display option to *Show field names at top of each page.*

9. Access the Summary tab. Apply the following summary formulas to the fields as indicated below.

FIELD	**Summary Formula**
STAFF	Sum
SALES	Sum
SALES	Average

10. Position the results at the end of the report, together in rows.

11. Preview the report.

12. Return to the Report Definition screen.

13. Preview your report.

– Modify the report as follows –

14. Move the title two columns to the left to center it.

15. Change the left and right margins to 1.75" to center the report.

16. Preview the report to see if the columns look centered.

17. Print one copy of the report.

18. Close the file; save the changes.

CREATE A STANDARD REPORT

1. Sort the report as desired.

2. Click **Tools**. .... `Alt`+`T`

3. Click **ReportCreator**. .... `R`

4. Type a name for your report............*text*

5. Click **OK**.................................... `Enter`

Add a Title to the Report

1. Access the **Title** tab.... `Alt`+`N` or `P`

2. In the **Report title** text box .... `Alt`+`R` type a one-line title.

3. Click **Done**.................... `Alt`+`O`

   OR

   Click on the tab .... `Alt`+`N` you wish to use next.

Select the Fields to Appear in the Report:

1. Access the **Fields** tab. `Alt`+`N` or `P`

2. In the **Fields available** .... `Alt`+`F` list box, click the field to be included in the report.

3. Click **Add** to include one field . `Alt`+`A`

Repeat steps 7 and 8 for each field you wish to include

OR

Click **Add All** .... `Alt`+`D` to include all fields.

4. Choose the desired field name display option.

   Show field names at............. `Alt`+`H` **top of each page**.

   OR

   Show summary..................... `Alt`+`H` **information only**.

5. Click **Done**............................ `Alt`+`O`

   OR

   Click the tab you......... `Alt`+`N` or `P` wish to use next.

Add Summary Statistics to the Report:

1. Access the **Summary**.. `Alt`+`N` or `P` tab.

2. In the **Select a field** list box... `Alt`+`F` click the field you wish to summarize.

3. In the **Summaries** area, choose the statistic you wish to apply to that field:

   - **Sum**.................................... `Alt`+`S`
   - **Average**............................... `Alt`+`A`
   - **Count**.................................. `Alt`+`C`
   - **Minimum** .... `Alt`+`M`
   - **Maximum**.............................. `Alt`+`X`
   - **Standard Deviation**............. `Alt`+`T`
   - **Variance**............................... `Alt`+`V`

4. In the **Display summary information area**, click where to position the statistics:

   - **At end of each group** .... `Alt`+`G`
   - **At end of report**................. `Alt`+`R`
   - **Under each column** .... `Alt`+`U`
   - **Together in rows**................. `Alt`+`W`

5. Click **Done**.......................... `Alt`+`O`

6. When prompted:

   - **Preview** your report. .... `Alt`+`P`

     OR

   - **Modify** your report. .... `Alt`+`M`

EXERCISE 22

■ **Modify a Report** ■ **Format a Report** ■ **Access a Report** ■ **Rename a Report** ■ **Delete a Report**

NOTES:

Modify a Report

- In most cases, the standard report is sufficient to present your data. You can, however, modify the report by changing the title, column headings or report instructions. You can also change the appearance of the data by using Works' formatting features. Changes are made in the Report Definitions Screen. This is referred to as Report view.

	A	B	C	D	E	
Title			TRI-STAR PUBLISHING COMPA			
Title			Equipment Assigments by Departm			
Title						
Headings	DEPARTMENT	ITEM	MODEL	MFG	SERIAL	
Headings	ASSIGNED TO				NUMBER	W
Headings						
Record	=ASSIGNED TO	=ITEM	=MODEL	=MFG	='SERIAL #	=V
Summary						
Summary						
Summary						

db inventory.20, Part II, Solution   Zoom 100%

Change a Column (Field) Heading

- The field headings in your database become the column headings in your report. You can change these headings to make them more descriptive. To change these headings in the Report view:

  - Select the cell containing the column heading you wish to change.

  - Type a new heading.

  - Press Enter.

    OR

    Press F2.

  - Edit the existing heading.

Insert a Subtitle or a Two-Line Column Heading

- When creating your report, Works only allows you to create a single-line title or column heading. You can add a row or rows in the Report Definition Screen and enter a multiple-line title and/or multiple-line column heading.

To insert a row into the report definition screen:

- Click in the row headers column where you wish the row to be inserted. The new row will appear directly above this row.

- Select Insert Row from the Insert menu.

  ```
  Insert
  ─────────────────
  Insert Row...
  Delete Row

  Insert Column
  Delete Column

  Field Name...
  Field Entry...
  Field Summary...
  ```

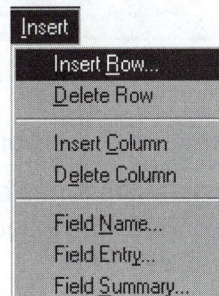

- In the Insert Row dialog box that follows, select the row type to be inserted.

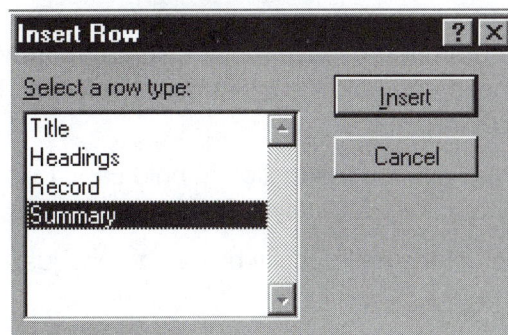

  ```
  Insert Row                    ? X
  Select a row type:
  ┌──────────────────┐  ┌──────────┐
  │ Title            │  │  Insert  │
  │ Headings         │  └──────────┘
  │ Record           │  ┌──────────┐
  │ Summary          │  │  Cancel  │
  │                  │  └──────────┘
  └──────────────────┘
  ```

- Click Insert.

Modify the Report Instructions

To change summary statistics instructions:

In the previous exercise you applied the SUM statistic to the staff column. Suppose you wanted to change the formula to a COUNT calculation. Rather than redo the report, you can modify the instruction in Report view by following these steps:

- Select the cell containing the instruction you wish to change.
- Click Insert.
- Click Field Summary.
- Select a field and statistic from the Insert Field Summary dialog box.

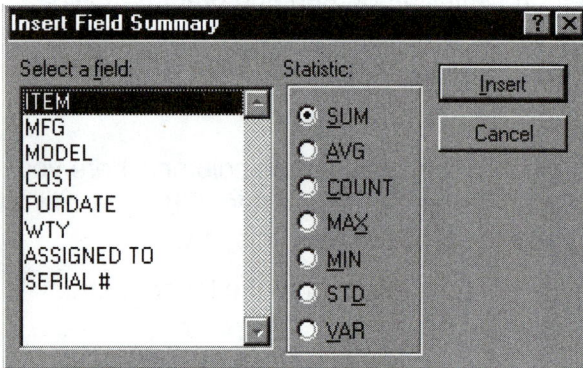

- Click Insert.

To delete a formula in the report Instructions:

You can delete one of the formulas by selecting the cell containing the formula you wish to delete and pressing the Delete key.

To add a formula to the report Instructions:

If you want to add a new summary statistic to a report, follow these steps:

- Add a summary row (or rows) if necessary. Remember to leave a blank summary row above and below each summary statistic for spacing.
- Type desired instruction in bold caps followed by a colon. Example: **SUM:**
- Select the cell directly below the one just created.
- Click Insert.
- Click Field Summary.
- Select a field and statistic from the Insert Field Summary dialog box.

✓ *NOTE: See illustration of Field Summary dialog box at the left.*

- Click Insert.
- Preview your report to view your new instruction.

To reposition summary statistics instructions:

In the previous exercise, you positioned the statistic summary results *together in rows*. Suppose you wanted to change this position to *under the column*. You can modify this instruction in the Report view by using cut and paste to move the instruction to the desired position.

Format a Report

- You can change the font size and style of text, column widths, alignments and margins to make your report more attractive using the same formatting methods learned in word processing and spreadsheets. Changes to the report are made in the Report Definitions Screen.

Font Size and Style

To change the font size and style of a cell, column or row of data:

- Click the cell, column or row to be changed.
- Click Format.
- Click Font and Style.
- Choose desired changes from the Font tab.

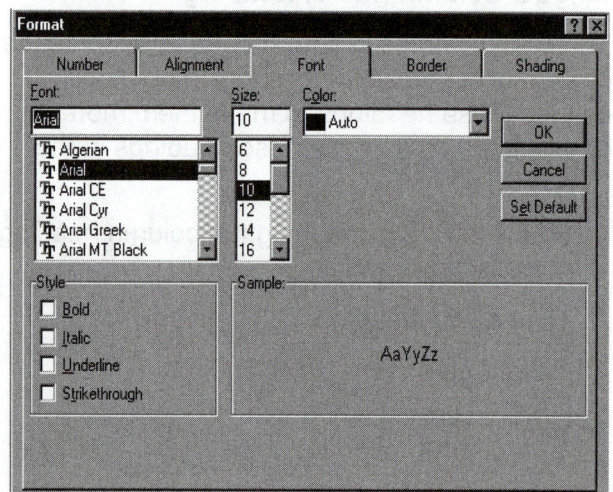

- Click OK.

OR

- Select desired options by using the Works toolbar.

To change the font and style for the entire report:

- Click the box to the left of the first column and above the first title row label.

Click here to highlight entire report screen

- Make the desired changes as noted above.

Column Widths

To change column widths using the mouse:

Drag column border wider or narrower as desired.

OR

To change column widths by a specific amount:

- Click on the header row of the column you wish to widen.

  OR

  Click, hold and drag the mouse across the column letters to highlight more than one column

- Click Format.
- Click Column Width.
- Specify the desired width in the dialog box.
- Click OK.

Margins

To change the margins:

- Select Page Setup from the File menu.
- Select the Margins tab.
- Make desired margin changes.
- Click OK.

Alignments

To center the title across the entire report:

- Select the cell containing the title.
- Use the cut and paste procedure to move the title to the first cell in the same row.
- Highlight this cell and drag the mouse across the report to the end of the last column.
- Click Format.
- Click Alignment.
- Click Center across selection.

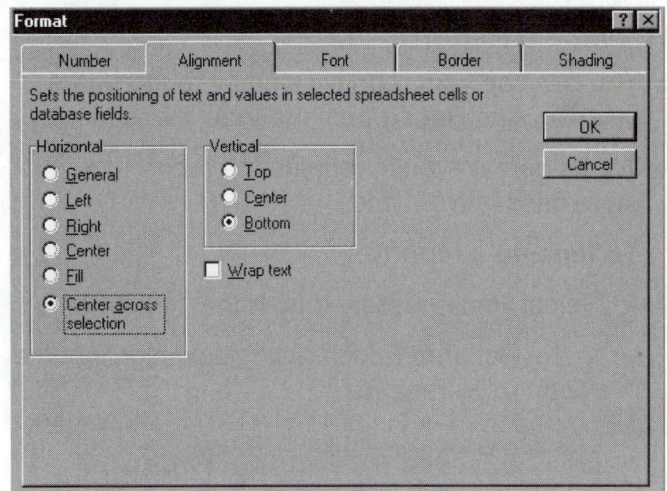

To align column heading:

- Select the column heading(s) to be aligned. Example: **ITEM**
- Select Alignment from the Format menu.
- Select the desired alignment in the Alignment tab.
- Click OK.

To align column data:

- Select the cell containing the formula representing the column data to be aligned. Example: **=ITEM**
- Select Alignment from the Format menu.
- Select the desired alignment in the Alignment tab.
- Click OK.

- After formatting a report, preview it before printing.

Access a Report

■ Once a report is created, it may be accessed at any time in the future. Remember, reports are part of the database. Therefore,

To access a report:

- Retrieve the database on which the report was based.
- Select Report from the View menu.
- Select the report name.
- Click Preview or Modify

Rename a Report

■ You can see your reports listed by report name by accessing Report from the View menu.

■ Works permits you to rename the report to a more descriptive name.

To rename a report:

- Select Rename Report from the Tools menu.
- In the Rename Report dialog box, highlight the report to be renamed.

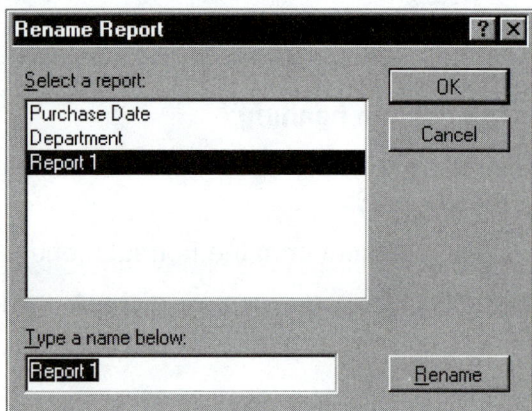

- Type desired name in *Type a name below:* text box.
- Click OK.

Delete a Report

■ Works permits you to create up to eight reports in a database. If you need to create more than eight reports, you must delete one or more existing reports.

To delete a report:

- Select Delete Report from the Tools menu.
- In the Delete Report dialog box, highlight the report to delete.

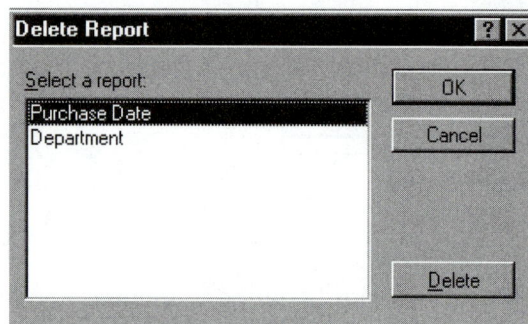

- Click Delete.
- Click OK.

  ✓ NOTE: *Works prompts you to confirm your deletion and alert you to the fact that this action cannot be undone. Click OK to confirm your deletion.*

EXERCISE DIRECTIONS:

PART I

1. Open the ⌨**INVENTORY**, or open 💾**DB INVENTORY.22**.

2. Sort the records alphabetically by ITEM and chronologically by PURDATE.

3. Create a report. Accept the default name of Report 1.

4. Access the Title tab. Enter the one-line title: TRI-STAR PUBLISHING COMPANY

5. Access the Fields Tab. Include the following fields in your report in this order.

   ITEM
   MFG
   MODEL
   PURDATE
   COST

6. Access the Summary tab. Apply the Sum statistic to total the COST field. Position the results at the end of the report, under each column.

Modify the report as directed below.

7. Insert a Title row.

8. Insert a subtitle for the report: Computer Equipment Inventory Purchase Dates

9. Change the column headings as indicated below:

ITEM		*no change*
MFG	to	MANUFACTURER
MODEL		*no change*
PURDATE	to	PURCHASED
COST	to	COST OF ITEM

10. Widen the columns widths to accommodate the longer column headings.

11. Move the title and subtitle to the first column. Use *Center across selection* to center the title and subtitle.

12. Set the title to 14-point bold.

13. Set the subtitle to italics.

14. Rename the report: Purchase Date

15. Preview the report.

16. Print one copy. Do not close the file.

PART II

1. Change to List view to modify the database.

2. Sort the records alphabetically by ASSIGNED TO and alphabetically by ITEM.

3. Create a report. Accept the default name of Report 1.

4. Assign a report title: TRI-STAR PUBLISHING COMPANY

5. Include the following fields in your report in this order:

   ASSIGNED TO
   ITEM
   MODEL
   MFG
   SERIAL #
   WTY
   PURDATE

6. Apply the Maximum formula to the PURDATE field to find the most recent purchase.

7. Position the results at the end of the report, under each column.

Modify the report as directed below.

8. Add a Title row.

9. Insert a subtitle for the report: Equipment Assignments by Department

10. Insert a Headings row.

11. Change the column headings to two-line column headings indicated below:

ASSIGNED TO	to	DEPARTMENT ASSIGNED TO
ITEM		*no change*
MODEL		*no change*
MFG		*no change*
SERIAL #	to	SERIAL NUMBER
WTY	to	UNDER WARRANTY
PURDATE	to	PURCHASE DATE

12. Widen the column widths to accommodate the longer column headings as needed.

13. Change the left and right margins to 0.5".

14. Center the title and subtitle.

   ✓ NOTE: *Remember to move the title and subtitle to the first column before centering it.)*

15. Set the title to 16 point bold.

16. Set the subtitle to 14 point italics.

17. Reformat the column headings as follows: center, set to bold italics and remove the underlining.

18. Rename the report: Department

19. Preview the report.

   ✓ NOTE: *Leave enough space between columns so the field data is easy to read.*

20. Print one copy of the report.

21. Close the file; save the changes.

DESIRED RESULT, PART I

TRI-STAR PUBLISHING COMPANY
Computer Equipment Inventory Purchase Dates

ITEM	MANUFACTURER	MODEL	PURCHASED	COST OF ITEM
Computer	IBM	PS2	6/95	$1,348
Computer	Canon	Notebook 486	1/96	$1,889
Computer	IBM	Thinkpad 500	6/96	$1,399
Computer	IBM	Thinkpad	6/96	$2,199
Computer	Canon	Notebook	8/96	$2,436
Computer	Canon	Notebook	8/96	$2,436
Hard Drive	Conner	CFS4 210MB	6/96	$200
Hard Drive	Quantum	LPS 40 170MB	6/96	$199
Modem	Intel	PCMCIA	1/96	$115
Monitor	NEC	FGE	12/96	$589
Monitor	NEC	FGE/3V	12/96	$539
Printer	Okidata	ML330RR	2/96	$295
Printer	IBM	ExecJet II	6/96	$335
Printer	HP	DeskJet	11/96	$429
Printer	HP	DeskJet	11/96	$429

SUM:

$14,837

DESIRED RESULT, PART II

TRI-STAR PUBLISHING COMPANY
Equipment Assignments by Department

DEPARTMENT ASSIGNED TO	ITEM	MODEL	MFG	SERIAL NUMBER	UNDER WARRANTY	PURCHASE DATE
Accounting	Computer	PS2	IBM	651198	Yes	6/95
Accounting	Computer	Thinkpad 500	IBM	671150	Yes	6/96
Accounting	Hard Drive	LPS 40 170MB	Quantum	54219	Yes	6/96
Accounting	Monitor	FGE	NEC	11112	No	12/96
Accounting	Printer	DeskJet	HP	99911	Yes	11/96
Personnel	Computer	Thinkpad	IBM	2059	Yes	6/96
Personnel	Computer	Notebook	Canon	98763	Yes	8/96
Personnel	Monitor	FGE/3V	NEC	87098	No	12/96
Personnel	Printer	ExecJet II	IBM	55211	Yes	6/96
Personnel	Printer	DeskJet	HP	22230	Yes	11/96
Purchasing	Computer	Notebook	Canon	76666	Yes	8/96
Purchasing	Hard Drive	CFS4 210MB	Conner	12345	No	6/96
Shipping	Computer	Notebook 486	Canon	1445	Yes	1/96
Shipping	Modem	PCMCIA	Intel	20098	No	1/96
Shipping	Printer	ML330RR	Okidata	98983	Yes	2/96

MAX: 12/96

CHANGE COLUMN HEADING
–In the Report Definition Screen–
1. Select the cell containing the heading to change.
2. Type a new title .... *text*
3. Press **ENTER** .... `Enter`

INSERT ROW
1. Click in Row Header column where row is to be inserted.
   OR
   Select a cell within the row where row is to be inserted.
2. Click **Insert** .... `Alt`+`I`
3. Click **Insert Row** .... `R`
4. **Select a row type** .... `Alt`+`S`, `↓` to be inserted.
   - Title
   - Headings
   - Record
   - Summary
5. Click **Insert** .... `Alt`+`I`

CHANGE A SUMMARY STATISTIC
1. Select the cell containing the instruction you wish to change.
2. Click **Insert** .... `Alt`+`I`
3. Click **Field Summary** .... `S`
4. Select a **field** and .... `Alt`+`F` statistic from the Insert Field Summary dialog box.
   - **SUM** .... `Alt`+`S`
   - **AVG** .... `Alt`+`A`
   - **COUNT** .... `Alt`+`C`
   - **MAX** .... `Alt`+`X`
   - **MIN** .... `Alt`+`M`
   - **STD** .... `Alt`+`D`
   - **VAR** .... `Alt`+`V`
5. Click **Insert** .... `Alt`+`I`

DELETE A SUMMARY STATISTIC INSTRUCTION.
1. Select the cell containing the formula you wish to delete.
2. Press the **Delete** key .... `Del`

ADD A SUMMARY STATISTIC INSTRUCTION.
1. Add a summary row or rows if necessary.
   ✓NOTE: See Insert Subtitle or Two Line Column Heading above.
2. Type desired **instruction** in bold **caps** followed by a **colon**. Example: **SUM:**
3. Select the cell directly below the one just created.
4. Click **Insert** .... `Alt`+`I`
5. Click **Field Summary** .... `S` *(See listing above).*
6. Select a **field** and .... `Alt`+`F` statistic from the Insert Field Summary dialog box.
7. Click **Insert** .... `Alt`+`I`

REPOSITION A SUMMARY STATISTIC

1. Select the cell containing the summary statistic to be repositioned.
2. Click **Edit** .... `Alt`+`E`
3. Click **Cut** .... `T`
4. Click the cell that you want to contain the summary statistic.
5. Click **Edit** .... `Alt`+`E`
6. Click **Paste** .... `P`

CHANGE FONT AND STYLE

1. Click the cell, column or row to be changed.
2. Click **Format** .... `Alt`+`O`
3. Click **Font and Style** .... `F`
4. Choose desired changes from the Font formatting tab.
   - **Font** .... `Alt`+`F`
   - **Size** .... `Alt`+`S`
   - **Color** .... `Alt`+`O`
   - Style
     - ◆ **Bold** .... `Alt`+`B`
     - ◆ **Italic** .... `Alt`+`I`
     - ◆ **Underline** .... `Alt`+`U`
     - ◆ **Strikethrough** .... `Alt`+`T`
5. Click **OK** .... `Enter`

CHANGE FONT AND STYLE FOR THE ENTIRE REPORT

1. Click the box to the left of the first column and above the first title row label.

2. Make the desired changes as noted above.

CHANGE COLUMN WIDTH

   –Using the Mouse–

Drag each column wider or narrower as desired.

   –To change column width by a specific amount–

1. Click on the header row of the column you wish to widen.

   OR

Click, hold and drag your mouse across the column letters to highlight more than one column.

2. Click **Format** .... `Alt`+`O`
3. Click **Column Width** .... `W`
4. Specify the desired .... *number* width in the dialog box.
5. Click **OK** .... `Enter`

CHANGE MARGINS

1. Click **File** .... `Alt`+`F`
2. Click **Page Setup** .... `G`
3. Select the **Margins** .... `Alt`+`M` formatting tab.
4. Make desired margin changes.
   - **Top** margin .... `Alt`+`T`
   - **Bottom** margin .... `Alt`+`B`
   - **Left** margin .... `Alt`+`L`
   - **Right** margin .... `Alt`+`R`
   - **Header** margin .... `Alt`+`A`
   - **Footer** margin .... `Alt`+`F`
5. Click **OK** .... `Enter`

CENTER TITLE OF REPORT

1. Select cell containing the title.
2. Click **Edit** .... `Alt`+`E`
3. Click **Cut** .... `T`
4. Select the first cell in the row.
5. Click **Edit** .... `Alt`+`E`
6. Click **Paste** .... `P`
7. With this cell selected, click, hold and drag your mouse across the report to the end of the last column.
8. Click **Format** .... `Alt`+`O`
9. Click **Alignment** .... `A`
10. Click **Center across selection** .... `A`
11. Click **OK** .... `Enter`

ALIGN COLUMN HEADING

1. Select column heading(s) to be aligned.
2. Click **Format** .... `Alt`+`O`
3. Click **Alignment** .... `A`
4. Select desired alignment
   - **General** .... `Alt`+`G`
   - **Left** .... `Alt`+`L`
   - **Right** .... `Alt`+`R`
   - **Center** .... `Alt`+`C`

   - **Fill** .... `Alt`+`F`
   - **Top** .... `Alt`+`T`
   - **Center** .... `Alt`+`E`
   - **Bottom** .... `Alt`+`B`
   - **Wrap text** .... `Alt`+`W`
5. Click **OK** .... `Enter`

To Align Column Data

1. Select the cell containing the formula to be aligned. Example: =**STAFF**
2. Click **Format** .... `Alt`+`O`
3. Click **Alignment** .... `A`
4. Select desired alignment as noted above.
5. Click **OK** .... `Enter`

ACCESS A REPORT

1. Open the database on which the report was based.
2. Click **View** .... `Alt`+`V`
3. Click **Report** .... `R`
4. Choose the report .... `↓` you wish to view from the list.
5. Click **Preview** .... `Alt`+`P`

   OR

   Click **Modify** .... `Alt`+`M`

RENAME REPORT

1. Open the database on which the report was based.
2. Click **Tools** .... `Alt`+`T`
3. Click **Rename Report** .... `M`
4. Type desired name. .... *text*
5. Click **OK** .... `Enter`

   OR

   Click **Rename** .... `Alt`+`R`
6. Click **OK** .... `Enter`

DELETE REPORT

1. Open the database on which the report was based.
2. Click **Tools** .... `Alt`+`T`
3. Click **Delete Report** .... `T`
4. **Select a report** to delete. .... `Alt`+`S`
5. Click **OK** .... `Enter`

   OR

   a. Click **Delete** .... `Alt`+`D`
   b. Click **OK** .... `Enter`

EXERCISE **23**

■ Sort and Group Report Data ■ Display Statistic Summaries within Each Group

NOTES:

- In the previous exercise, you sorted the records before you created your report. You can sort and group your records as you create your report using the ReportCreator's *Sorting* and *Grouping* tabs.

- **Grouping** shows related records together but set apart from records in different groups.

- Note the report below in which the data has been sorted and grouped by TYPE.

ILLUSTRATION A – REPORT GROUPED BY TYPE

SOFTWARE INVENTORY

TYPE	TITLE	PRICE
Accounting	Peaches	$115.95
Accounting	Quick	$42.50
Communication	BBS	$111.50
Database	Info Base	$488.88
Database	Accessor	$550.50
Database	Paradoxy	$144.95
Desktop	Pagemarker	$399.40
Graphics	Harword	$299.95
Integrated	Officemate	$479.95
Spreadsheet	Exceller	$594.20
Spreadsheet	Tulip 5	$594.20
Word Processing	Word-O-D	$499.85
Word Processing	Word-O-2	$499.85
Word Processing	Micro Words	$459.80
Word Processing	Word-O	$499.85

Sort and Group Report Data

As the Report is Created

- To group and sort your records as you create your database report:

  - Select the Sorting tab from the ReportCreator.

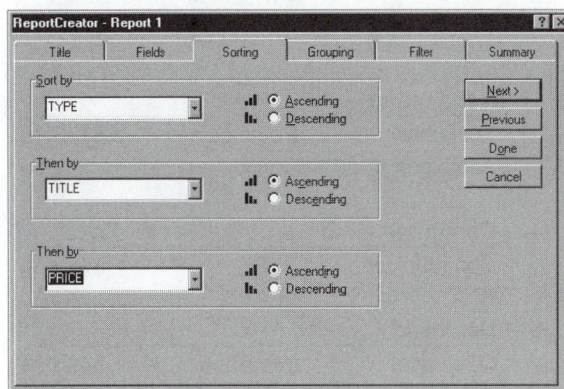

  - Sort your records by field name just as you did from in List view.

  - After choosing the desired options in the Sorting tab, click on the Grouping tab.

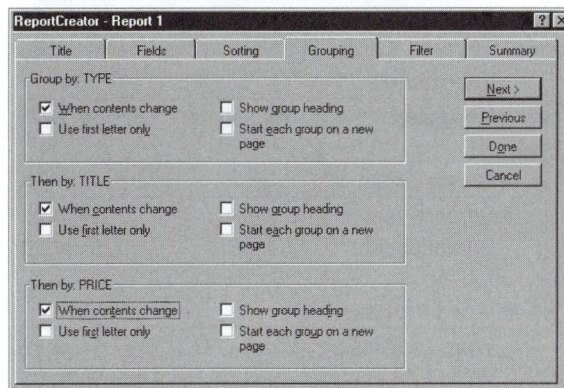

  - The field names you entered in the sorting tab now appear in the grouping tab. When you click *When contents change,* Works groups the records accordingly, producing the result shown in Illustration A on the left.

- Once *When contents change* has been selected, other options in the grouping tab may become available.

  - *Use first letter only* uses the first letter in each group.

  - *Show group heading* displays a heading for each group based on the sort instruction.

  - *Start each group on a new page* inserts a page break after each group.

- Note the report below in which the a group heading has been added for the TYPE field.

ILLUSTRATION B – REPORT WITH GROUP HEADINGS

SOFTWARE INVENTORY

TYPE	TITLE	PRICE
Accounting		
Accounting	Peaches	$115.95
Accounting	Quick	$42.50
Communication		
Communication	BBS	$111.50
Database		
Database	Info Base	$488.88
Database	Accessor	$550.50
Database	Paradoxy	$144.95
Desktop		
Desktop	Pagemarker	$399.40
Graphics		
Graphics	Harword	$299.95
Integrated		
Integrated	Officemate	$479.95
Spreadsheet		
Spreadsheet	Exceller	$594.20
Spreadsheet	Tulip 5	$594.20
Word Processing		
Word Processing	Word-O-D	$499.85
Word Processing	Word-O-2	$499.85
Word Processing	Micro Words	$459.80
Word Processing	Word-O	$499.85

Group Headings

Display Statistic Summaries within Each Group

- As your report is being created, you can position the summary formulas to display within each group by following these steps:

  ✓ NOTE: *These grouping options are only available as your report is being created.*

- Select the *Summary* tab from the ReportCreator.

- Click desired Display summary information options. An explantion of each appears below.

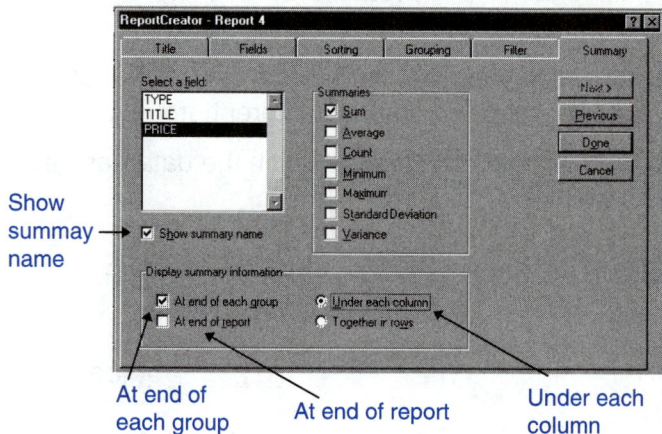

Show summary name

At end of each group   At end of report   Under each column

- **At end of each group** displays the formula as it is applied to each group.

- **At end of report** displays the formula as it is applied to the whole report. It displays a grand total of all the groups.

- **Together in rows** displays the formulas within each group at the left margin, listed one below the other.

- **Under each column** displays each formula under the field column.

- **Show summary name** displays the summary statistic name (SUM, COUNT, AVERAGE, etc.) along with the summary result. Click the check box to deselect it.

- Click Done.

- Note Illustration C, a report in which the summary statistics and summary name are displayed:
  - Under each column
  - At the end of each group
  - At the end of the report

ILLUSTRATION C

SOFTWARE INVENTORY

TYPE	TITLE	PRICE
Accounting	Peaches	$115.95
Accounting	Quick	$42.50
COUNT:		**SUM:**
1		$158.45
Communication	BBS	$111.50
COUNT:		**SUM:**
1		$111.50
Database	Info Base	$488.88
Database	Accessor	$550.50
Database	Paradoxy	$144.95
COUNT:		**SUM:**
3		$1,184.33
Desktop	Pagemarker	$399.40
COUNT:		**SUM:**
1		$399.40
Graphics	Harword	$299.95
COUNT:		**SUM:**
1		$299.95
Integrated	Officemate	$479.95
COUNT:		**SUM:**
1		$479.95
Spreadsheet	Exceller	$594.20
Spreadsheet	Tulip 5	$594.20
COUNT:		**SUM:**
2		$1,188.40
Word Processing	Word-O-D	$499.85
Word Processing	Word-O-2	$499.85
Word Processing	Micro Words	$459.80
Word Processing	Word-O	$499.85
COUNT:		**SUM:**
4		$1,959.35
COUNT:		**SUM:**
15		$5,781.33

Summary statistics at end of report. ↑

- Now, note Illustration D, a report in which the summary statistics are displayed:
  - At the end of each group
  - Together in rows
  - At the end of the report

ILLUSTRATION D

SOFTWARE INVENTORY

TYPE	TITLE	PRICE
Accounting	Peaches	$115.95
Accounting	Quick	$42.50
COUNT OF TYPE:		2
GROUP TOTAL PRICE:		$158.45
Communication	BBS	$111.50
COUNT OF TYPE:		1
GROUP TOTAL PRICE:		$111.50
Database	Info Base	$488.88
Database	Accessor	$550.50
Database	Paradoxy	$144.95
COUNT OF TYPE:		3
GROUP TOTAL PRICE:		$1,184.33
Desktop	Pagemarker	$399.40
COUNT OF TYPE:		1
GROUP TOTAL PRICE:		$399.40
Graphics	Harword	$299.95
COUNT OF TYPE:		1
GROUP TOTAL PRICE:		$299.95
Integrated	Officemate	$479.95
COUNT OF TYPE:		1
GROUP TOTAL PRICE:		$479.95
Spreadsheet	Exceller	$594.20
Spreadsheet	Tulip 5	$594.20
COUNT OF TYPE:		2
GROUP TOTAL PRICE:		$1,188.40
Word Processing	Word-O-D	$499.85
Word Processing	Word-O-2	$499.85
Word Processing	Micro Words	$459.80
Word Processing	Word-O	$499.85
COUNT OF TYPE:		4
GROUP TOTAL PRICE:		$1,959.35
COUNT OF TYPE:		15
GROUP TOTAL PRICE:		$5,781.33

↑ *Summary statistics at end of report*

Sort and Group Data

After the Report Has Been Created

- You can sort and group your records *after* the report is created by following these steps:

    - Click View, Report, Modify.

    - Click Report Settings

        ◆ Click the Sorting tab. Choose your sorting options.

        ◆ Click the Grouping tab. Choose your grouping options.

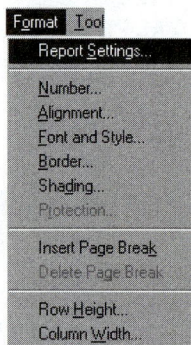

OR

- ◆ Click Tools from the Report view menu.

- ◆ Click Report Sorting.

    OR

    Click Report Grouping.

- Choose your sorting options.

- Click Done.

Report settings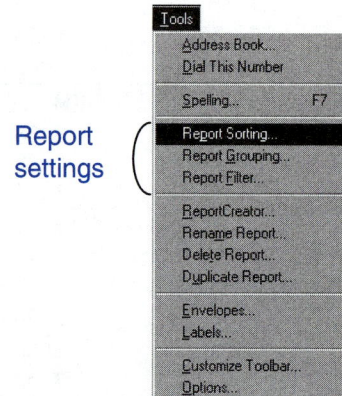

Before your company orders more software, they want to determine which products have been assigned to what departments, the cost of the packages they have purchased, and in what room they are stored. You have been asked to prepare two reports so that your manager can make an analysis.

EXERCISE DIRECTIONS:

PART I

To create the report in Illustration E (page 354):

1. Open 🖮**PROGRAM**, or open 🖫**DB PROGRAM.23**.

2. Create a report. Accept the default name of Report 1.

3. Title the report: SOFTWARE INVENTORY -- ROOM STORED

4. Include the following fields in your report in this order:

    TYPE
    TITLE
    STORED

5. Access the Sorting tab. Sort the records alphabetically by TYPE.

6. Access the Grouping tab. Group the TYPE field. Choose the *When contents change* option.

7. Access the Summary tab. Apply the Count formula to the TYPE field.

    a. Choose the At end of each group and Under each column option.

    b. Remove the check box in for the *At end of report* option.

    c. Eliminate the summary name from the count instruction by clicking the check box for the *Show summary name option* to deselect it.

8. Preview your report.

(Continued)

Modify the report as directed below:

9. Change all column widths to 17.

10. Move the title to the first cell and center it across the database. Set it to 12 point; leave it bolded.

11. Add a heading row and change the column headings to the new two-line column headings as follows:

PROGRAM	to	PROGRAM TYPE
TITLE	to	TITLE OF PROGRAM
STORED	to	ROOM WHERE STORED

12. Center both of the two-line column headings and set them to bold italics. Remove the underline from both rows.

13. Center the data below the ROOM WHERE STORED column.

   ✓ HINT: *The cell containing the data is preceded by an equal sign).*

14. Set 2.25" left and right margins.

15. Rename the report: Storage Room

16. Preview the report.

17. Save the report. *Do not close the file.*

PART II

To create the report in Illustration F (page 355):

1. Create a new report. Accept the default name.

2. Title the report: SOFTWARE INVENTORY BY OPERATING SYSTEM

3. Include the following fields in your report in this order.

   OS
   TYPE
   TITLE
   PRICE

4. Sort the records alphabetically by OS, alphabetically by TYPE and alphabetically by TITLE.

5. Group the OS field When contents change and Show group heading.

6. Include summary statistics as follows:

   a. Apply the Count formula to the TYPE field.

   b. Apply Sum, Average, Maximum and Minimum formulas to the PRICE field.

   c. Position the results at End of each group, Under each column.

   d. Allow *Show summary name* to remain selected.

   e. Click on the check box next to *At end of report* to deselect it.

7. Preview your report.

Modify the report as directed below

8. Change the column widths of columns A, B and C to 18. Change the column width of column D to 12.

9. Move the title to the first cell and center it across the report.

10. Set the title to 12 point italic. It should remain bold.

11. Add a heading row and change the column headings to the new two-line column headings indicated below:

OS	to	OPERATING SYSTEM
TYPE	to	PROGRAM TYPE
TITLE	to	PROGRAM TITLE
PRICE	to	PRICE OF PROGRAM

12. Reformat the column headings as follows: Center, set to bold and remove the underlining.

13. Rename the report: Type of OS

14. Preview the report.

15. Print one copy.

16. Close the file; save the changes.

SOFTWARE INVENTORY – ROOM STORED

PROGRAM TYPE	TITLE OF PROGRAM	ROOM WHERE STORED
Accounting	Peaches	B205
Accounting	Peaches	B205
Accounting	Quick	B205
	2	
Communication	BBS	D230
	1	
Database	Info Base	A114
Database	Accessor	A114
Database	Paradoxy	A114
	3	
Desktop	Pagemarker	A114
	1	
Graphics	Harword	D230
	1	
Integrated	Officemate	D238
	1	
Spreadsheet	Exceller	D238
Spreadsheet	Tulip 5	D238
	2	
Word Processing	Word-O-D	D238
Word Processing	Word-O-2	D238
Word Processing	Micro Words	D238
Word Processing	Word-O	D238
	4	

SOFTWARE INVENTORY BY OPERATING SYSTEM

OPERATING SYSTEM	PROGRAM TYPE	PROGRAM TITLE	PRICE OF PROGRAM
DOS			
DOS	Accounting	Peaches	$115.95
DOS	Accounting	Quick	$42.50
DOS	Database	Info Base	$488.88
DOS	Word Processing	Word-O-D	$499.85
	COUNT:		SUM:
		4	$1,147.18
			AVG:
			$286.80
			MIN:
			$42.50
			MAX:
			$499.85
OS/2			
OS/2	Communication	BBS	$111.50
OS/2	Database	Accessor	$550.50
OS/2	Word Processing	Word-O-2	$499.85
	COUNT:		SUM:
		3	$1,161.85
			AVG:
			$387.28
			MIN:
			$111.50
			MAX:
			$550.50
Windows			
Windows	Database	Paradoxy	$144.95
Windows	Desktop	Pagemarker	$399.40
Windows	Graphics	Harword	$299.95
Windows	Integrated	Officemate	$479.95
Windows	Spreadsheet	Exceller	$594.20
Windows	Spreadsheet	Tulip 5	$594.20
Windows	Word Processing	Micro Words	$459.80
Windows	Word Processing	Word-O	$499.85
	COUNT:		SUM:
		4	$3,472.30
			AVG:
			$434.04
			MIN:
			$144.95
			MAX:
			$594.20

SORT AND GROUP REPORT DATA

–As the report is being created–

1. Start to create a standard report.
   (See Exercise 21, Keystrokes.)

   ––IN THE REPORTCREATOR SCREEN–

2. Click the **Sorting** tab............... `Alt`+`N`

3. Choose the fields you wish to sort. Sort your fields just as you did in the database. *(See Exercise 17, Keystrokes)*

4. Click the **Grouping** tab.. `Alt`+`N` or `P`

5. Click **When contents change** `Alt`+`W` for each field you wish to group.

6. Choose any desired option that have now become available.

   • **Use first letter only**............. `Alt`+`Y`

   • **Show group heading**........... `Alt`+`G`

   • **Start each group**............... `Alt`+`E`
     on a new page.

7. Click the Summary tab. `Alt`+`A` or `P`

8. Choose summary statistic formulas you want included in the report. *(See Exercise 21, Keystrokes)*

9. Select a display summary information option.

10. Click **At end of each group**..... `Alt`+`G`

11. If you don't want a grand total printed at the end of the report (the default)

    OR

    • Click **At end of report**.......... `Alt`+`R`
      to deselect that option.

    • Click **Under** each column..... `Alt`+`U`

12. Click **Show summary name** .. `Alt`+`H` to not display summary name.

13. Click **Done**............................. `Alt`+`O`

–After the report has been created–

1. Access the report you wish to group. *(See Exercise 20, Keystrokes)*

2. Click **Modify**. .... `Alt`+`M`

3. Click **Format**........................ `Alt`+`O`

4. Click **Report Settings** .... `S`

   Click the **Sorting** tab .... `Alt`+`N`

   OR

   Click the **Grouping** tab .... `Alt`+`N` tab.

   OR

   Click **Tools**........................... `Alt`+`T`

      Click **Report Sorting** .... `P`

   OR

      Click **Report Grouping**.............. `G`

5. Choose desired options.

6. Click **Done**.......................... `Alt`+`O`

EXERCISE **24**

■ **Group and Sort Data** ■ **Use Shading in a Report**

NOTES:

- You can emphasize grouped summary data in the Report Definitions Screen by highlighting summary statistic formulas and applying the formatting features learned previously.

- Adding shading to the =BRANCH and =SUM(ANNSAL) statistics shown in Illustration A will result in shaded, grouped summary data shown in the report on page 359.

ILLUSTRATION A

	A	B	C	D
Title		KAO -- ANNUAL SALARIES BY BRANCH		
Title				
Headings				
Headings	BRANCH	DEPARTMENT	POSITION	ANNUAL
Headings				SALARY
Intr BRANCH	=BRANCH			
Record	=BRANCH	=DEPT	=POSITION	=ANNSAL
Summ BRANCH	COUNT:			SUM:
Summ BRANCH	=COUNT(BRANCH)			=SUM(ANN
Summary				
Summary	COUNT:			SUM:
Summary	=COUNT(BRANCH)			=SUM(ANN

Zoom 100%

ADD SHADING IN A REPORT

–IN THE REPORT DEFINITIONS SCREEN–

1. Select the cell that represents the cell or group of cells you want to shade.
2. Click **Format**. .... Alt + O
3. Click **Shading** .... D
4. Choose desired **Pattern**. . Alt + P , ↓
5. Click **OK**. .... Enter

REMOVE SHADING IN A REPORT

–IN THE REPORT DEFINITIONS SCREEN–

1. Select the cell that represents the cell or group of cells you want to shade.
2. Click **Format**. .... Alt + O
3. Click **Shading** .... D

4. Choose none. .... Alt + P , ↓
5. Click **OK**. .... Enter

> *The owners of the KAO Electronic Equipment Company need to evaluate their branch employees' salaries. You have been asked to prepare a report to assist this procedure.*

EXERCISE DIRECTIONS:

To create the report in Illustration B

1. Open ⌨**PROMOTE**, or open 💾**DB PROMOTE.24**

2. Create a report. Use any name you wish.

3. Title the report: KAO -- ANNUAL SALARIES BY BRANCH

4. Include the following fields in your report in this order:

    BRANCH
    DEPT
    POSITION
    ANNSAL

5. Sort the records in ascending order by BRANCH and ascending order by POSITION.

6. Group the records to change *When contents change* in the BRANCH sort. Select the option to *Show group heading*.

7. Apply the *Count* statistic to the BRANCH field.

8. Apply the *Sum* statistic to the ANNUAL SALARY field.

9. Position the results *At end of each group, At end of report, Under each column.*

10. Preview your report.

–Modify your report as directed below–

11. Change the column width of the BRANCH field to 20, the DEPT field to 15 and the ANNSAL field to 12.

12. If you changed the font of the database to 8 point in a previous exercise, change it to 10 point.

13. Move the title to the first cell and center it across the selection.

14. Set the title to 12 point. It should remain bold.

15. Add a headings row and change the column headings to the new two-line column headings below:

BRANCH		*no change*
DEPT	to	DEPARTMENT
POSITION		*no change*
ANNSAL	to	ANNUAL SALARY

16. Center, bold and underline the SALARY column heading. Remove the underlining from ANNUAL.

17. Remove the shading from the:

    =BRANCH cell in the RECORD row

    and the:

    =COUNT(BRANCH) cell in the Summ BRANCH row

    and the:

    =COUNT(BRANCH) cell in the Summary row

18. Add shading (20%) to the:

    =BRANCH cell in the Intr BRANCH row

    and the:

    =SUM(ANNSAL) cell in the Summ BRANCH row

19. Set the =SUM(ANNSAL) cell in the Summary row to bold.

20. Change the top margin to 0.5".

21. Change the left and right margins to 1.5".

22. Rename the report: Branch Salaries.

23. Preview the report.

24. Print one copy.

25. Close the file, save the changes.

KAO -- ANNUAL SALARIES BY BRANCH

BRANCH	DEPARTMENT	POSITION	ANNUAL SALARY
Bronx			
Bronx	Stock	Inventory Supervisor	$20,350
COUNT:			**SUM:**
1			$20,350
Brooklyn			
Brooklyn	Sales	Assistant Manager	$23,650
COUNT:			**SUM:**
1			$23,650
Fort Lee			
Fort Lee	Stock	Order Processing Clerk	$17,600
Fort Lee	Stock	Senior Stock Clerk	$17,650
COUNT:			**SUM:**
2			$35,250
Long Beach			
Long Beach	Admin.	Supervisor, Computer Operations	$24,600
COUNT:			**SUM:**
1			$24,600
Los Angeles			
Los Angeles	Stock	Assistant Coordinator	$19,021
Los Angeles	Admin.	Customer Service Rep	$16,500
Los Angeles	Admin.	Executive Assistant	$21,780
Los Angeles	Sales	Sales Rep, Level II	$13,500
Los Angeles	Sales	Senior Review Clerk	$15,670
Los Angeles	Sales	Vice President	$35,000
COUNT:			**SUM:**
6			$121,471
Manhattan			
Manhattan	Admin.	A/P Bookkeeper	$18,750
Manhattan	Admin.	Administrative Assistant	$20,267
Manhattan	Sales	Advertising Rep	$20,500
Manhattan	Stock	Assistant Supervisor	$18,500
Manhattan	Stock	Manager	$29,500
Manhattan	Sales	Sales Representative	$13,500
COUNT:			**SUM:**
6			$121,017
Queens			
Queens	Admin.	Payroll Supervisor	$27,500
Queens	Stock	Warehouse Coordinator	$26,500
COUNT:			**SUM:**
2			$54,000
San Francisco			
San Francisco	Admin.	A/R Bookkeeper	$21,000
San Francisco	Sales	Marketing Analyst	$22,500
COUNT:			**SUM:**
2			$43,500
COUNT:			**SUM:**
21			$443,838

■ **Create a Report Based on the Results of a Filter**

NOTES:

- In the previous exercises, you created a report using all the records in your database. You can, however, use a filter to select certain records and base your report on only those records. For example, in the inventory database shown below, you might want to include only items purchased before January 1996 or items that cost more than $50.00.

- You can access the Filter tab while in the Report Definitions Screen by accessing the ReportCreator.

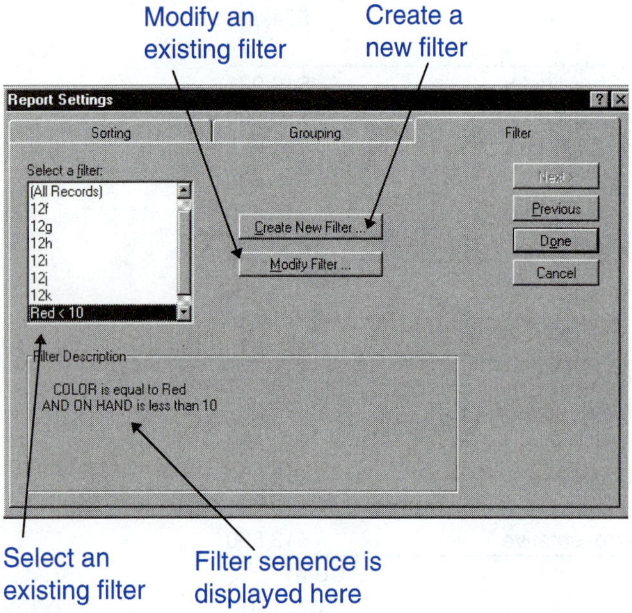

- On the Filter tab, you can:

  Select and apply a previously created filter.
  OR
  Create and apply a new filter.
  OR
  Modify and apply a previously created filter.

Modify an existing filter   Create a new filter

Select an existing filter   Filter senence is displayed here

In this exercise, you will modify the STOCK database and create a report based on the results of a filter. After taking inventory on March 1, 1996, your manager wants you to include the number of items you have on hand in each color. This will require that you modify the database to include the information. Your manager also wants to see several reports showing the data in different ways.

EXERCISE DIRECTIONS:

PART I

To create the report in Illustration B:

1. Open ⌨STOCK, or open 💾DB STOCK.25

2. Insert a new field, ON HAND. Enter the data shown in Illustration A.

ILLUSTRATION A

	STYLE	TYPE	COLOR	J5	J7	J9	J11	J13	PRICE	DATEORD	BU	ACC	ON HAND
1	J7455	Blazer	Black	23	32	21	34	32	$50.99	9/23/95	Yes	No	12
2	J8510	Skirt	Black	4	4	2	4	2	$26.00	10/18/95	Yes	No	3
3	P232	Skirt	Black	5	5	5	5	7	$29.50	2/10/96	Yes	No	4
4	P987	Skirt	Black	3	4	5	6	7	$30.75	2/10/96	Yes	Yes	2
5	J3254	Dress	Blue	4	15	16	12	14	$61.99	7/16/95	Yes	Yes	12
6	J3290	Dress	Blue	23	32	33	23	12	$56.88	11/17/95	No	Yes	23
7	J2121	Sweater	Brown	4	4	6	6	7	$29.99	2/7/96	Yes	No	2
8	J4230	Pants	Gray	24	4	6	7	13	$49.99	12/12/95	Yes	No	33
9	J5555	Blouse	Green	13	32	45	6	9	$19.99	6/19/95	No	No	13
10	J7654	Suit	Green	12	17	34	32	12	$85.50	9/18/95	Yes	Yes	12
11	P287	Blazer	Navy	7	9	11	14	14	$75.50	2/10/96	Yes	No	2
12	P998	Skirt	Navy	2	4	4	5	7	$35.40	2/10/96	Yes	Yes	1
13	J7699	Suit	Navy	12	10	10	8	7	$110.10	2/7/96	Yes	Yes	8
14	P999	Vest	Navy	6	6	7	7	7	$25.50	2/10/96	No	No	1
15	J2123	Sweater	Olive	5	5	6	7	9	$35.75	2/7/96	Yes	No	2
16	J5550	Blouse	Orange	12	24	43	25	4	$23.99	8/21/95	Yes	No	23
17	J5532	Skirt	Purple	12	21	32	12	21	$23.67	10/19/95	No	No	22
18	Q765	Blazer	Red	7	9	11	11	11	$60.99	2/10/96	Yes	Yes	9
19	P214	Blouse	Red	5	6	8	9	9	$25.50	2/10/96	Yes	No	5
20	J3291	Dress	Red	17	21	35	32	18	$48.25	10/8/95	No	Yes	8
21	J9090	Vest	Red	23	22	22	25	25	$20.00	2/7/96	No	No	14
22	J4309	Pants	Tan	2	12	12	3	4	$44.50	11/17/95	Yes	No	18
23	J5540	Blouse	White	5	6	6	4	3	$18.59	11/12/95	Yes	No	2
24	J3317	Dress	White	3	6	7	3	4	$62.65	1/7/96	Yes	Yes	2
25	J7676	Suit	White	9	6	5	3	7	$106.99	7/22/95	Yes	Yes	2

(Continued)

3. Change the column width of the STYLE, TYPE, COLOR, BU and ACC fields to 8. Change the column width of the J5, J7, J9 J11 and J13 fields to 5.

4. Change the left and right margins to 1.75".

5. Access the Filter dialog box from the Tools main menu and delete at least 2 filters.

6. Create a report. Name it: Red < 10.

7. Title the report. RED ITEMS -- LESS THAN 10 ON HAND.

8. Include the following fields in your report in this order:

    COLOR
    ON HAND
    DATEORD
    TYPE
    STYLE

9. Access the Filter tab. Create a new filter. Name the filter: Red < 10.

10. Define a filter sentence to list RED items that have less than 10 items

    ✔ HINT: COLOR is equal to RED and ON HAND is less than 10.

11. Apply the *Sum* statistic to the ON HAND field. Position the results at the end of the report together in rows.

12. Preview your report and then modify it as directed.

13. Change all the column widths to 15.

14. Move the title to the first cell and center it across the report. Set it to 12 point and leave it bolded.

15. Center all column data.

    ✔ HINT: Column data begins with an = sign.

16. Preview the report.

17. Print one copy.

18. Save the changes. *Do not close the file.*

ILLUSTRATION B – DESIRED RESULT PART I

RED ITEMS – LESS THAN 10 ON HAND				
COLOR	ON HAND	DATE ORD	TYPE	STYLE
Red	9	2/10/96	Blazer	Q765
Red	5	2/10/96	Blouse	P214
Red	8	10/8/95	Dress	J3291
TOTAL ON HAND		22	Dress	J3291

PART II

To create the report in Illustration C:

1. Create a report. Name it: Skirts & Suits

2. Give the report the title: SKIRTS AND SUITS -- ON HAND.

3. Include the following fields in your report in this order:

    TYPE
    COLOR
    STYLE
    PRICE
    ON HAND

4. Sort the records in ascending order by TYPE and subsort in alphabetical order by COLOR.

5. Create a new filter. Name it: Skirts & Suits

6. Define a filter sentence to list all Skirts and Suits. (TYPE *is equal to* SKIRT or TYPE *is equal to* SUIT).

7. Apply the *Average* statistic to the PRICE field. Position the results at the end of the report together in rows.

8. Preview the report and then modify as below.

9. Change all column widths to 15.

10. Move the title to the first cell and center it across the report. Set it to 12 point and leave it bolded.

11. Left align column headings and data for the TYPE, COLOR and STYLE columns.

12. Preview the report.

13. Print one copy.

14. Save the changes. Do not close the file.

ILLUSTRATION C – DESIRED RESULT, PART II

SKIRTS AND SUITS – ON HAND				
TYPE	COLOR	STYLE	PRICE	ON HAND
Skirt	Black	J8510	$26.00	3
Skirt	Black	P232	$29.50	4
Skirt	Black	P987	$30.75	2
Skirt	Navy	P998	$35.40	1
Skirt	Purple	J5532	$23.67	22
Suit	Green	J7654	$85.50	12
Suit	Navy	J7699	$110.10	8
Suit	White	J7676	$106.99	2
AVERAGE PRICE			$55.90	

(Continued)

PART III

1. Create a new report similar to the one shown in Illustration D based on the filter, Skirts & Suits created in Part II. Use the reporting and formatting features you have learned to create an exact copy of the desired result.

2. Preview your report.

3. Print one copy.

4. Close the file; save the changes.

ON HAND INVENTORY – MARCH 1, 1996

TYPE	COLOR	PRICE	ON HAND
Skirt	Black	$26.00	3
Skirt	Black	$29.50	4
Skirt	Black	$30.75	2
Skirt	Navy	$35.40	1
Skirt	Purple	$23.67	22
COUNT:		**SUM:**	
	5		32
Suit	Green	$85.50	12
Suit	Navy	$110.10	8
Suit	White	$106.99	2
COUNT:		**SUM:**	
	3		22

You have been hired by the Human Resources Department of Boynton College. One of your first jobs is to help organize information about the faculty. Once a database is created, you will be asked to update and modify the database as well as create several reports requested by the president. This summary exercise will review and apply all database concepts learned.

EXERCISE DIRECTIONS:

Creating and Saving the Database File

1. Create a new database file.

2. Use the field names indicated below:
   - TITLE
   - LAST
   - FIRST
   - DEPT
   - BUDGET
   - BLDG
   - NO. OF CLASSES
   - START
   - TENURE

3. Save the file; name it **TEACHER**.

Entering Records

4. Enter the records below into your database.

ILLUSTRATION A

	TITLE	LAST	FIRST	DEPT	BUDGET	BLDG	NO. OF CLASSES	START	TENURE
1	Dr.	Fernandez	Jose	Eng	200	M	5	9/16/86	Yes
2	Ms.	Marcus	Diana	Eng	250	M	4	9/16/86	Yes
3	Ms.	Hargrave	Sally	Eng	250	M	5	9/16/85	Yes
4	Mr.	Bergman	Paul	Math	150	A	3	9/16/84	No
5	Mr.	Pax	Robert	Sci	200	A	3	9/16/86	No
6	Mr.	Chassin	Matthew	Math	120	A	2	1/10/88	No
7	Ms.	Blane	Jaime	PE	120	M	3	9/16/88	No
8	Ms.	Chen	Julie	Sci	160	M	4	9/16/86	Yes
9	Ms.	Brown	Donna	Hist	200	A	5	2/1/89	Yes
10	Mr.	Anderson	Harvey	Hist	200	A	5	1/10/87	No
11	Dr.	Brown	Donald	Lang	140	M	3	2/1/87	Yes
12	Dr.	Mastresi	William	Sci	120	A	2	9/16/88	No
13	Ms.	Zhan	Rafu	Sci	200	M	5	9/9/84	Yes
14	Ms.	Browning	Paula	Eng	150	A	4	9/9/83	Yes
15	Dr.	Ng	Tom	Lang	180	M	3	9/9/88	No
16	Mr.	Greene	Ralph	Math	140	A	5	2/10/89	No
17	Ms.	Linn	Sarah	Bus	180	A	4	2/10/88	No
18	Ms.	Fernandez	Ricardo	Bus	180	A	3	1/20/88	No
19	Dr.	Keltz	Mel	Bus	200	A	5	2/10/91	No
20	Mr.	Grosso	Lenny	PE	140	M	2	9/16/86	Yes

5. Adjust the column widths to accommodate the longest entry in each field (including the field name).

   ✓ NOTE: Proofread your work carefully and correct all errors.

6. Change the left and right margins to 1".

7. Print one copy in Portrait orientation with the Gridlines and Field labels.

8. Save the changes.

Modifying the Form/Adding Records

9. Select List view.

10. To keep track of faculty members' teaching experience, add one new field to the database: EXP.

11. Enter the experience information into the database from Illustration B.

12. Change the left and right margins to 0.5".

ILLUSTRATION B

	TITLE	LAST	FIRST	DEPT	BUDGET	BLDG	NO. OF CLASSES	START	TENURE	EXP
1	Dr.	Fernandez	Jose	Eng	200	M	5	9/16/86	Yes	7
2	Ms.	Marcus	Diana	Eng	250	M	4	9/16/86	Yes	10
3	Ms.	Hargrave	Sally	Eng	250	M	5	9/16/85	Yes	11
4	Mr.	Bergman	Paul	Math	150	A	3	9/16/84	No	14
5	Mr.	Pax	Robert	Sci	200	A	3	9/16/86	No	10
6	Mr.	Chassin	Matthew	Math	120	A	2	1/10/88	No	8
7	Ms.	Blane	Jaime	PE	120	M	3	9/16/88	No	8
8	Ms.	Chen	Julie	Sci	160	M	4	9/16/86	Yes	10
9	Ms.	Brown	Donna	Hist	200	A	5	2/1/89	Yes	7
10	Mr.	Anderson	Harvey	Hist	200	A	5	1/10/87	No	8
11	Dr.	Brown	Donald	Lang	140	M	3	2/1/87	Yes	9
12	Dr.	Mastresi	William	Sci	120	A	2	9/16/88	No	8
13	Ms.	Zhan	Rafu	Sci	200	M	5	9/9/84	Yes	15
14	Ms.	Browning	Paula	Eng	150	A	4	9/9/83	Yes	15
15	Dr.	Ng	Tom	Lang	180	M	3	9/9/88	No	8
16	Mr.	Greene	Ralph	Math	140	A	5	2/10/89	No	6
17	Ms.	Linn	Sarah	Bus	180	A	4	2/10/88	No	7
18	Ms.	Fernandez	Ricardo	Bus	180	A	3	1/20/88	No	7
19	Dr.	Keltz	Mel	Bus	200	A	5	2/10/91	No	5
20	Mr.	Grosso	Lenny	PE	140	M	2	9/16/86	Yes	10

13. Several teachers' records were omitted from the database. Add the following records.

ILLUSTRATION C

	TITLE	LAST	FIRST	DEPT	BUDGET	BLDG	NO. OF CLASSES	START	TENURE	EXP
21	Dr.	Blanc	Pamela	Sci	200	M	5	9/9/81	Yes	15
22	Mr.	Talley	Charles	PE	140	A	3	2/10/86	No	11
23	Ms.	Goodcoff	Kayli	Lang	160	A	4	2/10/82	Yes	14
24	Mr.	Bergman	Thomas	Math	150	A	3	9/10/89	No	8
25	Dr.	Knossos	Joyce	Bus	200	A	5	2/10/83	Yes	13

14. Adjust the column widths to accommodate the longest entry if necessary.

(Continued)

Searching the Database/Using Filters

15. Using <u>E</u>dit, <u>F</u>ind (click All records), search the database for the answers to the following questions. *Write the answers in your notebook or print the displayed answers.*

    a. Which teachers work in the English Department?

    b. In which building does Ralph Greene work?

    c. Which teachers have doctoral degrees?

    d. Print one copy of this list.

16. Using Filters, search the database for answers to the following questions:

    a. Which teachers work in the main building and have more than 10 years experience?

    b. Which English teachers hold a doctoral degree?

    c. Which Math teachers work in the Annex and have a supply budget over $130?

Sorting the Database

17. Sort the file in ascending order by LAST name: subsort in ascending order by FIRST name. Print one copy.

18. Sort the file in ascending order by BLDG; subsort in ascending order by LAST name within each building.

Preparing Reports

Report 1

To create the report in Illustration D (page 367)

1. Create a report, name it Report 1. Use the report title: BOYNTON COLLEGE

2. Include the following fields in this order:

    START
    TITLE
    FIRST
    LAST
    EXP

3. Sort the data in descending order by START date.

4. Preview your report and then modify as below.

5. Add two title rows below the main title to include the following subtitles:

    Faculty List
    Seniority Order

6. Add a heading row and change the column headings as below:

START DATE	to	START
TITLE		*no change*
FIRST	to	FIRST NAME
LAST NAME	to	LAST
EXP	to	EXPERIENCE

7. Format the two-line column headings as follows:

    a. Set to bold.

    b. Center align.

    c. Remove the underline from any first-line heading.

    d. Add underline to all second-line headings.

8. Change the column widths of the START, TITLE, FIRST NAME AND LAST NAME fields to 10. Change the column width of the EXPERIENCE column to 13.

9. Move the title and subtitles to the first cell and center them across the report. Set the main title to14 point, leave it bold. Set the subtitles to 12-point bold italics.

10. Center align the column data in the TITLE and EXPERIENCE fields.

11. Change the left margin to 2".

12. Print one copy.

13. Save the changes.

BOYNTON COLLEGE

Faculty List

Seniority Order

START DATE	TITLE	FIRST NAME	LAST NAME	EXPERIENCE
2/10/91	Dr.	Mel	Keltz	5
9/10/89	Mr.	Thomas	Bergman	8
2/10/89	Mr.	Ralph	Greene	6
2/1/89	Ms.	Donna	Brown	7
9/16/88	Ms.	Jaime	Blane	8
9/16/88	Dr.	William	Mastresi	8
9/9/88	Dr.	Tom	Ng	8
2/10/88	Ms.	Sarah	Linn	7
1/20/88	Ms.	Ricardo	Fernandez	7
1/10/88	Mr.	Matthew	Chassin	8
2/1/87	Dr.	Donald	Brown	9
1/10/87	Mr.	Harvey	Anderson	8
9/16/86	Dr.	Jose	Fernandez	7
9/16/86	Ms.	Diana	Marcus	10
9/16/86	Mr.	Robert	Pax	10
9/16/86	Ms.	Julie	Chen	10
9/16/86	Mr.	Lenny	Grosso	10
2/10/86	Mr.	Charles	Talley	11
9/16/85	Ms.	Sally	Hargrave	11
9/16/84	Mr.	Paul	Bergman	14
9/9/84	Ms.	Rafu	Zhan	15
9/9/83	Ms.	Paula	Browning	15
2/10/83	Dr.	Joyce	Knossos	13
2/10/82	Ms.	Kayli	Goodcoff	14
9/9/81	Dr.	Pamela	Blanc	15

Report 2

To create the report in Illustration E (page 368)

1. Create Report 2. Use the title: DEPARTMENT BUDGETS

2. Include the following fields in this order.
   DEPT
   BUDGET
   BLDG

3. Sort the data in ascending order by DEPT and subsort it in ascending order by BUDGET.

4. Group the data by DEPT *When contents change*.

5. Apply the *Sum* statistic to the BUDGET data. Position the results *At end of each group, Under each column, At end of report*.

6. Preview your report and modify as below.

7. Add a title row and the subtitle: 1996

8. Change all column widths to 15.

9. Move the title and subtitle to the first cell and center them across the report. Set them to 12 point. Leave the main title bold and set the subtitle to bold italics.

10. Center align the DEPT and BLDG column data.

11. Shade the =SUM(BUDGET) statistic in the Summ DEPT row to 20%.

12. Shade the =SUM(BUDGET) statistic in the Summary row to 50%.

13. Format all money amounts to currency with two decimals.

14. Change the left margin to 2.5".

15. Preview the report.

16. Print one copy.

17. Save the changes.

ILLUSTRATION E, REPORT 2, DESIRED RESULTS

DEPARTMENT BUDGETS
1996

DEPT	BUDGET	BLDG
Bus	$180.00	A
Bus	$180.00	A
Bus	$200.00	A
Bus	$200.00	A
SUM:		
	$760.00	
Eng	$200.00	M
Eng	$250.00	M
Eng	$250.00	M
Eng	$150.00	A
SUM:		
	$850.00	
Hist	$200.00	A
Hist	$200.00	A
SUM:		
	$400.00	
Lang	$140.00	M
Lang	$180.00	M
Lang	$160.00	A
SUM:		
	$480.00	
Math	$150.00	A
Math	$120.00	A
Math	$140.00	A
Math	$150.00	A
SUM:		
	$560.00	
PE	$120.00	M
PE	$140.00	M
PE	$140.00	A
SUM:		
	$400.00	
Sci	$200.00	A
Sci	$160.00	M
Sci	$120.00	A
Sci	$200.00	M
Sci	$200.00	M
SUM:		
	$880.00	
SUM:		
	$4,330.00	

Report 3

To create the report in Illustration F

1. Create Report 3. Give it the title: BOYNTON COLLEGE

2. Include the following fields in this order:

   TITLE
   FIRST
   LAST
   BLDG
   NO. OF CLASSES
   DEPT

3. Create and apply a filter to list those who teach in the Main Building and who have four or more classes.

   ✔ NOTE: In the **BLDG** field, Main Building is represented by M and Annex is represented by A.

4. Apply the *Sum* statistic to the NO. OF CLASSES field. Position the results at the end of the report together in rows.

5. Preview the report and then modify as below:

6. Add two title rows be low the main title to include the following:

   More than Four Classes
   Main Building

7. Change the column heading NO. OF CLASSES to CLASSES.

8. Set all column widths to 12.

9. Move the title and the subtitle to the first cell and center them across the report. Set the main title to 12 point italics, leave it bolded. Set the two subtitles to 10 point bold.

10. Center the TITLE, BLDG, CLASSES and DEPT column data.

11. Set a 1" left margin and a .5" right margin.

12. Preview your report.

13. Print one copy, save the changes.

ILLUSTRATION F, REPORT 3, DESIRED RESULTS

BOYNTON COLLEGE
More than Four Classes
Main Building

TITLE	FIRST	LAST	BLDG	CLASSES	DEPT
Dr.	Jose	Fernandez	M	5	Eng
Ms.	Diana	Marcus	M	4	Eng
Ms.	Sally	Hargrave	M	5	Eng
Ms.	Julie	Chen	M	4	Sci
Ms.	Rafu	Zhan	M	5	Sci
Dr.	Pamela	Blanc	M	5	Sci

TOTAL NUMBER OF CLASSES: 28

Integration

Exercises 1 - 14

EXERCISE **1**

■ **Windowing** ■ **Maximize a Window** ■ **Minimize a Window** ■ **Resize a Window**
■ **Multiple Windows (Cascade Tile)** ■ **Restore a Window** ■ **Close a Document Window**

NOTES:

Windowing

■ Works lets you open and work with up to eight documents at one time. This is a convenient feature for moving and/or copying information from one document to another.

■ **Windowing** lets you view those documents as you work with them.

Maximize a Window

■ When you begin a new document for the Word Processor, Works provides the following window for you to begin typing.

Works close menu box · Title bar · Application buttons Minimize Restore Close · Document close menu box · Document title bar · Document buttons Close Maximize Minimize · Current document

■ The controls at the right of both the Works and document Title bars allow you to size, and close the application and/or current document window respectively. A window can be enlarged or **maximized** by clicking the **maximize button** ☐ at the right of the Title bar.

■ When a window is maximized, it is enlarged to its greatest possible size, and other open document windows are hidden behind it. In addition, the maximize button is replaced with the restore button ☐. See illustration of a maximized word processing window on the next page.

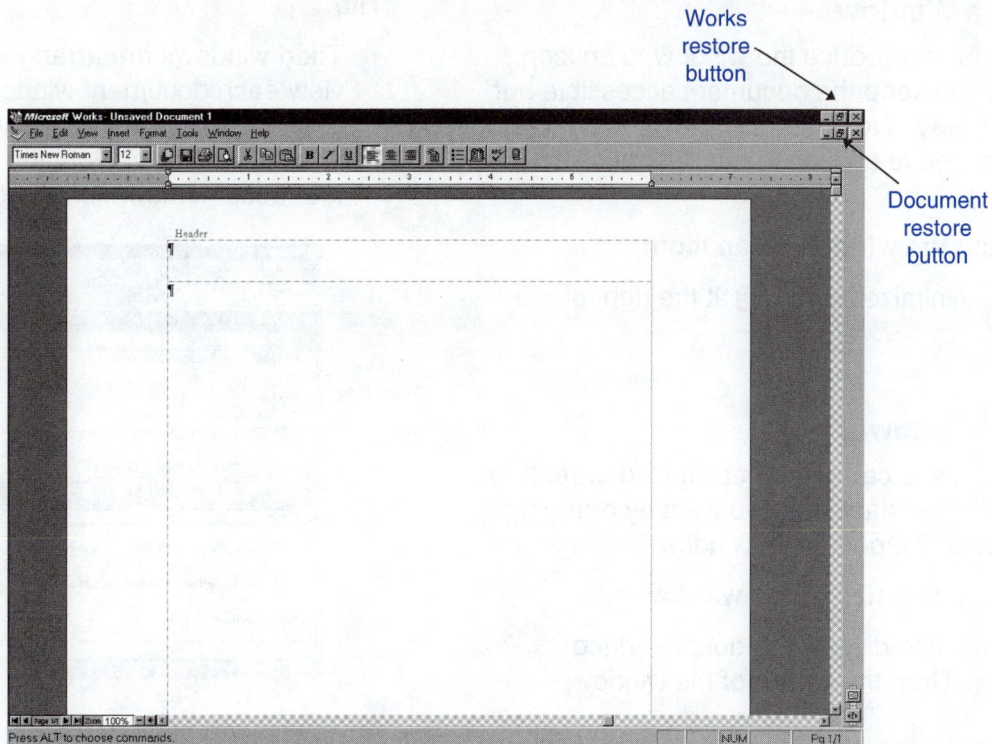

Document
restore
button

- If you maximze a window, all open windows are maximized.

Restore a Window

- **Restoring** a maximized window returns the window to its former size and location. When you restore a maximized window, you can view the title bars of all the open documents. To restore a maximized window, click the document restore button at the right of the Title bar shown in the illustration above.

  ✓ NOTE: Be sure to click on the document's restore button, not on the Works restore button. See the illustration above to distinguish between the two.

- When a document is restored, it is reduced to a small rectangle. Note the three minimized windows in the illustration below.

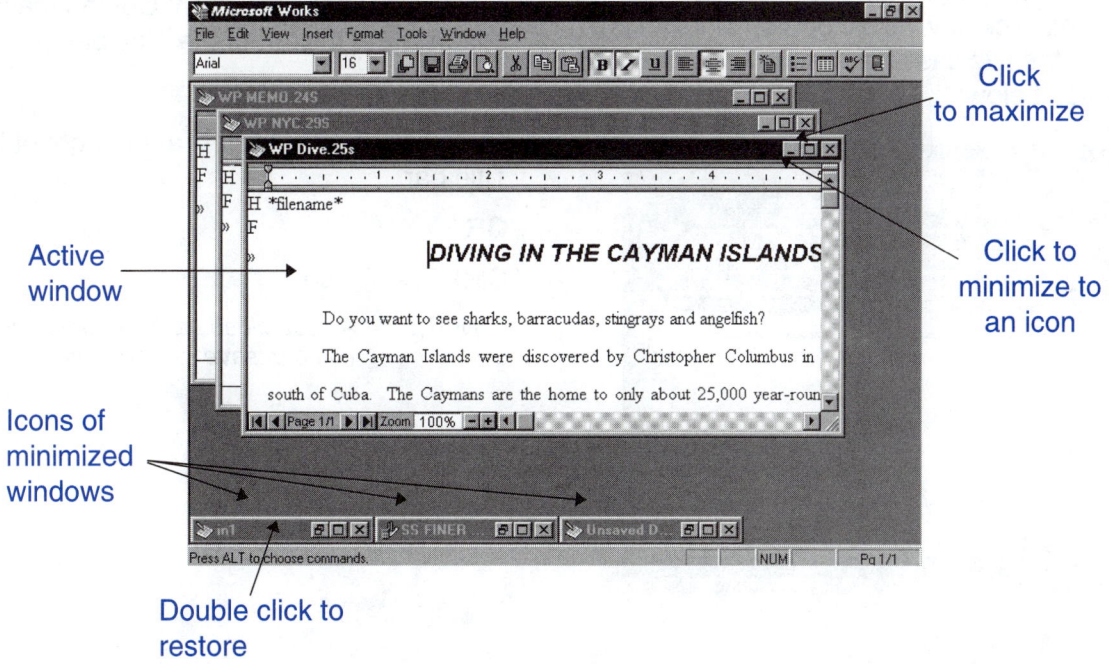

Click
to maximize

Click to
minimize to
an icon

Active
window

Icons of
minimized
windows

Double click to
restore

Minimize a Window

■ You can further reduce the window to an icon. This lets you keep the document accessible but out of the way. Note the documents that have been reduced to an icon in the illustration on the previous page.

To reduce the window to an icon:

Click the minimize button ▣ at the right of the Title bar.

Resize a Window

■ In addition, you can size a maximized or restored window to the exact size you want by dragging the frame of the document window.

To change the size of the window:

Move mouse to display the double-edged arrow ⬌. Drag the corner of the window.

Multiple Windows

■ Works offers several arrangements to organize and view your open documents.

Cascade

Cascaded windows allow you to view the Title bar of each open document. Cascaded windows are all equally sized and overlap so the Title bar of each window is displayed. The active window is indicated by the shaded Title bar. Click Window, Cascade to cascade the open windows. To make a window the active document, click any visible portion of a window. Note the the five cascaded windows in the illustration below:

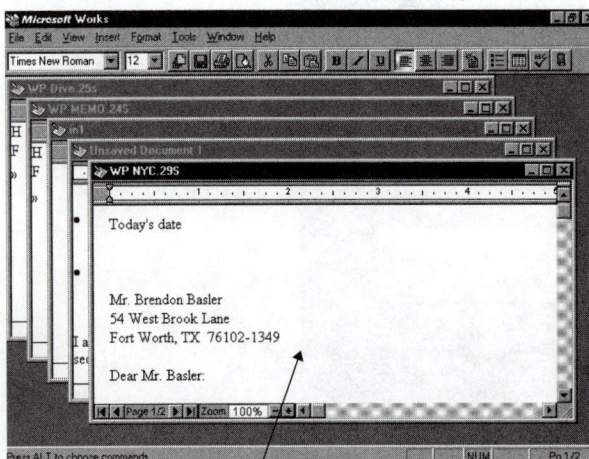

Active window

Tile

Tiled windows are arranged so that you can view each document window; they will not overlap. The active window is indicated by the shaded Title bar. Note the illustration below of four documents which are opened and tiled:

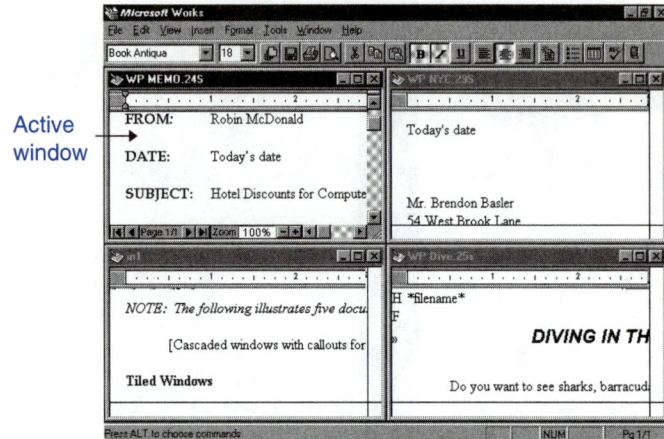

Active window

■ Any cascaded or tiled window can be maximized, restored or minimized by clicking the appropriate button at the right of the Title bar.

■ You can switch between document windows whether they are currently displayed or not by selecting Window from the main menu bar and choosing the document you want. You can also press Ctrl+F6 to switch to the next document.

Close a Document Window

■ You can close a document window several ways:

Double-click the Document Control menu button ▧ at the left of the Title bar.

OR

Click the Close button ☒ at the right of the Title bar.

OR

Click File, Close.

✓ NOTE: As you close each document window, you can save its contents.

EXERCISE DIRECTIONS:

1. Create a new document for the Word Processor.

2. Open 📠**DIVE**, or open 💾**IN DIVE.1**.

3. Open 📠**MEMO**, or open 💾**IN MEMO.1**.

4. Open 📠**NYC**, or open 💾**IN NYC.1**.

5. Cascade all the documents.

6. Make **DIVE** the active document.

7. Make **NYC** the active document.

8. Minimize **DIVE**.

   ✓ *NOTE: DIVE is reduced to an icon.*

9. Restore **DIVE**.

10. Tile all the documents.

11. Make **MEMO** the active document.

12. Close each window using a different method.

CASCADE DOCUMENTS

1. Click **Window**........................ `Alt`+`W`
2. Click **Cascade** ....`C`

TILE DOCUMENTS

1. Click **Window**........................ `Alt`+`W`
2. Click **Tile**..`T`

SWITCH AMONG OPEN DOCUMENTS

–USING MOUSE–

Click any visible portion of desired document.

OR

1. Click **Window**........................ `Alt`+`W`
2. Click name of desired document.

OR

Type document number.

–USING KEYBOARD–

1. Next Document command ..... `Alt`+`F6`
2. Previous Document command.................... `Ctrl`+`Shift`+`F6`

■ **Copy Text from One Word Processing Document to Another**

NOTES:

Copy Text from One Word Processing Document to Another

■ The procedure to copy text from one document to another is the same as copying text from one location to another in the same document.

■ Windowing makes it easy to copy text in one document and place it in another, since you can actually see where the text is coming from and where it is going.

■ You can use either copy and paste or drag and drop to copy text from one document to another.

> ✔ *REMINDER:* *Copying text leaves text in its original location and pastes a copy of it in its new location.*

■ When you have successfully copied all the text you want from a file, close that file. Then, tile your windows again to provide larger windows for the remaining documents.

■ If you wish to move text from one document to another, use the Cut and Paste commands from Edit menu or use drag and drop. However, when moving text between two documents, you must hold down the Shift key as you drag the text.

■ You can also move or copy text to a document in another program. For example, you can move or copy text from the Word Processor in Works to the Windows 95 WordPad found in Accessories. However, when tranferring text to some programs, you may lose the format of the document and will have to reformat the text after the transfer. To easily switch between Works and the other program, press Alt+Tab.

> *In this exercise, you will open several documents, tile them and copy some text from each to create a new document. This procedure may also be used for moving text from one document to another.*

EXERCISE DIRECTIONS:

1. Create a new document for the Word Processor.

2. Type the letter as shown on the right.

3. Use 1" left and right margins; begin the exercise approximately 2" from the top of the page.

4. Open 🖾**NYC**, 🖾**MEMO** and 🖾**DIVE**, or open 💾**IN NYC.2**, 💾**IN MEMO.2** and 💾**IN DIVE.2**.

5. Go to page 2 in the NYC document.

6. Tile all the documents.

7. Copy the indicated text in each document into the *new* document. Leave a double space before and after each insertion.

> ✔ *NOTE:* *The document to be copied from must be the active document. When you are ready to place the text, the NEW document must become the active document. Follow keystrokes carefully.*

8. Remove bullets and numbers from selected paragraphs before copying them.

9. Close all documents except the *new* document.

10. Maximize the *new* document window.

11. Insert an appropriate page 2 heading in the *new* document.

12. Format all hotel names in the same font and typestyle.

13. Spell check the *new* document.

14. Close and save the *new* document; name it **HOTELS**.

15. Print one copy of the new document.

16. Close the document window.

Today's date

Mr. Stephen Michaels
65 Penguin Way
Anchorage, AK 99508

Dear Mr. Michaels:

As you requested, I have compiled a list of hotels for the locations that you will be visiting on your upcoming trip.

Since you indicated that during your stay in San Francisco you would be attending the Computer Expo, I included hotels that are offering discounts to Expo attendees.
Paste San Franchisco hotels from MEMO.

For your stay in New York City, I chose hotels that are centrally located so you are within walking distance to your business meetings, restaurants and other attractions:
Paste New York hotels from NYC.

Finally, for your one week's vacation stay in the Cayman Islands, I specified hotels which offer free diving instruction.
Paste Cayman Island hotels from DIVE.

When you have decided upon the hotels, please let me know, and I will make your complete travel arrangements.

Sincerely,

David Craig
Travel Representative

dc/yo

MEMORANDUM

TO: All Managers Attending Computer Expo
FROM: Robin McDonald
DATE: Today's date
SUBJECT: Hotel Discounts for Computer Expo Attendees
****

The following *San Francisco* hotels have decided to offer special discounted rates to all attendees of Computer Expo. All hotels listed are within 20 minutes of the Convention Center.

- **Fairmont Hotel**
- **Holiday Inn Civic Center**
- **Hyatt Regency**
- **Grand Hyatt**
- **Villa Florence**
- **King George Hotel**
- **Mark Hopkins**
- **Nikko**
- **Westin St. Francis**

When you call to make your reservation at the Convention Center. There are preferred rates, so plan early.

Hotels listed below offer free parking:

- **Fairmont Hotel**
- **Nikko**
- **Westin St. Francis**

yo

Mr. Brendon Basler
Page 2
Today's date

shopping near your hotel. I have called the hotels to be certain they can accommodate you and your family. They all seem to have availability at the time you are planning to visit.

1. **Plaza Hotel** - located at 59th Street and Central Park South at the foot of Central Park. 1-800-555-3000.

2. **The Pierre Hotel** - located at 61st Street and Fifth Avenue across the street from Central Park. 1-800-555-3442.

3. **The Drake Swissotel** - located at 56th Street and Park Avenue. 1-212-555-0900.

Of course, you realize that there are many other hotel options available to you. If these are not satisfactory, let me know and I will call you with other recommendations.

DIVING IN THE CAYMAN ISLANDS

Do you want to see sharks, barracudas, stingrays and angelfish?

The Cayman Islands were discovered by Christopher Columbus in 1503 and are located south of Cuba. The Caymans are the home to only about 25,000 year-round residents. However, they welcome 200,000 visitors each year. Most visitors come with masks and flippers in their luggage.

Hotel/Diving Accommodations:

Anchorage View	PO Box 2123, East End, Grand Cayman, (809) 555-4209. Pool, four restaurants; check in 9 a.m., check out 2 p.m. Famous for outstanding view of the harbor from all rooms. Popular night spot among tourists and locals alike.
Cayman Diving Lodge	PO Box 11, East End, Grand Cayman, (809) 555-7555. No pool, room service available; check in 10 a.m., check out 4 p.m. Basic accommodations, low rates. Diving expeditions three times daily at extra cost.
Coconut Harbour	PO Box 2086, George Town, Grand Cayman; (809) 555-6468. Pool, two restaurants; check in 10 a.m., check out 4 p.m. Free scuba exhibitions nightly.
Red Sail Sports	PO Box 1588, George Town, Grand Cayman; (809) 555-7965. Pool, three restaurants; check in 11 a.m., check out 3 p.m. Wind surfing and parasailing available at extra cost.
Sunset House	PO Box 479, George Town, Grand Cayman, (800) 555-4767. Pool, three restaurants; check in 11 a.m., check out 3 p.m.

Hotels Offering Free Diving Instruction:

Cayman Diving Lodge	PO Box 11, East End, Grand Cayman, (809) 555-7555. No pool, room service available; check in 10 a.m., check out 4 p.m. Basic accommodations, low rates. Diving expeditions three times daily at extra cost.
Sunset House	PO Box 479, George Town, Grand Cayman; (809) 555-4767. Pool, three restaurants; check in 11 a.m., check out 3 p.m.

COPY/MOVE TEXT FROM ONE OPEN DOCUMENT TO ANOTHER

1. Open each file from which you are to copy or move text.

2. Open a new document to receive the moved/copied text.

✓ NOTE: To make the copy/move procedure easier, tile the open documents.

3. Click the window where text is to be moved/copied *from*.

4. Highlight text to be copied/moved.

5. **To copy text:**
   a. Click **Edit** .... Alt + E
   b. Click **Copy** C

   OR

   Click **Copy** button .... (toolbar)
   on Toolbar.

   OR

   Press **Ctrl+C** .... Ctrl + C

   To cut (move) text
   a. Click **Edit** .... Alt + E
   b. Click **Cut** .... T

   OR

   Click **Cut** button .... (toolbar)
   on Toolbar.

   OR

   Press **Ctrl+X** .... Ctrl + X

6. Click in window where text is to be moved/copied *to*.

7. Position insertion point where text is to be inserted.

8. Click **Edit** .... Alt + E

9. Click **Paste** .... P

   OR

   Click **Paste** button .... (toolbar)
   on the Toolbar

   OR

   Press **Ctrl+V** .... Ctrl + V

■ **Integrate Word Processing and Spreadsheet Files (Copy and Paste, Drag and Drop)**

NOTES:

Integrate Word Processing and Spreadsheet Files

- Just as you copied text from one word processing document to another in Exercise 2, you can copy information from one Works tool to another. This sharing or transferring of information between the tools is called **integration**.

- You can transfer between the Word Processor, Spreadsheet, Database and Communications tools.

- Because Works uses the same data format, it is not necessary to convert the file before transferring it.

- The **source** file is used to *send* data; the **destination** file is used to *receive* data.

- After information is placed in the destination document, you may have to adjust its placement by adding or deleting returns.

- The following procedures can be used to transfer information between the tools.

Cut and Paste	Moves the information to a temporary buffer area called the clipboard.
Copy and Paste	Duplicates the selected information and places it on the clipboard.
Drag and Drop	Moves the information between the tools, but you need to have both the source and destination documents visible. Use the tile arrangement if using drag and drop.
Linking	Connects two files so when you update the source document, the destination document is automatically updated.
Embedding	Allows you to copy information from another tool and use that tool's features within the Word Processor.

In this exercise, you will transfer an existing spreadsheet into an existing memorandum using copy and paste. You will save the newly created integrated document under a new name.

EXERCISE DIRECTIONS:

1. Open ▦**REPORT**, or open 🖫**IN REPORT.3**.

2. Open ▦**SALES**, or open 🖫**IN SALES.3**.

3. Copy the spreadsheet, **SALES**, Illustration B.

4. Switch to the word processing document, **REPORT**, Illustration A.

   ✓ *NOTE:* *You can use Ctrl + F6 or the Window menu to switch to the other document.*

5. Paste the spreadsheet where indicated.

6. Center the spreadsheet on the page.

7. Save as **REPSALES**.

8. Print one copy.

9. Close the open files.

MEMORANDUM

TO: Dennis Jones, Corporate Financial Manager

FROM: Susie Hand, Oceanview Branch Manager

DATE: Today's date

SUBJECT: Sales Comparison - Two Years

I have catalogued the sales figures for the last two years of all computer items we have in stock. I assembled these figures from the data I have in my computers. Please review the information for accuracy and completeness.

Paste SALES here.

I know you are anxious to assemble the sales results from all **Bit-Byte** computer stores to aid you in long-term planning for our organization. However, we must make sure our records are 100% correct before we can make any decisions concerning the future of our product lines.

Please let me know as soon as possible if any changes should be made.

sh/yo

SALES – ILLUSTRATION B

	A	B	C	D	E
1	BIT-BYTE COMPUTER COMPANY				
2	SALES INCOME - 2 YEARS				
3					
4	ITEM				NET
5	NO	ITEM	YEAR 1	YEAR 2	CHANGE
6					
7	184008	Computers	73246.98	88004.56	14757.58
8	181008	Monitors	20567.40	18755.31	-1812.09
9	183008	Printers	52349.76	55058.56	2708.80
10	180008	Scanners	35126.66	65845.90	30719.24
11	182008	Modems	7089.54	4800.00	-2289.54
12	188008	Drives	35876.07	54987.37	19111.30
13	189008	Keyboards	35156.30	38779.29	3622.99
14					
15	TOTAL		259412.71	326230.99	

INTEGRATE SPREADSHEET FILE WITH WORD PROCESSOR FILE

✓ NOTE: *Both the word processing document and the spreadsheet document must be created or opened (if they are existing files) before proceeding to integrate.*

–USING COPY AND PASTE–

1. Select desired range of cells in the spreadsheet document.
2. Click **Edit** .... `Alt`+`E`
3. Click **Copy** .... `Alt`+`C`
4. Click **Window** .... `Alt`+`W`
   OR
   Press **Ctrl + F6** .... `Ctrl`+`F6`
5. Click destination document.
6. Place insertion point at desired location.
7. Click **Edit** .... `Alt`+`E`
8. Click **Paste** .... `Alt`+`P`

–USING DRAG AND DROP–

1. Click **Window** .... `Alt`+`W`
2. Click **Tile** .... `Alt`+`T`
3. Click spreadsheet document.
4. Select desired range of cells.
5. Drag selected range of cells to copy to word processing document.
6. Click **No** .... `Alt`+`N`
   when asked "Create a link to the original data?"

■ Embed an Existing Spreadsheet

NOTES:

Embed an Existing Spreadsheet

■ When the spreadsheet is pasted into the word processing document, it is **embedded** in that document. This means that the information contained in the spreadsheet becomes a part of the word processing document.

■ You can make changes to the spreadsheet without having to leave the word processing document. Any changes made to the embedded spreadsheet will not be made to the original spreadsheet document.

✓ *NOTE:* *Changes can be made to the original spreadsheet only if a link is established. Links will be discussed in Integration, Exercise 7, p. 386.*

■ You must double-click the spreadsheet to edit it. This returns the spreadsheet to the spreadsheet tool providing you with a small window into the spreadsheet. The spreadsheet toolbar and all spreadsheet commands are available to make desired edits. Note the embedded spreadsheet in the illustration above right.

Word processing area

Click outside spreadsheet to return to word processing document.

The Finer Family of Funds is an excellent group of funds that has been performing at a consistently high level over a period of time. They are no load funds and have been under the same management for over ten years. I provided the following table to illustrate the funds' performance.

	A	B	C	D	E
4	FUND	LIFE OF FUND	FIVE YEARS	THREE YEARS	ONE YEAR
5					
6	Panorama	25.4	22.7	18.2	20.7
7	International	16.4	17.1	21.5	2.3
8	Finer Growth & Income	20.7	24.4	23.9	26.6
9	S & P 500	NO DATA	14.3	11.3	15.5
10	Emerging Growth	NO DATA	19.2	15.3	12.4

Choose Spreadsheet or Chart

If would also like to invite you to attend a seminar on mutual fund investments on October 5, 1999- at 7 p.m. Our investment group offers seminars on a variety of investment topics and since mutual funds are so popular we expect this session to be completely filled. We have limited

Embedded spreadsheet

■ When done editing, click outside the spreadsheet area to return to the word processing document.

■ If information has been added to the spreadsheet, you may need to resize the spreadsheet. To do this, return the highlight to cell A1 in the spreadsheet. Then, using the mouse, place the insertion point on one of the handles. *(The mouse pointer changes to a double-sided arrow.)* Drag the arrow until the desired data is displayed. When done, click outside the spreadsheet area to return to the word processing document.

In this exercise, you will create a letter and insert and edit an existing spreadsheet.

EXERCISE DIRECTIONS:

1. Create a new document for the Word Processor.

2. Type the letter in Illustration A using the following margins:

   • Top Margin   1.5"
   • Left Margin   1"
   • Right Margin   1"

3. Open **FINER FUNDS**, or open **IN FINER FUNDS.4**.

4. Copy the entire spreadsheet (cells A1:E9).

5. Paste where indicated in the letter.

6. Press the Enter key twice before and after the spreadsheet.

7. Double-click the spreadsheet and enter the following data for an additional fund:

| Emerging Growth | NO DATA | 19.2 | 15.3 | 12.4 |

✔ *NOTE:* *If you cannot see all the data in the spreadsheet, scroll to the top of the spreadsheet, then drag the double-sided arrow on the bottom middle handle to resize the window.*

8. Format data to be consistent with existing data.

9. Return to the word processing document.

10. Center the spreadsheet.

11. Preview the document and make any necessary adjustments to fit the document on one page.

12. Spell check the document.

13. Print one copy.

14. Save the document; name it **FINER INVEST**.

15. Close all files.

ILLUSTRATION A

Today's date

Mr. Joshua David
1923 Crandall Street
Binghamton, NY 13902

Dear Mr. David:

As we discussed on the phone last Wednesday, I recently met with your colleague, Mr. David Craig, to discuss the Finer Family of Funds. He was very impressed with their performance and suggested that you might be interested in investing.

The Finer Family of Funds is an excellent group of funds that has been performing at a consistently high level over a period of time. They are no-load funds and have been under the same management for over ten years. I provided the following table to illustrate the fund's performance.

→ *Insert spreadsheet here.*

If you are interested in discussing these or other funds, please contact me at 1-607-555-7543. I would also like to invite you to attend a seminar on mutual fund investments on October 5, 199- at 7 p.m. Our investment group offers seminars on a variety of investment topics and since mutual funds are so popular, we expect this session to be completely filled. We have limited seating, so please call to reserve a seat.

I look forward to seeing you on October 5.

Sincerely,

Joseph Aronow
Sales Representative

yo

ILLUSTRATION B

	A	B	C	D	E
1		FINER FAMILY OF FUNDS			
2		Average Annual Total Returns as of 3/31/95			
3					
4	FUND	LIFE OF FUND	FIVE YEARS	THREE YEARS	ONE YEAR
5					
6	Panorama	25.4	22.7	18.2	20.7
7	International	16.4	17.1	21.5	2.3
8	Finer Growth & Income	20.7	24.4	23.9	26.6
9	S & P 500	NO DATA	14.3	11.3	15.5

EMBED AN EXISTING FILE

1. In the source document, select the information you want to embed.

2. Click **Edit** .... Alt + E

3. Click **Copy** C

4. Switch to the destination document.

5. Place insertion point where you want to embed the spreadsheet.

6. Click **Edit** .... Alt + E

7. Click **Paste** .... P

8. Click **OK** .... Enter

EDIT AN EMBEDDED FILE

1. Double-click the embedded file to access other Works tool.

2. Make changes as if you were in the spreadsheet or other Works tool.

3. Click outside the emebedded area.

■ **Embed an Existing Chart**

NOTES:

Embed an Existing Chart

■ You can copy and embed an existing chart into a word processing document.

To embed an existing chart:

- Open both the source and destination documents.

- Place insertion point where the chart is to be placed.

- Click Insert.

- Click Chart.

- Select Use existing chart.

- Select desired spreadsheet in the Select a spreadsheet list box.

- Select desired chart in Select a chart list box.

- Click OK.

■ You can resize the chart as you did the spreadsheet in the last exercise. Click the chart to display the sizing handles, then drag a corner or middle handle to size the chart as desired.

✓ *NOTE:* *You can also resize your chart by using exact measurements. Once the sizing handles are displayed, click Format, Picture and make the desired changes in the Size tab of the Format Picture dialog box.*

EMBED AN EXISTING CHART

1. Open both source and destination documents.
2. Click **Insert** .... `Alt`+`I`
3. Click **Chart** .... `C`
4. Click **Use** existing chart .... `Alt`+`U`
5. Click desired spreadsheet .... `Alt`+`S`,`↓`
6. Click desired chart .... `Alt`+`C`,`↓`
7. Click **OK** .... `Enter`

RESIZE A CHART

1. Click on chart.
2. Position mouse pointer on a handle.

✓ *NOTE:* *The mouse pointer changes to the resize arrow.*

3. Drag to desired size.

   OR

a. Click **Format** .... `Alt`+`O`
b. Click **Picture/Object** .... `R`
c. Click **Size** .... `S`
d. Make desired changes.
e. Click **OK** .... `Enter`

EXERCISE DIRECTIONS:

1. Open ⌨**BONUS2**, or open 💾**IN BONUS2.5**.

2. Open ⌨**GOOD**, or open 💾**IN GOOD.5**.

3. Change the margins for **GOOD** as follows:
   - left and right margins   0.75"
   - top margin   2.00"
   - bottom margin   0.75"

   ✓ *NOTE:*   *Delete all returns so the date begins at the top of the screen.*

4. Make the revisions to the letter shown in Illustration A.

5. Insert the bar chart shown in Illustration B.

6. Press the Enter key twice before and after the chart.

7. Preview your document.

8. Resize the chart and make any other adjustments so that the letter fits on one page.

9. Spell check.

10. Print one copy.

11. Save the file as **GOODBAR**.

12. Close the document window.

ILLUSTRATION A

Today's date

Mr. Jack Smith, President
Bit-Byte Computer Company
481 Madison Avenue
New York, NY 10022

Dear Jack:

The sales promotion we ran from January - June was extremely profitable for the company and rewarded outstanding members of the sales staff as well. Total sales for the six-month period were $45,788.44. ← *Insert text here*

→ *Embed chart here*

We have provided a bar chart which shows the sales for each salesperson.

Three of our salespersons exceeded $9,000.00 in total sales, qualifying them for the higher 3 percent bonus. Janice Olson had the highest sales, followed by Hugh Robertson. Lois Chen did well also. We will honor these salespeople at our next board meeting.

Events like this motivate the staff to be more productive and reach higher sales levels. It is a pleasure to compensate these exceptional employees with this bonus.

Sincerely,

Deborah Wilson
Sales Manager

dw/yo

ILLUSTRATION B

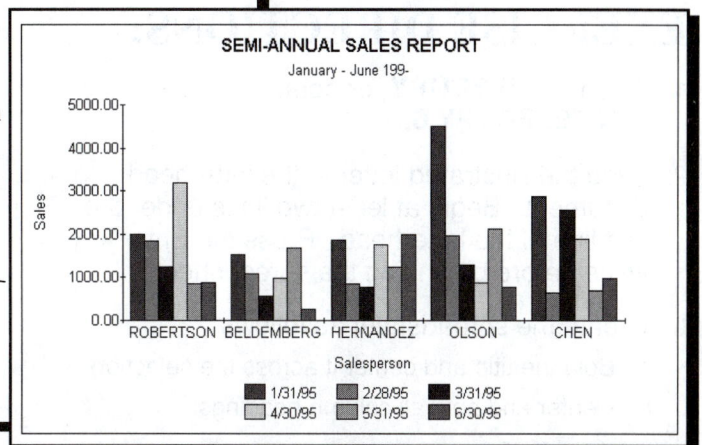

SEMI-ANNUAL SALES REPORT
January - June 199-

■ **Embed a New Spreadsheet**

NOTES:

Embed a New Spreadsheet

■ In Exercise 4 of the Integration section, you learned to embed an *existing* spreadsheet into a word processing document using the copy and paste procedure. However, you can also create a *new* spreadsheet from within the word processing document.

To embed a new spreadsheet:

- Click Insert.
- Click Spreadsheet.
- Click Create a new spreadsheet.
- Enter data into the embedded spreadsheet.
- Click outside the spreadsheet to return to the Word Processor.

■ If you need to widen the embedded spreadsheet, click the handles (white squares on the dark border) to display the double-sided arrows. See the embedded spreadsheet above right:

Place the double-sided arrows on the right, middle handle.

To display the desired number of columns and/or rows:

- Drag the middle handles on the left or right to display more columns.
- Drag the middle handles on the top or bottom to display more rows.
- Drag the corner handles to display more columns and rows.

■ Once the spreadsheet is accessed, you can use the same formatting and editing options you used when you created a spreadsheet directly in the Spreadsheet tool.

> *In this exercise, you will embed a new spreadsheet into a word processing document.*

EXERCISE DIRECTIONS:

1. Open ⌨**TELECOPY**, or open 💾**IN TELECOPY.6**.

2. Type the illustrated letter in the letterhead document. Begin at least two lines under the last line of the letterhead. Press the Enter key twice before beginning the spreadsheet.

3. Create the spreadsheet as follows:
   a. Bold the title and center it across the selection.
   b. Center and bold all column headings.

   c. Widen the columns to accommodate the longest line in each column.
   d. Format all money amounts to two decimal places.

4. Size the spreadsheet so only the three columns are displayed.

5. Press the Enter key twice after the spreadsheet.

6. Center the spreadsheet horizontally on the page.

7. Remove the gridlines.
   ✓HINT: *Access the spreadsheet and click View, Gridlines to remove the gridlines from the spreadsheet.*

8. Type the remainder of the document.

9. Spell check the document.

10. Preview your document and make any other adjustments necessary to fit the document on one page.

11. Print one copy.

12. Edit the spreadsheet as follows:

a. Change the spreadsheet title to serif 14 point bold.

b. Change the subtitle to serif 12 point bold and initial caps.

c. Center the data in columns B and C.

13. Preview your document.

14. Print one copy.

15. Save the document; name it **TELEMEMBER**.

TELECOPY CENTER

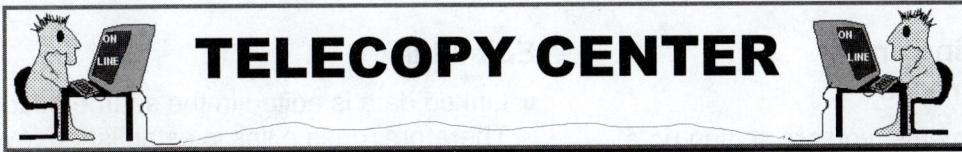

345 Northern Boulevard
Baldwin, NY 11755

Phone: 516-555-9843
Fax: 516-555-4596

Today's date

Dear Patrons:

We are delighted to announce that we are opening a new branch of the TELECOPY CENTER in Garden City.

In celebration of our grand opening, we are offering the following discounts.

SERVICE	REGULAR PRICE	CHART PRICE
TELECOPY CENTER ← *Change to serif 14 pt. bold*		
CHARTER MEMBERSHIP RATES ← *Change to serif 12 pt bold and initial caps.*		
Copies - B/W	0.06	0.04
Copies - Color	0.99	0.79
Fax - per sheet	1.29	1.10
On-line services - per hour*	20.00	15.00
Computer usage - per hour	10.00	8.00

*Includes Internet access

Center column data

We are offering a membership in our computer center which will entitle you to a discount on the copying rates as well as discounts on our other services. We have expanded to include Internet access and use of on-line databases.

Our grand opening celebration will be held at our new office at 341 Main Street, Garden City on July 31, from 12 noon to 5 p.m. We hope to see you there.

Sincerely,

Mr. Telly Camut
Branch Manager

yo

EMBED A NEW SPREADSHEET

1. Place insertion point at desired location.

2. Click **Insert** .... `Alt`+`I`

3. Click **Spreadsheet** .... `R`

4. Click **Create a new** .... `Alt`+`N` **spreadsheet**.

5. Click **OK** .... `Enter`

6. Resize spreadsheet as desired.

7. Enter data into new spreadsheet.

8. Click outside spreadsheet to return to the word processing document.

NOTES:

Link Word Processing and Spreadsheet Documents

■ When you link documents, you are setting up a connection between the source and destination documents. Whenever you update the information in the source document, the destination is *automatically* updated. This holds true for every destination document that is linked to the source document.

■ Information can be linked between any Works tools or a document created in another Windows-based application that supports linking. You can link pictures, drawings, text, spreadsheets, a range of cells within a spreadsheet and charts. The most popular use of the linking feature is incorporating a spreadsheet or chart into a word processing document.

■ The source document must be saved for linking to take place. A **link** is created when you copy data and paste it using the Paste Special command from the Edit menu. This command allows you to connect the two documents so that any changes made in the source document are also made in the destination document. Click Edit, Paste Special to access the following dialog box:

Edit a Link

■ Linked data is edited in the source document. Therefore, once a link is established, every time you make a change to the spreadsheet, the linked word processing document is updated. This is true even if the word processing document is not open. When you open the word processing document, you will be asked whether or not you want to update the link.

Change a Source

■ If you change the filename of the source document, you will break the link. However, the link can be reestablished between the word processing document and the renamed source document.

For example, you linked two files named MEMO1 and SS1. After updating the spreadsheet you saved it as SS2. There is no link between MEMO1 and SS2. You can now establish a link between MEMO 1 and SS2. From within the word processing dialog box click Edit, Links to display the following dialog box.

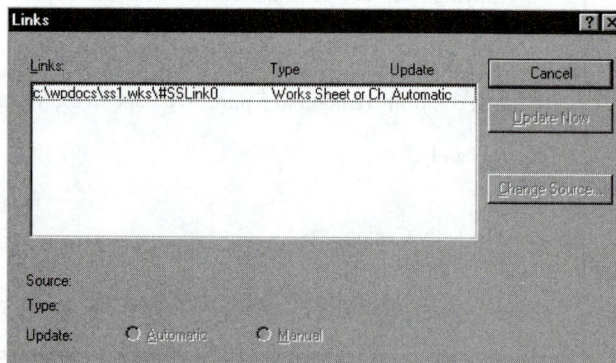

All links related to the active document are listed. Click the link you wish to change to display the following dialog box.

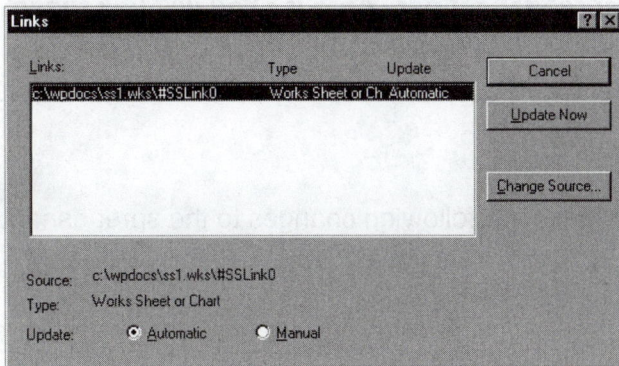

The dialog box now gives information on the source document. Click Change Source to display the following dialog box:

Enter a filename for the new source or select the desired file from the dialog box.

If you have other links to this source, Works will ask if you want to change all links to the new source file.

LINK WORD PROCESSOR AND SPREADSHEET

1. Open both word processing document and spreadsheet.

   ✓ NOTE: Spreadsheet must be saved in order to link.

2. Select spreadsheet data to copy.

3. Click **Edit**...............................Alt+E

4. Click **Copy**.......................................C

5. Switch to word processing document.

6. Click **Edit**...............................Alt+E

7. Click **Paste Special**........................S

8. Click **Paste Link**....................Alt+L

9. Click **As....Microsoft Works 4 Sheet or Chart Object**............Alt+A

10. Click **OK**......................................Enter

11. Make necessary additions and adjustments to the word processing document.

12. Save the word processing document.

13. Close both documents.

   ✓ NOTE: When prompted to save changes to the spreadsheet, click Yes.

EDIT A LINK

1. Open spreadsheet.

2. Make changes to spreadsheet.

3. Open linked word processing document.

4. Click **Yes** ....Alt+Y
   when prompted to update links.
   Note that data has been updated.

5. Close both documents.
   OR
   Save updated files under same names.
   OR
   Save updated files under different filenames.

CHANGE SOURCE OF A LINK

1. Open the word processing document.

2. Click the spreadsheet data to display the handles.

3. Click **Edit**...............................Alt+E

4. Click **Links** ....K

5. Click source file.

6. Click **Change Source** ....Alt+C

7. Type new source name
   OR
   Click filename from list box.

8. Click **OK** ....Enter

9. Click **Update now**.................Alt+U
   to accept new source file.

10. Click **Close.**

> *You are a teacher in the Business Education Department of New Meadows High School. Since you are a computer teacher, you record your grades in a spreadsheet. At the end of each quarter, you are required to submit your quarterly grades on a grade reporting form. This form is scanned into your computer so you can insert your spreadsheet data onto it. You will link these two documents so that the report is automatically updated when you record the new grades for the next quarter.*

EXERCISE DIRECTIONS:

1. Create a new document for the Word Processor.

2. Type the the word processing document shown in Illustration A. Begin the title at the top of the page.

3. Open **EXAM**, or open **IN EXAM.7**. See Illustration B.

4. Copy cells A1:G14.

5. Position the insertion point two lines below the divider line.

6. Paste link the spreadsheet.

7. Center the spreadsheet.

8. Save the file; name it **EXAM REP 3**.

9. Print **EXAM REP 3**.

10. Close both documents.
    - ✓ *NOTE: If prompted to save changes to Exam, click <u>Yes</u>.*

11. Assume it is now the fourth quarter and you need to submit your grades for the fourth quarter.

12. Open **EXAM**, or open **IN EXAM.7**.

13. Make the following changes to the spreadsheet:
    a. Change subtitle to FOURTH QUARTER EXAM GRADES
    b. Change the exam data for each student as shown in Illustration B.
    c. Change Daniels to Cohen.

14. Open **EXAM REP 3**.

15. Respond *YES* when asked to update the links.

16. Note that the changes were automatically made for the new quarter.

17. Save the new grade report sheet as **EXAM REP 4**.

18. Save the updated spreadsheet; name it **EXAM 4**.

19. Change the link to connect **EXAM REP 4** to **EXAM 4**.
    - ✓ *HINT: Make EXAM REP 4 the active document to select the inserted spreadsheet.*

20. Print one copy of **EXAM REP 4**.

21. Close both documents; save the changes.

GRADE REPORTING SHEET

TEACHER: Mr. Frank Proctor

DEPARTMENT: Business Education

TERM ENDING: June, 199-

↓ 2

Paste Link exam here

Fourth

	A	B		C		D		E		F	G
1		ADVANCED INFORMATION PROCESSING									
2		THIRD QUARTER EXAM GRADES									
3											
4										STUDENT	
5	STUDENT	EXAM 1		EXAM 2		EXAM 3		EXAM 4		AVERAGES	GRADE
6											
7	Burns	95	90	83	81	87	86	86	88	86.25	PASS
8	Daniels	71	71	67	67	72	65	38	38	60.25	FAIL
9	Edwards	55	65	62	78	71	81	65	87	77.75	PASS
10	Forbes	82	92	97	78	90	90	95	82	85.50	PASS
11	Garner	87	91	55	71	83	95	80	80	84.25	PASS
12	Hawkins	76	87	92	94	78	78	75	85	86.00	PASS
13	Lopez	92	98	90	83	87	91	89	78	87.50	PASS
14	Yaro	93	91	55	34	89	88	78	74	71.75	PASS

Cohen

■ **Integrate Database Files and Reports**

NOTES:

Integrate Database Files and Reports

- A database file or database report can be copied to either the Word Processor or the Spreadsheet. In either case, you use a simple copy and paste to accomplish the transfer.

- When you copy the database information to the Word Processor, the information is separated by tab stops rather than columns. Each line (or record) is ended with a paragraph mark.

  If the database is larger than the word processing margins, you may need to adjust the margins, tab stops or the font size to have the database display properly within the word processing document. The database file is NOT embedded using this method.

- When you copy the database information to the Spreadsheet tool, the information remains separated by columns. You can make adjustments to the column widths in the spreadsheet.

- Files transfer more easily into the Word Processor from the Spreadsheet. If a database file does not display correctly in the word processing document, copy it to the spreadsheet first, then bring it into the word processing document. Database files and reports copied in this way are embedded allowing you to easily make any editing or formatting changes.

COPY A DATABASE REPORT

1. Open the word processing document.

2. Open the desired database.

3. Create a report . (See Database, Lesson 4, Exercise 21.)

4. Click **Edit** .... `Alt`+`E`

5. Click **Copy Report Output** .... `Y`

6. Complete one of the following procedures:

a. Switch to the word processing document.

b. Click **Edit** .... `Alt`+`E`

c. Click **Paste** .... `P`

d. Adjust tab stops as needed to properly display report.

OR

a. Create new spreadsheet document.

b. Click **Edit** .... `Alt`+`E`

c. Click **Paste** .... `P`

d. Adjust column widths as necessary.

e. Select the spreadsheet.

f. Click **Edit** .... `Alt`+`E`

g. Click **Copy** .... `Alt`+`C`

h. Switch to the word processing document.

i. Click **Edit** .... `Alt`+`E`

j. Click **Paste** .... `P`

k. Make necessary adjustments to display properly.

EXERCISE DIRECTIONS:

1. Create a new document for the Word Processor.

2. Create the word processing document in Illustration B as follows:

   a. Use 1" left and right margins.

   b. Create a header with the header title DATABASE at the left and page number at the right. Do not print the header on the first page.

   c. Center the title and format attractively.

   d. Use single and double spacing as indicated.

      ✓NOTE: See Word Processing Lesson 4, Exercise 22 for changing line spacing within a document.

   e. Use the bulleted list feature as indicated.

3. Open the database ▦INVENTORY, or open ▦IN INVENTORY.8.

4. Create a report to include all fields as shown in Illustration A.

5. Title the report **HARDWARE INVENTORY**.

6. Copy the report to a new spreadsheet document.

7. Make adjustments to column widths as needed.

8. Change the spreadsheet to print with gridlines showing.

9. Copy the newly created spreadsheet to the word processing document where indicated. Adjust size to display properly.

10. Spell check.

11. Print preview. Make necessary adjusments to keep the database file on the first page of the report.

12. Print one copy.

13. Save the document; name it **DB INVENTORY**.

14. Close the documents.

ILLUSTRATION A

			HARDWARE INVENTORY				
ITEM	**MFG**	**MODEL**	**COST**	**PURDATE**	**WTY**	**SSIGNED T**	**SERIAL #**
Computer	IBM	PS2	$1,348	6/1/95	Yes	Accounting	651198
Computer	IBM	Thinkpad 5(	$1,399	6/1/96	Yes	Accounting	671150
Hard Drive	Quantum	LPS 40 170l	$199	6/1/96	Yes	Accounting	54219
Monitor	NEC	FGE	$589	12/1/96	No	Accounting	11112
Printer	HP	DeskJet	$429	11/1/96	Yes	Accounting	99911
Computer	IBM	Thinkpad	$2,199	6/1/96	Yes	Personnel	2059
Computer	Canon	Notebook	$2,436	8/1/96	Yes	Personnel	98763
Monitor	NEC	FGE/3V	$539	12/1/96	No	Personnel	87098
Printer	IBM	ExecJet II	$335	6/1/96	Yes	Personnel	55211
Printer	HP	DeskJet	$429	11/1/96	Yes	Personnel	22230
Computer	Canon	Notebook	$2,436	8/1/96	Yes	Purchasing	76666
Hard Drive	Conner	CFS4 210M	$200	6/1/96	No	Purchasing	12345
Computer	Canon	Notebook 4{	$1,889	1/1/96	Yes	Shipping	1445
Modem	Intel	PCMCIA	$115	1/1/96	No	Shipping	20098
Printer	Okidata	ML330RR	$295	2/1/96	Yes	Shipping	98983

ILLUSTRATION B

WHAT IS A DATABASE?

Have you ever . . .

- Searched frantically through your entire phone book for an important number because you can't remember the letter it was filed under?

- Had your supervisor ask you for information you know you have, and now can't find?

- Organized all your personal papers and financial information, only to have to search through pages upon pages to reach the information you need?

These situations are frustrating and a waste of valuable time. However, you can have the information you need at your fingertips if you record all the information into a **database.**

A database is a computer program that organizes your data. In addition, a database program allows you to manipulate the data so you can easily see trends and relationships to help you make important decisions. Once you record all your information into the database, you can access it at the touch of a button--no loss of time searching through file cabinets, phone books, or bureau drawers.

A good example of a database is an inventory database that keeps track of equipment, property, or assets and could be used in a school, business, club, or in the home. The following is an example of a typical inventory database for the offices of the Bit-Byte Computer Company.

The database organizes your information into categories or **fields**. Our inventory database is broken down into ITEM, MFG, MODEL, COST, PURDATE, WTY (Under Warranty), ASSIGNED TO and SERIAL #.

Information must be updated in the database over time. Obsolete items are deleted and new purchases are added to the database. Any transfer of equipment to another office must be recorded so the equipment can be easily traced.

Any item of information can be searched and quickly obtained. You may need to know how many pieces of hardware are under warranty. By setting up the correct conditions, the computer will easily give you the answer.

The information can be arranged in alphabetical, numerical, or chronological order in either ascending (A-Z or 1-9) or descending (Z-A or 9-1) order. You can sort the information by any category. In this database, you may want to arrange the inventory by PURDATE. This information would allow you to easily see which items are the oldest and in need of replacement.

Paste copy of database here..

DATABASE   2

In this exercise, you saw how an inventory database would help organize your equipment data.

From this illustration, you can easily see the benefits a database program offers and the effects it can have on all your informational needs.

■ Merge Word Processing and Database Documents ■ Create Form Letters ■ Print Merge

NOTES:

Merge Word Processing and Database Documents

■ **Merging** integrates a word processing document with a database file. The Merge feature allows you to mass produce letters, envelopes, mailing labels and other documents so they appear to be personalized.

■ A **form letter** is combined with a **database file** to produce multiple copies of the same letter with each letter containing information specific to the recipient. For example, the inside address, the salutation or an amount due would change on each letter.

■ The database file contains the variable information that will change in each printed letter. The database file *must* be created and saved before creating the letter. This same database file can be used to create envelopes and/or labels (see Exercises 11-13).

■ The form letter is created in the Word Processor. All formatting (margins, spacing, etc.), graphics and paper size information should be included in the form letter. When you create the form letter, codes known as **placeholders** are inserted where the variable information will be placed. These placeholders are the field names that identify where the data is located in the database file. When you print the form letters, the placeholders are replaced with the information provided in the database.

■ The following illustration shows the placeholders identifying the fields being used in the letter. Note the relationship between the placeholders in the form letter (Illustration 1) and the database fields (Illustration 2).

ILLUSTRATION 1

May 20, 199-

«TITLE» «FIRST» «LAST»
«ADDRESS»   ← Placeholders
«CITY», «ST» «ZIP»

Dear «TITLE» «LAST»: ←

Do you take time from your busy schedule to exercise and enjoy leisure activities? If you want to keep your energy up and your mind and body fit, then you know the value of a good exercise program.

One of the key elements in a good exercise program is good footwear. Whether you jog, play tennis, golf, softball, do aerobics, or get exercise by just thinking about working out, we, at **SOCK IT TO ME**, can offer you the best in sporting footwear to keep you at the top of your form. We carry the finest names in footwear in the latest styles, all at discounted prices.

Since you are a valued customer, we would like to extend a special invitation to attend our annual Marathon Sale on Saturday, June 5 from 8:00 a.m. to 10:00 p.m. Our entire inventory will be reduced with savings of 25-75% off regular prices.

If you haven't started an exercise program, now's the time. Hope to see you on the 5th.

Sincerely,

Cal E. Steniks
Vice President

yo

ILLUSTRATION 2
Field names – same as placeholders

	TITLE	LAST	FIRST	ADDRESS	CITY	ST	ZIP	PHONE	PROF
1	Ms.	Barnes	Leanne	808 Summer St.	Anaheim	CA	92803	555-4987	Student
2	Mr.	Brown	Miles	154 Newburg Rd.	Anaheim	CA	92804	555-4837	Accountant
3	Mr.	Griffith	Stuart	1551 Dean St.	Beverly Hills	CA	90210	555-3010	Lawyer
4	Mr.	Moon	Michael	32 Oak St.	Beverly Hills	CA	80210	555-8750	Teacher
5	Ms.	Smith	Trinia	3954 Wood Ave.	Anaheim	CA	92803	555-7283	Student
6	Ms.	Smith	Sheila	417 Specific Ct.	Anaheim	CA	92803	555-7284	Chiropractor
7	Ms.	Walker-Sim	Bette	1745 River St.	North Hollywood	CA	91615	555-8520	Lawyer
8	Mr.	Castillo	Carl	1956 Park Ave.	North Hollywood	CA	91615	555-5192	Banker
9	Mr.	Davis	John	P.O. Box 2333	North Hollywood	CA	91615	555-8129	Student
10	Ms.	Dixon	Amy	23 Albee St.	North Hollywood	CA	91615	555-8917	Orthopedist
11	Ms.	Kendall	Gale	15 Imperial Way	Beverly Hills	CA	90210	555-9888	Teacher
12	Ms.	Dagger	Janice	27 Ocean Ave.	Anaheim	CA	92804	555-7777	Orthopedist
13	Mr.	Chow	Michael	88 Riverside Dr.	Culver City	CA	90311	555-7655	Accountant
14	Mr.	Wagner	David	879 Beverly Dr.	Beverly Hills	CA	90210	555-6676	Banker
15	Ms.	Smith	Cleo	90 Rodeo Dr.	Beverly Hills	CA	90210	555-2222	Student
16	Ms.	Anderson	Carolyn	666 Santa Ana Dr.	Culver City	CA	90312	555-9988	Lawyer
17	Ms.	Ramaz	Naznine	9012 Wilshire Blvd.	Beverly Hills	CA	90210	555-2211	Teacher
18	Mr.	Yakar	Winston	776 Prince Lane	North Hollywood	CA	91615	555-0000	Student
19	Ms	Mancuso	Mary	12 Pacific Ct.	North Hollywood	CA	91615	555-7773	Banker

✓ NOTE: The same field can be inserted in the letter as many times as desired. Note that «LAST» is used twice, once in the inside address, and again in the salutation.

Create Form Letters

- Form letters are created through the Form Letters feature. This feature leads you through a series of steps which allow you to:
  - Choose the database.
  - Insert placeholders for the variable information.
  - Choose who will receive the letters (the recipients).
  - Type and edit the letter.
  - Preview and/or print the letters.

- You begin the process by creating a new word processing document. Type the letter until a placeholder has to be inserted. At this point, click Tools, Form Letters to access the Form Letters dialog box:

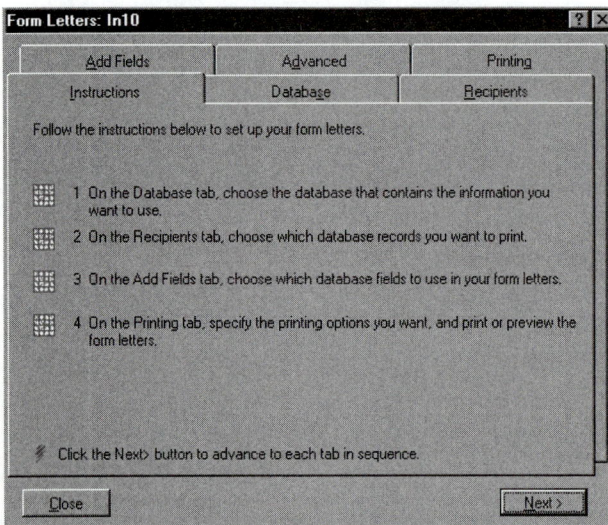

- This procedure leads you to each tab in the sequence listed below. Each tab of the dialog box offers a number of options.

Instructions	As you perform each step, a check is placed in the box.
Database	Allows you to choose the desired database for the merge.
Recipients	Allows you to specify which records you want to include in the merge. You can choose to print all the records, records that are currently visible, marked or filtered records. You can change the selected filters and mark additional records from this tab.
Add Fields	Provides a list of fields in the current database. Double click to insert the field into the letter.

Advanced	Minimizes the dialog box so you can type or edit the letter. Use this tab to edit the inside address and to insert proper line endings, punctuation and/or spaces. The Go Back box allows you to go back to the dialog box to add other fields.
Printing	Allows you to preview and print your document.

- After you choose your options in a tab, click Next to advance to the next tab in the sequence. As you complete a tab, a check is placed on the **Instructions** tab next to the completed step. However, if you choose not to follow the sequence, you can access a different tab at any time from within the Form Letters dialog box.

- Once you have chosen the database, you can select the recipients of the letters. In this lesson, you will send the letters to all the records in the database.

- Once the recipients have been selected, you need to supply the database fields (Add Fields tab). Double-click the desired fields in the correct order. For example, the «LAST» placeholder may be listed before the «FIRST» placeholder. However, when inserting the fields for the inside address, you will have to double-click the «FIRST» placeholder before the «LAST» placeholder. The placeholders are inserted in paragraph form. Therefore, you will need to edit the format of the inside address once the fields have been inserted.

- The **Advanced** tab is next in the sequence. Format the inside address in this area. Click Edit to return to the form letter where you can add returns, spaces and punctuation marks to format the address correctly. Insert a comma after the «CITY» placeholder and insert an additional space after the «ST» placeholder. See the correct format below:

«TITLE» «FIRST» «LAST»
«ADDRESS»
:«CITY», «ST» «ZIP»

Insert comma   *Insert 2 spaces*

Continue to type and/or edit the letter in the Advanced tab. You will need to click Go Back when you need to add other fields or are finished typing the letter.

Remember to insert the colon in the salutation *immediately* after the placeholder for «LAST» . See illustration below:

Dear «TITLE» «LAST»:
↑
Insert colon

■ The final step in the sequence is printing the merged letters. The **Printing** tab allows you to either preview or print the document. If you detect errors in the preview, click the Advanced tab to edit the letter. Once the letter is edited, return to the Printing tab to preview the document again. When everything is correct, print the letters. One letter will be printed for each record in the database.

■ After the letters are printed, click Close to end the procedure. Save the form letter upon completing the merge procedure.

✓ *NOTE:* *Only the form letter is saved; the merged documents are not and can only be recreated by reprinting.*

Print Merge

■ Once a form letter has been created, you can preview or print it again as you would in any other word processing document. Click File, Print to access the Print dialog box below:

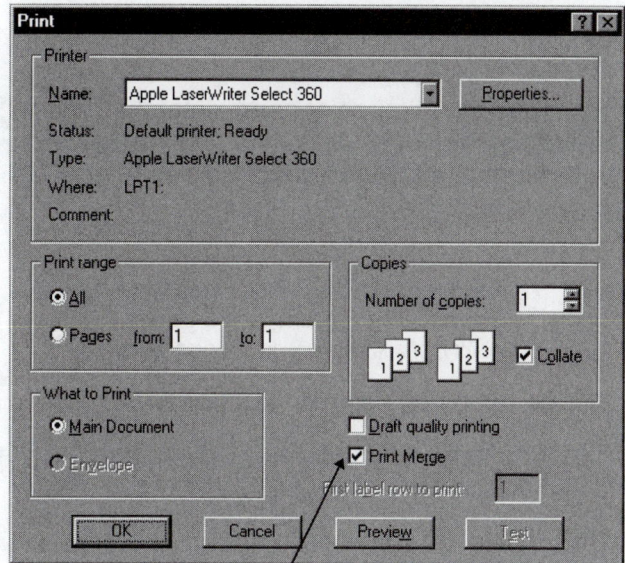

This option prints all letters in the merge.

■ Note the Print Merge box is selected. This means you will either preview or print all the letters in the merge. Deselect the Print Merge check box if you wish to preview or print only the form letter showing the placeholders.

To avoid wasting paper, you should always preview a merge before printing. In this way, you can detect any errors and make the necessary adjustments to the form letter. Failure to do this will result in the same error appearing in each letter.

■ The printing can be canceled by pressing ESC.

> *In this exercise, you will create a form letter announcing a sale to valued customers of the SOCK IT TO ME Sporting Footwear store. You will merge the letter with the all the records in the MEMBER database. All copies will be printed on the store's letterhead.*

EXERCISE DIRECTIONS:

1. Open 🖶**SOCK**, or open 🖫**IN SOCK.9** – Illustration B.

2. Place the insertion point approximately 2" from the top of the page. Make sure you are at least two returns below the letterhead before you begin typing.

   ✔ *NOTE:* *If the border continues when you press the Enter key, you need to press Ctrl+Q to discontinue the border feature. You also need to select a serif 12 point font and deselect bold to type the letter.*

3. Create the letter shown in Illustration C.

4. Type the letter until you are ready to insert the first placeholder.

5. Click Tools, Form Letters.

6. Click Next to access the Database tab.

   ✔ *NOTE:* *The Form Letters procedure leads you through a series of tabs, automatically advancing you to the next tab when you press Next. If the Next key does not bring you to the desired tab, or if it is unavailable, click the desired tab to select it manually.*

7. Choose 🖶**MEMBER** or 🖫**IN MEMBER.9** as the desired database.

8. Click Next to access the Recipients tab.

9. Click All records in the database.

10. Click Next to access the Add Fields tab. Double-click all the fields you need for the inside address.

    ✔ *NOTE:* *Works will automatically insert a space between each field if you choose more than one field at a time.*

11. Click Next to access the Advanced tab.

12. Click Edit.

13. Move the dialog box by dragging the Title bar.

14. Edit the address to add spaces, returns and appropriate punctuation.

15. Continue to type the letter until you need to enter the next placeholder.

16. Click Go Back to return to the Form Letters dialog box and click the Add Fields tab to add new fields.

17. Return to the Advanced tab and click Edit to continue typing and/or editing the letter. Repeat steps 10-17 until the letter is completed.

18. Proofread and spell check the letter while in the Advanced tab.

19. Click Go Back to return to the Form Letters dialog box.

20. In the Printing tab, click Print Preview.

    ✔ *NOTE:* *If the procedure does not automatically advance you to the Printing tab, click it.*

21. Click the Advanced tab to edit the letter if needed.

22. When you are ready to print, access the Printing tab and click Print.

23. Compare your results with the letters in Illustration D.

24. When the sequence is completed, click Close to exit the Form Letters procedure.

25. Save the document; name it **SPORTS**.

    ✔ *NOTE:* *Make sure you save under a new name. You do not want to replace the letterhead file.*

26. Close the document window.

Member

TITLE	LAST	FIRST	ADDRESS	CITY	ST	ZIP	PHONE	PROF
Ms.	Barnes	Leanne	808 Summer St.	Anaheim	CA	92803	555-4987	Student
Mr.	Brown	Miles	154 Newburg Rd.	Anaheim	CA	92804	555-4837	Accountant
Mr.	Griffith	Stuart	1551 Dean St.	Beverly Hills	CA	90210	555-3010	Lawyer
Mr.	Moon	Michael	32 Oak St.	Beverly Hills	CA	80210	555-8750	Teacher
Ms.	Smith	Trinia	3954 Wood Ave.	Anaheim	CA	92803	555-7283	Student
Ms.	Smith	Sheila	417 Specific Ct.	Anaheim	CA	92803	555-7284	Chiropractor
Ms.	Walker-Sim	Bette	1745 River St.	North Hollywood	CA	91615	555-8520	Lawyer
Mr.	Castillo	Carl	1956 Park Ave.	North Hollywood	CA	91615	555-5192	Banker
Mr.	Davis	John	P.O. Box 2333	North Hollywood	CA	91615	555-8129	Student
Ms.	Dixon	Amy	23 Albee St.	North Hollywood	CA	91615	555-8917	Orthopedist
Ms.	Kendall	Gale	15 Imperial Way	Beverly Hills	CA	90210	555-9888	Teacher
Ms.	Dagger	Janice	27 Ocean Ave.	Anaheim	CA	92804	555-7777	Orthopedist
Mr.	Chow	Michael	88 Riverside Dr.	Culver City	CA	90311	555-7655	Accountant
Mr.	Wagner	David	879 Beverly Dr.	Beverly Hills	CA	90210	555-6676	Banker
Ms.	Smith	Cleo	90 Rodeo Dr.	Beverly Hills	CA	90210	555-2222	Student
Ms.	Anderson	Carolyn	666 Santa Ana Dr.	Culver City	CA	90312	555-9988	Lawyer
Ms.	Ramaz	Naznine	9012 Wilshire Blvd.	Beverly Hills	CA	90210	555-2211	Teacher
Mr.	Yakar	Winston	776 Prince Lane	North Hollywood	CA	91615	555-0000	Student
Ms	Mancuso	Mary	12 Pacific Ct.	North Hollywood	CA	91615	555-7773	Banker

SOCK IT TO ME
SPORTING FOOTWEAR
777 Mercedes Drive
Los Angeles, CA 90210
310 555-4398

May 20, 199-

Sock

«TITLE» «FIRST» «LAST»
«ADDRESS»
«CITY», «ST» «ZIP»

ILLUSTRATION C

Sports

Dear «TITLE» «LAST»:

Do you take time from your busy schedule to exercise and enjoy leisure activities? If you want to keep your energy up and your mind and body fit, then you know the value of a good exercise program.

One of the key elements in a good exercise program is good footwear. Whether you jog, play tennis, golf, softball, do aerobics, or get exercise by just thinking about working out, we, at **SOCK IT TO ME**, can offer you the best in sporting footwear to keep you at the top of your form. We carry the finest names in footwear in the latest styles, all at discounted prices.

Since you are a valued customer, we would like to extend a special invitation to attend our annual Marathon Sale on Saturday, June 5 from 8:00 a.m. to 10:00 p.m. Our entire inventory will be reduced with savings of 25-75% off regular prices.

If you haven't started an exercise program, now's the time. Hope to see you on the 5th.

Sincerely,

Cal E. Steniks
Vice President

yo

Merged
documents

CREATE FORM LETTERS

✔ *NOTE:* *The database file must be created first and saved.*

1. Open a previously stored letter.
   OR
   Create a new file for the Word Processor.
2. Click **Tools** .... `Alt`+`T`
3. Click **Form Letters** .... `F`
4. Click **Next** .... `Alt`+`N`
   OR
   Click **Database** tab .... `Alt`+`S`
5. Click **Choose a database** .... `Alt`+`H`
6. Click desired database
   OR
   Click **Open a** .... `Alt`+`O`
   database not listed here.
7. Click **Next** .... `Alt`+`N`
   to return to Instructions tab.
8. Click **Next** .... `N`
   to advance to the next tab.
   OR
   Click **Recipients** tab .... `Alt`+`R`
9. Click one of the following options:
   - **All records in the database** `Alt`+`L`
   - **Current records** .... `Alt`+`U`
     visible in the database.
   - **Currently marked** .... `Alt`+`K`
     records in the database.
   - **Filtered records** .... `Alt`+`F`
     in the database.
     Click **Current Filter** .... `Alt`+`T`
     OR
     Click **Change Filter** .... `Alt`+`H`
     to create a new filter.

10. Click **Next** .... `Alt`+`N`
    to return to Instructions tab.
11. Click **Next** .... `N`
    to advance to the next tab.
    OR
    Click **Add Fields** tab .... `Alt`+`A`
12. Click **Choose a field** .... `Alt`+`H`
13. Double-click desired fields.
14. Click **Next** .... `Alt`+`N`
    to return to Instructions tab.
15. Click **Next** .... `N`
    to advance to the next tab.
    OR
    Click **Advanced** tab................ `Alt`+`D`
16. Click **Edit** .... `Alt`+`E`
17. Edit the document to include correct line endings, spacing and punctuation between placeholders.
18. Click **Go Back** .... `Alt`+`G`
    to access Form Letters dialog box
19. Repeat steps 11 - 18 above to insert additional fields and edit text.
20. Click **Next** .... `Alt`+`N`
    to return to Instructions tab.
21. Click **Next** .... `N`
    to advance to the next tab.
    OR
    Click **Printing** .... `Alt`+`G`
    when letter is complete
22. Click **Preview** .... `Alt`+`V`
    OR
    Click **Print**............................... `Alt`+`P`
23. Click **Next** .... `Alt`+`N`
    to return to Instructions tab.
24. Click **Close** .... `Alt`+`C`

PRINT MERGE

Ctrl + P

To Print the Merge from the File Menu

1. Open the form letter.
2. Click **File** .... `Alt`+`F`
3. Click **Print**.............................. `Alt`+`P`
4. Click **Preview** .... `Alt`+`W`

   ✔ *NOTE:* *Click OK to preview all records.*

5. Click **Print** .... `Alt`+`P`
   on the preview screen if no editing is needed.
   OR
   Click **Cancel** .... `Esc`
   and return to edit the letter.
6. Click **OK**................................... `Enter`
   to print merged letters
   OR
   Deselect **Print Merge** .... `Alt`+`I`
   to print form letter showing placeholders.

   ✔ *NOTE:* *You may be prompted to confirm that the correct database file is selected.*

7. Click **OK** to print all records......... `Enter`

EXERCISE **10**

■ **Merge Selected Records**

NOTES:

Merge Selected Records

■ There may be occasions when you need to merge only certain records with a word processing document. For example, in this exercise you will be sending a letter only to the parents or guardians of students who have been accepted to the National Honor Society.

■ There are a number of options available in the Recipients tab of the Form Letters dialog box to limit the merge to specific records within the database. You can hide unwanted records, mark desired records or create a filter to find those records you wish to include.

■ When using the Form Letters feature, click the Recipients tab to access the following dialog box.

■ The main advantage of this feature is you do not have to leave the Recipients tab to select your records. You can access the database from within the Recipients tab and mark the records you want to print. In addition, you can change the current filter to select different records to print with your letter. All this can be accomplished from the Recipients tab. Once the desired records have been chosen, you can continue with the Merge procedure.

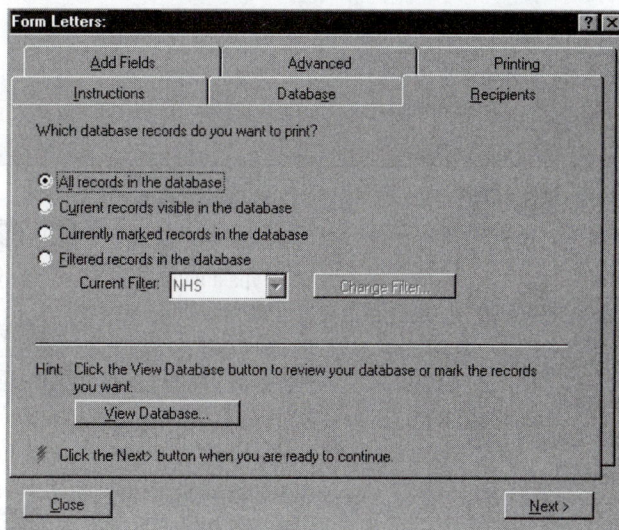

> *In this exercise, you will use the Form Letters feature to create a letter notifying selected students from the STUDENT database of their acceptance into the National Honor Society. All letters will be printed on the school's stationery.*

EXERCISE DIRECTIONS:

1. Open ⌨**JETS**, or open 💾**IN JETS.10**.

2. Place the insertion point approximately 2" from the top of the page. Make sure you are at least two returns below the letterhead.

3. Change to left alignment.

4. Create the form letter shown in Illustration A.

5. Type the letter until you are ready to insert the first placeholder.

6. Click Tools, Form Letters.

7. Follow all steps in the Form Letters dialog box until you are in the Recipients tab.

8. Make the following change in the Recipients tab.
   a. Click Filtered records in database.
   b. Click Change Filter.
   c. Create a new filter; name it NHS. Create a new filter definition to find those students who are in the NHS.

9. Select the appropriate fields in the Add Fields tab.

✓ NOTE: *Works will automatically insert a space between each field if you choose more than one field at a time.*

10. Perform the following in the Advanced tab:
    a. Format the inside address correctly.
    b. Type the remainder of the letter.
    c. Edit the letter to ensure correct placement and spacing before and after placeholders.
    d. Proofread and spell check the letter.

11. Preview your document in the Printing tab.

12. Return to the Advanced tab to make any corrections or adjustments.

13. Return to the Printing tab to print the form letters.

14. Click Close when the procedure is completed.

15. Save the file; name it **ACCEPT**.

16. Close the document window.

MERGE SELECTED RECORDS

Select Merge Using Form Letter Procedure

1. Open a previously stored letter.
   OR
   Create a new file for the Word Processor.

2. Click **Tools** .... Alt + O

3. Click **Form Letters** .... Alt + F

4. Follow keystrokes in Exercise 9 to select desired database and advance to Recipients tab.
   OR
   Select **Recipients** tab .... Alt + R

5. In the Recipients tab, click one of the following options:

   All records .... Alt + L
   in the database
   OR

   Current records .... Alt + U
   visible in the database.
   OR
   Currently marked .... Alt + K
   records in the database.

   To Select Currently marked records in the database.
   a. Click **View Database** Alt + V
   b. Click desired records.
   c. Click **Go Back** .... Alt + G
      to return to Recipients tab.
   OR
   Filtered records................. Alt + F
   in the database.
   Click **Current Filter** ...... Alt + T
   OR
   Click **Change Filter** ...... Alt + H
   to create a new filter

   To Change a Filter
   a. Click **New Filter**....... Alt + F
   b. Type a name .... *name*
      for the filter.
   c. Click **OK**...................... Enter
   d. Select **Field name** .. Alt + L
   e. Select the comparison from list
   f. Type compare to data ..... *data*
   g. Click **OK**................. Enter
   ✓ NOTE: *The new filter appears in the Current Filter text box.*

6. Click **Next**.......................... Alt + N

7. Follow keystrokes in Exercise 9 to complete the merge procedure.

8. Click **Close** when done.

- As in the Form Letters procedure, you can click <u>N</u>ext to advance to the next tab, or you can click a desired tab from any location within the Envelopes dialog box.

- Once the envelope is created, it appears at the top of the word processing document and is separated by a hard page break that cannot be deleted. The envelope data would have to be deleted before you can delete the page break.

In this exercise you will create two envelopes. One envelope will be attached to an accompanying letter and the other will be a single self-addressed envelope.

EXERCISE DIRECTIONS:

1. Open 📠**BLOCK**, or open 💾**IN BLOCK.11**.

2. Select the inside address.

3. Create the envelope shown in the illustration below as follows:

   a. Select a #10 envelope.

   b. Choose NO DATABASE.

   c. Do not add a return address.

   d. Since the address for the letter was preselected, it should appear in the Main address text box. If not, type the address as it appears on the inside address of the letter.

   e. Print preview the envelope.

   ✓NOTE: *If there is a return address from a previous document, delete it.*

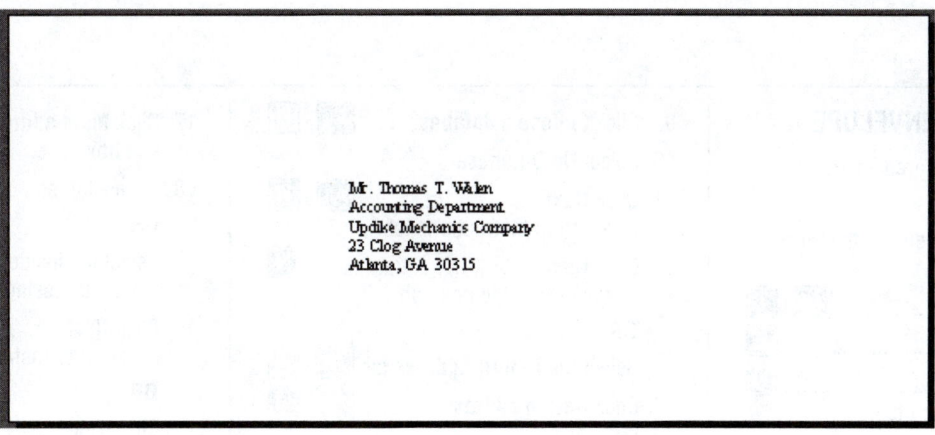

4. Print the envelope.

5. Resave the file.

6. Close the document window.

7. Create a new document for the Word Processor.

8. Create a self-addressed envelope following the directions in the keystroke section.

9. Use your home address for the delivery address *and* the return address.

10. Print the envelope.

11. Save the file; name it **SELF**.

12. Close the document window.

Mr. Thomas T. Walen
Accounting Department
Updike Mechanics Company
23 Clog Avenue
Atlanta, GA 30315

CREATE A SINGLE ENVELOPE

1. Open a previously stored letter.

   OR

   Create a new document for the Word Processor.

2. Click **Tools** .... `Alt`+`T`

3. Click **Envelopes**............................. `E`

4. Click **Next** .... `N`
   to advance to the next tab.

   OR

   Select the **Envelope Size** tab.. `Alt`+`Z`

5. Click **Choose an** .... `Alt`+`H`
   Envelope size.

6. Click desired size.

7. Click **Next**.............................. `Alt`+`N`
   to return to Instructions tab.

8. Click **Next** .... `N`
   to advance to the next tab.

   OR

   Select the **Database** tab .... `Alt`+`S`

9. Click **Choose a database** .... `Alt`+`H`

10. Select **No Database**.

11. Click **Next**.............................. `Alt`+`N`
    to return to Instructions tab.

12. Click **Next** .... `N`
    to advance to the next tab.

    OR

    Select the **Return Address** tab `Alt`+`A`

13. Click **Return address** .... `Alt`+`U`
    text box.

14. Type the return address . *return address*

15. Click **Next** .... `Alt`+`N`
    to return to Instructions tab.

16. Click **Next** .... `N`
    to advance to the next tab. ....

    OR

    Select the **Main Address** tab .. `Alt`+`M`

17. Click **Main address** .... `Alt`+`E`
    text box.

18. Type address ....*address*

    OR

    Select the inside address on the letter before accessing the Tools menu.

19. Click **Next**.............................. `Alt`+`N`
    to return to Instructions tab.

    OR

    Click **Next**...................................... `N`
    to advance to the next tab.

20. Select the **Printing** tab............ `Alt`+`G`

21. Click **Print**.............................. `Alt`+`P`

22. Click **Next**.............................. `Alt`+`N`
    to return to Instructions tab.

23. Click **Close** .... `Alt`+`C`

■ **Create and Merge Envelopes**

NOTES:

Create and Merge Envelopes

■ As mentioned in Exercise 11, Works allows you to create an envelope for each letter in a merged document.

■ To create an envelope for a print merge, open the form letter and click <u>T</u>ools. Click <u>E</u>nvelopes to access the Envelopes dialog box. Click <u>N</u>ext to advance to the tabs you need to use.

✓ NOTE: *If you are merging envelopes with a form letter, you must use the Database, Recipients and Main Address tabs to successfully complete the procedure.*

Select the Databa<u>s</u>e tab to access the area shown below:

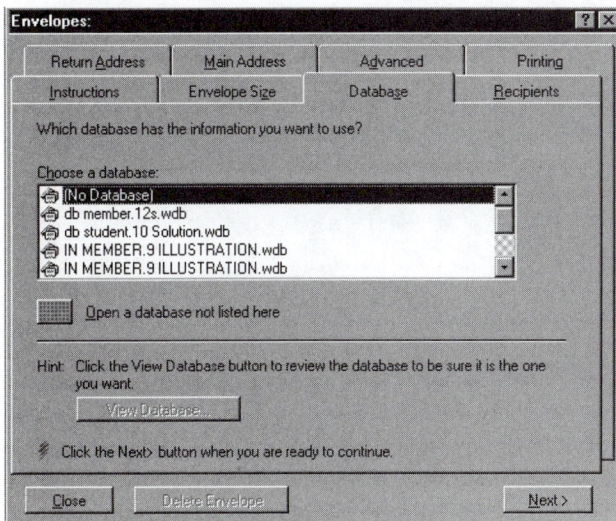

■ The **Database** tab displays a list of database files. Click the file with which you want to merge the envelope. If the desired file is not listed, click <u>O</u>pen a database not listed here to view additional database files.

■ The **Recipients** tab allows you to choose the records you want for the envelopes.

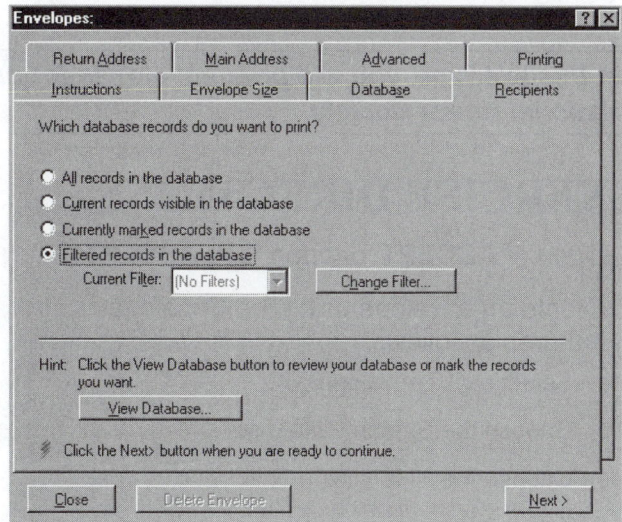

■ You can select the entire database or specific records. In this exercise, you will use the **Filtered records in the database** option.

■ The **Main Address** tab allows you to select those fields you need to create the envelope.

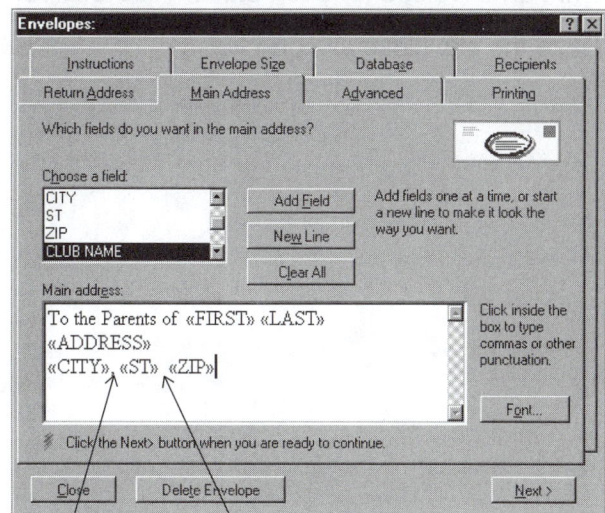

Insert comma and space

Insert two spaces betweem state and zip

■ You can edit the placeholders in the Main address text box. Be sure to include the correct number of spaces and/or punctuation marks between the various placeholders in the envelope as you did when you prepared the inside address for the form letter. (*See Integration, Exercise 9, p. 393*). For example, type a comma and space after the CITY placeholder.

■ The envelope will appear on the top of the form letter in Normal view and on a separate page in Page Layout view. You can alter the margin and indent settings as well as select other print options for the envelope independently of the letter.

Merge Printing an Envelope

■ Once the envelope has been created, you print as you would any other document. Both the Envelope radio button and the Print merge check box should be selected.

> *In this exercise, you will print envelopes for only those students who are accepted into the National Honor Society.*

EXERCISE DIRECTIONS:

1. Open ⌨**ACCEPT**, or open 💾**IN ACCEPT.12**.

2. Create an envelope using the Envelopes features as follows:

   a. Select a #10 envelope.

   b. Choose the Student database.

   c. Choose the NHS filter.

   d. Add a return address. Refer to the letterhead for address information.

   e. Add the necessary fields for the envelope. Refer to the inside address of the letter to see the wording and required fields.

   f. Print preview the envelope.

3. Print an envelope for each student in the NHS.

4. Save the file; close all open files.

CREATE AN ENVELOPE FOR A PRINT MERGE

1. Open a previously stored letter.

   OR

   Create a new document for the Word Processor.

2. Click **Tools** .... `Alt`+`T`
3. Click **Envelopes** .... `Alt`+`E`
4. Click **Next**..`N`
   to advance to the next tab.

   ✓ *NOTE:* *If a tab has previously been selected, as evidenced by a check mark in the Instructions tab, Works automatically opens the next unchecked tab. You can click any tab to select it without clicking Next.*

   OR

   Select the **Envelope size** tab.. `Alt`+`Z`

5. Click **Choose an** .... `Alt`+`H`
   Envelope size.
6. Click desired size.
7. Click **Next**.............................. `Alt`+`N`
   to return to the Instructions tab.
8. Click **Next**.......................................`N`
   to advance to the next tab.

   OR

   Select the **Database** tab......... `Alt`+`S`

9. Click **Choose a database** .... `Alt`+`H`
10. Click desired database
11. Click **Next**.............................. `Alt`+`N`
    to return to the Instructions tab.

    ✓ *NOTE:* *If using a form letter that has been previously associated with a database, the database is checked on the Instructions tab. Works will automatically open the next unchecked tab. Click the Database tab if you wish to use a different database.*

12. Click **Next**......................................`N`
    to advance to the next tab.

    OR

    Select the **Recipients** tab ...... `Alt`+`R`
13. Select one of the following options
    - **All records in** .... `Alt`+`L`
      the database
    - **Current records**................... `Alt`+`U`
      visible in the database
    - **Currently marked**................ `Alt`+`K`
      records in the database
    - **Filtered records**.................. `Alt`+`F`
      in the database
14. Click **Current Filter** .... `Alt`+`T`

    OR

    Click **Change Filter**................ `Alt`+`H`
    to create a new filter

15. Click **Next** .... `Alt`+`N`
    to return to the Instructions tab.
16. Click **Next** ....`N`
    to advance to the next tab.

    OR

    Select the **Return Address** tab `Alt`+`A`
17. Click **Return address** .... `Alt`+`U`
    text box.
18. Type the return address.
19. Click **Next**.............................. `Alt`+`N`
    to return to the Instructions tab.
20. Click **Next**......................................`N`
    to advance to the next tab.

    OR

    Select the **Main Address** tab.. `Alt`+`M`
21. Click **Main address**............... `Alt`+`E`
    text box.
22. Type address.

    OR

    Select the inside address on the letter before accessing the Tools menu.

23. Click **Next** .... `Alt`+`N`
    to return to the Instructions tab.
24. Click **Next** ....`N`
    to advance to the next tab.

    OR

    Select the **Printing** tab .... `Alt`+`G`
25. Click **Print Preview** .... `Alt`+`W`
26. Click **Print** .... `Alt`+`P`
27. Click **Next**.............................. `Alt`+`N`
    to return to the Instructions tab.
28. Click **Close**........................... `Alt`+`C`

NOTES:

Create and Print Labels

■ You can create a single label or merge multiple labels for each record in a database file. In addition, you can create mailing labels for your form letters in much the same way you created envelopes in the previous exercise. The database file must be created before you can create mailing labels.

- Click Tools, Labels to display the dialog box below:

■ Once you make your choice, the following dialog box displays:

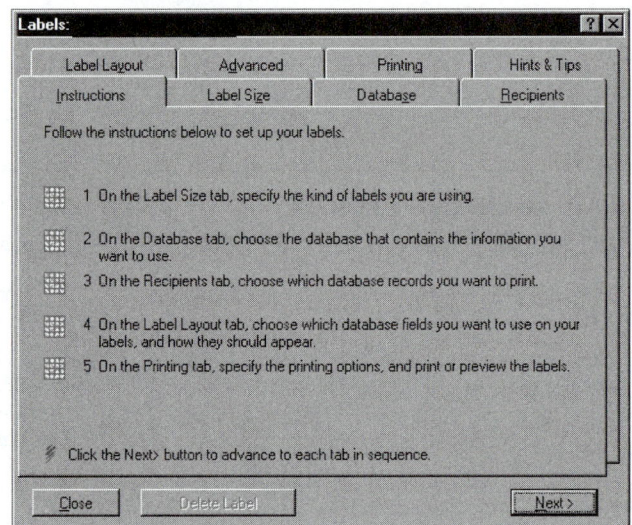

■ The **Labels** feature works in exactly the same way as the envelopes feature. Follow the steps on the Instructions tab and click Next to advance to each tab or click a tab and select the desired options for the labels.

The options are:

Label Size	Provides a list of label definitions. Select the appropriate definition from the Choose a label size list box. If you need special dimensions, select the Custom button to access the Custom Labels dialog box. Enter your label's dimensions to create your own label definition.
Database	Allows you to choose the database that contains the information you need for the labels.
Recipients	Provides options to specify the records for which you want labels.

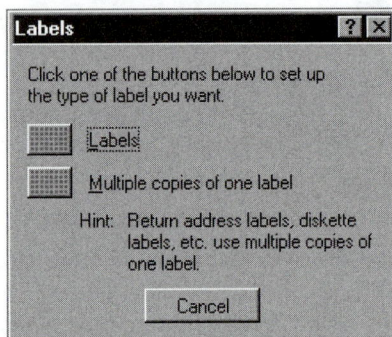

- Choose Labels to create mailing labels from a database file. However, if you want a single label, return address labels or disk labels, choose Multiple copies of one label.

Label Layout	Lists the fields associated with the desired database. Click the fields you want to use on your labels. Make changes to the position, spacing and punctuation between the fields in the Label layout text box. If you are not using a database, just type your label information in the Label layout textbox.
Advanced	Allows you to go back and edit the document.
Printing	Allows you to preview, test and print the labels.
Hints & Tips	Offers helpful advice on creating, editing and enhancing labels.

- As with envelopes, once the label is created for an accompanying letter, Works inserts the label placeholders at the top of the word processing document in Normal view and on a separate page in Page Layout view.

- If the information is too big for the label, try reducing the font size.

- Before printing all the labels, run a print test to see if the information aligns correctly with the label form. A print test takes up two rows on the label form. However, you do not have to discard the test label and start the print job from the beginning since Works allows you to specify which row to begin printing the labels. Click Printing, First row to print to specify a starting row.

- Works provides a variety of standard size labels. You will need to decide which ones work best with your printer. If you get an error message stating the labels will not print correctly, follow the instructions to correct the problem. You may need to change the label size or the dimensions of the label page. Preview the labels before printing. Whichever label you select for the document will become the default label.

In this exercise, you will create mailing labels for the merge of the SPORTS letter and the MEMBER database that was created in Exercise 9.

EXERCISE DIRECTIONS:

1. Open **SPORTS**, or open **IN SPORTS.13**.

2. Create the mailing labels shown in the illustration for the merged documents using a preset definition.

3. Preview the labels.

4. Print the labels.

5. Resave the file.

6. Close the document window.

Ms. Leanne Barnes
808 Summer St.
Anaheim, CA 92803

Mr. Miles Brown
154 Newburg Rd.
Anaheim, CA 92804

Mr. Stuart Griffith
1551 Dean St.
Beverly Hills, CA 90210

Mr. Michael Moon
32 Oak St.
Beverly Hills, CA 80210

Ms. Trinia Smith
3954 Wood Ave.
Anaheim, CA 92803

Ms. Sheila Smith
417 Specific Ct.
Anaheim, CA 92803

Ms. Bette Walker-Sim
1745 River St.
North Hollywood, CA 91615

Mr. Carl Castillo
1956 Park Ave.
North Hollywood, CA 91615

Mr. John Davis
P.O. Box 2333
North Hollywood, CA 91615

Ms. Amy Dixon
23 Albee St.
North Hollywood, CA 91615

Ms. Gale Kendall
15 Imperial Way
Beverly Hills, CA 90210

Ms. Janice Dagger
27 Ocean Ave.
Anaheim, CA 92804

Mr. Michael Chow
88 Riverside Dr.
Culver City, CA 90311

Mr. David Wagner
879 Beverly Dr.
Beverly Hills, CA 90210

Ms. Cleo Smith
90 Rodeo Dr.
Beverly Hills, CA 90210

Ms. Carolyn Anderson
666 Santa Ana Dr.
Culver City, CA 90312

Ms. Nazmine Ramaz
9012 Wilshire Blvd.
Beverly Hills, CA 90210

Mr. Winston Yakar
776 Prince Lane
North Hollywood, CA 91615

Ms Mary Mancuso
12 Pacific Ct.
North Hollywood, CA 91615

CREATE AND PRINT LABELS

1. Create the database first.
2. Create or Open the word processing document
3. Click **T**ools .... `Alt`+`T`
4. Click **L**abels .... `Alt`+`L`
5. Click **L**abels .... `Alt`+`L`
6. Click **OK** .... `Enter`
7. Click **N**ext .... `N`
   to advance to the next tab

✓ NOTE: If a tab has previously been selected, as evidenced by a check mark in the Instructions tab, Works automatically opens the next unchecked tab. You can select any tab in the dialog box without pressing Next.

In the **Label size** tab .... `Alt`+`Z`
a. Click **Choose a** .... `Alt`+`H`
   Label size.
b. Click desired size.
   OR
   Click **Custom** .... `Alt`+`U`
c. Click **N**ext .... `Alt`+`N`

8. Click **N**ext .... `N`
   to advance to the next tab.
   In the **Database** tab .... `Alt`+`S`
   a. Click **Choose a database** ... `Alt`+`H`
   b. Click desired Database
   c. Click **N**ext .... `Alt`+`N`

✓ NOTE: If you are using a form letter that has been previously associated with a database, the database checkbox is checked on the Instructions tab. Works will automatically open the next unchecked tab. Click the Database tab if you wish to use a different database.

9. Click **N**ext .... `N`
   to advance to the next tab.
   In the **Recipients** tab .... `Alt`+`R`
   a. Click one of the following options:
   - **All records in** .... `Alt`+`L`
     the database
   - **Current records** .... `Alt`+`U`
     visible in the database
   - **Currently marked** .... `Alt`+`K`
     records in the database

   - **Filtered records** .... `Alt`+`F`
     in the database
   b. Click **Current Filter** .... `Alt`+`T`
      OR
      Click **Change Filter** .... `Alt`+`H`
      to create a new filter
   c. Click **N**ext .... `Alt`+`N`
10. Click **N**ext .... `N`
    to advance to the next tab.
    In the **Label Layout** tab .... `Alt`+`Y`
    a. Click desired fields
    b. Click **Label layout** .... `Alt`+`B`
    c. Edit placeholders as needed.
    d. Click **N**ext .... `Alt`+`N`
11. Click **N**ext .... `N`
    to advance to the next tab.
    In the **Printing** tab .... `Alt`+`G`
    a. Click **Preview** .... `Alt`+`W`
       OR
       Click **T**est .... `Alt`+`E`
       OR
       Click **Print** .... `Alt`+`P`
    b. Click **N**ext .... `Alt`+`N`
12. Click **Close** .... `Alt`+`C`

EXERCISE **14**

Integration – Summary

In this exercise you will work with three documents:
* Create a letterhead for the GLOBAL COMMUNICATIONS COMPANY
* Edit the PROMOTE database.
* Create a letter with mailing labels to merge print with the PROMOTE database.
You will send out letters to all employees on company letterhead informing them of their promotions and new salaries. You will print a label for each letter.

EXERCISE DIRECTIONS:

Letterhead Directions

1. Create a letterhead for the GLOBAL COMMUNICATIONS COMPANY to include the following information:

   GLOBAL COMMUNICATIONS COMPANY
   COMPANY HEADQUARTERS
   150 Broadway
   Abilene, TX 79603
   Phone: (217) 555 - 4343
   Fax: (217) 555 - 4400

2. Format the letterhead as desired using any combination of ClipArt, WordArt, Borders, Fonts, and Header/Footers. Compare your results with the letterhead in Illustration A.

   ✓ NOTE: *Create the letterhead in the header or decrease the top margin.*

3. Print one copy.

4. Save the letterhead; name it **LH COMM**.

Database Directions

1. Open **PROMOTE**, or open **IN PROMOTE.14**.

2. Insert a new field at the beginning of the database; name it **TITLE**.

3. Enter the field data as shown on Illustration B.

4. Sort the database in alphabetical order by the **LAST** name of each employee.

5. Change the information for the employees listed in the table below to reflect their promotions:

6. Mark the records of these employees.

7. Print one copy of the newly edited database in Landscape orientation. Make any changes necessary to make the database print on one page.

8. Resave the database.

LAST	FIRST	POSITION	WKSAL	ANNSAL
Gregonis	Dimitri	Customer Service Manager	$408.65	$21,250
Lee	Chin	Sr. Vice President	$769.23	$40,000
Palmieri	Marie	Floor Manager	$423.07	$22,000

Letter Directions

1. Open the **LH COMM** letterhead.

2. Type the letter in Illustration C on the letterhead form. Format appropriately.

3. Insert placeholders as indicated.

4. Preview the letter and make any changes necessary to make it fit on one page.

5. Create mailing labels to merge with all the records in the database.

6. Print one copy of the mailing labels.

7. Go back to the Form letters and change the recipients to the *currently marked records* in the database.

8. Print the three form letters.

9. Create envelopes for these three letters. *NOTE: The envelopes will replace the labels.*

10. Print one copy of the envelopes.

11. Close the file, save the changes. Name it **PROMOTE 2**.

ILLUSTRATION A

ILLUSTRATION C

GLOBAL COMMUNICATIONS COMPANY

Phone: (217) 555-4343
Fax: (217) 555-4400

COMPANY HEADQUARTERS
150 Broadway
Abilene, TX 79603

Today's date

«TITLE» «FIRST» «LAST»
«ADDRESS»
«CITY», «ST» «ZIP»

Dear «FIRST»:

Congratulations on your promotion. It is the policy of the Global Communications Company to promote from within. The reasons are two-fold: To reward those employees who have excellent performance records, and to maintain an outstanding work force which is the backbone of our company. We thank you for your past contributions, and look forward to working with you in your new position.

As we discussed at your last semi-annual review, you will be assuming the position of «POSITION» in the «DEPT» Department at the «BRANCH» store. You will begin on January 1 with a new annual salary of «ANNSAL», breaking down to «WKSAL» weekly. If you have any questions concerning the above, please do not hesitate to call me.

As we discussed previously, all promotions become effective on the first of the year. Prior to beginning your new responsibilities, you will participate in a two-week training seminar. Additional information will be forthcoming.

You have been a member of our staff since «HIRED», and we look forward to many more years of valued service. Again, congratulations on your promotion and a job well done.

Sincerely,

Phil A. Busta
Personnel Director

yo

ILLUSTRATION B
Insert field and add data
↓

	TITLE	LAST	FIRST	ADDRESS	CITY	ST	ZIP	BRANCH	ID NO	HIRED	POSITION	DEPT	WKSAL	ANNSAL
1	Mr.	Accosta	Anthony	1314 13th Avenue	Brooklyn	NY	11219	Brooklyn	13929	1/3/90	Assistant Manager	Sales	$454.81	$23,650
2	Mr.	Carson	George	2505 Benson Avenue	Brooklyn	NY	11236	Manhattan	14078	4/1/92	Administrative Assistant	Admin.	$389.76	$20,267
3	Mr.	Carson	Laurence	34 Flower Avenue	Merrick	NY	11566	Manhattan	14356	9/30/91	Assistant Supervisor	Stock	$355.77	$18,500
4	Mr.	Carson	Penn	2234 Montgomery Street	Brooklyn	NY	11213	Manhattan	14399	8/25/93	Sales Representative	Sales	$259.62	$13,500
5	Mr.	Gregonis	Dimitri	7200 Moore Avenue	Los Angeles	CA	90066	Los Angeles	14395	5/15/93	Customer Service Rep	Admin.	$317.31	$16,500
6	Mr.	Hopkins	George	35 Gates Place	Tappan	NY	10983	Bronx	14396	5/30/92	Inventory Supervisor	Stock	$391.35	$20,350
7	Mr.	Lee	Randy	8234 Cigna Lane	Laguna Beach	CA	92650	Los Angeles	13298	5/15/91	Assistant Coordinator	Stock	$365.80	$19,021
8	Mr.	Lee	Chin	62 Orange Court	LaHabra	CA	90631	Los Angeles	13254	1/6/89	Vice President	Sales	$673.08	$35,000
9	Mr.	Lee	Michael	34 Woodrow Road	Staten Island	NY	10312	Queens	14295	5/1/90	Warehouse Coordinator	Stock	$509.62	$26,500
10	Mr.	Martino	John	1001 Costa Drive	Berkley	CA	94704	San Francisco	14289	3/5/91	A/R Bookkeeper	Admin.	$403.85	$21,000
11	Mr.	Naidle	Adam	334 Roxbury Drive	Beverly Hills	CA	90210	Los Angeles	14321	7/25/91	Senior Review Clerk	Sales	$301.35	$15,670
12	Ms.	Palmieri	Marie	2044 Waterview Drive	Edgewater	NJ	07020	Fort Lee	14367	11/1/91	Senior Stock Clerk	Stock	$339.42	$17,650
13	Mr.	Parsons	Kyle	876 Rocky Point Drive	Yorktown Heights	NY	10598	Manhattan	14398	8/12/93	A/P Bookkeeper	Admin.	$360.58	$18,750
14	Mr.	Rogers	Jane	346 La Vista Road	Berkley	CA	94704	San Francisco	14024	2/15/90	Marketing Analyst	Sales	$432.69	$22,500
15	Mr.	Samtanai	Perkash	67 Main Street	Los Angeles	CA	90012	Los Angeles	14354	9/1/91	Sales Rep, Level II	Sales	$259.62	$13,500
16	Ms.	Sawyer	Harriet	354 Marisol Road	Los Angeles	CA	90020	Long Beach	13290	5/1/89	Supervisor, Computer Operations	Admin.	$473.08	$24,600
17	Ms.	Tommie	Lori	344 Van Buren Drive	Baldwin Harbor	NY	11510	Manhattan	13852	11/1/89	Manager	Stock	$567.31	$29,500
18	Ms.	Valdez	Lina	344 Woodland Lane	Denby	CT	06418	Queens	14385	2/1/92	Payroll Supervisor	Admin.	$528.85	$27,500
19	Ms.	Viacomma	Maria	25433 Crown Street	Woodland Hills	CA	91365	Los Angeles	14397	7/15/93	Executive Assistant	Admin.	$418.85	$21,780
20	Ms.	Watterson	Cathy	456 Adrienne Road	Staten Island	NY	10305	Manhattan	14269	12/15/90	Advertising Rep	Sales	$394.23	$20,500
21	Mr.	Wilson	Robert	34 Oak Place	E. Brunswick	NJ	08816	Fort Lee	14235	11/1/90	Order Processing Clerk	Stock	$338.46	$17,600

TaskWizards and Templates

Exercises 1 - 5

■ **Create a Letterhead with a TaskWizard**
■ **Integrate a Letterhead with a Letter** ■ **Create a Template**

NOTES:

Create a Letterhead with a TaskWizard

■ This lesson introduces two features, TaskWizards and Templates, that help you to produce professional looking documents easily and quickly. A wizard creates the document offering you options in the process, while a template is already designed.

■ A **TaskWizard** is a time-saving feature which allows you to customize common documents, such as letterheads and form letters, as well as phone book, database and inventory files.

■ The TaskWizard asks you a series of questions concerning the layout of the document. As you make your choices, the wizard displays a preview of the document. After you make all your selections and approve the final format, the wizard creates the document.

■ You can create a TaskWizard document at any time while you are in Works. You can access TaskWizards from the Works Task Launcher dialog box shown below:

■ From the list in the dialog box, choose the type of document you wish to produce. In this exercise, you will create a TaskWizard letterhead. Once you select the desired wizard, the following dialog box displays:

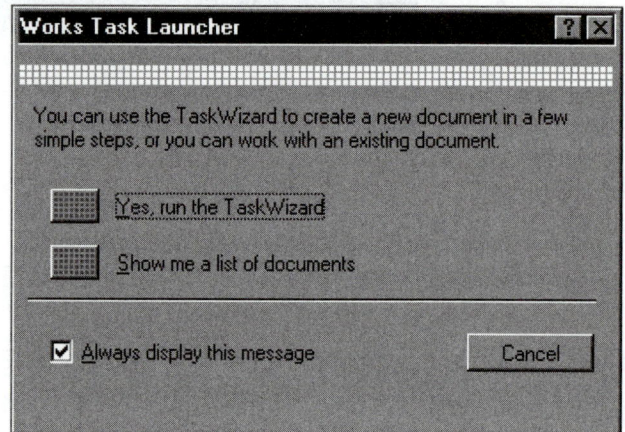

You will be asked to choose between running the wizard or selecting a document from a list of documents that have been previously created by the wizard.

■ Most wizard pages contain three buttons: Back, Cancel and Next.

Back button	Allows you to return to a previous screen to make changes.
Cancel button	Cancels the wizard.
Next button	Brings you to the next step in the process.
CREATE IT! button	On the last screen in the process, you click this button to ask Works to create the document type specified.

414

- The Letterhead wizard also creates a letter to accompany the letterhead. You can create your letter by selecting one or more of the following options.

  - Specify a single address or merge the letter with a database file.

  - Choose from a list of letters written by professional writers or choose to write your own.

  - Choose the text style of the letter.

  - Specify additional letter elements to be included in the letter.

- Works automatically creates an accompanying letter with the letterhead. You may use this letter, or if you wish to use only the letterhead, you may delete the letter and save the letterhead. In this way, you can reuse the letterhead with other letters. You will delete the accompanying letter for this exercise.

Create a Template

- A **template** is a predesigned file that provides a quick way to produce your documents because the formats, layout and formulas are already in place. Once you retrieve the appropriate template, all you have to do is enter your information. After your information is entered, save the file with a new filename that identifies the data in the template. The template itself is not changed and can be used over and over again.

- You can save any document as a template. Click Save As, Template to access the following dialog box:

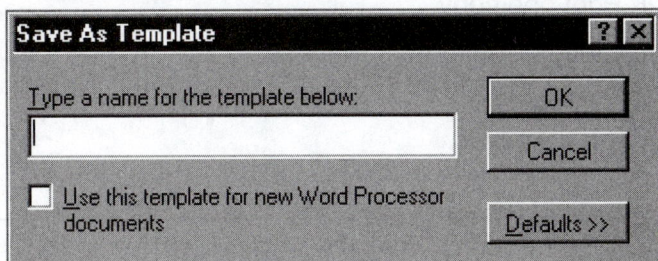

Save As Template	?	X
Type a name for the template below:	OK	
	Cancel	
☐ Use this template for new Word Processor documents	Defaults >>	

Supply a filename for the template. You can also designate the template as the default document. Choose this option only if you want to have the same document automatically opened every time you create a new document. You can specify one default template for each Works tool.

- In other words, when you open a template, you open a copy. Feel free to make changes. The original template remains intact, even saving with the same filename does not destroy the template.

Integrate a Letterhead with a Letter

- You can type a letter directly on the letterhead page, or you can open a previously saved letter and copy and paste it onto the letterhead page. If you are copying from one document to another you can press Ctrl+F6 to toggle back and forth between documents, or you can click Window to access the documents you need to use.

> *In this exercise, you will create a letterhead and save it. You will then open a letter and integrate it with the letterhead. The new document containing the letterhead and the letter will be saved under a different name.*
>
> ✓ *NOTE: Only the first page of a multiple-page letter is on a letterhead. The second and succeeding pages of a multiple-page letter should contain a header with the name of the addressee, the page number and the date. All subsequent pages are on plain paper which should match the color and texture of the letterhead paper.*

EXERCISE DIRECTIONS:

1. Click the TaskWizards tab in the Works Task Launcher dialog box.

2. Double-click on Letterhead and choose Yes to run the TaskWizard.

3. Select Professional style.

4. Click Next button.

5. Click the Letterhead button.

6. Choose I want to design my own.

7. Click Next.

8. Choose the Art Deco option.

9. Click Next.

10. Supply the following company name: GLOBAL TRAVEL GROUP

11. Click Next.

12. Use the Tab key to advance to each box in this section and enter the following information:

Address Line 1	485 Madison Avenue
City, State/Province, Postal Code	New York, NY 10034

    ✓ *NOTE: Delete any data from the address lines you are not including in your letterhead.*

13. Click Next.

14. Enter the following phone information:

Work phone number:	(212) 555-4566
Fax number:	(212) 555-9877

15. Click Next.

16. View the letterhead in the sample box. If you need to make changes, click the left arrow to go back.

17. Once everything is correct, click OK.

18. Click Create It!

19. Read the checklist. If everything is correct, click Create Document.

20. Delete the text from the date through the closing.

21. Save the letterhead as a template; name it **LHGLOBAL**.

22. Do not close the document window.

23. Open **DIVING**, or open **WW DIVING.1**.

24. Copy the entire document.

25. Switch to the letterhead window and position the insertion point where the date should appear.

26. Paste **DIVING** into the letterhead document.

    ✓ *NOTE: Make all necessary adjustments to the placement of the letter. Keep the letter two pages in length, and adjust the placement of the second page heading so it remains at the top of the second page.*

27. Save the file; name it **LHDIVE**.

28. Print one copy.

29. Close all document windows.

TASKWIZARD LETTERHEAD

1. Click **TaskWizards**................ `Alt`+`K`
   from Works Task Launcher dialog box.

2. Click **Letterhead**.
   OR
   Use arrow keys to locate selection bar on letterhead.

3. Click **OK**.................................. `Enter`

4. Follow instructions provided by the Wizard.

   –FROM WITHIN WORKS –

1. Click **File** .... `Alt`+`F`

2. Click **New** .... `N`

3. Repeat steps 2-4 above.

CREATE A TEMPLATE

1. Click **File** .... `F`

2. Click **Save As** .... `A`

3. Click **Template** .... `T`

4. Enter a template name.................*name*

5. Click **OK**.................................. `Enter`

GLOBAL TRAVEL GROUP

◆ ◆ ◆

485 Madison Avenue
New York, NY 10034
◆
Phone (212) 555-4566
Fax (212) 555-9877

Today's date

Mr. Kenyatta Belcher
80 Avenue C
Cambridge, MA 01238

Dear Ken:

SUBJECT: Diving in the Cayman Islands

Do you want to see sharks, barracudas, stingrays and angelfish?

The Cayman Islands were discovered by Christopher Columbus in 1503 and are located south of Cuba. The Caymans are the home to only about 25,000 year-round residents. However, they welcome 200,000 visitors each year. Most visitors come with masks and flippers in their luggage.

Before you descend the depths of the ocean, it is important that you have a few lessons on the do's and don'ts of diving. Don't touch the coral, and don't come up to the surface too fast holding your breath. Now, you are ready to jump in.

Here are some hotel suggestions:

Hotel/Diving Accommodations:

Anchorage View
PO Box 2123, East End, Grand Cayman; (809) 555-4209. Pool, four restaurants; check in 9 a.m., check out 2 p.m. Famous for outstanding view of the harbor from all rooms. Popular night spot among tourists and locals alike.

Cayman Diving Lodge
PO Box 11, East End, Grand Cayman; (809) 555-7555. No pool, room service available; check in 12 noon, check out 4 p.m. Basic accommodations, low rates. Diving expeditions three times daily at extra cost.

Coconut Harbour
PO Box 2086, George Town, Grand Cayman; (809) 555-6468. Pool, two restaurants; check in 12 noon, check out 4 p.m. Free scuba exhibitions nightly.

PO Box 1588, George Town, Grand Cayman; (809) 555-7965. Pool, three restaurants; check in 11 a.m., check out 3 p.m. Wind surfing and parasailing available at extra cost.

PO Box 479, George Town, Grand Cayman; (809) 555-4767. Pool, three restaurants; check in 11 a.m., check out 3 p.m.

Diving Instruction:

PO Box 11, East End, Grand Cayman; (809) 555-7555. No pool, room service available; check in 12 noon, check out 4 p.m. Basic accommodations, low rates. Diving expeditions three times daily at extra cost.

Sunset House
PO Box 479, George Town, Grand Cayman; (809) 555-4767. Pool, three restaurants; check in 11 a.m., check out 3 p.m.

This is a great vacation spot. Let me know when you are ready to make reservations. Meanwhile, if you have any questions, please give me a call.

Yours truly,

John Rogers
Travel Agent

jr/yo

■ **Address Book TaskWizard**

NOTES:

- The **address book** created by the Address Book TaskWizard is a database which contains names, addresses and additional related information.

- Click the TaskWizards tab from the Works Task Launcher and choose Address Book from the Common Tasks category. The following screen displays:

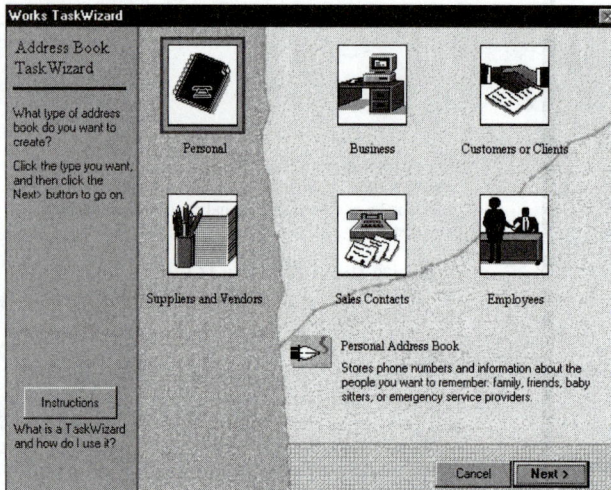

- The wizard allows you to choose the type of address book that is best suited to your needs. In the Address TaskWizard screen shown above, click each address book type to see a brief description. In this lesson, we will create a personal address book.

- Works offers options to include additional pre-defined fields, and to add your own fields to customize your address book.

- The wizard also can generate reports based on the information in your database. Choose this feature if you want Works to define the report format. There are two formats: Alphabetized directory or Categorized directory. A **categorized directory** involves a secondary sort which lists your information according to a specific field and then alphabetizes within the category. Note the illustration of the alphabetized report created by the wizard.

- You can designate the address book as the default address book. The default address book can be opened from any of the Works tools: Word Processor, Spreadsheet, Database and Communications. This is akin to having a Rolodex® right on your desktop. You automatically access the address book when you click the Address Book button 🖳 on the Toolbar.

- To make an address book the default, select the **Yes, I want this to be my default address book** option from within the Wizard. If you do not designate a default address book, Works automatically asks if it should run the Address Book TaskWizard when you click the Toolbar button.

- Remember, the address book is actually a database and each page is a record. To enter information in a field, use the arrow keys to highlight the field, then enter your data. Use the Tab key to advance to the next field.

- Decrease the Zoom factor to see the entire record, and Press Ctrl+PageDown to access the next record.

- If you want to enter data into a protected field, you must unprotect it. You will need to do this to the REMINDER field for Birthdays and Anniversaries. Follow these steps to allow entry into the field:

  - Click View, Form Design.
  - Click Format, Protection.

- Deselect the Protect check box.
- Click OK.
- Click View, Form.
- Enter your data.

- Sort the address book using the same procedure presented in the database section. (*See Database Lesson 4, Exercise 19*).

In this exercise, you will create a small personal address book using the names, addresses and other information provided below. Once you are familiar with the procedure, you will create your own personal address book.

EXERCISE DIRECTIONS:

1. Click the TaskWizards tab on the Works Task Launcher dialog box.

2. Choose Address Book from the Common Tasks category.

3. Click Yes, run the TaskWizard.

4. Click each type of address book and read the description.

5. Select Personal Address Book.

6. Click Next.

7. After reading the fields contained in the address book, click Next.

8. Click Additional Fields:
   a. Click Personal information.
   b. Click OK.

9. Click Reports.
   a. Click Alphabetized directory.
   b. Click OK.

10. Click Create It!

11. Read the checklist and check to see you have the following:

    Address book type: Personal
    Additional fields: Personal information
    Reports: Alphabetized directory

12. Click *No, don't change my default address book.*

13. Click Create Document.

14. Enter the information for the two illustrated records using the Tab key to advance to each field.

    ✓ NOTE   *Remove protection to enter data into protected cells.*

15. Press Ctrl+PageDown to access the second record.

16. Enter the information.

17. Press Ctrl+PageDown to access the third record.

18. Enter your personal information.

19. Print each record from Form View.

20. Click View, Report to see the report created by the Wizard.

21. Click Preview.

22. Print the report.

23. Save the file; name it **SAMPLE ADDRESS BOOK**.

24. Create another personal address book using the Address Book Wizard as follows:
    a. Use the personal address book format.
    b. Choose Personal Information for the additional fields.
    c. Choose Your Own Fields and create a field for Emergency No.
    d. Choose alphabetized report.
    e. Enter the information for your friends, family members, emergency numbers, etc.

25. Designate this address book to be the default address book.

26. Print the file.

27. Save the file; name it **ADDRESS BOOK**.

28. Close the document window.

PERSONAL ADDRESS BOOK

March 21, 1996

REMINDER: Birthdays this month? | Yes

REMINDER: Anniversary this month? | Yes

Title: Mr.   *Mr. Mrs. Ms. Miss*

Last name: Stephens

First name: David

Middle name: Craig

Home phone: (516) 555-7899

Entry date: February 01, 1996

Category: Friend

Company: New Meadows Schools

Position: Teacher

Business type: Education

ADDRESS

Address1: 786 Western Avenue

Address2:

City: New Meadows

State or Prov: NY

Postal code: 11554

Country:

PERSONAL AND FAMILY INFORMATION

	Children	Birth Dates
Nickname: Prof	Wendy	7/6/73
Birthday: November 05, 1945	Horace	5/26/76
Anniversary: February 03, 1968		
Spouse's name: Dorothy		
Spouse bday: October 19, 1947		

PERSONAL ADDRESS BOOK

April 01, 1996

REMINDER: Birthdays this month? | No

REMINDER: Anniversary this month? | No

Title: Mr.   *Mr. Mrs. Ms. Miss*

Last name: Rogers

First name: John

Middle name:

Home phone: (212) 555-3454

Entry date: March 01, 1996

Category: Travel Agent

Company: Global Travel Group

Position: Agent

Business type: Travel Agency

ADDRESS

Address1: 485 Madison Avenue

Address2:

City: New York

State or Prov: NY

Postal code: 10034

Country:

PERSONAL AND FAMILY INFORMATION

	Children	Birth Dates
Nickname:		
Birthday:		
Anniversary:		
Spouse's name:		
Spouse bday:		

EXERCISE 3

■ Grade Book TaskWizard

NOTES:

Grade Book TaskWizard

- Works has created a TaskWizard to help record and compile test data for the classroom teacher.

- The Grade Book TaskWizard creates a spreadsheet to tally, average and provide weighted averages.

- The Wizard offers three types of grade books:

- **Standard** - Calculates averages and grades based on the combined scores for the class assignments and tests.

- **Modified** - Calculates separate grades and averages for class assignments and tests.

- **Weighted** - Tallies grades based on tests and the weighted average of assignments.

- Again, you must turn off the cell protection to enter data into a protected cell.

In this exercise, you will use the Grade Book TaskWizard to create a grade book. You will then enter student information and grades and compute the 2nd quarter averages for the Computer Literacy class.

EXERCISE DIRECTIONS:

1. From the Works Task Launcher, access the Tas<u>k</u>Wizards.

2. Select Grade Book from the Students and Teachers category.

3. Choose the Standard Grade Book option.

4. Click Create It!

5. Enter the following information in the designated cell locations:

C3:	Computer Literacy - Period 1
E10:	SS1
F10:	CONSS1

G10:	SS2
H10:	CONSS2
I10:	SS3
J10:	CONSS3

✓ NOTE: *The column headings SS1 and ConSS1 refer to the type of test. SS1 is an actual spreadsheet and ConSS1 is a short answer test evaluating spreadsheet concepts. These headings apply to the second and third series of tests as well.*

6. Enter the illustrated student names beginning in cell A12 and their grades beginning in cell E12.

7. Format all test grades as a general number with no decimal places.

STUDENTS	SS1	CONSS1	SS2	CONSS2	SS3	CONSS3
Torey Johnson	95	85	98	92	94	78
Donny Haber	75		88	82	88	75
Lenny Stone	85	90	98	88	90	80
Nicole Neifer	70	75	80	78	78	67
Jennifer Sooth	90	80	85	92	90	88
Andy West	87	78	80	85	90	72
Philip Washington	78	83	84	77	80	75
Victor Hernandez	82	72	77	76	78	76
Yu Chang	88	90	92	80	84	80
Jasmine Yee	60	58	52		65	
Helen Anderson	68	70	67	71	75	68
Corey Henderson	55	62	54	63	60	52
Katie O'Hara	72	83	70	78	87	72
Erica Green	98	100	95	96	95	95

8. Save the file; name it **COMPUTER LITERACY PER. 1**.

9. Print one copy.

   ✓ NOTE: *Check your document in Print Preview to see how many pages have been created. Print only those pages that contain data.*

10. Close the document window.

11. Answer the following based on the spreadsheet results:

   a. Who had the highest score on the first test?

   b. Who had the lowest grade on the last test?

   c. Who missed two tests?

   d. Which function was used to compute the letter grades?

■ **Brochure TaskWizard**

NOTES:

Brochure TaskWizard

■ The TaskWizards take the worry out of designing documents. The Brochure Wizard from the Correspondence or Business Management group, for example, offers you three options to set up an advertising brochure. They are:

Two Panel This is a simple folded brochure you can use to advertise your product.

Jazzy Three-Panel This option adds pictures and borders to a three-panel layout.

Simple Three Panel This option is a simple layout without graphic elements. It works well with a border.

■ The document is created with placeholder text that you will replace with your information. Use the Overtype mode to replace the placeholder text.

■ Once the text is replaced, highlight the text to be reformatted and make the desired changes. In addition to font, font size and typestyle changes, you can add lines between the columns, alter the spacing between the columns and add graphics as desired.

> *In this exercise, you will create a three-panel brochure to advertise the Business Department course offerings at New Meadows High School.*

EXERCISE DIRECTIONS:

1. Access the Brochure TaskWizard.

2. Choose Jazzy Three Panel.

3. Click Create It!

4. Make the following changes:

   left and right margins   0.5"
   top and bottom margins   0.7"

5. Copy the text from the illustration to replace placeholder text.

6. Format the brochure to duplicate the illustration as closely as possible.

7. Change all fonts and point sizes as indicated on the illustration.

8. All body text should be set to serif 10 point.

9. Make necessary adjustments to font, font size and graphics elements to fit the document on two pages.

10. Save the file; name it **BROCHURE**.

11. Print one copy.

12. Close the document window.

Sans serif 16 point bold.

Sans serif 20 point bold. Delete underline from template

NEW MEADOWS HIGH SCHOOL
BUSINESS DEPARTMENT

◆ Mind Your Business

The Business Education Department offers a series of courses that can help you succeed in the future. Take a business course to explore a possible career, or to learn skills that will help you compete in today's global economy. Here's a sampling of what we offer:

- Keyboarding - This 1/2 year course is the *key* to success. Learn touch typing to do your school papers and future business reports. All computers use a keyboard--learn to use it the right way.

- Computer Literacy/Applications - Learn the most popular computer applications used in business today. Become familiar with word processing, spreadsheets, database and desktop publishing.

- Accounting - Explore an accounting career. Enter the world of high finance and join many of our programs' graduates who have become successful CPA's.

Serif 12 point bold

■ Room 104
■ New Meadows High School

Sans serif 14 point bold

◆ Much Much More.....

We offer many additional courses. Take a variety of electives ranging from Marketing and Advertising to Hotel and Restaurant Management. You can even get a head start on your college credits. Take advanced placement courses in accounting and business law and graduate high school with up to 9 college credits.

Do you need to work while you are attending high school? We have the answer. Enroll in our Cooperative Education program and get school credit in addition to your salary. We also offer paid and non-paid internships in many fields. We have students working for the cable TV company, in the hospital pharmacy and in local businesses.

Interested in extracurricular activities? As a business student, you can join the Future Business Leaders of America and participate in charity drives, contests and scholarship programs.

We offer so many options and the space on this brochure is limited. **Sooo**, if you are interested or have any questions, please see your guidance counselor or make an appointment to see Mr. Kenneth Ilocis, Chairperson of the Business Department in Room 401.

Sans serif 14 point bold

◆ Need a Job?

Have a lot of expenses and your allowance just doesn't make it? Come into our placement office in Room 403 and see Mrs. DeMoler. She may have a job for you.

Serif 14 point bold

Mind your business and take a business course. Pay attention to your future needs and be prepared. Sign up today!!!!!

TaskWizards and Templates– Summary

In this exercise, you will send a letter of application for a position in industrial sales and marketing to four different companies. Using the TaskWizards, you will create a database file of the companies you are applying to as well as a form letter to merge with the database.

EXERCISE DIRECTIONS:

1. Access the Start From Scratch TaskWizard from the Works Task Launcher.

2. Choose Yes, run the TaskWizard.

3. Choose Database. Click Next.

4. Click Fields. Click Name and Address fields. Click OK.

5. Click Text Style. Click Contemporary. Click OK.

6. Click Create It!

7. Compare your results with the following:

TOOL:	Database
FIELDS:	Name and Address Fields
TEXT STYLE:	Contemporary

8. Click Create Document.

9. Switch to List view and from the illustrated source documents on the next page, enter the data for each company in the appropriate fields. (Use the Tab key to advance to each field.)

10. Save the file; name it **PAPER COMPANY**.

11. Access the Correspondence category from the TaskWizards tab in the Works TaskLauncher and choose Form Letter.

12. Chose Yes, run the TaskWizard.

13. Choose Simple style. Click Next.

14. Click Letterhead and select: I want to design my own. Click Next.

15. Choose the Contemporary option and click Next.

16. Deselect Company name, click the Personal name checkbox and enter your name. Click Next.

17. Provide your personal information for the letterhead. Use the Tab key to advance to each field.

18. Deselect work phone number and enter your home phone and fax number for the phone information. Click Next.

19. When prompted that you are finished designing the letterhead, review the letterhead and click OK.

20. Click Content and choose the Resume cover letter. Click OK.

21. Click Extras and choose the Enclosure option. Type 1 in the text box. Click OK.

22. Click Text Style and choose Contemporary. Click OK.

23. Click Address.

24. Click I want to use addresses from a Works database. Click Next.

25. Click The file I want to use checkbox.

26. Choose the **PAPER COMPANY** from the list. Click Next.

27. Click the appropriate fields in the correct order for the address box. Click New Line to place a field on a new line and click comma after the City field is placed. Click Next.

28. Add the Title and Last Name field for the Greeting line. Click Next.

29. When prompted: You are finished addressing your letter, click OK.

30. Cick Create It!

31. Check to see you have the following options:

   Simple
   Wizard-designed Letterhead
   Addresses from **PAPER COMPANY**
   Resume cover letter
   Contemporary
   Enclosures 1

32. Click Create document.

33. Delete the LETTER WRITING TIPS.

34. Make the following changes in the letter:

- Change the comma after the salutation to a colon.

- Change the phone number in the third paragraph to your home phone number.

- Type your name to replace the name placeholder in the closing.

35. Make sure the closing is a double space below the last line of the body.

36. View the letter in the Print Preview and make any adjustments necessary to attractively format the letter. Pay particular attention to the vertical placement of the letter. There should be approximately the same amount of space between the letter and the top and bottom margins.

✓ NOTE: If you have any questions concerning the spacing between the various parts of the letter, refer to Word Processing, Ex. 7 illustration. You must make adjustments to the letter before merging the letter with the database; otherwise, you will need to make the adjustments on each letter in the merge.

37. Save the file; name it **COVER LETTER**.

38. Print the letter. You should have four copies with each one addressed to a different company.

39. Close the document window.

NAMES AND ADDRESSES

Title: *Mr.*

Last Name: *Hanover*

First Name: *Charles*

Middle Name:

Relationship: *President*

ADDRESS

Address Line 1: *CCG, Incorporated*

Address Line 2: *110 Newbridge Avenue*

City: *Merrick*   State or Prov: *NY*

Postal Code: *11522*   Country:

Home Phone:

NAMES AND ADDRESSES

Title: Ms.

Last Name: Tarangello

First Name: Trisha

Middle Name:

Relationship: Vice President, Marketing

ADDRESS

Address Line 1: Write Right

Address Line 2: 345 Wakefield Road

City: Stony Brook   State or Prov: NY

Postal Code: 11794   Country:

Home Phone:

NAMES AND ADDRESSES

Title: Mr.

Last Name: Ortiz

First Name: Louis

Middle Name:

Relationship: Sales Manager

ADDRESS

Address Line 1: International Paper Products

Address Line 2: 875 Fifth Avenue

City: New York   State or Prov: NY

Postal Code: 10034   Country:

Home Phone:

NAMES AND ADDRESSES

Title: Ms.

Last Name: Henley

First Name: Teresa

Middle Name:

Relationship: Director of Marketing

ADDRESS

Address Line 1: Stationers Unlimited

Address Line 2: 896 East 36th Street

City: New York   State or Prov: NY

Postal Code: 10014   Country:

Home Phone:

Communications

Exercises 1 - 5

■ **Introduction to Communications** ■ **Begin a Communications Session**

Save   Paste

Copy

NOTES:

Introduction to Communications

■ **Communications** is a tool that allows your computer to communicate with other computers.

■ You can exchange mail with friends, colleagues or business associates from any location. You can send your messages locally or internationally.

■ You can connect to **bulletin boards**, which are services that allow the interchange of information with other users who have similar interests and/or avocations. Depending upon the bulletin board you may be able to send and receive messages, transfer files, obtain software and computer games. Many bulletin boards are free.

■ You can access the Internet using the Works communications tool. However, in most cases, you will have to pay a fee for this service.

■ You can also subscribe, for a monthly fee, to a **communications service**. These services provide information on entertainment, sports, travel, education, the stock market and other specialized interest. They also provide access to the Internet.

■ The information you obtain through the use of the Works Communications tool can be printed, saved or both. It can then be used in a report, letter or any other document you need to create.

■ In addition to your computer, you will need the following in order to communicate:

Modem

Computers communicate over phone lines using a device called a **modem**. A modem converts the signals so the computers can send or receive the information via the phone lines.

Phone line

You do not need a separate phone line. However, your phone line will be busy and you cannot receive or make any other calls while you are communicating on line. Be sure to disable your call waiting; otherwise, you will have a signal disruption.

Communications Software

In addition to the modem and phone line, you also need communications software. This is the program that allows you to send or receive information. The Communications tool in Works is your communications software.

Begin a Communications Session

■ When communicating for the first time using Works, the program starts the Modem Wizard. Follow the directions to install your modem. This procedure detects the appropriate settings and makes the modem available for use. You must configure your dialing properties to tell the computer where you are dialing from and how you want the call dialed. You can specify such items as: an area code, dial prefix (9 for an outside line), tone or pulse, disable call waiting (dial *70) or use of the computer from a different location.

- For communication to take place, your computer must recognize the signals sent by the other computer. Both computers must have the same settings to share information, just as two people must speak the same language to understand each other.

- When you start up Works, you are given standard settings that are generally used to establish a connection. These settings can be changed at any time if your communication does not work. (*See Adjust Settings, Exercise 2, p. 433*).

- To begin a communications session, your computer must dial the number you wish to reach. These numbers can be saved so that you do not have to redial them each time.

- Works offers a feature that allows you to easily access frequently used numbers. When you begin a new communications session, the Easy Connect dialog box appears.

- Fill in the information for the phone number and name of service. Works supplies information for the area code and country based on your dialing properties. The number you entered is dialed when you click OK. The name of the service appears in the Services list box whenever you open a new communications session. Click the name to reconnect to the service. Save the file to retain the names you entered. You can save up to eight frequently used names.

  ✓NOTE: *Be sure to enter all digits of the phone number. You may use hyphens or spaces to separate the parts of the number.*

- The Communications Toolbar, as shown at the top of page 430, is on the top of every communications screen. The Works Task Launcher buttons, Save, Copy and Paste are the same in all the tools. The other buttons will be introduced in later lessons.

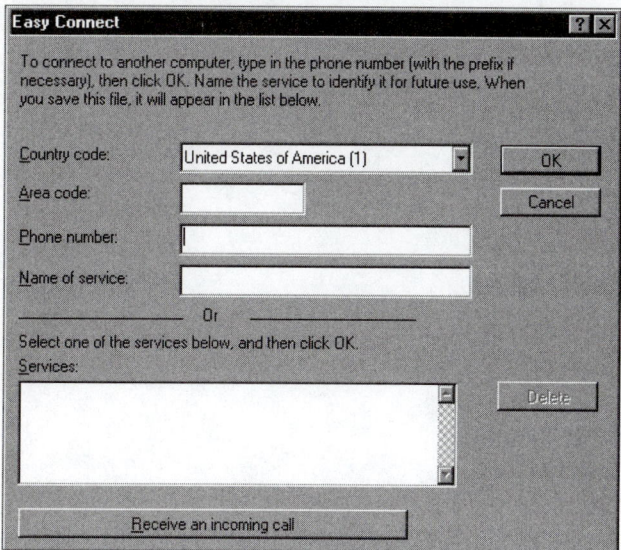

Easy Connect   ? ☒

To connect to another computer, type in the phone number (with the prefix if necessary), then click OK. Name the service to identify it for future use. When you save this file, it will appear in the list below.

Country code: United States of America (1) ▼   OK

Area code: [   ]   Cancel

Phone number: [   ]

Name of service: [   ]

——————————— Or ———————————

Select one of the services below, and then click OK.

Services:
[   ]   Delete

[Receive an incoming call]

> *In this exercise, you will simulate starting a communications session to communicate with B & B Talk, a bulletin board. You will enter a phone number and the name of the service in the Easy Connect dialog box.*

EXERCISE DIRECTIONS:

1. Click Communications from the Works Task Launcher dialog box.

2. Enter the following information in the Easy Connect dialog box.

   Phone number: 555-555-1234
   Name of service: B & B Talk

   ✓ *NOTE: B & B Talk is not a real bulletin board. It is being used for practice purposes only.*

3. Click Cancel.

   ✓ *NOTE: If you were running a real communications session, you would press OK and the number you entered would be dialed. For this exercise, however, click the Cancel button.*

4. Close the document window.

BEGIN A COMMUNICATIONS SESSION

Enter a Phone Number

✓ *NOTE: If the Easy Connect dialog box is on the screen, skip to step 4.*

1. Click **Communications** .... `Alt`+`C` from the Works Task Launcher

2. Click **Phone** .... `Alt`+`P`

3. Click **Easy Connect** .... `C`

4. Click **Phone number** .... `Alt`+`P`

5. Enter a phone number .... *phone number* (including area code).

6. Click **Name of service** .... `Alt`+`N`
   OR
   Press **Tab** .... `Tab`

7. Enter name of service .... *name*

✓ *NOTE: Execute step 8 only if you are beginning an actual Communications session. If this is a practice session, click the Cancel button.*

8. Click **OK** .... `Enter`
   OR
   Click **Cancel** .... `Esc`

9. Click **File** .... `Alt`+`F`

10. Click **Close** .... `C`

■ **Adjust Settings** ■ **Save Settings**

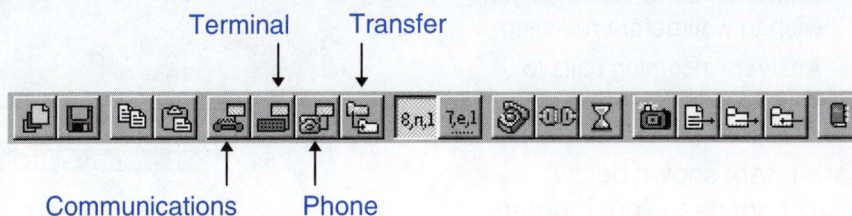

Terminal   Transfer

Communications   Phone

NOTES:

Adjust Settings

■ In the last exercise, you used the Easy Connect dialog box to connect quickly by just supplying a phone number. This type of connection uses the default settings which are usually compatible with most other computers. These settings are instructions that the computer needs to communicate with other computers or services. Although the default settings Works provides are compatible with most other computers and on-line services, you may need to make adjustments if you are not able to establish a connection. Changes to settings are made in the Settings dialog box.

To access the Settings dialog box:

Click the appropriate Toolbar buttons as shown above.

OR

Click Settings and access the desired pull-down menu as shown below.

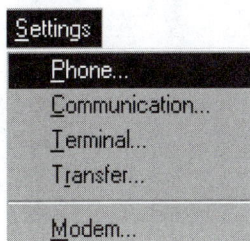

Settings
Phone...
Communication...
Terminal...
Transfer...
Modem...

■ There are four tabs on the Settings dialog box: Phone, Communication, Terminal and Transfer. On each tab, you can make changes to a number of options and settings.

• The **Phone** tab allows you to make adjustments to the dialing and answering options:

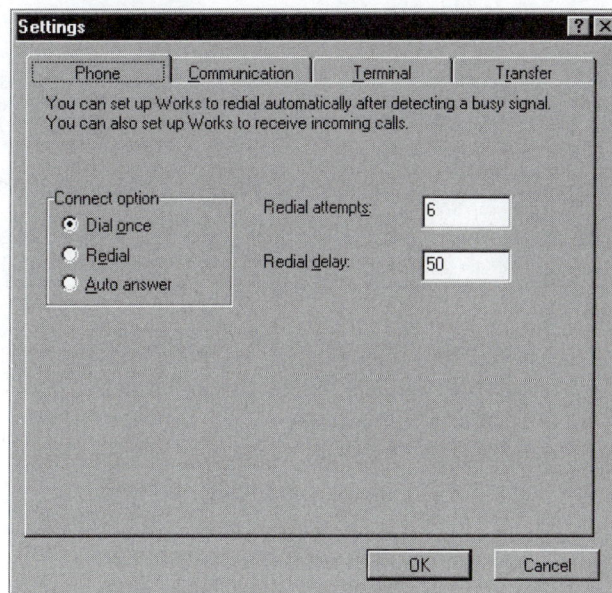

You can change the following settings:

Dial once   Instructs Works to dial only once to connect to another computer.

Redial   Allows you to call again automatically if you get a busy signal.

Redial attempts	Used if Redial is selected. Enter the number of times Works will redial a number. You can specify between 3 and 120.
Redial delay	Used if Redial is selected. Enter number of seconds you wish to wait before redialing.
Auto answer	Answers incoming calls to your modem.

- The **Communication** tab, shown below, allows you to make changes to your modem and tell your computer how to communicate with another computer. It is advisable to determine the other party's settings *before* beginning a session. If the settings do not match, you will not be able to connect.

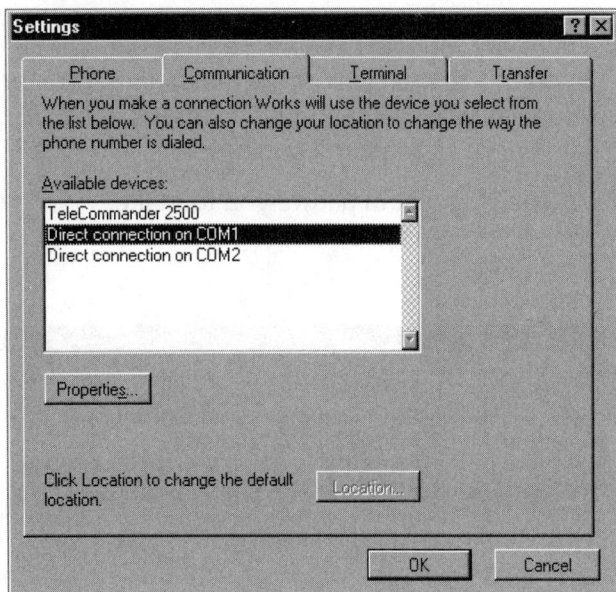

You can change the following setings:

Available devices	Lists the modems that are available.
Properties	Displays additional dialog boxes where you can configure the selected modem. The number of tabs and options displayed depends upon the modem you selected in the Available devices list box. Following is a brief explanation of the more commonly displayed options. For more information, click the Help button in the dialog box and click the item you wish to research.

The **General** tab, shown below, allows you to make changes to the connection port, speaker volume and available connection speeds.

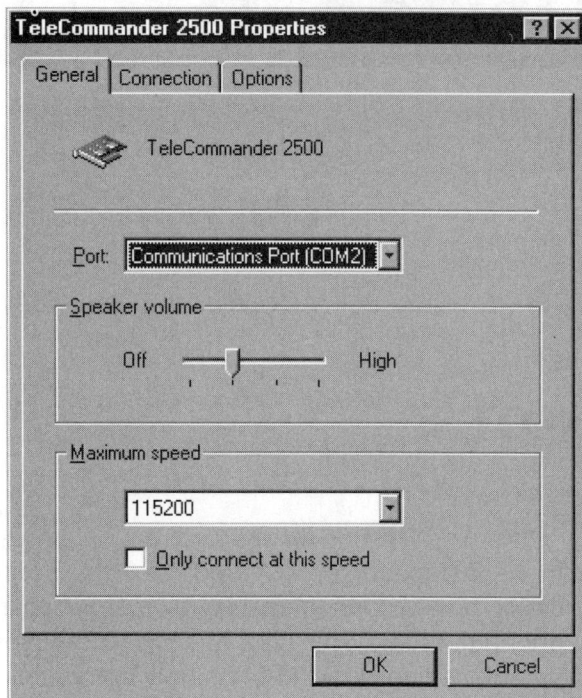

The **Connection** tab, shown below, allows you to make changes to connection and call preferences.

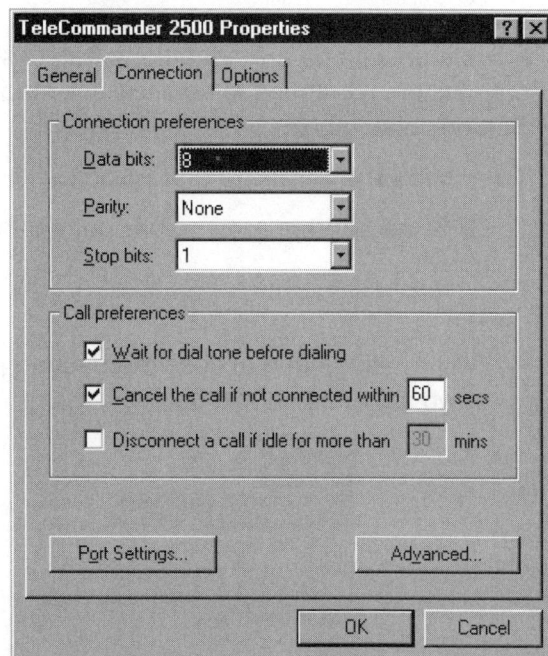

The connection preferences are described below and on the following page.

Data Bits	Determines the number of bits sent per byte. Your computer's setting must match the distant computer's.

Parity   Checks for errors in the transmission. The setting should match the other computer's parity parameter.

Stop Bits   Determines how many stop bits at the end of each byte. The distant computer needs to know how many stop bits to identify the end of a byte.

✓ *NOTE:*   *The available options vary with the selected modem.*

The **Options** tab, shown below, allows you to determine the connection and dialing controls.

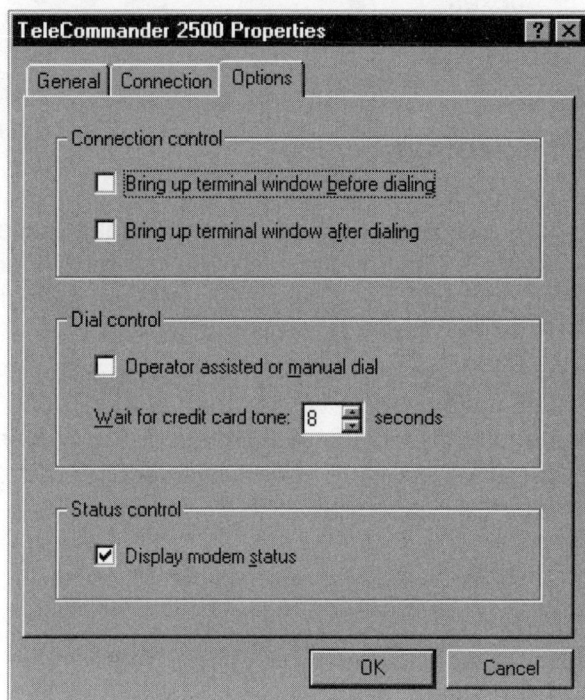

TeleCommander 2500 Properties

General | Connection | Options

Connection control
- ☐ Bring up terminal window *b*efore dialing
- ☐ Bring up terminal window *a*fter dialing

Dial control
- ☐ Operator assisted or *m*anual dial
- *W*ait for credit card tone: 8 seconds

Status control
- ☑ Display modem *s*tatus

OK   Cancel

- **Terminal** settings, shown below, determine how your computer will accept and display the data it is receiving. Again, the default settings are usually compatible with most other computers; however, if the data is incorrectly displayed, you may have to make adjustments in the Terminal Settings tab.

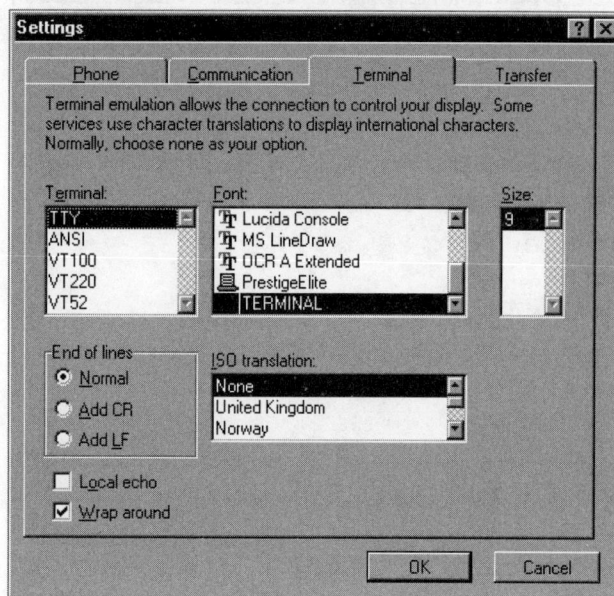

Settings

Phone | Communication | Terminal | Transfer

Terminal emulation allows the connection to control your display. Some services use character translations to display international characters. Normally, choose none as your option.

Terminal:
- TTY
- ANSI
- VT100
- VT220
- VT52

Font:
- Lucida Console
- MS LineDraw
- OCR A Extended
- PrestigeElite
- TERMINAL

Size: 9

End of lines
- ● Normal
- ○ Add CR
- ○ Add LF

ISO translation:
- None
- United Kingdom
- Norway

- ☐ Local echo
- ☑ Wrap around

OK   Cancel

The following options are available in Terminal Settings dialog box:

Terminal   Lists the settings available to emulate most common data terminals. The default is set to TTY. Change if necessary to match the other computer's terminal.

Font   Lists fonts you can use on your screen.

End of lines   Is set to **Normal**. Change to add a carriage return (Add CR) or line feed (Add LF) if your incoming data appears on one line.

ISO translation   Is set to **None**. If communicating internationally, you can click on the appropriate country to have any special characters translated.

Local echo   Is set to off. If your typing does not appear on the screen, turn this feature on.

Wrap around   Is set to on. Provides an automatic return. Change to off if you don't want text to wrap to the next line.

- **Transfer** settings determine the language or protocol the computers use to communicate. Again, check with the person whose computer you are connecting with to make sure you are both using the same language. Note the options available in the **Transfer** tab below:

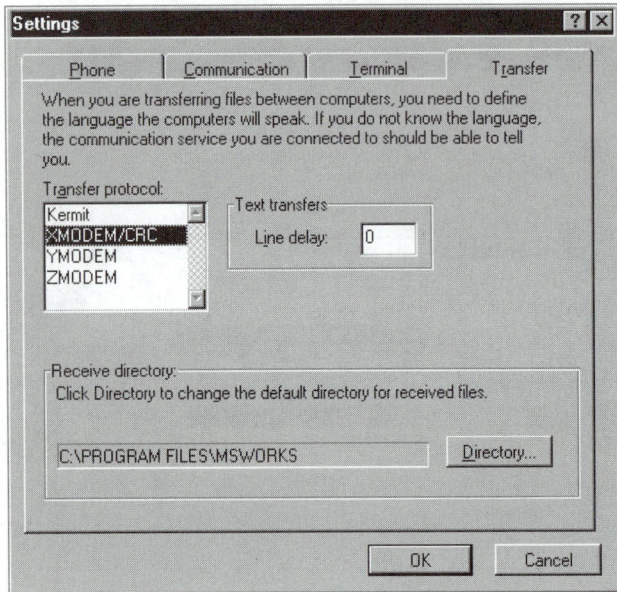

Settings

Phone | Communication | Terminal | Transfer

When you are transferring files between computers, you need to define the language the computers will speak. If you do not know the language, the communication service you are connected to should be able to tell you.

Transfer protocol:
Kermit
XMODEM/CRC
YMODEM
ZMODEM

Text transfers
Line delay: 0

Receive directory:
Click Directory to change the default directory for received files.

C:\PROGRAM FILES\MSWORKS   Directory...

OK   Cancel

Transfer protocol	Allows you to choose the correct protocol for transferring files. Both computers must use the same protocol.
Line Delay	Creates a pause between each line of text your computer sends in an ASCII text file. The number entered represents a tenth of a second.
Directory button	Allows you to select a directory where you will save any files that have been transmitted. Saving transmitted files is called **downloading**.

To make changes in any of the settings:

- Begin a communications session.
- Cancel the Easy Connect dialog box.
- Click the appropriate Toolbar button as indicated above.

  OR

  Click Settings.

  Click appropriate menu item (Phone, Communication, Terminal, Transfer).

- Make desired changes in the appropriate dialog boxes.
- Click OK.

Save Settings

- If you need to adjust the settings to connect to a particular computer, you need to make those changes only the first time you connect. Once the connection is successful, you can save the changes. When the settings are saved, the name of the person or service allied with those settings appears at the bottom of the Phone menu and in the Easy Connect dialog box under Services. All you need do is select the name to start the connection.

In this exercise, you will simulate a Communications session with a friend who just bought a new computer system with a modem and communications software. After several failed attempts at connecting, you discover that you need to adjust your settings to insure compatibility with your friend's computer. You will make and save the changes to the phone, communication, terminal and transfer settings.

✓ NOTE: All students can do this assignment. You do not need a modem to do this assignment.

EXERCISE DIRECTIONS:

1. Create a new Communications document.

2. Cancel the Easy Connect dialog box.

3. Click Settings menu and access the Phone dialog box.

4. Make the following changes:

Connect option:	Redial
Redial attempts:	3
Redial delay:	30

5. Make the following change to the Communication tab:

Bits per second:	9600

✓ NOTE: This value represents the baud rate for the port. If the connecting computer cannot communicate at the same rate, you will have to lower your rate.

✓ HINT: You need to access Properties to make this change.

6. Make the following changes to the Terminal settings:

Terminal:	ANSI
End of lines:	Add CR
Local echo:	on

7. Make the following change to the Transfer settings:

Transfer protocol:	ZMODEM

8. Click Easy Connect on the Phone menu.

9. Enter the following information in the Easy Connect dialog box:

Phone number:	1-908-555-2318
Name of service:	Felicia Snow

10. Click Cancel.

11. Close the document window.

✓ NOTE: If this were an actual communications session and you proceeded to connect, the file would automatically save under the Name of service. All changes to the settings would be saved along with the file.

PHONE SETTINGS

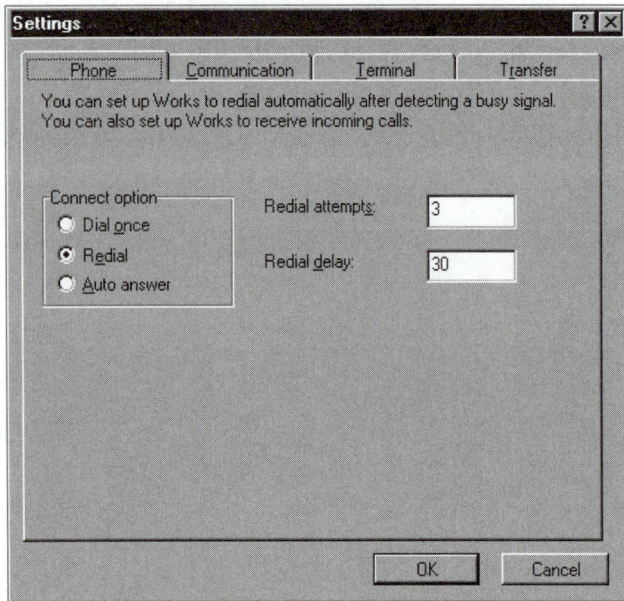

Settings

Phone | Communication | Terminal | Transfer

You can set up Works to redial automatically after detecting a busy signal. You can also set up Works to receive incoming calls.

Connect option
- Dial once
- ● Redial
- Auto answer

Redial attempts: 3

Redial delay: 30

OK | Cancel

COMMUNICATION SETTINGS

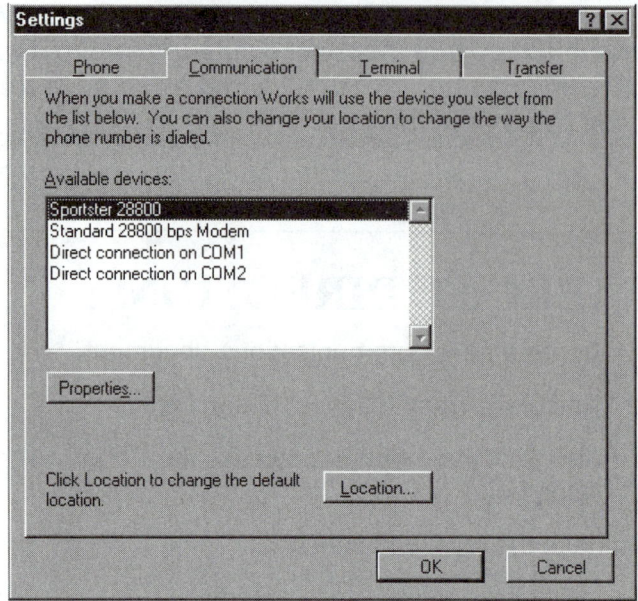

Settings

Phone | Communication | Terminal | Transfer

When you make a connection Works will use the device you select from the list below. You can also change your location to change the way the phone number is dialed.

Available devices:

Sportster 28800
Standard 28800 bps Modem
Direct connection on COM1
Direct connection on COM2

Properties...

Click Location to change the default location.

Location...

OK | Cancel

TERMINAL SETTINGS

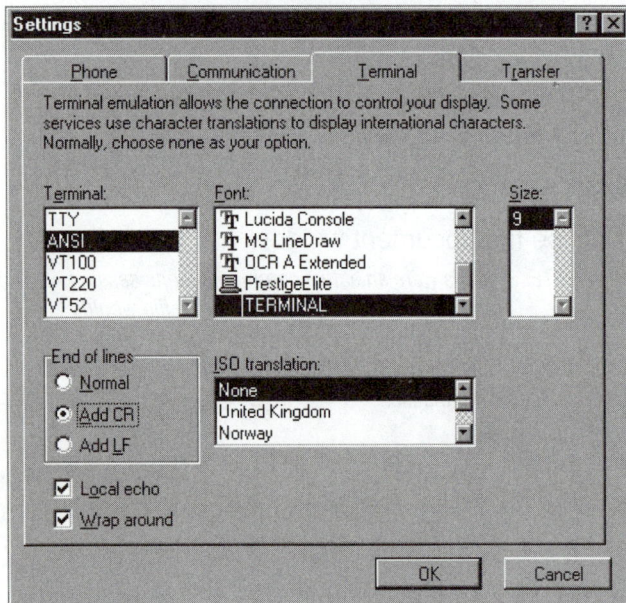

Settings

Phone | Communication | Terminal | Transfer

Terminal emulation allows the connection to control your display. Some services use character translations to display international characters. Normally, choose none as your option.

Terminal:
TTY
ANSI
VT100
VT220
VT52

Font:
Lucida Console
MS LineDraw
OCR A Extended
PrestigeElite
TERMINAL

Size: 9

End of lines
- Normal
- ● Add CR
- Add LF

ISO translation:
None
United Kingdom
Norway

☑ Local echo
☑ Wrap around

OK | Cancel

TRANSFER SETTINGS

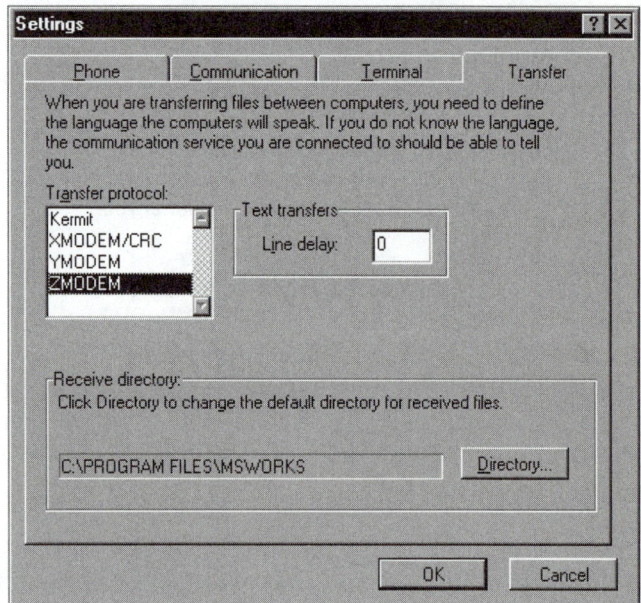

Settings

Phone | Communication | Terminal | Transfer

When you are transferring files between computers, you need to define the language the computers will speak. If you do not know the language, the communication service you are connected to should be able to tell you.

Transfer protocol:
Kermit
XMODEM/CRC
YMODEM
ZMODEM

Text transfers
Line delay: 0

Receive directory:
Click Directory to change the default directory for received files.

C:\PROGRAM FILES\MSWORKS

Directory...

OK | Cancel

CHANGE SETTINGS

1. Click **Communications** .... Alt + C
   from the Works Task Launcher.
2. Cancel Easy Connect dialog box.
3. Click **Settings** .... Alt + S
4. Choose one of the following options:
   - **Phone** .... P
   - **Communication** C
   - **Terminal** .... T
   - **Transfer** .... R

5. Make desired changes.
6. Click **OK** .... Enter

SAVE SETTINGS

1. Make desired changes to settings.
2. Click **Phone** .... Alt + P
3. Click **Easy Connect** .... Alt + Y
4. Click **Phone number** .... Alt + P
5. Enter number .... *number*

6. Click **Name of service** .... Alt + N
7. Type name of service .... *name*
8. Click **OK** .... Enter
9. Click **Dial** .... Alt + D
10. File is automatically saved under the name of service.

EXERCISE **3**

■ **Send Information** ■ **Send Text** ■ **Send Files** ■ **Send a Fax** ■ **End a Session**

Send text   Send binary file

NOTES:

Send Information

■ There are two ways you can send information using the Communications tool in Works:

- You can send messages to another computer by typing the text on your Communications screen. The receiver views your message and can type a message back to you. This is similar to a telephone conversation except the interchange is written with all conversations appearing on both parties' screens.

- You can send entire files that are stored on disk. When sending files, the contents of the files do not appear on the screen. The transferred file is stored on the receiving computer. Once it is received, the file can be opened and edited like any other file. If you are sending the file, you are **uploading**. If you are receiving the file, you are **downloading**.

Send Text

■ Once you are connected, you can send messages directly from your Communications screen. You can send messages directly to a friend, communicate with a bulletin board or transmit a message to a mailbox, (a location on the computer where messages are stored). A mailbox may be available on a network or on an on-line service. As you type, your text is automatically transmitted to the receiving computer.

■ If the information you are typing is not visible on the screen, or if lines of text overwrite each other as you type, you will need to make adjustments in the Terminal tab of the Settings dialog box. Access Terminal from the Settings menu and turn on Local echo, and/or select Add LF (line feed) in the Terminal dialog box.

   ✓ *NOTE:*   *If you get a double of each character as you type, then turn Local echo to off.*

■ You can also copy text from any document created in Works (word processing, spreadsheet or database), paste it onto the Communications screen and send it to the other computer. This procedure can save you money because it reduces the time spent on-line. When you send text this way only the text is sent; Works does not transfer the format of the document. The copied information is transmitted as soon as it is pasted onto the Communications screen.

■ While you are connected, the bottom right-hand portion of the Status bar shows that you are on-line and how many minutes have elapsed.

Send Files

■ In addition to holding a conversation with the person operating the remote computer, you will most likely want to transmit a file. When you send a file, the receiving computer saves that file directly to a folder on the hard drive or a floppy disk.

   ✓ *NOTE:*   *When sending files make sure the transfer protocols are the same.*

■ Works sends its files as binary files. A binary file can be a word processing, database or spreadsheet file and contains character and paragraph formatting.

You can send binary files by choosing the Send Binary File button on the Toolbar, or choosing the Send File command from the Tools menu. The Send File dialog box appears:

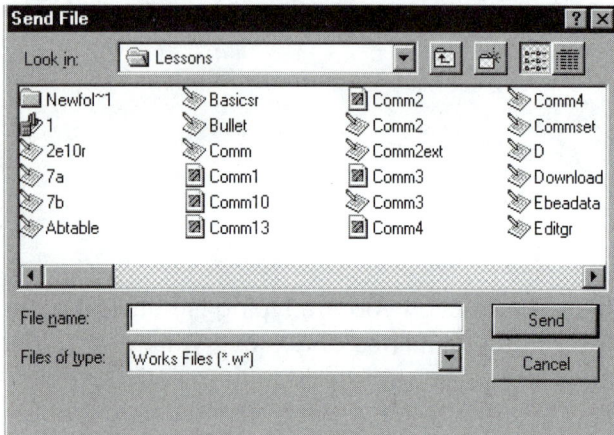

✓ *NOTE:*   *The file is transmitted to a disk or folder and will not appear on the receiving computer's Communications screen. If the receiving computer has Works installed, the operator must open the file in the appropriate tool (word processing, spreadsheet, database).*

■ **Text files** contain the text but do not contain the original formatting instructions. You would transmit a file as a text file if the sending and receiving computers do not have the same program. For example, you wish to transmit a document that was created in Works to your friend's computer. Your friend does not have Works and will not be able to call up the document. However, if you change your file to a text file before the transfer, you avoid the incompatibility and your friend will be able to call up the document. Remember, only the text is sent without the format; therefore, your friend will have to reformat the document after it is received.

✓ *NOTE:*   *You may see formatting codes amongst the text.*

• You can send text files by choosing the Send Text button on the Toolbar, or choosing the Send Text command from the Tools menu. The following dialog box displays:

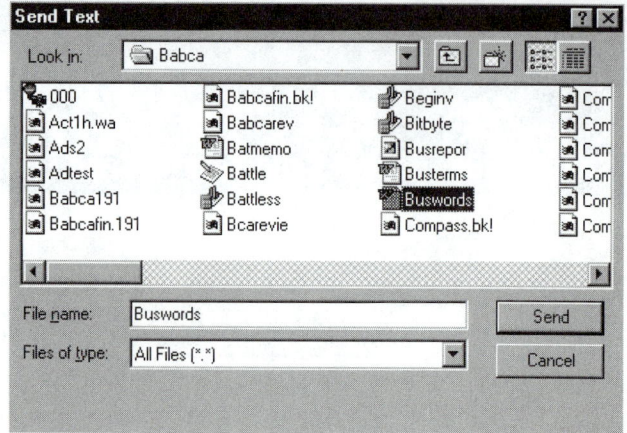

■ During the actual transmission, you will see the following message:

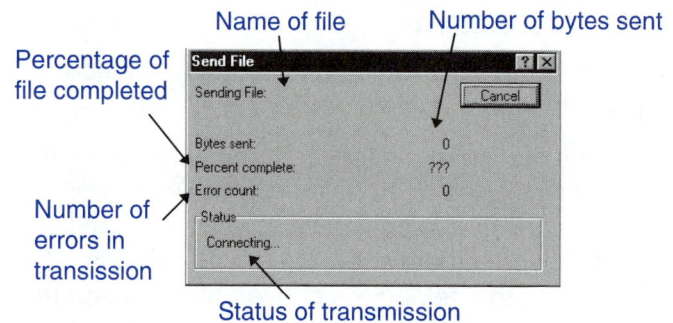

✓ *NOTE:*   *You can cancel a file transfer by pressing the ESC key.*

Send a Fax

■ If you have a fax modem you can send a document as a fax. However, if you are sending a fax from Works for the first time using Microsoft Fax, you must follow the instructions **To install Microsoft Exchange and Microsoft Fax**. These instructions can be found in the Help feature. Click Help, Index and type Fax in the text box. Press the Enter key and the instructions will be listed to the right of the Help window.

■ Once Microsoft Fax is installed, you can send any Works document as a fax.

✓ *NOTE:*   *You can use fax programs other than Microsoft Fax to send or receive a fax in Works.*

To send a fax:

- Click File, Print.

- Select Microsoft Fax (or other fax program) in the Name box.

- Click OK.

  The document begins printing to the fax modem and the following dialog box displays.

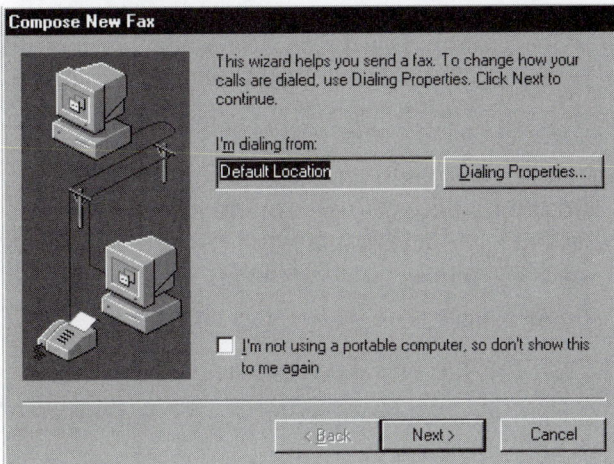

- Verify that the sending location is correct and click Next to advance to the following dialog box.

Name of recipient

Fax number

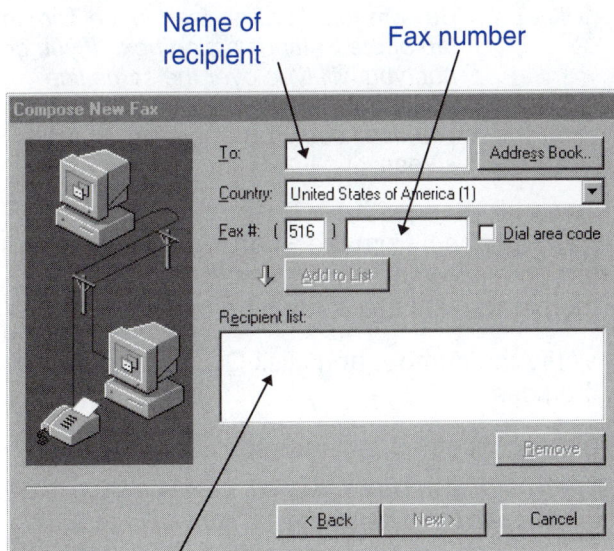

Click name if listed

- Type the name of the recipient in the To box and type the recipient's fax number in the Fax # box.

- Click Next to continue and follow instructions to choose a cover page and type a brief note. When all selections are made, click Finish to send the fax.

End a Session

■ Once the session is over, click the Dial/Hangup button on the Toolbar, or choose Hang up from the Phone menu. A message will appear asking whether you wish to disconnect; click OK. After you disconnect, the Status bar reads OFFLINE.

> *In this exercise, you are working on a group project on using the Internet. One of the members of your group needs information from you. You decide to send this information through the computer. However, since this is the first time you are communicating with this particular computer, you need to make adjustments to the settings. Once all adjustments are made, you will send information directly from your screen and then you will send a file saved on your disk.*

EXERCISE DIRECTIONS:

✓ *NOTE:* *You will complete two of the three sections in this exercise.*

PART A is for everyone to complete.

PART B is for those who have a modem and another computer to connect to.

PART C is for those who have a modem and can connect to someone who has a fax machine or a fax modem.

PART A

In this portion of the exercise, you will practice changing the options available in each of the tabs in the Settings dialog box.

1. Create a new communications document.

2. Cancel the Easy Connect dialog box.

3. Practice making the following changes to the various settings.

   Phone Settings:
Connect option:	Redial
Redial attempts:	3

   Communications Settings:
   Change the Bits per second to 9600.
   Transfer Settings
   Choose Kermit as your file
   Transfer protocol.
   Terminal Settings
   Turn on local echo
   Add a line feed.

4. Practice entering information in the Easy Connect dialog box as follows:

Country Code	Supply correct country code
Area code	Supply your area code
Phone number:	718 555-1234
Name of service:	PS

5. Cancel the Easy Connect dialog box.

   ✓ *NOTE:* *If you were beginning an actual communications session, you would click OK to commence dialing. When you save the file, the settings are saved along with the file, and Works uses the name of the service as the filename.*

PART B

✓ *NOTE:* *You must have a modem and remote computer to complete this portion of the exercise. If you do not have the equipment to complete this part, read through it to familiarize yourself with the communications process.*

1. Before continuing, contact the operator of the remote computer to determine the correct settings. Write them down if necessary to avoid wasting valuable time on line.

2. Open ⌨**INFO**, or open 💾**CO INFO.3**.

3. Copy the title and the first paragraph.

4. Create a new communications document.

5. Check all settings to make sure they are compatible with the computer to which you will connect.

6. Make any necessary adjustments in any of the Settings dialog box tabs.

   ✓ *NOTE:* *Be sure to add a line feed in the Terminal tab of the Settings dialog box. If you do not, you will type over the same line repeatedly. Also, turn on Local echo if you don't see your typed text on the screen .*

7. Once all changes have been made, choose Easy Connect from the Phone menu. Type in the phone number and the name of service of the person you are contacting and click OK.

8. Verify the number and click Dial to commence the session.

9. Once connected, type the following message:

   Hi, I am glad we connected. I am going to send you part of a file. This should be coming onto your screen in just a few seconds.

10. Paste the paragraph from the **INFO** file.

    ✓ *NOTE:* *This file is transmitted as soon as it is placed on your Communications screen.*

11. If you have trouble communicating, you may need to make further adjustments to the various settings.

12. Type the following message:

    *Now I am going to send you an entire file named **ETIQUETTE**. Here goes and good luck!*

13. Send ⌨**ETIQUETTE**, or 💾**CO ETIQUETTE.3**.

   ✔*NOTE: If the receiving computer has Works installed, send the file as a binary file. If not, then you will have to send **ETIQUETTE** as a text file.*

14. If you have difficulty sending the file, check to see that the Transfer protocol matches the remote computer's.

15. Type this message:

   Hope this information is helpful. I'll talk, really talk, to you soon. Bye.

16. End the Communications session. Click Dial/Hangup on the Toolbar or Click <u>H</u>angup from the <u>P</u>hone menu.

17. Close all open files. Save if desired.

PART C

1. Make arrangements to send a fax to another party.

2. Open ⌨**ETIQUETTE**, or open 💾**CO ETIQUETTE.3**.

3. Print it to the Microsoft Fax or whatever fax you are using on your computer.

4. Follow all instructions and supply the necessary information for the specific fax program.

SEND TEXT FROM COMMUNICATIONS SCREEN

A.   To Type a Message directly onto the Communications Screen:

1. Click <u>F</u>ile .... `Alt`+`F`

2. Click <u>O</u>pen .... `O`
   to open existing communications file.
   OR
   a. Click <u>N</u>ew .... `N`
   b. Click Works <u>T</u>ools tab .... `Alt`+`T`
      on the Works Task Launcher.
   c. Click <u>C</u>ommunications .... `C`

   ✔*NOTE: If you are connecting for the first time, check to see that all settings are compatible with those of the remote computer.*

3. Once connected, type a greeting on screen.

4. Type message you want to send.

B.   To Send Text Copied from another Works Tool:

1. Before beginning a communications session
   a. Click <u>F</u>ile .... `Alt`+`F`
   b. Click <u>O</u>pen .... `O`
   c. Choose desired file.
   d. Select text to copy.
   e. Click <u>E</u>dit .... `Alt`+`E`
   f. Click <u>C</u>opy .... `Alt`+`C`

2. Repeat steps 1-4 above to begin communications session

3. Click <u>E</u>dit............................... `Alt`+`E`

4. Click <u>P</u>aste .... `P`

SEND A BINARY FILE

1. Start a Communications session.

2. Click <u>T</u>ools .... `Alt`+`T`

3. Click <u>S</u>end File .... `S`
   OR
   Click Send binary file button . ... 📇
   on Toolbar.

4. Select file to send .... *filename*

5. Click **OK** .... `Enter`

SEND A TEXT FILE

✔*NOTE: Save the file as a text file before transmitting it.*

1. Start a Communications session.

2. Click <u>T</u>ools .... `Alt`+`T`

3. Click <u>S</u>end Text .... `Alt`+`T`
   OR
   Click Send text button. .... 📄
   on Toolbar

4. Select file to send .... *filename*

5. Click **OK** .... `Enter`

SEND A FAX

✔*NOTE: The following instructions are for Microsoft Fax in Windows 95. If you are using another fax program, follow the instructions for that program.*

1. Open or create document you want to send.

2. Click <u>F</u>ile............................... `Alt`+`F`

3. Click <u>P</u>rint .... `P`

4. Select Microsoft Fax in the list box.

5. Click **OK** .... `Enter`

6. Verify the sending location in the Compose New Fax dialog box.

7. Click **Next**.

8. Do one of the following:
   a. Click <u>A</u>ddress Box .... `Alt`+`S`
      if recipient is previously entered.
   b. Double-click desired recipient
   c. Click **OK**............................... `Enter`
   d. Click **Next** .... `Enter`
   OR
   e. Click <u>T</u>o box...................... `Alt`+`T`
   f. Type name of recipient. .... *name*
   g. Click <u>F</u>ax # box................. `Alt`+`F`
   h. Type recipient's fax number ..*number*
   i. Click **Add to list** .... `Alt`+`A`
   j. Click **Next**.

14. Choose if you want a cover page.

15. Click **Next**

16. Click <u>S</u>ubject box .... `Alt`+`S`

17. Type a subject, if desired. .... *subject*

18. Click <u>N</u>ote .... `Alt`+`N`

19. Type a note, if desired................... *note*

20. Click **Next**

21. Click **Finish** to send the fax.

END A COMMUNICATIONS SESSION

1. Click <u>P</u>hone........................... `Alt`+`P`

2. Click <u>H</u>ang Up .... `H`

3. Click **OK** .... `Enter`
   when message box appears.

■ **Answer a Call** ■ **Receive and Save Incoming Text**
■ **Capture Text** ■ **Receive Files** ■ **Information Services/Bulletin Boards**

Pause   Receive binary file

NOTES:

Answer a Call

■ Either you or the remote computer can initiate the call to begin a communications session. However, just as you adjusted the settings before dialing a remote computer, you must make sure that your settings match the computer that is calling you.

■ If you expect an incoming call, click Receive an incoming call in the Easy Connect dialog box. In addition, your computer must be set to Auto Answer to accept the call. Click the Auto Answer check box in the Phone tab of the Settings dialog box shown below.

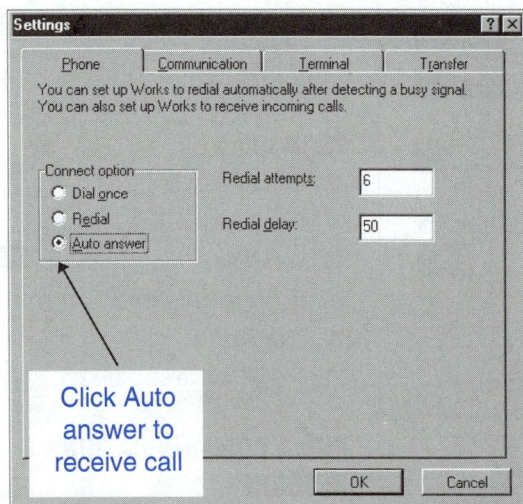

Click Auto answer to receive call

Receive and Save Incoming Text

■ Once the connection is established, you can receive text directly to your screen from another computer. Text received in this manner is held in a temporary storage area called a buffer. This buffer can hold up to 256,000 lines.

■ You can review the incoming text in a number of ways.

• You can read it as it is transmitted. However incoming text may transmit quickly and may scroll off the screen before you have a chance to read it.

• You can pause the transmission to read the text. Click the Pause button on the Toolbar to stop the transmission then click the button again to continue.

• The buffer can hold a large amount of information; however, if the transmission is larger than the buffer's capacity, you may lose text. Pause the transmission and copy the text in the buffer to a word processing document. Once the text is pasted into the new document, switch back to the communications screen and resume the transmission.

CAUTION: *Using the pause feature can become costly. Even though you have paused the transmission, you are not disconnected, and continue to accumulate on-line and phone charges.*

- The most cost-efficient method is to read the incoming text after it is received. Save the incoming text to **another document**. Saving your communications document will only save the settings; it will not save the buffer. You need to copy the contents of the communications screen to a word processing document in order to save it.

Capture Text

- Capturing text allows you to retain all incoming text and eliminates the need to copy text from the buffer to another document. As the text is coming in, it is **automatically** saved to a file you select.

- Click the Capture button on the Toolbar to access the Capture Text dialog box:

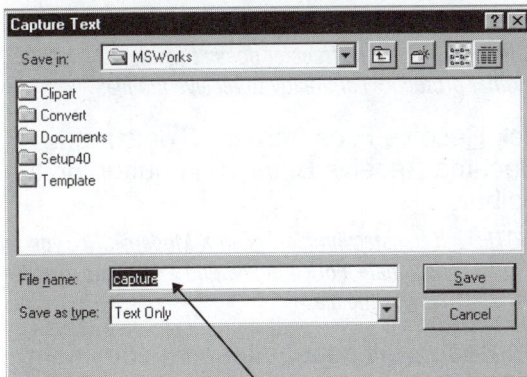

Saves file to *capture*

- You can create a new file or select an existing file. If you choose to capture text to an existing file, you need to specify whether to append the incoming text or overwrite existing data.

- Once the communications session is over, you can open the file and view the contents of the transmission. You are now viewing the text off-line, thereby eliminating any additional charges you would have accumulated had you taken time to read the text while connected.

Receive Files

- When you receive files directly to your computer, the files are sent to a disk or a directory on your hard drive. The process of obtaining files is called downloading. You can download files from another computer, bulletin board or on-line service.

- You can download all types of files: word processing, graphics, spreadsheets, databases, and shareware programs that have the author's permission to be copied.

- Make sure that all your settings are compatible with the computer you are connecting to. In order for files to be transferred, both computers must use the same protocol.

  ✓ *NOTE:* *If you want to receive a file from an information service, select the file you wish to download and follow the downloading directions provided by the service.*

- After you are connected and ready to receive the file, choose <u>R</u>eceive File from the <u>T</u>ools menu, or select the Receive Binary File button on the Toolbar as shown above. As the file is being transferred, the Receive File dialog box gives the status of the transfer.

- If you are using XMODEM, you must enter a filename. All other transfer protocols use the same filename used on the remote computer.

  ✓ *NOTE:* *A transfer can be canceled at any point by pressing the ESC key. Click OK to confirm the cancel.*

Information Services/Bulletin Boards

- Connecting to an **information service** or **bulletin board** is a little different than connecting to a friend's, employer's or classmate's computer. You may use the Works communications software to connect to a bulletin board or other service such as an Internet provider. However, once you are connected, you must follow the directions to access information. You will probably have a **username** or **password** or both. You cannot gain access without them, so keep them in a safe place.

  ✓ *NOTE:* *The more popular commercial on-line services provide their own software to connect directly to the service. If you wish to subscribe to a specific service, you will need to install that service's software on your system.*

- Once you gain access to the service, you are **logged on**. When you exit the service, you are **logged off**. In addition to the time being recorded in your Works Status bar, the service may keep a record of the time you were on-line with their system.

- You can download files and capture text from an information service or bulletin board just as you would from another computer.

- Some services have E-Mail where you can leave and receive personal messages. The **Works Forum** is a bulletin board you can access directly from Works. This service allows you to communicate with other Works users. Click Help, Launch Works Forum. Once you are connected, you can get answers to questions concerning Works, download templates and additional software, and obtain some handy tips and tricks to help you operate more successfully in Works. In order to use the Works Forum, you need to subscribe to the Microsoft Network which is an on-line service built into Windows 95.

> *In this exercise, you will change settings, capture text and transfer files from a remote computer and/or information service or bulletin board.*

EXERCISE DIRECTIONS:

✓ *NOTE:* *There are two sections to this exercise: **PART A** is for those who have a modem and another computer to connect to. **PART B** is for those who have a modem and access to a bulletin board or information service.*

PART A

✓ *NOTE:* *You must have a modem and a remote computer to connect to in order to complete this portion of the exercise. If you do not have the equipment to complete this part, read through it to familiarize yourself with the communications process.*

1. Before beginning this exercise, make arrangements to connect to someone's computer for practice in exchanging text and files. Arrange for the remote computer to call you.

2. Make all necessary changes to the settings to connect to another computer.

3. From Settings menu, select Phone and turn on Auto Answer.

4. After connecting and reading any message transmitted by the remote computer, type the following message (or a similar one):

   Hi, this is a practice session to learn the Communications tool in Works. Can you read this message?

5. Wait for a response, then begin capturing all messages.

   ✓ *NOTE:* *If you cannot see your text on the screen, go to the Terminal tab of the Settings dialog box and turn on Local echo. Also, you may need to type additional messages so the remote computer is kept informed of your intentions and problems you may be having.*

6. Designate a drive and/or folder and a filename for the capture.

7. Type the following (or similar) message:

   I need to try out a file transfer. Can you send me a file? Let me know if you can and what type of file it is.

8. Once you receive a response to the previous message, type a message back informing the remote user that you are using XMODEM/CRC as the file transfer protocol. You can type the following (or similar) message:

   Make sure that you set your protocol or transfer setting to XModem/CRC. If the transfer doesn't work, we can try another protocol. I am ready to receive the file.

9. Click Receive Files from the Tools menu or select the Receive Binary File button on the Toolbar.

   ✓ *NOTE:* *If transferring files using X Modem-CRC, you must designate a drive, folder and a filename in order to receive the file.*

10. A message will appear keeping you informed of the transfer status.

11. Once the file is received, type the following back to the remote computer:

    I received the file. Thanks. Signing off for now. Bye, (supply your name).

    ✓ *NOTE:* *If there was an error in the file transmission, communicate with your remote partner to try other protocols to effect a successful transfer.*

12. Stop the capture. Click Tools, End Capture text.

13. End your communications session.

14. Close the document window.

15. Open the capture. View the contents.

    ✓ *NOTE:* *Captures are generally located in the Works folder. Choose All Files in the Files of type text box to view the entire contents of the folder.*

16. Close the document window.

17. Open the transmitted file. View the contents.

18. Close the document window.

PART B:

✔ NOTE: *The following part of this exercise can only be completed if you have a modem and access to a bulletin board or information service. Please note that the following steps may vary according to the bulletin board or service you are using.*

1. Contact the bulletin board to confirm correct settings.

2. Begin a new Communications session and cancel the Easy Connect dialog box.

3. Make all necessary changes to the settings to connect to the service or bulletin board.

4. Access the Easy Connect dialog box and enter the number and name of service.

5. Once connected, follow the instructions to obtain access to the service.

6. Find an area or article of interest on this service.

7. Once you have information on the screen, begin a capture.

8. Designate a drive, folder and filename for the capture.

9. End the capture as desired.

10. Find a file you wish to receive.

   ✔ NOTE: *Your service or bulletin board may have additional instructions for downloading.*

11. Follow your bulletin board's or service's instructions to download a file.

12. Click Receive File from the Tools menu.

13. Give an appropriate filename for the file being transmitted, and designate a drive or folder.

14. End your on-line session by following the service's instructions to log out.

15. End your Communications session.

16. Open the capture and read the contents.

17. Close the document window.

18. Open the file and view the contents.

19. Close the document window.

ANSWER A CALL

1. Click **Settings** .... `Alt`+`S`
2. Click **Phone** .... `P`
3. Select **Auto Answer** .... `Alt`+`A`
4. Click **OK** .... `Enter`

PAUSE A SESSION

1. Click **Phone** .... `Alt`+`P`
2. Click **Pause** .... `P`

   OR

   Click Pause button . ... `⧗`
   on Toolbar.

To turn off Pause:

   Repeat the command.

SAVE INCOMING TEXT

1. End your Communications session.
2. Click **File** .... `Alt`+`F`
3. Click **Save As** .... `A`
4. Enter a filename. .... *filename*

5. Click **Save File as Type** .... `Alt`+`T`
6. Select **Session Data**.
7. Click **OK** .... `Enter`

CAPTURE TEXT

1. Click **Tools** .... `Alt`+`T`
2. Click **Capture Text** .... `Alt`+`X`
3. Specify a drive, and/or folder and filename.
4. Click **OK** .... Enter

To end a capture:

1. Click **Tools** .... `Alt`+`T`
2. Click **End Capture Text** .... `C`

RECEIVE FILES

1. Verify that both computers are using the same protocols.
2. Click **Tools** .... `Alt`+`T`
3. Click **Receive File** .... `R`

   OR

   Click Receive Binary File . ... `⊞`
   button on Toolbar.

   ✔ NOTE: *You only need to specify a filename if using XMODEM. Otherwise, it is automatically named with the same filename it has on the other computer.*

4. Specify a filename .... *filename* if using XMODEM.

5. Message appears giving status of transfer.

To cancel a transfer:

   Press Esc .... `Esc`

In this exercise, you will review the basics of communications by using both the Works Help feature and the information provided in this lesson. You will create a word processing document where you will respond to a series of questions.

EXERCISE DIRECTIONS:

Part A

1. Create a new document for the Word Processor.

2. Type your name at the top of the page. Press the Enter key twice before beginning the exercise.

3. Follow the instructions listed in the next section and answer all questions in the Word Processor as follows:

   • Type each question in bold.

   • Press the Enter key twice after each question.

   • Type your answers in full sentences. Do not bold the answers.

   • Press the Enter key twice before typing the next question.

Part B

1. Click Help, click Index

2. Type *communications* in the textbox provided.

3. Click Communications documents: connection by modem.

4. Click to connect to another computer for the first time CM.

5. Click More Info tab, click Quick Tour. Take the tour and click Done when finished.

6. After taking the Quick Tour, answer the following questions:

   a. What does a computer with a modem allow you to do?

   b. What does the Easy Connect dialog box do?

7. In the Index textbox:

   • Type *settings*

   • Click settings, communications: described

   • Click changing communication settings, CM

   • Read the Overview and click Done when finished. Answer the following:

   c. What are communication settings?

   d. What do they enable the computers to do?

8. Close the Help Index screen and choose to hide Help.

9. Create a new communications session, cancel the Easy Connect dialog box. Click on each of the tabs in the Settings menu and use the Help button (the question mark on each dialog box) to aid in researching the solutions to the following situations:

   e. You cannot see the text you are typing on the screen.

   f. All the text stays on one line.

   g. You are transferring files to another computer and are not successful.

   h. It is taking very long to connect and receive information from the remote computer.

   i. What you type appears twice.

   j. You are receiving incoming text and it is coming in so fast you can't possibly read it. What are your options to correct this situation?

   k. Assume you have a computer with communications capabilities. Be imaginative and discuss how you would use this feature. List and discuss three ways you would use communications.

10. Save the file; name it **COMM SUMMARY**.

11. Print one copy.

12. Close all document windows.

INDEX

A

absolute
    reference 230
absolute condition
    in Spreadsheet 209
absolute value
    in Spreadsheet 209
ACCESS A REPORT
    in Database 348
active cell
    Spreadsheet 187, 188, 197
add a field
    Database 291, 297
ADD A SUMMARY STATISTIC
    in Database Report 347
Add Fields
    Form Letters 394
ADD SHADING IN A REPORT 357
address book 418
ADJUST COLUMN WIDTH 147
Advanced options
    labels 409
align column data
    in Database report 343, 348
align column heading
    in Database report 343, 348
alignment 143
    center 201
    general 201
    left 201
    right 201
    vertical 201
alignment options 46
    center 46
    left 46
    right 46
alignments
    in Database 324, 326
All Caps 28
And
    logical operator 314
answer a call 444
Apply Filter 314
arguments
    function 212
ascending sort
    in Spreadsheet 245
    in Database 333
asterisk
    wildcard 313
Auto answer
    communications 434
Autofill
    Spreadsheet 216

AutoFormat 253
automatic page break 104
Automatically enter a default value check box ... 323
Autosum button 214
Average
    summary statistic 340
AVG function 212
axes
    chart 257
    horizontal 257
    vertical 257
    x-axis 257
    y-axis 257

B

background color 155
Backspace key 16
bar chart 257
    stacked 264
Best Fit
    Database 308
    WordArt 175
binary files 440
block business letter 28
body text 164
bold 52, 54
bookmark 107
    delete 108
    locate 108
    set 108
Border feature
    Spreadsheet 250
Borders 151, 275
    in Database 324, 326
brochure
    TaskWizard 423
buffer (communications) 444
built-In functions
    Spreadsheet 219, 220
bullet 52
    change shape and size 54
    create bulleted lists 54
    remove 54
    style 53
bulletin boards 430, 445
business letter
    block 28
    body 24
    closing 24
    inside address 24
    modified-block 43
    reference initials 24

✓ NOTE: Index entries in all captial letters indicate keystroke procedures.

salutation 24
   signature line 24
   title line 24
byline 164

C

cancel selection 39
caption 179
capture text
   communications 445
cascade
   windows 374
categorized directory
   address book 418
category labels
   chart 257
   font characteristics 273
cell
   Spreadsheet 187
   width 189
cell address
   Spreadsheet 188, 207
cell protection
   grade book 421
cell reference area
   Spreadsheet 187
center 46, 47
   Database alignment 324
   Spreadsheet alignment 201
Center across selection
   in Database report 343, 348
   in Spreadsheet 201
center tab 133
   in headers and footers 116
CENTER TITLE OF REPORT
   in Database 348
CHANGE A CHART TYPE 266
CHANGE A SUMMARY STATISTIC
   in Database Report 347
CHANGE BULLET SHAPE AND SIZE 54
CHANGE COLORS, PATTERNS AND MARKERS ... 275
CHANGE COLUMN HEADING
   in Database report 347
CHANGE COLUMN WIDTH
   in Database Report 348
CHANGE FIELD WIDTH 290
CHANGE FONT AND STYLE
   in Database Report 348
CHANGE MARGINS
   in Database Report 348
CHANGE PAGE SETUP 266
CHANGE RECORD HEIGHT 290
change titles
   chart 260
CHANGE VIEW MODES 290
   database 284
change views 259
chart
   3-D 273
   change type 264
   duplicate 268
   multiple series 263

rename 260
save 260
Spreadsheet 257
stacked bar 264
check box 11
check mark 10
ClipArt 157, 167, 171
Clipboard 82
CLOSE 18
Close 17
Close a New Document 16
Close button 7, 9
closing
   business letter 24
color 58
   chart 273
   font 56
   Spreadsheet 250
color pattern 155
Column (Field) Heading
   modify in Database 341
column headings 141
Column Layout 131
Column number 230
column width
   adjust 146
   adjust in Spreadsheet 193
   change in Spreadsheet 219, 220
   Spreadsheet 227
   in Database report 343
columns 131
   delete from Spreadsheet 238
   insert in Spreadsheet 238
   move in Spreadsheet 238
   Spreadsheet 187
Columns feature 128
Combine Two Paragraphs 41
Comma
   Number tab 204
command button 10
communications 430
Compare To
   filter 314
Control menu button 7, 9
COPY
   ClipArt 173
   Draw object 173
   Spreadsheet columns/rows 238
copy and paste 86, 87
   from one document to another 376
   in Database 293
   in List view 297
   in Spreadsheet 207, 208
   integration 378
copy data
   in Database 292, 297
Copy Formats 86, 87
copy notation 57, 107
Copy Text 86
COPY/PASTE
   in Spreadsheet 239
Count
   summary statistic 340

COUNT function 216
cover page 154
CREATE A STANDARD REPORT 340
CREATE BULLETED LISTS 54
CREATE CHART FROM MULTIPLE SERIES 266
CREATE DATABASE FILE 282
Currency
   Number tab 204
Customize an Indent 89
Customize the Toolbar 19, 20
cut and paste 81, 82, 124
   integration 378
   move a field 292
   using Go To 123

D

data
   edit in Database cell 303
Data Bits 434
Data Entry tab
   Database 290
data labels
   chart 257, 270
   font characteristics 273
data markers
   chart 273
database
   create a file 281
   Form Letters 394
   format 322
   introduction 280
   labels 408
   merge 393
   open a file 287
   plan 281
   save a file 281
Database tab
   envelope merge 405
Date
   format in Database 323
   Number tab 205
Date and Time Feature 28
dateline 164
Day
   Spreadsheet 216
Decimal places increment box 322
decimal-aligned tab 133
default
   address book 418
   field width 289
   bullet 53
   communications 433
   font 16, 57, 58
      Spreadsheet 248
   font size 57
   footnote position 113
   margins 16
   tabs 16
   text alignment 16
   type size 16
   tab 19
   top margin 24

record height in Database 289
delete 39
   characters 41
   columns/rows
      Spreadsheet 239
   contents of record or field 303
   field 297
   file 124
   filter 320
   graphic 158
   range name 244
   report 344
   report
      from Database 348
      Spreadsheet columns/rows 238
   summary statistic
      in Database Report 347
   tabs 41, 135
   text 37
descending sort
   in Database 333
   in Spreadsheet 245
destination document/file 378, 379, 382, 386
dialog box 10
dimmed options 10
DISPLAY ALL RECORDS
   after filter 314
   in Database 302, 317
document screen 7
downloading 439. 445
drag and copy
   in Spreadsheet 238
drag and drop 81, 82, 86, 87
   from one document to another 376
   in Database 293
   in List view 297
   in Spreadsheet 207, 208, 238
   integration 378
   move a field 292
DRAW OBJECT
   edit 173
drive letter 17
drop-down list 11
DUPLICATE A CHART 269
duplicate chart 268

E

Easy Calc feature 227, 229, 231
Easy Connect
   communications 431
Easy Format 61, 77
   edit 84
Easy Text 60
edit
   Spreadsheet data for charts 267
EDIT A LEGEND 269
EDIT A SERIES RANGE 269
Edit an Easy Format 84
EDIT CLIPART 173
Edit Record or Field Data 303
EDIT THE SPREADSHEET DATA 269
ellipsis (...) 10

embed
    existing chart 382
    existing spreadsheet 380
    new spreadsheet 384
embedding
    integration 378
enclosure 107
End of lines
    communications 435
enter records 290
    Database 288
entry bar 191, 200
    Spreadsheet 187, 193, 197
enumeration 77
envelope 393
    merge 405
    print 402
explode a Pie Chart 271
Exponential
    Number tab 204
Extend Selection mode 37

F

F8 key 200
fax modem
    communications 440
field
    add in Database 291, 297
    database 280
    delete in Database 292, 297
    move in Database 292, 297
    overlapping 292
field contents
    Database 280
field data
    delete in Database 303
    edit in Database 303
field entry
    correct in Database 288
field labels
    print in Database 299, 302
field name
    database 280
    filter 314
field name border
    Database 289
Field Size
    Database 290
field width
    change in Form Design view 289, 290
    change in List view 289, 290
    correct in Database 288
    Database 290
filename extension 17, 84
File Menu 8
File name 34
Files of type 34
Files of Type options 287
fill
    in Database 293
    Spreadsheet 201

Fill Down
    button 207
    in Database 293
    in List view 297
    in Spreadsheet 207, 208
Fill mouse shape
    in Spreadsheet 207
Fill Right
    button 207
    in Database 293
    in List view 297
    in Spreadsheet 207, 208
Fill Series
    in Database 293
    in List view 297
    Spreadsheet 216
filter
    apply 314, 317
    apply previously created 326
    base Database report on 360
    create 317
    Database records for merge 399
    delete 319
    display all records 314
    in Database 313
    previously created 322
    rename 319
    results 314
    search in Database 317
    view 319
Filter dialog box 319
filter sentence
    in Database 313
Filter using formula 319
Filtered records
    envelope merge 405
final copy 33
find
    specific record in Database 312
find and replace 100
    in Database 313, 317
find special characters 97
find text 97
Find whole words only 100
First Record button
    Database 304
first-ine indent 73, 75
first-line indent marker 69, 73
Fixed
    Number tab 204
folder 16, 17, 123
    create 123, 124
font 56, 58
    appearance in Database 324, 326
    change in Database 324
    chart 273
    color 56
    communications 435
    defaults 57
    points 56
    size 56
    Spreadsheet 248
    True Type 56

font color
   chart 273
Font Face List 12
FONT SIZE 58
   chart 273
   Spreadsheet 248
   in Database report 116
footer 110
footnotes 110
   at end of document 113, 114
   automatic superscript 120
   default position 113
   edit 114
   Normal view 110
   on separate page 114
   Page Layout view 110, 113
foreground color 155
form
   database 283
   modify in Database 291
Form Design view
   add a field 291, 297
   database 283, 288
   delete in Database 297
   delete in field 292
   move a field 292, 297
Form Letters feature 394
Form view
   create a filter 313
   database 283, 287
   delete a record 304
   enter records 288, 290
   insert a record in Database 304
   print gridlines in Database 302
format
   database 281, 326
FORMAT DATA
   Spreadsheeet 206
formula
   add to Database report 342
   delete from Database report 342
   Spreadsheet 186, 197
Fraction
   Number tab 205
freeform tool
   Microsoft Draw 167
freeze titles
   row and column headings 225
function
   =HLOOKUP 230
   =VLOOKUP 230
   arguments 212
   Autosum button 214
   AVG 212
   built-in 219
   COUNT 216
   IF statement 221
   MAX 216
   MIN 216
   Spreadsheet 212
   SUM 214

function name 212

G

general
   Number tab 204
   Spreadsheet alignment 201
general alignment
   in Database 324
Go To 123, 124
grade book
   TaskWizard 421
graphic 158
   delete 158
   move 158
   resize 157
grid
   Microsoft Draw 168
gridlines 141
   chart 270
   print in Database 299, 302
   print in Spreadsheet 194
group 171
group feature
   Microsoft Draw 168
grouped summary data
   in Database report 357
Grouping
   report data in Database 349
Grouping tab 349
guide words 57

H

hanging indent 73, 75, 93
hard page break 104
hard return 40
header 116
headers and footers 16, 128
   avoid printing on first page 118
   center tab 116
   create 118
   edit 118
   in Database 300, 302
   left-aligned text 116
   Normal view 116
   Page Layout view 116
headings
   report in Database 339
headline 164
Help feature
   about Microsoft Works 13
   access 15
   contents 13
   first-time feature 14
   hide 13
   how to use 13
   index 13
   introduction to Works 13
   launch Works Forum 13
   More Info tab 14

Help window 13
hide
   Database records for merge.................................399
hide columns and rows
   Spreadsheet 227, 229
HIDE/RESTORE A LEGEND 269
highlighted 200
horizontal axis 257
HORIZONTAL LOOKUP 234
horizontal scroll arrows.......................................22
horizontal scroll bar 7, 22
horizontal scroll box..22
Hot zone 101
hyphenation...101

I

I beam 81, 86
   Spreadsheet 191
IF statement 221
Increase/Decrease Indent Levels.................74, 76
indent..73
   first line 73, 75
   hanging 73, 75, 93
   increase/decrease 76
   levels
      increase/decrease 74
   nested paragraph 74
   quotation style 74, 75
   undo 74
insert
   Spreadsheet columns/rows 238
INSERT DATE...30
INSERT A RANGE NAME......................................244
INSERT COLUMNS/ROWS
   Spreadsheet 239
Insert mode 7, 35
INSERT ROW
   in Database Report 347
INSERT TEXT...36
Insert/ Overtype Text..35
insertion point 7, 16, 21, 97, 140, 143
INSERTION POINT MOVEMENT KEYSTROKES 23
inside address 24
Instructions
   Form Letters 394
integrate 379
   letterhead and letter 415
integration..378
Internet 430
ISO Translation
   communications...435
italics 52. 54

J

justify text 50

K

kerning...176

L

label 186
   as outcome of IF statement 221
   chart 257
   create and print 408
   merge..408
   Spreadsheet 189
   width in Spreadsheet 193
Label Layout 409
Label Size 408
landscape
   orientation in Database....................................302
   orientation in Spreadsheet.............................193
Last Record button
   Database 304
leaders
   with tabs..137
Leading Zeros
   Number tab 205
left
   Spreadsheet alignment....................................201
LEFT ALIGN 47
left aligned..143
   labels 189
left alignment..46
   in Database 324
left indent marker 69
left-aligned tab 133
legend 263
   delete 267
   display 268
   edit 267
   hide 267, 268
legends
   chart 257
   font characteristics..273
letter of application...93
letterhead...162
   TaskWizard 415
letters
   business letter..24, 43
   advanced form letters 394
   business letter..24, 43
   copy notation 107
   enclosure 107
   subject 107
   with special notations......................................107
line
   Microsoft Draw..167
line chart 257
line spacing...69, 70
link 380
   word processing and spreadsheet..................386
linked
   data in charts 267
linking
   integration 378
list box 11
List view
   add a field 291, 297
   copy data in Database 297
   create a filter 313
   database 283, 287

delete a record...304
delete in Database..297
delete in field..292
enter records 288, 290
insert a record in Database 303
move a field 292, 297
print gridlines in Database 302
Local echo
    communications...435
LOCATE A SPECIFIC RECORD
    in Database 317
locked
    cells 234
logged off
    communications...445
logged on
    communications...445
Logical Operators
    filter 314
Look in 34
Lookup function 230
Lookup value 230, 234

M

mailbox
    communications...439
mailing labels 393
main address
    envelope 402
Main Address tab
    envelope merge...405
manual page break 104
margins 68
    bottom.. 69
    for Database report 343
    left 68
    right 68
    top 69
mark record
    for merge 399
    in Database 301
    show in Database 301
Match case 100
MAX function 216
maximize 7
    window..372
Maximum
    summary statistic 340
memorandum 57
menu... 9
    access 8
    main menu 8
    main pull-downmenu 8
Menu bar 6, 7
merge envelopes 405
Merge feature 393
merge selected records 399
merged documents...395
Microsoft Draw..167
Microsoft Network..446
MIN function 216

minimize 7
    window..374
Minimum
    summary statistic 340
modem 430
Modem Wizard...430
modified-block
    business letter 24, 43
Month
    Spreadsheet...216
MOVE A FIELD
    in Database 297
move a graphic 158
MOVE AND COPY INFORMATION
    in Spreadsheet..239
Move selection after Enter
    Database...290
Move Text 81
move to next row with Enter
    set in List view 290
moving..171
multiple windows 372
multiple-level sort 245
Multiple-series charts 263

N

NAME A RANGE 244
named range 242
nameplate 164
Negative numbers in red box 323
nested paragraph 74
newsletter...164
next record
    Ctrl+PageDown...288
Next Record button
    Database...304
non-breaking hyphen 89
Normal view 110, 128, 135
    headers and footers 116
Note-It 179
number format
    Database...322, 326
Number of digits increment box 322
Number tab 204
numbered list.. 77
numeric data as a fraction
    format in Database...323
numeric data as text
    format in Database...323
numeric data in serialized form
    format in Database...323

O

One-Page Report.. 68
OPEN A DATABASE FILE...290
Open a Previously Stored Document.................................... 33
OPEN A SAVED DOCUMENT 36
Open dialog box...123
Options
    Database...290

Or
    logical operator 314
orientation
    Spreadsheet 193
Other Options
    Page Setup in Database 299
Oval/Circle
    Microsoft Draw 167
overlapping fields 292
Overtype mode 7, 35, 36
    in brochure 423
overwrite
    Spreadsheet 191

P

page borders 154
page break
    automatic 104
    hard 104
    insert in Database 299
    manual 104
    soft 104
Page Layout
    default view mode 16
Page Layout view 113, 128
    headers and footers 116
PAGE NUMBERS 118, 120
Page Setup 24, 68, 131
    change 266
    Database 302
    in Database 299
paper orientation
    in Database 299
paper size
    in Database 299
paper source
    in Database 299
Parity 435
password 445
Paste Special 386
    in Spreadsheet 238, 239
patterns 175
    Spreadsheet 250
percentage
    Spreadsheet 197
pie chart 257
    explode 271
placeholder 167, 175, 219, 395
    in envelope merge 406
plan
    database 281
pointer
    Microsoft Draw 167
points 56
Portrait
    orientation in Database 302
preview
    report in Database 339
PREVIEW OPTIONS 26
previous record
    Ctrl+PageUp 288

Previous Record button
    Database ....30∢
primary sort
    in Database ....33∃
PRINT ....3∁
    in Database ....300, 30∂
    no header or footer on first page 118
    selected pages ....10∢
Print a Document ....2∁
Print Area
    deselect 231
    set 231
Print Merge box ....39∃
print multiple records
    in Database ....30∁
Print Preview ....24, 2∁
    in Database ....300, 30∂
print test
    labels ....40∃
printer ....2∃
    copies ....2∃
    print range ....2∃
    properties ....2∃
    what to print ....2∃
Printing tab
    Form Letters ....39∃
    labels ....40∃
Proofreaders' marks ....3∃
Properties 434
protect data 234
    Spreadsheet 234
protocol ....43∁
pull-down menu 8
pull-down submenu 10

Q

question mark wildcard 313
quotation style 74, 75

R

radio button 11
RANGE ....20∃
    chart 258
    for pattern or color 250
    NAME 244
    named 242
Range Name 242
    delete 244
    insert in a formula 244
Range reference 230, 234
read-only 34
receive files 445
receive text 444
Recipients
    Form Letters 394
    labels 408
Recipients tab
    envelope merge 405
record 287
    database 280, 287
    delete in Database 304

insert anywhere in Database 304
insert at end of Database 303, 304
insert in Database 303
locate in Database 312
record data
delete in Database 303
edit in Database 303
record height
change in List view 289, 290
Database 289, 290
record number
Database 289
record row
report in Database 339
records
show all in Database 302
Recycle Bin 124
Redial 433
reference initials
business letter 24
relational operators
filter 314
in Database 318
relative reference
in Spreadsheet 207
remove bullets 53, 54, 64
REMOVE INDENTS 76
REMOVE SHADING IN A REPORT 357
Remove Typestyles 64
Rename a File 84
RENAME A FILTER 320
Rename Report 344
in Database 348
Report
access in Database 344
create in Database 337, 340
delete from Database 344
format in Database 342
modify in Database 341
one-page 68
preview in Database 339
rename in Database 344
title in Database 337
statistics in Database 337
Report Definition Screen 339
Report view
in Database 339
ReportCreator
in Database 338
REPOSITION A SUMMARY STATISTIC
in Database Report 348
RESET THE TOOLBAR 20
resize
embedded chart 382
window 374
RESIZE A TABLE 147
restore 7, 39
window 373
resume 93
return address 402
right
Spreadsheet alignment 201

RIGHT ALIGN 47
right aligned 143
values 191
right alignment 46
in Database 324
right mouse button 84
right-aligned tab 133
headers and footers 116
right-click 124
rotate 175
rough-draft 33
row
delete from Spreadsheet 238
insert in Database report 341
insert in Spreadsheet 238
move in Spreadsheet 238
Spreadsheet 187
Row Height
Database 289, 290
Spreadsheet 227
Row number 234
rule 128
Ruler bar 7, 73, 89, 133

S

salutation 24, 395
sample window 11
sans serif 56
Save a New Document 16
SAVE AND CLEAR SCREEN 18
SAVE AND CONTINUE 18
SAVE AND EXIT MICROSOFT WORKS 18
SAVE CHANGES 36
SAVE DATABASE FILE 282
scale
chart 257
scroll 23
horizontal scroll arrows 22
horizontal scroll bar 22
horizontal scroll box 22
vertical scroll bar 21
vertical scroll box 21
with frozen titles 225
Scroll a Document 21
Scroll bars 7, 21
scrolling
Spreadsheet 188
SEARCH
specific field 317
search value
in Database 312
second page headings 104
select text 37, 39
SELECTED RECORD
show and print in Database 302
selected records
envelope merge 405
show and print in Database 301
send a file 123, 124
series range
edit 267

serif...56
SET OPTION TO MOVE TO NEXT ROW WITH ENTER..290
Set Print Area...231
shading...154
shading patterns
   in Database.....................................325, 326
shadow option..151
SHOW ALL CHARACTERS................................41
Show All Records
   in Database...317
SHOW HIDDEN COLUMNS/ROWS
   Spreadsheet...229
signature line...24
   business letter..24
sizing handles...382
soft page break...104
sort
   Database records....................................333
   report data in Database........................349
Sort and Group
   after report is created...........................352
   in Database report.................................352
   report data in Database........................349
SORT AND GROUP REPORT DATA..................356
Sort feature..245
   Spreadsheet...245
SORT RECORDS
   in Database...335
source file..378, 382, 386
Source, Size and Orientation tab
   in Database...302
space..40
special characters...................................40, 43
   * asterisk wildcard................................313
   ? question mark wildcard......................313
   =HLOOKUP function........................230, 234
   =VLOOKUP function........................230, 234
   3-D chart..273
   hard return...40
   space...40
   tab...40
spell check...49, 50
Spreadsheet
   Fill Series...216
Spreadsheet tool..186
stacked bar chart...264
Standard Deviation
   summary statistic...................................340
standard settings
   communications.....................................431
statistic summaries
   for grouped data in report....................350
Status bar...7, 14
Step By
   Spreadsheet...216
Stop Bits..435
subject
   letters..107
subscripts..120
subsort
   in Database...333
subtitle
   insert in Database report.......................341

Sum
   summary statistic...................................340
SUM function..214
summary rows
   report in Database.................................339
summary statistics
   add to Database report..........................340
   for report in Database............................338
   modify in Database report......................342
   reposition in Database report.................342
superscripts...120

T

Tab key..19, 20, 40
table...146
   resize..146
Table feature..186
tabs...133, 140
   centered...133
   database document in Word Processor.........390
   decimal-aligned.....................................133
   leaders..137
   left-aligned..133
   right-aligned..133
TABS DIALOG BOX...135
tabular columns..134
Task Launcher..33
Taskbar...7
   task button..7
TaskWizard..414
   address book...418
   brochure...423
   grade book...421
   letterhead.......................................414, 416
template...415
   create..416
Terminal settings..435
Text
   Number tab...205
text area...7
text box...10
text capture
   communications.....................................445
thesaurus...60, 62
three-digit extension..84
tile
   windows...374
Time
   format in Database.................................323
   Number tab...205
Title bar...6, 372
   document name...7
title of report
   in Database...338
title rows
   report in Database.................................339
titles
   change in chart......................................260
   chart..258
toggle
   between documents...............................415

Toolbar 7, 9, 17, 134
   buttons 19
   Spreadsheet 187
   WordArt 175
Transfer protocol 436
Transfer settings 435
True Type fonts 56
True/False
   Number tab 205
two-line column heading
   insert in Database report 341
typeface 56
typestyle
   bold 52
   chart 273
   italics 52
   Spreadsheet 248
   underline 52
Typing Replaces Selection 40

U

underline 52, 54
Undo
   Editing 38, 39
   Indents 74
unmarked records
   show in Database 301
unprotect cells 234
uploading 439
UPPERCASE 50
username 445

V

value
   keep constant 209
   Spreadsheet 189, 191
value (Y) series 263
value series in chart 259
variable information
   merge 393
Variance
   summary statistic 340
vertical
   Spreadsheet alignment 201
vertical axis 257
vertical scroll bar 7, 21
vertical scroll box 21
View
   normal 12
   Page Layout 12, 110
view a filter 319
VIEW A FILTER SENTENCE 320
view magnification
   Print Preview 300

view modes
   database 283, 287
views
   change 259, 260

W

Weekday
   Spreadsheet 216
Width
   Database 290
wildcard 312, 313
windowing 372
word count 60
word processing screen 6
Word Processor
   access 6
word wrap 16
WordArt 175, 176
Works Forum 446
Works Task Launcher 6, 9, 16
Wrap around 435
Wrap Text option
   in Spreadsheet cell 201
   in Database 324
wrapping text 164

X

x- and y-axis titles
   font characteristics 273
x-axis 257
x-series
   edit 267

Y

y-axis 257
y-axis scale
   font characteristics 273
Year
   Spreadsheet 216
y-series
   data labels 270
   edit 267

Z

zoom factor 7
Zoom Feature 14, 15
   in Microsoft Draw 167
Zoom In 25
Zoom Out 25

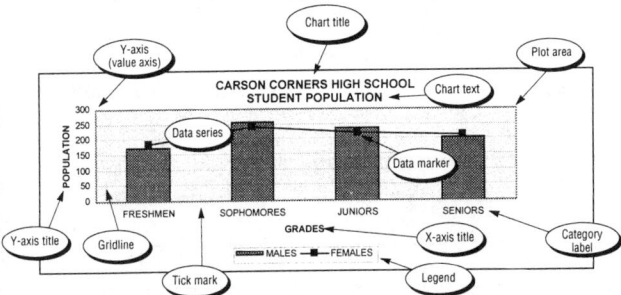

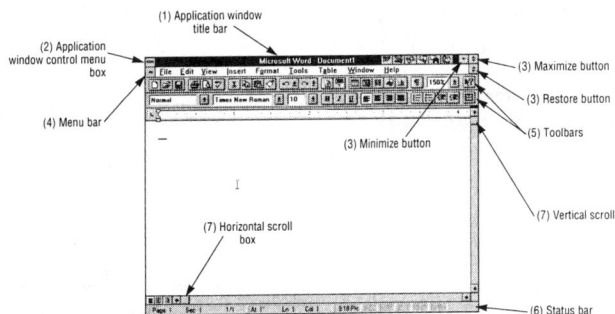

More Fast-teach Learning Books

Did we make one for you?

Title	Cat. No.
Corel WordPerfect 7 for Win 95	Z12
DOS 5–6.2 (Book & Disk)	D9
DOS + Windows	Z7
Excel 5 for Windows	E9
Excel 7 for Windows 95	XL7
INTERNET	Z15
Lotus 1-2-3 Rel. 2.2–4.0 for DOS	L9
Lotus 1-2-3 Rel. 4 & 5 for Windows	B9
Microsoft Office	M9
Microsoft Office for Windows 95	Z6
Windows 3.1 – A Quick Study	WQS-1
Windows 95	Z3
Word 2 for Windows	K9
Word 6 for Windows	1-WDW6
Word 7 for Windows 95	Z10
WordPerfect 5.0 & 5.1 for DOS	W9
WordPerfect 6 for DOS	P9
WordPerfect 6 for Windows	Z9
WordPerfect 6.1 for Windows	H9
Works 3 for Windows	1-WKW3
Works 4 for Windows 95	Z8

DESKTOP PUBLISHING LEARNING BOOKS

Word 6 for Windows	Z2
WordPerfect 5.1 for DOS	WDB
WordPerfect 6 for Windows	F9
WordPerfect 6.1 for Windows	Z5

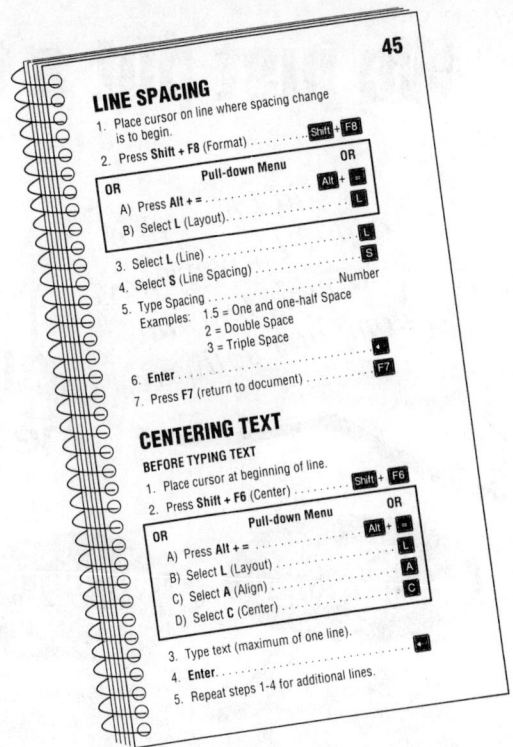

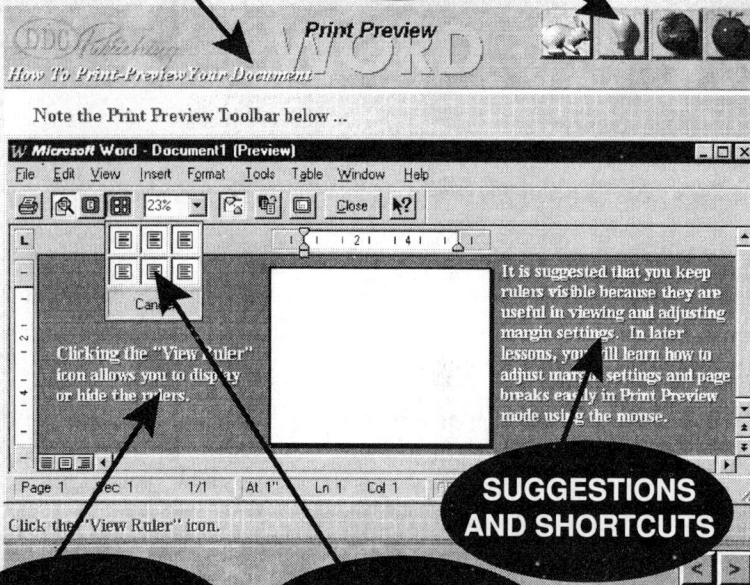